M000111149
L'ASIE
la Pologne
la Belgique
le Luxembourg
la Moldavie
la France
L'EUROPE
la Suisse
la Roumanie
la Bulgarie
Monaco
l'Albanie
la Macédoine
la Tunisie
le Liban
Israël
le Maroc
le Sahara occidental
l'Algérie
L'AFRIQUE
l'Égypte
la Syrie
la Mauritanie
le Mali
le Niger
le Tchad
le Laos
le Sénégal
la Guinée-Bissau
la Guinée
la République centrafricaine
Djibouti
le Cambodge
Pondichéry
le Vietnam
le Burkina-Faso
le Togo
le Bénin
la Cameroun
le Ruanda
le Burundi
la République Démocratique du Congo
L'océan Indien
le Gabon
la Côte-d'Ivoire
le Congo
les Comores
les Seychelles
l'Angola
Mayotte (COM)
Madagascar
l'île Maurice
la Réunion (DOM)
le Mozambique
L'AUSTRALIE
les îles St. Paul et Amsterdam
Terres australes et antarctiques françaises (COM)
l'archipel Crozet
l'archipel Kerguelen
N
O
E
S
Le monde francophone
Terre-Adélie
L'ANTARCTIQUE

La France
La Mer Du Nord
L'ANGLETERRE
Londres
LES PAYS-BAS
L'ALLEMAGNE
Bonn
LA BELGIQUE
Bruxelles
LE LUXEMBOURG
Luxembourg
La Manche
Calais
Lille
NORD-PAS DE CALAIS
Amiens
PICARDIE
Cherbourg
Le Havre
HAUTE-NORMANDIE
Rouen
Caen
BASSE-NORMANDIE
la Seine
Paris
ÎLE-DE-FRANCE
Reims
la Marne
CHAMPAGNE-ARDENNE
Troyes
la Meuse
Metz
LORRAINE
Nancy
la Moselle
Chaumont
Strasbourg
le Rhin
LES VOSGES
ALSACE
Mulhouse
Brest
BRETAGNE
Rennes
Le Mans
PAYS DE LA LOIRE
Angers
Nantes
Orléans
Tours
CENTRE
la Loire
Dijon
BOURGOGNE
FRANCHE-COMTÉ
Besançon
Berne
le Lac Léman
LA SUISSE
N
O
E
S
Poitiers
POITOU-CHARENTES
La Rochelle
Limoges
LIMOUSIN
Vichy
Clermont-Ferrand
AUVERGNE
la Saône
Lyon
Genève
Annecy
Chamonix
Mont Blanc
RHÔNE-ALPES
St-Étienne
Grenoble
L'ITALIE
L'océan Atlantique
Bordeaux
la Dordogne
la Garonne
LE MASSIF CENTRAL
le Rhône
AQUITAINE
MIDI-PYRÉNÉES
Toulouse
LANGUEDOC-ROUSSILLON
Nîmes
Montpellier
Avignon
PROVENCE-ALPES-Côte d'Azur
MONACO
Aix-en-Provence
Nice
Cannes
Marseille
Toulon
Bayonne
Perpignan
L'ANDORRE
L'ESPAGNE
La Mer Méditerranée
Bastia
CORSE
Ajaccio
0 50 100 150 200
Kilomètres

Intrigue

Second Edition

Langue, culture et mystère dans le monde francophone

Intrigue

Second Edition

Langue, culture et mystère dans le monde francophone

Elizabeth Blood
Salem State College

Yasmina Mobarek
The Johns Hopkins University

Upper Saddle River, NJ 07458

Library of Congress Cataloging-in-Publication Data

Blood, Elizabeth.
Intrigue : langue, culture et mystère dans le monde francophone /
Elizabeth Blood, Yasmina Mobarek.— 2nd ed.
p. cm.
Includes index.
ISBN 0-13-221378-8
1. French language—Textbooks for foreign speakers—English. I. Mobarek, Yasmina. II. Title.

PC2129.E5B56 2006
448.2'421—dc22 2006041615

Acquisitions Editor: Rachel McCoy
Publishing Coordinator: Claudia Fernandes
Executive Director of Market Development: Kristine Suárez
Director of Editorial Development: Julia Caballero
Production Supervision: Nancy Stevenson
Project Manager: Assunta Petrone, Preparé
Assistant Director of Production: Mary Rottino
Supplements Editor: Meriel Martínez Moctezuma
Media Editor: Samantha Alducin
Media Production Manager: Roberto Fernandez
Prepress and Manufacturing Buyer: Brian Mackey
Prepress and Manufacturing Manager: Nick Sklitsis
Interior Design: Emilcomp/Preparé
Director, Image Resource Center: Melinda Reo
Interior Image Specialist: Beth Boyd Brenzel
Manager, Rights & Permissions IRC: Zina Arabia
Senior Marketing Manager: Jacquelyn Zautner
Marketing Coordinator: William J. Bliss
Publisher: Phil Miller
Cover image: AP Wide World

Photo acknowledgments appear on p. 427, which constitutes a continuation of the copyright page.
This book was set in 10/12 Palatino typeface by Emilcomp/Preparé and was printed and bound by Courier Westford.
The cover was printed by Phoenix Color.

Printed in the United States of America
10 9 8 7 6 5 4 3 2 1

ISBN 0-13-221378-8

Pearson Education LTD., *London*
Pearson Education Australia PTY, Limited, *Sydney*
Pearson Education Singapore, Pte. Ltd
Pearson Education North Asia Ltd., *Hong Kong*
Pearson Education Canada, Ltd., *Toronto*
Pearson Educación de México, S.A. de C.V.
Pearson Education—Japan, *Tokyo*
Pearson Education Malaysia, Pte. Ltd
Pearson Education, *Upper Saddle River*, New Jersey

Brief Contents

Table des Matières

À EXPLORER

À APPRENDRE
Fonctions

À EXPLORER

To the Instructor

Overview

> **intrigue** *n.* **1.** The quality or power of arousing curiosity or interest. **2.** The events and situations that complicate the plot of a story. **3.** A plotting or scheming by secret or underhand means. **4.** A secret or illicit love affair. (*Funk & Wagnall's Standard College Dictionary*)
>
> **intrigue** *n.f.* **1.** Menées secrètes pour faire réussir ou échouer une affaire. **2.** Liaison secrète. **3.** Combinaison des différents incidents qui forment le sujet d'une pièce, d'un roman, d'un film. (*Dictionnaire Hachette*)

Intrigue is essentially a mystery story. It is the story of a Frenchman named Jean-Louis and a Québécoise graduate student named Claire who meet, seemingly coincidentally, in New Orleans. One in search of a rare original manuscript written by a famous eighteenth-century author, and the other with hidden motives, the two become entangled in a web of adventures that take them from Louisiana to the Caribbean, West Africa, Europe, and Canada. The protagonists discover, in the course of these travels, that their meeting was not entirely coincidental and that they themselves are part of a larger international scheme of intrigue and deception.

This mystery story, however, is not written in a traditional narrative format. Rather, it evolves through the chapter dialogues, listening comprehension selections, communicative activities, and even grammar exercises in the textbook. With each episode in each chapter, the story progresses, and the students learn more about the characters' motives as they pick up clues related to the twists and turns of the story line. As they become interested in the evolving mystery story, they become engaged in learning the French language and in discovering French-speaking cultures around the globe. As the title indicates, **Intrigue** aims to arouse the students' curiosity by offering a complex mystery plot in which characters use underhanded means to accomplish their objectives. By offering continuity between readings, student listening recordings, classroom activities, and homework exercises, **Intrigue** draws students into using the French language in meaningful situations and into learning about the cultures of the French-speaking world. In **Intrigue**, readings, activities, and cultural content are contextualized and relevant to the story line.

The innovative mystery-story textbook arouses student curiosity and encourages students to participate actively in understanding the story and related authentic documents, to discuss the content of chapter readings, to write about their opinions and reactions, and even to complete grammar review activities—all of which advance the plot and offer clues to solving the mystery. Students engage with the material as they work through the contextualized activities, which foster active communication and collaborative learning while lowering the affective filter.

Intrigue is a comprehensive and flexible intermediate-level textbook that develops the four basic communicative skills: reading, writing, speaking, and listening. Its proficiency-oriented methodology focuses on communication, linguistic functions, and interactive exchanges. **Intrigue** incorporates a range of grammar review and communicative activities into the textbook, and offers additional grammar review and expansion activities in both the *Student Activities Manual* (*Cahier d'activités*) and the textbook's Companion Website (*Cahier électronique*). The plot of the mystery story ties together the numerous objectives of an intermediate-level French textbook and provides a meaningful context for the presentation of language functions, vocabulary, grammar explanations, authentic literary excerpts, student audio listening activities, and cultural information. Students are introduced first to plot events of the story and then to the vocabulary, grammar structures, idiomatic expressions, and cultural information needed to fully comprehend what they are reading and to imagine themselves functioning in similar linguistic situations. Student learning is natural, as the text builds skills and recycles grammar points and functions in order to reinforce learning.

In each chapter, personal opinion questions help the students to relate to the information presented, allow them to express ideas, encourage them to adapt vocabulary to their own circumstances, and foster critical thinking. Authentic materials are presented in conjunction with various episodes in the mystery story, and challenging literary readings also relate to the mystery story or chapter themes. These help to prepare intermediate-level language students for future upper-level courses in French literature or culture. Vocabulary pools build upon the basics (work, travel, food, family life, clothes) and introduce some new topics (introductory business French, describing political movements, *québécismes*). Process-writing activities, plus pre-reading and post-reading exercises, foster improvement in reading and writing skills.

Each chapter offers several "Comment dire" sections that present idiomatic expressions and common phrases needed to achieve the communicative goals of the chapter, as well as "Comment faire" sections that explain the formation and use of various grammatical structures or verb tenses needed for the chapter's language functions. Interspersed throughout the chapters are "Information" boxes that provide grammar tips, explain idiomatic expressions, present vocabulary, or offer cultural/historical background information. Also sprinkled throughout the chapters are prompts for the online "Pour aller plus loin" activities and for the "Point de vue" video and its related workbook activities.

The *Student Activities Manual* (*Cahier d'activités*) presents additional aural/oral and written review activities that target language functions, grammatical structures, vocabulary, and verb conjugations, as well as culture and literature review and expansion activities. It offers activities to accompany the lab audio program and the textbook video. The lab audio program introduces students to secondary characters from the various cultures encountered in the textbook's fictional story line and includes a challenging short dictée, while the video offers interesting personal interviews with real Francophones from each of the target cultures. The online Companion Website (*Cahier électronique*) offers "Pour réviser" self-correcting grammar and vocabulary review activities, "Pour aller plus loin" content-based expansion activities, "Pour agir" experiental learning suggestions, and "Pour vous aider" links to good online bilingual dictionaries and verb conjugation resources.

The "Pour aller plus loin" expansion activities may be Internet search activities or the study of additional literary texts, works of art, radio programs, news, music, films, or other cultural texts. These online content-based activities offer endless opportunities for student interaction with authentic texts in French. The "Pour agir" section, also explained on the Companion Website, suggests related experiential, community-based, or service-learning projects. The idea of encouraging students to get out of the classroom and act on what they have learned is a unique feature of **Intrigue**. The aim of these projects is as much to enrich the overall educational experience of the students as to reinforce the learning of French language and Francophone cultures. While **Intrigue** prepares students for upper-level French courses, for many, the intermediate language course is merely a college requirement. Ten years after taking Intermediate French in college, most students will not remember how to conjugate the subjunctive. However, they may remember a volunteer project or a group outing of which they were a part. Experiential learning, which requires students to act on the knowledge and skills they have developed, not only makes learning French something "real" but also helps to instill more fundamental concepts such as awareness of cultural differences, openness to new ideas . . . and perhaps even the desire to continue studying French at the upper levels.

The activities in the textbook are designed to reach a broad range of learners, addressing those with diverse learning styles, those with varying levels of preparation in French, and nontraditional adult students. Activities to practice each function or grammar point are scaled to different levels—each one including inductive activities, discrete activities, open-ended and interactive exercises—and are varied to reach students who may be visual or tactile learners, linear thinkers, or inductive reasoners. Instructors may choose the activities that best address the needs of their students.

Both the design and content of the textbook are geared toward college-level and adult students, partly in response to the growing number of non-traditional older students in today's universities and partly to offer traditional-age college students material that they will find challenging and interesting. Not cluttered with cartoons or irrelevant visual material that can be distracting, the story is what will draw the students to the page. The text assumes an intellectually mature and perceptive reader hindered only by his or her limited knowledge of French. The material presented to students in **Intrigue** aims to incite lively interaction and critical reflection, encouraging students to draw on their own life experiences, thereby rendering the subject of the course personally relevant to them.

Intrigue may be used for a full-year intermediate course or compressed into an intensive one-semester grammar review. The text and workbook together offer opportunities for a basic intermediate course. Or the text and workbook can be used with a selection of the texts and activities suggested in "Pour aller plus loin" or "Pour agir," as a more challenging intermediate French course. The "Interlude" section in the middle of the textbook—which offers short synopses of the plot events, a time line, and brief descriptions of the main characters—may be used as a mid-year review for a two-semester course. This way, a student who is beginning language study at the second-semester intermediate level can quickly get up to speed on the plot and skills reviewed in the first five chapters, or a student returning from a long break can refresh his or her memory.

As concerned educators in an age dominated by pop culture, true crime stories, action-adventure mysteries, and courtroom dramas, we want to reach out to our students and help them engage with the course material. **Intrigue** allows us to offer our students the best of both worlds: all of the fun of a mystery story combined with all of the educational value of a communicative French textbook.

Important Features of ***Intrigue***

- The textbook is designed to meet the "**five C's**" of the standards for foreign language learning:
  - **Communication** (accurate language use, achieved through contextualized language activities)
  - **Cultures** (understanding different cultural perspectives, achieved through contextualized cultural information and authentic texts)
  - **Connections** (interdisciplinary explorations, presented in the text and expanded in the "Pour aller plus loin" activities)
  - **Comparisons** (insight into the nature of language/culture, achieved through comparative questions in the text and workbook)
  - **Communities** (use of language beyond the classroom setting, targeted by the "Pour agir" experiential learning suggestions)
- Vocabulary-building activities in the first episode of each chapter encourage students to draw on their knowledge of basic vocabulary and add new vocabulary pools, including *québécismes*, literary analysis, and an introduction to business French.
- Process-writing activities in each chapter, at the end of each episode, guide students through the writing process. The "À l'écrit" activities successively target vocabulary development, question formation, and practical writing. These first three activities in the three "Épisodes" of each chapter lead to a more formal essay or letter-writing assignment in the "Dénouement" final section of each chapter.
- Pre-reading and post-reading activities assist students in developing strategies for understanding meaning from context. Original readings that expose the plot of the mystery story are accompanied by realia and other authentic texts such as songs, poems, or literary excerpts. Readings become progressively more complex in each subsequent chapter and include examples of the grammatical structures or language functions learned in the chapter.
- Grammar review and language function activities are designed to address the needs of students with varying levels of language preparation and diverse learning styles. Grammar explanations in English ensure that students will have a clear understanding of the structures, but students are also exposed to grammatical terminology in French to facilitate in-class discussions of grammar in the target language.

- Students are drawn into the vibrancy and diversity of cultures in the French-speaking world through the characters presented in the context of the mystery story. The "Information" boxes offer historical and cultural background information about Francophone cultures or useful tips about French language usage.

New to this Edition

- **Video:** The "Points de vue" video provides interviews with French speakers from each of the textbook's ten target cultures. The interview questions are related to each chapter's vocabulary and grammar structures, as well as to the cultural theme. A wealth of related activities are found in the Student Activities Manual (SAM).
- **Revised Student Activities Manual:** You will now find not only workbook and lab manual activities, but also video-related activities, vocabulary crossword puzzles, and more recycling of grammar structures.
- **Revised grammar explanations and student activities:** In the text we now have more models and examples, allowing for more productive classroom time for communicative activities.
- **Reformatted cultural and literary analysis activities:** These are targeted to the unique aspects of each culture/literary excerpt.
- **Verb conjugation charts (*Conjugaisons de verbes*):** This new appendix is a wonderful resource for students, as they need to reference verb conjugations in various forms and tenses.
- **Expanded French–English/English–French glossary:** Students now have access to more useful vocabulary for completing activities.
- **Revised testing program:** This instructor resource now offers a greater variety of question types and topics.
- **Two-color design:** This new design creates an appealing page layout, allowing students more visual support for learning. You will also notice that the pages are a little looser, which will make reading easier on the eyes.

Chapter Organization

Each of the ten chapters is composed of a one-page preview called "Avant-propos," three main sections or "Épisodes," and a "Dénouement" (synthesis) section. Each section develops the story and all four language skills, while focusing on particular skills and/or language functions. Interspersed throughout the four sections are relevant visuals to aid in learning, "Information" boxes that offer cultural background or language tips, the "Pour aller plus loin" prompts that suggest optional but closely related content-based expansion activities found on the text's Companion Website, and the "Point de vue" prompts for the companion video.

As you read through the text, notice that the story line develops principally in the main reading/listening texts in each section of each chapter—the "À lire" paragraph on the chapter opener, the "Lecture" written dialogue in Épisode 1; the "À l'écoute" dialogue in Épisode 2; the "Correspondance" letter or e-mail in Épisode 3; and the "À suivre" paragraph at the end of the chapter. While there are some additional clues and plot developments in many of the student activities, the textbook is designed such that the main reading/listening sections are the only ones essential to following the mystery story plot. The plot developments in the grammar review and communicative activities are not absolutely necessary to follow the story. This way, instructors and students are not obliged to complete *all* of the textbook activities in class, and instructors may select the activities that work best in their particular classrooms.

Chapter Structure

Avant-propos : Introduction

This ***preview to the chapter*** begins with a proverb, saying, or quotation that serves the dual purpose of ***introducing the cultural context*** of the chapter and providing a clue to the story. The *Instructor's Resource Manual* (IRM) suggests ways to use the proverb to introduce the cultural context and pique student interest. It also offers pronunciation work, as students may repeat aloud or memorize the saying. The chapter opener also offers a synopsis of the developments of the mystery story in each chapter, without giving away the plot twists, to give students a ***pre-reading context*** and to entice them to read on. Further, communicative goals are listed on this page to highlight the chapter's language functions.

Épisode 1 : Exposition

The first section introduces a new episode in the development of the mystery story, a cultural context, and a pool of vocabulary. Activities practice all four skills, but the ***focus is on reading skills and vocabulary building,*** including a quick writing activity to brainstorm vocabulary for upcoming writing assignments. The opening episode in the story also introduces all of the grammar tools and language functions that will be the focus of the chapter, thereby providing rich inductive material.

Épisode 2 : Développement

In this section, students will draw on the vocabulary presented in the first episode and concentrate on developing correct usage of the ***grammatical tools*** (articles, pronouns, and so on) that are needed for the chapter language functions. Again, activities span all four skills, but the ***focus in this section is on aural/oral skills***. A listening comprehension dialogue on the audio program (full text available in the IRM only) continues the mystery story and requires attentive listening. Oral and written activities are designed to target listening, conversational speaking, and informal writing.

Épisode 3 : Nœud

The third section also emphasizes structures needed for the language functions of the chapter, with a particular ***focus on verb conjugations and accurate use of verb tenses in practical speaking/writing contexts***. Some activities in this section of each chapter will intermingle tenses, ensuring that students remember how to form those learned earlier in the course and can demonstrate proper usage in realistic situations. A short reading in this section in the form of real-life correspondence (a letter, e-mail, fax) brings the action of the mystery story to a peak, further involving the students in the mystery plot, and serves as an example for a practical writing activity that includes the vocabulary and structures practiced in the two earlier episodes.

Dénouement : Synthèse

The final section of each chapter offers ***activities that synthesize the material*** presented in the chapter (vocabulary, grammar structures, language functions, cultural information). Interactive activities, such as games, role-playing, and debates, recycle chapter functions and themes in a meaningful and fun way. Writing activities, including a more formal essay-writing assignment, also recycle the material learned in this and previous episodes. A ***literary excerpt*** related to the chapter material further expands students' reading and speaking skills while introducing them to major authors of the Francophone world. A final short conclusion to the chapter's mystery story episode is an open-ended "À suivre" section with questions that allow students to reflect critically on the character's actions thus far and to hypothesize about upcoming events or scenarios.

Program Components

Student Activities Manual (SAM)

This workbook, also called the *Cahier d'activités*, comprises three parts: Workbook, Lab Manual, and Video Manual. The "Pour réviser" oral and written review activities target vocabulary, language functions, grammar structures, culture, and literature. The "Activités orales" help the students with listening comprehension. The "Activités écrites" provide written review and expansion activities. The "Point de vue" provides video-related activities. There are also special activities that relate to the "Interlude" section of the text, ideal for mid-year review.

Audio Program to Accompany the Text

Here you will find recordings related to the dialogues that correspond to the "À l'écoute" section in Épisode 2 of each chapter and the "Comment dire" section.

Audio Program to Accompany the SAM:

This contains recordings related to the oral review sections of the SAM ("Pour réviser: activités orales").

Video

The *Points de vue* video offers a series of ten personal interviews with French-speakers from each of the ten cultures highlighted in the textbook (Louisiana, Haiti, France/Vietnam, Algeria, Paris, Martinique, Senegal, Switzerland, Provence, Québec) The video offers personal insights into the interviewee's native culture, and interview questions are targeted to each chapter's vocabulary and grammar structures, offering provocative and useful authentic input. Video-related activities can be found in the *Student Activities Manual.*

Companion Website

The textbook's Companion Website, or *Cahier électronique*, has four components: the "Pour réviser" self-correcting vocabulary and grammar review activities; the "Pour aller plus loin" content-based expansion activities; the "Pour agir" experiential, community-based, or service-learning suggestions; and the "Pour vous aider" online French–English and English–French dictionaries and verb conjugation tools. The Web address is: **http://www.prenhall.com/intrigue**.

Instructor's Resource Manual (IRM)

The manual contains sample syllabi, cultural history synopses for each chapter, rationales for each activity in the textbook, teaching suggestions, text audio dialogue tapescripts, a complete testing program, and additional resources to assist instructors in using the **Intrigue** program.

Acknowledgments

We would like to express our appreciation to the people at Prentice Hall who continue to devote time, talent, and interest in making **Intrigue** a success. Thanks to Rachel McCoy, Acquisitions Editor, for her enthusiasm and endless efforts to talk with adopters of **Intrigue** to learn how to make this program a more useful curriculum. We also express thanks to Phil Miller, Publisher for World Languages, and to the rest of the team: Mary Rottino, Assistant Director of Production; Nancy Stevenson, Senior Production Editor; Samantha Alducin, Media Editor, for her guidance in producing an excellent video for the second edition; Meriel Martínez Moctezuma, Supplements Editor; Roberto Fernandez, Media Production Manager; and Claudia Fernandes, Publishing Coordinator.

Thanks to our families and to all of our friends for their support and encouragement. A special thanks to Ben Jackson (story consultant), Dan O'Sullivan, Renee Cardona, Ann Damoiseaux, Karen Schneider RSM, Brian Thompson, Thierry Gustave, Louissa Abdelghany, Betsy Lynch, Ariane Duffy, Dana Hale, and Jeff Haus.

We finally wish to thank the following reviewers for their thoughtful comments and suggestions:

Susanne Akins, *San Antonio College*
Dr. Debra L. Bell, *University of Georgia*
Anne L. Birberick, *Northern Illinois University*

Sylvie E. Blum, *University of Florida*
Maureen Gillespie Dawson, *University of Kansas*
Antoinette Drouart, *Rivier College, NH*
Karen Kelton, *University of Texas at Austin*
Cheryl Krueger, *University of Virginia*
Glyn P. Norton, *Williams College, MA*
Jin Lu, *Purdue University, Calumet*
Daniel E. O'Sullivan, *University of Mississippi*
Isabel Roche, *Bennington College, VT*
Aurora Schlegel, *Monmouth University, NJ*
Scott Sheridan, *Illinois Wesleyan University*
Homer B. Sutton, *Davidson College, NC*
Brian Thompson, *University of Massachusetts, Boston*
Kelle S. Truby, *University of California, Riverside*

Elizabeth Blood
Yasmina Mobarek

To the Student

Three Keys to Success in the Second-Language Classroom
Five Simple Tips to Improve Fluency
Ten Reasons to Become Fluent in French

> *"I didn't learn anything in my high school French class."*
> *"It's been so long since I took a French class. I've forgotten everything."*
> *"I'm just not good with languages. I don't understand anything."*
> *"I've only had one year of French. The other students seem more advanced."*

Excuses! We've heard them all! The fact is that language is one of the most natural things that human beings learn to use, and everyone is good at languages on some level. If you can read this and you can speak English, you can also learn to read and speak a second language. However, you are still in the early stages of learning French, and you will often feel that you are in over your head. Be assured that this is completely normal! You will not understand every word you read or hear using this program. In the second-language classroom, you are always presented with language that is above your level. We do this on purpose so that you always have room to grow and improve your use of the language. So, no more excuses! Dive in and do what you can to stay afloat. Soon, you'll be swimming laps with ease.

Three Keys to Success in the Second-Language Classroom

Here are three key techniques to learning a second language, like French, that may help you to stay afloat at this post-beginner level: (1) memorization and practice, (2) trial and error, and (3) curiosity and open-mindedness.

Memorization and Practice

Learning vocabulary, grammar, and good pronunciation always starts with memorization and practice. If you devote the time to memorizing vocabulary, verb conjugations, and grammar rules, and you practice the structures presented in class by speaking and writing as often as possible, you will improve your French. In this book, you will be re-introduced to the basic structures you learned in your beginning French classes. If you don't remember them well, now is the time to focus on learning them more thoroughly. Memorization requires time and self-discipline, but if you are in college, you've already proven you can do it. So, get those index cards ready and start reviewing!

Trial and Error

Don't be afraid to make mistakes! In fact, if you are not making any mistakes, you are not being a good student of French. No mistakes usually means no attempts to use new words or structures. Don't worry about crafting a perfect sentence every time you speak, just try to communicate as best you can. And, take risks! You must make assumptions from context and try to use the words and grammar you know in order to improve.

The worst that can happen is that someone corrects you . . . and then, you've learned something new! Even people who have no knowledge of French can grasp the meaning of simple phrases by looking for English cognates. The fact is that many French vocabulary words are derived from English, and in English we use a great number of French-derived words as well. Think about the French words "le marketing," "le pull-over," "le week-end," or the English words "cuisine," "port," "lingerie," or "camouflage." There are also many cognates, or words that are spelled the same or similarly in both languages, like "adoration," "balance," "canal," "double," "déclaration," etc. They are often pronounced differently—and sometimes you may come across "false friends" (*faux amis*) that look the same but mean something entirely different—but generally you'll find that cognates have similar root meanings. Even the title of this book, "Intrigue," is both a French word and an English word, pronounced differently and with similar meanings, though "une intrigue" in French also means "a plot or story line."

■ CURIOSITY AND OPEN-MINDEDNESS

Consider yourself a detective! In order to really excel at learning a second language, you must engage with the material and be curious about the things you will learn—about how language works and how cultural perspectives differ. This book centers on a mystery story involving characters from French-speaking countries. The readings, dialogues, listening comprehension, and even grammar activities are all parts of the story that give you clues to what is happening. We hope that as you become interested in the characters and the story, you will learn vocabulary, grammar, and communication skills, but you will also learn about a variety of French-speaking (Francophone) cultures. Keep an open mind as you learn about the way of life, traditions, and customs in those cultures. The materials suggested in the "Pour aller plus loin" activities, found on the text's Companion Website, are related to the cultures and situations in the story and will give the curious student the opportunity to take his or her French skills to an even higher level.

Five Simple Tips to Improve Fluency

You know some French, you can get the gist from reading or listening, but you have problems producing sentences and expressing yourself accurately. This is normal for an intermediate learner and easy to change. Here are five tips to improve your fluency in French.

■ DON'T TRANSLATE!

The impulse to translate from English to French, or vice versa, is natural in the early stages of language learning, but real fluency will begin once you abandon translation and begin communicating directly in the language. The emphasis here is on understanding others and making yourself understood. Don't get hung up on trying to find the exact word you would have used in English. When speaking, use the French words and phrases you know instead of searching to translate more difficult words or sentence structures from English.

Also, when writing, don't ever use online translators—they simply do not work well. Trust us on this! Most translation programs translate sentences literally, and therefore inaccurately, creating utterances which are absolutely incomprehensible to native speakers. If you need to know a word, look it up in a bilingual dictionary that offers multiple options according to context, part of speech, and intended meaning (use one of the free excellent online dictionaries linked to the "Pour vous aider" section of our Companion Website!).

■ USE CIRCUMLOCUTION!

What *is* circumlocution, you ask? It's finding a way to express an idea with words you know. You will not always be able to say exactly what you want to say in French (or the way you would say it in English) because you may lack some grammar or vocabulary or because French sentences are just constructed differently than English ones. Instead of giving up and using English or asking for a translation, try to communicate your idea in another way—with easier words you already know, gestures, or even facial expressions.

Example:

You want to say "I go to the laundromat every morning" (= "*Je vais à la laverie automatique tous les matins*"). However, you don't know the words for "laundromat" or how to say "every morning." Don't give up! Maybe you do know "I wash," "clothes," and "morning." You could simply say "*Je lave les vêtements le matin.*" Or, if you don't know the word for "clothes," you could even just say "*Je lave . . . le matin*" while pointing to your clothes. It is not exactly what you wanted to say (because the listener doesn't know where you wash your clothes), but it is close enough to communicate the essential idea. Your listener may respond by asking if you wash your clothes at home or at the laundromat, and you will learn the vocabulary that you were lacking. As you continue to speak and listen, you will pick up more vocabulary and you will find you can construct sentences more easily. Soon, you will realize that you don't need to use circumlocution as often as you did at first.

■ ASK QUESTIONS AND REPEAT!

Use every activity in the target language to learn new words and phrases. At first, you may find that you can understand more words than you can actually generate yourself. One way to rectify that situation is by active "listening and repeating" in classroom conversations with your teacher and your peers . . . or out in French-speaking communities. You will remember the words better if you take action and say them aloud, rather than just passively hearing them in conversation. If someone uses a word or phrase you don't know, or don't understand, ask her to repeat it. Listen attentively. Ask what it means. Repeat it yourself (out loud!) to be sure you have grasped the phrase. Use the same technique when reading. If you come across a word or phrase you don't know, look it up in a dictionary, say it out loud, and repeat it several times.

Useful phrases:

Qu'est-ce que c'est?	*What is that?*
Que veut dire ___________?	*What does ___________ mean?*
Comment dit-on ___________?	*How do you say ___________?*
Répétez, s'il vous plaît.	*Please repeat that.* (formal)
Excusez-moi, je n'ai pas compris.	*I'm sorry, I didn't understand that.* (formal)
Encore une fois?	*One more time?*
Comment?	*Huh? What?* (less formal)

■ READ OUT LOUD!

Reading aloud at home is good practice for pronunciation and a great way to build your vocabulary. Your friends and family may think you're nuts, but if you read out loud in French for 10–15 minutes a day, your accent, vocabulary, and overall fluency *will* improve. Some hints for reading out loud: try to focus on the pronunciation of difficult letters (like "u" or "r") as well as intonation. Read your homework aloud to kill two birds with one stone!

■ LISTEN TO THE NEWS IN FRENCH!

Check out news on the Web! Try **www.rfi.fr** (Radio France Internationale has world news in French; look for the "Infos en français facile," which offers a simplified version, if you're having difficulty understanding the main broadcast) or **www.tv5.org** (TV5 has streaming live video of TV news broadcasts from France and Africa downloadable with RealPlayer). Listen for just ten minutes a day. Not only will your listening comprehension and vocabulary improve, you'll learn about what's going on in the Francophone world!

Ten Reasons to Become Fluent in French

You're wondering if it's worth it to continue your studies of French? The answer is "oui"! French is not only a beautiful language that allows you access to a rich heritage of culture, literature, and philosophy, it is also a valuable asset in today's global marketplace. Here are ten reasons to keep studying French until you become truly fluent in the language.

✔ **Proficiency in French increases your job prospects!** A U.S. State Department study of the international job market at the turn of the millennium indicates that **over 50%** of international jobs require or prefer candidates to speak French.

✔ **French is the second most influential language in the world!** *Language Today*, a publication for language professionals, ranked French second only to English at the turn of the millennium.

✔ **French is an official language in the United States!** The State of Louisiana's official languages are French and English.

✔ **Canada, whose official languages are French and English, is the primary trading partner of the United States!** And, with NAFTA, more and more products will be marketed in Canada and companies will require French-speaking employees.

✔ **France is the #1 tourist destination in the world!** The number of people visiting France per year is *greater than* its entire population. Oh là là!

✔ **In over 20 African countries, French is used for government and business!** There is a strong French influence in North Africa, West Africa, and Central Africa.

✔ **French is an official language of many international organizations!** It is an official language at the United Nations, the Red Cross, the International Monetary Fund, the World Health Organization, UNESCO, and the International Olympic Committee!

- ✔ **French is spoken on dozens of islands all over the globe!** Including islands in the South Pacific, the Caribbean, the Indian Ocean, and the Mediterranean.
- ✔ **France ranks 4th in the world in terms of Gross National Product!** Plus, over 1,200 French companies have investments in the U.S., and these French companies employ over 400,000 Americans annually.
- ✔ **All three branches of the European Union are headquartered in French-speaking countries!** EU headquarters are located in Brussels (Belgium), Strasbourg (France), and Luxembourg City (Luxembourg).

(Source: The American Association of Teachers of French **http://www.frenchteachers.org***)*

Chapitre 1

Un séjour en Louisiane

Un musicien joue devant le Royal Café, un restaurant dans le Vieux Carré à la Nouvelle-Orléans.

Épisode *1* *L'arrivée*

Épisode *2* *L'excursion*

Épisode *3* *La bourse*

Dénouement

Les haricots sont pas salés.
—expression cajun-créole

À apprendre

- Comment saluer et se présenter
- Comment parler de ses préférences
- Comment poser des questions
- Comment décrire sa routine quotidienne
- Comment écrire une lettre

Culture

Le **Vieux Carré** est l'ancien quartier français à la Nouvelle-Orléans, une ville fondée par les Français en 1718. La rue la plus célèbre du Vieux Carré est la rue Bourbon. On y fête Mardi gras chaque année vers la fin de l'hiver.

À lire

Dans le foyer de l'Hôtel Le Moyne, situé rue Dauphine, dans le Vieux Carré, à la Nouvelle-Orléans, dans l'état de la Louisiane, au sud des États-Unis, en Amérique du Nord, une jeune femme québécoise rencontre un Français. C'est le mois d'août, et il fait très, très chaud. Claire, la Québécoise, fait de la recherche littéraire pour la thèse de doctorat qu'elle prépare à l'Université de Sainte-Foy au Québec. C'est une bonne raison de braver la chaleur humide et oppressive de l'été louisianais. Mais Jean-Louis, le Français, pourquoi est-il là ? Que fait-il à la Nouvelle-Orléans ?

Épisode 1

L'arrivée

Avant de lire

1.1 Vos voyages **Répondez aux questions suivantes.** Discutez de vos réponses avec vos camarades de classe et n'hésitez pas à poser des questions supplémentaires si vous voulez en savoir plus.

1. Est-ce que vous voyagez souvent ? de temps en temps ? rarement ? jamais ?
2. Quand vous voyagez, est-ce que vous prenez la voiture, le train, l'avion ou un autre mode de transport ?
3. Quand vous voyagez, partez-vous avec votre famille, vos amis, un groupe de touristes que vous ne connaissez pas, ou préférez-vous voyager tout(e) seul(e) ?
4. Où aimez-vous aller ? à une grande ville ? à la plage ? à la campagne ? à la montagne ? en Europe ? en Afrique ? en Asie ? en Amérique (du Nord ou du Sud) ? aux Antilles ? Préférez-vous des voyages actifs ou reposants ?
5. Que faites-vous pour vous amuser ? Est-ce que vous faites du sport ? du tourisme ? du shopping ? du camping ? Aimez-vous visiter des musées ou des sites historiques ?
6. Où préférez-vous vous loger ? dans un hôtel (de luxe ou modeste) ? chez des amis ? dans un terrain de camping ? dans une pension ? dans une chambre d'hôte ? dans une auberge de jeunesse ?

i Langue

Une **auberge de jeunesse** est une résidence pour les touristes, souvent jeunes, qui offre des lits à un prix raisonnable. Souvent, dans les auberges de jeunesse, il faut partager une chambre et une salle de bains avec d'autres touristes. Une **pension** est un petit hôtel où on est logé et nourri. Une **chambre d'hôte** est une chambre louée dans une maison privée.

1.2 Le Vieux Carré Regardez le plan de la Nouvelle-Orléans que Claire apporte dans son sac à dos et répondez aux questions d'après vos observations. Discutez de vos réponses avec la classe.

1. Où est le Vieux Carré ? Où est la rue Dauphine ?
2. Quelles sont les rues du Vieux Carré ? Leurs noms sont-ils tous français ?
3. Pouvez-vous identifier l'influence d'autres cultures en observant les noms des rues ? À votre avis, quelles autres cultures ont contribué à la culture créole de la Nouvelle-Orléans ?
4. Quels sont les monuments, musées, parcs ou sites historiques proches du Vieux Carré ?

Pour aller plus loin : CULTURE

ACTIVITÉ A : Apprenez un peu sur l'histoire de la Louisiane et de la Nouvelle-Orléans. Consultez votre cahier électronique !

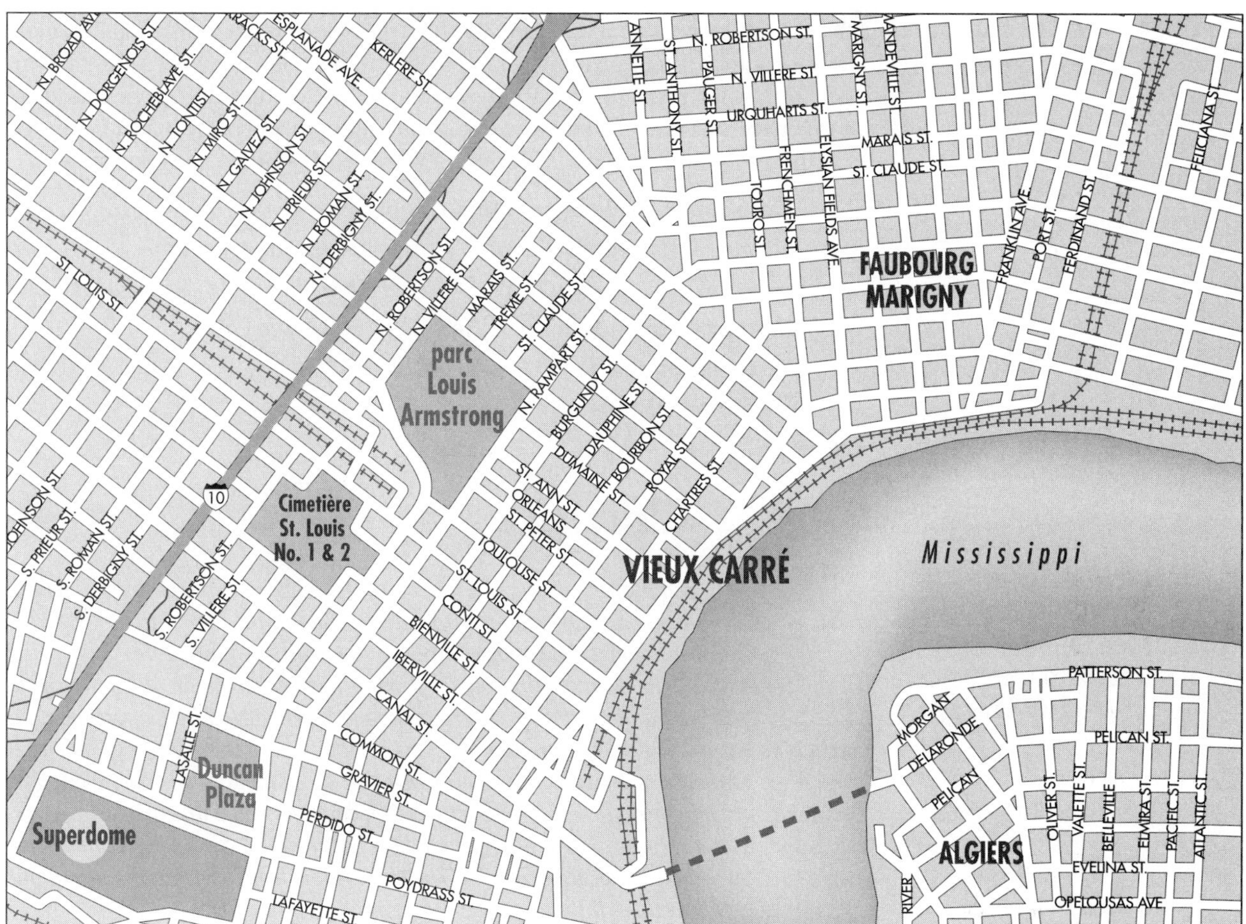

Un plan de la Nouvelle-Orléans.

1.3 Les rencontres Quand on voyage, on rencontre beaucoup de gens. Parfois, les rencontres sont heureuses, parfois elles sont désagréables. En groupes, lisez les phrases suivantes et indiquez si les phrases sont (a) formelles ou familières ? et (b) polies ou impolies ? (N'oubliez pas que le «vous» peut indiquer une situation formelle ou le pluriel.)

1. Bonjour ! Comment allez-vous aujourd'hui ?
2. Salut, toi ! Quoi de neuf ?
3. Je vous connais, non ? Vous êtes le chauffeur de taxi.
4. Très heureux de faire votre connaissance, madame.
5. Permettez-moi de me présenter. Je m'appelle Jean-Louis Royer. Et vous ?
6. Salut, les filles. Venez boire un coup avec nous !

1.4 Le bavardage Quand on parle avec une personne que l'on vient de rencontrer, il faut être poli(e) et parler de sujets légers (c'est à dire, bavarder). Lisez les phrases suivantes et indiquez si le sujet de conversation est **convenable** ou **non convenable** pour une première rencontre avec quelqu'un. Donnez votre avis personnel et discutez-le avec des camarades de classe.

1. Quel temps ! Il fait chaud aujourd'hui, n'est-ce pas ?
2. Oh là là ! Il faut être riche pour porter un costume Armani.
3. Vous avez un accent bizarre. D'où venez-vous ?
4. Ma sœur va bientôt divorcer. Je suis bouleversée.
5. Que pensez-vous de la Nouvelle-Orléans ?
6. Aimez-vous la cuisine créole ?

lisez

L'arrivée

La porte du taxi s'ouvre devant l'Hôtel Le Moyne. Une jeune femme descend et attend devant l'entrée pendant que le chauffeur vient retirer du coffre ses bagages, une valise et un sac à dos. Il les dépose près d'elle pendant qu'elle fouille dans son sac à main à la recherche de son portefeuille. Elle lui donne de l'argent et se dirige vers le foyer de l'hôtel. Elle s'approche de la réception, mais il n'y a personne derrière le comptoir. Claire examine la grande salle aux murs jaunes; des ventilateurs rotatifs pendent du plafond et des portes en verre donnent sur une cour ensoleillée. Au centre de la cour se trouve une piscine entourée de palmiers et de chaises longues. Un paradis ! Les meubles dans la salle intérieure semblent dater du 18ème siècle. Un homme en costume bleu, assis dans un fauteuil, lit un guide touristique. Il lève les yeux et regarde la jeune Québécoise.

JEAN-LOUIS : Bonjour.

CLAIRE : Bonjour.

JEAN-LOUIS : Bienvenue à la Nouvelle-Orléans. Vous êtes touriste comme moi ? *Il montre la couverture de son guide Michelin.*

CLAIRE : Non, pas exactement, mais je compte visiter la ville pendant mon séjour.

JEAN-LOUIS : Moi aussi. Je viens de Paris. Je fais un voyage d'affaires, mais je profite de quelques jours de congé pour visiter la Nouvelle-Orléans. Je trouve cette ville fascinante. Qu'est-ce qu'on dit ? «Laissez les bons temps rouler», hein ? *Il se lève et tend la main à la jeune femme.* Permettez-moi de me présenter. Je m'appelle Jean-Louis Royer.

CLAIRE : Enchantée. Je suis Claire Plouffe. *Elle lui serre la main un peu brusquement.*

JEAN-LOUIS : C'est un plaisir de faire votre connaissance. Ne vous inquiétez pas. Philippe. . . euh, c'est l'hôtelier. . . il reviendra dans un instant.

CLAIRE : Excusez-moi si j'ai l'air un peu énervé. Ça fait des heures que je voyage, le vol a été retardé de deux heures à cause d'orage, et je suis un peu fatiguée.

JEAN-LOUIS : Ce n'est pas grave. Vous avez un petit accent. . . peut-être martiniquais ? algérien ? suisse ? acadien ? canadien ?

CLAIRE : Je suis Québécoise.

À ce moment, l'hôtelier arrive à la réception, et Jean-Louis retourne à son fauteuil.

PHILIPPE : Bonjour, madame.

CLAIRE : Bonjour, monsieur.

PHILIPPE : Bienvenue à l'Hôtel Le Moyne. Excusez-moi de vous avoir fait attendre. Avez-vous réservé une chambre ?

CLAIRE : Oui, oui. C'est au nom de Plouffe. Claire Plouffe.

PHILIPPE : Pouvez-vous épeler votre nom de famille ?

CLAIRE : P-L-O-U-F-F-E. Comme le son d'une pierre qui tombe dans l'eau.

PHILIPPE : Ah, oui ! Je vois. Vous voulez une chambre pour une personne, non fumeur, avec salle de bains et balcon. Vous restez combien de nuits ?

CLAIRE : Six, je crois. Mais il y a une petite possibilité que ça change si je ne trouve pas ce que je cherche. Enfin, serait-il possible de rester plus longtemps, si nécessaire ?

PHILIPPE : Aucun problème. L'hôtel n'est pas au complet. On est loin du Mardi gras et cette saison humide décourage la plupart des touristes. Il faut faire attention. Il y a déjà eu trois morts à cause de la chaleur en Louisiane cet été. Mais ne vous inquiétez pas, madame, je vous assure que toutes les chambres sont climatisées. Comment désirez-vous payer ?

CLAIRE : Par carte de crédit. Voilà.

PHILIPPE : Très bien, et voici votre clé. La femme de ménage a déjà préparé votre chambre. Le petit déjeuner est servi ici dans la grande salle le matin de 7h30 à 10h, et on sert du champagne et des hors-d'œuvre dans la cour le soir de 6h à 8h. Je m'appelle Philippe Aucoin, et si vous avez des questions ou si je peux vous rendre service, n'hésitez pas à m'appeler.

CLAIRE : Merci. Au fait, cela coûte combien en supplément, le petit déjeuner ?

PHILIPPE : Mais, c'est compris dans le prix de la chambre, ainsi que le champagne. C'est gratuit.

CLAIRE : Quel luxe !

PHILIPPE : Mais nous sommes ravis de vous servir, madame. Allez ! Je vous accompagne à votre chambre. Votre valise a l'air assez lourd et il n'y a pas d'ascenseur dans ce vieux bâtiment. Nous prendrons l'escalier. *Ils se dirigent vers l'escalier.* Ah, monsieur Royer ! Je vous présente Claire Plouffe, une autre francophone qui vient juste d'arriver du Québec.

JEAN-LOUIS : On s'est déjà rencontré.

CLAIRE : Oui. *Elle sourit.* Bonne journée, monsieur Royer.

JEAN-LOUIS : Au revoir, madame. À la prochaine !

Il continue à regarder la jeune femme alors qu'elle monte l'escalier de fer forgé. — Voilà une jeune femme bien intéressante, pense-t-il.

i Langue

En français, on dit «plouf» pour indiquer le son de quelque chose qui frappe l'eau. En anglais, on dit «*plop*» ou «*splosh*». Il y a d'autres **onomatopées** en français qui sont assez différentes de l'anglais. Pouvez-vous deviner l'usage des mots suivants : **cliquetis, glouglou, toc toc, pan, coin coin** ? (Les équivalents en anglais, pas dans le même ordre, sont : *knock-knock, click, bam, glug-glug, quack-quack.*)

VOCABULAIRE

Les voyages

fouiller (dans)	*to search (through)*
se diriger (vers)	*to head (towards)*
être retardé(e) (de deux heures)	*to be delayed (by two hours) (flight, transportation)*
le vol	*flight*
la valise	*suitcase*
le sac à dos	*backpack*
le sac à main	*handbag*
le portefeuille	*wallet*
le guide (touristique)	*guidebook*
l'orage (*m.*)	*storm*
la chaleur	*heat*

À l'hôtel

épeler	*to spell*
se serrer la main	*to shake hands*
rendre service (à)	*to be of service (to)*
être au complet	*to be full, have no vacancy*
le/la client(e)	*hotel guest, client*
la femme de ménage	*cleaning woman*
l'hôtelier/l'hôtelière	*innkeeper, hotel owner*
la grande salle	*great room, main room*
le mur	*wall*
le foyer	*entranceway, lobby*
les meubles	*furniture*
le fauteuil	*living-room chair*
la réception, le comptoir	*check-in desk, counter*
la cour	*courtyard*
le balcon	*balcony*
l'escalier (*m.*)	*stairs*
l'ascenseur (*m.*)	*elevator*
la piscine	*pool*
le fer forgé	*wrought iron*
la clé	*key*
fumeur, non fumeur	*smoking, nonsmoking*
climatisé(e)	*air-conditioned*
gratuit(e), compris(e)	*free, included*

Après avoir lu

1.5 Avez-vous compris ? Répondez aux questions suivantes. Justifiez vos réponses en citant le texte.

1. Qui sont Claire et Jean-Louis ? Quelles sont leurs nationalités ? Quelles sont leurs professions ?
2. Comment est-ce que Jean-Louis se présente à Claire ? Que dit-il ? Que fait-il ? Est-ce une rencontre typique ?
3. Pourquoi Jean-Louis est-il assis dans le foyer de l'hôtel quand Claire arrive ? Pensez-vous qu'il s'apprête à faire du tourisme ou non ? Pourquoi ?
4. Comment trouvez-vous cet hôtel ? Décrivez l'ambiance. Voudriez-vous être un(e) client(e) dans cet hôtel ? Pourquoi ou pourquoi pas ?
5. Qui est Philippe Aucoin ? Quelle est sa profession ? sa nationalité ? Que dit-il pour saluer (*to greet*) Claire quand elle arrive à l'hôtel ?
6. Pourquoi est-ce que Philippe et Jean-Louis disent «madame» à Claire ? Est-ce qu'elle est mariée ou est-ce un signe de respect (comme «*Ms.*» au lieu de «*Miss*» en anglais) ?
7. Pour combien de temps Claire va-t-elle rester dans cet hôtel ? Est-elle contente d'être à la Nouvelle-Orléans ?

1.6 D'accord ou pas d'accord ? Indiquez si vous êtes d'accord ou pas avec les phrases suivantes, d'après votre compréhension du récit. Justifiez votre opinion en citant le texte, **si possible. Discutez de vos réponses avec la classe.**

	D'accord	Pas d'accord
1. Claire Plouffe a voyagé à la Nouvelle-Orléans en voiture.	_______	_______
2. Claire et Jean-Louis se connaissent très bien.	_______	_______
3. En été, il y a beaucoup de touristes dans cet hôtel.	_______	_______
4. L'hôtel est très chic et très moderne.	_______	_______
5. Claire est intelligente et opiniâtre (*opinionated*).	_______	_______
6. Jean-Louis est détendu (*relaxed*) et gentil.	_______	_______
7. Claire a l'habitude de loger dans des hôtels de luxe.	_______	_______
8. Philippe Aucoin est un hôtelier très professionnel.	_______	_______

i Langue

Vous rappelez-vous les conjugaisons des **verbes irréguliers** suivants : **être, avoir, aller, faire, venir, vouloir** et **pouvoir** ? Si non, mémorisez leurs conjugaisons avant de continuer !

- **être** (*to be*) : je suis, tu es, il/elle/on est, nous sommes, vous êtes, ils/elles sont
- **avoir** (*to have*) : j'ai, tu as, il/elle/on a, nous avons, vous avez, ils/elles ont
- **aller** (*to go*) : je vais, tu vas, il/elle/on va, nous allons, vous allez, ils/elles vont
- **faire** (*to do, to make*) : je fais, tu fais, il/elle/on fait, nous faisons, vous faites, ils/elles font
- **venir** (*to come*) : je viens, tu viens, il/elle/on vient, nous venons, vous venez, ils/elles viennent
- **vouloir** (*to want*) : je veux, tu veux, il/elle/on veut, nous voulons, vous voulez, ils/elles veulent
- **pouvoir** (*to be able, can*) : je peux, tu peux, il/elle/on peut, nous pouvons, vous pouvez, ils/elles peuvent

1.7 Vous êtes d'où ? Jean-Louis essaie de deviner la nationalité de Claire, et il mentionne plusieurs possibilités. **Devinez la nationalité, la langue ou le nom du lieu** qui manquent dans le schéma suivant. Ne vous inquiétez pas si vous ne savez pas toutes les réponses. Vous en apprendrez plus au sujet de ces cultures dans les prochains chapitres. Discutez de vos réponses avec la classe.

Nationalité ou identité	Langue(s) parlée(s)	Pays/région
français(e)	le français	la France
américain(e), acadien(ne)/créole	? ? ?	? ? ?
? ? ?	? ? ?	le Québec
martiniquais(e)	? ? ?	? ? ?
? ? ?	le wolof, le français	le Sénégal
algérien(ne)	l'arabe, le français	? ? ?
? ? ?	le français, l'italien, l'allemand	? ? ?

1.8 Votre identité **Posez des questions** à un partenaire et **répondez** à votre tour.

1. Quel est votre nom ?	—Je m'appelle. . .
2. Pouvez-vous l'épeler, s'il vous plaît ?	—Oui, c'est. . .
3. D'où venez-vous ?	—Je viens de (+ *nom d'une ville*). . .
4. Quelle est votre nationalité ?	—Je suis. . .
5. Quelles langues parlez-vous ?	—Je parle. . .

1.9 Les voyages Regardez les mots de vocabulaire qui suivent. Dans chaque ligne, il y a un mot qui n'appartient pas au groupe de mots. **Entourez le mot qui ne va pas** avec les autres et essayez d'expliquer pourquoi. Attention : il y a parfois plusieurs bonnes réponses. Il faut justifier votre choix !

1. la valise	le sac à dos	le livre	les bagages
2. le taxi	le train	la voiture	l'avion
3. l'escalier	l'ascenseur	le trottoir (*sidewalk*)	le remonte-pentes (*ski lift*)
4. l'appareil photo	le billet d'avion	le passeport	le permis de conduire
5. une chambre	une salle de bains	un balcon	une salle d'exercices
6. un restaurant	un monument	un musée	une boutique
7. luxueux	gratuit	bon marché	cher
8. des espèces (*cash*)	un chèque	une carte de crédit	un chèque de voyage

Pour aller plus loin : CULTURE

ACTIVITÉ B : Trouvez un hôtel de luxe à la Nouvelle-Orléans ! Consultez votre cahier électronique !

1.10 Le courriel (*e-mail*) Dans sa chambre, Claire prend une douche rafraîchissante et puis branche (*plug in*) son ordinateur portable (*laptop computer*). Elle connecte facilement à son fournisseur d'accès à l'internet (*Internet service provider*) en composant un des numéros de téléphone locaux que la compagnie fournit aux clients voyageant à l'étranger. Elle écrit un petit message au courriel (un e-mail) à sa sœur pour la rassurer qu'elle est bien arrivée à sa destination. **Remplissez les blancs** avec un mot ou une expression convenable de la liste suivante.

bagages	**balcon**	**chambre**	**client**	**climatisée**	**cour**
gratuit	**hôtel**	**hôtelier**	**salle**	**taxi**	

Chère Marie,

Salut ! Je suis bien arrivée à la Nouvelle-Orléans ! Air Canada n'a pas perdu mes ______________, et j'ai facilement trouvé un ______________ à l'aéroport pour venir en ville. L'______________ est adorable ! Un vrai bâtiment historique du 18ème siècle. Il y a une grande ______________ jaune et une ______________ ensoleillée au rez-de-chaussée. Ma ______________ est au 2ème étage, et j'ai un ______________ avec vue sur les rues du Vieux Carré. Les gens ici sont gentils. L'______________, qui s'appelle Philippe Aucoin, est très sympa. Il y a un Français qui est aussi un ______________ et loge dans cet hôtel comme moi. Ici, il fait très chaud, mais ma chambre est ______________. Ce soir, je vais boire du champagne dans la cour (imagine, c'est ______________ !) et je vais me reposer. Si je reçois du courrier (*regular mail*) de l'université, dis-le-moi tout de suite.

J'attends une réponse à propos de ma bourse (*scholarship/fellowship*) pour l'année prochaine. Amuse-toi à la campagne et embrasse Maman et Papa pour moi. À bientôt !

Gros bisous, Claire

1.11 Vocabulaire personnel Pensez à vos voyages (passés ou futurs) et, pour chaque catégorie, **faites une liste de cinq à dix mots** importants que vous pouvez utiliser pour décrire vos propres voyages. Consultez un dictionnaire si nécessaire.

1. Les moyens de transport : comment voyagez-vous ?
2. Les bagages : qu'apportez-vous quand vous voyagez ?
3. Le logement : où vous logez-vous ? comment est votre logement ? comment le payez-vous ?
4. Le tourisme : que faites-vous pour vous amuser ? où allez-vous ?

la Louisiane

Rencontrez une Louisianaise ! Regardez la vidéo et consultez votre cahier d'activités !

1.12 L'heure du champagne Claire descend à la cour à 7h du soir pour prendre un verre de champagne avec les autres clients de l'hôtel. Là, elle revoit Jean-Louis qui parle avec un homme aux cheveux gris. Choisissez un des mots ou une des expressions entre parenthèses et **lisez le dialogue à haute voix** par groupes de trois personnes. Quand vous voyez « ? ? ?», vous pouvez imaginer votre propre expression.

JEAN-LOUIS : Bonsoir, Madame Plouffe ! Quelle coïncidence !
CLAIRE : (Bonsoir ! / Vous encore !) Je vous dérange ?
JEAN-LOUIS : Pas du tout ! Claire Plouffe, (je vous présente / permettez-moi de vous présenter) Henri Hébert. C'est un vrai Cajun qui vient de Lafayette pour affaires.
CLAIRE : (Très heureuse de faire votre connaissance. / Enchantée.)
HENRI : (Bonsoir, madame. / Enchanté, madame.)
JEAN-LOUIS : Madame Plouffe est ici pour faire des recherches, c'est ça ?
CLAIRE : Enfin, oui, mais comment. . . ?
HENRI : Excusez-moi. J'ai un rendez-vous à 7h30. Il faut vraiment que je parte. C'était un plaisir (de faire votre connaissance / de vous parler). Amusez-vous bien en Louisiane !
CLAIRE : (Au revoir / Bonne soirée !)
JEAN-LOUIS : (Au revoir / À bientôt !) *Il regarde Claire.* Vous allez bien ce soir ?
CLAIRE : (Très bien, merci. / Pas mal. / Je suis un peu fatiguée, mais ça va.) Et vous ?
JEAN-LOUIS : Ça va bien. Il fait (chaud/froid/beau) ce soir, non ?
CLAIRE : Oui. C'est (rafraîchissant/insupportable/ ? ? ?).
JEAN-LOUIS : Que pensez-vous de (cet hôtel / la Nouvelle-Orléans) ?
CLAIRE : C'est (charmant/passionnant/intéressant). J'adore (voyager / visiter les monuments historiques / ? ? ?).

Langue

Pour **être poli(e)**, on emploie parfois **le conditionnel** et non l'indicatif. Par exemple, au lieu de dire «je veux» (impoli), on dit «je voudrais» (poli). Voici quelques verbes souvent utilisés au conditionnel pour exprimer la politesse :

- **vouloir** (*want → would like*) : je voudrais, tu voudrais, il/elle/on voudrait, nous voudrions, vous voudriez, ils/elles voudraient
  — Je voudrais aller à la rue Dauphine.
- **pouvoir** (*can → could*) : je pourrais, tu pourrais, il/elle/on pourrait, nous pourrions, vous pourriez, ils/elles pourraient
  — Pourriez-vous m'aider ?
- **savoir** (*know → would know*) : je saurais, tu saurais, il/elle/on saurait, nous saurions, vous sauriez, ils/elles sauraient
  — Sauriez-vous où se trouve la rue Dauphine ?

N'oubliez pas que pour être poli, il faut employer souvent **des expressions** comme **merci**, **excuse(z)-moi** et **s'il vous/te plaît**. En plus, il faut vous adresser aux gens que vous ne connaissez pas bien en employant **monsieur** ou **madame**, et en les vouvoyant ! Vous allez en apprendre plus sur le conditionnel au Chapitre 7.

JEAN-LOUIS : Moi aussi. Mais je déteste (visiter les musées / aller aux bars / ? ? ?). Écoutez, je vais dîner chez Olivier ce soir. C'est un très bon restaurant créole. Voudriez-vous m'accompagner ?

CLAIRE : (C'est tentant / J'aimerais beaucoup / ? ? ?), mais j'ai déjà mangé et je voudrais (me reposer / être seule / ? ? ?) ce soir.

JEAN-LOUIS : Ah, bon. Une autre fois, peut-être ?

CLAIRE : Oui, (bien sûr / peut-être / faut pas rêver).

JEAN-LOUIS : Écoute, je n'aime pas trop les formalités. On se tutoie ?

CLAIRE : (D'accord ! / Pourquoi pas ?)

JEAN-LOUIS : Alors, puis-je t'offrir un autre verre de champagne ?

CLAIRE : Non, merci. Je suis (très fatiguée / déjà ivre / un peu malade / ? ? ?). Je vais monter à ma chambre, mais je te souhaite (une bonne soirée / un bon dîner / ? ? ?). Bonsoir.

JEAN-LOUIS : Salut, Claire. À demain.

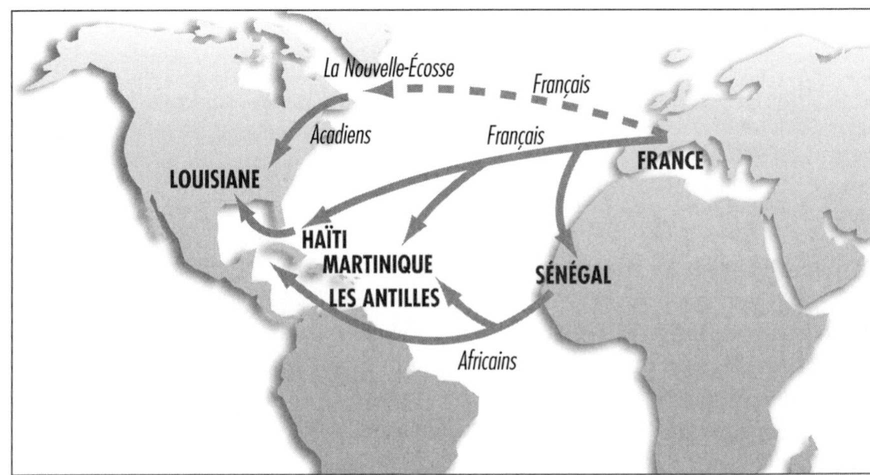

L'immigration en Louisiane au 18ème siècle.

Culture

Créole ou Cajun ? Les **Acadiens**, que beaucoup de gens appellent les **Cajuns**, habitent les paroisses acadiennes et sont les descendants des Français-Acadiens qui ont été exilés de l'Acadie (aujourd'hui la Nouvelle-Écosse, au Canada) en 1755 par les Anglais. Ils ont des traditions, une musique et un dialecte français qui leur sont particuliers. Il y a 22 paroisses acadiennes qui se trouvent à l'est et au nord-est de la Nouvelle-Orléans, près de la ville de Lafayette. Les Acadiens ont des origines françaises, mais culturellement ils se distinguent des Créoles. Les **Créoles** étaient pour la plupart les descendants des Français venus directement de la France pour établir la colonie de la Louisiane et la ville de la Nouvelle-Orléans en 1718. Parmi eux, il y avait des gouverneurs, des entrepreneurs, des criminels et des prostituées (envoyés en exil comme châtiment), des réfugiés des îles antillaises (aux Caraïbes) et des esclaves africains. Les Créoles, alors, peuvent être d'origine française aussi bien que d'origine espagnole, africaine, allemande, anglaise ou bien amérindienne. Bien sûr, les **Amérindiens** vivaient en Louisiane bien avant la «découverte» de cette terre par les Européens.

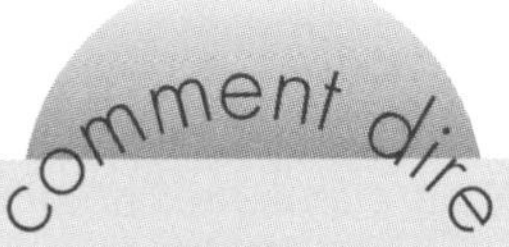

les rencontres

	Formal	Informal
Greetings	Bonjour/Bonsoir, monsieur/ madame/mademoiselle.	Salut !/Bonjour./Bonsoir.
Small talk	Comment allez-vous ? Vous allez bien ?	Ça va ? Tu vas bien ?
	Très bien, merci. Et vous ?	Ça va. Pas mal. Et toi ?
	Il fait beau/chaud/froid/frais/mauvais, n'est-ce pas ? Quel(le) chaleur/vent/pluie !	Quoi de neuf ? Qu'est-ce qui se passe ?
	Voudriez-vous. . . ?	Ça te dit de. . . ?
	Pourriez-vous me dire si. . . ?	Tu peux me dire si. . . ?
Introductions	Permettez-moi de me présenter. Je m'appelle. . . , et vous ?	Salut, je suis. . . , et toi ?
	Je vous présente. . . (mon collègue, etc.)	Voici. . . (mon ami, etc.)
	Enchanté(e). Très heureux/se de faire votre connaissance.	Salut. Ça va ?
	On s'est déjà rencontré.	On se connaît déjà.
Fillers	Eh. . . Alors. . . En somme. . . Enfin. . .	Eh. . . Alors. . . Bon, ben. . .
Good-byes	Au revoir, monsieur/madame/ mademoiselle.	Salut ! Ciao ! Au revoir !
	À bientôt ! À la prochaine ! À demain !	À bientôt ! À la prochaine ! À demain !

Culture

Tutoyer ou vouvoyer ? Le verbe **tutoyer** veut dire utiliser le «tu» familier avec quelqu'un. L'autre possibilité est de **vouvoyer**, ou utiliser le «vous» formel. En général, on tutoie les amis, la famille et les parents, et les enfants. On vouvoie les personnes qu'on ne connaît pas très bien (les inconnus et les gens qu'on vient de rencontrer dans une situation formelle) et les personnes à qui on veut témoigner du respect en raison soit de leur âge soit de leur statut social soit de la distance que l'on veut imposer (les professeurs, les policiers, les juges, les gens qui travaillent dans les magasins, etc.). Bien sûr, il n'y a pas de règle fixe, et l'usage du «tu» ou du «vous» dépend des circonstances de chaque rencontre (des traditions culturelles de la région, des goûts individuels, etc.). Si vous n'êtes pas sûr(e), utilisez le «vous» ou écoutez bien et utilisez ce que l'autre personne utilise avec vous.

1.13 À vous Imaginez que vous êtes dans les situations suivantes. Que dites-vous ? Avec un(e) partenaire, **écrivez des petits dialogues** pour chaque situation. Jouez des scènes pour la classe.

1. Vous êtes dans l'avion en direction de la Nouvelle-Orléans. Présentez-vous au passager assis près de vous.
2. Bavardez avec le chauffeur de taxi qui vous amène à l'hôtel.
3. Parlez à un enfant qui joue dans la cour de votre hôtel.
4. Parlez à l'hôtelier que vous croisez dans l'escalier.
5. Vous allez au restaurant avec Jean-Louis quand vous voyez un ami que vous avez perdu de vue depuis longtemps. Présentez-vous et bavardez.

1.14 Circulez et bavardez Imaginez que vous êtes dans la cour de l'Hôtel Le Moyne à l'heure du champagne. Chaque étudiant dans la classe est un client de l'hôtel (vous pouvez inventer des personnages si vous voulez). Vous ne connaissez personne, sauf l'hôtelier Philippe Aucoin (joué par le professeur), mais vous voulez rencontrer des gens et vous faire des amis. Circulez dans la salle, présentez-vous aux gens, faites des présentations et bavardez. Soyez poli(e), mais vous pouvez être formel(le) ou familier(ère) ! **Essayez de rencontrer toutes les personnes** à la soirée.

MODÈLE : Bonsoir, madame. Permettez-moi de me présenter.
Je m'appelle. . .

ou Il fait chaud ce soir, n'est-ce pas ?

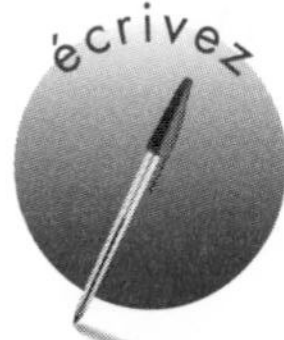

À l'écrit *première étape*

1.15 Une carte postale Vous êtes à la Nouvelle-Orléans. Choisissez un étudiant dans votre classe de français et écrivez-lui sur une feuille de papier **le texte d'une carte postale** que vous allez lui envoyer. N'oubliez pas de :

- saluer.
- parler du temps qu'il fait.
- donner votre opinion de l'hôtel.
- dire ce que vous aimez, ce que vous détestez à la Nouvelle-Orléans.
- terminer avec un adieu.

Échangez vos cartes postales. Offrez des corrections possibles et écrivez une courte réponse à votre camarade de classe.

L'excursion

Épisode 2

Le célèbre Café du Monde à la Nouvelle-Orléans.

Structures *les articles définis et indéfinis*

1.16 Au petit déjeuner Au petit déjeuner, le matin après son arrivée, Claire discute avec l'hôtelier Philippe Aucoin. Lisez le dialogue en analysant l'usage des **articles définis** (le, la, les) et **indéfinis** (un, une, des). Dans quelles circonstances utilise-t-on les articles définis ? et les articles indéfinis ? Essayez de décrire les circonstances vous-mêmes. Ensuite, lisez l'explication **(Comment faire)** ci-dessous et analysez encore l'usage des articles.

PHILIPPE : Bonjour, madame. Vous avez bien dormi ?

CLAIRE : Bonjour. Oui, très bien ! **Le** lit dans ma chambre est parfait, et **la** vue du balcon est superbe.

PHILIPPE : Je peux vous servir **un** café, **un** thé ou **un** jus de fruit ?

CLAIRE : **Un** café au lait, s'il vous plaît. Je ne peux pas me réveiller sans café **le** matin. J'adore **le** café.

PHILIPPE : Très bien. Voudriez-vous **des** beignets ? **Les** beignets sont **une** spécialité nouvelle-orléannaise. Ou bien voudriez-vous **des** œufs ? **une** omelette ?

CLAIRE : Je déteste **les** œufs, mais j'aimerais bien essayer **un** beignet. Et qu'avez-vous comme fruits ?

Culture

Un **beignet** est une pâte frite qui ressemble à un *doughnut* rectangulaire et sans trou. C'est une spécialité qu'on trouve partout à la Nouvelle-Orléans. Au **Café du Monde**, près du fleuve Mississippi, on mange des beignets couverts de sucre en poudre avec un bon café au lait, et on écoute les musiciens qui jouent sur la place Jackson.

PHILIPPE : Nous avons beaucoup de fruits ce matin. Comme vous voyez, il y a **des** oranges, **des** poires, et il me reste **une** pêche. Pourtant, il n'y a plus de bananes.

CLAIRE : Je prendrai **la** pêche, s'il vous plaît.

PHILIPPE : Excellent. Vous parlez très bien français, madame. Est-ce votre langue maternelle ?

CLAIRE : Oui, **le** français est **la** langue officielle du Québec, mais nous avons **un** accent un peu différent de celui des Français, et nous employons **des** mots différents de temps en temps.

PHILIPPE : Ah, oui ! **Le** Québec, c'est comme **la** Louisiane. C'est **une** ancienne colonie française, n'est-ce pas ?

CLAIRE : Oui, c'est vrai. Connaissez-vous bien **l'**histoire des francophones de la Louisiane ?

PHILIPPE : Pas très très bien, mais c'est **un** sujet qui m'intéresse. Allez ! Je vais vous chercher votre petit déjeuner. Je reviens tout de suite.

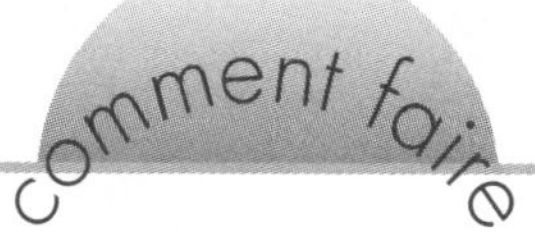

les articles définis et indéfinis

Articles are used differently in French than in English and often do not translate easily. In choosing between the *definite article* **(l'article défini : le, la, les)** and the *indefinite article* **(l'article indéfini : un, une, des)**, it may be useful to think about two concepts: (1) whether the noun is *identifiable* in a given context and (2) whether the noun represents *the generic whole group* or a subset of a group.

Is it *identifiable*?

Yes! Use the *definite article* **(le, la, les)** to talk about *identifiable* nouns. A noun is *identifiable* if you can point to it in front of you, if it has been referred to previously in conversation, or if it is simply known to the speakers in a particular context. For example, in the conversation above, the following nouns *are readily identifiable* by the two speakers:

- **Le** lit dans ma chambre. . . **la** vue du balcon
- Je prendrai **la** pêche

No! Use the *indefinite article* **(un, une, des)** to talk about nouns that are *not identifiable* in the context and exist only as an abstract concept in the minds of the speakers. For example:

- Je peux vous servir **un** café, **un** thé ou **un** jus de fruit ?
- **Un** café au lait
- Voudriez-vous **des** beignets. . . ? **une** omelette ?

Does it represent *the generic whole group*?

Yes! Use the *definite article* **(le, la, les)** to talk about *the whole group* or *whole class* in a generic sense. In other words, use the *definite article* to refer to all of the members of the group or all of the elements of the class in general. For example, in the conversation above, the following nouns represent the *generic whole group*:

- J'aime **le** café (*all coffee, in general*)
- Je déteste **les** œufs (*all eggs, in general*)

No! Use the *indefinite article* **(un, une, des)** to talk about nouns that represent a subset of a generic whole group. For example:

- Il y a **des** oranges (*not the whole generic group of oranges, but a subset of oranges*)
- Nous employons **des** mot différents (*not all the different words that exist, but a subset of different words*)

Note some special uses of the *definite article*!

The *definite article* is often used:

- with reference to *times or seasons*: Je ne peux pas me réveiller sans café **le** matin (*every morning, in the morning in general*). C'est **l'**été (*It's summer*).
- with reference to *languages*: **Le** français est la langue officielle. However, *no article* is used before a language with the verb **parler**: Vous parlez français.
- with reference to *geographic locations*: **le** Québec (the province), **la** Louisiane, **la** Nouvelle-Orléans, **les** États-Unis, **la** France. However, normally, cities *do not* take an article: je vais à Paris, je vais à Québec (the city). Often geographic locations require prepositions: Je vais en Louisiane, j'habite au Canada. You will review the use of prepositions with geographic locations in Chapter 5.
- in contractions *with the prepositions* **à** (*to/at* → **au, aux**) and **de** (*from/of* → **du, des**): un accent différent **des** Français, **au** petit déjeuner. Do not confuse the contraction **des** (**de** + **les**, *of the* / *from the*) with the *indefinite article* **des** (*some*): Nous venons **des** États-Unis. Nous avons **des** beignets.

Note some special uses of the preposition *de*!

The preposition **de** is used:

- *after a negative*, in place of an *indefinite article*: Il n'y a **pas de** bananes. (However, the *definite article* does not change after the negative: Je n'aime pas **le** café.)
- *after expressions of quantity* **(beaucoup de, un peu de, un kilo de, un verre de)**: Nous avons beaucoup **de** fruits.
- *after a noun*, to specify *a particular variety or type* of something: un jus **de** fruits.
- *before a plural noun that is qualified by a preceding adjective*: Ce sont **de grands** beignets. (vs. Ce sont **des** beignets énormes.)

The *partitive* **(le partitif : du, de la, de l')** is used exclusively with mass nouns; that is, nouns that cannot be counted and exist in mass or as an idea only: **du** sucre, **de la** joie, etc. You will review the use of the partitive in Chapter 2.

For more examples, analyze the use of articles in Activity 16 (above) or in the opening dialogue in Episode 1.

1.17 Au petit déjeuner (*suite*) Le petit déjeuner continue... Remplissez les blancs avec un **article défini** (**le, la, les**), un **article indéfini** (**un, une, des**) ou **de** tout seul.

PHILIPPE : Voici trois beignets, __________ pêche et __________ café au lait.

CLAIRE : Merci bien, monsieur. Est-ce que je pourrais avoir __________ jus d'orange aussi ?

PHILIPPE : Oui, certainement.

CLAIRE : Où sont __________ autres clients ce matin ?

PHILIPPE : Ils ne se lèvent pas de si bonne heure. __________ clients aiment dormir tard, en général, parce que __________ bars ferment très tard et on fait la fête toute __________ nuit.

CLAIRE : Pas moi. Je dois travailler.

PHILIPPE : Ah, ouais ! Si je me souviens bien, vous cherchez quelque chose.

CLAIRE : Oui, je cherche __________ livre.

PHILIPPE : C'est simple, alors. Vous trouverez __________ livres de toute sorte à __________ bibliothèque municipale. Ils ont beaucoup __________ livres là-bas.

CLAIRE : Non, je cherche __________ manuscrit très rare du 18ème siècle qui ne se trouve pas à __________ bibliothèque. Je crois qu'__________ personne créole qui habite ici à la Nouvelle-Orléans possède __________ seule copie qui existe au monde. À __________ bibliothèque, je vais faire de la recherche généalogique et étudier __________ famille de François Fontenot, __________ homme qui a immigré en Louisiane en 1792. C'est __________ homme qui a apporté le manuscrit aux États-Unis. Enfin, c'est ce que je crois.

PHILIPPE : Ça a l'air bien intéressant, votre histoire. J'espère que vous réussirez à trouver __________ manuscrit que vous cherchez.

1.18 Et vous ? Imaginez que vous prenez le petit déjeuner à l'Hôtel Le Moyne aussi. Que dites-vous pour bavarder avec Philippe Aucoin ? Faites des questions ou des phrases avec les verbes et les noms suivants. Attention à l'usage des articles définis et indéfinis !

MODÈLES : J'aime **la** piscine.
Je voudrais **un** guide touristique.

J'aime. . .	chambre
J'ai beaucoup. . .	taxi
Je voudrais. . .	valises
Il y a. . .	livres
Je déteste. . .	musées
Je n'ai pas. . .	balcon
C'est. . .	musique jazz
Voilà. . .	clés
Avez-vous. . . ?	piscine
Ce sont. . .	portefeuille
	guide touristique
	? ? ? (à vous !)

Structures *la négation*

1.19 Les haricots sont salés Deux jours plus tard, Claire parle avec Philippe Aucoin. Elle n'a pas encore réussi à trouver les descendants de François Fontenot. Mais Philippe est optimiste. Il voit toujours le bon côté des choses. **Transformez ces phrases** négatives en phrases affirmatives en éliminant la négation. Ajoutez des mots, s'il le faut. En analysant vos changements, pouvez-vous décrire comment fonctionnent les expressions négatives avec (a) le présent, (b) l'impératif, (c) les verbes réfléchis, (d) l'infinitif et (e) l'inversion ?

MODÈLE : Ce **n'**est **pas du tout** facile ! →
C'est très facile !

1. Vous **n'**allez **pas** trouver le manuscrit.
2. **Ne** mangez **ni** beignets **ni** fruits de mer !
3. Jean-Louis **n'**est **plus** ici.
4. Vous **ne** vous connaissez **pas encore**.
5. Je préfère **ne jamais** travailler le week-end.
6. Il **n'**y a **rien** à faire à Lafayette ce week-end.
7. **Personne ne** peut louer de voiture.
8. **Ne** vous souvenez-vous **pas** de notre devise : Laissez les bons temps rouler ?
9. Vous **ne** passez **que** six jours à la Nouvelle-Orléans.

la négation

To make a phrase *negative*, add a negative expression to the phrase. Common negatives are:

ne. . . pas	*not*
ne. . . pas encore	*not yet* (*opposite:* **déjà**, *already*)
ne. . . pas du tout	*not at all* (*opposite:* **très** *or* **tout à fait**, *quite/completely*)
ne. . . plus	*no longer* (*opposite:* **toujours**, *still*)
ne. . . jamais	*never* (*opposite:* **toujours**, *always* or **souvent**, *often*)
ne. . . personne	*nobody, no one* (*opposite:* **tout le monde**, *everyone*)
ne. . . rien	*nothing* (*opposite:* **tout**, *everything* or **beaucoup**, *a lot*)
ne. . . ni. . . ni	*neither . . . nor* (*opposite:* **et**, *and*)
ne. . . que	*only* (*opposite: a quantity*)

Placement of negative expressions:

- With a *simple verb phrase*, place the **ne** before the verb and the **pas**, or other expression, just after the verb: Tu **ne** travailles **pas**. Tu **ne** connais **personne**.
- With *neither . . . nor*, place the **ne** before the verb and each **ni** before the term it modifies, without using any articles: Tu **ne** veux **ni** beignets **ni** café au lait. Il **ne** veut **ni** parler **ni** chanter.
- With *inversion*, place the **ne** before the verb and the **pas**, or other expression, after the subject: **Ne** travailles-tu **pas** ?
- With *pronominal verbs* (reflexives) *or verbs that are preceded by object pronouns*, place the **ne** after the subject and the **pas**, or other expression, after the verb: Tu **ne** te lèves **pas** tôt. Il **ne** vous embête **pas**.
- With *inverted pronominal verbs*, place the **ne** before the pronoun and the **pas**, or other expression, after the subject: **Ne** te lèves-tu **pas** tôt ?
- With *compound verbs or infinitives*, place the negative expression *around* the conjugated verb, following the usual rules above, or *before* the infinitive (or before the pronoun + infinitive), depending on which verb you want to negate: Je **ne** veux **pas** travailler demain (*I don't want to work tomorrow*), Je veux **ne pas** travailler (*I want not to work at all*), Je **ne** décide **pas** de me lever tard (*I don't decide to get up late*), Je décide de **ne pas** me lever tard (*I decide not to get up late*).
- When the negatives **personne** or **rien** are the *subject* of the sentence, they precede the **ne** and verb: **Personne ne** travaille ici (*Nobody works here*), **Rien ne** se passe ici (*Nothing is happening here*).

1.20 Un autre matin Un jour, Jean-Louis arrive pour le petit déjeuner et s'assied près de Claire. Il essaie de bavarder avec elle, mais elle est préoccupée par son projet de recherche. Alors, il commence une conversation avec un autre client qui est de mauvaise humeur ce matin. **Transformez les phrases** à la forme négative en employant une expression négative. Variez les expressions négatives.

MODÈLE : Il fait déjà trop chaud aujourd'hui. →
Il ne fait pas encore trop chaud.

1. Je voyage souvent.
2. J'aime me promener dans le Vieux Carré.
3. Le prix de ma chambre est tout à fait raisonnable.
4. Les chambres sont grandes et climatisées.
5. L'hôtelier connaît tout le monde.
6. Aimez-vous les beignets ?
7. Philippe se réveille toujours à 5h du matin.
8. Il sert 50 beignets chaque matin.
9. J'adore bavarder et discuter avec les autres clients.
10. Vous levez-vous toujours aussi tôt ?

1.21 Ne faites pas ça ! **Faites une liste de six activités** qu'on ne fait pas normalement quand on voyage. Puis, **transformez vos phrases en questions** et posez les questions à un partenaire.

MODÈLE : Quand on voyage, on ne travaille pas.
—Ne travaillez-vous pas quand vous voyagez ?
—Non, je ne travaille jamais quand je voyage. *ou*
—Si, je travaille tout le temps quand je voyage !

Structures *l'interrogatif*

1.22 Claire pose des questions Vendredi, après une semaine de travail à la bibliothèque, toujours sans succès, Claire rentre à l'hôtel. Elle pose des questions à Philippe. Bien sûr, Jean-Louis, qui arrive à la réception au même moment, écoute attentivement. **Transformez chaque question en une phrase déclarative**. Vous pouvez simplement rayer (*cross out*) des mots ou des signes de ponctuation, ou vous pouvez récrire la phrase. En analysant vos changements, pouvez-vous décrire **cinq façons de poser une question simple ?**

MODÈLE : Ne travaillez-vous pas quand vous voyagez ? →
Vous ne travaillez pas quand vous voyagez.

1. Est-ce qu'il y a un guichet automatique (*ATM*) près d'ici ?
2. Le guichet automatique n'est pas dans la rue Bourbon ?
3. Il va pleuvoir demain, n'est-ce pas ?
4. Y a-t-il un festival à Lafayette ce week-end ?
5. Est-ce que l'agence de location de voitures (*car rental agency*) est loin d'ici ?
6. Vous êtes né à la Nouvelle-Orléans, n'est-ce pas ?
7. Ne connaissez-vous pas quelqu'un qui s'appelle Fontenot ?
8. Je peux laisser mes affaires dans ma chambre, non ?

l'interrogatif (questions simples)

To form a *yes/no question*, you may use one of the following methods:

- Use *intonation* by adding a question mark at the end of the sentence and raising your intonation near the end: Vous savez l'heure ? Il parle français ? Note that in casual conversation, most speakers use simple *intonation* to ask a question.
- Use *inversion* by placing the subject pronoun after the verb and connecting the two with a hyphen: Avez-vous l'heure ? Parle-t-il français ? (Remember that if a verb ends in a vowel and the subject begins with a vowel, you must add a **-t-** to facilitate pronunciation.) Note that *inversion* is often used in written French or formal conversations but is less frequently used in casual conversation (except with certain formulaic phrases like **Comment allez-vous ?**).
- Use **est-ce que** by inserting it at the beginning of the sentence: **Est-ce que** vous savez l'heure ? **Est-ce qu'**il parle français ?
- Use **n'est-ce pas** by adding it onto the end of the sentence: Il est huit heures, **n'est-ce pas ?** Il parle français, **n'est-ce pas ?** Note that **n'est-ce pas** is used when asking for confirmation (yes or no) and would be inappropriate after an information question.
- Use *informal expressions* like **hein ?** or **non ?** in very casual speaking situations by adding one to the end of the sentence: Il est huit heures, **non ?** Il parle français, **hein ?**

In Chapter 2, you will review the use of the interrogative expressions in forming information questions with **qui, que, quand, où, pourquoi,** and **comment**.

1.23 L'interrogatoire Samedi matin, au petit déjeuner, Jean-Louis pose des questions à Claire juste avant son départ pour la ville de Lafayette. Avec un partenaire, **jouez une scène entre Jean-Louis et Claire**.

a. **Vous êtes Jean-Louis**. Changez les mots donnés en questions. (N'oubliez pas les articles !) Variez la forme de chaque question que vous posez à votre partenaire.
b. **Vous êtes Claire**, et vous n'aimez pas les questions de Jean-Louis. Répondez à chaque question par une autre question. Variez la forme de vos questions.

MODÈLE : Tu / aimes / beignets →

a. **Tu aimes les beignets, non ?**
b. **Oui. Est-ce que tu aimes les beignets, toi ?**

1. Tu / aimes / cuisine / créole
2. Tu / restes / à / bibliothèque / toute la journée
3. Tu / étudies / littérature française
4. Tu / cherches / livre particulier
5. Ton séjour / est / agréable

la Louisiane

Quelles questions poseriez-vous à une Louisianaise ? Regardez la vidéo et consultez votre cahier d'activités !

1.24 Et vous ? Est-ce que vous avez des questions à poser à Philippe Aucoin ? Par groupes de deux ou trois personnes, **écrivez six questions** à propos de l'hôtel, des clients (Claire, Jean-Louis ou Henri Hébert), ou bien de la Nouvelle-Orléans. **Échangez vos questions avec un autre groupe et répondez** aux questions que vous recevez. Utilisez votre imagination !

MODÈLE : **—Est-ce que Jean-Louis est agréable ?**

—Oui, il est assez agréable.

Avant d'écouter

1.25 Avant l'excursion En petits groupes, posez les questions suivantes et répondez selon vos goûts personnels.

1. Aimez-vous la musique ? Quel type de musique : le rock, le hip-hop, le jazz, le blues, la musique classique, la techno, le rap, la musique alternative, le reggae, le zydeco ? Pourquoi ?
2. Aimez-vous danser ? Pourquoi ou pourquoi pas ? Sur quelle musique aimez-vous danser ?
3. Où est-ce que vous dansez ? Peut-on danser à une fête, à une fête de mariage, dans un bar, en boîte de nuit, dans les rues, dans la salle de classe, à la bibliothèque. . . ?
4. Pourquoi est-ce qu'on danse : pour rencontrer des gens, pour se détendre, pour bouger, pour s'amuser. . . ?
5. Aimez-vous lire ? Quels types de livres préférez-vous : des romans d'amour, des romans policiers, des romans de suspense, de la science-fiction, des biographies ?
6. Quel est le titre de votre roman préféré ? Pourquoi aimez-vous ce livre ?

Culture

Un **fais do-do** est une fête traditionnelle dans le sud de la Louisiane où on écoute de la musique cajun et **zydeco**, et on danse le «two-step» et la valse. Selon la tradition, les familles viennent à la fête avec des petits enfants qui «font do-do» (qui s'endorment) pendant que les parents et les jeunes adultes dansent et s'amusent. Le zydeco est une musique créole influencée par la musique traditionnelle cajun. Le nom **zydeco** vient d'une chanson célèbre, «Les haricots sont pas salés», et «le zydeco» est dérivé de la prononciation cajun de «les haricots».

écoutez

L'excursion

Après une semaine aux archives de la bibliothèque municipale, Claire n'a toujours pas de succès. Elle n'arrive pas à trouver les documents nécessaires pour identifier les descendants vivants de François Fontenot, un homme qui a immigré à la Nouvelle-Orléans en 1792 et la dernière personne à posséder le manuscrit. Quelle malchance ! Pour se changer les idées, Claire décide de faire une excursion à la ville de Lafayette pour mieux connaître la culture acadienne. Elle loue un «char» (le mot québécois pour une voiture) et conduit deux heures et demie pour arriver à Lafayette, une ville au centre des paroisses acadiennes. C'est au moment de la Fête des Acadiens, et il y a un «fais do-do» ce soir. Pourquoi ne pas rester la nuit, pense-t-elle. Ça pourrait être amusant. Ce qu'elle ne sait pas, c'est que Jean-Louis a eu la même idée qu'elle. . .

Maintenant, **écoutez le dialogue sur votre CD**. Consultez le vocabulaire, lisez les notes culturelles pour mieux comprendre le dialogue, et puis répondez aux questions suivantes.

VOCABULAIRE

Les voyages	
se détendre	*to relax, unwind*
se reposer	*to relax, rest*
faire une excursion	*to take a short trip*
faire do-do	*to go night-night (fam.)*
un fais do-do	*a dance party (reg. Louisiana)*
louer	*to rent*
conduire	*to drive*
une paroisse	*a parish; a county (in Louisiana)*

La littérature	
écrire une thèse	*to write a thesis*
lire	*to read*
un descendant	*descendant*
la recherche	*research*
un auteur	*author*
un siècle; le 18ème siècle	*a century; the 18th century*
la littérature	*literature*
un bouquin	*book (slang)*
un livre	*book*
un roman	*novel*
un roman policier	*detective novel*
un roman épistolaire	*epistolary novel (novel composed of letters)*
la science-fiction	*science fiction*

Le travail et les vacances	
s'ennuyer (de)	*to get bored (with)*
danser	*to dance*
la chanson	*song*
se tromper (de)	*to be mistaken (about)*
être bien habillé(e)	*to be well-dressed*
un boulot	*job, work (slang)*
les grandes vacances	*summer vacation*
exprès	*on purpose*
le costume	*(man's) suit*
les affaires (*f. pl.*)	*business*
les yeux (*m. pl.*), un œil	*eyes, an eye*
un copain, une copine	*friend; boy/girlfriend*
ravissant(e)	*ravishing, beautiful*
un(e) fan(atique)	*fan, lover of something*

Langue

En principe, les étudiants de français langue étrangère apprennent à parler et à écrire un **français standard**. Or, en réalité, il existe plusieurs **registres linguistiques** et **niveaux de langue**, et il faut savoir choisir ses mots selon le contexte dans lequel on se trouve. Vous savez déjà, par exemple, qu'il existe une différence entre la conversation **formelle** et **familière** (l'usage du **vous** ou du **tu**, des formules de politesse, des gestes différents, etc.), mais il y a beaucoup d'autres situations sociolinguistiques où il faut faire attention à votre façon de vous exprimer. En lisant ce manuel, vous allez trouver des mots de vocabulaire et des expressions qu'on n'utilise que dans certains contextes spécifiques. Afin de vous aider à ne pas vous tromper, on va vous indiquer les mots et les expressions qui font partie de l'**argot** (*slang*), qui sont **vulgaires** (*vulgar*) ou qui sont des **régionalismes** (une expression louisianaise, québécoise, antillaise, sénégalaise, maghrébine, provençale, suisse, etc.). Alors, quand vous apprenez un nouveau mot ou une nouvelle expression, faites attention aux limites de son usage !

Culture

Pierre-Ambroise **Choderlos de Laclos** est un écrivain français du 18ème siècle. Son chef-d'œuvre est le roman épistolaire *Les Liaisons dangereuses*. Dans ce roman à lettres, il y a beaucoup d'histoires d'amour et de trahisons. Hollywood a fait plusieurs films basés sur ce roman, y compris le film populaire *Cruel Intentions*. Vous pouvez lire un extrait de ce roman dans la dernière partie de ce chapitre. *Les Liaisons dangereuses* est connu comme le seul roman que Laclos ait écrit et publié de sa vie.

Après avoir écouté

1.26 Avez-vous compris ? Répondez aux questions après avoir écouté le dialogue entre Claire et Jean-Louis au fais do-do. Discutez de vos réponses en classe.

1. Où sont Claire et Jean-Louis ? Pourquoi ?
2. Quelle est la réaction de Claire quand elle rencontre Jean-Louis ?
3. Quels types de questions est-ce que Jean-Louis pose à Claire ? Est-ce qu'elle répond à toutes ses questions ?
4. Comment est-ce que Claire s'excuse à la fin ?

1.27 D'accord ou pas d'accord ? Après avoir écouté le dialogue entre Claire et Jean-Louis au fais do-do, lisez les phrases suivantes **et donnez votre opinion**. Discutez-en en petits groupes.

	D'accord	Pas d'accord
1. Jean-Louis est vraiment surpris de voir Claire.	_______	_______
2. Claire est contente de voir Jean-Louis.	_______	_______
3. Claire écrit une thèse sur un auteur du 18ème siècle.	_______	_______
4. Laclos a écrit des romans policiers.	_______	_______
5. Jean-Louis adore la littérature française.	_______	_______
6. Jean-Louis va bientôt retourner à Paris.	_______	_______
7. Claire a un petit ami au Québec.	_______	_______

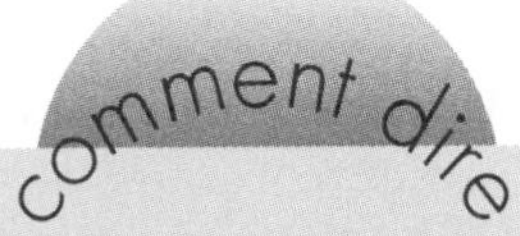

les rencontres (suite)

Talking about habits — normalement, en général, souvent, parfois, quelquefois, de temps en temps, rarement, jamais

Stating preferences — adorer, aimer, être fanatique de, avoir envie de, préférer, ne pas trop aimer, ne pas aimer du tout, détester, avoir horreur de

	Informal	**Formal**
Expressing surprise	Tiens ! C'est toi !	Tenez ! C'est vous !
	Ça me fait plaisir de te voir !	Ça me fait plaisir de vous voir !
	Je suis content(e) de te revoir !	Je suis content(e) de vous revoir !
	Qu'est-ce que tu fais ici ?	Qu'est-ce que vous faites ici ?
	Quelle surprise ! Quelle coïncidence !	
	C'est chanceux, n'est-ce pas ?	
	En effet ! Absolument !	
Breaking the ice	Tu viens ici souvent ?	Vous venez ici souvent ?
	T'as une cigarette ? T'as l'heure ?	Auriez-vous une cigarette ? Auriez-vous l'heure ?
	Je te connais, non ?	Je vous connais, non ?
	On s'est déjà rencontré ?	
	Tu aimes cette chanson ?	Aimez-vous cette chanson ?
	Tu veux danser ? Danse avec moi !	Voudriez-vous danser avec moi ?
	Tu as l'air ravissant ce soir.	Vous êtes ravissant(e).
	Tu as de beaux yeux.	Vous avez de beaux yeux.
	Quel beau sourire !	

Pour aller plus loin : CULTURE

ACTIVITÉ C : Voulez-vous mieux connaître la musique acadienne et créole de la Louisiane ? Consultez votre cahier électronique !

1.28 Vos préférences Utilisez une expression de chaque colonne pour former des phrases. Puis, avec un partenaire, **exprimez vos préférences** et posez des questions.

MODÈLE : **—Normalement, je déteste danser. Et toi ?**
—Moi, j'adore danser.

Normalement	j'aime	écouter de la musique
En général	je déteste	porter un jean
De temps en temps	j'ai envie de	travailler dans un hôtel
	j'adore	lire des romans d'amour
	je n'aime pas trop	aller aux musées
	j'ai horreur de	chanter sous la douche
		me détendre
		me lever très tôt
		? ? ? (Utilisez votre imagination !)

1.29 Rompez la glace Imaginez que vous êtes au fais do-do et que vous voulez rencontrer des gens. Qu'est-ce que vous pourriez dire aux personnes suivantes **pour commencer une conversation** ? N'oubliez pas de les saluer et de vous présenter (révisez Épisode 1, si nécessaire) avant de commencer à parler ou à poser des questions.

MODÈLE : Un étudiant qui était dans votre cours de français l'année dernière. →
—Tiens, c'est toi ! Quelle coïncidence !

1. Deux vieilles dames qui vendent des beignets
2. Une jolie jeune femme qui danse toute seule
3. Un beau jeune homme qui lit un roman
4. Vos amis de l'université (quelle surprise !)
5. Des enfants qui ne peuvent pas dormir
6. Vos parents et leurs amis (quelle surprise !)
7. Votre professeur de français (quelle coïncidence !)
8. Les musiciens pendant leur break

Langue

Plusieurs expressions québécoises, ou **québécismes**, sont marquées par l'influence de l'anglais. Par exemple : un char (une voiture), une toune (une chanson), c'est le fun (c'est amusant), la face (la figure), rusher (être pressé ou stressé), le change (la monnaie), toffe (difficile), cute (mignon).

1.30 Quelle surprise ! Sur une feuille de papier, écrivez une phrase **pour indiquer quelque chose que vous aimez ou que vous détestez** qui est surprenante. N'y mettez pas votre nom ! Échangez vos papiers au hasard. Lisez la phrase sur le papier que vous recevez et circulez dans la classe pour trouver l'auteur. Ne montrez pas le papier, et posez des questions *sans* utiliser les mots de vocabulaire sur le papier. Trouvez l'auteur, et vous gagnez !

MODÈLE : «De temps en temps, j'aime chanter sous la douche.»
—Est-ce que tu aimes la musique ? *ou*
—Tu aimes écouter, danser ou autre chose ?

À l'écrit *deuxième étape*

1.31 Ne faites pas do-do ! Imaginez que vous êtes à Lafayette au fais do-do avec Claire et Jean-Louis. **Écrivez un dialogue** dans lequel :

- vous vous présentez à Claire ou à Jean-Louis.
- vous posez des questions afin de savoir s'il/si elle est là pour travailler ou pour s'amuser.
- vous posez des questions afin de savoir ce qu'il/qu'elle aime ou n'aime pas.
- vous imaginez les réponses (polies ou impolies !).

Finalement, avec un partenaire, révisez vos dialogues et lisez-les à haute voix.

Épisode 3

La bourse

Structures *l'infinitif et le présent*

1.32 Le travail Faites correspondre la profession (à gauche) avec son activité professionnelle (à droite). Pour chaque activité professionnelle, indiquez si le verbe est **régulier** ou **irrégulier**. Quelle en est la différence ?

Profession

1. le boulanger, la boulangère
2. le policier, la policière
3. l'infirmier, l'infirmière
4. le pompier
5. le professeur
6. l'avocat, l'avocate
7. le médecin
8. l'acteur, l'actrice
9. le boucher, la bouchère
10. l'aviateur, l'aviatrice
11. l'homme/la femme d'affaires
12. le chauffeur
13. l'ingénieur
14. l'auteur
15. le danseur, la danseuse
16. le/la secrétaire

Activité professionnelle

a. danse
b. combat les feux et les incendies; conduit un camion rouge avec des pompes à eau
c. prépare et vend de la viande
d. vole en avion; synonyme de pilote
e. joue un rôle dans une pièce de théâtre ou dans un film
f. utilise ses compétences techniques et scientifiques pour concevoir ou organiser des projets et des machines
g. prépare et vend du pain
h. aide le médecin, surtout dans un hôpital
i. écrit des romans, des poèmes ou des pièces de théâtre
j. travaille dans le commerce, la gestion, l'administration, ou à la direction d'une compagnie et s'occupe de questions financières
k. répond au téléphone, fait des photocopies, tape des documents à l'ordinateur
l. protège les gens et arrête les criminels
m. s'occupe de gens malades et les soigne
n. enseigne à l'université et fait de la recherche
o. conduit une grande voiture ou un taxi
p. étudie les lois et défend les cas en justice

Pour aller plus loin : CULTURE

ACTIVITÉ D : Trouvez l'emploi de vos rêves dans un pays francophone ! Consultez votre cahier électronique !

1.33 Questions personnelles **Répondez aux questions suivantes.** Vous pouvez mentionner d'autres professions qui ne sont pas sur la liste ci-dessus !

1. Quelles professions vous intéressent ? Êtes-vous capable d'exercer ces professions ? Pourquoi ou pourquoi pas ?
2. Quelles professions ne vous intéressent pas du tout ? Pourquoi pas ?
3. Quelles professions sont dangereuses ? ennuyeuses ? amusantes ? respectées ?
4. Que pensez-vous de la décision prise par Claire de devenir professeur de littérature ? Est-ce que les professeurs font des choses intéressantes ? Est-ce qu'ils sont bien payés ? Ont-ils beaucoup de temps libre ?

1.34 Travailler c'est trop dur Au fais do-do à Lafayette, Claire entend une chanson zydeco de Zachary Richard qu'elle aime beaucoup parce que la chanson exprime la fatigue d'une personne qui travaille trop. Elle commence à douter de la possibilité de trouver le manuscrit. Bref, elle perd aussi l'envie de travailler. **Faites les activités suivantes avec un partenaire :**

1. *Avant* de lire les paroles de la chanson, faites une liste de tous les verbes que vous associez à la profession de musicien.
2. Lisez la chanson à haute voix.
3. Soulignez tous les verbes à l'infinitif (non conjugués). Peut-on traduire tous les infinitifs en anglais comme «*to* —» ? Si non, quels sont les autres possibilités ? Pouvez-vous décrire comment/quand utiliser l'infinitif ? (Bonus : Pouvez-vous trouver un infinitif réfléchi ?)
4. Entourez tous les verbes au présent. Pouvez-vous donner l'infinitif de chaque verbe ? Est-il un verbe régulier ou irrégulier ? Comment le savez-vous ?
5. Comparez votre liste de verbes associés aux musiciens avec les verbes que vous avez soulignés et entourés. Combien sont les mêmes ?
6. Discutez : Quand ce musicien travaille, que fait-il ? Est-ce qu'il gagne beaucoup d'argent ? Est-ce qu'il aime son travail ? Est-ce que vous aimez travailler ? Étudier, c'est travailler, à votre avis ? Quand vous voulez éviter le travail, qu'est-ce que vous aimez faire ?

Pour aller plus loin : CULTURE

ACTIVITÉ E : Qui est Zachary Richard ? Apprenez un peu sur sa vie, sa musique et sa philosophie quant à son bilinguisme en Louisiane. Consultez votre cahier électronique !

Travailler c'est trop dur

■ Zachary Richard

Travailler c'est trop dur,° — *hard*
Et voler° c'est pas beau; — *to fly (to take off, slang)*
Demander la charité
C'est quelque chose que je peux pas faire

Chaque jour que moi je vis° — *I live*
On me demande de quoi moi je vis
Je dis que je vis sur l'amour,
Et j'espère de vivre vieux.

Moi je prends mon violon,
Et j'attrape mon archet,° — *bow*
Et je joue ma vieille valse,° — *waltz*
Pour faire mes amis danser.
Vous connaissez mes chers amis
La vie est bien, bien trop courte
Pour se faire des misères° — *to trouble oneself*
Allons danser ce soir.

Moi je fais la musique
C'est presque tous les soirs.

Trainer° tout par tout — *to hang around*
Chanter dans les wiskies-bars.
Et des fois,° tu connais, — *sometimes*
J'aimerais lâcher,° pis° m'en aller,° — *to give up/then (reg. Louisiana)/ take off*
Mais je suis venu ce soir
Pour le plaisir de chanter.

l'infinitif et le présent

A. The *infinitive* (**l'infinitif**) is the unconjugated form of the verb. As you see above, the infinitive can be used to talk about a concept in an abstract way: **Travailler** c'est trop dur ; pour le plaisir de **chanter**. It is also used to refer to an action or state, often in conjunction with other verbs (Allons **danser**). The French infinitive often does not translate into English as "to —," which is commonly given as its only translation.

- Note that some verbs require a preposition when followed by an infinitive: J'essaie **de** chanter, N'hésitez pas **à** me contacter. You will learn more about verbs that require prepositions in Chapter 7.
- Note also that, if you have a pronominal verb in infinitive form, you must make the pronoun agree with the subject of the main verb in the sentence even though you are not conjugating the verb: Nous aimons **nous lever** tôt. Je veux **me coucher**.

B. The *present tense* (**le présent**) of regular verbs (**-er**, **-ir**, **-re**) is formed by adding the appropriate endings for each subject to the verb stem. The present tense of regular pronominal verbs (**se** + verb) is conjugated in the same way, but also involves adding the correct form of pronoun before the verb: **je me, tu te, il/elle se, nous nous, vous vous, ils/elles se** + verb.

- **-er** verbs like **travailler** or **se réveiller**: Add endings **-e, -es, -e, -ons, -ez, -ent**

  Other common **-er** verbs are **aimer, détester, adorer, (se) parler, marcher, chanter, danser, visiter, préparer, penser, apprécier, arriver, discuter, donner, jouer, sembler, (se) téléphoner, se contenter de, s'habiller, se réveiller, se raser, se brosser (les dents), se coiffer, se coucher**.
- **-ir** verbs like **finir**: Add endings **-is, -is, -it, -issons, -issez, -issent**

  Other common **-ir** verbs are **choisir, grandir, grossir, maigrir, obéir, (se) réunir, réfléchir, réussir, rougir, vieillir, réjouir, accomplir, fleurir, aboutir**.
- **-re** verbs like **attendre**: Add endings **-s, -s, —, -ons, -ez, -ent**

  Other common **-re** verbs are **défendre, descendre, (s')entendre, fondre, répondre, vendre, rendre, rendre visite à, se rendre compte, pendre, perdre, se détendre**.

C. The *present tense* (**le présent**) *of slightly irregular* **-er**, **-ir**, and **-re** verbs is formed with minor deviations from the regular conjugation. Usually, these changes are required to maintain proper pronunciation of the verb forms.

- **-ger** verbs (like **manger**) require the addition of an **e** before the ending in the **nous** form to preserve the pronunciation of the soft **g** sound (**nous mangeons**). Otherwise, they are conjugated like regular **-er** verbs. Some other **-ger** verbs are **changer, voyager, nager, ranger, venger**.

- **-cer** verbs (like **commencer**) require the addition of a cedilla (**ç**) on the **c** in the **nous** form to preserve the pronunciation of the soft **c** sound (**nous commençons**). Otherwise, they are conjugated like regular **-er** verbs. Some other **-cer** verbs are **avancer, balancer, placer, remplacer**.
- **-yer** verbs (like **essayer**) require that you change the **y** to an **i** in all forms *except* the **nous** and **vous** forms, which require the stronger **y** sound. Otherwise, the endings are regular **-er** endings. Some other **-yer** verbs are **ennuyer, envoyer, nettoyer, payer**.
- **-eler** and **-eter** verbs (like **appeler**) require that you double the **l** or the **t** in all forms *except* the **nous** and **vous** forms. Note that a word cannot end in the combination **e-consonant-e** in French; sometimes the consonant is doubled and other times an **accent grave** is added (see below) to aid pronunciation. These verbs have regular **-er** endings. Some other **-eler** and **-eter** verbs like this are **s'appeler, rappeler, jeter, rejeter**.
- Verbs like **lever** require that you add an **accent grave** to the middle **e** (**è**) in all forms *except* the **nous** and **vous** forms. Otherwise, the endings are regular **-er** endings. Other verbs like this are **se lever, acheter, élever, mener, amener, emmener, (se) promener**.
- Verbs like **préférer** require that you change the accent on the middle **é** to an **accent grave** (**è**) in all forms *except* the **nous** and **vous** forms. Otherwise, the endings are regular **-er** endings. Other verbs like this are **répéter, espérer, considérer, posséder**.
- Verbs like **ouvrir** are conjugated with the regular **-er** endings *instead* of the **-ir** endings. Other verbs like this are **découvrir, offrir, souffrir**.
- Verbs like **prendre** are conjugated like regular **-re** verbs in the singular, but have different plural forms, in which the **-d** in all plural stems is dropped and the **n** in the third person plural is doubled (**nous prenons, vous prenez, ils/elles prennent**). Other verbs like this are **apprendre, comprendre, entreprendre, s'éprendre de**.

1.35 Le travail de Philippe Quand Claire rentre à l'Hôtel Le Moyne après son week-end à Lafayette, elle rencontre Philippe dans la grande salle. Il travaille à la réception. **Conjuguez** les verbes entre parenthèses **au présent**.

Les verbes en -er

CLAIRE : Bonjour, Philippe. Vous (travailler) ________________ toujours !

PHILIPPE : Oui, mais j'(adorer) ________________ cette vie. Je (se lever) ________________ à 5h, je (visiter) ________________ mes amis au marché, et j'(acheter) ________________ des produits frais. Puis, mon assistant et moi, nous (préparer) ________________ le petit déjeuner et nous (discuter) ________________ des nouvelles. Les clients (arriver) ________________ dans la salle et tout est prêt ! Nous (s'amuser) ________________ beaucoup à faire ce travail.

CLAIRE : Et nous (apprécier) ________________ votre hospitalité.

Les verbes en -ir

PHILIPPE : Cela me (réjouir) ____________________ le cœur d'avoir des clients satisfaits. Est-ce que vous avez fini vos travaux de recherche à la bibliothèque ?

CLAIRE : Ah, mais, les travaux de recherche (ne pas s'achever) ____________________ si facilement !

PHILIPPE : Hélas, c'est vrai. Tout de même, il faut profiter du moment. La vie passe vite. . . les fleurs (fleurir) __________________, les enfants (grandir) ___________________ et vous (vieillir) __________________ ! Laissez les bons temps rouler, hein !

CLAIRE : Vous avez raison. Même si je ne trouve pas le manuscrit ici, au moins je (découvrir) ________________ un tas de choses intéressantes sur l'histoire de cette ville merveilleuse.

Les verbes en -re

JEAN-LOUIS : (*arrivant brusquement*) Quoi ? Qu'est-ce que j'(entendre) __________________ ? Tu as réussi à trouver le manuscrit ?

CLAIRE : Non, non, pas encore.

JEAN-LOUIS : Tu (ne pas perdre) _____________ confiance en toi, j'espère.

CLAIRE : Non, mais aujourd'hui, je (se détendre) ________________. Je (ne pas descendre) ____________________ aux archives de la bibliothèque quand il fait si beau dehors.

PHILIPPE : Allez, vous deux ! Il ne fait pas trop chaud et vous (perdre) ____________________ votre temps ici. Vous (s'entendre) ____________________ assez bien. Pourquoi pas aller faire un tour des marécages (*swamps*) ensemble ? Ils (vendre) ________________ des billets à demi-tarif cet après-midi. Je peux vous arranger ça très facilement. Qu'est-ce que vous en dites ? Que me (répondre) ___________________-vous ?

JEAN-LOUIS : Je (répondre) ____________________ «oui !». Et toi, Claire ?

CLAIRE : D'accord. Cet après-midi vers 3h ?

JEAN-LOUIS : Parfait. À cet après-midi, alors.

1.36 Aux marécages À trois heures pile (*on the dot*), Claire et Jean-Louis quittent l'hôtel pour aller aux marécages. Lors de leur tour en bâteau dans les marécages, ils se parlent de leurs vies. Choisissez un des verbes donnés et **conjuguez** ce verbe **au présent** pour remplir les blancs.

attendre	**commencer**	**essayer**	**finir**	**prendre**
se coucher	**se lever**	**s'intéresser**	**travailler**	**visiter**

JEAN-LOUIS : Alors, parle-moi de tes recherches. C'est fascinant.

CLAIRE : Quoi ? Normalement, les gens ne ____________________ pas trop à la littérature du 18ème siècle.

JEAN-LOUIS : Ouais, mais, tu ____________________ beaucoup de villes exotiques et tu ____________________ de résoudre le mystère du manuscrit perdu de Laclos.

CLAIRE : Ma vie au Québec n'est pas aussi intéressante. Quand je suis chez moi, c'est la routine. Mais, Jean-Louis, qu'est-ce que tu fais comme travail ?

JEAN-LOUIS : Oh, moi, je suis barman. Je ____________________ à Mulligan's, un bar irlandais à Paris. C'est une vie assez déréglée. On dort tard et on ____________________ tard, vers 1h de l'après-midi. On ____________________ le petit-déjeuner à l'heure du déjeuner et le déjeuner à l'heure du dîner.

CLAIRE : Ça doit être un peu bizarre.

JEAN-LOUIS : En effet, et mon partenaire et moi, nous ____________________ à travailler vers 6h du soir, et nous ____________________ le travail vers 3h du matin. Je rentre chez moi et je ____________________ à 6h du matin, quand tout le monde se réveille. C'est une vie assez difficile.

CLAIRE : Et tu ____________________ patiemment toute l'année le mois d'août parce que le bar ferme pendant le mois des grandes vacances ?

JEAN-LOUIS : Non, le bar est ouvert au mois d'août, mais j'aime voyager en été. Je suis comme la cigale (*cicada/grasshopper*) qui chante tout l'été.

CLAIRE : Mais attention, c'est la fourmi travailleuse qui triomphe à la fin de cette fable.

JEAN-LOUIS : Tu as raison, mais c'est la cigale qui s'amuse le plus, n'est-ce pas ?

Pour aller plus loin : LITTÉRATURE

ACTIVITÉ F : Lisez la fable de La Fontaine : «La Cigale et la fourmi». Il s'agit de diverses opinions sur le travail. Consultez votre cahier électronique !

1.37 Et vous ? Que faites-vous dans les situations suivantes ? **Interviewez quelqu'un** dans la classe.

MODÈLE : —Que fais-tu quand tu n'as pas envie de travailler ?
—Quand je n'ai pas envie de travailler, je téléphone à mes amis.

1. Quand je n'ai pas envie de travailler. . .
2. Quand je veux faire de l'exercice. . .
3. Quand je suis à la plage. . .
4. Quand je veux contacter un ami. . .
5. Quand j'ai besoin d'argent. . .
6. Quand je voyage. . .
7. Quand je veux me détendre. . .
8. Quand il pleut. . .
9. Le matin, avant de quitter la maison. . .
10. Le soir, avant de m'endormir. . .

la Louisiane

Que fait notre Louisianaise quand elle voyage ? Que fait-elle comme travail ? Regardez la vidéo et consultez votre cahier d'activités !

1.38 Une carrière intéressante Avec un partenaire, choisissez une profession bizarre ou intéressante. Sur une feuille de papier, écrivez plusieurs phrases courtes pour décrire les activités typiques d'une personne qui fait ce travail. Échangez vos papiers et **essayez de deviner les carrières décrites** par vos camarades de classe.

MODÈLE : Il voyage en camion rouge. Il combat les feux. Il prépare le dîner pour ses collègues. Il est toujours prêt à partir.

—C'est un pompier ?

Quand Claire retourne à l'hôtel, elle y trouve un fax qui vient d'être transmis. Ce fax a l'air assez important...

La bourse

Québec, le 26 août 2003

Mademoiselle Claire PLOUFFE

Hôtel Le Moyne, rue Dauphine

La Nouvelle-Orléans, Louisiane 70130 USA

FAX : 504-525-8422

Chère Mademoiselle,

J'ai le grand plaisir de vous annoncer la décision du Département de Lettres Modernes de vous nommer bénéficiaire d'une bourse° de recherche pour l'année universitaire 2003/2004. Cette somme considérable vous permettra d'achever° votre ambitieux projet de recherche sur le manuscrit perdu de Laclos. C'est aussi une distinction importante accordée par les membres du Département qui pensent, comme moi, que votre projet a du mérite. La découverte de ce manuscrit sera une vraie contribution à l'histoire littéraire.

stipend, fellowship
to complete

Je suis très heureux de pouvoir vous attribuer cette bourse, car° je pense que vous la méritez pleinement et je vous félicite° sincèrement. Je souhaite° que vos projets aboutissent° comme vous l'espérez. Vous recevrez une lettre des Services Financiers avec tous les détails sur le versement° de l'argent sur votre compte.° N'hésitez pas à me contacter si vous avez des questions. Je serai en France cet automne, et j'espère que nous aurons l'occasion de nous rencontrer.

for
to congratulate/to wish
to finish
deposit/bank account

Je vous prie de croire, chère Mademoiselle, à l'assurance de mes sentiments les meilleurs.

P.F. Thuillier

Directeur de la Recherche et des Études littéraires

L'Université de Sainte-Foy

Après avoir lu

1.39 D'accord ou pas d'accord ? Après avoir lu la lettre ci-dessus, lisez les phrases suivantes et **donnez vos opinions personnelles**. Discutez-en en petits groupes.

	D'accord	Pas d'accord
1. Claire et Monsieur Thuillier sont de très bons amis.	______	______
2. Claire va recevoir beaucoup d'argent de son université.	______	______
3. Le projet de recherche de Claire est intéressant.	______	______
4. Monsieur Thuillier a confiance en Claire.	______	______
5. Claire n'a pas le soutien (*support*) de tout le département.	______	______
6. Claire va aller en France pour continuer ses recherches.	______	______

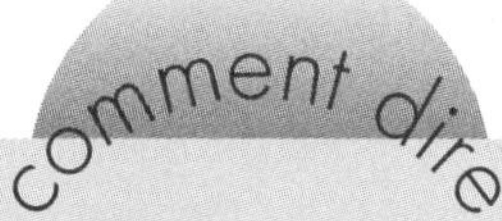

écrire une lettre

	Formal	Informal
Greetings	Monsieur/Madame/ Mademoiselle	Cher/Chère (prénom), Salut (prénom)
Wishes	Je suis très heureux/euse pour vous	Ça va ? Tu vas bien ?
	Je pense que vous méritez. . .	Je suis très content(e) d'apprendre que. . .
	Je vous félicite sincèrement. . .	Félicitations !
	Je pense / Je crois / J'espère que vous. . .	Je pense / Je crois / J'espère que tu. . .
	N'hésitez pas à me contacter si. . .	Écris-moi / Téléphone-moi si. . .
Closings	Je vous prie de croire, Monsieur/ Madame/Mademoiselle, à l'assurance de mes sentiments respectueux / les meilleurs / les plus cordiaux	En espérant te voir bientôt Amitiés/Amicalement Je t'embrasse (affectueusement) Gros bisous / Grosses bises
	Je vous prie de recevoir, cher/chère Monsieur/Madame/Mademoiselle, mes salutations respectueuses/distinguées.	Je pense bien à toi À très bientôt / Au plaisir de te lire

1.40 Formalités Cette lettre est assez formelle. **Transformez les phrases** suivantes pour rendre le ton plus familier. Attention : Il faut changer les **vous** en **tu**, mais vous pouvez aussi changer des mots ou introduire des expressions plus familières.

1. Chère Mademoiselle,
2. J'ai le grand plaisir de vous annoncer la décision du Département de Lettres Modernes de vous nommer bénéficiaire d'une bourse de recherche.
3. Je souhaite que vos projets aboutissent comme vous l'espérez.
4. N'hésitez pas à me contacter si vous avez des questions.
5. Je vous prie de croire, chère Mademoiselle, à l'assurance de mes sentiments les meilleurs.

1.41 Le courriel ou le courrier ? Avec un partenaire, **choisissez une salutation, des vœux** (*wishes*) **et un adieu** qu'on peut employer pour chacune des situations suivantes. En plus, décidez s'il faut envoyer chaque lettre **par courriel** (courrier électronique, *e-mail*) **ou par courrier** (*mail*) normal.

1. Pour féliciter une amie qui vient d'avoir un bébé
2. Pour souhaiter «joyeux anniversaire» à votre oncle qui va avoir 50 ans
3. Pour remercier une collègue québécoise qui vous invite à un dîner (malheureusement, vous n'êtes pas libre !)
4. Pour souhaiter «bon voyage» à vos voisins avant leur départ pour Paris

Langue

Dans une **lettre formelle** à quelqu'un que vous avez déjà rencontré, vous pouvez commencer avec «Cher Monsieur» ou «Chère Madame» ou «Chère Mademoiselle». L'usage du mot **cher** indique que vous connaissez assez bien le destinataire. Alors, «Monsieur» est plus formel que «Cher Monsieur», et on utilise le premier pour les gens qu'on ne connaît pas personnellement ou à qui on veut témoigner un plus grand respect.

À l'écrit *troisième étape*

1.42 Vos vacances de rêve à la Nouvelle-Orléans Imaginez que vous êtes en vacances à la Nouvelle-Orléans. Un camarade de classe décide de visiter la ville la semaine prochaine et veut savoir comment vous contacter pendant la journée. Écrivez-lui une brève lettre ou un courriel avec votre emploi du temps pour la journée. Faites une liste de huit activités. Échangez votre liste avec celle d'un de vos camarades de classe (par courriel, si vous voulez !) et offrez-lui une réponse et quelques corrections possibles.

Dénouement

Une enseigne historique à la Nouvelle-Orléans.

Activités de révision

1.43 Votre ville Imaginez qu'un groupe de Français viennent dans votre ville pour faire du tourisme. Ils ont seulement une journée pour découvrir la ville et/ou la région. Ils arrivent à 7h et partent à 21h. En petits groupes, **imaginez un itinéraire** et quelques activités. N'oubliez pas de suggérer des restaurants pour les repas. Comparez votre itinéraire avec ceux de vos camarades !

1.44 Compatibilité Vous cherchez un compagnon de voyage qui a les mêmes goûts que vous. C'est à vous de le choisir ! Répondez aux questions suivantes (des vérités ou des mensonges sont acceptables). Puis, circulez dans la salle de classe et posez des questions à vos camarades. **Vous voulez trouver quelqu'un qui soit compatible avec vous !**

MODÈLE : —Moi, quand je voyage, je préfère me loger dans un hôtel de luxe. Et toi ?
—Moi, je préfère un terrain de camping.

1. Quand vous voyagez, vous préférez vous loger où ?
2. Vous avez un après-midi à passer à la Nouvelle-Orléans, que faites-vous ?
3. Quelle cuisine ethnique préférez-vous ?
4. Comment aimez-vous voyager ? (en avion, en voiture, . . . ?)
5. Quelle musique aimez-vous ?
6. Dans le monde francophone, vous voulez absolument aller où ?

Pour aller plus loin : CINÉMA

ACTIVITÉ G : Regardez le film *L'ami de mon amie* d'Éric Rohmer. Il s'agit de deux jeunes femmes et de deux jeunes hommes qui se rencontrent et se trouvent dans des situations délicates. Consultez votre cahier électronique !

Avant de lire *Les Liaisons dangereuses*

1.45 Les contraires s'attirent Imaginez deux personnes complètement incompatibles : une femme traditionnelle (qui aime la vie sage et a des mœurs strictes) et un homme libertin (qui aime laisser les bons temps rouler). En gros, ce sont les caractères des deux personnages principaux du texte de Laclos que vous allez lire. Regardez les activités suivantes et, avec un partenaire, décidez si ce sont les activités d'une femme traditionnelle ou celles d'un homme libertin. **Conjuguez** les verbes **au présent**. Justifiez vos choix.

MODÈLE : se coucher à 9h du soir →
Une femme traditionnelle se couche à 9h du soir.

1. assister à la messe à 8h du matin
2. se confesser au prêtre
3. rencontrer des amis dans un bar
4. rendre visite à des parents âgés
5. danser toute la nuit
6. se promener tout(e) seul(e) à la campagne
7. jouer au poker avec des hommes riches
8. jouer aux cartes avec une vieille dame
9. ne pas se marier
10. donner de l'aide aux pauvres
11. acheter des vêtements très chic et très chers
12. rester dans un hôtel de luxe

1.46 Premières impressions **Lisez l'extrait** suivant, tiré d'une lettre du roman *Les Liaisons dangereuses* de Pierre-Ambroise Choderlos de Laclos, sans essayer de comprendre chaque mot. Après votre première lecture du texte, répondez aux questions. Ensuite, relisez le texte une deuxième fois, plus attentivement.

1. Est-ce un homme ou une femme qui écrit cette lettre ?
2. Qui va recevoir cette lettre, un homme ou une femme ? un(e) ami(e) ou un(e) inconnu(e) ?
3. Est-ce que le ton de la lettre est formel ou familier ? Est-ce qu'on se vouvoie ou est-ce qu'on se tutoie ?
4. Est-ce que le ton est plutôt passionné ou plutôt mélancolique ?
5. Où se situe l'action ? à Paris ou à la campagne ?

lisez

Les Liaisons dangereuses

L'intrigue du roman de Pierre-Ambroise Choderlos de Laclos se passe en France au 18ème siècle, période pendant laquelle l'aristocratie est en déclin. Deux aristocrates, le Chevalier de Valmont et son ancienne maîtresse la Marquise de Merteuil, se livrent à un libertinage plus ou moins déclaré. Dans cette lettre adressée à sa complice, Valmont décrit son projet de séduire une femme dévote et mariée qu'il a rencontrée dans la maison de campagne de sa vieille tante. La Marquise de Merteuil, elle, veut que Valmont séduise une jeune femme qu'elle connaît à Paris, mais Valmont l'informe de son intention de rester chez sa tante. Voici ce que Valmont écrit à son amie la Marquise...

■ Pierre-Ambroise Choderlos de Laclos

Les Liaisons dangereuses (extrait)

Ne vous fâchez pas et écoutez-moi. Dépositaire de tous les secrets de mon cœur, je vais vous confier° le plus grand projet que j'aie jamais formé. Que me proposez-vous ? de séduire une jeune fille qui n'a rien vu, ne connaît rien. . . Vingt autres peuvent y réussir comme moi. Il n'en est pas ainsi° de l'entreprise qui m'occupe. [. . .]

Vous connaissez la présidente° de Tourvel, sa dévotion, son amour conjugal, ses principes austères. Voilà ce que j'attaque; voilà l'ennemi digne° de moi; voilà le but° où je prétends° atteindre.° [. . .]

Vous saurez donc que le président° est en Bourgogne, à la suite d'un grand procès° (j'espère lui en faire perdre un plus important). Son inconsolable moitié° doit passer ici tout le temps de cet affligeant° veuvage.° Une messe chaque jour, quelques visites aux pauvres du canton,° des prières du matin et du soir, des promenades solitaires, de pieux° entretiens° avec ma vieille tante, et quelquefois un triste wisk,° devaient être ses seules distractions. Je lui en prépare de plus efficaces.° Mon ange m'a conduit ici, pour son bonheur et le mien. Insensé !° je regrettais vingt-quatre heures que je sacrifiais à des égards d'usage.° Combien on me punirait, en me forçant de retourner à Paris ! Heureusement il faut être quatre pour jouer au wisk; et comme il n'y a ici que le curé° du lieu, mon éternelle tante m'a beaucoup pressé° de lui sacrifier quelques jours. Vous devinez° que j'ai consenti.

to confide
it is not the case
wife of a judge
worthy/goal/to aspire to/to reach
judge
trial
(other) half/sorrowful/widowhood
district
pious/conversations
a card game
more efficient (sarcasm)
madman
social obligations
parish priest
to urge/to guess

Après avoir lu

1.47 Avez-vous compris ? En petits groupes, **discutez** de vos réponses aux questions suivantes.

1. Quel est le «plus grand projet» de Valmont ? Que pensez-vous de ce projet ?
2. Pourquoi est-ce que Valmont rejette la jeune fille innocente et choisit la présidente de Tourvel ?
3. Où est le président de Tourvel (le mari de la présidente de Tourvel) ? Pourquoi ?
4. Quelles sont les activités habituelles de la présidente de Tourvel lorsqu'elle elle est à la campagne ? Est-ce que ce sont les activités d'une personne dévote ? Est-ce que ce sont les activités habituelles de Valmont ? Est-ce que Valmont a du respect pour la présidente de Tourvel ?
5. Pourquoi est-ce que la tante invite Valmont à rester quelques jours de plus ? Valmont est-il heureux d'accepter ou non ?
6. Quelle est votre réaction à cette lettre ? Que pensez-vous de Valmont ? Que pensez-vous de la présidente de Tourvel ?

1.48 D'accord ou pas d'accord ? Réfléchissez sur l'extrait du roman de Laclos. Ensuite, lisez les phrases suivantes et **donnez votre opinion**. Discutez de vos réponses en petits groupes.

	D'accord	Pas d'accord
1. La présidente de Tourvel est une femme malheureuse.	_______	_______
2. Valmont est amoureux de la présidente de Tourvel.	_______	_______
3. Valmont est un homme respectable.	_______	_______
4. On s'amuse bien à la maison de campagne de cette tante.	_______	_______
5. La vieille tante a beaucoup d'amis.	_______	_______

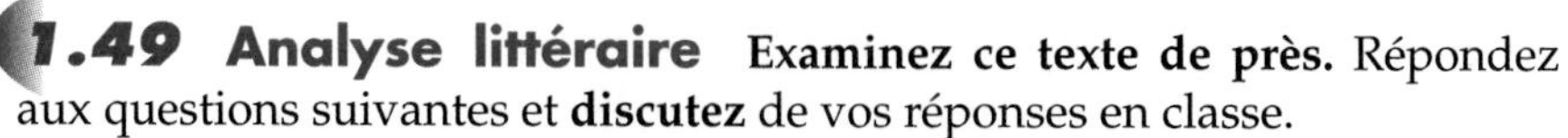

1.49 Analyse littéraire **Examinez ce texte de près.** Répondez aux questions suivantes et **discutez** de vos réponses en classe.

1. L'écrivain de cette lettre, le personnage du Vicomte de Valmont, a-t-il l'air d'être sûr de soi (*self-confident*) ou est-il incertain ? Qu'est-ce qui contribue à ce ton (le vocabulaire, les temps de verbes, le style d'écriture) ?
2. Quand Valmont parle de son «plus grand projet», il évoque l'image de la guerre (*war*). Quels mots associe-t-on à la guerre ? Comment est-ce que cette image a influencé votre lecture du texte ?
3. Dans le troisième paragraphe où l'on parle de la vie quotidienne de la présidente de Tourvel, l'auteur décrit ses activités en forme de liste («une messe chaque jour, quelques visites aux pauvres. . .»). Il n'emploie pas le présent («Elle assiste à la messe chaque jour, et elle rend visite aux pauvres. . .»). Récrivez cette liste d'activités en ajoutant un sujet et un verbe au présent pour chaque activité et comparez votre paragraphe avec des verbes à l'original. Quel est l'effet de l'usage de la liste (c'est à dire de l'omission du sujet qui agit) ? Comment influence-t-elle le portrait de la présidente de Tourvel ?
4. Y a-t-il d'autres éléments structurels (ponctuation, répétitions, phrases longues ou courtes, contrastes, etc.) que l'auteur emploie systématiquement ? Regardez, par exemple, la répétition du mot «voilà» au deuxième paragraphe. Quels sont les effets de l'emploi des éléments comme celui-ci ?

Pour aller plus loin : CINÉMA

ACTIVITÉ H : Regardez les films américains *Dangerous Liaisons* et *Cruel Intentions* et comparez les scènes de la rencontre entre Valmont et Tourvel avec l'original que vous avez lu ! Consultez votre cahier électronique !

Synthèses

1.50 Réfléchissons à la culture Voici quelques éléments de la culture louisianaise que vous avez étudiés dans ce chapitre. En petits groupes, répondez aux questions et **discutez de vos impressions** avec vos camarades.

les Cajuns | **un fais do-do** | **le Mardi gras**

1. Définissez ou décrivez chaque élément.
2. Pourquoi chaque élément est-il important dans cette culture ? Y a-t-il un phénomène historique ou social qui explique son importance ?
3. À votre avis, est-ce que ces éléments témoignent de la richesse et de la diversité de la culture louisianaise de nos jours, ou sont-ils au contraire stéréotypiques ? Pourquoi ?
4. Est-ce que votre impression de la culture louisianaise est différente maintenant que vous avez commencé à l'étudier ? Si oui, comment et pourquoi ? Si non, pourquoi pas ?

1.51 À débattre Lisez les questions suivantes et **discutez-les en groupes**. Si possible, parlez de vos expériences personnelles relatives aux questions.

1. **Les stéréotypes !** Les Français accusent les Américains d'être superficiels quand il s'agit des rapports d'amitié. On dit que les Américains, en général, sont très amicaux à la première rencontre et posent tout de suite des questions personnelles, mais deux jours après, ils peuvent être distants ou même «oublier» de vous avoir parlé. Par contre, on dit que les Français semblent être plus distants et plus réservés à la première rencontre, mais quand ils se font des amis, ils sont plus constants. Qu'en pensez-vous ?

2. **Pourquoi voyage-t-on ?** Michel de Montaigne, un grand philosophe français, a écrit la phrase suivante : «Je réponds ordinairement à ceux qui me demandent raison de mes voyages : que je sais bien ce que je fuis (*flee*), et non pas ce que je cherche.» Êtes-vous d'accord ? Quand on voyage, est-ce qu'on fuit quelque chose ou est-ce qu'on cherche quelque chose ?
3. **Travailler, c'est trop dur ?** On dit que les jeunes gens aujourd'hui ne veulent plus travailler. Tout le monde a envie d'être riche, mais on ne veut pas sacrifier son énergie et son temps libre pour réussir. Les jeunes rêvent de gagner à la loterie ou de recevoir de l'argent en héritage ou d'un procès entamé contre une grande entreprise. Ils ne rêvent pas d'un bon emploi stable et permanent. La nouvelle génération n'a pas la même éthique de travail que l'ancienne. Êtes-vous d'accord ? Pourquoi ou pourquoi pas ?

la Louisiane

Comment est-ce que la culture de la Nouvelle-Orléans est différente de la vôtre ? Regardez la vidéo et consultez votre cahier d'activités !

1.52 À l'impromptu Voici des situations de rencontre. Avec une ou deux autres personnes, choisissez une scène et **improvisez** devant la classe. Si vous ne voulez pas improviser, écrivez votre dialogue avant et puis jouez-le pour la classe.

1. Un rencontre à la terrasse d'un café
   (a) Vous êtes à la terrasse d'un café à la Nouvelle-Orléans quand vous remarquez un touriste francophone à la table d'à côté. Dites-lui bonjour et essayez d'entamer une conversation. Ne vous découragez pas si, d'abord, la personne semble un peu distante. Vous savez que la compagnie lui manque et qu'il aimerait bavarder avec quelqu'un.
   (b) Vous êtes touriste français(e) dans un café à la Nouvelle-Orléans. Vous êtes fatigué(e). Il fait trop chaud et l'hôtel où vous êtes descendu(e) est minable (*seedy*). La seule chose que vous voulez faire, c'est de lire votre guide touristique en paix. Un(e) Américaine, qui souhaite pratiquer son français avec vous, essaie d'attirer votre attention. Vous n'avez aucune envie de lui parler.
2. Le premier jour de travail au bureau
   (a) Vous travaillez dans un bureau à Lafayette. Votre poste est important. Votre emploi de temps est très chargé. Vous êtes assailli(e) par de nombreuses questions que vous pose l'équipe avec laquelle vous collaborez. Malheureusement, le temps vous manque. En effet, vous avez rendez-vous d'affaires avec des collègues très haut-placés dans votre société (*company*) cet après-midi.
   (b) Vous voulez présenter le nouvel employé (personne «c») à votre patron (personne «a»). Vous savez que votre patron est très occupé, mais vous devez interrompre son travail pour faire les présentations.

(c) Vous venez d'être engagé(e) dans un bureau francophone à Lafayette. Vous allez rencontrer votre patron pour la première fois. Vous voulez discuter de vos responsabilités professionnelles, mais vous voulez aussi faire la connaissance de vos nouveaux collègues. Asseyez-vous et bavardez avec eux.

3. Un malentendu à l'hôtel
   (a) Vous êtes dans le foyer d'un hôtel à Lafayette au cœur du pays acadien. Vous remarquez un homme qui ressemble fort au chanteur louisianais Zachary Richard. Présentez-vous et essayez d'établir son identité. Le chanteur est là incognito, mais soyez persistent(e) ! Lâche pas la patate !
   (b) Vous êtes réceptionniste dans un hôtel à Lafayette. Vous êtes acadien(ne) et vous adorez la musique zydeco, mais vous n'êtes pas musicien(ne). Un touriste vous prend pour un(e) musicien(ne) célèbre et vous pose un tas de questions ! Restez poli(e) et répondez à toutes ses questions. Vous ne voulez pas perdre votre pourboire (*tip*).

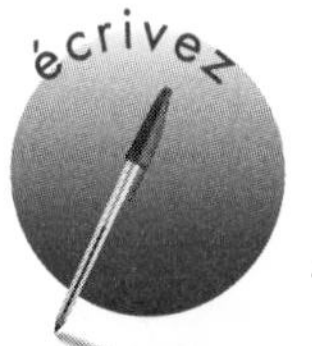

À l'écrit *étape finale*

1.53 Une lettre de la Nouvelle-Orléans Vous êtes en vacances à la Nouvelle-Orléans, et vous restez à l'Hôtel Le Moyne. Révisez et élaborez vos travaux d'écriture de ce chapitre (Activités 15, 31 et 42). **Rédigez une lettre formelle** à votre professeur de français. Utilisez le **présent** autant que possible. N'oubliez pas les éléments suivants :

- Salutation
- Déscription des activités pendant une journée typique
- Discussion des gens que vous connaissez (Claire, Jean-Louis, Philippe)
- Questions sur vos camarades de classe ou votre université (vous ne voulez pas avoir l'air complètement égoïste !)
- Vœux (c'est l'anniversaire de votre professeur !)
- Adieu

Pour aller plus loin : LITTÉRATURE

ACTIVITÉ 1 : Lisez un extrait du roman *Manon Lescaut* de l'Abbé Prévost. C'est un roman français du 18ème siècle. Dans l'extrait, Manon et son fiancé décrivent leur arrivée à la Nouvelle-Orléans.

À suivre

Le matin suivant, Claire retourne à la bibliothèque. Les bibliothécaires annoncent qu'ils ont trouvé le nom et l'adresse de la seule descendante vivante de François Fontenot. Elle s'appelle Sandrine Fontenot-Chardin, et elle habite à la Nouvelle-Orléans ! François Fontenot, son parent éloigné, n'est pas venu directement de la France, après tout. C'est un homme de couleur qui a immigré en Louisiane de Saint-Domingue (l'île qui est aujourd'hui partagée entre Haïti et la république Dominicaine) au moment de la Révolution haïtienne. Il est possible que Sandrine Fontenot-Chardin possède le manuscrit inédit de Laclos sans savoir son importance. Claire décide de lui rendre visite le lendemain. . .

1.54 Qu'est-ce qui va se passer ? Imaginez ce qui va se passer dans le prochain chapitre. Écrivez six phrases et parlez de vos idées avec vos camarades de classe.

Pour agir : LA LOUISIANE !

Si vous voulez bouger et faire quelque chose pour mieux connaître la Nouvelle-Orléans et la Louisiane, ou pour aider les autres à mieux comprendre l'influence française aux États-Unis, consultez la section **Pour agir** dans votre cahier électronique ! Il y a tant de choses à faire :

- **Vendez des beignets** et du café au lait sur votre campus et contribuez l'argent que vous gagnez à une organisation qui préserve les maisons et bâtiments historiques ou les cimetières historiques de la Nouvelle-Orléans.
- **Enseignez** ce que vous savez de la culture de la Louisiane à des enfants de l'école primaire.
- **Entrez en contact** avec des Francophones d'Amérique du Nord.
- **Écrivez une brochure touristique** en français pour attirer des touristes francophones à votre communauté.
- **Organisez un voyage** à la Nouvelle-Orléans pour les vacances de printemps.
- **Cuisinez !** Préparez un vrai repas créole avec vos camarades de classe.

VOCABULAIRE UTILE

Les voyages

auberge (*f.*) de jeunesse	*youth hostel*
chaleur (*f.*)	*heat*
chambre (*f.*) d'hôte	*guest room*
conduire	*to drive*
espèces (*m. pl.*)	*cash*
être retardé(e) (de deux heures)	*to be delayed (by two hours) (flight, transportation)*
faire do-do	*to go night-night (slang)*
faire une excursion	*to take a short trip*
fais do-do (*m.*)	*dance party (reg. Louisiana)*
fouiller (dans)	*to search through*
guide (touristique) (*m.*)	*guidebook*
louer	*to rent*
orage (*m.*)	*storm*
paroisse (*f.*)	*parish; county (in Louisiana)*
permis (*m.*) de conduire	*driver's license*
portefeuille (*m.*)	*wallet*
remonte-pente (*m.*)	*ski lift*
sac (*m.*) à dos	*backpack*
sac (*m.*) à main	*handbag*
se détendre	*to relax, unwind*
se reposer	*to relax, rest*
terrain (*m.*) de camping	*camp ground*
trottoir (*m.*)	*sidewalk*
valise (*f.*)	*suitcase*
vol (*m.*)	*flight*

À l'hôtel

ascenseur (*m.*)	*elevator*
balcon (*m.*)	*balcony*
clé (*f.*)	*key*
client(e)	*hotel guest; client*
climatisé(e)	*air-conditioned*
comptoir (*m.*)	*counter, hotel desk*
cour (*f.*)	*courtyard*
courriel (*m.*)	*e-mail*
épeler	*to spell*
escalier (*m.*)	*stairs*
être au complet	*to be full, have no vacancy*
fauteuil (*m.*)	*armchair*
femme (*f.*) de ménage	*chambermaid*
fer (*m.*) forgé	*wrought iron*
foyer (*m.*)	*entranceway, lobby*
fumeur, non fumeur	*smoking, nonsmoking*
grande salle (*f.*)	*great room, main room*
gratuit(e), compris(e)	*free, included*
hôtelier (*m.*), hôtelière (*f.*)	*innkeeper, hotel owner*
meubles (*m. pl.*)	*furniture*
mur (*m.*)	*wall*
pension (*f.*)	*bed-and-breakfast*
piscine (*f.*)	*pool*
réception (*f.*)	*check-in desk*
rendre service (à)	*to be of service (to)*
se serrer la main	*to shake hands*

La littérature

auteur (*m.*)	*author*
bouquin (*m.*)	*book (slang)*
descendant(e)	*descendant*
écrire une thèse	*to write a thesis*
littérature (*f.*)	*literature*
recherche (*f.*)	*research*
roman (*m.*)	*novel*
roman épistolaire (*m.*)	*epistolary novel (novel composed of letters)*
roman policier (*m.*)	*detective novel*
science-fiction (*f.*)	*science fiction*
siècle (*m.*); le 18ème siècle	*century; the 18th century*

Le travail et les vacances

affaires (*f. pl.*)	*business*
boulot (*m.*)	*job, work (slang)*
chanson (*f.*)	*song*
copain (*m.*), copine (*f.*)	*friend; boy/girlfriend*
costume (*m.*)	*(man's) suit*
danser	*to dance*
être bien habillé(e)	*to be well-dressed*
exprès	*on purpose*
fan(atique) (*m. / f.*)	*fan, a lover of something*
grandes vacances (*f. pl.*)	*summer vacation*
ravissant(e)	*ravishing, beautiful*
s'ennuyer	*to get bored*
se tromper de	*to be mistaken about*
yeux (*m. pl.*); un œil	*eyes; an eye*

Chapitre 2

Une recette créole

Un restaurant louisianais à la Nouvelle-Orléans.

Épisode 1 *Chez les Fontenot*

Épisode 2 *L'invitation*

Épisode 3 *Un mot de Sandrine*

Dénouement

L'okra ne se mange pas d'un seul doigt.

—proverbe haïtien

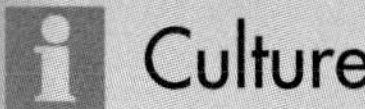

Culture

La France a colonisé la **Saint-Domingue** (aujourd'hui **Haïti**) en 1697. La Saint-Domingue, c'était la partie occidentale de l'île qu'on appelait Hispaniola. La partie orientale a été colonisée par l'Espagne. Les Français ont transplanté à Saint-Domingue des esclaves issus de plusieurs pays d'Afrique, comme le Bénin et le Congo, pour travailler sur les plantations. En 1792, suivant l'exemple des révolutionnaires français et américains, les populations d'esclaves, de personnes de couleur libres (*free people of color*) et d'esclaves affranchis (*freed slaves*) se sont unies et se sont révoltées contre l'oppression des Français. Cette violente et complexe **révolution** a été un succès. En 1804, les révolutionnaires ont expulsé les troupes françaises du nouvel empereur Napoléon, et ils ont renommé le pays Haïti, qui veut dire «île montagneuse» en **arawak**, la langue d'un peuple indigène à l'île. La première «république noire» était fondée au Nouveau Monde. Le pays est aujourd'hui une république indépendante, malgré deux siècles de problèmes économiques et politiques — y compris une série de dictateurs violents, plusieurs régimes militaires, des crises agriculturelles et l'occupation militaire du pays par les États-Unis de 1915 à 1934.

À apprendre

- Comment inviter quelqu'un et comment accepter ou refuser une invitation
- Comment dîner au restaurant
- Comment poser des questions (suite)
- Comment décrire une situation
- Comment donner des ordres, encourager ou avertir quelqu'un

À lire

Claire rend visite à Sandrine Fontenot-Chardin, descendante de François Fontenot, un homme de couleur qui a échappé à la violence de la Révolution haïtienne en immigrant à la colonie française de la Louisiane. Claire croit que Fontenot a transporté à la Nouvelle-Orléans le manuscrit inédit d'un deuxième roman de l'écrivain Choderlos de Laclos. Elle espère que Sandrine possède toujours ce manuscrit important ou encore qu'elle sait où le trouver. Pourtant, le rendez-vous avec Sandrine ne va pas comme prévu, et ensuite Claire doit prendre une décision difficile.

Épisode 1

Chez les Fontenot

Avant de lire

2.1 Vos préférences gastronomiques **Répondez aux questions suivantes.** Discutez de vos réponses avec vos camarades de classe et n'hésitez pas à poser des questions supplémentaires si vous voulez en savoir plus.

1. Quel type de cuisine préférez-vous ? la cuisine américaine ? italienne ? chinoise ? Quel est votre plat (*dish*) préféré ?
2. À quelle heure est-ce que vous prenez le petit déjeuner ? le déjeuner ? le dîner ? Quel est votre repas (*meal*) préféré ?
3. Aimez-vous la viande (*meat*), la volaille (*poultry*), le poisson ou les fruits de mer (*seafood*) ?
4. Que buvez-vous le plus souvent : de l'eau ? du coca ? du jus de fruit ? du lait ?
5. Est-ce que vous dînez au restaurant souvent ? de temps en temps ? rarement ? jamais ? Avec qui allez-vous au restaurant ? Préférez-vous aller au restaurant ou dîner chez vous ?
6. Préférez-vous un restaurant élégant, un bistro ou un café ? Pourquoi ? Quel est l'aspect le plus important dans votre choix de restaurant : le prix ? l'ambiance ? la distance ? la qualité de la nourriture ? Pourquoi ?

Langue

Un **restaurant** est d'habitude plus formel qu'un **bistro**. Le bistro sert de bons repas à un prix raisonnable et à une ambiance animée. Au **café**, on peut prendre une boisson ou bien un petit repas. On y trouve aussi une ambiance animée, mais les plats sont d'habitude plus simples.

2.2 Êtes-vous gastronomes ? En petits groupes, **écrivez une liste de types de nourriture** dans chaque catégorie suivante. Ne regardez ni dans le dictionnaire ni dans le glossaire de ce livre. Pensez à des mots de vocabulaire que vous connaissez déjà !

1. types de viandes
2. types de volaille (*poultry*)
3. types de fruits de mer
4. types de légumes
5. types de produits laitiers (*dairy*)
6. types de fruits
7. types de boissons
8. types de desserts

lisez

Chez les Fontenot

Claire arrive à l'adresse que les bibliothécaires lui ont donnée, une jolie maison rouge avec un balcon de fer forgé, pas loin du cimetière Saint-Louis au nord du Vieux Carré. Elle sonne, et une femme potelée et aux yeux vifs ouvre la porte. C'est Sandrine Fontenot-Chardin. Claire se présente et explique pourquoi elle est là... qu'elle cherche un manuscrit du 18ème siècle et qu'elle a des questions à poser à propos de François Fontenot. Sandrine, qui doit avoir la cinquantaine d'après Claire, l'invite à entrer. Elles s'assoient autour d'une table dans la cuisine, où Sandrine est en train de préparer le dîner.

SANDRINE : Je peux vous servir quelque chose à boire ? Un café ?

CLAIRE : Volontiers. Merci. Qu'est-ce que vous cuisinez ? Comme ça sent bon !

SANDRINE : Je prépare une étouffée. C'est une ancienne recette de famille. Vous savez, ma famille habite la Nouvelle-Orléans depuis 1792, quand François Fontenot est arrivé de Saint-Domingue. Il était restaurateur, et il a fait fortune ici avec son restaurant créole. C'est à cause de lui que toute ma famille adore la nourriture créole piquante !

CLAIRE : Qu'est-ce qu'on met dans une étouffée ? Comment est-ce qu'on la prépare ?

SANDRINE : Oh, c'est facile ! On achète des écrevisses ou du poisson chat, des tomates, des oignons et beaucoup d'épices. Dans une grande poêle ou une marmite, mettez tous les ingrédients sauf les fruits de mer, faites-les sauter quelques minutes, ajoutez un peu de farine et remuez. Puis, ajoutez les écrevisses ou le poisson et faites mijoter. Et vous, mademoiselle, je devine que vous mijotez quelque chose aussi, non ? Vous voulez acquérir ce manuscrit ?

CLAIRE : Vous avez raison. Est-ce que vous sauriez si ce manuscrit existe parmi les affaires laissées en héritage par François ?

SANDRINE : Répondez-moi franchement. Pourquoi voulez-vous ce manuscrit ?

CLAIRE : Enfin, il est très important à mon projet de recherche sur la littérature française du 18ème siècle.

SANDRINE : Dites-moi la vérité. Est-ce la seule raison ?

CLAIRE : Oui, je vous assure. Je veux l'étudier, c'est tout. Trouver un manuscrit non publié d'un auteur comme Laclos, qui a publié un seul roman de sa vie, ce serait une grande découverte intellectuelle. Vous pensez que le manuscrit existe ? Savez-vous où il se trouve ?

SANDRINE : Vous avez l'air très sincère. Alors, je vais vous dire ce que je sais, mais je vous avertis que ce manuscrit porte malheur. À mon avis, il vaut mieux le laisser tomber dans l'oubli. Je ne l'ai jamais vu moi-même, mais mon grand-père l'avait dans sa bibliothèque privée. Des hommes l'ont menacé. Une nuit, ils ont même essayé de voler ce manuscrit. Pendant le vol, mon grand-père a eu une crise cardiaque, et il est mort sur le coup. Les voleurs se sont échappés, sans avoir trouvé le manuscrit. Mon père a vendu toute la bibliothèque le lendemain à un bouquiniste (*bookseller*) parisien qu'il connaissait depuis ses jours en France comme soldat pendant la Seconde Guerre mondiale. Figurez-vous que mon père n'avait rien dit à propos de l'auteur du manuscrit, et le bouquiniste ne savait même pas qu'il était parmi les livres achetés.

CLAIRE : Quelle histoire ! Et les voleurs ? On les a arrêtés ?

SANDRINE : Non, jamais. Mais le lendemain, ma grand-mère a fait une offrande au Baron Samedi, un des loas (*Vodun spirits*) les plus puissants, et les voleurs n'ont jamais essayé de recontacter notre famille. En fait, vous êtes la première personne à nous parler de ce manuscrit depuis ce temps-là.

CLAIRE : Connaissez-vous le nom de ce bouquiniste ? On dit que les familles de bouquinistes à Paris vendent leurs livres du même endroit au bord de la Seine pendant des générations. Il est possible que le manuscrit perdu de Laclos y soit encore ! Pourriez-vous me donner l'adresse du bouquiniste ?

SANDRINE : D'accord, mais méfiez-vous, mademoiselle ! Soyez prudente et gardez pour vous ce que je viens de vous confier. Soyez prudente !

Claire accepte les conseils de Sandrine et quitte sa petite maison avec la recette de l'étouffée et le nom d'un bouquiniste parisien. L'air triomphant, en route pour l'hôtel, elle traverse le cimetière Saint-Louis, numéro 1. Elle s'arrête un petit moment près du tombeau de Marie Laveau, la célèbre reine du vaudou à la Nouvelle-Orléans au 19ème siècle, et elle repense à l'histoire que Sandrine lui a racontée. Elle achète une fleur blanche à une vieille femme qui a le visage caché par un grand foulard noir. Claire met la fleur devant le tombeau et repart. Bizarrement, la femme suit Claire jusqu'à la porte du cimetière et lui crie «Méfiez-vous des voleurs, mademoiselle !»

Culture

Dans les **cimetières historiques** de la Nouvelle-Orléans, on enterre les corps dans des tombeaux au-dessus du sol (*above ground*) à cause des fréquentes inondations qui agiteraient les cercueils (*caskets*) sous terre. Le tombeau de **Marie Laveau**, une vaudouiste très célèbre à la Nouvelle-Orléans dans les années 1880, est très ancien. Beaucoup de gens gravent des croix sur le tombeau et demandent de l'aide à l'esprit de Marie Laveau. Pourtant, cette pratique n'est pas une tradition acceptée et elle détruit le tombeau historique. Selon les traditions du vaudou, il vaut mieux laisser une offrande (*offering*) comme des fleurs, du rhum ou de l'argent.

Le tombeau de Marie Laveau dans le cimetière Saint-Louis, numéro 1, à la Nouvelle-Orléans.

Culture

Le **vaudou** est une religion d'origine africaine pratiquée en Afrique, à Haïti, à la Nouvelle-Orléans et dans beaucoup d'autres lieux dont la population est d'origine africaine ou haïtienne. Cette religion est souvent mal-représentée par les média. En réalité, les pratiquants de vaudou font des prières aux esprits (qu'on appelle les loas) et leur font des offrandes afin de demander du bonheur pour leurs familles et leurs amis. À Haïti, la plupart des gens (80 pour cent) pratiquent le catholicisme, mais la moitié (50 pour cent) pratiquent le vaudou en même temps, sans y voir de contradiction.

VOCABULAIRE

Dans la cuisine		Décrire une personne ou un événement	
boire	*to drink*	avoir la cinquantaine	*to be in one's 50s*
faire cuire	*to cook*	s'asseoir	*to sit down*
sentir	*to smell*	potelé(e)	*portly*
ajouter	*to add*	un(e) bouquiniste	*bookseller*
faire sauter	*to sauté*	un(e) bibliothécaire	*librarian*
faire mijoter	*to simmer*	mijoter un projet	*hatch a scheme*
remuer	*to stir*	voler	*steal*
une écrevisse	*crawfish*	s'échapper	*escape*
un poisson chat	*catfish*	se méfier de	*beware of*
une recette	*recipe*	confier	*confide, disclose*
une épice	*spice*	sur le coup	*on the spot, instantly*
une poêle	*frying pan*	une offrande	*offering*
une marmite	*pot*	un endroit	*place*
piquant(e)	*spicy/sharp*	le lendemain	*the next day*
		parmi	*among*

Après avoir lu

2.3 Avez-vous compris ? **Répondez** aux questions suivantes. **Justifiez vos réponses** en citant le texte.

1. Pourquoi est-ce que François Fontenot a quitté Saint-Domingue ?
2. Comment est-ce que le grand-père de Sandrine est mort ?
3. Quand est-ce que le père de Sandrine a vendu la bibliothèque familiale ? À qui l'a-t-il vendue ? Qu'est-ce qui était parmi les livres ? Pourquoi est-ce qu'il n'a rien dit au bouquiniste à propos du manuscrit ?
4. Qu'est-ce que la grand-mère de Sandrine a fait pour protéger sa famille des voleurs ? Croit-elle aux êtres surnaturels ?
5. Comment trouvez-vous Sandrine Fontenot-Chardin ? Voudriez-vous dîner chez elle un soir ? Pourquoi ou pourquoi pas ?
6. Quels conseils est-ce que Sandrine donne à Claire ?

Pour aller plus loin : CULTURE

ACTIVITÉ A : Apprenez un peu sur la religion vaudou. Consultez votre cahier électronique !

2.4 D'accord ou pas d'accord ? Indiquez si vous êtes **d'accord ou pas d'accord** avec les phrases suivantes, d'après votre compréhension du récit. Justifiez votre opinion en citant le texte, si possible. Discutez de vos réponses avec la classe.

	D'accord	Pas d'accord
1. Sandrine a fait bon acceuil à Claire.	_______	_______
2. Claire a bu un café et a mangé de l'étouffée.	_______	_______
3. Il est facile de faire cuire une étouffée.	_______	_______
4. Sandrine a vendu le manuscrit de Laclos.	_______	_______
5. Le manuscrit était maudit (*cursed*).	_______	_______
6. La visite chez Sandrine a été un succès pour Claire.	_______	_______

Langue

Dérouillez-vous la mémoire ! Rappelez-vous les mots pour **la nourriture**. S'il y a des aliments que vous adorez qui ne sont pas là, cherchez les mots dans le dictionnaire !

- **Viandes et volaille :** du bœuf, du porc, du jambon (*ham*), du veau (*veal*), du poulet (*chicken*), de la dinde (*turkey*), du canard (*duck*), du lapin (*rabbit*), des saucissons, du pâté de foie gras
- **Poissons et fruits de mer :** de la sole, du saumon (*salmon*), du thon (*tuna*), des moules (*mussels*), des palourdes (*clams*), des crevettes (*shrimp*), des écrevisses (*crawfish*), des huîtres (*oysters*), du homard (*lobster*)
- **Légumes :** une carotte, une tomate, un oignon, un concombre, des brocoli, du céleri, de la salade (*lettuce*), une aubergine (*eggplant*), une courgette (*zucchini*), une pomme de terre (*potato*), un poivron (*bell pepper*), des haricots (*beans*), du maïs (*corn*)
- **Fruits :** une orange, une banane, une pomme, une pêche, une poire (*pear*), un ananas (*pineapple*), du raisin (*grapes*), un citron (*lemon*), une fraise (*strawberry*), une framboise (*raspberry*), une myrtille (*blueberry*), un bleuet (*blueberry, Québec*), une canneberge (*cranberry*), des fruits des bois (*berries*)
- **Produits laitiers :** du lait, du fromage, du yaourt, du beurre, de la crème, de la glace (*ice cream*), des œufs (*eggs*)
- **Assaisonnements et produits de première nécessité :** du sel, du poivre, de l'ail (*garlic*), du basilic (*basil*), du persil, de l'huile, du vinaigre, de la moutarde, de la mayonnaise, du sucre, du miel (*honey*), de la cannelle (*cinnamon*), de la farine (*flour*), du riz (*rice*), des pâtes (*pasta*), une pâte (*dough or pie crust*), des nouilles (*noodles*)

2.5 La nourriture américaine Pendant son séjour à la Nouvelle-Orléans, Claire remarque que les Américains mangent toutes sortes de plats ethniques. **Faites correspondre le plat (à gauche) avec la description du plat (à droite).**

1. les sushi	a. une spécialité allemande faite de saucisses sur un lit de choux cuits
2. le pain perdu	b. un plat chinois fait avec des œufs, du porc, des petits pois, des oignons et du riz
3. les spaghetti	c. un pain mexicain rempli de viande hâchée épicée et garni de tomates, d'oignons et de fromage
4. le riz frit au porc	d. un rouleau japonais rempli de riz et de poisson cru, entouré d'une feuille d'algue et coupé en morceaux
5. les tacos	e. une spécialité du moyen-orient, faite de pois chiches moulus avec du citron, de l'huile d'olive et de l'ail
6. la choucroute (*sauerkraut*)	f. une spécialité du sud des États-Unis, faite de viande grillée couverte d'épices
7. le barbecue	g. un plat italien où des pâtes sont couvertes d'une sauce à la tomate, à l'ail et au basilic, servi avec du fromage râpé
8. le hummus	h. un plat français qu'on sert souvent aux États-Unis pour le petit déjeuner, fait de tranches de pain trempées (*dipped*) dans des œufs battus, cuites au beurre et servies avec du sirop d'érable

2.6 Le bien manger Regardez les mots de vocabulaire qui suivent. Dans chaque ligne, il y a **un mot qui ne va pas** avec les trois autres. Entourez ce mot et essayez d'expliquer pourquoi. Attention : Il y a parfois plusieurs bonnes réponses. Il faut justifier votre choix !

1. une table	une chaise	un four (*oven*)	un meuble à tiroirs (*cabinet*)
2. une poêle	une assiette	une marmite	un bol (*bowl*)
3. un couteau	une cuillère	une fourchette	des baguettes (*chopsticks*)
4. un hamburger	un po'boy	un beignet	une étouffée
5. mijoter	sauter	ajouter	rôtir (*to roast*)
6. doux (*sweet*)	épicé	amer (*bitter*)	crémeux
7. du bœuf	du porc	du poulet	du saumon
8. des tomates	des citrons	des ananas	des œufs

Haïti

Rencontrez un Haïtien-Américain !
Regardez la vidéo et consultez votre cahier d'activités !

Culture

Beaucoup d'Haïtiens ont immigré en Louisiane à la fin du 18ème et au début du 19ème siècle, pendant et après la Révolution haïtienne. Pendant le 20ème siècle aussi, beaucoup d'Haïtiens ont quitté leur pays afin de se faire une vie ailleurs, de trouver des emplois ou de chercher l'asile politique.
On trouve des communautés de cette **diaspora haïtienne** en France (surtout à Paris), au Canada (surtout à Montréal), dans plusieurs pays francophones de l'Afrique, et bien sûr, aux États-Unis (surtout à Miami, à New York et à Boston).

2.7 Le courriel De retour à l'Hôtel Le Moyne, Claire branche son ordinateur portable. Elle écrit un petit message au courriel à sa sœur pour parler de sa rencontre avec Sandrine. **Remplissez les blancs** avec un mot ou expression convenable de la liste suivante.

bourse	**cuisine**	**épices**	**ingrédients**
marmite	**mijoter**	**poisson**	**recette**

Chère Marie,

Salut ! Aujourd'hui j'ai rencontré Sandrine Fontenot-Chardin, la descendante de l'homme qui a transporté le manuscrit de Laclos en Louisiane ! Elle était très gentille. Elle m'a accueillie dans sa maison et nous avons parlé dans la __________________ pendant qu'elle préparait une étouffée. Elle m'a donné la __________________ de ce plat traditionnel. Il paraît qu'on met tous les __________________, des oignons, des poivrons et des tomates, dans une grande __________________. Puis on ajoute beaucoup d'__________________ pour que le plat ait un goût piquant. Et finalement, il faut laisser __________________ l'étouffée quelque temps. Sandrine a fait ce plat avec des écrevisses, mais on peut aussi utiliser du poulet ou du __________________. Ça a l'air délicieux, non ? Oui, je sais, tu veux savoir si j'ai trouvé le manuscrit. Hélas, le père de Sandrine l'a vendu à un bouquiniste parisien, il y a trente ans (*thirty years ago*). Je ne sais pas s'il vaudra la peine d'être lu, mais comme je viens de recevoir cette ______________ de l'université et que j'ai assez d'argent, je pense y aller moi-même pour parler avec la famille du bouquiniste. Au pire, je perds un peu de temps. Enfin, je vais réfléchir un peu avant de prendre une décision. Autrement, tout va bien ici. Et toi ? Tu te reposes à la campagne ?

Bisous, Claire

Pour aller plus loin : CULTURE

ACTIVITÉ B : Apprenez à préparer des recettes françaises ! Consultez votre cahier électronique !

Vocabulaire

Vous rappelez-vous les mots pour **parler des repas** et **pour faire la cuisine** ? Révisez ceux qui suivent !

Pour parler des repas : le petit déjeuner, le déjeuner, le goûter, l'apéritif (*before-dinner drink*), un hors-d'œuvre, un amuse-gueule (*appetizer*), le dîner, l'entrée (*first course*), le plat principal, le dessert, le digestif (*after-dinner drink*) (Attention : au Québec, le repas du matin est «le déjeuner», le repas du midi est «le dîner», et le repas du soir est «le souper» !)

Pour préparer les repas : une poêle, une marmite, une casserole (*saucepan*), une grande cuillère (*big spoon*), une cuillerée (*spoonful*), une pincée (*pinch*), la cuisinière (*stove*), le four (*oven*), le four à micro-ondes, le réfrigérateur (un frigo), le congélateur (*freezer*), décongeler, remuer, mélanger, ajouter, faire cuire (au four), faire sauter, faire mijoter, faire griller, faire bouillir (*to boil*), faire dorer (*to brown*), faire rôtir

Pour mettre la table : une cuillère (à thé, à café, ou à soupe), une fourchette, un couteau, une assiette (*plate*), un plat (*platter*), un saladier (*large salad serving bowl*), un bol, un verre, une tasse, servir, débarrasser la table (*to clear the table*), faire la vaisselle (*to do the dishes*)

2.8 Vocabulaire personnel Pensez à vos préférences culinaires et, pour chaque catégorie, **faites une liste de cinq à dix mots** importants que vous pouvez utiliser pour décrire vos propres repas. Consultez un dictionnaire si nécessaire.

1. Les plats que vous mangez le plus souvent à la maison : au petit déjeuner, au déjeuner, au goûter, au dîner
2. Vos boissons préférées
3. Les ingrédients que vous adorez : les protéines, les légumes, les fruits, les produits à base de céréales (*carbohydrates*), les assaisonnements
4. Les ingrédients que vous détestez ou auxquels vous êtes allergique
5. Vos restaurants préférés et les plats ou les boissons que vous y prenez souvent

2.9 L'heure du champagne Claire descend à la cour à 19h pour prendre un verre de champagne avec les autres clients de l'hôtel, comme d'habitude. Là, elle revoit Jean-Louis qui l'invite à dîner au restaurant. **Choisissez** une des expressions entre parenthèses et **lisez le dialogue** à haute voix avec un partenaire. Quand vous voyez «? ? ?», imaginez votre propre expression.

JEAN-LOUIS : Bonsoir, Claire. Comment ça va ?

CLAIRE : Bonsoir. (Je vais bien. / Pas mal. / ? ? ?) Et toi ?

JEAN-LOUIS : Ça va. Je te conseille de goûter ces (hors-d'œuvre / amuse-gueule) que notre hôtelier vient de préparer. Ils sont vraiment (extraordinaires / délicieux) !

CLAIRE : (Merci / Bonne idée) !

JEAN-LOUIS : Ce fromage me rappelle la fondue de ma grand-mère.

CLAIRE : (Vraiment ? / Pas possible ! / ? ? ?) La fondue est une spécialité suisse, non ?

JEAN-LOUIS : Tu as raison. Ma famille vient d'une petite ville près de la frontière suisse. On y trouve (le meilleur fromage / beaucoup de vaches) ! Écoute, j'ai (très faim / une faim de loup). Ça te dit de dîner au restaurant avec moi ce soir ?

CLAIRE : Eh, j'aimerais bien, mais j'allais souper ici dans ma chambre. . .

JEAN-LOUIS : Allez ! (Laisse-toi convaincre ! / Viens avec moi au restaurant créole.) Je n'ai pas envie de dîner seul ce soir.

CLAIRE : Bon, d'accord. À vrai dire, j'ai très envie de découvrir une étouffée, mais apporte ton parapluie ! Il va (pleuvoir / neiger) ce soir.

JEAN-LOUIS : (Super ! / Formidable ! / ? ? ?) Essayons ce petit restaurant à côté de l'hôtel. Il a l'air intéressant.

CLAIRE : Entendu.

JEAN-LOUIS : Et puis, tu me parleras de ta journée ! Tu as réussi à trouver ton manuscrit ?

CLAIRE : Oh, ça ! Ne m'embête pas avec des questions sur mon travail. Allons souper et parlons d'autres choses !

les invitations

	Formal	**Informal**
Invitations	Voudriez-vous m'accompagner à. . . ?	Tu veux venir. . . ?
	Seriez-vous libre de. . . ?	Tu es libre ? Je t'invite à. . . !
	Je vous invite à. . .	Ça t'intéresse ? Ça te dit ?
Acceptances	Merci, j'aimerais bien. . .	D'accord ! Bien sûr !
	J'accepte avec plaisir.	Pourquoi pas ! Allons-y !
Refusals	C'est très gentil, mais. . .	Zut ! Je ne suis pas libre.
	Je voudrais bien, mais. . .	Je suis pris(e).
	Je ne peux pas me libérer.	Désolé(e) ! Je ne peux pas.
	Malheureusement, je suis pris(e).	Ce n'est pas mon truc.
	Je suis très occupé(e) en ce moment.	Va te faire cuire un œuf ! (*impoli*)
Encouragements	Venez avec moi !	Viens avec moi ! S'il te plaît !
	Laissez-vous convaincre !	Laisse-toi convaincre !
	Ne me laissez pas seul(e) !	Ne me laisse pas tomber !
	Allez ! J'insiste !	Allez ! J'insiste !

2.10 À vous **Imaginez que vous êtes dans les situations suivantes. Que dites-vous ?** Avec un partenaire, choisissez des expressions pour chaque situation.

1. Vous voulez inviter Claire et Jean-Louis à dîner avec vous.
2. Vous ne voulez pas aller au cinéma avec votre cousin, un homme contrariant (*annoying*).
3. Vos amis ne veulent pas aller au café avec vous. Il faut les convaincre !
4. Un petit garçon que vous rencontrez dans le parc veut de la glace au chocolat. Refusez d'en acheter une pour lui.
5. Votre copain/copine veut aller à un concert de jazz, mais vous êtes fatigué(e). Essayez de refuser.
6. Une personne mystérieuse vous invite à visiter les marécages (*swamps*). Acceptez.

2.11 Samedi soir Sur une feuille de papier, écrivez une phrase pour décrire une activité que vous ne voudriez *pas* faire le samedi soir ! Puis, **circulez** dans la salle de classe et **invitez vos camarades** à faire cette activité avec vous. **Essayez de convaincre** autant de personnes que possible !

MODÈLE : Aller au cirque

—Je t'invite à aller au cirque samedi soir. Ça te dit ?

—Désolée, mais ce n'est pas mon truc.

—Mais, c'est amusant ! Allons, laisse-toi convaincre !

Langue

Vous rappelez-vous les conjugaisons des **verbes irréguliers** suivants : **boire, croire, devoir , recevoir** et **voir** ? Si non, mémorisez leurs conjugaisons avant de continuer !

- **boire** (*to drink*) : je bois, tu bois, il/elle/on boit, nous buvons, vous buvez, ils/elles boivent
- **croire** (*to believe*) : je crois, tu crois, il/elle/on croit, nous croyons, vous croyez, ils/elles croient
- **devoir** (*to have to, must, to owe*) : je dois, tu dois, il/elle/on doit, nous devons, vous devez, ils/elles doivent
- **recevoir** (*to receive*) : je reçois, tu reçois, il/elle/on reçoit, nous recevons, vous recevez, ils/elles reçoivent
- **voir** (*to see*) : je vois, tu vois, il/elle/on voit, nous voyons, vous voyez, ils/elles voient

2.12 À la carte Claire et Jean-Louis décident de manger au Restaurant Bienville ensemble. Voici le menu ! Consultez-le et puis **répondez aux questions** suivantes.

Entrées	
Soupe à l'oignon gratinée	$6
Gumbo maison	$7
Escargots à l'ail (8)	$8
Crabe farci (*stuffed*)	$9
Salade au chèvre chaud	$8
Salade verte	$5
Plats	
Saumon en sauce blanche avec moules	$18
Crevettes créoles et riz	$16
Rôti de porc avec sauce piquante et pommes sautées	$17
Poulet à l'étouffée et riz	$16
Filet de sole au citron avec haricots verts et courgettes	$18
Alligator sauté avec des pommes de terre rôties	$19
Bœuf bourguignon	$17
Riz et haricots rouges	$10
Desserts	
Mousse au chocolat	$6
Glaces au choix (chocolat, vanille, fruits des bois)	$5
Fromages au choix (brie, chèvre, camembert, bleu)	$5
Tarte du jour	$6
Boissons	
Eaux minérales	$2
Apéritifs et digestifs	$5
Carafe de vin (litre/demi-litre)	$18/$11
Café ou thé	$3

1. Sur le menu, il y a des spécialités créoles et des plats plus traditionnellement français. Pouvez-vous les identifier ?
2. Voyez-vous des fruits de mer sur le menu ? Nommez-les.
3. Qu'est-ce qu'on peut commander (*order*) si on est végétarien(ne) ?
4. Quels plats aimeriez-vous goûter ? Pourquoi ? Y a-t-il des plats qui vous dégoûtent ? Pourquoi ?

5. Croyez-vous que le menu présente un bon choix de plats ? Quelles modifications voudriez-vous faire ?
6. Est-ce que vous recevez souvent des amis chez vous ? Si non, pourquoi pas ? Si oui, servez-vous des plats comme ceux qu'on trouve dans ce restaurant ? Pourquoi ou pourquoi pas ?
7. Imaginez que vous dînez dans ce restaurant ce soir. Qu'est-ce que vous prendriez comme entrée ? comme plat principal ? comme dessert ?
8. Qu'est-ce que vous buvez avec le dîner ? et après ?
9. Combien devez-vous payer pour votre dîner ? Et combien allez-vous laisser comme pourboire (*tip*) au serveur ?

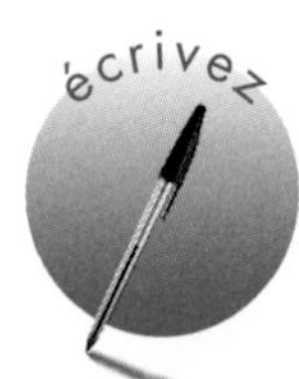

À l'écrit *première étape*

Pour aller plus loin : CULTURE
ACTIVITÉ C : Soyez «critique gastronomique» ! Consultez votre cahier électronique !

2.13 Un dîner élégant Vous invitez des amis francophones à dîner chez vous. **Choisissez les plats que vous allez servir et faites une liste des ingrédients** que vous devez acheter au supermarché. N'oubliez pas qu'il vous faut des hors-d'œuvre, une entrée (*first course*), un plat principal (*main course*) avec des légumes, une salade, un dessert et des boissons. Ensuite, échangez votre menu et votre liste d'ingrédients avec un camarade de classe. Vérifiez que votre partenaire a pensé à tous les ingrédients nécessaires. Ajoutez des ingrédients ou faites des suggestions si nécessaires.

L'invitation

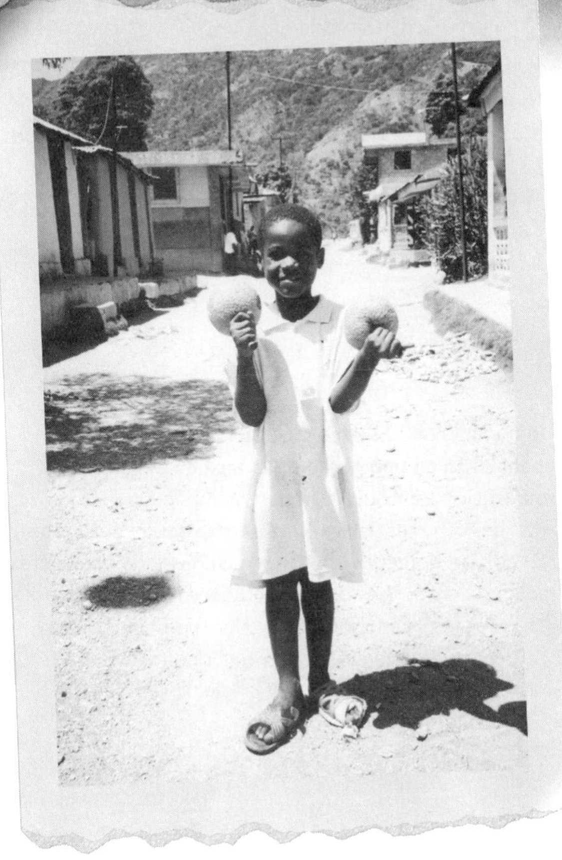

Une jeune Haïtienne avec des fruits.

Structures *le partitif*

2.14 Au restaurant créole Claire et Jean-Louis s'assoient à une petite table au Restaurant Bienville. Le serveur leur décrit les plats du jour. Réfléchissez à l'usage des articles (voir Chapitre 1). Dans quelles circonstances utilise-t-on les articles définis ? les articles indéfinis ? Quand est-ce qu'on emploie **de** tout seul ? **Lisez le petit dialogue et faites attention à l'usage du *partitif*** (en caractères gras) : **du, de l', de la**. Pouvez-vous décrire les conditions pour l'usage du *partitif* par rapport aux autres articles ?

SERVEUR : Bonsoir, madame et monsieur. Bienvenu au Restaurant Bienville. Aujourd'hui, nous avons plusieurs plats du jour. Notre chef vous propose comme entrée des bananes des Antilles (*plantains*), qui sont frites et servies avec une sauce piquante. C'est une spécialité haïtienne. Et comme plat principal, nous vous proposons également **du** poulet Port-au-Prince avec une salsa antillaise.

JEAN-LOUIS : Qu'est-ce que c'est que le poulet Port-au-Prince ?

SERVEUR :	C'est **du** poulet rôti aux épices haïtiennes, servi avec **du** riz et **de la** salsa. Dans la salsa antillaise, il y a de belles tomates fraîches, des oignons, **de l'**ail, **de la** mangue, **du** maïs et **du** jus de citron vert. C'est très léger et très savoureux. Nous avons aussi **du** homard farci accompagné d'un beurre au citron. Il est servi avec des légumes à la vapeur (*steamed*).
CLAIRE :	Est-ce possible de commander l'étouffée avec des écrevisses au lieu du (*instead of the*) poulet ?
SERVEUR :	Oui, oui. Pas de problème, madame. Vous êtes prêts à commander ?
JEAN-LOUIS :	Non, donnez-nous encore quelques minutes, s'il vous plaît. Je n'ai pas encore choisi.

Culture

La ville de **Port-au-Prince** est la capitale de la République d'Haïti. Haïti et la République dominicaine occupent chacune une partie de la même île située aux Antilles, dans la mer des Caraïbes. Haïti se trouve à l'ouest et la République dominicaine se trouve à l'est de l'île. D'autres îles voisines sont Cuba au nord-ouest et la Jamaïque au sud-ouest. La **cuisine haïtienne** représente un mélange de cultures qui ont influencé la culture créole haïtienne : des peuples indigènes (les Caraïbes), des colonisateurs européens (la France et l'Espagne), des cultures africaines, des influences antillaises des îles voisines, aussi bien que de la culture américaine. Aujourd'hui, cependant, la sous-alimentation (*malnutrition*) reste un problème sérieux à Haïti où la situation économique demeure précaire.

Pour aller plus loin : CULTURE

ACTIVITÉ D : Pour en savoir davantage sur l'histoire et la culture d'Haïti, consultez votre cahier électronique !

le partitif

The *partitive* (**le partitif : du, de l', de la**), much like the *indefinite article* (**l'article indéfini : un, une, des**), is used to refer to nouns that are not identifiable in a given context (review *Comment faire : les articles définis et indéfinis* in Épisode 2 of Chapter 1). The partitive, however, is used to talk about an *unspecified quanitity* of a noun (an unspecified part of a whole) or a noun that exists in a form that is *uncountable* (therefore always an unspecified quantity). By this definition, the *partitive* can never be plural (plural nouns are countable or whole units). When deciding whether to use the partitive, keep the following two questions in mind.

Is the noun *countable*?

Uncountable nouns, also called *mass nouns*, require the *partitive* when not identifiable. Examples of mass nouns are liquids, foods with very small grains, or abstract concepts: **de l'**eau, **du** sel, **du** beurre, **de la** joie. Examples of *count nouns*, which take an indefinite article, are foods that are consumed in individual pieces or ones that can be separated into countable pieces: **une** pomme, **un** homard, **des** crevettes (une crevette, deux crevettes), **des** petits pois (un pois, deux pois, trois pois). So, is the noun countable?

Yes! It is countable. Use the *indefinite article* (**un, une, des**): **une** sauce piquante, **des** bananes, **des** légumes.

No! It is an uncountable noun. Use the *partitive* (**du, de la, de l'**) to refer to mass nouns: **du** riz, **de la** salsa, **du** maïs.

Is there a *specific quantity* of the noun indicated?

Unspecified quantities of nouns also require the *partitive*. Count nouns can take the partitive when they exist in an unspecified quantity, that is, when you are referring to a part of a whole. Use the partitive when talking about an unspecified portion of a noun: **du** café (vs. un café), **du** homard (vs. un homard). Is the quantity specified?

Yes! It is specified. Use the *indefinite article* (**un, une, des**) or an expression of quantity: **une** salsa antillaise, **beaucoup de** fruits.

No! It is an uncountable or an unspecified quantity. Use the *partitive* (**du, de la, de l'**): **du** poulet rôti, **de la** mangue.

Remember!

- Some nouns can only be *mass nouns*, but some can be either mass nouns or count nouns, depending on the context: one does not usually speak of "a rice" or "a salt," but one can speak of "a coffee" or "a sauce." For example, **sauce** is a mass noun (**de la** sauce), but can also exist in countable quantities when referring to types or to a canned product: **une** sauce piquante, **deux** sauces piquantes, etc.
- You can specify a quantity of an obligitory mass noun by using an *expression of quantity*: **une cuillerée de** sel, **un bol de** riz. Expressions of quantity are always followed by **de** and never by the partitive or the indefinite article.
- Note that the *partitive* resembles the contraction of the preposition **de** (*of/from*) with the *definite article* **le, la** (*the*): **du, de la** (*of the/from the*). Be careful to distinguish between the two. Some examples of contractions with the preposition **de** are: plats **du** jour (specials *of the* day), au lieu **du** poulet (instead *of the* chicken), bananes **des** Antilles (bananas *from the* Antilles).
- Also remember that **de** alone is used after a negative (il n'y a pas **de** problème), before a plural noun qualified by a preceding adjective (**de** belles tomates), with an expression of quantity (beaucoup **de** fruits), or when specifying a variety of something (du jus **de** citron vert).

2.15 Au restaurant créole (*suite*) Le dîner continue... **Remplissez les blancs** avec un **article défini (le, la, les)** pour les noms identifiables ou génériques, un **article indéfini (un, une, des)** pour les noms non identifiables et contables, le **partitif (du, de l', de la)** pour les noms non indentifiables et en quantité non spécifique ou **de** tout seul (avec un négatif, une expression de quantité, etc.). Il y a parfois plus d'une bonne réponse d'après votre interprétation du contexte.

JEAN-LOUIS : Alors, vous aimez ________ écrevisses ?

CLAIRE : Je ne sais pas, mais je voudrais essayer ________ écrevisses à l'étouffée.

JEAN-LOUIS : On étouffe (*smother*) les écrevisses avec ________ oignons et ________ tomates, c'est ça ?

CLAIRE : Oui, et beaucoup ________ épices créoles.

JEAN-LOUIS : Moi, je voudrais ________ fruits de mer aussi. Je mange souvent ________ poisson. C'est très bon pour la santé. Je ne veux pas ________ poulet, mais ________ poulet Port-au-Prince a l'air très bon.

CLAIRE : C'est vrai. Il y a trop ________ choix ! Moi, je veux commencer avec ________ salade. Je crois que je vais prendre ________ salade comme entrée, et puis je prendrai ________ écrevisses à l'étouffée.

JEAN-LOUIS : C'est dommage qu'il n'y ait pas ________ ratatouille au menu. C'est un de mes plats favoris. Ma mère fait une ratatouille exceptionnelle avec ________ aubergines, ________ oignons, ________ tomates, ________ ail et ________ champignons. Mais on est en Louisiane, alors il faut manger ________ fruits de mer !

2.16 Des fêtes américaines Imaginez que vous parlez avec Claire et Jean-Louis. Ils veulent savoir **ce que les Américains mangent** pour célébrer leurs jours de fête. **Décrivez tous les plats** que vous préparez pour célébrer les fêtes suivantes chez vous, et parlez des principaux ingrédients qu'il faut acheter afin de les préparer ! N'oubliez pas les boissons et les desserts. Attention à l'usage des articles !

MODÈLE : son anniversaire →

On mange son plat préféré, et puis on mange du gâteau et de la glace !

1. le jour de Thanksgiving (en novembre)
2. la fête nationale américaine (le 4 juillet)
3. la veille de la Toussaint (le 31 octobre)
4. la fête de la Saint-Valentin (le 14 février)
5. la fête des mères (en mai)

Langue

À Haïti, le **français** et le **kreyòl** (le créole haïtien) sont les deux langues officielles, mais moins de 15 pour cent de la population parle français à la maison. La plupart parle kreyòl, une langue distincte du français, qui comprend des mots français, africains, arawaks, espagnols et américains. Beaucoup d'expressions en kreyòl ressemblent phonétiquement à leurs cousins français. Pouvez-vous deviner le sens des expressions suivantes ? : (a) tanzantan, (b) soivouplé, (c) li fè chô, (d) i pa bon, (e) an nou zouké, (f) ka ki là ? Lequel veut dire «s'il vous plaît», «ce n'est pas bon», «de temps en temps», «Qui est là ?», «allons danser» (de la musique zouk, très populaire aux Antilles) et «il fait chaud» ? Voyez-vous des similarités et des différences ?

2.17 Votre repas préféré Avec un partenaire, **faites la liste des ingrédients** d'un de vos plats préférés (une pizza, une lasagne, des burritos, des biscuits, etc.). Puis, lisez votre liste à haute voix. Vos camarades de classe vont deviner (*to guess*) de quel plat il s'agit !

MODÈLE : On y met du beurre, du sucre, des œufs, de la farine et des petits morceaux de chocolat

—Ce sont des biscuits «chocolate chip» !

Haïti

Découvrez un plat typique haïtien. Regardez la vidéo et consultez votre cahier d'activités !

Structures *l'interrogatif*

2.18 Quoi ? Pendant le dîner, Claire écoute les gens qui parlent à la table d'à côté, et elle entend beaucoup de questions. **Faites correspondre** la question (à gauche) à sa réponse logique (à droite). Marquez la lettre appropriée à gauche.

_______	1. **Qu'est-ce que** vous voulez boire ?	a. La semaine prochaine. (*time*)
_______	2. **Qui est-ce que** tu as rencontré ?	b. À 6h30. (*time*)
_______	3. **Qui est-ce qui** travaille à la réception ?	c. J'ai rencontré Jean-Louis. (*person*)
_______	4. **Où est-ce qu'**on trouve ce musée ?	d. Philippe travaille ce soir. (*person*)
_______	5. **Pourquoi est-ce que** tu ne manges pas ?	e. De ma sœur Marie. (*person*)
_______	6. **Qu'est-ce qui** s'est passé ?	f. C'est dans le Vieux Carré. (*place*)
_______	7. **Comment** était le concert ?	g. Un jus d'orange. (*thing*)
_______	8. **Que** voudriez-vous comme dessert ?	h. De la glace au chocolat. (*thing*)
_______	9. **Quand est-ce que** tu pars ?	i. On a dîné ensemble. (*event*)
_______	10. De **quoi** parles-tu ?	j. C'était un concert super ! (*event*)
_______	11. De **qui** parlez-vous ?	k. De la révolution haïtienne. (*event*)
_______	12. **À quelle heure est-ce que** tu te lèves ?	l. Parce que j'ai déjà dîné. (*explanation*)

Regardez bien les questions et réponses ci-dessus (*above*) et puis **répondez** aux questions suivantes sur l'interrogatif.

- Quelle est la différence entre «Quand» et «À quelle heure» ?
- Quelle est la différence entre «Qu'est-ce que» et «Qu'est-ce qui» ? entre «Que» et «Qu'est-ce que» ?
- Quelle est la différence entre «Qui est-ce que» et «Qui est-ce qui» ? entre «Qui» et «Qui est-ce qui» ?
- Quelle est la différence entre «de quoi» et «de qui» ? quelles en sont les similarités ?
- Quelles expressions peuvent se traduire avec le mot anglais «*what*» ?

l'interrogatif

To form an *information question*, use an interrogative expression. Common interrogatives are:

Qui ? **Qui** (+ *verb*) *or* **Qui est-ce qui** (+ *verb*) →
Qui est-ce qui travaille ce soir ?

Qui est-ce que (+ *subject* + *verb*) →
Qui est-ce que tu as rencontré ?

(*Preposition*) + **qui** (+ est-ce que *or inverted verb-subject*) →
À qui penses-tu ?

Quoi ? **Qu'est-ce qui** (+ *verb*) →
Qu'est-ce qui ne va pas ?

Que (+ *inverted verb-subject*) *or* **Qu'est-ce que** (+ *subject* + *verb*) →
Qu'est-ce que tu veux ?

(*Preposition*) + **quoi** (+ est-ce que *or inverted verb-subject*) →
À quoi penses-tu ?

Quand ? **Quand** (+ est-ce que *or inverted verb-subject*) →
Quand part-elle ?

À quelle heure (+ est-ce que *or inverted verb-subject*) →
À quelle heure part-elle ?

Où ? **Où** (+ est-ce que *or inverted verb-subject*) →
Où va-t-elle ?

Pourquoi ? **Pourquoi** (+ est-ce que *or inverted verb-subject*) →
Pourquoi part-elle ?

Pour quelle raison (+ *inverted verb-subject*) →
Pour quelle raison veut-elle partir ?

Comment ? **Comment** (+ est-ce que *or inverted verb-subject*) →
Comment s'appelle-t-elle ?

Combien ? **Combien** (+ est-ce que *or inverted verb-subject*) →
Combien coûte le sandwich ?

Combien de (+ noun + est-ce que *or inverted verb-subject*) →
Combien de livres a-t-elle ?

Remember!

- The question *who?* usually begins with **qui** and the question *what?* usually begins with **que**, unless there is a preposition involved; however, the endings of the interrogative expressions are determined by their grammatical function in the sentence. When the interrogative expression is a subject, it ends with **qui** (followed directly by a verb): **Qui est-ce qui** travaille ? **Qu'est-ce qui** sent bon ? When the interrogative expression is a direct object of a verb, it ends in **que** (followed by a subject and verb): **Qui est-ce que** tu cherches ? **Qu'est-ce que** tu prépares ?
- The term **quoi** can be used after a preposition (**De quoi** te mêles-tu ?), or it can be used alone to ask *what?* in familiar situations if you did not clearly hear someone or understand something (**Quoi ?**).
- When asking about *time*, **quand** refers to a general time-frame, while **à quelle heure** is used to ask the specific hour something occurs.
- The term **comment ?** means *how?* but can also be translated as *what?* in certain English contexts (**Comment** était le voleur ? → *What did the robber look like?*). It can also be used alone to ask *what?* if you did not hear someone or understand something (**Comment** ?). The term **combien ?** means *how much?* (**Combien** coûte le vin ?) or *how many?* when followed by **de** (**Combien de** touristes visitent Haïti chaque année ?).
- Most *interrogative expressions* are followed by either **est-ce que** or inversion of the subject and verb.

You will learn more about the interrogative adjective **quel(le)** (*which/what*) in Chapitre 4, Épisode 2.

2.19 Claire pose des questions Claire pose des questions personnelles à Jean-Louis. Remplissez les blancs avec **une expression interrogative**.

1. _______________ est-ce que tu es né ?

   Jean-Louis : Je suis né à Annecy, une petite ville près de la frontière suisse.

2. _______________ ta famille a-t-elle déménagé (*moved*) à Paris ?

   Jean-Louis : Parce que la famille de mon père habite la région parisienne.

3. _______________ est-ce que tu as commencé à travailler au bar irlandais ?

   Jean-Louis : L'année dernière.

4. _______________ tu vas faire demain ?

   Jean-Louis : Je ne sais pas. Je pense aller au musée du Mardi gras pour voir les masques.

5. Avec _______________ vas-tu au musée ?

   Jean-Louis : J'y vais tout seul. Tu veux m'accompagner ?

6. _______________ tu connais à la Nouvelle-Orléans ?

   Jean-Louis : Je connais bien Henri Hébert, mais il habite à Lafayette.

7. ______________ est-ce que tu as trouvé l'Hôtel Le Moyne ?

   Jean-Louis : Un ami m'a dit que c'était un bon hôtel au cœur du Vieux Carré.

8. À ______________ t'intéresses-tu ? à la politique ? à la musique ?

   Jean-Louis : Je m'intéresse à tout. En ce moment, je m'intéresse beaucoup à la littérature.

2.20 Qu'est-ce qui se passe ? **Faites une liste de huit questions** que vous voulez poser à quelqu'un que vous venez de rencontrer afin de mieux le connaître. Puis, **posez vos questions** à un(e) partenaire qui joue la rôle de l'autre personne, et répondez à votre tour.

MODÈLE : Où est-ce que vous habitez ?

—J'habite à la résidence universitaire. Et vous ?

—Moi, j'ai un appartement en ville.

Avant d'écouter

2.21 Avant l'invitation Regardez les questions suivantes et décidez si c'est un **serveur** ou **un client** qui pose la question. Ensuite, **imaginez une courte réponse** polie.

1. Vous avez déjà choisi ?
2. Est-ce que vous voudriez voir la carte de vins ?
3. Qu'est-ce que vous nous conseillez comme entrée ?
4. Aimeriez-vous encore du pain ?
5. Quel vin utilisez-vous dans votre bœuf bourguignon ?
6. Vous désirez autre chose ?
7. L'addition (*bill*), s'il vous plaît ?
8. Encore un peu de café, madame ?

écoutez

L'invitation

Au Restaurant Bienville, Claire et Jean-Louis commandent leurs repas. Ensuite, Jean-Louis pose des questions à Claire, et Claire reçoit une invitation inattendue. . .

Maintenant, écoutez le dialogue sur votre CD. Consultez le vocabulaire ci-dessous et lisez les notes culturelles pour mieux comprendre le dialogue, et puis répondez aux questions suivantes.

VOCABULAIRE

Discuter au restaurant

commander	*to order*
apporter	*to bring (things)*
valoir	*to be worth*
ça vaut la peine	*it's worth the trouble*
il vaut mieux	*it's better, it would be better*
perdre confiance en	*to lose confidence in*
on verra	*we'll see*
ça dépend	*it depends*
remercier	*to thank*

Après avoir écouté

2.22 Avez-vous compris ? En petits groupes, **répondez aux questions** suivantes.

1. Quand est-ce que Claire va quitter la Nouvelle-Orléans ? et Jean-Louis ?
2. Où vont-ils aller ? Pourquoi est-ce qu'ils vont partir ?
3. Décrivez le problème en face de Claire. À votre avis, doit-elle abandonner son projet de recherche ?
4. Quelle est l'invitation de Jean-Louis ? Que pensez-vous de cette invitation ?
5. Qu'est-ce que Claire et Jean-Louis commandent (*order*) ? Est-ce qu'ils ont bien choisi leurs repas ?
6. Que pensez-vous du dîner en général ? Est-ce que Claire et Jean-Louis s'amusent ?

i Culture

Vous connaissez déjà quelques **expressions et proverbes culinaires** comme «Les haricots sont pas salés» et «L'okra ne se mange pas d'un seul doigt». Une autre expression louisianaise est «Lâche pas la patate !». Il y a aussi beaucoup de proverbes français, parmi lesquels : «La caque (*barrel*) sent toujours le hareng (*herring*)», «Faute de grives (*thrush, a delicacy*) on mange des merles (*blackbirds*)», «Vieille viande fait bonne soupe» et «On ne fait pas d'omelette sans casser d'œufs». Pouvez-vous expliquer leur sens sans traduire en anglais ? Connaissez-vous des proverbes culinaires en anglais ?

2.23 D'accord ou pas d'accord ? Après avoir écouté le dialogue entre Claire et Jean-Louis au restaurant, lisez les phrases suivantes et **donnez votre opinion**. Discutez en petits groupes.

	D'accord	Pas d'accord
1. Jean-Louis aime les fruits de mer.	_______	_______
2. Personne ne mange de bœuf.	_______	_______
3. Claire préfère l'eau minérale et ne boit pas de vin.	_______	_______
4. Claire ne veut pas entendre les conseils de Jean-Louis.	_______	_______
5. Jean-Louis et Claire vont bientôt quitter la Louisiane.	_______	_______
6. Claire va rester chez Jean-Louis à Paris.	_______	_______

dîner au restaurant

Ordering food	Je prends. . . Je voudrais essayer. . . J'aimerais. . . Apportez-moi. . . Donnez-moi. . .
Asking questions	Qu'est-ce que vous me conseillez ? Qu'avez-vous comme entrées / fruits de mer / desserts / etc. ? Est-ce que nous pourrions avoir encore du pain / de l'eau / etc. ? Quels sont les ingrédients dans le/la. . . ? Comment est-ce qu'on prépare le poisson / le poulet / etc. ? Où sont les toilettes ? Est-ce que nous pourrions avoir l'addition (*the bill*), s'il vous plaît ? Est-ce que le service est compris (*included*) ?

Pour aller plus loin : CINÉMA

ACTIVITÉ E : Regardez le film *Le Dîner de cons*, une comédie basée sur l'idée de réunir amis et inconnus pour un dîner un peu spécial. Consultez votre cahier électronique !

2.24 Que dites-vous ? Qu'est-ce qu'on peut dire pour se faire comprendre **dans les situations suivantes** ? Avec un partenaire, décidez quelles questions vous pouvez poser.

MODÈLE : Vous hésitez entre deux plats et vous voulez savoir l'opinion du serveur. →

—Qu'est-ce que vous me conseillez comme plat principal, le poulet ou le poisson ?

1. Vous voulez savoir les ingrédients qui figurent dans le gumbo.
2. Vous voulez vous laver les mains avant de commencer à manger.
3. Vous voulez un cendrier (*ashtray*) pour fumer votre cigare. (*ou* : Vous ne voulez plus vous asseoir à côté de ces gens qui fument !)
4. Vous voulez payer et vous voulez savoir si le restaurant accepte les cartes de crédit.
5. Vous voulez savoir si le poisson est frais ou congelé (*frozen*).
6. Vous ne voulez pas de dessert aux noix (*nuts*) à cause de votre allergie.
7. Vous voulez savoir combien coûte le plat du jour.
8. Vous voulez une autre tasse de café.

demander et donner une opinion

	Formal	**Informal**
Asking for an opinion	Que pensez-vous de. . . ?	Que penses-tu de. . . ?
	Qu'en pensez-vous ?	Qu'en penses-tu ?
	Qu'est-ce que vous me suggérez ?	Qu'est-ce que tu me suggères ?
	Qu'en dites-vous ?	Qu'en dis-tu ?
	Que me conseillez-vous ?	Qu'est-ce que tu me conseilles ?
	Dites-moi ce que vous pensez de. . .	Dis-moi ce que tu penses de. . .
	Dites-moi la vérité !	Dis-moi la vérité !
	Soyez honnête !	Sois honnête !
	Parlez franchement.	Parle franchement.
Giving your opinion: encouragements & warnings	Je crois/pense que. . .	Je crois/pense que. . .
	Vous devriez. . .	Tu devrais. . .
	Ne perdez pas confiance !	Ne perds pas confiance !
	Allez, il faut essayer/persévérer !	Allez, il faut essayer/persévérer !
	Soyez prudent(e)/patient(e) !	Sois prudent(e)/patient(e) !
	Ayez du courage !	Aie du courage !
	Ne vous inquiétez pas !	Ne t'inquiète pas !
	Méfiez-vous de. . . !	Méfie-toi de. . . !
	Attention ! Réfléchissez bien à. . . !	Attention ! Réfléchis bien à. . . !

Langue

Rappelez-vous l'usage de l'**impératif**. Pour donner des ordres ou des directions, pour encourager ou avertir quelqu'un ou bien pour suggérer une solution, on emploie l'impératif.

- Pour les **verbes réguliers**, les formes sont souvent les mêmes que le **tu, nous** et **vous** au temps présent, mais sans sujet. Notez qu'il faut omettre la lettre **-s** après **e** ou **a** (surtout avec les verbes en **-er**) à la 2ème personne du singulier (tu vas → Va !). Exemples : Mange ! Mangeons ! Mangez ! Finis ! Finissons ! Finissez ! Attends ! Attendons ! Attendez !
- Il y a quelques **verbes irréguliers** à l'impératif, comme **être** (sois, soyons, soyez), **avoir** (aie, ayons, ayez) et **savoir** (sache, sachons, sachez). Exemples : Soyons patients ! Ayez du courage ! Sache que je vais t'aider !
- Quand il y a **un pronom**, le pronom suit le verbe à la forme affirmative et les pronoms **me** et **te** deviennent **moi** et **toi**. En plus, on n'omet pas le **-s** des verbes en **-er** si le pronom commence avec une voyelle. À la forme négative, le pronom précède le verbe. Exemples : **Donnez-moi** un café ! **Ne me donnez pas** de beignets ! **Écoutons-le** ! **Ne l'écoutons pas** ! **Manges-en** ! **N'en mange pas** ! **Vas-y** ! **N'y va pas** !

Pour aller plus loin : LITTÉRATURE

ACTIVITÉ F : Lisez un extrait du livre comique *Gargantua* de François Rabelais dans lequel l'auteur décrit un festin bizarre. Consultez votre cahier électronique !

2.25 À vous Imaginez que vous déjeunez chez un(e) ami(e). Avec un partenaire, **jouez de petites scènes** pour chaque situation suivante. Attention à l'usage de l'impératif !

1. Votre ami(e) veut savoir comment préparer le repas que vous venez de lui servir. Vous expliquez la recette et donnez des suggestions pour des plats complémentaires.
2. Votre ami(e) gagne beaucoup d'argent mais déteste son travail. Il y a beaucoup de chômage (*unemployment*) en ce moment ! Donnez votre opinion. Avertissez ou encouragez votre ami(e).
3. Votre ami(e) cherche un bon restaurant. Dites-lui ce que vous savez des restaurants du coin (*in your neighborhood*).
4. Votre ami(e) veut faire un voyage en Louisiane et vous invite à l'accompagner. Cela vous intéresse ?
5. Votre ami(e) est allergique aux fruits de mer et commence à manger votre bouillabaisse (une soupe aux fruits de mer). Avertissez-le/la !

2.26 Quel dilemme ! Avec un partenaire, **imaginez un dilemme ou une situation difficile**. Sur une feuille de papier, décrivez cette situation (n'y mettez pas votre nom). Échangez vos papiers au hasard, donnez votre opinion et écrivez des encouragements ou des avertissements.

MODÈLE : Mon dilemme, c'est que je n'ai jamais le temps de manger le petit déjeuner et alors je n'ai pas beaucoup d'énergie le matin.

—Vous devriez acheter des yaourts buvables et des fruits et mangez en route. Réfléchissez à votre santé. Il faut essayer !

À l'écrit *deuxième étape*

2.27 Un dîner élégant Vous êtes en train d'organiser un dîner chez vous pour vos amis francophones. Un(e) ami vous pose des questions afin d'avoir plus de renseignements sur votre soirée. **Imaginez un dialogue** où il/elle vous pose huit questions à propos du dîner (où allez-vous dîner ? à quelle heure ? pourquoi ?, etc.) et donnez vos réponses aux questions. Finalement, avec un(e) partenaire, révisez vos dialogues et lisez-les à haute voix.

Un mot de Sandrine

Structures *le passé composé et l'imparfait*

2.28 Une recette de famille Claire et Jean-Louis continuent à bavarder au Restaurant Bienville. Claire parle de la recette de l'étouffée que Sandrine Fontenot-Chardin lui a donnée. Remarquez que les verbes dans la recette sont à l'**impératif** (voir Épisode 2) et que les verbes dans la description de Claire sont au **passé composé** et à l'**imparfait**. Donnez l'**infinitif** de chaque verbe en caractères gras dans le dialogue. Pouvez-vous décrire comment fonctionnent le passé composé et l'imparfait en analysant ces verbes ?

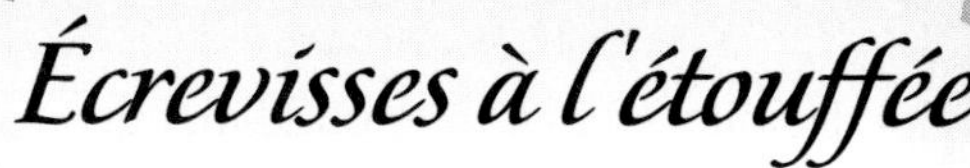

Écrevisses à l'étouffée

1 livre d'écrevisses
1/2 tasse de beurre
1 oignon coupé en dés
2 gousses d'ail émincées
1 cuillère à thé de farine
1 cuillère à thé de sel
1/4 cuillère à thé de poivre de cayenne
1 tomate en cubes
le jus d'un citron
de l'eau
des épices créoles

***Faites** fondre le beurre dans une casserole, **ajoutez** l'oignon et **faites sauter** quelques minutes.*
*Ajoutez la farine et **remuez**. Faites votre sauce en ajoutant la tomate, l'ail, le sel, le poivre de cayenne, les épices créoles, le jus de citron et un peu d'eau. Puis, **mijotez** 20 minutes. Ajoutez encore de l'eau si nécessaire. Finalement, **mettez** les écrevisses dans la casserole et faites cuire encore 8 minutes. **Assaisonnez** et **servez** avec du riz. **Buvez** un bon vin blanc ou de la bière avec ce plat.*

JEAN-LOUIS : Alors, pourquoi ce désir de manger des écrevisses ce soir ? Tu **n'as jamais mangé** d'écrevisses ?

CLAIRE : Non, jamais. Mais aujourd'hui, Sandrine Fontenot-Chardin **préparait** une étouffée pendant que nous **parlions**, et j'**étais** inspirée par le fumet (*smell*) de cuisine... toutes ces épices qui **mijotaient** ensemble ! Et elle m'**a enseigné** comment préparer ce plat selon une ancienne recette de famille.

JEAN-LOUIS : Bon, raconte-moi comment elle l'**a préparée**.

CLAIRE : D'abord, Sandrine **a fait** fondre du beurre, et puis elle **a ajouté** un oignon et elle **a fait** sauter l'oignon quelques minutes. Puis, elle **a ajouté** de la farine, une tomate, de l'ail, des épices et de l'eau. Tous ces ingrédients **ont mijoté** quelques minutes, et finalement Sandrine **a mis** des écrevisses dans la casserole. Elle m'**a dit** que, quand elle **était** petite, sa grand-mère **servait** toujours l'étouffée avec du riz et qu'ils **buvaient** du vin blanc ou de la bière avec ce plat.

JEAN-LOUIS : Alors, ce sauvignon blanc **était** un bon choix comme vin, non ?

2.29 À vous Vous voulez mieux connaître les goûts de vos camarades de classe. En petits groupes, **répondez aux questions** suivantes.

1. Quand vous étiez petit(e), qu'est-ce que vous aimiez manger ?

   —J'aimais...

2. Est-ce qu'il y avait des plats que votre famille mangeait souvent ?

   —Nous mangions souvent...

3. Alliez-vous aux restaurants quand vous étiez petit(e)s ? Auxquels ? Dans les restaurants ethniques, des restaurants fast-food, des restaurants élégants ?

   —Nous allions souvent à... Une ou deux fois, nous sommes allé(e)s à... Nous n'allions jamais à...

4. Connaissez-vous des recettes de famille qui ont passé d'une génération à l'autre ? Si oui, décrivez comment préparer un de ces plats. (Si non, décrivez comment préparer un plat que vous aimez maintenant et utilisez l'impératif).

   —Chez nous, on préparait toujours...

5. Est-ce que vous avez essayé de préparer un repas élégant récemment ? Si oui, dites quand et décrivez le repas. Si non, dites pourquoi pas.

   —J'ai préparé... Je n'ai pas préparé de repas élégant récemment parce que...

6. Qu'est-ce que vous avez mangé hier ?

   —Au petit déjeuner, j'ai mangé... Au déjeuner, j'ai mangé... Au goûter (*snack*), j'ai mangé... Au dîner, j'ai mangé...

le passé composé

The **passé composé** is used to describe a completed past event or series of events. It is composed of two parts: (1) the *auxiliary verb* (**l'auxiliare**) **avoir** or **être** in the present tense and (2) the *past participle* (**le participe passé**) of the verb you are conjugating.

Choosing **avoir** *or* **être** *as the auxiliary verb*:

- Most verbs take **avoir**, except the following *motion verbs* that take **être**: **aller**, **arriver**, **descendre**, **devenir**, **entrer**, **monter**, **mourir**, **naître**, **partir**, **passer**, **rentrer**, **rester**, **retourner**, **revenir**, **sortir**, **tomber**, **venir**. All *reflexive verbs* (**se** + ***verb***) also take **être** in the passé composé.

Forming the past participle (**le participe passé**):

- The *past participle* of regular **-er**, **-ir**, and **-re** verbs is simple to form. Drop the infinitive ending and add the following endings:

-er verbs → **é**	**parler** → j'ai **parlé**
-ir verbs → **i**	**choisir** → j'ai **choisi**
-re verbs → **u**	**vendre** → j'ai **vendu**

- Some verbs have *irregular past participles* that must be memorized. Some common irregular past participles are:

être → j'ai **été**	**faire** → j'ai **fait**	**avoir** → j'ai **eu**
vouloir → j'ai **voulu**	**pouvoir** → j'ai **pu**	**boire** → j'ai **bu**
venir → je suis **venu(e)**	**croire** → j'ai **cru**	**devoir** → j'ai **dû**
voir → j'ai **vu**	**recevoir** → j'ai **reçu**	**prendre** → j'ai **pris**
mettre → j'ai **mis**	**ouvrir** → j'ai **ouvert**	**offrir** → j'ai **offert**
naître → je suis **né(e)**	**mourir** → je suis **mort(e)**	

Examples of verbs conjugated in the ***passé composé***:

vendre	**partir**	**se lever**
j'ai vendu	je suis parti(e)	je me suis levé(e)
tu as vendu	tu es parti(e)	tu t'es levé(e)
il/elle/on a vendu	il/elle/on est parti(e)	il/elle/on s'est levé(e)
nous avons vendu	nous sommes parti(e)s	nous nous sommes levé(e)s
vous avez vendu	vous êtes parti(e)(s)	vous vous êtes levé(e)(s)
ils/elles ont vendu	ils/elles sont parti(e)s	ils/elles se sont levé(e)s

Agreement of the past participle with subjects and preceding direct objects:

- *Motion verbs*: the past participle must agree with the feminine or plural *subject* of motion verbs that take **être**: **Ils** sont parti**s**, et **elle** est allé**e** au café où **ces femmes** sont entré**es**.

- *Reflexive verbs*: the past participle must agree with the feminine or plural *reflexive pronoun* of reflexive verbs that take **être** (when the reflexive is a direct object): Nous **nous** sommes couché**s** au moment où elle **s'**est réveillé**e**.
- *Verbs that take **avoir***: the past participle agrees with the *preceding direct object* of verbs that take **avoir**: Elle a donné ses valises à Jean-Louis, et il **les** a donné**es** à Philippe. Voilà **la femme** qu'ils ont vu**e** hier.

Remember!

- *Dual auxiliaries*: verbs like **descendre**, **monter**, and **passer** usually take **être**, *unless* they are followed by a *direct object*, in which case they take **avoir**: Je **suis passé(e)** par l'hôtel, BUT J'**ai passé** une semaine à la Nouvelle-Orléans.
- *The verb **quitter***: Although the verb **quitter** means *to leave*, it is always followed by a *direct object* and therefore always takes **avoir** in the **passé composé**: **J'ai quitté la Louisiane** en septembre.
- *Negatives*: In the **passé composé**, the negative expression surrounds the *auxiliary verb* and *not* the past participle: Je **n'**ai **jamais** chanté. Ils **ne** se sont **pas encore** couchés.

2.30 Qu'est-ce qui s'est passé ? Pendant le dîner au restaurant, Jean-Louis continue à poser des questions à propos du manuscrit perdu de Laclos. Finalement, Claire décrit sa visite chez Sandrine Fontenot-Chardin, mais sans divulguer tous les détails parce qu'elle se rappelle l'avertissement de Sandrine : «Méfiez-vous, mademoiselle !» Conjuguez les verbes entre parenthèses au **passé composé**. (Attention : c'est une femme qui parle ! Faites l'accord !)

Bon, ce matin, je (se lever) ________________ à 8h et je (descendre) ________________ à la grande salle. Je (prendre) ________________ le petit déjeuner à l'hôtel. Philippe (servir) ________________ des beignets et du café au lait à moi et à deux autres clients. Est-ce que tu (rencontrer) ________________ ce couple marocain qui est à l'hôtel depuis hier ? Non ? Enfin, ensuite des touristes italiens (arriver) ________________ à la reception et Philippe (partir) ________________. Alors, nous (boire) ________________ nos cafés, et je (quitter) ________________ l'hôtel vers 9h.

Je (décider) ________________ d'aller d'abord à la bibliothèque pour parler à nouveau avec les bibliothécaires. Ils (ne... jamais, trouver) ________________ le volume d'enregistrement des naissances (*birth registry*) qui manquait. Pourtant, une bibliothécaire (découvrir) ________________ le nom et l'adresse de Sandrine Fontenot-Chardin dans un site généalogique sur Internet. Je (rester) ________________ à la bibliothèque quelques heures. Puis, je (décider) ________________ d'aller directement à l'adresse, car je n'avais pas le numéro de téléphone. Je (frapper) ________________ à la porte. Une femme m'(inviter) ____________________ à entrer, et nous (parler) __________________. Nous (s'entendre) ___________________ bien __________________. Et voilà, elle (raconter) ________________ comment son père avait vendu les livres de François Fontenot il y a 30 ans. Sandrine ne sait pas où se trouve le manuscrit aujourd'hui. Après, on (discuter) _______________ de la préparation des plats créoles. Et voilà toute l'histoire.

l'imparfait

The **imparfait** is also a past tense, but unlike the passé composé, which describes completed actions, it is used to describe habitual, ongoing, or incomplete actions: to describe feelings; or to give description or background information.

Formation of the imparfait:

- The **imparfait** is formed by adding the imperfect endings (**-ais**, **-ais**, **-ait**, **-ions**, **-iez**, **-aient**) to the **nous** form of the verb minus the **-ons**: je faisais, tu faisais, il/elle/on faisait, nous faisions, vous faisiez, ils/elles faisaient.
- Irregular stem: Only **être** has an irregular imperfect stem, **ét-**. It still takes the regular imperfect endings: j'étais, tu étais, il/elle/on était, nous étions, vous étiez, ils/elles étaient.

Usage of the imparfait:

- To describe *habitual actions* in the past or things you *used to do*: Je **voyageais** beaucoup quand j'étais jeune. (*I **used to travel** a lot when I was young.*)
- To describe *ongoing* or *incomplete actions* in the past: Je **voyageais** en Louisiane quand j'ai rencontré Jean-Louis. (*I **was traveling** in Louisiana when I met Jean-Louis.*)
- To describe *feelings* in the past: **J'avais** faim et **j'étais** fatiguée. (*I **was** hungry and I **was** tired.*)
- To give *background information* or *description*: Il **faisait** chaud et l'hôtel **était** vide. (*It **was** hot, and the hotel **was** empty.*)

Remember!

- *Slightly irregular -er verbs*: **-ger** and **-cer** verbs that normally take an extra **e** (nous mang**e**ons) or a cedilla **ç** (nous commen**ç**ons) in the third person plural form take these changes in *all* the **imparfait** forms *except* the **nous** and **vous**: je mang**e**ais, tu mang**e**ais, il/elle/on mang**e**ait, nous mangions, vous mangiez, ils/elles mang**e**aient; je commen**ç**ais, tu commen**ç**ais, il/elle/on commen**ç**ait, nous commencions, vous commenciez, ils/elles commen**ç**aient.

2.31 Comment était-elle ? Claire continue à raconter ce qui s'est passé chez Sandrine Fontenot-Chardin parce que Jean-Louis veut savoir comment était cette femme. Conjuguez les verbes entre parenthèses à l'**imparfait**.

Sandrine (être) _______________ très gentille et très ouverte. Il (faire) _______________ un peu chaud dans sa cuisine parce qu'elle (préparer) _______________ le dîner. Comme je viens de t'expliquer, il y (avoir) _______________ une étouffée qui (mijoter) _______________ sur la cuisinière. Je (ne. . . pas, se préoccuper) _______________ de la chaleur parce que j'(avoir) _______________ tellement envie d'entendre parler du manuscrit. Sandrine m'a dit que ses grands-parents (parler) _______________ de temps en temps d'un manuscrit inédit quand elle (être) _______________ petite. Elle (prendre) _______________ le manuscrit en question pour un manuscrit authentique de Pierre-Ambroise Choderlos de Laclos. Pourtant, son père l'avait vendu et elle ne l'a jamais lu. De toute façon, elle (commencer) _______________ à s'ennuyer de mes questions sur le manuscrit, et je ne (vouloir) _______________ pas l'embêter, alors on a parlé de la cuisine créole. Et voilà.

2.32 Et vous ? Qu'est-ce que vous avez fait hier soir ? Comment était votre soirée ? Avec un partenaire, **écrivez une liste** de six activités que vous avez terminées (utilisez **le passé composé**), et **écrivez six phrases** pour décrire le temps, le lieu ou vos sentiments (utilisez **l'imparfait**).

MODÈLE : **Activités : J'ai dîné chez ma mère. J'ai regardé la télé. Je suis allé(e) au gymnase. . .**

Description : Il faisait froid. J'étais fatigué(e). Je ne voulais pas faire mes devoirs. . .

Pour aller plus loin : LITTÉRATURE

ACTIVITÉ G : Lisez un extrait de *Madame Bovary*, un roman de Gustave Flaubert. Dans l'extrait, Emma Bovary décrit un dîner élégant chez des amis très riches. Consultez votre cahier électronique !

2.33 Philippe pose des questions Après le dîner, Claire et Jean-Louis rentrent à l'hôtel où ils rencontrent Philippe Aucoin. Jean-Louis s'excuse et monte à sa chambre lorsque Philippe pose des questions à Claire à propos du Restaurant Bienville. **Imaginez ses questions.** Utilisez des **expressions interrogatives** (voyez Épisode 2) et choisissez le **passé composé** ou **l'imparfait** selon la réponse.

MODÈLE : Vous avez bien mangé ?

Claire : Oui, nous **avons** très bien **mangé**, merci.

1. ____ ?

   Claire : Le restaurant **était** fantastique.

2. ____ ?

   Claire : Nous **avons pris** des fruits de mer.

3. ____ ?

   Claire : Nous **sommes partis** du restaurant il y a dix minutes.

4. ____ ?

   Claire : Nous **sommes rentrés** parce que j'étais fatiguée.

5. ____ ?

Claire : Oui, nous **nous sommes** très bien **entendus**.

6. ____ ?

Claire : Non, je ne **savais** pas qu'il y **avait** une lettre pour moi à la réception. Un petit garçon a remis cette lettre cet après-midi, vous dites ? C'est un peu bizarre.

Haïti

Connaissez-vous un peu de l'histoire d'Haïti ? Regardez la vidéo et consultez votre cahier d'activités !

Un mot de Sandrine

La Nouvelle-Orléans, le 29 août 2003
Mademoiselle Claire PLOUFFE
aux bons soins de l'Hôtel Le Moyne
rue Dauphine

Chère Mademoiselle Plouffe,

C'était un vrai plaisir pour moi de vous rencontrer cet après-midi. Après votre départ, mon mari est rentré. Je lui ai raconté comment vous étiez venue me parler à la maison. Puis, j'ai décrit votre projet de recherche parce qu'il voulait savoir pourquoi vous poursuivez ce manuscrit. Deux heures plus tard, quand vous avez téléphoné, je faisais la vaisselle° et je ne pouvais pas répondre au téléphone. C'est pour cette raison que mon mari a répondu et qu'il savait tout sur votre visite. Enfin, il m'a communiqué votre question, et je me suis souvenue° que vous étiez descendue à l'Hôtel Le Moyne. Nous partons en vacances demain et donc je ne vais pas pouvoir recevoir votre appel.° Alors, je vous écris avec la réponse au lieu° d'attendre que vous me rappeliez.°

to do the dishes

to remember

a call

instead of/ to call back (again)

Vous vouliez savoir le nom de mon père et les dates de son service militaire ? Je vous ai déjà dit, je crois, que mon père s'appelait Henri Pierre Fontenot. Il était dans l'armée américaine de 1941 à 1945, et il était en garnison à Paris pendant le printemps de 1945. Il a rencontré Monsieur Gustave, le bouquiniste, le lendemain de son arrivée à Paris et ils se sont vus souvent pendant que mon père était en France.

J'espère que vous trouverez ce dont vous avez besoin à Paris, et je vous répète encore de faire attention. Méfiez-vous des personnes sournoises° et réfléchissez bien à ce que vous faites. Je serai très contente de recevoir de vos nouvelles, que vous réussissiez ou non à trouver ce manuscrit. Je vous prie de croire, chère Mademoiselle, à l'assurance de mes sentiments les meilleurs.

sly, shifty

Sandrine Fontenot-Chardin

Après avoir lu

2.34 D'accord ou pas d'accord ? Après avoir lu la lettre ci-dessus, lisez les phrases suivantes et **donnez vos opinions personnelles**. Discutez en petits groupes.

	D'accord	Pas d'accord
1. Claire est partie de chez Sandrine avant le retour de son mari.	_______	_______
2. Quand il a répondu au téléphone, le mari de Sandrine ignorait que Claire avait parlé avec sa femme plus tôt dans la journée.	_______	_______
3. Pendant sa visite chez Sandrine, Claire a dit qu'elle descendait à l'Hôtel Le Moyne.	_______	_______
4. Claire a téléphoné parce qu'elle ne se souvenait plus du nom du grand-père de Sandrine.	_______	_______
5. Henri Pierre Fontenot était un soldat français.	_______	_______
6. Claire ne va plus contacter Sandrine.	_______	_______

parler du passé

To indicate a point in time

- aujourd'hui, ce matin, cet après-midi, ce soir, plus tôt dans la journée (*earlier today*)
- hier, avant-hier (*the day before yesterday*), la veille (*the day before*), l'avant-veille (*two days before*)
- le jour où... (*the day when/that...*), le lendemain (*the day after*), le surlendemain (*two days after*)
- la semaine dernière, la semaine d'avant/précédente (*the week before*), la semaine d'après/suivante (*the week after*)
- le mois dernier, l'année dernière
- il y a un an / voilà un an / cela fait un an / ça fait un an (*one year ago*)

To advance the plot (commonly used with the **passé composé***)*

d'abord, puis, ensuite, alors, tout d'un coup, tout de suite, soudain (*suddenly*), quand, un jour, une fois, peu après, plus tard

To describe habits (commonly used with the **imparfait***)*

tous les jours, normalement, généralement, habituellement, d'habitude, parfois, de temps en temps, pendant ce temps

To relate actions in the recent past

venir de (+ *infinitive*)

2.35 Comme c'est curieux ! En lisant la lettre de Sandrine, Claire devient toute rouge. Philippe Aucoin, qui remarque ce changement, lui demande ce qui ne va pas. Voici son explication. Récrivez le récit de Claire et **ajoutez des expressions** de la liste ci-dessus (*above*) pour indiquer le moment précis dans le passé, pour avancer l'histoire, et/ou pour souligner qu'il s'agit d'habitudes.

CLAIRE : Comme c'est curieux ! Je viens de recevoir cette lettre de la femme que j'ai vue aujourd'hui. Dans la lettre, elle parle d'un coup de téléphone, mais je ne lui ai jamais téléphoné. J'ai quitté sa maison vers 5h. J'étais très contente de moi. J'ai traversé le cimetière. Il y avait une femme bizarre. Je suis rentrée à l'hôtel. Je suis montée à ma chambre. Quand j'étais à Québec, je travaillais beaucoup. Je faisais la sieste de 6h à 7h. Je lisais un peu avant la sieste. J'ai lu quelques pages d'un roman de Flaubert. J'ai fait une petite sieste. J'ai envoyé un e-mail à ma sœur. Je suis descendue à la cour. Je suis sortie avec Jean-Louis. Je viens de rentrer. Pensez-vous que quelqu'un lui ait téléphoné en faisant semblant d'être moi ? Je vais téléphoner à Sandrine demain pour résoudre ce mystère.

Langue

Pour parler du **passé récent**, on emploie le verbe **venir** au présent ou à l'imparfait avec **de** et l'infinitif du verbe d'action : Je **viens de recevoir** cette lettre. (*I **just received** this letter.*) Pour parler du **futur proche** ou, plus proprement dit, d'un événement futur assez certain, on emploie le verbe **aller** au présent avec l'infinitif du verbe d'action : Je **vais téléphoner** à Sandrine demain. (***I'm going to call** Sandrine tomorrow.*)

2.36 La réponse de Marie De nouveau dans sa chambre, Claire trouve une réponse de sa sœur Marie. Choisissez un des verbes donnés et conjuguez ce verbe au **passé composé (PC)** ou à **l'imparfait (I)**, selon les indications entre parenthèses. Chaque verbe ne peut être utilisé qu'une seule fois.

être	**faire**	**aller**	**vouloir**	**avoir**	**manger**
adorer	**préparer**	**demander**	**acheter**	**retourner**	**servir**

Chère Claire,

Salut ! Je suis contente de savoir que ton rendez-vous avec Madame Fontenot-Chardin s'est bien passé. La recette pour l'étouffée a l'air intéressant. Cet après-midi, il ______________ (I) un peu froid, alors je ______________ (PC) à maman de nous préparer une tourtière. Elle a dit «oui», et alors je ______________ (PC) au supermarché pour acheter les ingrédients. Puis, quand j' ______________ (I) en ville, j' ______________ (PC) une poutine. J'______________ (I) très faim, et elle ______________ (I) délicieuse. Te souviens-tu de combien nous ______________ (I) la poutine quand nous ______________ (I) petites ? J'aime toujours ces frites garnies. C'est comme la madeleine de Proust, la poutine me rappelle les beaux jours de notre enfance. Enfin, je ______________ (PC) à la maison avec les ingrédients pour la tourtière, et maman l'______________ (PC). Après le dîner, Papa ______________ (PC) de la glace au sirop d'érable, sa favorite. Enfin, maman, papa et moi, nous ______________ (PC) tous nos plats préférés aujourd'hui ! J'avais l'impression d'être dans la cabane à sucre au mois de mars. Et maintenant je n'en peux plus (*I'm stuffed*) ! Tu nous manques beaucoup ! À demain !

Bisous, Marie

Culture

La **cuisine québécoise** est marquée par les traditions françaises et anglaises et fortement influencée par les produits régionaux. La **tourtière** (*a meat pie*), un plat traditionnel québécois, est une tarte salée qu'on prépare avec du porc, du veau et/ou du bœuf hâché. La **poutine**, c'est des frites avec du fromage en grain (*white cheddar cheese curds*) et de la sauce brune (*gravy*). Le **sirop d'érable** (*maple syrup*) est abondant au Québec à la fin de l'hiver et au printemps. Beaucoup de familles à la campagne ont des **cabanes à sucre** et font leur propre sirop d'érable chaque année. Les **madeleines**, pourtant, sont une spécialité française. Ce sont de petits gâteaux au citron que l'auteur Marcel Proust a rendus célèbres dans son œuvre *À la recherche du temps perdu* (vous pouvez en lire un extrait à la fin de ce chapitre !).

2.37 Où étiez-vous ? Avec un partenaire, posez les questions suivantes et répondez à votre tour. Attention à l'usage du **passé composé** (pour décrire des actions terminées) ou de l'**imparfait** (pour décrire vos émotions, l'ambiance ou la situation).

MODÈLE : —À quelle heure avez-vous pris le petit déjeuner hier ? Quel temps faisait-il ? →

—J'ai pris le petit déjeuner à 7h30 du matin. Il faisait assez froid.

1. Qu'est-ce que vous avez mangé hier matin ? Comment était ce repas ?
2. Où est-ce que vous avez dîné hier ? et avant-hier ?
3. Où étiez-vous la veille du jour de l'an 2000 ? Quel temps faisait-il ? Qui était avec vous ?
4. Où étiez-vous l'avant-veille du jour de l'an 2000 ? et le lendemain du jour de l'an 2000 ?
5. Quand est-ce que vous avez commencé vos études universitaires ? Comment étiez-vous pendant votre première semaine à l'université ? et pendant la semaine suivante ?
6. Qu'avez-vous fait pendant l'été il y a quatre ans ? et l'été dernier ?

2.38 Une soirée mémorable **Pensez à une soirée intéressante, bizarre ou amusante de votre passé.** Quand s'est passée cette soirée ? Où ? Comment était le décor ? Qui était invité ? Qu'est-ce que vous avez fait ? Qu'avez-vous mangé ? Puis, circulez dans la classe et posez des questions à vos camarades de classe à propos de leurs soirées mémorables. Essayez d'interviewer au moins trois ou quatre personnes !

MODÈLE : Pour mon anniversaire, j'ai dîné chez McDo avec mes neveux. J'ai pris un Big Mac et des frites, et mes neveux ont joué avec leurs jouets en plastique. Puis, le clown Ronald a chanté «Joyeux Anniversaire» avec mes neveux !

Questions : Pourquoi êtes-vous allés chez McDo ? Comment était le clown ? Aviez-vous peur du clown ?

À l'écrit *troisième étape*

Pour aller plus loin : CULTURE

ACTIVITÉ H : Apprenez un peu plus sur la culture et la nourriture québécoises. Consultez votre cahier électronique !

2.39 Votre invitation **Imaginez** que vous continuez les préparations pour votre dîner avec des amis francophones. Vous avez déjà décidé de votre menu, du lieu, de la date et de l'heure et des amis qui vont venir. Maintenant, **écrivez une lettre d'invitation** à envoyer à vos amis. Soyez formel(le) parce que le dîner va être élégant ! Échangez votre invitation avec celle d'un de vos camarades de classe (par courriel, si vous voulez !) et offrez-lui une réponse et quelques corrections possibles.

Dénouement

Activités de révision

2.40 La chronologie Voici un résumé des événements qui ont culminé avec la visite de Claire Plouffe chez Sandrine Fontenot-Chardin. Avec un partenaire, **faites un récit** — à l'écrit ou à l'oral — en mettant les verbes au **passé composé** (actions terminées) ou à **l'imparfait** (description). Ajoutez des mots pour lier des phrases, indiquer le moment ou avancer l'histoire.

1782 Pierre-Ambroise Choderlos de Laclos **finit** d'écrire *Les Liaisons dangereuses* ; le roman **est** un best-seller en France ; François Fontenot **arrive** à Paris pour faire des études culinaires.

1789 Laclos **écrit** un deuxième roman ; la Révolution française **commence**.

1790 François Fontenot **retourne** à Saint-Domingue.

1792 C'**est** le début de la Révolution haïtienne ; François Fontenot ne **veut** pas mettre sa famille en danger ; ils **quittent** Saint-Dominque et **vont** en Louisiane ; Laclos **envoie** son nouveau manuscrit à son ami François Fontenot.

1803 Laclos **meurt** en France ; son manuscrit **reste** dans la bibliothèque privée de François Fontenot en Louisiane ; il n'**est** jamais publié.

1806 François Fontenot **ouvre** un restaurant créole à la Nouvelle-Orléans ; il **aime** lire ; il **achète** beaucoup de livres.

1822 François Fontenot **meurt** en Louisiane ; il **a** une famille nombreuse ; ils **sont** tristes.

1941 Henri Pierre Fontenot **fait** son service militaire ; c'**est** la Deuxième Guerre mondiale.

1945 Henri Pierre Fontenot **rencontre** Lionel Gustave ; il **est** bouquiniste à Paris ; ils **deviennent** amis.

1972 Le père d'Henri Pierre Fontenot **meurt** d'une crise cardiaque pendant une tentative de vol (*attempted robbery*) ; le père de Sandrine Fontenot **a** peur ; il **vend** tous les livres de François Fontenot à Monsieur Gustave.

2001 Claire **fait** des études supérieures en lettres françaises au Québec ; elle **lit** un article au sujet d'un manuscrit inédit de Laclos.

2002 Claire **découvre** le nom de François Fontenot dans les archives de la Bibliothèque nationale à Paris ; le nom **figure** dans une lettre écrite à la main par Laclos mais jamais envoyée ; la lettre **décrit** un «paquet» donné à François Fontenot ; Claire **photocopie** la lettre.

2003 Claire **reprend** ses recherches avec une bourse de l'université ; elle **rend** visite à Sandrine Fontenot-Chardin à la Nouvelle-Orléans.

2.41 Vos menus, vos recettes Imaginez que vous êtes traiteurs (*caterers*) et que vous devez inventer des menus pour les événements suivants. En petits groupes, proposez des plats, décrivez vos recettes pour ces plats, demandez les opinions de vos partenaires et prenez des décisions. Si vos clients sont satisfaits, vous ferez de bonnes affaires !

1. un pique-nique pour une réunion de famille
2. un déjeuner d'affaires pour des clients importants
3. le mariage d'un jeune couple
4. une fête pour célébrer le nouvel an
5. une fête pour un couple d'un certain âge qui prennent leur retraite

Avant de lire À la recherche du temps perdu

2.42 Les souvenirs gastronomiques Vous écrivez un article pour un magazine culinaire. Le sujet est «Les souvenirs gastronomiques». Circulez dans la salle de classe et **posez des questions** à vos camarades. Essayez de trouver les réponses les plus intéressantes !

1. Quelle est votre nourriture préférée ? Vous souvenez-vous de la première fois (*the first time*) que vous avez essayé cette nourriture ? Où ? Quand ? Avec qui ? Pourquoi ?
2. Quels aliments détestez-vous ? Quelle était la dernière fois (*the last time*) que vous avez goûté cet aliment ? Où ? Pourquoi ? Comment était-il ?
3. Quelle nourriture vous rappelle le plus votre enfance ? de la glace ? des bonbons ? un dessert ? des hot dogs. . . ?

Langue

On utilise souvent **le passé simple** dans la narration littéraire ou historique pour parler d'actions accomplies au passé. On ne l'utilise pas normalement en français parlé, et (ne vous inquiétez pas !) on ne vous demandera pas d'écrire au passé simple ! Pourtant, quand vous lisez des textes littéraires ou historiques, il est utile de pouvoir reconnaître ce temps. Les formes du passé simple sont assez simples :

- **Pour les verbes en -er :** On laisse tomber le **er** et on ajoute : **-ai, -as, -a, -âmes, -âtes**, **-èrent**.
- **Pour les verbes en -ir et en -re :** On laisse tomber le **-ir** ou le **-re** et on ajoute : **-is, -is, -it, -îmes, -îtes, -irent**.
- **Pour les verbes irréguliers :** Au radical irrégulier, on ajoute les mêmes terminaisons qu'on utilise pour les verbes en **-ir/-re** ou bien on ajoute les terminaisons suivantes : **-us, -us, -ut, -ûmes, -ûtes, -urent**.

Pouvez-vous identifier l'infinitif des verbes au **passé simple** dans l'extrait littéraire qui suit ?

2.43 Premières impressions **Lisez l'extrait** suivant, qui vient du recueil *À la recherche du temps perdu* de Marcel Proust, sans essayer de comprendre chaque mot. Après votre première lecture du texte, **répondez aux questions**. Ensuite, relisez le texte une deuxième fois, plus attentivement.

1. Qui parle ? un petit garçon ? un homme adulte ? un vieillard ?
2. Où se passe l'histoire ? Quand ?
3. Qu'est-ce que le narrateur mange ? Pourquoi ?
4. Analysez l'expérience du narrateur. Est-elle positive ou négative ? amusante ? mystérieuse ? intéressante ? agaçante (*annoying*) ? désagréable. . . ?
5. Est-ce qu'il y a des goûts, des parfums, des vues ou des sons qui vous font penser à votre jeunesse ?

Pour aller plus loin : LITTÉRATURE

ACTIVITÉ 1 : Qui est Marcel Proust ? Apprenez un peu sur sa vie et son œuvre. Consultez votre cahier électronique !

lisez

À la recherche du temps perdu

Cet extrait vient du roman de Marcel Proust, Du côté de chez Swann, *un des romans de son recueil qui s'intitule* À la recherche du temps perdu. *Ici, il s'agit d'un homme qui rend visite à sa mère au village de Combray, en France, où il a grandi. Dans cet extrait, le narrateur décrit comment la nourriture l'aide à ressentir des impressions de son enfance qu'il croyait avoir perdues.*

■ Marcel Proust

À la recherche du temps perdu (extrait)

Il y avait déjà bien des années que, de Combray, tout ce qui n'était pas le théâtre et le drame de mon coucher,° n'existait plus pour moi, quand un jour d'hiver, comme je rentrais à la maison, ma mère, voyant que j'avais froid, me proposa de me faire prendre, contre mon habitude, un peu de thé. Je refusai d'abord et, je ne sais pourquoi, me ravisai.° Elle envoya chercher un de ces gâteaux courts et dodus° appelés Petites Madeleines qui semblent avoir été moulés° dans la valve rainurée° d'une coquille de Saint-Jacques.° Et bientôt, machinalement,° accablé° par la morne° journée et la perspective d'un triste lendemain, je portai à mes lèvres une cuillerée° du thé où j'avais laissé s'amollir° un morceau de madeleine. Mais à l'instant même où la gorgée° mêlée de miettes° de gâteau toucha mon palais,° je tressaillis,° attentif à ce qui se passait d'extraordinaire en moi. Un plaisir délicieux m'avait envahi,° isolé, sans la notion de sa cause. Il m'avait aussitôt rendu les vicissitudes de la vie indifférentes, ses désastres inoffensifs, sa brièveté illusoire, de la même façon qu'opère l'amour, en me remplissant° d'une essence précieuse : ou plutôt cette essence n'était pas en moi, elle était moi. J'avais cessé° de me sentir médiocre, contingent, mortel. D'où avait pu me venir cette puissante° joie ? Je sentais qu'elle était liée au goût° du thé et du gâteau, mais qu'elle le dépassait infiniment, ne devait pas être de même nature. D'où venait-elle ? Que signifiait-elle ? Où l'appréhender ? Je bois une seconde gorgée où je ne trouve rien de plus que dans la première, une troisième qui m'apporte un peu moins que la seconde. Il est temps que je m'arrête, la vertu du breuvage° semble diminuer. Il est clair que la vérité que je cherche n'est pas en lui, mais en moi.

bedtime
to change one's mind
plump
to mould/grooved
scallop shell/automatically/overwhelmed/gloomy
spoonful/to soften
gulp, mouthful/crumbs
the palate/to tremble
to invade
to fill
to stop
powerful
the taste
a beverage

Après avoir lu

2.44 Avez-vous compris ? En petits groupes, **discutez** des questions suivantes.

1. Quand le narrateur retourne chez sa mère à Combray, c'est en quelle saison ? Qu'est-ce qu'on associe à cette saison ? Quelle est la suggestion de la mère du narrateur ?
2. Le narrateur dit que le «drame du coucher» est le seul souvenir de son enfance. Est-ce que l'heure du coucher était un moment agréable pour le narrateur ? Est-ce qu'il a eu une enfance heureuse ?
3. Quels sont les sentiments que le goût du thé avec de la madeleine provoque chez le narrateur ? Est-ce que ce sont des sentiments ou des souvenirs détaillés ou imprécis ?
4. Le goût du thé mélangé avec des madeleines déclenche (*unleashes*) des sentiments et des souvenirs qui étaient cachés (*hidden*) dans la mémoire du narrateur. Il veut préciser d'où viennent ces émotions puissantes. Que fait-il pour en savoir plus ? Est-ce que ça marche ?
5. Pourquoi est-ce que le narrateur dit que la solution au mystère du lien entre le goût et les émotions n'est pas dans le thé mais «en lui» ? La solution, est-elle dans son passé ou dans son imagination ?

2.45 D'accord ou pas d'accord ? Après avoir lu l'extrait du roman de Proust, lisez les phrases suivantes et **donnez votre opinion**. **Discutez** de vos réponses en petits groupes.

	D'accord	Pas d'accord
1. Le narrateur boit du thé tous les jours.	_______	_______
2. Les madeleines sont des fruits de mer.	_______	_______
3. Le narrateur se sent immortel à cause du goût du thé mélangé avec des miettes de gâteaux.	_______	_______
4. Les goûts provoquent toujours des souvenirs d'enfance.	_______	_______
5. Les souvenirs sont rarement indéfinis et abstraits.	_______	_______

2.46 Analyse littéraire **Examinez ce texte** de près. **Répondez** aux questions suivantes et **discutez** de vos réponses en classe.

1. La première phrase de l'extrait de Proust est très très longue. Divisez-la en phrases plus courtes et plus simples et comparez les deux. Quel est l'effet de l'usage des phrases très longues ? Y a-t-il un rapport entre les longues phrases et le thème de la mémoire ?
2. Pensez à l'image du petit gâteau qui s'appelle la madeleine. La madeleine, est-elle dure ou molle (*soft*) ? douce ou piquante ? petite ou grande ? Comparez cette image avec l'idée d'un enfant. Quelles en sont les similarités ?
3. Analysez l'usage des noms et des adjectifs descriptifs employés pour décrire les sentiments du narrateur. Quels noms et adjectifs dominent dans la première partie de l'extrait ? Et dans la deuxième ? Quel est l'effet de ce renversement ?

4. Dans la dernière partie de l'extrait, le narrateur se pose des questions. Analysez l'emploi des questions ici. Quel en est l'effet ?
5. Pensez au titre de ce recueil de romans, *À la recherche du temps perdu*. Quel est le rapport entre le titre et cet extrait, qui est le plus célèbre de tous les romans de Proust ?

Haïti

Découvrez des plats mémorables de plusieurs pays francophones ! Regardez la vidéo et consultez votre cahier d'activités !

2.47 Un dîner très mémorable Imaginez que vous dînez au restaurant avec des gens que vous ne connaissez pas très bien. En petits groupes, asseyez-vous autour d'une table, saluez les gens, **présentez-vous** et **commandez** votre dîner (utilisez le menu de l'Épisode 1 de ce chapitre, ou imaginez votre propre menu avant de commencer). Puis, pendant le repas, **chaque personne raconte un souvenir** provoqué par le plat qu'il/elle est en train de manger. Les autres posent des questions supplémentaires.

MODÈLE : **—Cette soupe à l'oignon me rappelle le jour où j'ai appris à faire de la bicyclette.**

—Où avez-vous grandi ?, etc.

Pour aller plus loin : CULTURE

ACTIVITÉ J : En France, beaucoup de fermiers agriculteurs résistent à la mondialisation. Ils font des manifestations contre les restaurants internationaux à succursales multiples (*chain restaurants*). Apprenez pourquoi. Consultez votre cahier électronique !

Synthèses

2.48 Réfléchissons à la culture **Voici quelques plats typiques** de plusieurs cultures francophones que vous avez étudiées dans ce chapitre. En petits groupes, **répondez** aux questions et **discutez** de vos impressions avec vos camarades.

les bananes des Antilles (Haïti)	**les madeleines (la France)**
l'étouffée aux écrevisses (la Louisiane)	**la tourtière (le Québec)**
la fondue (la Suisse)	

1. Décrivez chaque plat. Quels en sont les ingrédients principaux ?
2. Pourquoi chaque plat est-il important à sa culture ? Y a-t-il un phénomène historique ou une raison géographique qui explique son importance culturelle ?
3. Aujourd'hui, dans les sociétés développées, on a très peu de contraintes en ce qui concerne l'accès aux ingrédients exotiques ou étrangers, mais les gens continuent à préparer des repas traditionnels. Pourquoi ?
4. À votre avis, est-ce que ces plats témoignent de la richesse et de la diversité des cultures francophones de nos jours ou sont-ils stéréotypiques ? Pourquoi ?

Pour aller plus loin : LITTÉRATURE

ACTIVITÉ K : Lisez des articles haïtiens en français ou en kreyòl. Consultez votre cahier électronique !

2.49 À débattre Lisez les questions suivantes et **discutez**-les en groupes. Si possible, parlez de vos expériences personnelles relatives aux questions.

1. **Le fast-food !** On dit que les Américains, en général, mangent mal. Ils mangent trop de fast-food trop vite et n'apprécient pas la bonne cuisine. Par contre, les Français ont la réputation d'être gastronomes et de prendre du plaisir à dîner lentement et avec beaucoup de cérémonie. Pourtant, les Français commencent à manger plus souvent dans des restaurants de fast-food et les Américains commencent de plus en plus à apprécier la bonne cuisine. Est-ce que ces stéréotypes sont démodés ? Qu'en pensez-vous ?
2. **Vivre pour manger ou manger pour vivre ?** Georges Jacques Danton, un des leaders de la Révolution française, a dit, «Après le pain, l'éducation est le premier besoin du peuple». Êtes-vous d'accord ? Pourquoi ou pourquoi pas ?
3. **Qui dort dîne ?** La pauvreté et la sous-alimentation (*malnutrition*) sont de grands problèmes à Haïti aujourd'hui, comme dans beaucoup de pays en voie de développement qui ont été colonisés par les états européens. Est-ce que ce sont des problèmes mondiaux, nationaux ou régionaux ? Est-ce que les jeunes Américains d'aujourd'hui font assez pour combattre la sous-alimentation chez nous ? Et chez nos voisins ? Et aux pays pauvres qui se trouvent loin des États-Unis ? Pourquoi ou pourquoi pas ?

2.50 À l'impromptu Voici des situations interactives. Avec une ou deux autres personnes, **choisissez une scène et improvisez** devant la classe. Si vous ne voulez pas improviser, écrivez votre dialogue avant et puis jouez-le pour la classe.

1. Un inconnu au restaurant !
   (a) Vous dînez dans un restaurant qui est plein à craquer. Une personne entre et vous demande de bien vouloir partager la table que vous et votre ami(e) occupez. Vous aimez faire de nouvelles connaissances. Acceptez donc et essayez d'en savoir davantage sur la vie de cette personne.
   (b) Vous êtes l'ami(e) de la personne assise à cette table et au contraire vous êtes fatigué(e) et vous n'avez pas du tout envie de rencontrer quelqu'un que vous ne connaissez pas. Soyez poli(e), mais essayez de convaincre votre ami(e) de ne pas accepter une autre personne à votre table.
   (c) Vous êtes un voleur(-se), et une des personnes assises à cette table a un sac à dos qui a attiré votre attention. Essayez de vous faire accepter à leur table et de savoir ce que le sac contient.
2. Un changement d'emploi !
   (a) Vous dînez dans ce même restaurant. Vous venez de quitter un job que vous détestiez pour ouvrir une librairie dans le Vieux Carré de la Nouvelle-Orléans. Demandez à votre ami(e) son opinion sur ce changement récent.

(b) Vous êtes en train de dîner avec un(e) ami(e) qui vient de démissionner afin d'ouvrir une librairie à la Nouvelle-Orléans. Demandez à votre ami(e) la raison de cette décision sans oublier de l'encourager dans son entreprise.

(c) Vous travaillez comme serveur(-se) dans le restaurant, mais vous n'aimez pas trop cet emploi. Annoncez à vos clients les plats du jour et prenez leurs commandes. Vous les entendez parler d'ouvrir une librairie. Vous êtes intéressé(e). Posez-leur des questions discrètement afin de savoir s'ils ont besoin de quelqu'un.

3. Une enquête !

(a) Vous êtes un agent de police que l'on vient d'appeler pour enquêter (*to investigate*) un vol dans un restaurant à la Nouvelle-Orléans. On a volé le porte-monnaie d'un client. Menez votre enquête en interrogeant les clients du restaurant.

(b) Vous êtes le gérant (*manager*) du restaurant. Vous parlez du vol dont vous venez d'être témoin (*witness*) à un agent de police. Aidez-le en décrivant la scène du vol. Aussi, offrez-lui quelque chose à boire ou à manger. Vous êtes, après tout, dans un restaurant !

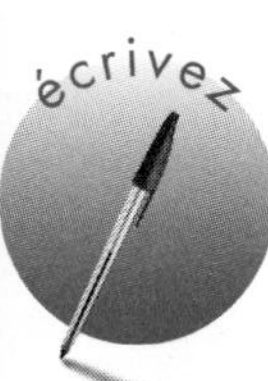

À l'écrit *étape finale*

2.51 Le lendemain de votre dîner Votre dîner élégant avec vos amis francophones était hier soir. Révisez et élaborez vos travaux d'écriture de ce chapitre (Activités 13, 27 et 39) et rédigez une lettre formelle à votre professeur de français. Décrivez comment était votre soirée. Utilisez le **passé composé** et **l'imparfait**. N'oubliez pas les éléments suivants :

- Saluez
- Parlez de ce que vous avez servi
- Décrivez les gens que vous avez invités
- Parlez de ce que vous avez fait avant et après le dîner
- Donnez votre opinion du dîner
- Invitez votre professeur à venir chez vous la prochaine fois (enouragez-le !)

À suivre

Le lendemain de sa visite chez Sandrine, Claire se lève très tôt et essaie de téléphoner à Sandrine pour parler de la lettre qu'elle a reçue la veille. Pas de réponse. Elle essaie encore quelques heures plus tard, mais toujours sans succès. Sandrine et son mari sont déjà partis en vacances. Alors, Claire doit prendre une décision : aller à Paris à la recherche du manuscrit, ou rentrer chez elle et trouver un nouveau sujet de thèse ? Finalement, elle décide d'aller à Paris. Elle trouve une place sur un vol qui part le jour suivant à 8h du soir. Elle passe ses dernières 24 heures à se promener dans le Vieux Carré, et le jour de son départ, elle règle son compte avec Philippe Aucoin et quitte l'Hôtel Le Moyne sans voir personne. Elle laisse un petit mot pour Jean-Louis à la réception : «Ça a été un plaisir de te rencontrer. Je te souhaite une bonne fin de séjour à la Nouvelle-Orléans. Claire.» Le taxi arrive. Claire s'en va, direction Paris. . .

2.52 Qu'est-ce qui s'est passé ? Pensez à ce qui s'est passé depuis le début de l'histoire. **Écrivez six phrases au passé** pour décrire les événements les plus importants. **Parlez** de vos idées avec vos camarades de classe.

MODÈLE : Claire est allée chez Sandrine Fontenot-Chardin. C'est important parce que. . .

2.53 Qu'est-ce qui va se passer ? Imaginez ce qui va se passer dans le prochain chapitre. **Écrivez six phrases** et **parlez** de vos idées avec vos camarades de classe.

MODÈLE : Jean-Louis va être triste parce que Claire est partie sans dire «au revoir» !

Pour agir :
HAÏTI !

Si vous voulez bouger et faire quelque chose pour mieux connaître Haïti, ou pour aider les autres à mieux connaître les cultures francophones, consultez la section **Pour agir** dans votre cahier électronique ! Il y a tant de choses à faire :

- **Vendez des livrets de recettes** et contribuez l'argent que vous gagnez à une organisation qui préserve les forêts ou qui aide les pauvres à Haïti.
- **Cliquez et aidez** des gens pauvres qui meurent de faim. Visitez des sites sur Internet qui font un don d'argent pour chaque personne qui visite leur site (pour vous, c'est gratuit !).
- **Enseignez** ce que vous savez de la culture de Haïti à des enfants de l'école primaire. Lisez-leur des contes haïtiens traduits en anglais ou faites-les danser sur de la musique de Wyclef Jean, un chanteur haïtien-américain.
- **Entrez en contact** avec des haïtiens qui vivent dans votre communauté ou ailleurs aux États-Unis.
- **Organisez un voyage** au Québec pour les vacances de printemps.
- **Cuisinez !** Préparez un vrai repas québécois ou antillais avec vos camarades de classe.

VOCABULAIRE UTILE

Dans la cuisine

ajouter	*to add*
amère	*bitter*
baguettes (*f. pl.*)	*chopsticks*
boire	*to drink*
bol (*m.*)	*bowl*
casserole (*f.*)	*saucepan*
congélateur (*m.*)	*freezer*
cuillère (*f.*)	*spoon*
cuillerée (*f.*)	*spoonful*
cuisinère (*f.*)	*stove*
doux, douce	*sweet*
épice (*f.*)	*spice*
épicé(e)	*spicy*
faire cuire	*to cook*
faire mijoter	*to simmer*
faire sauter	*to sauté*
four (*m.*)	*oven*
goûter	*to taste*
goûter (*m.*)	*snack*
livre (*f.*)	*pound*
marmite (*f.*)	*pot*
meuble (*m.*) à tiroirs	*cabinet*
pincée (*f.*)	*pinch*
piquant(e)	*spicy/sharp*
poêle (*f.*)	*frying pan*
recette (*f.*)	*recipe*
remuer	*to stir*

rôtir	*to roast*
sentir	*to smell*
souper (*m.*)	*supper*
tasse (*f.*)	*cup*

Viandes et volailles

bœuf (*m.*)	*beef*
canard (*m.*)	*duck*
dinde (*f.*)	*turkey*
foie (*f.*)	*liver*
jambon (*m.*)	*ham*
lapin (*m.*)	*rabbit*
pâté (*m.*)	*pâté*
porc (*m.*)	*pork*
poulet (*m.*)	*chicken*
veau (*m.*)	*veal*

Poissons et fruits de mer

crevette (*f.*)	*shrimp*
écrevisse (*f.*)	*crawfish*
homard (*m.*)	*lobster*
huître (*f.*)	*oyster*
moules (*f. pl.*)	*mussels*
palourdes (*f. pl.*)	*clams*
poisson chat (*m.*)	*catfish*
saumon (*m.*)	*salmon*
sole (*f.*)	*sole*
thon (*m.*)	*tuna*

Légumes

aubergine (*f.*)	*eggplant*
brocoli (*m.*)	*broccoli*
carotte (*f.*)	*carrot*
céleri (*m.*)	*celery*
concombre (*m.*)	*cucumber*
courgette (*f.*)	*zucchini*
haricot (*m.*)	*bean*
maïs (*m.*)	*corn*
oignon (*m.*)	*onion*
poivron (*m.*)	*bell pepper*
pomme (*f.*) de terre	*potato*
salade (*f.*)	*lettuce/salad*
tomate (*f.*)	*tomato*

Fruits

ananas (*m.*)	*pineapple*
banane (*f.*)	*banana*
bleuets (*m.pl.*)	*blueberries (reg. Québec)*
canneberge (*m.*)	*cranberry*
citron (*m.*)	*lemon*
fraise (*f.*)	*strawberry*
framboise (*f.*)	*raspberry*
fruits des bois (*m. pl.*)	*berries*
myrtille (*f.*)	*blueberry*
orange (*f.*)	*orange*
pêche (*f.*)	*peach*
poire (*f.*)	*pear*
pomme (*f.*)	*apple*
raisin (*m.*)	*grapes*

Produits laitiers

beurre (*m.*)	*butter*
crème (*f.*)	*cream*
fromage (*m.*)	*cheese*
glace (*f.*)	*ice cream*
lait (*m.*)	*milk*
œuf (*m.*)	*egg*
yaourt (*m.*)	*yogurt*

Assaisonnements et produits de première nécessité

ail (*m.*)	*garlic*
basilic (*m.*)	*basil*
canelle (*f.*)	*cinnamon*
farine (*f.*)	*flour*
huile (*f.*)	*oil*
mayonnaise (*f.*)	*mayonnaise*
miel (*m.*)	*honey*
moutarde (*f.*)	*mustard*
noix (*m.pl.*)	*nuts*
nouilles (*f.pl.*)	*noodles*
pâte (*f.*)	*pastry dough/crust*
pâtes (*f.pl.*)	*pasta*
persil (*m.*)	*parsley*
poivre (*m.*)	*pepper*
riz (*m.*)	*rice*
sel (*m.*)	*salt*
sucre (*m.*)	*sugar*
vinaigre (*f.*)	*vinegar*

Décrire un événement

confier	*to confide/disclose*
endroit (*m.*)	*place*
lendemain (*m.*)	*the next day*
mijoter un projet	*to hatch a scheme*
offrande (*f.*)	*offering*
parmi	*among*
se méfier de	*to beware of*
s'échapper	*to escape*
sur le coup	*on the spot/instantly*
voler	*to steal*

Discuter au restaurant

addition (*f.*)	*bill*
apporter	*to bring (things)*
ça dépend	*it depends*
commander	*to order*
il vaut la peine	*it's worth the trouble*
il vaut mieux	*it's better, it would be better*
on verra	*we'll see*
perdre confiance en	*to lose confidence in*
pourboire (*m.*)	*tip*
remercier	*to thank*
valoir	*to be worth*

Chapitre 3

En vogue à Paris

La flânerie parmi les livres des bouquinistes à Paris.

Épisode 1 *Au voleur !*

Épisode 2 *L'aveu*

Épisode 3 *Une lettre à Sandrine*

Dénouement

Il ne faut pas vendre
la peau de l'ours
avant de l'avoir tué.
—proverbe français

Culture

Le **Quartier latin** est le quartier des étudiants de la Sorbonne, qui fait partie aujourd'hui de l'Université de Paris. L'Université de Paris a été fondée en 1215. À cette époque les professeurs enseignaient encore en latin. Le **Quartier latin** se trouve sur la rive gauche de la **Seine**. La cathédrale de **Notre-Dame** de Paris se trouve sur l'**île de la Cité**, une des deux îles sur la Seine. L'autre s'appelle l'**île Saint-Louis**. De chaque côté du fleuve on trouve des **bouquinistes** qui vendent des bouquins (des livres), des affiches, des gravures (*engravings*) et des souvenirs.

À apprendre

- Comment décrire les gens, les vêtements et les objets
- Comment s'excuser et pardonner à quelqu'un
- Comment décrire une situation

À lire

Claire arrive à Paris, mais il y a un problème avec ses bagages à l'aéroport Charles-de-Gaulle. Donc, elle va à l'Hôtel Quasimodo dans le Quartier latin, près de la cathédrale de Notre-Dame, sans valise. En se promenant à côté des bouquinistes qui longent les bords de la Seine près de Notre-Dame, Claire rencontre son ami Jean-Louis Royer. Cette fois, ce n'est pas une coïncidence, et Jean-Louis lui fait un aveu. Jean-Louis aussi travaillait pendant son séjour à la Nouvelle-Orléans. . .

Au voleur !

Avant de lire

3.1 Vous et vos affaires **Répondez** aux questions suivantes. **Discutez** de vos réponses avec vos camarades de classe et n'hésitez pas à poser des questions supplémentaires si vous voulez en savoir plus.

1. Est-ce que vous pensez beaucoup à vos vêtements ? Combien de fois par an achetez-vous de nouveaux vêtements ? Où ? Au centre commercial ? Dans de petites boutiques ? Dans les grands magasins ?
2. Quand vous vous habillez le matin, est-ce que vous changez de vêtements plusieurs fois pour trouver le bon «look» ? Ou décidez-vous de vos vêtements la veille avant de vous coucher ?
3. Portez-vous des vêtements de couleurs plutôt vives (jaune, orange, rouge, vert, violet) ou de couleurs plutôt sombres (noir, gris, brun, bleu marine) ? Pourquoi ?
4. Quand vous sortez le matin ou le soir, apportez-vous des affaires (*possessions/things*) personnelles avec vous, comme un portefeuille, un sac à main, un sac à dos, un porte-documents (*briefcase*) ? Qu'est-ce que vous apportez avec vous régulièrement ?
5. Êtes-vous plutôt grand(e), moyen(ne) ou petit(e) ? Avez-vous les cheveux noirs, bruns, blonds ou roux ? Avez-vous les yeux marron, bleus, gris ou verts ?

3.2 Les grands magasins Il y a beaucoup de petites boutiques à Paris, mais il y a aussi de grands magasins (*department stores*) où on peut trouver tout pour s'habiller, pour décorer la maison et pour se divertir. Pendant son vol en avion de la Nouvelle-Orléans à Paris, Claire lit une brochure qu'elle trouve dans la pochette en face d'elle. Elle y trouve le plan d'un grand magasin parisien qui a cinq étages, un rez-de-chaussée et un sous-sol. **Consultez le plan et répondez aux questions suivantes.**

1. Où est-ce qu'on achète une poupée (*doll*) pour une petite fille ? des CD du rappeur français MC Solaar ? des sandales ? des ustensiles de cuisine ? un aspirateur (*vacuum cleaner*) ? un dessus de lit (*bedspread*) ? une nouvelle montre (*watch*) ? un imperméable (*raincoat*) ?
2. Où pouvez-vous trouver quelque chose à porter pour une soirée élégante à l'Opéra ? et pour une journée à la plage ?
3. Où va-t-on pour prendre quelque chose à boire ? pour acheter des billets d'avion ?
4. À quel service s'adresse-t-on quand on va se marier et on veut préparer une liste de cadeaux possibles ? quand on veut se faire rembourser pour un pull qu'on vous a acheté mais qui est trop petit ? quand on veut laisser son manteau et ses sacs quelque part pendant qu'on fait du shopping ? quand on a perdu quelque chose dans le magasin ?
5. Avez-vous besoin de quelque chose ? Pouvez-vous le trouver quelque part dans ce magasin ? Où ?

Pour aller plus loin : CULTURE

ACTIVITÉ A : Apprenez un peu sur la mode et faites une visite virtuelle d'un des grands magasins à Paris. Consultez votre cahier électronique !

Guide du Magasin Lutèce

5ème Restaurant Panoramique

Ameublement - Linge de Table - Arts de la Table
Literie - Tapis - Éclairage - Encadrement - Bagages

4ème Mode Femme

Chemisiers - Jupes - Pantalons - Pulls - Robes
Tailleurs - Lingerie - Bas et Collants
Couturiers - Robes de Mariée

3ème Mode Homme

Costumes - Vestes - Pantalons - Chemises - Pulls
Pyjamas - Sous Vêtements - Manteaux
Pardessus - Fourrure

2ème Mode Enfant

La Future Maman - Mode Ado - Jeux et Jouets
Accessoires Enfants

1er Sport Femme - Sport Homme

Maillots de bain - Espace Jean - Chaussures

RdC Espace Beauté

Accessoires - Cravates - Foulards - Maroquinerie
Bijouterie - Horlogerie - Parfumerie

SS Café

Loisirs - Librairie - Papeterie - Disques -
Électroménager

Services

Acceuil (RdC)
Agence de voyage (SS)
Change bébé (2)
Listes de Mariage (5)
Objets trouvés (SS)
Réclamations (SS)
Toilettes (SS, 1, 3, 5)
Vestiaire (RdC)

3.3 Plan de Paris Claire trouve aussi un petit plan de Paris dans la pochette en face d'elle. Elle le consulte afin de trouver l'hôtel que Philippe Aucoin lui a suggéré : l'Hôtel Quasimodo, dans le 5ème arrondissement, sur la rive gauche. **Regardez le plan** ci-dessous et **répondez** aux questions.

1. L'Hôtel Quasimodo, dans le 5ème arrondissement, est près de quels monuments parisiens ?
2. La place de la Bastille, où la Révolution française a commencé, est dans quel arrondissement ?
3. La tour Eiffel est dans quel arrondissement ?
4. Le fleuve, la Seine, traverse quels arrondissements ?
5. Quels monuments sont sur la rive gauche ? Lesquels trouve-t-on sur la rive droite ?
6. À votre avis, quel arrondissement semble être le plus intéressant ? Où voudriez-vous habiter si vous alliez à Paris ?

Culture

La ville de Paris est divisée en **20 arrondissements**, ou secteurs urbains. Le premier arrondissement est au centre de la ville, près de l'île de la Cité, et les numéros des arrondissements augmentent selon une spirale. Alors, plus le numéro est petit, plus on est proche du centre-ville. Le Quartier latin, par exemple, s'étend du 5ème au 6ème arrondissements.

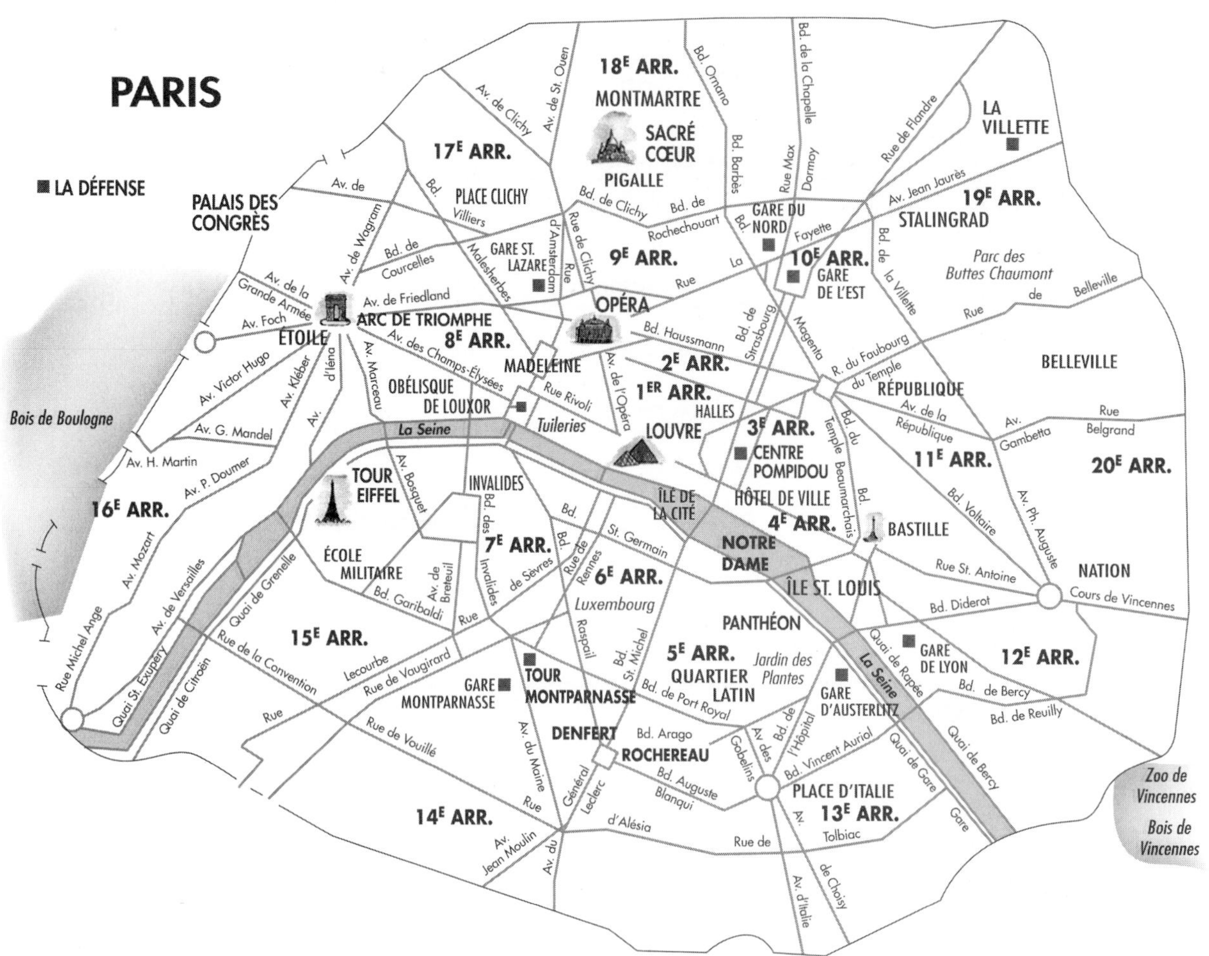

Au voleur !

L'avion atterrit à l'aéroport Charles-de-Gaulle à Paris vers 8h du matin. Claire, fatiguée, n'ayant pas pu dormir pendant le vol, se dirige vers la livraison des bagages enregistrés. Elle y trouve une grande foule de gens qui attendent leurs bagages. Elle se met loin de la sortie des bagages pour éviter qu'on lui marche sur les pieds, et elle regarde les valises qui tombent l'une après l'autre sur le tapis roulant. Après quelques minutes, elle voit sa grande valise verte et s'avance pour la prendre. Pourtant, avant de pouvoir d'en saisir, un homme la prend et s'en va, disparaissant dans la foule. Étonnée, Claire croit d'abord avoir mal identifié sa valise. Il se peut que d'autres gens aient des valises presque identiques à la sienne. Mais après avoir attendu une heure, nulle trace de sa valise, elle commence à penser que cet homme l'a volée. Tout d'un coup, comme si elle venait de voir le vol, elle crie à haute voix : «Au voleur ! Au voleur !» Un agent de sécurité arrive, et ne voyant rien de suspect, essaie de calmer la jeune Québécoise.

L'AGENT : Madame, madame, calmez-vous. Qu'est-ce qui se passe ?

CLAIRE : Quelqu'un a volé ma valise ! La valise verte, c'était la mienne, pas la sienne ! Arrêtez-le !

L'AGENT : Je ne vois personne, et je ne vois pas de valise verte.

CLAIRE : Non, ça s'est passé il y a une heure ! Mais il est peut-être toujours dans l'aéroport !

L'AGENT : Calmez-vous, madame. Racontez-moi ce qui s'est passé.

CLAIRE : Bon, d'accord. *Elle respire un peu.* Excusez-moi.

L'AGENT : Allez, racontez ce que vous avez vu.

CLAIRE : Bon, je suis descendue de l'avion et je suis arrivée à la livraison des bagages enregistrés. Il y avait une grande foule, alors je suis restée là, un peu plus loin, mais près du tapis roulant. J'ai vu sortir une valise verte que j'ai prise pour la mienne. Pourtant, un homme s'est avancé, et il l'a prise. J'ai pensé au début que je m'étais trompée et que c'était la sienne. Mais, maintenant, toutes les valises sont sorties de l'avion et la mienne n'est toujours pas là !

L'AGENT : Est-ce que vous pouvez décrire votre valise ?

CLAIRE : Oui, oui. Ma valise est verte, rectangulaire, assez grande, avec de petites roulettes. Il y avait un ruban rose attaché à la poignée et une fiche d'identité aussi.

L'AGENT : Et l'homme que vous avez vu, comment était-il ?

CLAIRE : Je l'ai vu avant le vol. J'avais remarqué qu'il était assez beau. Il était de taille moyenne, un peu mince, et il avait les cheveux blonds. Il portait des lunettes, et il avait le visage carré. Il avait de petits yeux bleus, un nez pointu et des lèvres minces aussi. Ses oreilles étaient assez petites aussi. Il n'avait ni moustache ni barbe.

L'AGENT : Des cicatrices ? Des tatouages ?

CLAIRE : Non, je ne crois pas.

L'AGENT : Qu'est-ce qu'il portait comme vêtements ?

CLAIRE : Enfin, un pantalon beige et un t-shirt gris, des tennis blancs aux pieds, sans chaussettes, et une ceinture en cuir. En plus, il avait un porte-documents noir.

L'AGENT : Et dans votre valise, qu'est-ce qu'il y avait ?

CLAIRE : Rien d'extraordinaire — des vêtements, des chaussures, des articles de toilette, du maquillage, quelques souvenirs des États-Unis et un dossier avec des notes et des papiers pour mes recherches — mais il n'y avait rien d'important. J'ai apporté mon ordinateur portable et mes disquettes avec moi dans l'avion, et j'ai mis tout mon argent, mes documents, mon appareil photo et mon baladeur dans mon sac à dos.

L'AGENT : Vous n'aviez pas de bijoux dans votre valise ?

CLAIRE : Non, je ne porte pas de bijoux avec moi quand je voyage . . . au cas où, vous savez.

L'AGENT : Alors, nous allons probablement trouver vos affaires quelque part dans l'aéroport. Les voleurs cherchent des bijoux, de l'argent ou des appareils électroniques de grande valeur, et s'ils n'en trouvent pas, normalement ils abandonnent la valise avant de quitter l'aéroport. Tout de même, il nous faudra une liste détaillée du contenu de votre valise avec une description de vos vêtements. Remplissez cette fiche et n'oubliez pas d'y mettre votre nom aussi bien que le nom et l'adresse de votre hôtel à Paris. Comme ça, nous pourrons vous contacter si nous trouvons vos affaires.

Claire remplit la fiche et quitte l'aéroport. Elle décide de prendre un taxi pour aller à son hôtel, l'Hôtel Quasimodo, dans le 5ème arrondissement. . .

VOCABULAIRE

À l'aéroport	
atterrir	*to land*
se diriger	*to make one's way*
la livraison des bagages enregistrés	*baggage claim area*
la foule	*crowd*
le tapis roulant	*conveyor belt*
ramasser	*to pick up/gather up*
disparaître	*to disappear*
crier	*to yell/shout*
le/la mien(ne)	*mine*
le/la sien(ne)	*his/hers*
se tromper	*to be mistaken*
les roulettes (*f.*)	*little wheels*
le ruban	*ribbon*
la poignée	*handle*
la fiche	*form, sheet*
au cas où	*just in case*
Les gens	
la taille	*size, height*
moyen(ne)	*medium*
mince	*thin*
les cheveux (*m. pl.*)	*hair*
les lunettes (*f. pl.*)	*glasses*
le visage	*face*
carré(e)	*square*
les yeux (*m. pl.*)	*eyes*
le nez	*nose*
pointu(e)	*pointy*
les lèvres (*f. pl.*)	*lips*
les oreilles (*f. pl.*)	*ears*
la cicatrice	*scar*
le tatouage	*tattoo*
la moustache	*mustache*
la barbe	*beard*
Les affaires personnelles	
le pantalon	*pants*
le t-shirt	*tee-shirt*
les tennis	*sneakers*
les chaussettes	*socks*
la ceinture	*belt*
le cuir	*leather*
du maquillage	*makeup*
le dossier	*file*
un appareil photo	*camera*
un baladeur	*Walkman™*
les bijoux (*m. pl.*)	*jewels, jewelry*

Après avoir lu

3.4 Avez-vous compris ? **Répondez** aux questions suivantes. Justifiez vos réponses en citant le texte.

1. Immédiatement après avoir vu le vol, qu'est-ce que Claire a fait ? Qu'a-t-elle fait une heure plus tard ? À votre avis, pourquoi est-ce qu'elle a attendu avant de crier ?
2. Comment était le voleur ? Décrivez cette personne.
3. Qu'est-ce qu'il y avait dans la valise de Claire ? Qu'est-ce que Claire a apporté avec elle dans l'avion ? À votre avis, est-ce qu'elle avait trop de bagages ?
4. Est-ce que l'agent de sécurité était gentil ? Que pensez-vous de sa réaction au vol des bagages ?
5. Qu'est-ce que Claire a dû faire après avoir parlé avec l'agent et avant de pouvoir quitter l'aéroport ?

i Langue

Vous rappelez-vous les conjugaisons des **verbes irréguliers** suivants : **mettre**, **partir**, **sortir** et **tenir** ? Si non, mémorisez leurs conjugaisons avant de continuer.

- **mettre** (*to put, to put on*) : je mets, tu mets, il/elle/on met, nous mettons, vous mettez, ils/elles mettent ; participe passé = mis (j'ai mis, etc.) ; d'autres verbes conjugués comme **mettre** sont **admettre**, **omettre**, **permettre**, **promettre**, **remettre** et **soumettre**. Notez qu'on utilise **mettre** pour l'acte de s'habiller et qu'après s'être habillé, on emploie le verbe **porter**.

- **tenir** (*to hold*) : je tiens, tu tiens, il/elle/on tient, nous tenons, vous tenez, ils/elles tiennent ; participe passé = tenu (j'ai tenu, etc.). Notez qu'on utilise **apporter** pour dire *to carry* et que **tenir à** quelque chose veut dire *to value something* or *to hang onto an idea.*
- **partir** (*to leave*) : je pars, tu pars, il/elle/on part, nous partons, vous partez, ils/elles partent ; participe passé = parti (je suis parti/e, etc.) ; un synonyme est l'expression **s'en aller**.
- **sortir** (*to go out*) : je sors, tu sors, il/elle/on sort, nous sortons, vous sortez, ils/elles sortent ; participe passé = sorti (je suis sorti/e, etc.).

3.5 D'accord ou pas d'accord ? Indiquez si vous êtes **d'accord ou pas d'accord** avec les phrases suivantes, d'après votre compréhension du récit. Justifiez vos opinions en citant le texte, si possible. Discutez de vos réponses avec la classe.

	D'accord	Pas d'accord
1. Claire est très fatiguée quand elle arrive à Paris.	_______	_______
2. Claire a vu le voleur de sa valise.	_______	_______
3. Le voleur était un vieil homme aux cheveux gris.	_______	_______
4. Le voleur portait un short beige et une chemise grise.	_______	_______
5. Le voleur a pris l'ordinateur et les disquettes de Claire.	_______	_______
6. L'agent de sécurité va trouver la valise bientôt.	_______	_______

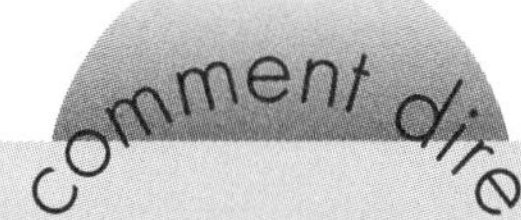

décrire les vêtements et les affaires personnelles

Unisex clothes	un pantalon, un jean, un short, un t-shirt, un jogging, un pull-over, des sous-vêtements, un pyjama, des pantoufles, un maillot de bain, un manteau, un anorak, un imperméable, des chaussettes, des chaussures, des bottes, des tennis, des sandales, un chapeau, une écharpe
Women's clothes	un chemisier, un haut (*top*), un foulard, une tenue, une jupe, une robe, un gilet (*cardigan*), un soutien-gorge (*bra*), un collant (*pantyhose*), des talons hauts/plats (*high/low heels*)
Men's clothes	une chemise, une cravate, un costume, une veste (*suit jacket*), un slip (*briefs*)
Textile patterns	à fleurs (*floral*), à rayures (*striped*), tartan/écossais (*plaid*), solide
Toiletries	une brosse à dents, du dentifrice, une brosse à cheveux, un peigne, du shampooing, un sèche-cheveux, du savon, du maquillage (*makeup*), un rasoir, du parfum, du déodorant, des médicaments
Jewelry	une bague, un collier, un bracelet, une broche, des boucles d'oreille, une montre
Miscellaneous	un parapluie, un portefeuille, un porte-documents, un sac à main, un sac à dos, un baladeur, un téléphone mobile (un portable), un ordinateur portable, un appareil photo, une pellicule (*film*), des lunettes
Materials	en cuir (*leather*), en coton, en rayonne, en laine (*wool*), en polyester, en soie (*silk*), en paille (*straw*), en feutre (*felt*), en plastique, en or (*gold*), en argent (*silver*)

3.6 Les affaires Regardez les mots de vocabulaire qui suivent. Dans chaque ligne, il y a **un mot qui cloche avec les trois autres**. Entourez le mot qui ne va pas avec les autres et essayez d'expliquer pourquoi. Attention : il y a parfois plusieurs bonnes réponses. Il faut justifier votre choix !

1. des tennis	des chaussettes	des chaussures	un chapeau
2. les yeux	le nez	les oreilles	les mains
3. grand	mince	petit	moyen
4. se tromper	atterrir	se diriger	s'en aller
5. une cicatrice	une moustache	une boucle d'oreille	un tatouage
6. une fiche	un plan	un passeport	un dossier

3.7 Qu'est-ce qu'on met ? À l'aéroport, Claire voit beaucoup de gens qui partent en voyage partout dans le monde. **Imaginez les vêtements** que portent les gens suivants et **décrivez-les** ! Faites des dessins, si vous voulez, pour illustrer vos idées.

MODÈLE : Un enfant qui va chez ses grand-parents en Provence. →
Un short rouge, un t-shirt bleu, des chausettes blanches et des tennis rouges et bleus.

1. Un homme d'affaires qui part pour une réunion d'affaires à Genève en Suisse.
2. Deux femmes d'un certain âge qui passent leurs vacances à Tahiti, une île tropicale française en Polynésie.
3. Une jeune femme très branchée qui voyage à Milan en Italie.
4. Des étudiants universitaires qui vont au Québec pour un stage (*internship*) de six mois, jusqu'au mois de février.
5. Une famille de touristes américains qui viennent d'arriver à Paris.
6. Un jeune couple BCBG qui est en lune de miel (*honeymoon*) en Tunisie en Afrique du nord.

i Langue

Vous connaissez déjà les **couleurs fondamentales** : blanc(-che), jaune, orange, rouge, rose, vert(e), bleu(e), violet(te), brun(e), gris(e), noir(e). Il y a plein d'autres **couleurs plus nuancées** comme : **ivoire**, **beige**, **bronzé(e)**, **moutarde**, **lavande**, **mauve**, **turquoise**, **olive**, **saumon**. On peut aussi qualifier les couleurs de **clair** (*light*) ou de **foncé** (*dark*) : **une chemise bleu clair**, **une cravate bleu foncé**. Notez que les couleurs qualifiées d'adjectifs sont invariables (les mêmes formes au masculin et au féminin) et que les couleurs qui sont aussi des noms (**une olive**, **une orange**, **de la lavande**, **de la moutarde**, **du saumon**, **un marron**, etc.) sont toujours invariables. Remarquez aussi qu'on emploie des mots différents quand on parle des couleurs des parties du corps. On dit «**les cheveux roux**» (pas rouges !) ou «**les yeux marron**» (pas bruns !).

Culture

En France, pour décrire **le look** ou **le style vestimentaire** d'une personne, on emploie plusieurs adjectifs descriptifs. Voici quelques expressions courantes. Vous identifiez-vous avec un de ces styles vestimentaires ?

- **BCBG** (Prononcez «**bécébégé**» ; acronyme de «bon chic, bon genre») : vêtements bien fabriqués et de grandes marques connues (*brand names*), contours d'une grande netteté, souvent portés par la classe bourgeoise qui habite les quartiers chic
- **baba-cool :** vêtements larges et de style décontracté, parfois froissés (*wrinkled*), inspirés par les hippies des années 60 ou par des motifs ethniques, souvent portés par les jeunes, les artistes ou les bohémiens
- **branché(e) :** vêtements modernes et toujours à la mode, changeants à chaque saison, souvent portés par les jeunes gens qui sortent en ville dans les clubs également branchés
- **classique :** vêtements conservateurs et de styles traditionnels qui ne sont jamais démodés, souvent portés par les cadres ou les professionnels
- **sportif(-ive) :** vêtements confortables et de style actif et fonctionnel, souvent portés par les jeunes, les étudiants et bien sûr tous ceux qui font du sport

3.8 Le témoin Après avoir interviewé Claire, l'agent de sécurité est abordé par un homme asiatique, bien habillé, qui pense avoir vu un voleur dans les toilettes de l'aéroport. L'agent lui pose des questions. Avec un partenaire, **lisez le dialogue à haute voix**. Où vous voyez des expressions entre parenthèses, choisissez celle qui vous intéresse le plus.

L'AGENT : (Comment vous appelez-vous / Quel est votre nom), monsieur ?

M. PHAN : Phan, François Phan.

L'AGENT : Monsieur Phan, est-ce que vous êtes (citoyen français / touriste) ?

M. PHAN : Je suis né (à Paris / à Marseille / à Lyon). Mes parents ont immigré en France du Vietnam dans les années 50. Je viens de rentrer d'un séjour chez mes grands-parents.

L'AGENT : Très bien. Alors, racontez-moi ce que vous avez vu dans (les toilettes / l'aéroport).

M. PHAN : Ben, il y avait un homme qui fouillait les affaires d'une grande valise. J'ai pensé que c'était bizarre parce que (il n'y avait que des vêtements de femme / l'homme avait l'air nerveux).

L'AGENT : C'était à quelle heure ?

M. PHAN : C'était vers (8h30 / 9h) du matin.

L'AGENT : Pouvez-vous décrire (l'homme / la valise) ?

M. PHAN : Oui. C'était (un homme blond et mince qui portait un pantalon beige et un t-shirt gris / une grosse valise verte avec de petites roulettes).

Pour aller plus loin : CULTURE

ACTIVITÉ B : Apprenez un peu sur la culture vietnamienne. Consultez votre cahier électronique !

Culture

En France, surtout dans les grandes villes comme Paris, on trouve une **société multiculturelle**. En effet, environ 4 pour cent de la population immigrée en France est **d'origine vietnamienne**. Le Vietnam a été une colonie française pendant cent ans : depuis l'invasion militaire par les forces de Napoléon III en 1857 jusqu'à la bataille de **Dien Bien Phu** en 1954, dernière bataille de la guerre d'Indochine, où beaucoup de soldats français sont morts. À cette époque, à Genève, la France a signé un traité de paix avec le Vietnam et la plupart des Français qui y vivaient sont rentrés en France. Aussi, un grand nombre de Vietnamiens ont immigré en France depuis cette époque à cause de la situation politique au Vietnam et à cause des liens culturels entre les Vietnamiens et la France.

L'AGENT : Pouvez-vous décrire (le visage de l'homme / la couleur des yeux de l'homme) ?

M. PHAN : Non, malheureusement, je n'ai vu cet homme que (de dos / très rapidement).

L'AGENT : Habitez-vous à Paris ?

M. PHAN : Oui, dans le 4ème. J'ai une épicerie vietnamienne dans la rue de Turenne et moi et ma famille, nous habitons (au-dessus / à côté) du magasin.

L'AGENT : Écrivez votre adresse et votre numéro de téléphone ici au cas où on aurait besoin (de plus de détails / de vous poser encore des questions). Et merci beaucoup de votre témoignage. En effet, une valise verte a été volée ce matin.

M. PHAN : Je suis content de pouvoir vous aider. (Au revoir / Bonne chance) !

L'AGENT : Au revoir, et merci encore.

la France multiculturelle

Rencontrez une Française et un Asiatique francophone et écoutez lorsqu'ils décrivent les vêtements qu'on porte au travail en France ! Regardez la vidéo et consultez votre cahier d'activités !

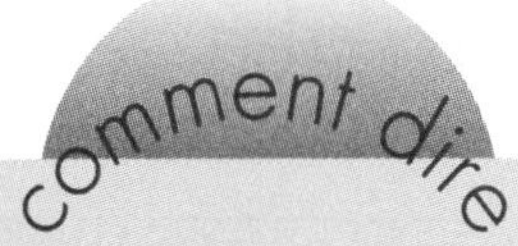

décrire les objets

Expressions	C'est/Ce sont. . . C'est une chose/un truc/un objet/un machin qu'on utilise pour. . . C'est une espèce/un type/une sorte de. . . C'est un lieu/un endroit où. . .
Shapes	rond(e), ovale, carré(e), rectangulaire, triangulaire, voûté (*vaulted*), en spirale
Sizes	grand(e), gros(se), énorme, moyen(ne), normal(e), petit(e), mince, minuscule, comme ça (Montrez avec vos mains !)
Materials	en bois (*wood*), en verre, en pierre (*stone*), en fer (*iron*), en aluminium, en métal, en plastique, en tissu (*cloth*), en papier, en liquide
Feel	mou/molle (*soft*), dur(e), tranchant(e) (*sharp*), inégal(e) (*uneven*), lisse (*smooth*)

Culture

La conquête romaine de **la Gaule** (territoire qui ressemble à la France d'aujourd'hui) était au premier siècle avant J.-C. (*first century B.C.*). Les Romains ont donné le nom de **Lutèce** à la ville principale (aujourd'hui Paris). Les **Arènes de Lutèce**, un amphithéâtre au style romain qui se trouve aujourd'hui près du Quartier latin à Paris, datent de cette époque. Lors des invasions des **Francs** (un peuple germanique) au 3ème siècle, les Gaulois se sont réfugiés sur l'île de la Cité, ancien site de la capitale de la tribu **Parisii** (vaincu par les Romains). C'étaient au 4ème siècle qu'on a renommé la ville «Paris» et au 5ème siècle, sous le règne de Clovis Ier (le premier roi catholique), que les Francs se sont unis au peuple gaulois. Clovis Ier a nommé le pays la **France** et a choisi la ville de **Paris** comme capitale.

3.9 Les monuments parisiens À Paris, il y a beaucoup de monuments très connus. Regardez la liste de monuments suivants et les descriptions des monuments en bas. Pour chaque description, **décidez de quel monument il s'agit**. (Si vous ne connaissez pas les monuments de Paris, consultez l'Internet avant de faire cette activité !)

l'arc de Triomphe	**les Arènes de Lutèce**
la basilique du Sacré-Cœur	**l'Obélisque de la place de la Concorde**
le Pont des Arts	**la pyramide du Louvre** **la tour Eiffel**

1. C'est une grande structure carrée, construite de pierre, avec des sculptures sur la façade. Il y a une voûte au centre pour laisser passer des défilés militaires.
2. C'est une assez grande structure faite en verre avec des soutiens en fer. Elle a quatre côtés triangulaires.
3. C'est une énorme structure blanche, construite de pierre, avec des toits arrondis, mais pas tout à fait ronds.
4. C'est une structure en bois avec des soutiens en fer qui est très longue et large, mais pas très haute.
5. C'est une structure en fer très célèbre qui est grande en bas et devient plus petite en haut.
6. C'est une très ancienne structure en pierre, très grande, avec une pointe tout en haut. Il y a des dessins égyptiens gravés sur les quatres côtés rectangulaires.
7. C'est une grande structure circulaire, faite en pierre, qui a des côtés assez hauts (avec des trous en bas) et un espace ouvert au centre.

Pour aller plus loin : CULTURE

ACTIVITÉ C : Participez à un jeu afin de mieux connaître les monuments, les musées et l'histoire de la ville de Paris. Consultez votre cahier électronique !

Culture

Paris est connue pour et par ses **monuments**. La **tour Eiffel** a été construite entre 1887 et 1889 pour l'Exposition universelle de 1889. Son ingénieur, Gustave Eiffel, était spécialiste de l'architecture métallurgique. Eiffel a aussi travaillé sur l'armature métallique de la Statue de la Liberté donnée aux États-Unis. La tour Eiffel, aujourd'hui le symbole de la ville de Paris, est reconnue partout dans le monde, mais elle a été critiquée à l'époque de sa construction. On disait que la tour était laide et abominable. La situation était pareille à l'époque où I.M. Pei a construit la **Pyramide** dans la cour du musée du Louvre dans les années quatre-vingts. Au début, on la détestait. Aujourd'hui la Pyramide est aussi un symbole de la ville de Paris dont les Parisiens sont fiers.

3.10 Des achats Imaginez que vous avez besoin d'acheter les choses suivantes à Paris, mais que vous ne connaissez pas les mots de vocabulaire suivants. Que dites-vous pour vous faire comprendre dans les grands magasins ? Avec des partenaires, **écrivez des descriptions des choses suivantes**. Puis, lisez des descriptions à haute voix et vos camarades de classes devineront l'objet que vous décrivez.

MODÈLE : des boules Quiès® (*earplugs*) →

—Ce sont des petites choses rondes et molles qu'on met dans les oreilles pour dormir en paix.

1. une brosse à dents
2. des pansements adhésifs (*Band-Aids®*)
3. un portefeuille
4. des lunettes de soleil
5. un petit réveil-matin (*alarm clock*)
6. de nouveaux écouteurs (*earphones*) pour votre baladeur
7. un pull-over
8. ??? (à vous de choisir ! Utilisez votre imagination !)

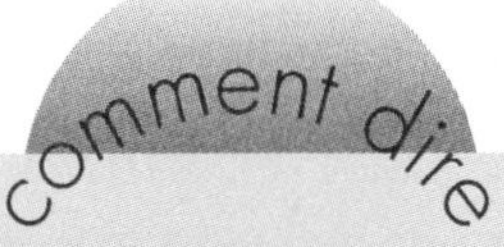

décrire les gens (l'aspect physique)

Expressions	C'est quelqu'un qui est. . . (+ *adjectif*) Il/Elle a. . . (+ *nom* + *adjectif*)
Size	grand(e), moyen(ne), petit(e) gros(se), fort(e), potelé(e), costaud, musclé(e), normal(e), bien proportionné(e), mince
Facial features	le visage (rond, ovale, carré), les yeux (marron, gris, verts, bleus), les sourcils (épais, minces), les cheveux (noirs, bruns, châtain, roux, blonds, gris ; frisés, bouclés, raides ; longs, courts, moyens), le nez (pointu, épais), les oreilles (décollées), la bouche, les lèvres (minces, épaisses), le menton (carré, fuyant), le front (large, fuyant), le cou (mince, épais, long, court)
Body parts	la tête, les épaules (*shoulders*), le bras, le coude (*elbow*), le poignet (*wrist*), la main, les doigts, les ongles, la poitrine (*chest*), le ventre (*stomach*), le dos, la jambe, le genou (*knee*), la cheville (*ankle*), le pied, les doigts de pied

Langue

L'adjectif **décollées**, utilisé pour décrire des oreilles qui ne restent pas contre la tête, vient du verbe **coller** (*to glue, to stick*) et du nom **la colle** (*glue*). On voit l'influence de cette racine dans le mot **collant** ; les collants «collent» aux jambes des femmes. On parle aussi d'une robe **décolletée** (*low-cut*) qui ne «colle» pas au cou. On remarque aussi le **décollage** d'un avion ; c'est-à-dire, le moment où l'avion quitte la terre et commence à voler. Et vous avez, peut être, fait des **collages** artistiques où l'on rassemble des images variées et les colle sur un papier.

3.11 Vocabulaire personnel Pensez à vos affaires et à votre apparence physique et, pour chaque catégorie, **faites une liste de cinq à dix mots** importants que vous pouvez utiliser pour décrire vos propres vêtements, affaires, objets et vous-même. Consultez un dictionnaire si nécessaire.

1. Vos vêtements préférés pour se reposer : types, couleurs, tissus, styles
2. Vos vêtements préférés pour travailler ou pour sortir : types, couleurs, tissus, styles
3. Les affaires personnelles que vous apportez avec vous quand vous voyagez
4. Vos objets les plus précieux que vous gardez à la maison
5. Votre description physique personnelle

3.12 Circulez et bavardez Hier, il y a eu un vol (*robbery*) sur votre campus ! Quelqu'un a volé tous les livres du bureau de votre professeur de français. Vous avez vu une personne très agitée près de son bureau hier juste avant le vol. Imaginez cette personne, et puis circulez dans la salle et **décrivez la personne** (physiquement, vêtements et les affaires qu'il/elle portait) aux autres étudiants. En même temps, **posez des questions** aux autres «témoins» que vous rencontrez. Essayez de trouver quelqu'un qui a vu la même personne que vous.

MODÈLE : J'ai vu une jeune femme blonde et mince qui portait une robe noire. Et vous ?

—Moi aussi j'ai vue une jeune femme, mais elle était brune.

Pour aller plus loin : LITTÉRATURE

ACTIVITÉ D : Lisez un extrait des *Caractères* de La Bruyère, un auteur français du 17ème siècle, dans lequel il décrit un homme qui est l'esclave de la mode. Consultez votre cahier électronique !

À l'écrit *première étape*

3.13 Des préparatifs Vous avez besoin de vacances et vous décidez de faire un petit voyage. Choisissez une destination et **faites une liste de toutes les choses que vous mettez dans votre valise.** N'oubliez pas :

- les documents nécessaires.
- des vêtements appropriés pour le climat.
- des appareils électroniques.
- d'autres articles personnels.

Échangez votre liste avec celle d'un camarade de classe. Suggérez des choses que votre partenaire a peut-être oubliées et écrivez un petit message en bas de page pour lui souhaiter un bon voyage !

Épisode 2

L'aveu

Un magasin dans le Marais, le 4ème arrondissement de Paris.

Structures *les adjectifs descriptifs*

3.14 Un coup de téléphone Claire arrive finalement à l'Hôtel Quasimodo, fatiguée et sans valise. Elle dîne dans sa chambre et se couche tôt. Le matin, elle est réveillée par le téléphone qui sonne très fort. C'est l'agent de sécurité de l'aéroport. Lisez le dialogue et puis décidez si les adjectifs en **caractères gras** sont (a) **masculins ou féminins**, (b) **singuliers ou pluriels**. En plus, décidez si ces adjectifs sont placés (c) **avant ou après** le nom qu'ils modifient. Pouvez-vous décrire comment fonctionnent les adjectifs en analysant ces exemples ?

CLAIRE : Allô ?

L'AGENT : Bonjour, Madame Plouffe. C'est Étienne Duroc, et j'ai de **bonnes** nouvelles.

CLAIRE : Bonjour, Monsieur Duroc. Avez-vous trouvé ma valise ?

L'AGENT : Tout à fait. Grâce à un témoin **scrupuleux** qui a repéré le voleur dans les toilettes, on a pu récupérer la plupart de vos affaires.

CLAIRE : Un témoin ?

L'AGENT : Oui, oui, un homme qui tient une épicerie **vietnamienne** dans le 4ème. Il a vu un **jeune** homme **blond** qui fouillait dans vos affaires. En effet, deux minutes plus tard, nous avons cherché et nous avons trouvé votre **grande** valise **verte** dans les toilettes.

CLAIRE : Et vous avez dit qu'on a récupéré *la plupart* de mes affaires ?

L'AGENT : Eh, oui. D'après votre liste, tout est là sauf la **petite** tasse à café et le gilet **rouge**.

CLAIRE : Bizarre. Et mon dossier **précieux** avec mes notes de recherche ?

L'AGENT : Oui, oui. Enfin, j'espère que tous vos papiers sont là. Il y a six pages de notes écrites à la main. Elles étaient dans la poubelle (*garbage can*).

CLAIRE : Et les deux pages photocopiés d'un **vieux** manuscrit des *Liaisons dangereuses* de Laclos ?

L'AGENT : Désolé, madame, mais on n'a pas cherché des photocopies. Sur la fiche de déclaration, vous avez marqué seulement des notes écrites à la main et un dossier. C'étaient des photocopies d'un manuscrit **ancien**, vous dites ? Elles étaient **importantes** ?

CLAIRE : Non, pas tellement. Mon **ancien** professeur de littérature me les avait données. C'était juste pour voir comment était l'écriture de Laclos. Je cherche un **autre** manuscrit qu'il a écrit, mais enfin, je suis **heureuse** de pouvoir récupérer la plupart de mes affaires **personnelles**. Merci beaucoup, monsieur.

L'AGENT : Je vous en prie, madame. On envoie vos affaires à votre hôtel cet après-midi.

la France multiculturelle

Comment sont Véronique et Richard ? Décrivez-les. Regardez la vidéo et consultez votre cahier d'activités !

les adjectifs descriptifs

Descriptive adjectives (**les adjectifs descriptifs**) are used to modify nouns and must agree in *number* and *gender* with the nouns they modify.

To make an adjective agree with the *gender*:

- Usually add an **-e** to make a masculine adjective *feminine*: un sac **vert**, une valise **verte**.
- Some adjectives are *invariable* (those ending in an unaccented **-e** in the masculine and feminine forms AND those derived from nouns): un **jeune** homme/une **jeune** femme, des yeux **marron**.

- Some adjectives require the *doubling of a final consonant* in the feminine form (**-ien/-ienne, -el/-elle, -il/-ille, -os/-osse, bon[s]/bonne[s]**) or the *addition of an accent* (**-er/-ère**): des papiers **personnels**/des affaires **personnelles**, le mois **dernier**/la semaine **dernière**.
- Some adjectives follow *slightly irregular* patterns (such as those ending in **-eux/-euse** or **-aux/-ausse**): **heureux/heureuse(s), précieux/précieuse(s), faux/fausse(s)**.
- Some adjectives are *completely irregular*, such as: **beau(x)/belle(s), nouveau(x)/nouvelle(s), vieux/vieille(s)**. Note that **beau, nouveau,** and **vieux** all have irregular masculine singular forms when placed before a noun that begins with a vowel or **silent h**: un **bel** ami, un **nouvel** ami, un **vieil** hôtel.

To make an adjective agree in *number*:

- Usually add an **-s** to make an adjective *plural*: une **petite** tasse, de **petites** tasses (unless the singular form already ends in **-s** or **-x**).
- Sometimes add an **-x** to form the *masculine plural*: un **nouveau** sac/de **nouveaux** sacs.

Descriptive adjectives are placed in a sentence according to the following rules:

- The adjective is normally placed *after a noun it modifies*: un gilet **rouge**
- The adjective is placed after **être** if it *modifies a subject*: elles étaient **importantes.**
- A limited number of specific adjectives that describe *beauty* (**beau, joli**), *age* (**jeune, vieux, nouveau**), *goodness* (**bon, mauvais**), and *size* (**petit, grand, gros, autre**), normally *precede the noun*: un **jeune** homme blond. Numbers also *precede the noun*: la **première** fois, la **deuxième** fois.
- Some adjectives may be used either *before or after the noun*, depending on meaning (see table below):

	BEFORE the noun	**AFTER the noun**
ancien/ancienne	mon ancien prof *old, former*	un manuscrit ancien *old, ancient*
cher/chère	mon cher ami *dear, cherished*	un ordinateur cher *dear, expensive*
dernier/dernière	la dernière fois *last in a series*	le mois dernier *last, previous*
grand/grande	un grand auteur *great, famous*	un homme grand *tall*
pauvre	le pauvre touriste *poor, unfortunate*	un touriste pauvre *poor, broke*
prochain/prochaine	la prochaine fois *next, following*	le mois prochain *next, coming up*
propre	ma propre chemise *own* (*property*)	une chemise propre *proper, clean*

3.15 Le courriel Après avoir raccroché le téléphone, Claire branche son ordinateur, utilisant l'adapteur qu'elle a acheté lors de son dernier voyage à Paris et le numéro de téléphone local fourni par sa compagnie internet au Québec. Elle écrit un petit message à sa sœur au Québec. **Remplissez les blancs avec un adjectif descriptif** de la liste suivante (vous pouvez utiliser un adjectif plus d'une fois). N'oubliez pas de faire l'accord (masculin/féminin, singulier/pluriel) et de bien placer l'adjectif (avant/après un nom) !

blond	**cher**	**gris**	**important**	**jeune**	**noir**	**pauvre**
petit	**prochain**	**propre**	**sympathique**			

Paris, le 2 septembre 2003

Ma ________________ Marie,

Comment vas-tu ? Je suis bien arrivée à Paris. Il y a eu un ________________ problème à l'aéroport. Quelqu'un a volé ma valise ! Le voleur était un ________________ homme ________________. Je l'ai vu prendre ma valise, mais j'ai pensé que sa valise devait être exactement comme la mienne. Mais non, c'était ma ________________ valise ! Alors, j'ai beaucoup crié. Le ________________ agent de sécurité a dû me calmer. Il était très ________________. Je suis arrivée à mon hôtel sans valise et sans autres vêtements que ceux que je portais : un pantalon ________________, un t-shirt, un gilet en soie, et des chaussures ________________. Heureusement que je portais tout mon argent et toutes les choses ________________ avec moi dans l'avion. Donc, au moins, je ne suis pas une victime ________________. Et de toute façon, on a retrouvé ma valise et on me l'envoie à l'hôtel. Je sais que la famille est rentrée à Montréal. Est-ce que tes cours ont déjà commencé ? Dis bonjour à tout le monde pour moi. Je téléphonerai à Maman et Papa la semaine ________________ !

Je t'embrasse, Claire

3.16 Le monde à l'envers Imaginez que c'est le monde à l'envers : C'est Jean-Louis qui s'est fait voler à l'aéroport, et tout était le contraire de ce qui s'est passé avec le vol de la valise de Claire. Pour chaque expression suivante, **remplacez chaque adjectif donné avec un adjectif opposé** ou très différent.

1. une grande valise verte et rectangulaire
2. un jeune homme blond et mince
3. un bon témoin honnête
4. un pantalon beige et un t-shirt gris
5. une nouvelle chambre propre

3.17 Vingt questions **Pensez à un objet qu'on voit tous les jours** et écrivez ce mot sur une feuille de papier. Puis, pliez et gardez le papier. Vos camarades de classe peuvent poser jusqu'à vingt (20) questions «oui ou non» pour essayer de deviner l'objet auquel vous pensez. À votre tour, écoutez les questions des autres et répondez «oui» ou «non» à leurs questions. Attention à l'usage des adjectifs descriptifs. À la fin, montrez votre feuille de papier avec la bonne réponse !

MODÈLE : un DVD

—C'est un grand objet ?

—Non !

—C'est un objet dur ?

—Oui !

Structures *l'adjectif possessif et le pronom possessif*

3.18 Une promenade En attendant sa valise, Claire décide de faire une petite promenade sur les bords de la Seine pour voir ce qu'on vend chez les bouquinistes. Elle ne va pas chercher le bouquiniste qui a acheté les livres de la famille Fontenot aujourd'hui. Aujourd'hui, elle se repose. Pourtant, en se promenant, elle croise Jean-Louis Royer, le Français qu'elle a rencontré à la Nouvelle-Orléans. Lisez le dialogue et puis décidez si les mots en **caractères gras** sont **des adjectifs** (qui décrivent un nom) ou **des pronoms** (qui remplacent un nom). Quelle est la différence ? Pouvez-vous décrire comment fonctionnent les adjectifs et les pronoms possessifs en analysant ces exemples ?

CLAIRE : Jean-Louis ? C'est toi ?

JEAN-LOUIS : Tiens ! Claire ! Quelle surprise ! Je ne savais pas que tu étais à Paris.

CLAIRE : Je viens d'arriver. Voilà **mon** hôtel, juste en face. Et toi, tu habites ce quartier ? Est-ce que **ton** appartement est près d'ici ?

JEAN-LOUIS : Non, **mes** cousins habitent près d'ici. **Leur** appartement est sur le boulevard Saint-Michel. **Le mien** est en banlieue. Ils ont un grand téléviseur. **Le mien** est très petit. Donc, je préfère **le leur** quand il y a un match de foot. Il te plaît, **ton** hôtel ?

CLAIRE : Oui, oui. C'est correct. Il n'est pas aussi luxueux que **notre** hôtel à la Nouvelle-Orléans, mais ça va. Et quand **ma** valise arrivera, je serai plus contente.

JEAN-LOUIS : Où est **ta** valise ?

CLAIRE : On l'avait volée, mais les agents de sécurité l'ont trouvée très rapidement. J'ai vu le vol de **mes** propres yeux. Un homme blond a pris **ma** valise du tapis roulant et j'ai pensé que c'était **sa** valise à lui. Mais, ce n'était pas **la sienne**. C'était **la mienne** !

JEAN-LOUIS : J'espère qu'on ne t'a rien pris de grande valeur. Écoute, j'ai très faim. **Mes** cousins ont un téléviseur super, mais **leur** frigo est toujours vide. Je connais un petit restaurant vietnamien près d'ici qui s'appelle Le Petit Saïgon. C'est **mon** restaurant préféré dans ce quartier. Ça te dit ?

CLAIRE : Oui, d'accord. Je n'ai rien mangé aujourd'hui. Allons-y.

Pour aller plus loin : CINÉMA

ACTIVITÉ E : Voulez-vous mieux connaître l'histoire du Vietnam pendant l'occupation française ? Regardez le film *Indochine*. Consultez votre cahier électronique !

Culture

La ville de **Saïgon** est aujourd'hui la ville de **Ho Chi Minh**, au sud du Vietnam. Pendant l'occupation française de l'Indochine (les colonies du **Vietnam**, du **Cambodge** et du **Laos**), la ville de Saïgon était la ville principale pour les colons. Après la réunification du Vietnam sous le régime communiste qui gouverne le pays encore aujourd'hui, on a renommé cette ville en l'honneur de Ho Chi Minh, qui était président de la république du Vietnam en 1945, fondateur du parti communiste indochinois, chef du mouvement nationaliste du Viêt-Minh et un homme politique important durant la guerre contre les Français. La capitale du Vietnam, pourtant, est la ville de Hanoi qui se trouve au nord du pays. Aujourd'hui, il ne reste qu'une minorité de la population vietnamienne qui parle français. Pourtant, le Vietnam fait partie de l'Organisation internationale de la francophonie et entretient des rapports avec les autres pays francophones du monde.

l'adjectif possessif et le pronom possessif

The *possessive adjective* (**l'adjectif possessif**) indicates ownership or possession of a noun and, like descriptive adjectives, agrees in number and gender with the noun being modified.

- There are *six types of possessive adjectives* that correspond to the six *subjects* that can own the noun (je, tu, il/elle/on, nous, vous, ils/elles). Each type has *several forms* (masculine singular, feminine singular, plural) that agree in gender/number with the *noun that is owned* by the subject:

my	mon, ma, mes	*our*	notre, notre, nos
your	ton, ta, tes	*your*	votre, votre, vos
his/her	son, sa, ses	*their*	leur, leur, leurs

- Choose the *type of possessive adjective* based on the subject that is showing ownership or possession of the noun and choose the *form of the adjective* based on the gender/number of the noun itself: **mes cousins** habitent près d'ici (je = *owner*; cousins = *plural noun*), c'était **sa valise** (le voleur/il = *owner*; valise = *feminine singular noun*).
- *Possessive adjectives* are always placed immediately *before the noun* they modify.
- Note: always use the forms **mon**, **ton**, **son** before a singular feminine noun that begins with a vowel or silent **h**: c'est **mon amie**.

The *possessive pronoun* (**le pronom possessif**) also indicates ownership or possession of a noun but replaces the *possessive adjective and noun* in a sentence.

- The *possessive pronoun* also has *six types* that each have *four forms* (masculine singular, feminine singular, masculine plural, feminine plural) to agree in number and gender with the noun being replaced:

mine	le mien, la mienne, les miens, les miennes	*ours*	le nôtre, la nôtre, les nôtres, les nôtres
yours	le tien, la tienne, les tiens, les tiennes	*yours*	le vôtre, la vôtre, les vôtres, les vôtres
his/hers	le sien, la sienne, les siens, les siennes	*theirs*	le leur, la leur, les leurs, les leurs

- Choose the *type of possessive pronoun* based on the owner and the *form* based on the gender/number of the *noun* being replaced: je préfère **le leur** (les cousins/ils = *owners*; téléviseur = *masculine singular noun*), ce n'était pas **la sienne** (le voleur/il = *owner*; valise = *feminine singular noun*).

3.19 Nos affaires Quand François Phan rentre chez lui, ses enfants sont en train de ranger leurs affaires dans l'appartement avec leur grand-mère. Ils demandent à qui sont les affaires suivantes. Remplissez les blancs avec un **adjectif possessif**.

MODÈLE : Les chaussettes sont à Mai. →
Ce sont ses chaussettes.

1. La chemise est à Papa. C'est _______________ chemise.
2. Les jouets sont à nous. Ce sont _______________ jouets.
3. La brosse à dents est à Hanh. C'est _______________ brosse à dents.
4. Les brosses à cheveux sont à Mai et à Kim. Ce sont _______________ brosses à cheveux.
5. Les parapluies sont à toi et à grand-père. Ce sont _______________ parapluies.
6. Les chaussures sont à moi. Ce sont _______________ chaussures.
7. Le livre est à toi. C'est _______________ livre.

3.20 Non, c'est le sien ! François Phan arrive au bon moment. Il corrige ses enfants, qui attribuent la plupart des affaires aux mauvaises personnes. Remplissez les blancs avec un **pronom possessif**.

MODÈLE : Les chaussettes sont à Hanh. →
Ce sont les siennes !

1. La chemise est à grand-père. C'est _______________.
2. Les jouets sont à vous. Ce sont _______________.
3. La brosse à dents est à moi. C'est _______________.
4. Les brosses à cheveux sont à Hanh et à moi. Ce sont _______________.
5. Les parapluies sont à Mai et à Kim. Ce sont _______________.
6. Les chaussures sont à toi. Ce sont _______________.
7. Le livre est à Maman. C'est _______________.

3.21 Ce sont vos affaires ? Choisissez un ou deux objets personnels (un stylo, un livre, un parapluie, une clé, un CD, une casquette de base-ball, une vidéo, etc.) et mettez-le(s) sur un bureau devant la salle de classe. À votre tour, approchez-vous au bureau et choisissez un objet (attention, ne choisissez pas le vôtre !). Puis, **décidez qui est le propriétaire de l'objet** et **posez une question** à cette personne afin de savoir si l'objet est à elle. La personne va répondre «oui» (si c'est le sien) ou «non» (et identifier le vrai propriétaire).

MODÈLE : C'est ta vidéo ?
—Oui, c'est la mienne.
—Non, c'est la sienne !

Avant d'écouter

3.22 Avant l'aveu (*the confession*) En petits groupes, posez les questions suivantes et répondez selon vos goûts personnels.

1. Est-ce que vous dites toujours la vérité ? Si non, dans quelles situations est-il permis de mentir (*to lie*), à votre avis ?
2. On dit que les étudiants américains mentent souvent à leurs professeurs. Êtes-vous d'accord ? Pourquoi ou pourquoi pas ? Donnez un exemple des mensonges (*lies*) typiques des étudiants.
3. Si un ami vous confie un secret, est-ce que vous gardez ce secret ? Dans quelles situations est-il permis de raconter un secret aux autres ?
4. Quand vous faites une gaffe (*blunder, mistake*), est-ce que vous avouez (*admit, confess*) toujours ce que vous avez fait ? Pourquoi ou pourquoi pas ?
5. Si un ami vous demande pardon d'avoir menti ou d'avoir fait une gaffe, est-ce que vous pardonnez facilement à cette personne ? Ou êtes-vous plutôt rancunier(-ère) (*vindictive*) ?

écoutez

L'aveu

Claire et Jean-Louis s'installent dans le restaurant Le Petit Saïgon. Ils commandent des rouleaux de printemps suivis de deux grands bols de soupe aux nouilles. Claire pose une question à propos du bar irlandais où Jean-Louis travaille, et il a l'air très mal à l'aise. Finalement, il décide de lui faire un aveu. . .

Maintenant, écoutez le dialogue sur votre CD. Consultez le vocabulaire pour mieux comprendre le dialogue, et puis répondez aux questions suivantes.

VOCABULAIRE

Décrire un événement

rouleau(x) de printemps	*spring roll(s)*
mal à l'aise	*uneasy*
dérangé(e)	*deranged*
forcément	*necessarily*
un(e) antiquaire	*antique dealer*
prendre un pot	*to have a drink*
au hasard	*by chance*
exprès	*on purpose*
un patron, une patronne	*boss*
un mensonge	*lie*
mentir	*to lie*
supplier	*to beg*
en vouloir à quelqu'un	*to be mad at someone*
s'en faire	*to worry/get upset*

Après avoir écouté

3.23 Avez-vous compris ? Après avoir écouté le dialogue entre Claire et Jean-Louis au restaurant vietnamien, lisez les questions suivantes et donnez votre opinion. Discutez-les en petits groupes.

1. Où sont Claire et Jean-Louis ? Pourquoi ont-ils choisi ce restaurant ?
2. Quelles sont les questions que Claire pose à Jean-Louis ? Quelles sont ses réponses ?
3. Quel était le mensonge de Jean-Louis ? À votre avis, pourquoi est-ce que Jean-Louis a menti ? Est-ce un mensonge pardonnable ou impardonnable ?
4. Pourquoi est-ce que Jean-Louis choisit ce moment pour avouer qu'il a menti à Claire ?
5. Si c'était vous à la place de Claire, est-ce que vous accepteriez ou refuseriez de lui pardonner ? Pourquoi ?

Pour aller plus loin : CULTURE

ACTIVITÉ F : Voulez-vous mieux connaître la cuisine vietnamienne ? Consultez votre cahier électronique !

3.24 D'accord ou pas d'accord ? Après avoir écouté le dialogue entre Claire et Jean-Louis au restaurant vietnamien, lisez les phrases suivantes et **donnez votre opinion**. Discutez-les en petits groupes.

	D'accord	Pas d'accord
1. Claire aime la cuisine vietnamienne.	_______	_______
2. Jean-Louis ne travaille pas dans un bar irlandais.	_______	_______
3. Jean-Louis est vraiment désolé d'avoir menti à Claire.	_______	_______
4. Claire pardonne à Jean-Louis trop facilement.	_______	_______
5. Claire n'a jamais menti à Jean-Louis.	_______	_______

s'excuser et pardonner

	Formal	Informal
Admitting wrongdoing	Écoutez, j'ai quelque chose à vous dire.	J'ai quelque chose à te dire.
	J'ai fait une gaffe/une bêtise.	J'ai fait une gaffe/une bêtise.
	Ne vous fâchez pas.	Ne te fâche pas.
	Ne m'en voulez pas.	Ne m'en veux pas
	J'avoue/admets que. . .	J'avoue/admets que. . .

Apologizing	Je suis désolé(e)/navré(e).	Je suis désolé(e)/navré(e).
	C'est/était de ma faute.	C'est/était de ma faute.
	Excusez-moi. Pardonnez-moi.	Excuse-moi. Pardonne-moi.
	Je vous présente mes excuses.	Je te présente mes excuses.
Accepting an apology	Je vous pardonne.	Je te pardonne.
	Ne vous en faites pas.	Ne t'en fais pas.
	Ce n'est pas si grave que ça.	Ce n'est pas si grave que ça.
	N'y pensez plus.	N'y pense plus.
Expressing resentment	Il est trop tard pour vous excuser.	Il est trop tard pour t'excuser.
	Vous avez eu tort.	Tu as eu tort.
	Vous n'avez pas honte !	Tu n'as pas honte !

3.25 Pardonnez-moi ! Imaginez que vos amis troublés vous demandent pardon de leurs fautes. Pour chaque situation suivante, **acceptez ou refusez de leur pardonner**, selon votre humeur ! Avec un partenaire, donnez votre réponse à chaque aveu.

1. Excuse-moi d'avoir menti à propos de mon travail. J'avais peur de te dire la vérité. C'est que je suis avocat(e) et je sais que tu les détestes.
2. Je te demande pardon d'être allé(e) au cinéma sans toi, mais tu étais si en retard !
3. J'ai honte de te dire que j'ai vendu ta montre Cartier pour m'acheter une nouvelle bicyclette. C'était vraiment bête, et je suis complètement navré(e). Tu m'en veux ?
4. Écoute, j'ai quelque chose à te dire. J'ai fait une gaffe. En téléchargeant (*downloading*) une chanson sur ton ordinateur, j'ai eu un petit problème. Bref, ton ordinateur ne marche plus, mais ce n'est pas vraiment de ma faute !

3.26 Avouez-le, vous avez mal agi ! Imaginez que vous avez mal agi et qu'il faut présenter vos excuses. Que dites-vous pour **admettre votre faute** et pour **demander pardon** dans les situations suivantes ? Que dit-on pour vous pardonner ? Avec un partenaire, inventez des dialogues pour les situations suivantes.

1. Votre ami a très faim, mais vous avez mangé son sandwich pendant qu'il cherchait une boisson.
2. Vous avez essayé le pantalon de votre frère/sœur et maintenant il est tout déchiré (*ripped*).
3. Vous avez emprunté le pull-over blanc de votre ami et maintenant il y a une grosse tache rouge sur la manche (*sleeve*).
4. Hier soir, vous êtes sorti(e) avec vos amis et vous n'avez pas fait vos devoirs pour la classe de français. Votre professeur veut savoir ce qui se passe !

3.27 C'est à vous ? Sur une feuille de papier, **écrivez une phrase pour décrire un de vos objets préférés**. Utilisez beaucoup d'adjectifs descriptifs. N'y mettez pas votre nom ! Échangez vos papiers au hasard. Lisez la phrase sur le papier que vous recevez, et circulez dans la classe pour trouver l'auteur. Ne montrez pas le papier, et posez des questions *sans* utiliser les mots de vocabulaire sur le papier. Quand vous **trouvez l'auteur**, donnez-lui son «objet préféré» en vous excusant de l'avoir pris sans demander sa permission !

MODÈLE : Mon grand chapeau de paille est jaune avec un ruban rouge et bleu.

—Est-ce que tu aimes la mode ? Portes-tu souvent des choses sur la tête ? Ah, bon ! Enfin, je crois que j'ai ton chapeau de paille. C'est le tien ? Je suis désolé(e). Excuse-moi !

À l'écrit *deuxième étape*

3.28 Désolé(e), madame ! Imaginez que vous arrivez à votre destination de vacances, mais que vous prenez la mauvaise valise du tapis roulant. Il faut retourner à l'aéroport et admettre votre faute à la personne au comptoir. **Écrivez un dialogue** dans lequel :

- vous avouez d'avoir pris la mauvaise valise et vous demandez pardon.
- vous décrivez les affaires qui sont dans votre valise.
- vous posez des questions afin de savoir si on a trouvé votre valise.
- vous imaginez les réponses (polies ou impolies !) de la personne au comptoir.

Finalement, avec un partenaire, révisez vos dialogues et lisez-les à haute voix.

Une lettre à Sandrine

Épisode 3

Structures *le participe présent*

3.29 C'est en forgeant qu'on devient forgeron Après leur déjeuner, Claire et Jean-Louis font une promenade dans le Quartier latin. Claire lui demande comment on devient antiquaire, et Jean-Louis répond avec le proverbe «c'est en forgeant qu'on devient forgeron» (*blacksmith*). **Faites correspondre l'état ou la profession** (à gauche) **avec les activités** qui mènent à cet état ou profession (à droite).

État/Profession	Activités
1. On devient professeur. . .	a. en travaillant l'or et l'argent et en faisant des bijoux.
2. On devient vendeuse. . .	b. en préparant des plats.
3. On devient touriste. . .	c. en apprenant une deuxième langue et en le parlant.
4. On devient couturier. . .	d. en vendant beaucoup de choses.
5. On devient bijoutier. . .	e. en achetant un billet d'avion, en réservant une chambre et en voyageant.
6. On devient musicienne. . .	f. en dessinant des robes et en cousant (*sewing*).
7. On devient bilingue. . .	g. en allant aux concerts, en écoutant de la musique et en jouant d'un instrument tous les jours.
8. On devient cuisinier. . .	h. en étudiant, en faisant de la recherche et en enseignant.

3.30 Un sonnet pour Hélène Claire et Jean-Louis s'arrêtent dans une librairie de livres anciens. Là, Jean-Louis trouve une vieille édition des sonnets de Pierre de Ronsard, un poète français de la Renaissance. Voici un poème du recueil *Sonnets pour Hélène*, écrit en 1578, où le poète imagine la vie d'Hélène qui sera très triste si elle rejette l'amour de Ronsard. Faites les activités suivantes avec un partenaire.

1. *Avant de lire* les paroles du poème, faites une liste de tous les verbes que vous associez à la vie d'une vieille femme qui habite toute seule dans une grande maison.
2. *Lisez l'extrait* à haute voix et puis donnez l'infinitif de chaque verbe en **caractères gras**. Ce sont des participes au présent. Pouvez-vous décrire comment fonctionne le participe présent en analysant ces exemples ?
3. *Comparez* votre liste de verbes associés à la vie d'une vieille femme avec les verbes en caractères gras. Combien sont les mêmes ?
4. *Discutez* : Comment est la vie d'Hélène à l'avenir ? Que fait-elle tous les soirs ? Comment est-ce que Ronsard imagine l'aspect physique d'Hélène à l'avenir ? Où est Ronsard pendant ce temps ? Comment imaginez-vous cette femme pendant sa jeunesse ? Comment imaginez-vous le poète ? Quand Ronsard demande à Hélène de «cueillir les roses de la vie», qu'est-ce que cela veut dire ? Est-ce que vous avez jamais écrit ou reçu un poème d'amour ? Que pensez-vous de cette manière de faire la cour (*to court*) à quelqu'un ?

Pour aller plus loin : CULTURE

ACTIVITÉ G : Qui est Pierre de Ronsard ? Apprenez un peu sur sa vie, ses poèmes et la Renaissance en France. Consultez votre cahier électronique !

Littérature

Les grandes époques de la littérature française se divisent plus ou moins par siècles : le Moyen Âge (12ème–15ème siècles), la Renaissance (16ème siècle), l'Époque Classique (17ème siècle), le Siècle des Lumières (*Enlightenment*) (18ème siècle), l'Âge Romantique (19ème siècle), l'Époque Moderne (20ème siècle). Chaque époque est nommée pour un mouvement littéraire ou intellectuel dominant. Qui sait comment on nommera le 21ème siècle ? Avez-vous des idées ?

Sonnets pour Hélène

■ Pierre de Ronsard

Quand vous serez° bien vieille, au soir à la chandelle,°
Assise auprès du feu,° **dévidant**° et **filant**,°
Direz, **chantant** mes vers,° en **vous émerveillant** :
«Ronsard me célébrait du temps que j'étais belle.»

Lors° vous n'aurez° servante oyant° telle nouvelle,
Déjà sous le labeur à demi **sommeillant**,°
Qui au bruit° de Ronsard ne s'aille **réveillant**,
Bénissant° votre nom de louange° immortelle.

Je serai° sous la terre, et fantôme sans os°
Par les ombres myrteux° je prendrai mon repos :
Vous serez au foyer° une vieille accroupie,°

Regrettant mon amour et votre fier dédain.°
Vivez, si m'en croyez, n'attendez à demain :
Cueillez° dès aujourd'hui° les roses de la vie.

will be/candlelight
fire/spooling/spinning thread
verses
at that time/will not have/hearing (inf. ouïr)
to doze off
sound (of Ronsard's name)
to bless/praise
will be/bones
shadows of myrtle (a plant)
hearth/crouched, hunched over
proud disdain
gather, pick/starting today

le participe présent

The *present participle* (**le participe présent**) is used to express ongoing actions in the present and corresponds to words that end in *-ing* in English (walking, talking, etc.). It is often used with the preposition **en** (*while*).

Formation of the present participle:

- Drop the **-ons** from the **nous** form of the verb in the present tense and add the ending **-ant**: nous finissons → en **finissant**.
- There are three *irregular present participles*: **étant** (être), **ayant** (avoir), **sachant** (savoir).
- The reflexive pronoun of *reflexive verbs* should agree with the main subject of the sentence: en **me réveillant**.
- Verbs that have *slightly irregular spellings* in the **nous** form (like verbs that end in **-ger** or **-cer**) retain their irregular spellings as present participles: en commen**ç**ant, en mang**e**ant.
- To make a present participle negative, place the negative around the verb: en **ne chantant pas**.

The *present participle* can be used to describe:

- *ongoing actions*: **chantant** mes vers, vous dites. . .
- *simultaneous actions*: je m'habille en **regardant** la télé
- *cause-and-effect events*: j'ai déchiré mon pantalon en **m'habillant**

3.31 En passant par le Marais Après le déjeuner, Claire et Jean-Louis continuent à se balader dans les rues de Paris. Ils suivent les quais jusqu'au Marais, le 4ème arrondissement, et montent la rue Saint-Paul. Mettez les verbes entre parenthèses au **participe présent**.

1. En (passer) ____________________ par le Marais, Claire voit beaucoup de petites boutiques et de petits magasins.
2. Jean-Louis, (parler) ____________________ toujours du vol de la valise, demande comment était le voleur.
3. Claire, ne (vouloir) ____________________ pas trop parler de la situation et (être) ____________________ un peu fatiguée, répond vaguement à ses questions.
4. En (voyager) ____________________, dit-elle, on risque toujours d'être victime d'un crime.
5. Puis, (voir) ____________________ une épicerie vietnamienne, Claire se demande si ce n'est pas le magasin du témoin et y entre.
6. En (attendre) ____________________ que la jeune femme à la caisse en termine avec son coup de fil, Claire raconte à Jean-Louis comment le témoin a trouvé ses affaires dans l'aéroport.
7. Malheureusement, la jeune femme ne sait rien de cette histoire du vol et, (insister) ____________________ que la leur est la seule épicerie vietnamienne dans le quartier, conseille à Claire et Jean-Louis de chercher ce monsieur ailleurs.
8. Donc, ils partent, tout en (s'excuser) ____________________ d'avoir dérangé (*to have bothered*) la jeune femme.

Culture

Le **Marais** est un quartier ancien qui se trouve dans les 3ème et 4ème arrondissements. À l'origine de la ville de Paris, ce quartier était un vrai marais, un marécage. Mais au cours des siècles, le quartier est devenu un endroit chic et beaucoup d'écrivains célèbres y ont habité : Racine, Molière, Voltaire, Victor Hugo et Madame de Sévigné. On trouve le Musée Carnavalet (musée de l'histoire de la ville de Paris) dans l'ancienne maison de Madame de Sévigné, et on peut visiter l'appartement de Victor Hugo (auteur des *Misérables* et de *Notre-Dame de Paris*, parmi d'autres) à la Place des Vosges. Dans le Marais, surtout autour de la rue des Rosiers, on trouve aussi une grande communauté juive qui, depuis des siècles, a contribué à la vie culturelle du quartier.

3.32 La vie urbaine Claire et Jean-Louis s'arrêtent dans un café du Marais où ils entendent des gens qui parlent des événements de leurs vies urbaines chargées. Imaginez toutes les choses que les gens peuvent faire simultanément. Terminez les phrases avec des **participes au présent**.

MODÈLE : On lit le journal tout en. . . →
en prenant un café et en parlant à ses amis.

1. Je me réveille en. . .
2. Il a répondu au téléphone tout en. . .
3. Nous travaillons en. . .
4. Tu as fini ton café tout en. . .
5. Vous prenez le métro tout en. . .

Structures *l'infinitif passé*

3.33 Que savez-vous ? Beaucoup de choses bizarres se sont passées depuis le début du projet de recherche de Claire. Vous rappelez-vous tous les événements ? **Terminez les phrases suivantes** avec un événement qui s'est passé ou que vous inventez (si vous n'avez pas une bonne mémoire !). Employez le passé composé (pour les actions terminées) ou l'imparfait (pour les émotions ou les descriptions).

MODÈLE : Avant d'arriver à la Nouvelle-Orléans. . . →

Claire a demandé une bourse à son université. En plus, elle a trouvé son sujet de thèse. Elle était très occupée.

Langue

Rappel ! Rappel ! Si vous ne vous souvenez pas de la formation du **participe passé** ou de quels verbes prennent **être** au passé composé, révisez l'Épisode 3 du Chapitre 2 !

1. Avant de rencontrer Sandrine Fontenot-Chardin. . .
2. Après avoir rencontré Sandrine Fontenot-Chardin. . .
3. Avant de partir de la Nouvelle-Orléans. . .
4. Après être partie de la Nouvelle-Orléans. . .
5. Avant de revoir Jean-Louis à Paris. . .
6. Après avoir revu Jean-Louis à Paris. . .

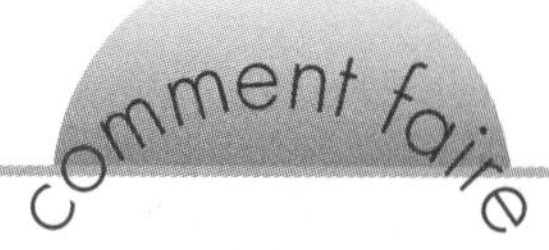

l'infinitif passé

The *past infinitive* (**l'infinitif passé**) is the equivalent of the infinitive (the unconjugated verb) in the past. The *past infinitive* is simply the infinitive of **avoir** or **être** followed by the past participle (**le participe passé**). Remember the following in forming the past infinitive:

- Choose **avoir** or **être** and form the **past participle** by following the same guidelines for the **passé composé**.
- Note that the past participle of a verb that takes **être** must agree with the main subject of the sentence, even though it is part of an infinitive.
- To make a past infinitive negative, as with the present infinitive, place the negative before the verb: Après **ne pas avoir dit** la vérité, Jean-Louis a demandé pardon.
- The past infinitive is often used with the preposition **après** or with the preposition **de** (when apologizing for having done something in the past): **Après être allée** chez Sandrine, Claire a traversé le cimetière. Excuse-moi **d'avoir déchiré** ton pantalon. J'ai honte **d'avoir mangé** ton sandwich.

3.34 En rentrant Finalement, Jean-Louis accompagne Claire à son hôtel, mais il n'arrête pas de s'excuser de son comportement à la Nouvelle-Orléans. Remplissez les blancs avec **l'infinitif passé** du verbe entre parenthèses.

JEAN-LOUIS : Encore une fois, Claire, excuse-moi de t'(mentir) _______________. Après (entendre) _______________ ton sujet de recherche, j'étais fasciné de ce manuscrit perdu. J'ai honte de ne pas (mentionner) _______________ mon association à l'antiquaire. Pardonne-moi d'(être) _______________ si méfiant. Après (retourner) _______________ à Paris, j'ai téléphoné à mon patron qui m'a dit de chercher ce manuscrit. Je suis vraiment navré de ne pas t'(confier) _______________ ce secret dès le jour de notre rencontre. Et après (apprendre) _______________ qu'on a volé ta valise à l'aéroport, j'ai eu peur. Si quelqu'un d'autre cherchait ce même manuscrit ! Mais, après (sortir) _______________ avec toi aujourd'hui, je suis rassuré. C'était peut-être une coïncidence.

3.35 La réponse de Marie Après avoir pardonné à Jean-Louis plusieurs fois, Claire monte dans sa chambre de l'Hôtel Quasimodo, où sa valise l'attend déjà. Elle branche encore son ordinateur et voit que Marie avait répondu à son message. Choisissez un des verbes donnés pour remplir les blancs et mettez ce verbe à **l'infinitif passé** ou au **participe présent**.

aller écrire finir mettre rentrer retrouver voyager

Chère Claire,

Je suis désolée d'entendre qu'on a volé ta valise ! Quelle chance d'_______________ la valise tout de suite après l'incident. En _______________ en avion, il y a toujours la possibilité de perdre ses bagages. Tu as eu de la chance d'_______________ toutes tes choses importantes dans ton sac à dos. J'espère que la suite de ton séjour à Paris sera plus heureuse. Quant à moi, je reprends mes études à l'université. Après _______________ à Montréal la semaine dernière, toute la famille a repris son travail. J'ai parlé avec un de tes profs hier. En _______________ à l'université, j'ai rencontré ton directeur de thèse de Sainte-Foy, le Professeur Thuillier, dans le métro. Il s'excuse de ne pas _______________ beaucoup de messages récemment, mais il est très occupé en _______________ son travail administratif afin de pouvoir partir en congé sabbatique à la fin du mois. Enfin, Maman et Papa attendent ton appel, et moi aussi. Amuse-toi bien à Paris, mais fais attention aussi !

Bisous, Marie

lisez

Une lettre à Sandrine

Paris, le 2 septembre 2003
Madame Sandrine Fontenot-Chardin
22 Saint Philip Street
New Orleans, Louisiana 70130 USA

Chère Madame,

Je vous écris d'abord pour vous remercier de votre accueil° chaleureux et de m'avoir donné le nom du bouquiniste à Paris qui a acheté les livres de votre famille. Je suis actuellement à Paris, et je continue ma recherche du manuscrit perdu de Laclos. La deuxième raison pour cette lettre est de vous informer des développements du projet. À vrai dire, je commence un peu à m'inquiéter, et je ne sais pas à qui faire confiance. Je me souviens de votre histoire des voleurs qui ont provoqué la mort de votre grand-père. Moi aussi, après être arrivée à Paris, j'ai été la victime d'un vol. J'attendais à la livraison des bagages enregistrés, où il y avait une grande foule, quand un homme blond est parti avec ma valise. J'étais bouleversée !° Bêtement, j'ai attendu une heure avant de contacter les agents de sécurité. Heureusement, les agents de sécurité ont retrouvé ma valise une heure après le vol.

welcome · *upset*

Pourtant, il y a eu pas mal° de choses bizarres qui se sont passées depuis notre rendez-vous. Vous m'avez envoyé une lettre à l'Hôtel Le Moyne après avoir reçu un coup de téléphone que je n'ai pas passé. Je vous ai téléphoné deux fois le lendemain pour savoir ce que cette personne vous avait dit pour vous faire croire que c'était moi, mais vous étiez déjà partis en vacances. Ensuite, après avoir rencontré un touriste français sympa à la Nouvelle-Orléans, je le revois à Paris et j'apprends qu'il travaille pour un antiquaire qui s'intéresse au même manuscrit de Laclos. Et en arrivant à Paris, on a volé ma valise. Est-ce que ce sont des coïncidences ? Enfin, je ne crois pas aux malédictions,° mais votre avis de «me méfier des voleurs» fait écho dans ma tête. Quand j'étais à la Nouvelle-Orléans, je parlais trop de mon projet aux gens que je ne connaissais pas bien. Dès aujourd'hui, je serai plus prudente. Je suis à l'Hôtel Quasimodo encore pour quelques semaines, si vous voulez m'écrire ou me téléphoner ici. Je vous remercie encore de votre gentillesse.°

quite a few · *curses* · *kindness*

En attendant de vous lire ou de vous parler, je vous prie de croire à l'assurance de mes sentiments les plus cordiaux.

Claire Plouffe

Après avoir lu

3.36 D'accord ou pas d'accord ? Après avoir lu la lettre ci-dessus, lisez les phrases suivantes et donnez vos opinions personnelles. Discutez en petits groupes.

	D'accord	Pas d'accord
1. Claire écrit à Sandrine pour la remercier de sa gentillesse.	_______	_______
2. Claire ne s'inquiète pas du tout de la malédiction du manuscrit.	_______	_______
3. Claire n'a plus confiance en Jean-Louis.	_______	_______
4. Il faut toujours se méfier des voleurs.	_______	_______
5. Sandrine va venir à Paris pour aider Claire avec ses recherches.	_______	_______

Structures *le passé composé et l'imparfait (suite)*

3.37 Qu'est-ce qu'elle a dit ? Relisez la lettre que Claire envoie à Sandrine dans laquelle elle parle de ce qui s'est déjà passé. Soulignez tous les verbes qui sont au **passé composé** ou à l'**imparfait**, et essayez de décrire pourquoi Claire a choisi l'un ou l'autre.

le passé composé et l'imparfait (suite)

Remember that the **passé composé** and the **imparfait** are both used for descriptions in the past. They have different uses depending on the context in which they are used or on the meaning intended by the person speaking. In general, use the **passé composé** for completed actions or states of being. More precisely, it is used for actions or states that occurred at a specific moment in time, for a specific number of times, or for a duration of time with a specific beginning and end. Use the **imparfait** for actions or states which were habitual or ongoing (no specified beginning or end), or provide background information or description.

For example, the following are verb tenses used in the letter to Sandrine (above):

Passé composé

- *Action or state occurring at a specific moment in time*: un homme blond est parti, vous m'avez envoyé, je n'ai pas passé le coup de téléphone
- *Actions or states occurring a specific number of times*: je vous ai téléphoné deux fois
- *Actions or states occurring during a specific period of time*: j'ai attendu une heure

Imparfait

- *Habitual actions or states*: je parlais trop
- *Ongoing actions or states*: j'attendais
- *Emotions*: j'étais bouleversée
- *Background information/description*: il y avait une grande foule

Note that the *imperfect* can also be used *to make suggestions* when it follows **si** (*if*): **Si on dînait** ensemble ce soir ? (What if we had dinner together tonight?)

Langue

Rappel ! Rappel ! Révisez la formation et l'usage du **passé composé** et de **l'imparfait** (dans l'Épisode 3 du Chapitre 2) si vous en avez besoin. Rappelez-vous aussi que plusieurs verbes prennent un sens légèrement différent s'ils sont au **passé composé** ou à l'**imparfait**. Par exemple :

vouloir	j'ai voulu (*I wanted* [*attempt made*])	je voulais (*I wanted* [*no attempt made*])
pouvoir	j'ai pu (*I was able, I succeeded*)	je pouvais (*I could, I was capable of*)
devoir	j'ai dû (*I had to, I must have*)	je devais (*I was supposed to*)
savoir	j'ai su (*I realized*)	je savais (*I knew*)
connaître	j'ai connu (*I met* [*a person*])	je connaissais (*I used to know, I knew*)

3.38 Tu as bien dormi ? Sa deuxième nuit à l'Hôtel Quasimodo se passe assez tranquillement. Le matin, Claire se lève de bonne heure et va au café Le Clou de Paris, sur la place Saint-André-des-Arts, pour rencontrer Jean-Louis. Il lui demande si elle a bien dormi et ce qu'elle a fait hier soir. Voici sa réponse. Mettez les verbes entre parenthèses au **passé composé** ou à l'**imparfait**.

CLAIRE : Hier soir ? Voyons, ma soirée (être) _______________ assez tranquille. Je (monter) _______________ à ma chambre vers 8h. Il (faire) _______________ assez frais dehors, alors je (fermer) _______________ les fenêtres. Ensuite, je (défaire) _______________ ma valise, qui (être) _______________ là quand je (revenir) _______________. Je (choisir) _______________ de laver plusieurs vêtements à la main et d'envoyer les autres au pressing (*dry cleaner*). Puis, je (commander) _______________ un petit repas dans ma chambre. En effet, je (prendre) _______________ mon souper quand je (recevoir) _______________ un message par courriel de ma sœur Marie. Elle (avoir) _______________ peur pour moi à cause de cette histoire de vol. Quand nous (être) _______________ petites, elle (s'inquiéter) _______________ toujours de tout.

	Donc, je lui (envoyer) ______________ un message pour la rassurer. Et puis, je (s'endormir) ______________ en regardant un film à la télé.
JEAN-LOUIS :	Alors, tu (ne pas voir) ____________ le bossu (*hunchback*) ?
CLAIRE :	Non, pas hier soir, mais je l'ai vu au Grand Théâtre de Québec l'année dernière.

3.39 La soirée de Jean-Louis Imaginez la soirée de Jean-Louis. Décrivez tout ce qu'il a fait après avoir laissé Claire à son hôtel hier soir. **Écrivez dix à douze phrases** avec un partenaire. Puis, échangez vos papiers avec un autre groupe et lisez leur version des événements. Faites des commentaires en bas de page !

MODÈLE : Après avoir laissé Claire à l'hôtel, Jean-Louis est allé au bar où il travaillait comme barman avant de devenir antiquaire.

—Vraiment ? Pourquoi est-il allé au bar ? Avec qui a-t-il parlé ?

la France multiculturelle

Racontez les passés de Véronique et Richard. Regardez la vidéo et consultez votre cahier d'activités !

3.40 Et vous ? **Interviewez** quelqu'un dans la classe et demandez-lui ce qu'il/elle faisait ou ce qu'il/elle a fait aux moments suivants. À votre tour, répondez aux questions en fournissant beaucoup de détails. Attention à l'usage du passé composé, de l'imparfait et d'autres temps des verbes !

1. hier soir
2. l'été dernier
3. l'hiver dernier
4. en 2001

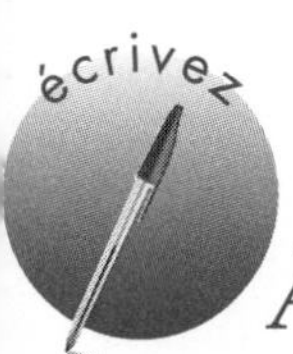

À l'écrit *troisième étape*

3.41 À propos de votre valise Imaginez que vous avez rendu la valise que vous avez prise par erreur à l'aéroport, mais que votre propre valise est toujours disparue. **Écrivez une brève lettre ou un e-mail** à l'agence de sécurité de l'aéroport avec une description du problème, votre version des événements, des excuses et une description de votre valise et de son contenu. Échangez votre lettre avec celle d'un de vos camarades de classe (par courriel, si vous voulez !) et offrez-lui une réponse et quelques corrections possibles.

Culture

Notre-Dame de Paris est un des plus grands romans de **Victor Hugo**, un écrivain parisien du 19ème siècle. L'intrigue du roman se passe au Moyen Âge, et il s'agit d'un bossu nommé **Quasimodo** qui habite la tour de la cathédrale de Notre-Dame. Ce bossu tombe amoureux d'une belle femme qui s'appelle Esmeralda. Cette histoire très populaire a souvent été adaptée pour des publics variés, y compris en dessin animé pour le cinéma par Disney (aux États-Unis) et en pièce musicale pour le théâtre par une troupe québécoise (au Canada).

Pour aller plus loin : CULTURE

ACTIVITÉ H : Lisez un extrait du roman *Notre-Dame de Paris* de Victor Hugo. Consultez votre cahier électronique !

Dénouement

Activités de révision

3.42 Comment sont-ils ? Avec un partenaire, **décrivez les gens suivants** : leur aspect physique, leurs vêtements, et les objets personnels qu'ils apportent souvent avec eux.

1. votre professeur de français
2. le Président des États-Unis
3. une femme dans votre classe de français
4. un homme dans votre classe de français
5. Claire Plouffe (*imaginez !*)
6. Philippe Aucoin, l'hôtelier à la Nouvelle-Orléans (*imaginez !*)
7. Sandrine Fontenot-Chardin, la femme créole (*imaginez !*)
8. François Phan, le témoin vietnamien (*imaginez !*)

Pour aller plus loin : CULTURE

ACTIVITÉ 1 : Voulez-vous vous habiller comme un parisien ou une parisienne ? Consultez votre cahier électronique !

3.43 Vos magasins Imaginez qu'un couple français arrive dans votre région pour un week-end de vacances. Pourtant, la ligne aérienne a perdu leurs bagages, et ils ont besoin d'acheter de nouveaux vêtements et d'autres affaires personnelles pour leur séjour aux États-Unis. En petits groupes, **écrivez une liste** des vêtements et des affaires personnelles que vous leur suggérez (attention que tout soit approprié au climat en cette saison) et indiquez dans quels magasins ils peuvent trouver toutes ces choses. Comparez vos suggestions avec celles de vos camarades.

Avant de lire *La Parure*

3.44 À la mode Imaginez qu'on vous invite à une soirée élégante. Pourtant, vous n'avez pas de vêtements élégants à la mode et vous n'avez pas d'argent pour en acheter. Il faut emprunter des choses à vos camarades de classe. Circulez dans la salle de classe et **posez des questions** à vos camarades. Vous voulez trouver des gens qui peuvent vous prêter les vêtements, les accessoires dont vous avez besoin !

MODÈLE : **—Est-ce que vous avez un pantalon noir à la taille (*size*) 8 que je pourrais emprunter ?**

—Désolé(e), ce n'est pas ma taille ! Mais avez-vous des chaussures marron à la pointure (*shoe size*) 7 ?

3.45 Sans un sou Votre ami n'a pas de job mais dépense beaucoup d'argent avec ses cartes de crédit. Il ne comprend pas pourquoi il est toujours sans le sou. Vous expliquez pourquoi ! Terminez les phrases avec des verbes au **participe présent**.

1. On devient pauvre en. . .
2. On accumule des dettes en. . .
3. On ne trouve pas de job en. . .
4. On dépense trop d'argent en. . .
5. On repaie ses dettes en. . .
6. On devient riche en. . .

3.46 Premières impressions Lisez l'extrait suivant, tiré du conte *La Parure* (*The Jewels*) de Guy de Maupassant, sans essayer de comprendre chaque mot. Après votre première lecture du texte, répondez aux questions. Ensuite, relisez le texte une deuxième fois, plus attentivement.

1. Est-ce que les Loisel sont riches ? Comment le savez-vous ?
2. Comment est Madame Loisel après dix ans de travail ?
3. Est-ce que Madame Loisel et Madame Forestier se connaissent bien ?
4. Quel est le sujet de discussion entre les deux femmes ?
5. Où se situe l'action ?

lisez

La Parure

L'intrigue de ce conte de Guy de Maupassant se situe à Paris, au 19ème siècle, dans une société où il est important de paraître riche et de bon goût, même si on mène une vie modeste. Madame Loisel, qui s'est mariée avec un fonctionnaire, emprunte un collier de diamants (une parure) à une amie plus riche pour aller à une fête. En revenant de la fête, elle perd le collier. Ne voulant pas avouer sa faute à son amie, elle achète un autre collier qui ressemble au premier et le laisse passer pour l'original. Pourtant, ce collier coûte très très cher, et Monsieur et Madame Loisel passent dix ans à rembourser leur dette. . .

■ Guy de Maupassant

La Parure (extrait)

Elle connut les gros travaux du ménage, les odieuses° besognes° de la cuisine. Elle lava la vaisselle, usant ses ongles roses sur les poteries grasses et le fond des casseroles. Elle savonna le linge sale, les chemises et les torchons,° qu'elle faisait sécher sur une corde ; elle descendit à la rue, chaque matin, les ordures,° et monta l'eau, s'arrêtant à chaque étage pour souffler.° Et, vêtue comme une femme du peuple, elle alla chez le fruitier, chez l'épicier, chez le boucher, le panier° au bras, marchandant,° injuriée,° défendant sou à sou son misérable argent.

odious, hateful/task

dishcloth

trash/to catch one's breath

basket/to haggle/insulted

Il fallait chaque mois payer des billets, en renouveler d'autres, obtenir du temps. Le mari travaillait, le soir, à mettre au net les comptes d'un commerçant, et la nuit, souvent, il faisait de la copie à cinq sous la page. Et cette vie dura dix ans.

Au bout de dix ans, ils avaient tout restitué, tout, avec le taux de l'usure,° et l'accumulation des intérêts superposés. Madame Loisel semblait vieille, maintenant. Elle était devenue la femme forte, et dure, et rude, des ménages pauvres. Mal peignée, avec les jupes de travers° et les mains rouges, elle parlait haut, lavait à grande eau les planchers. Mais parfois, lorsque son mari était au bureau, elle s'asseyait auprès de la fenêtre, et elle songeait à cette soirée d'autrefois, à ce bal où elle avait été si belle et si fêtée. Que serait-il arrivé si elle n'avait point perdu cette parure ? Qui sait ? qui sait ? Comme la vie est singulière, changeante ! Comme il faut peu de chose pour vous perdre ou vous sauver !

Or, un dimanche, comme elle était allée faire un tour aux Champs-Élysées pour se délasser° des besognes de la semaine, elle aperçut tout à coup une femme qui promenait un enfant. C'était Madame Forestier, toujours jeune, toujours belle, toujours séduisante. Madame Loisel se sentit émue°. Allait-elle lui parler ? Oui, certes. Et maintenant qu'elle avait payé, elle lui dirait tout. Pourquoi pas ?

Elle s'approcha.

«Bonjour, Jeanne.»

L'autre ne la reconnaissait point, s'étonnant° d'être appelée ainsi familièrement par cette bourgeoise. Elle balbutia° : «Mais. . . Madame !. . . Je ne sais. . . Vous devez vous tromper.»

—Non. Je suis Mathilde Loisel.»

Son amie poussa un cri :

«Oh !. . . ma pauvre Mathilde, comme tu es changée !. . .

—Oui, j'ai eu des jours bien durs, depuis que je ne t'ai vue ; et bien des misères. . . et cela à cause de toi !. . .

—De moi. . . Comment ça ?

—Tu te rappelles bien cette rivière de diamants que tu m'as prêtée pour aller à la fête du ministère.

—Oui. Eh bien ?

—Eh bien, je l'ai perdue.

—Comment ! puisque tu me l'as rapportée.

—Je t'en ai rapporté une autre toute pareille.° Et voilà dix ans que nous la payons. Tu comprends que ça n'était pas aisé pour nous, qui n'avions rien. . . Enfin, c'est fini, et je suis rudement contente.

—Tu dis que tu as acheté une rivière de diamants pour remplacer la mienne ?

—Oui. Tu ne t'en étais pas aperçue,° hein ? Elles étaient bien pareilles.»

Et elle souriait d'une joie orgueilleuse° et naïve. Madame Forestier, fort émue, lui prit les deux mains.

«Oh ! ma pauvre Mathilde ! Mais la mienne était fausse.° Elle valait au plus cinq cents francs !»

interest — *the wrong way* — *to relax* — *moved* — *to be shocked* — *to stammer* — *similar* — *to realize* — *proud* — *fake*

Après avoir lu

3.47 Avez-vous compris ? En petits groupes, **discutez de vos réponses** aux questions suivantes.

1. Qu'est-ce que Mathilde Loisel a avoué à son amie à la fin de l'histoire ? Lui demande-t-elle de la pardonner ?

2. Comment a été la vie de Mathilde Loisel pendant les dix ans de travail ? Comment imaginez-vous sa vie quotidienne avant de perdre le collier de son amie ? Et après ?
3. Décrivez Mathilde Loisel (physiquement). Pourquoi est-ce que Madame Forestier ne la reconnaît pas ? Imaginez comment elle était avant l'incident.
4. Est-ce que la fin de l'histoire est ironique, amusante ou triste, à votre avis ? Pourquoi ?
5. Pourquoi est-ce que Madame Loisel n'a pas voulu avouer à son amie la perte de son collier au moment où elle l'a perdu ?
6. À votre avis, est-ce que Madame Forestier va lui pardonner ? Pourquoi ou pourquoi pas ?

3.48 D'accord ou pas d'accord ? Après avoir lu l'extrait, lisez les phrases suivantes et **donnez votre opinion**. Discutez de vos réponses en petits groupes.

	D'accord	Pas d'accord
1. Madame Loisel a eu une vie difficile.	_______	_______
2. Monsieur Loisel voulait quitter sa femme après la perte du collier.	_______	_______
3. En dix ans, Madame Loisel a beaucoup changé physiquement.	_______	_______
4. Madame Forestier n'était pas plus riche que son amie.	_______	_______
5. Madame Loisel a fait une bêtise de ne pas avouer sa faute au début.	_______	_______

3.49 Analyse littéraire Examinez ce texte de près. Répondez aux questions suivantes et **discutez de vos réponses** en classe.

1. Quels temps de verbe trouvez-vous dans les deux premiers paragraphes où l'auteur décrit comment les Loisel ont pu repayer leur dette ?
2. Relisez le portrait de Madame Loisel au début du 3ème paragraphe. Quels adjectifs descriptifs sont employés ? Quelle est votre réaction à ce portrait ? La trouvez-vous méchant, réaliste, pathétique ? Comparez ce portrait avec celui de Madame Forestier au 4ème paragraphe.
3. À la fin du 3ème paragraphe, dans lequel on trouve le portrait de Madame Loisel, elle pense à comment était sa vie avant d'avoir perdu le collier de son amie. Quelle ponctuation est employée pour décrire ce moment de nostalgie ? Quel en est l'effet ?
4. Dans la 4ème paragraphe, quand Madame Loisel voit son ancienne amie, où se trouve cette rencontre ? Quand ? Quelle est la signification de ce contexte ? Qu'est-ce qu'il contribue au ton de la rencontre ?
5. Quand les deux femmes parlent du collier, elles l'appellent «une rivière de diamants». Pensez à cette image. À quoi associe-t-on une rivière ? Quel est l'effet de choisir cette image pour parler du collier ?
6. Regardez la ponctuation dans la conversation entre les deux femmes. Quel est l'effet de l'alternance entre les points d'interrogation et les points d'exclamation ? Est-ce que l'effet de la ponctuation à la fin du 3ème paragraphe présage (*foreshadows*) l'effet de la ponctuation à la fin de cette histoire ?

Synthèses

3.50 Réfléchissons à la culture Voici quelques éléments de la culture parisienne que vous avez étudiés dans ce chapitre. En petits groupes, répondez aux questions et discutez de vos impressions avec vos camarades.

l'immigration **la mode** **la tour Eiffel**

1. Définissez ou décrivez chaque élément.
2. Quand les Américains pensent à la ville de Paris, auxquels de ces éléments pensent-ils ? Lesquels contribuent à l'image internationale de Paris et lesquels contribuent à la vie quotidienne dans la ville ? Expliquez.
3. Les styles vestimentaires et les styles architecturaux changent souvent, et la population immigrante d'une grande ville comme Paris est aussi fluide. Comment est-ce qu'on réagit différemment à ces changements ? Comment influencent-ils la vie dans une grande ville ?
4. À votre avis, est-ce que ces éléments sont stéréotypiques ou font-ils vraiment partie de la culture parisienne ? Pourquoi ?

la France multiculturelle

Comment décrit-on la ville de Paris ? Regardez la vidéo et consultez votre cahier d'activités !

3.51 À débattre Lisez les questions suivantes et **discutez** en groupes. Si possible, parlez de vos expériences personnelles relatives aux questions.

1. **Les stéréotypes !** Les Français ont la réputation d'être très chic et très à la mode. Pourtant, les couturiers s'inspirent souvent d'autres cultures pour créer leur nouveau «look» chaque saison. Est-ce que les Français sont plus chic que les autres ? Si oui, pourquoi ? Si non, comment explique-t-on ce stéréotype ?
2. **Est-ce que l'habit fait le moine ?** Le proverbe «L'habit ne fait pas le moine» enseigne une leçon universelle. Il y a un proverbe vietnamien similaire qui dit : «Bonne réputation vaut mieux que beaux habits». Pourtant, même si on sait que l'extérieur ne reflète pas toujours l'intérieur d'une personne, on juge souvent les gens par leurs vêtements, leurs coiffures, leurs voitures, etc. (avouons-le !). À votre avis, a-t-on parfois raison de juger les gens sur leurs apparences ?
3. **Achetez-vous de la fourrure (*fur*) ?** Il y a souvent des manifestations contre l'usage de la fourrure pour faire des vêtements ou des manteaux. On veut protéger ces pauvres animaux. En même temps, il y a des gens qui souffrent en travaillant dans les usines de l'industrie textile dans les pays en voie de développement (comme Haïti ou le Vietnam) : leurs journées de travail sont extrêmement longues, ils sont mal payés et mal nourris, et ce sont souvent des jeunes. Ils fabriquent des vêtements en coton ou en soie qu'on achète tous les jours dans les grands magasins dans les pays de l'ouest. Pourtant, on ne manifeste pas souvent pour eux. À votre avis, est-ce que les animaux sont mieux protégés par la presse et l'opinion publique que les êtres humains ? Pourquoi ou pourquoi pas ?

Pour aller plus loin : CULTURE

ACTIVITÉ J : Découvrez l'œuvre de Thich Nhat Hanh, un célèbre bouddhiste vietnamien. Consultez votre cahier électronique !

3.52 À l'impromptu Voici des situations de rencontres. Avec une ou deux autres personnes, **choisissez une scène** et **improvisez-la** devant la classe. Si vous ne voulez pas improviser, écrivez votre dialogue en avance et puis jouez-le pour la classe.

1. Un rendez-vous romantique !
   (a) Vous êtes dans un café du Quartier latin après avoir quitté l'homme ou la femme avec qui vous sortez. Vous êtes bien habillé(e). Vous y rencontrez un ami et vous lui racontez votre rendez-vous romantique à l'Opéra de la Bastille et combien vous êtes amoureux(-euse). Décrivez la personne avec qui vous êtes sorti(e) !
   (b) Vous vous promenez dans les rues de Paris et vous rencontrez par hasard un vieil ami. Vous remarquez une énorme tache (*stain*) sur son manteau, et ses cheveux sont ébouriffés (*messed up*). Vous essayez de savoir ce qui lui est arrivé.
2. Au service des objets perdus !
   (a) Vous travaillez au service des objets perdus à l'aéroport Charles-de-Gaulle à Paris. Une longue file de gens attendent pour réclamer ce qu'ils ont perdu. Écoutez chacun d'eux à son tour et restituez-leur leurs biens quand vous serez convaincu(e) de leurs descriptions.
   (b) Vous venez de perdre votre valise lors d'un vol transatlantique. Vous êtes en colère. Vous allez trouver les services adéquats. Allez vous plaindre et faites une description détaillée du contenu de votre valise.
3. Un vol au Marais !
   (a) Vous êtes un(e) touriste américain(e) qui se promène dans les rues du Marais à Paris quand vous êtes le témoin d'un vol. Imaginez les circonstances et répondez aux questions d'un agent à la poursuite du voleur.
   (b) Vous êtes aussi un témoin du vol dans les rues du Marais à Paris. Mais la personne que vous avez vue commettre ce crime ne ressemble pas du tout à la personne que le/la touriste américain(e) est en train de décrire. En fait, le voleur que vous avez vu ressemble beaucoup à ce(tte) touriste américain(e) ! Décrivez-le/la pour l'agent de police.
   (c) Vous êtes l'agent de police qui mène l'enquête sur le vol dans les rues du Marais. Interrogez les deux témoins et essayez de trouver le voleur parmi les gens dans la rue (vos camarades de classe !).

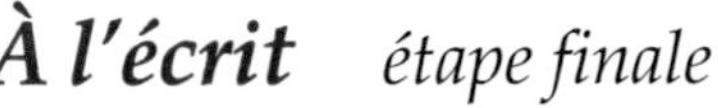

À l'écrit *étape finale*

3.53 Le vol de votre valise Finalement, en réponse à votre lettre, l'agence de sécurité vous envoie son rapport sur le vol de votre valise. Tout était enregistré sur le magnétoscope (*video recorder*) dans la livraison des bagages enregistrés ! Imaginez la scène du vol, la personne qui a volé votre valise et la chaîne des événements. **Révisez et élaborez vos travaux d'écriture de ce chapitre (Activités 13, 28 et 41) et rédigez le rapport officiel** qui décrit le vol. Soyez aussi descriptifs que possible et faites attention à l'usage des verbes au passé composé ou à l'imparfait.

Pour agir :
LA FRANCE

Si vous voulez bouger et faire quelque chose pour mieux connaître la France et la ville de Paris, ou pour aider les autres à mieux comprendre l'influence française aux États-Unis, consultez la section **Pour agir** dans votre cahier électronique ! Il y a tant de choses à faire :

- **Vendez des croissants** et du café au lait sur votre campus et contribuez l'argent que vous gagnez à une organisation qui restaure le parc du château de Versailles, ou bien vendez des rouleaux de printemps et offrez l'argent à une organisation qui aide les immigrés en France.
- **Organisez une collection** de vêtements usagés et offrez ces vêtements à une organisation caritative qui aide les gens des pays pauvres aux Antilles ou en Asie du sud-est.
- **Allez dans un restaurant** français ou vietnamien dans votre région.
- **Entrez en contact** avec des Vietnamiens francophones.
- **Organisez un voyage** à Paris.
- **Cuisinez !** Préparez un vrai repas français ou vietnamien avec vos camarades de classe.

À suivre

Malgré ses appréhensions, Claire accepte de collaborer avec Jean-Louis, et elle avoue que Sandrine Fontenot-Chardin lui a donné le nom de l'acheteur de la bibliothèque familiale. Donc, ils partent ensemble à la recherche de Monsieur Gustave, le bouquiniste qui aurait acheté le manuscrit, peut-être sans le savoir, il y a plus de 30 ans. Ne sachant pas si ce bouquiniste possède toujours le manuscrit ou même s'il est toujours en vie, les deux gardent quand même un certain espoir. . .

3.54 Qu'est-ce qui s'est passé ? Pensez à ce qui s'est passé dans ce chapitre. **Écrivez six phrases aux temps passés** pour décrire les événements que vous pensez être les plus importants. Parlez de vos idées avec vos camarades de classe.

MODÈLE : On a volé la valise de Claire à l'aéroport. C'est important parce que. . .

3.55 Qu'est-ce qui va se passer ? Imaginez ce qui va se passer dans le prochain chapitre. **Écrivez six phrases** et parlez de vos idées avec vos camarades de classe.

MODÈLE : Claire et Jean-Louis vont trouver le manuscrit chez le bouquiniste !

VOCABULAIRE UTILE

À l'aéroport

au cas où	*just in case*
crier	*to yell/shout*
disparaître	*to disappear*
fiche (*f.*)	*form, sheet*
foule (*f.*)	*crowd*
livraison (*f.*) des bagages enregistrés	*baggage claim area*
mien(ne)	*mine*
poignée (*f.*)	*handle*
ramasser	*to pick up/gather up*
roulettes (*f. pl.*)	*little wheels*
ruban (*m.*)	*ribbon*
se diriger	*to make one's way*
se tromper	*to be mistaken*
sien(ne)	*his/hers*
tapis (*m.*) roulant	*conveyor belt*

Les gens

barbe (*f.*)	*beard*
carré(e)	*square*
cheveux (*m. pl.*)	*hair*
cicatrice (*f.*)	*scar*
lèvres (*f. pl.*)	*lips*
lunettes (*f. pl.*)	*glasses*
mince	*thin*
moustache (*f.*)	*mustache*
moyen(ne)	*medium*
nez (*m.*)	*nose*
oreilles (*f. pl.*)	*ears*
pointu(e)	*pointy*
taille (*f.*)	*size, height*
tatouage (*m.*)	*tattoo*
visage (*m.*)	*face*
yeux (*m. pl.*)	*eyes*

Les vêtements

anorak (*m.*)	*winter jacket*
bottes (*f. pl.*)	*boots*
ceinture (*f.*)	*belt*
chapeau (*m.*)	*hat*
chaussette (*f.*)	*sock*
chaussures (*f. pl.*)	*shoes*
chemise (*f.*)	*shirt*
chemisier (*m.*)	*blouse*
collant (*m.*)	*pantyhose*
costume (*m.*)	*men's suit*
cravate (*f.*)	*tie*
foulard (*m.*)	*scarf*

gilet (*m.*)	*cardigan*
imperméable (*m.*)	*raincoat*
jean (*m.*)	*jeans*
jogging (*m.*)	*sweats*
jupe (*f.*)	*skirt*
maillot (*m.*) de bain	*swimsuit*
manteau (*m.*)	*overcoat*
pantalon (*m.*)	*pants*
pull-over (*m.*)	*sweater*
robe (*f.*)	*dress*
sandales (*f. pl.*)	*sandals*
short (*m.*)	*shorts*
slip (*m.*)	*briefs*
sous-vêtements (*m. pl.*)	*underwear*
soutien-gorge (*m.*)	*bra*
talons (*m. pl.*) hauts/plats	*high/low heels*
tennis (*m. pl.*)	*sneakers*
tenue (*f.*)	*women's suit*
t-shirt (*m.*)	*tee-shirt*
veston (*m.*)	*men's sport jacket*

Les couleurs

à fleurs	*floral*
à rayures	*striped*
beige	*beige*
blanc(he)	*white*
bleu(e)	*blue*
bronzé(e)	*bronze*
brun(e)	*brown*
clair	*light*
foncé	*dark*
gris(e)	*grey*
ivoire	*ivory*
jaune	*yellow*
lavande	*lavender*
mauve	*mauve*
moutarde	*mustard yellow*
noir(e)	*black*
olive	*olive*
orange (*inv.*)	*orange*
rose	*pink*
rouge	*red*
roux, rousse	*red (hair)*
saumon	*salmon*
tartan/écossais(e)	*plaid*
turquoise	*turquoise*
vert(e)	*green*
violet(te)	*purple*

Les matériaux

argent (*m.*)	*silver*
coton (*m.*)	*cotton*
cuir (*m.*)	*leather*
feutre (*m.*)	*felt*
laine (*f.*)	*wool*
or (*m.*)	*gold*
paille (*f.*)	*straw*
plastique (*f.*)	*plastic*
polyester (*m.*)	*polyester*
rayonne (*f.*)	*rayon*
soie (*f.*)	*silk*

Les affaires personnelles

appareil photo (*m.*)	*camera*
bague (*f.*)	*ring*
baladeur (*m.*)	*Walkman®*
bijoux (*m. pl.*)	*jewels, jewelry*
boucles (*m. pl.*) d'oreille	*earrings*
bracelet (*m.*)	*bracelet*
brosse (*f.*) à cheveux	*hairbrush*
brosse (*f.*) à dents	*toothbrush*
collier (*m.*)	*necklace*
dentifrice (*m.*)	*toothpaste*
déodorant (*m.*)	*deodorant*
dossier (*m.*)	*file*
maquillage (*m.*)	*makeup*
médicament (*m.*)	*medicine*
montre (*f.*)	*watch*
ordinateur (*m.*) portable	*laptop computer*
parapluie (*m.*)	*umbrella*
parfum (*m.*)	*perfume*
peigne (*m.*)	*comb*
pellicule (*f.*)	*film*
porte-documents (*m.*)	*briefcase*
portefeuille (*m.*)	*wallet*
rasoir (*m.*)	*raser*
sac (*m.*) à dos	*backpack*
sac (*m.*) à main	*handbag*
savon (*m.*)	*soap*
sèche-cheveux (*m.*)	*hairdryer*
shampooing (*m.*)	*shampoo*
téléphone (*m.*) mobile/portable	*cell phone*

Décrire un événement

antiquaire (*m.*)	*antiques dealer*
au hasard	*by chance*
dérangé(e)	*deranged*
en vouloir à quelqu'un	*to be mad at someone*
exprès	*on purpose*
forcément	*necessarily*
mal à l'aise	*uneasy*
mensonge (*m.*)	*lie*
mentir	*to lie*
patron (*m.*), patronne (*f.*)	*boss*
prendre un pot	*to have a drink*
rouleau(x) (*m.*) de printemps	*spring rolls*
s'en faire	*to worry/get upset*
supplier	*to beg*

Chapitre 4

Une famille francophone

Une mosquée en Afrique.

Épisode 1 *Au kiosque*

Épisode 2 *L'anecdote*

Épisode 3 *Un courriel énigmatique*

Dénouement

En restant entre deux mosquées, on revient sans avoir prié.
—proverbe arabe

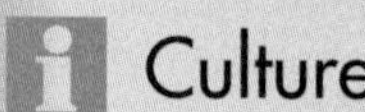

Culture

La France a colonisé l'**Algérie** et a imposé des protectorats sur la **Tunisie** et le **Maroc** au 19ème siècle. Ces trois pays font partie de la région de l'Afrique du Nord qu'on appelle **le Maghreb**. Malgré des différences nationales et culturelles, les pays du Maghreb sont généralement liés par le patrimoine arabe, la religion islamique, la présence des peuples berbères (indigènes aux régions montagneuses du Maghreb) et l'héritage de la colonisation française. Les immigrés d'origine maghrébine forment le plus grand groupe de minorités ethniques en France aujourd'hui où l'islam est la deuxième religion du pays.

À apprendre

- Comment décrire la famille et le caractère des gens
- Comment exprimer son désaccord et se réconcilier
- Comment poser des questions
- Comment exprimer la nostalgie
- Comment décrire une situation

À lire

Claire et Jean-Louis cherchent le bouquiniste Monsieur Gustave à Paris, et ils apprennent des nouvelles troublantes de quelqu'un qui le connaît très bien, un homme maghrébin qui travaille dans le kiosque en face de l'étalage du bouquiniste de la famille Gustave. Après cette rencontre, Claire et Jean-Louis ne savent pas quoi faire. Il faut prendre une décision, s'organiser et agir. Pourtant, ils ne sont pas du même avis, et ils sont distraits par une autre rencontre surprise et un message déconcertant. . .

Épisode 1

Au kiosque

Avant de lire

4.1 Vous et votre famille **Répondez** aux questions suivantes. **Discutez** de vos réponses avec vos camarades de classe et n'hésitez pas à poser des questions supplémentaires si vous voulez en savoir plus.

1. Êtes-vous marié(e) ou célibataire ? Êtes-vous plutôt optimiste ou pessimiste ? timide ou ouvert(e) ? stressé(e) ou détendu(e) ?
2. Êtes-vous enfant unique ? Avez-vous des frères ou des sœurs ? Si vous en avez, êtes-vous l'aîné(e) (*the oldest*) ou le cadet / la cadette (*the youngest*) ? Aimez-vous les familles nombreuses ou les petites familles ? Pourquoi ?
3. Avez-vous beaucoup de tantes et d'oncles ? Combien ? Quels sont leurs noms ? Ce sont des frères et sœurs de votre mère ou de votre père ? Avez-vous des cousins ?
4. Avez-vous des nièces ou des neveux ? Quel âge ont-ils ? Où habitent-ils ?
5. Quelle est la personne qui a eu la plus grande influence sur vous quand vous étiez petit(e) ? vos parents ? vos grands-parents ? un beau-père ou une belle-mère ? une sœur ou un frère ? une tante ou un oncle ? Décrivez ces personnes (physiquement).

Langue

Pour décrire la **famille**, on peut parler de la **famille nucléaire** : les parents (la mère et le père) et les enfants (les fils et les filles, les frères et les sœurs). On peut aussi parler des parents (*relatives*) en général, comme les grands-parents, les grand-tantes, les grands-oncles, les tantes, les oncles, les cousins, les arrière-grands-parents. Aujourd'hui, la définition de la famille est parfois beaucoup plus complexe. En France, on se marie civilement (à la mairie). Certains gens décident aussi d'avoir une cérémonie religieuse (dans une église, une synagogue ou une mosquée). Depuis 1999, au lieu de se marier, deux individus peuvent décider de «se pacser» (signer le PACS, un pacte civil de solidarité, sans se marier traditionnellement). Voici des liens de parenté créés par des cérémonies civiles ou religieuses typiques en France :

- **À cause du remariage de votre père ou de votre mère :** la belle-mère, le beau-père, la demi-sœur, le demi-frère
- **À cause de votre mariage :** la fiancée, le fiancé, la mariée (*bride*), le marié (*groom*), la femme, le mari, les enfants (les filles, les fils), les jumeaux/jumelles (*twins*), la belle-famille (la famille de votre époux/épouse), la belle-mère, le beau-père, la belle-sœur, le beau-frère
- **À cause de votre remariage :** la belle-fille, le beau-fils, l'ex-femme, l'ex-mari
- **À cause d'un baptême :** la marraine (*godmother*), le parrain (*godfather*), la filleule (*goddaughter*), le filleul (*godson*)
- **À cause du mariage de votre frère ou sœur :** le beau-frère, la belle-sœur, le neveu, la nièce
- **À cause du mariage de vos enfants :** la belle-fille, le beau-fils, la petite-fille, le petit-fils
- **À cause d'un PACS (pacte civile de solidarité) :** un(e) partenaire

Notez qu'en français, il n'y a pas de distinction au niveau du vocabulaire entre, par exemple, une belle-mère (*stepmother*) et une belle-mère (*mother-in-law*). Pour préciser, on peut dire «la femme de mon père» ou «la mère de mon mari».

4.2 La famille de Jean-Louis La famille de Jean-Louis vient de fêter le 80ème anniversaire de son grand-père. Voici la liste des parents qui étaient à la fête. En petits groupes, dites qui sont ces personnes par rapport à Thomas, le cousin de Jean-Louis.

MODÈLE : la sœur de son père

—C'est sa tante.

1. les fils de son frère
2. la femme de son frère
3. la fille de sa tante
4. la deuxième femme de son père
5. les deux filles nées de son père et de la deuxième femme de son père
6. le frère de sa grand-mère

l'Algérie

Rencontrez un Algérien et écoutez lorsqu'il parle de sa famille. Regardez la vidéo et consultez votre cahier d'activités !

lisez

Au kiosque

Claire et Jean-Louis se rencontrent à la place Saint-Michel et se promènent sur les quais de la Seine en direction du musée du Louvre. En passant près du Pont des Arts, ils voient un vieillard avec une grosse barbe blanche et des lunettes noires, assis sur un banc. Ce vieillard a la tête baissée, et au moment où Jean-Louis et Claire vont le croiser, il commence à bégayer en disant : «Ce... ce... c'est là..., mais i... i... il n'est pas là». Claire se demande si l'homme s'adresse à eux. Mais non, il semble parler tout seul, pense-t-elle. Tout d'un coup, Jean-Louis, qui regarde attentivement un bout de papier, annonce qu'ils s'approchent de l'adresse que Sandrine Fontenot-Chardin a donnée à Claire avant son départ de la Nouvelle-Orléans. Ils s'arrêtent près d'un kiosque où un homme maghrébin est en train de vendre des journaux et des magazines.

JEAN-LOUIS : Je pense que c'est ici. Mais, il y a plusieurs étalages de bouquiniste ici. Quel est celui de Monsieur Gustave ?

CLAIRE : Je vais demander à cet homme-là.

JEAN-LOUIS : Quel homme ? Celui qui travaille au kiosque ? Bonne idée.

CLAIRE : Bonjour, monsieur. Excusez-nous de vous déranger. Est-ce que vous pourriez nous donner un petit renseignement ?

TALAL LATEEF : Je ferai de mon mieux.

CLAIRE : Connaissez-vous un Monsieur Gustave qui est bouquiniste dans ce quartier ?

TALAL LATEEF : Oui, oui. Je le connais très bien. C'est un ami.

JEAN-LOUIS : Savez-vous quel étalage lui appartient ?

TALAL LATEEF : Lequel est le sien ? C'est cet étalage-là, en face de nous !

JEAN-LOUIS : Celui qui est fermé ? Mais, ce n'est pas vrai !

TALAL LATEEF : En effet, c'est assez curieux. Nicolas Gustave est un jeune homme très énergique et très consciencieux. C'est un homme d'affaires efficace et infatigable. Normalement, il est là tous les jours, sauf le lundi. Il est très fiable, celui-là. L'année dernière, il n'a même pas raté un jour ! Il était là quand il neigeait, quand il pleuvait, quand il y avait des grèves de métro. Il était là même quand il était enrhumé ! Et il était toujours de bonne humeur. Pourtant, hier il était tout nerveux, tout agité, et hier soir, il est parti sans s'arrêter pour acheter un journal et bavarder, comme d'habitude.

JEAN-LOUIS : Qu'est-ce qui s'est passé hier ?

TALAL LATEEF : Hier matin, une voiture grise s'est arrêtée devant son étalage. J'ai cru reconnaître l'homme qui était assis à l'arrière. La veille, il était venu avec un autre homme. Ils avaient acheté un journal ici au kiosque, et puis ils avaient traversé la rue pour parler à Nicolas. Ils avaient parlé longuement, et l'homme principal, celui qui était dans la voiture hier, avait eu l'air fâché. Finalement, ils ont fini de discuter, et les deux hommes sont partis. J'allais demander à Nicolas qui étaient ces clients désagréables, mais comme j'ai dit, il est parti tout de suite après avoir fermé son étalage hier.

CLAIRE : Ce Nicolas est un jeune homme, vous avez dit ?

TALAL LATEEF : Oui, enfin, il a la trentaine, quoi.

CLAIRE : Est-ce qu'il est le fils d'un Monsieur Gustave qui était soldat pendant la Seconde Guerre mondiale ?

TALAL LATEEF : Non, non. Celui-là c'est son oncle. Nicolas est le fils aîné du frère cadet de Lionel Gustave, celui qui était soldat. Comme Lionel n'a pas eu d'enfants avant la mort de sa femme, il a proposé à Nicolas d'être son apprenti. Ce que Lionel avait de la chance de travailler avec son neveu et de passer du temps avec lui ! Le temps qu'on passe avec les siens est si important. Ma femme et moi, nous avons une fille et un fils. L'aîné, mon fils Ahmed, il veut devenir médecin, et la cadette, Karine, elle fait des études en sciences politiques. Je suis très fier d'eux, mais je les vois trop peu ces jours-ci. Enfin, vous le connaissez bien, Lionel Gustave ? C'est un de vos parents ?

CLAIRE : Non, pas vraiment. C'est un ami d'une amie.

JEAN-LOUIS : Nous allons revenir cet après-midi et peut-être que Nicolas Gustave sera là. Monsieur, nous vous remercions de votre aide. Allons-y, Claire.

CLAIRE : Attends, Jean-Louis, une dernière chose. (*à Talal Lateef*) Est-ce que Monsieur Gustave, l'oncle, habite toujours à Paris ?

TALAL LATEEF : Dans le 18ème, oui. Il habite près de Montmartre dans la rue des Trois-Frères.

CLAIRE : Ah, bon ! Merci beaucoup. Et, avant de partir, je voudrais acheter un *Pariscope*, s'il vous plaît, et un de ces petits plans de Paris par arrondissement. (*Elle lui donne de l'argent.*)

TALAL LATEEF : Très bien, madame. Voilà. (*Il lui donne le petit magazine et le plan de Paris.*)

CLAIRE : Merci bien. Au revoir, monsieur.

VOCABULAIRE

Décrire une personne			
bégayer	*to stutter*	(l')aîné(e)	*(the) oldest*
faire de son mieux	*to do one's best*	(le/la) cadet(te)	*(the) youngest*
énergique	*energetic*	fier/fière	*proud*
consciencieux/-euse	*conscientious*	**Divers**	
efficace	*efficient*	un quai	*embankment, walkway or roadway next to the river*
infatigable	*tireless*		
fiable	*reliable*	un renseignement	*piece of information*
être enrhumé(e)	*to have a cold*	sauf	*except*
nerveux/-euse	*nervous*	rater	*to miss (a day, a bus, an event, etc.)*
agité(e)	*agitated*	une grève	*workers' strike*
avoir la trentaine	*to be in one's 30s*	le siège arrière	*backseat*

Langue

Pour décrire l'âge approximatif d'une personne ou pour faire une approximation en général, on peut employer des **nombres collectifs**, comme «la trentaine». Pour former un nombre collectif, on ajoute la terminaison **-aine** au nombre en laissant tomber le **-e** final, s'il y en a un. Par exemple, «une douzaine» est à peu près douze. Il y a quelques exceptions, comme : **une dizaine** (environ dix) et **un millier** (environ mille). D'autres nombres collectifs utilisés souvent sont : **une quinzaine**, **une vingtaine**, **une trentaine**, **une quarantaine**, **une cinquantaine** et **une centaine**. Pour décrire l'âge, on emploie le verbe **avoir** et l'article défini (par exemple : «il a la cinquantaine»), mais pour être discret, on dit que les gens qui ont plus de quarante ans sont **d'un certain âge**.

Après avoir lu

4.3 Avez-vous compris ? Répondez aux questions suivantes. Justifiez vos réponses en citant le texte.

1. Pourquoi est-ce que Claire et Jean-Louis parlent avec Talal Lateef ?
2. Décrivez Nicolas Gustave. Comment est-il ?
3. Qu'est-ce qui s'est passé il y a deux jours ? Qu'est-ce qui s'est passé hier ?
4. Décrivez la famille de Talal Lateef. Est-ce une famille typique ?
5. Pourquoi est-ce que Jean-Louis voulait partir ?
6. Qu'est-ce que Claire a acheté avant de partir ? Pourquoi ?

4.4 D'accord ou pas d'accord ? Indiquez si vous êtes d'accord ou pas avec les phrases suivantes, d'après votre compréhension du récit. Justifiez vos opinions en citant le texte, si possible. Discutez de vos réponses avec la classe.

	D'accord	Pas d'accord
1. Claire et Jean-Louis ont trouvé le bon endroit.	_______	_______
2. Talal Lateef ne connaît pas Monsieur Gustave.	_______	_______
3. Nicolas Gustave est le neveu de Lionel Gustave.	_______	_______
4. Nicolas est un homme paresseux (*lazy*) et frivole.	_______	_______
5. Talal Lateef est trop ouvert et trop amical.	_______	_______

Culture

Les pays du **Maghreb** ont regagné leur **indépendance** de la France au milieu du 20ème siècle. Le Maroc et la Tunisie sont devenus indépendants en 1956, mais en Algérie une guerre d'indépendance a duré huit ans. Ce n'est qu'en 1962 que l'Algérie devient un pays indépendant. Ce changement politique a provoqué le départ pour la France de la plupart des colons français vivant en Algérie ainsi qu'un nombre d'immigrants algériens. Parmi ces gens, il y avait des **harkis**, c'est-à-dire des Maghrébins qui ont combattu avec les Français contre le Front de libération nationale (FLN) algérien. Il y avait aussi des **pieds noirs**, — des Français qui sont nés et qui ont grandi en Algérie française.

Pour aller plus loin : CULTURE

ACTIVITÉ A : Apprenez un peu plus au sujet des cultures et de l'histoire du Maghreb. Consultez votre cahier électronique !

4.5 Suite au kiosque Regardez les mots de vocabulaire qui suivent. Dans chaque ligne, il y a un mot qui cloche avec les trois autres. Entourez le mot qui ne va pas avec les autres et essayez d'expliquer pourquoi. **Attention** ! Il y a parfois plusieurs bonnes réponses. Il faut justifier votre choix.

1. l'aîné	le cadet	le frère	la sœur
2. énergique	prudent	sociable	impulsif
3. bavarder	bégayer	débattre	murmurer
4. le Marais	le Louvre	Montmartre	le Quartier latin
5. le beau-frère	la belle-mère	la marraine	la femme
6. généreux	franc	sincère	fiable

4.6 Les gens de toutes sortes Pendant son séjour à Paris, Claire se rend compte qu'il y a des Parisiens de toutes sortes. **Faites correspondre** le type de personnalité (à gauche) avec la description des actions (à droite).

1. une personne pessimiste	a. elle fait ce qu'elle veut, elle compte sur elle-même, elle suit son propre chemin
2. une personne fiable	b. elle voit toujours et seulement le mauvais côté des choses, elle est peureuse (*fearful*), elle redoute d'apprendre de mauvaises nouvelles
3. une personne paresseuse	c. elle conduit sa voiture sagement, elle suit toujours les règles, elle est toujours disponible à offrir de l'aide
4. une personne stressée	d. elle change d'avis souvent, elle fuit une situation sans y penser pour en trouver une autre au goût du moment
5. une personne indépendante	e. elle se lève tard, elle n'a jamais envie de travailler, elle se plaint toujours d'être fatiguée
6. une personne impulsive	f. elle conduit rapidement, elle est très occupée, elle est émotive, elle fait trop de choses en même temps

Langue

Vous rappelez-vous les conjugaisons des **verbes irréguliers suivre, fuir** et **conduire** ? Si non, mémorisez leurs conjugaisons avant de continuer !

- **suivre** (*to follow*) : je suis, tu suis, il/elle/on suit, nous suivons, vous suivez, ils/elles suivent (*participe passé :* suivi)
- **fuir** (*to flee*) : je fuis, tu fuis, il/elle/on fuit, nous fuyons, vous fuyez, ils/elles fuient (*participe passé :* fui)
- **conduire** (*to drive*) : je conduis, tu conduis, il/elle/on conduit, nous conduisons, vous conduisez, ils/elles conduisent (*participe passé :* conduit)

décrire les gens (le caractère)

Expressions Il/Elle est vraiment / complètement / vachement (*familiar*) / tout à fait (+ *adjectif*)
Normalement / En général / Parfois / De temps en temps, il/elle est. . . (+ *adjectif*)
Il y a des moments où il/elle est. . . (+ *adjectif*)
Que tu es (+ *adjectif*) ! / Que vous êtes (+ *adjectif*) !
Sans mentir ! Je n'exagère pas ! C'est vrai !
Peut-être que j'exagère un peu. J'amplifie ses fautes/qualités.

Adjectives aimable, ambitieux/-euse, amusant/e, avare (*greedy*), bavard/e (*talkative*), bête, bon/ne, calme, chaleureux/-euse, consciencieux/-euse, courageux/-euse, créateur/créatrice, crédule, désagréable, diligent/e, discret/-ète, drôle (*funny*), dynamique, égoïste, émotif/-ive, ennuyeux/-euse, énergique, exigeant/e (*demanding*), fiable (*trustworthy*), fier/fière (*proud*), franc(-che), froid/e, fou/folle (*crazy*), généreux/-euse, gentil/le, honnête, idéaliste, indépendant/e, impatient/e, impulsif/-ive, incrédule, insupportable, intelligent/e, irritable, loyal/e, mauvais/e, méchant/e, modeste, naïf/-ive, nerveux/-euse, obstiné/e, optimiste, ouvert/e, paresseux/-euse (*lazy*), passif/-ive, patient/e, pessimiste, poli/e, prudent/e, réaliste, réservé/e, sensible (*sensitive*), sérieux/-euse, sincère, snob, sociable, sympathique, têtu/e (*stubborn*), timide, tolérant/e, vaniteux/-euse (*vain*), vertueux/-euse

4.7 Comment sont-ils ? Décrivez le caractère des gens suivants en employant des adjectifs descriptifs.

MODÈLE : Julia Child (*The French Chef*) →
—Elle était très drôle, sympathique, bavarde et un peu nerveuse !

1. les professeurs de français (en général)
2. le président des États-Unis
3. la mère Thérèse
4. les amis de l'émission «Friends» (ou une autre émission télévisée populaire)
5. les membres de la famille de Bart Simpson (ou une autre famille à la télé)
6. Superman (et Clark Kent)

4.8 Vocabulaire personnel Pensez à votre famille et pour chaque catégorie, **faites une liste** de cinq à dix mots importants que vous pouvez utiliser pour décrire votre famille, votre caractère et les caractères des autres. Consultez un dictionnaire si nécessaire.

1. Les membres de votre famille nucléaire.
2. Les membres de votre famille étendue que vous voyez de temps en temps.
3. Votre caractère personnel.
4. Les caractéristiques que vous admirez aux gens.
5. Les caractéristiques que vous détestez aux gens.

Langue

Rappel ! Rappel ! N'oubliez pas qu'il faut toujours faire l'accord entre l'adjectif et le nom qu'il décrit. Révisez la formation et l'ordre des **adjectifs descriptifs** dans l'Épisode 2 du Chapitre 3, si vous en avez besoin !

Pour aller plus loin : CULTURE

ACTIVITÉ B : Qu'est-ce qui se passe à Paris cette semaine ? Consultez votre cahier électronique !

4.9 Au Palais-Royal Claire et Jean-Louis continuent de marcher jusqu'aux jardins du Palais-Royal, près du métro du Louvre. Là, ils s'arrêtent pour discuter de ce qui s'est passé et de ce qu'il faut faire maintenant. **Choisissez une des expressions** entre parenthèses et **lisez le dialogue** à haute voix avec un partenaire. Quand vous voyez «? ? ?», vous pouvez imaginer votre propre expression.

JEAN-LOUIS : Il était (sympa / gentil / utile), ce monsieur au kiosque.

CLAIRE : Oui, mais qu'est-ce que nous allons faire maintenant ?

JEAN-LOUIS : Évidemment, on va attendre jusqu'à (l'après-midi / 3h) et on reviendra parler avec le bouquiniste. On n'a pas (de choix / d'autre possibilité).

CLAIRE : Que tu es (timide / prudent / bête) ! On pourrait trouver l'adresse de Monsieur Gustave sur Internet et aller directement chez lui.

JEAN-LOUIS : Mais non, on ne peut pas faire ça ! Est-ce que tu es complètement (folle / naïve / ? ? ?) ?

CLAIRE : Qu'est-ce que tu veux dire ?

JEAN-LOUIS : Si nous allons directement chez Monsieur Gustave sans invitation, il va se méfier de nous. Tu devrais être un peu plus (patiente / prudente / réaliste / ? ? ?).

CLAIRE : Je ne suis pas tout à fait d'accord. À quoi bon (perdre notre temps / attendre l'après-midi / parler au neveu) ? C'est le vieux Gustave qui a acheté le manuscrit, le jeune n'y est pour rien.

JEAN-LOUIS : Je vois ce que tu veux dire, mais il faut considérer ce problème sous tous ses aspects. Nous ne connaissons ni Lionel Gustave ni son (neveu / apprenti / ? ? ?) Nicolas, mais nous savons où travaille le deuxième. Et, à vrai dire, il vaut mieux aborder un jeune bouquiniste (ouvert / énergique / ? ? ?) au travail qu'un vieillard (réservé / nerveux / ? ? ?) chez lui.

CLAIRE : Il ne s'agit pas de cela ! (L'essentiel / L'important) est de prendre contact avec la famille Gustave au plus tôt.

JEAN-LOUIS : C'est bien dit. Tu as peut-être raison. Mais, ne leur disons pas que nous cherchons un manuscrit écrit par Laclos. Si jamais ils savaient le nom de l'auteur de ce manuscrit anonyme, ils ne nous vendraient pas ce manuscrit !

CLAIRE : (Bon / Très bien / ? ? ?) ! Allons chercher l'adresse exacte de la maison familiale à Montmartre.

JEAN-LOUIS : Entendu. Mais, j'ai des commissions à faire pour mon patron. Est-ce que tu pourrais chercher l'adresse et (puis / ensuite / ? ? ?) nous pourrions nous rejoindre ici dans deux heures ?

CLAIRE : D'accord, mais sais-tu où je pourrais trouver un ordinateur près d'ici ? Je n'ai pas envie de retourner à mon hôtel.

JEAN-LOUIS : Je pense avoir vu un café-internet près d'ici. Sinon, tu peux toujours utiliser un Minitel à la poste. Il y en a une pas trop loin d'ici.

exprimer son désaccord et se réconcilier

	Informal	Formal
Expressing disagreement	Attends, je ne suis pas d'accord !	Excusez-moi, je ne suis pas d'accord !
	Tu as tort ! Mais, ce n'est pas vrai !	Vous avez tort ! Mais, ce n'est pas vrai !
	Il ne s'agit pas de cela ! Cela ne sert à rien !	Il ne s'agit pas de cela ! Cela ne sert à rien !
	Qu'est-ce que tu veux dire ?	Que voulez-vous dire ?
	À quoi bon (faire quelque chose) ?	À quoi bon (faire quelque chose) ?
	À la rigueur, on peut dire que. . .	À la rigueur, on peut dire que. . .
Making a compromise	Je vois ce que tu veux dire.	Je vois ce que vous voulez dire.
	J'apprécie ton point de vue / franchise.	J'apprécie votre point de vue / franchise.
	Cette idée a ses bons côtés / du mérite.	Cette idée a ses bons côtés / du mérite.
	Tu as peut-être raison.	Vous avez peut-être raison.
	C'est bien dit./C'est bien parlé.	C'est bien dit./C'est bien parlé.
	D'accord, je m'y rends.	D'accord, je m'y rends.
	C'est un bon compromis.	C'est un bon compromis.

4.10 À vous Imaginez que vous êtes dans les situations suivantes. Que dites-vous ? **Exprimez le désaccord et puis faites la paix**. Avec un partenaire, jouez une petite scène pour chaque situation.

1. Votre ami veut aller voir un mauvais film d'épouvante (*horror film*). Vous voulez faire vos devoirs pour la classe de français.
2. Un de vos parents décide de vous rendre visite ce week-end (sans être invité), mais vous avez un rendez-vous avec une personne dynamique et intéressante que vous venez de rencontrer.
3. Votre sœur ne veut pas aller au restaurant avec vous parce qu'elle est trop économe et ne dépense jamais son argent.
4. Vous voulez conduire votre vieille voiture de la Californie jusqu'à l'état de Maine. C'est une aventure ! Vos amis pensent que vous êtes fou/folle.

i Langue

Connaissez-vous les **verbes irréguliers connaître** et **savoir** ? Si non, mémorisez leurs conjugaisons et remarquez les sens différents des verbes au passé composé :

- **connaître** (*to know*) : je connais, tu connais, il/elle/on connaît, nous connaissons, vous connaissez, ils/elles connaissent (*participe passé* : j'ai connu, *I met*)
- **savoir** (*to know*) : je sais, tu sais, il/elle/on sait, nous savons, vous savez, ils/elles savent (*participe passé* : j'ai su, *I heard / found out*; *participe présent* : sachant)

Comment choisir entre ces deux verbes ? En général, on emploie **connaître** pour parler des gens ou des endroits avec lesquels on est familier. On utilise **savoir** pour parler des idées, des directions, des conseils, des pensées ou des faits qu'on a appris ou qu'on a en tête.

4.11 Connaissez-vous les gens suivants ? Avec un partenaire, regardez la liste suivante des gens célèbres. Chaque personne est liée soit au monde arabe soit à la religion musulmane. Dites si vous connaissez ces personnes, décrivez-les et racontez ce que vous savez de leurs vies. Vous pouvez parler des faits donnés entre parenthèses ou bien ajouter d'autres faits. Si vous n'êtes pas d'accord avec votre partenaire, exprimez le désaccord et dites ce que vous en savez. (Si vous voulez en savoir plus, consultez l'Internet avant de faire l'activité en classe !)

MODÈLE : Isabelle Adjani (actrice, Française, père maghrébin) →

—Je connais Isabelle Adjani. Je ne la connais pas personnellement, bien sûr, mais je sais qu'elle est actrice en France et qu'elle est très jolie. Elle est grande et mince et brune. Je sais que son père est d'origine maghrébine.

1. Isabelle Adjani (actrice, Française, père maghrébin)
2. Christiane Amanpour (journaliste, Américaine, née en Iran)
3. Naguib Mahfouz (écrivain, Égyptien, Prix Nobel)
4. Zinédine Zidane (joueur de foot, Français, parents maghrébins)
5. Dodi Al-Fayed (homme riche, petit ami de la Princesse Diane, mort à Paris)
6. la Reine Noor (habite en Jordanie, née aux États-Unis, parents libanais, musulmane)
7. Tahar Ben Jelloun (écrivain, Marocain, Prix Goncourt)
8. Assia Djebar (écrivain et cinéaste, Algérienne, feministe)

4.12 Des étudiants désagréables Sur une feuille de papier, écrivez une phrase pour décrire une opinion que vous avez sur la vie ou les études à votre université. Puis, circulez dans la salle de classe et exprimez votre opinion. À votre tour, écoutez les opinions des autres et exprimez votre désaccord (même si vous êtes d'accord en réalité). Puis, faites la paix et passez au prochain étudiant. Essayez de parler avec autant de personnes que possible !

MODÈLE : Je pense que nos professeurs ne sont pas assez exigeants !

—Qu'est-ce que tu veux dire ? À la rigueur, on peut dire qu'ils sont un peu trop indulgents.

4.13 Des portraits de gens célèbres Sur une feuille de papier, décrivez une vedette ou une personne très connue. . . historique ou vivante. Faites le portrait de cette personne en décrivant l'aspect physique et le caractère et sa situation familiale. Ne dites pas ce qu'elle fait comme travail. Puis, lisez votre description à haute voix. Vos camarades de classe vont essayer de deviner de qui il s'agit.

MODÈLE : C'est une belle femme française. Elle est grande et élégante et sophistiquée, mais elle est très égoïste, paresseuse et vaniteuse. Elle est mariée et elle a des enfants. Elle est morte et son mari est mort aussi.

—C'est Marie-Antoinette ?

Pour aller plus loin : CULTURE

ACTIVITÉ C : Connaissez-vous bien les gens qui sont célèbres en France ? Lisez leurs portraits. Consultez votre cahier électronique !

4.14 L'homme ou la femme de vos rêves Faites une interview avec un(e) camarade de classe afin de savoir comment est l'homme ou la femme de ses rêves. Posez des questions à propos de l'aspect physique, du caractère, du type de travail, des goûts en musique, des passe-temps, etc. !

MODÈLE : Comment est l'homme de tes rêves, physiquement ? Et comment est son caractère ?

—**Il est brun et de taille moyenne. Il a les yeux verts. Il est assez sportif et indépendant. Il est honnête, intelligent et très drôle.**

Pour aller plus loin : CULTURE

ACTIVITÉ D : Participez à un sondage afin de découvrir le genre de personne qui pourrait être votre partenaire idéal. Consultez votre cahier électronique !

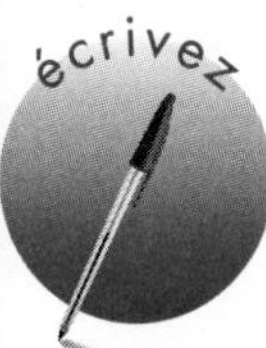

À l'écrit *première étape*

4.15 Votre arbre généalogique Faites un arbre généalogique de trois ou quatre générations de votre famille. Pour chaque membre de la famille mentionné, écrivez leur position familiale par rapport à vous (par exemple : c'est mon cousin) et choisissez un adjectif pour décrire cette personne (par exemple : il est ennuyeux). Ensuite, échangez votre arbre généalogique avec un camarade de classe. Vérifiez que les liens de parenté sont clairs, posez des questions à votre camarade à propos des membres de sa famille ou faites des suggestions.

Épisode 2

L'anecdote

Structures *l'adjectif et le pronom démonstratif*

4.16 Une petite manifestation En retournant de la poste, Claire traverse une rue où il y a une grande foule de jeunes gens qui manifestent contre le racisme. Elle s'y arrête et parle avec une jeune femme qui distribue des pamphlets. Lisez le dialogue et dites si les mots en **caractères gras** sont (1) **des adjectifs ou des pronoms**, (2) **masculins ou féminins** et (3) **singuliers ou pluriels**. Pouvez-vous décrire comment fonctionnent les adjectifs et les pronoms démonstratifs en analysant ces exemples ?

Pour aller plus loin : CULTURE

ACTIVITÉ E : Apprenez plus au sujet du racisme et de la politique de l'immigration en France. Consultez votre cahier électronique !

CLAIRE : Qu'est-ce que c'est que **cette** manifestation ?

UNE JEUNE FEMME : **Celle-ci** est une manif contre le racisme. Le groupe qui organise **cet** événement s'appelle SOS Racisme.

CLAIRE : Ah, oui ! **Celui** que j'ai vu à la télé hier soir. J'ai entendu parler de **ce** groupe.

UNE JEUNE FEMME : Exact. Nous essayons de combattre le racisme et les inégalités sociales. Vous voyez **ces** affiches-là ?

CLAIRE : **Celles** qui ont le slogan «Touche pas à mon pote» (*pal*) ? Oui, **cette** devise est bien connue parmi les jeunes activistes.

UNE JEUNE FEMME : **Ces** problèmes intéressent surtout les jeunes, mais aussi tous **ceux** et toutes **celles** qui sont idéalistes. **Ces** gens-ci qui manifestent cherchent à créer une meilleure société pour les prochaines générations. Voulez-vous prendre **cette** brochure ?

CLAIRE : D'accord. Merci bien pour l'information.

l'adjectif et le pronom démonstratif

The *demonstrative adjective* **(l'adjectif démonstratif)** is used to point out people or things (*this/that, these/those*) and agrees in number and gender with the noun it modifies. The forms of the demonstrative adjectives are:

	singular	*plural*
masculine	**ce** **cet** (before vowel or silent **h**)	**ces**
feminine	**cette**	**ces**

- To specify whether you are talking about *this/these* or *that/those*, add **-ci** (over here) or **-là** (over there) to the adjective being modified: **cette** affiche-**là**, **ces** gens-**ci**.

The *demonstrative pronoun* (**le pronom démonstratif**) replaces the demonstrative adjective and noun, and it is also used to point out people and things (*this one / that one, these ones / those ones*) that have already been referred to in conversation. Demonstrative pronouns also agree in gender and number with the noun they replace:

	singular	*plural*
masculine	**celui**	**ceux**
feminine	**celle**	**celles**

- To specify whether you are talking about this one / these ones or that one / those ones, add **-ci** or **-là** to the pronoun: **Celle-ci** est une manif contre le racisme.
- To specify ownership, add **de** plus a person/noun to the pronoun: cet étalage-là, c'est **celui de** Monsieur Gustave.
- To specify other details, add **qui** (+ *verb* + *clause*) or **que** (+ *subject* + *verb* + *clause*): **celles qui** sont idéalistes, **celui que** j'ai vu à la télé.

Les jardins du Palais-Royal.

4.17 De nouveau au Palais-Royal Claire arrive au lieu du rendez-vous au Palais-Royal, mais Jean-Louis n'est pas encore là. Elle s'assoit sur un banc au soleil et commence à parler avec une vieille dame. Remplissez les blancs avec un **adjectif ou pronom démonstratif**.

LA VIEILLE DAME : Quelle belle journée ! Regardez ______________ belles fleurs, mademoiselle.

CLAIRE : Ah, oui ! ______________-là sont très jolies.

LA VIEILLE DAME : Et __________ fontaine-ci, elle est magnifique, n'est-ce pas ?

CLAIRE : C'est vrai, mais je préfère __________ qui est sur la place de la Concorde. __________ -là est vraiment impressionnante avec toutes __________ sculptures de poissons.

LA VIEILLE DAME : Mais, __________ jardin-ci est beaucoup plus tranquille.

CLAIRE : C'est vrai. Avec tous __________ jardins à Paris, comment arrive-t-on à en choisir un ?

LA VIEILLE DAME : C'est une bonne question. Normalement, on choisit __________ qui est le plus proche de chez soi. Moi, j'habite tout près d'ici avec mon mari et mes trois filles, qui sont toutes célibataires. Je n'ai pas encore de petits-enfants.

4.18 Admirez votre environnement Avec un partenaire, décrivez les objets dans votre salle de classe ou bien les objets que vous voyez à travers les fenêtres. Une personne va admirer une chose, et l'autre ne va pas être d'accord. Suivez le modèle et variez les adjectifs que vous employez. Faites attention à l'usage des adjectifs et pronoms démonstratifs !

MODÈLE : Regarde ce joli bureau !

—Celui-là ? Mais, ce bureau-là est très laid !

Structures *l'adjectif et le pronom interrogatif*

4.19 Quel beau jardin ! La vieille dame et Claire continuent à bavarder. Décidez si les mots en **caractères gras** sont (1) **des adjectifs ou des pronoms**, (2) **masculins ou féminins** et (3) **singuliers ou pluriels**. Pouvez-vous décrire comment fonctionnent les adjectifs et les pronoms interrogatifs en analysant ces exemples ?

LA VIEILLE DAME : **Quel** beau jardin ! Alors, mademoiselle, vous êtes étudiante ? Vous allez à **quelle** université ?

CLAIRE : Je fais un doctorat à l'Université de Sainte-Foy, au Québec, et j'étudie des auteurs français.

LA VIEILLE DAME : **Lesquels** préférez-vous ?

CLAIRE : Je fais de la recherche sur les œuvres de Laclos.

LA VIEILLE DAME : Ah, oui ! **Quel** était le nom de son roman ?

CLAIRE : **Lequel** ? Celui que tout le monde connaît s'appelle *Les Liaisons dangereuses*. J'ai une bourse pour faire de la recherche sur ses romans cette année.

LA VIEILLE DAME : **Quelle** coïncidence ! Une de mes filles a une bourse cette année aussi. Elle étudie cet auteur algérien.

CLAIRE : **Duquel** parlez-vous ? de Kateb Yacine ?

LA VIEILLE DAME :	Non, c'est une femme-auteur. Elle fait aussi du cinéma. Ah, oui ! C'est Assia Djebar. Vous la connaissez ?
CLAIRE :	Oui, bien sûr, elle est très connue... (*Claire regarde sa montre*) Mon ami est en retard. Pourriez-vous me donner un renseignement ? **Quelles** lignes de métro prend-t-on pour aller à Montmartre ?
LA VIEILLE DAME :	Il y a plusieurs stations de métro près de Montmartre. **À laquelle** voulez-vous descendre ?
CLAIRE :	Je veux descendre à Abbesses, je crois.
LA VIEILLE DAME :	Enfin, c'est assez compliqué. Il vaut mieux consulter le plan du métro à l'entrée de la station.
CLAIRE :	Merci bien. Au revoir et bonne journée !

Pour aller plus loin : LITTÉRATURE

ACTIVITÉ F : Lisez un poème d'un poète algérien. Consultez votre cahier électronique !

l'adjectif et le pronom interrogatif

The *interrogative adjective* (**l'adjectif interrogatif**) is used to distinguish between people or things when asking questions (*which?* or *what?*) and agrees in number and gender with the nouns it modifies. The forms of the interrogative adjectives are:

	singular	*plural*
masculine	**quel**	**quels**
feminine	**quelle**	**quelles**

- The *interrogative adjective* usually directly precedes the noun it modifies or precedes the verb **être**: À **quelle** université ? **Quel** était le nom de son roman ?
- The *interrogative adjective* can also be used in exclamations referring to people or things: **Quelle** coïncidence !

The *interrogative pronoun* (**le pronom interrogatif**) replaces the interrogative adjective and noun combined. This type of pronoun is also used to distinguish between nouns (*which one? / which ones?*) that have already been referred to in conversation. It must also agree in gender and number with the noun it replaces:

	singular	*plural*
masculine	**lequel**	**lesquels**
feminine	**laquelle**	**lesquelles**

- The *interrogative pronoun* is often preceded by a preposition (**à**, **de**, **sur**, **avec**, **dans**, etc.).
- When **lequel, lesquels** or **lesquelles** is preceded by the preposition **à** or **de**, the preposition contracts with the masculine or plural definite article (**auquel, auxquelles, duquel, desquels**). The feminine form does not change: **Duquel** parlez-vous ? **À laquelle** voulez-vous descendre ?

l'Algérie

Quelles questions peut-on poser à propos de la famille de Smain ? Regardez la vidéo et consultez votre cahier d'activités !

4.20 Le voilà ! En sortant de l'arcade du Palais-Royal, Claire aperçoit Jean-Louis qui court vers elle. **Remplissez les blancs** avec la forme appropriée de **quel** ou **lequel**. N'oubliez pas de faire les accords en genre et en nombre, si nécessaire.

CLAIRE : ____________________ chance ! J'allais partir sans toi.

JEAN-LOUIS: Je suis désolé. Mon patron m'a retenu au bureau un bon petit moment. J'espère que je ne t'ai pas fait attendre trop longtemps.

CLAIRE : Ce n'est pas grave. Je parlais avec une vieille dame qui était très gentille.

JEAN-LOUIS: (*Il surveille le jardin.*) Ah, oui ? Il y en a beaucoup. Avec ____________________ parlais-tu ?

CLAIRE : Celle en bleu qui est assise sur le banc, près de la fontaine.

JEAN-LOUIS: ____________________ est son nom ?

CLAIRE : Je ne sais pas. On ne s'est pas présenté. ____________________ est le problème ?

JEAN-LOUIS: Rien, mais avec toutes ces histoires de bagages volés et de gens menaçants, il faut faire attention.

CLAIRE : De ____________________ gens menaçants parles-tu ?

JEAN-LOUIS: Ben. . . de ces autres personnes qui cherchent le manuscrit de Laclos.

CLAIRE : ____________________ autres personnes cherchent le manuscrit ? De quoi parles-tu, enfin ?

JEAN-LOUIS: Je parle de ces hommes qui sont venus voir le bouquiniste hier, ceux qui l'ont un peu bouleversé.

CLAIRE : Et pour ____________________ raison penses-tu qu'ils cherchent le même manuscrit que nous ?

JEAN-LOUIS: Enfin, je l'imagine peut-être. Alors, tu as eu du succès à la poste, sans doute. ____________________ est l'adresse de ce Monsieur Gustave ?

4.21 Vos préférences personnelles **Posez vos questions** à un partenaire afin de connaître ses préférences personnelles, suivant le modèle. Puis, **répondez** à votre tour. Attention à l'usage de **quel** et **lequel** !

MODÈLE : Quelles sont tes couleurs préférées ? →
—J'aime le bleu et le vert.
—Laquelle préfères-tu ?
—Je préfère le bleu.

1. couleurs préférées
2. émissions (*TV shows*) préférées
3. livres préférés
4. écrivains préférés
5. villes préférées
6. musiciens préférés
7. films préférés
8. parfums (*flavors*) de glace préférés

4.22 Il faut choisir ! À Paris, il y a beaucoup d'endroits intéressants. Imaginez que vous êtes à Paris et que vous avez le choix entre les deux endroits suivants. Avec un partenaire, discutez de vos choix. Attention à l'usage des **pronoms démonstratifs** et des **pronoms interrogatifs**.

MODÈLE : Ce café-ci est très tranquille, mais ce café-là est plus chic. →
—Lequel préfères-tu ?
—Je préfère celui qui est plus chic !

1. Ce restaurant-ci est très bon, mais ce restaurant-là est moins cher.
2. Ces magasins-ci sont bon marché, mais ces magasins-là sont plus intéressants.
3. Ces tours en haut de la cathédrale de Notre-Dame sont très anciennes, mais cette grande tour en fer est très célèbre.
4. Cette cathédrale-ci a de beaux vitraux (*stained-glass windows*), mais cette cathédrale-là a de belles mosaïques.
5. Ces maisons-ci sont jolies, mais ces maisons-là sont plus grandes.
6. Ce petit boulevard est très tranquille, mais ces grands boulevards sur la rive droite sont très animés.

Culture

Sur la rive droite de Paris, on trouve plusieurs **grands boulevards** comme les **Champs-Élysées** et le boulevard Haussmann. C'était Georges Eugène **baron de Haussmann**, un administrateur et homme politique au 19ème siècle, qui a aggrandi les boulevards, favorisé la construction de parcs et de gares et dirigé la transformation de la capitale qui s'est effectuée à la fin du siècle.

4.23 Faisons un tour du campus ! Faites un petit tour de votre campus et admirez les choses autour de vous. Demandez à vos camarades ce qu'ils aiment ou ce qu'ils préfèrent, et répondez à votre tour. Attention à l'usage des **adjectifs descriptifs** (avant ou après le nom), des **adjectifs et pronoms démonstratifs** et des **adjectifs et pronoms interrogatifs**.

MODÈLE : —**Quel** bel arbre !
—**Duquel** parles-tu ?
—De **celui** qui est à côté du bâtiment.
—Ah, oui ! **Cet** arbre-**là** est très beau.

Avant d'écouter

4.24 Avant l'anecdote Répondez aux questions suivantes avant d'écouter le dialogue.

1. Quels membres de votre famille sont gentils ? Décrivez-les.
2. Lesquels sont indiscrets ? De quoi parlent-ils ?
3. Lesquels sont amusants ? Comment ? Donnez un exemple.
4. Lesquels sont sérieux ? De quoi parlent-ils ?
5. Quand les parents âgés parlent du «bon vieux temps», de quoi parlent-ils ?
6. Comment étiez-vous quand vous étiez petit(e) ? Est-ce que votre caractère a beaucoup changé ou non ?

écoutez

L'anecdote

En sortant du métro à la station Abbesses, Jean-Louis et Claire rencontrent par hasard une des parentes de Jean-Louis : c'est sa tante Émilie. Jean-Louis présente sa tante à Claire, qui est très contente de faire sa connaissance. Comme la tante est un peu indiscrète et un peu bavarde, elle pose toutes sortes de questions à Claire et elle raconte une anecdote embarrassante concernant l'enfance de Jean-Louis. . .

Maintenant, **écoutez le dialogue sur votre CD**. Consultez le vocabulaire pour mieux comprendre le dialogue, et puis répondez aux questions suivantes.

VOCABULAIRE

La vie en famille

amener	*to bring (someone)*
un jeu	*game*
n'importe quoi	*anything at all*
attirer	*to attract*
se réunir	*to get together*
la messe	*mass (Catholic)*
la magie	*magic*
le souvenir	*memory*
apparaître	*to appear*
un lapin	*rabbit*
un animal familier	*pet*
charmant(e)	*charming*
la chasse	*hunting*
la bête	*animal*
le ragoût	*stew*
pleurer	*to cry*
fichu(e)	*ruined*

Après avoir écouté

4.25 Avez-vous compris ? Après avoir écouté le dialogue entre Claire et Jean-Louis et la tante Émilie, répondez aux questions suivantes. Discutez en petits groupes.

1. Où habite la famille de Jean-Louis ?
2. Qu'est-ce que Jean-Louis voulait faire le jour de la réunion familiale que tante Émilie a décrite ?

3. Pourquoi est-ce que Jean-Louis pleurait le jour de la réunion familiale ? Qu'est-ce qui est arrivé au lapin ?
4. Comment est le caractère de tante Émilie ? Décrivez-la.
5. Comment était Jean-Louis quand il était petit ? A-t-il beaucoup changé ?

4.26 D'accord ou pas d'accord ? Après avoir écouté le dialogue entre Claire et Jean-Louis et la tante Émilie, lisez les phrases suivantes et donnez votre opinion. Discutez en petits groupes.

	D'accord	Pas d'accord
1. Claire connaît tous les endroits touristiques à Paris.	_______	_______
2. La tante Émilie est timide.	_______	_______
3. La tante Émilie a une bonne mémoire.	_______	_______
4. Autrefois, la famille Royer se réunissait plus souvent.	_______	_______
5. Jean-Louis a eu une enfance heureuse.	_______	_______
6. Jean-Louis était un garçon très sérieux.	_______	_______

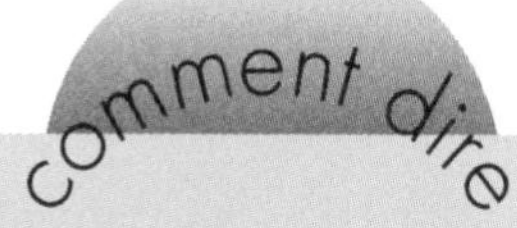

exprimer la nostalgie

To express nostalgia

Ah, le bon vieux temps ! / Quels beaux jours ! / Quels beaux souvenirs !
Il fut un temps où. . . / Ça, c'était l'époque où. . . / C'était la belle époque !
Dans le temps / Autrefois / Jadis / À cette époque-là, je/on/nous. . .
Il y a bien des années. . . / Vingt ans bien comptés. . .
Je me souviens bien du jour où. . . / Je m'en souviens bien.
C'était toujours comme ça. / Ce n'en était pas ainsi.
Que le temps passe vite ! / Le temps fuit !

Culture

L'expression **Je me souviens** est devenue une devise importante pour le Québec et les Québécois. On trouve cette expression sur les plaques d'immatriculation québécoises, sur les monuments et les objets officiels, et sur les affiches touristiques. Pour beaucoup de francophones québécois, cette devise rappelle l'histoire politique et l'oppression des Québécois francophones par les Anglais. Pourtant, elle rappelle aussi des moments plus simples de la vie quotidienne d'autrefois. On se souvient des fêtes traditionnelles et familiales, des cabanes à sucre, des calèches (*sleighs*) sur la neige, des chansons populaires. Cette devise exprime une nostalgie collective aussi bien qu'une solidarité politique et culturelle.

Pour aller plus loin : CINÉMA

ACTIVITÉ G : Regardez le film *Outremer* dans lequel il s'agit de la vie d'une grande famille française qui habite en Algérie juste avant la guerre d'indépendance. Consultez votre cahier électronique !

4.27 Que dites-vous ? Qu'est-ce qu'on peut dire pour **exprimer la nostalgie** dans les situations suivantes ? Avec un partenaire, décidez ce que vous pouvez dire.

1. Vous montrez des photos de votre famille et de vous-même quand vous étiez petit(e) à une amie.
2. Vous écoutez des personnes âgées qui décrivent comment était la vie familiale avant l'invention des ordinateurs.
3. Vous écoutez un vieil homme qui raconte une anecdote de la vie en Alger avant la révolution en Algérie.
4. Vous expliquez à des jeunes gens ce que vous faisiez pendant les vacances d'été quand vous étiez petit(e).
5. Vous regardez le vieux film *Casablanca* et vous parlez du bon vieux temps quand on faisait de vrais films classiques !

4.28 Soyez nostalgiques ! Avec un partenaire, imaginez comment était le bon vieux temps à l'époque de vos grands-parents (ou de vos arrière-grands-parents). Sur une feuille de papier, écrivez **six à huit phrases utilisant l'imparfait** pour décrire comment était la vie au temps jadis (*olden days*). Puis, circulez dans la salle de classe et comparez vos idées du bon vieux temps avec celles de vos camarades. Si vous n'êtes pas d'accord, exprimez le désaccord (et puis faites la paix !). Si vous êtes d'accord, exprimez la nostalgie de ce beau temps passé.

MODÈLE : —Au temps jadis, on ne regardait pas la télévision. Toute la famille dînait ensemble chaque soir. Les gens s'amusaient en racontant des contes et des histoires.

—Mais, tu as tort ! On écoutait la radio. C'était presque la même chose !

—Je vois ce que tu veux dire. Tu as peut-être raison.

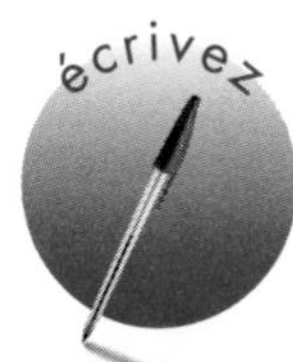

À l'écrit *deuxième étape*

4.29 Une réunion familiale Vous organisez une réunion familiale et tous les membres de votre famille que vous avez invités sont présents (ceux qui sont sur votre arbre généalogique). Votre ami(e), qui ne connaît pas tous les membres de votre famille, regarde vos photos de la famille et vous pose des questions afin d'avoir plus d'information sur chaque personne invitée. Imaginez un dialogue où il/elle vous pose huit à dix questions à propos des différents membres de votre famille (Qui est cette dame blonde ? Lequel est son mari ? etc.) et donnez vos réponses aux questions. Finalement, avec un partenaire, révisez vos dialogues et lisez-les à haute voix.

Un courriel énigmatique

La sortie de la station de métro Abbesses, à Montmartre.

Structures *le plus-que-parfait*

4.30 Dans la rue des Trois-Frères Claire et Jean-Louis arrivent à la maison de Monsieur Lionel Gustave qui se trouve dans la rue des Trois-Frères. Ils se présentent à Monsieur Gustave et Claire explique les événements qui l'ont menée à sa maison. D'abord, soulignez les verbes qui sont au passé composé ou à l'imparfait. Ensuite, donnez l'infinitif de chaque verbe en **caractères gras**. Ce sont les verbes au plus-que-parfait. Pouvez-vous décrire comment former et comment employer le **plus-que-parfait** en analysant ces exemples ?

CLAIRE : Ce matin, nous sommes allés à l'étalage de bouquiniste de votre neveu. Il n'était pas là, mais on a parlé avec un de ses amis. Enfin, à vrai dire, nous ne cherchions pas votre neveu. Nous voulions vous parler. Une amie américaine m'**avait donné** votre nom. J'**étais allée** à la Nouvelle-Orléans au mois d'août à la recherche d'un manuscrit ancien. C'est un manuscrit inédit (*unpublished*) qu'un de ses ancêtres **avait reçu** d'un auteur français à la fin du

18ème siècle. Avant de venir à Paris, j'**avais rencontré** Sandrine Fontenot-Chardin, et elle m'**avait parlé** de vous et de l'histoire de la bibliothèque de son grand-père. C'est la bibliothèque que vous **aviez achetée** juste après la mort de son grand-père. Si seulement ils **avaient gardé** ce manuscrit ! Mais hélas, ils l'ont vendu avec les autres livres. Enfin, nous sommes partis de la Louisiane tout de suite après avoir appris cette nouvelle et nous sommes venus ici pour demander si vous l'aviez toujours parmi vos livres à vendre.

l'Algérie

Comment était la vie du père de Smain ? Regardez la vidéo et consultez votre cahier d'activités !

Culture

Montmartre est un quartier pittoresque qui se trouve sur une colline dans le 18ème arrondissement. La rue des Trois-Frères monte le long de la colline, près de la place des Abbesses, et mène à des escaliers qui vont au sommet, mais ceux qui n'aiment pas marcher peuvent prendre le funiculaire de la rue Steinkerque. Au sommet de la colline, on trouve la place du Tertre où il y a beaucoup d'artistes et de cafés. À côté de la place, on trouve la **Basilique du Sacré-Cœur**, une immense église blanche avec des mosaïques très jolies à l'intérieur. De la coupole, on a une belle vue sur tout Paris. Le peintre Utrillo a peint beaucoup de beaux tableaux dans lesquels il représente le bon vieux temps dans ce quartier parisien.

le plus-que-parfait

The *pluperfect* (**le plus-que-parfait**) can be described as the "past of the past" and is often used in the context of other past tenses to refer to something that happened prior to the past moment being discussed.

Formation of the ***plus-que-parfait*****:**

- The *pluperfect* (**le plus-que-parfait**) is composed of *the imperfect* (**l'imparfait**) of the auxiliary verb (**avoir/être**) followed by the *past participle*. The choice of auxiliary verb and the formation of the past participle follow the same rules as the **passé composé**; past participles in the **plus-que-parfait** also follow the same rules concerning agreement with the subject (verbs conjugated with **être**), the personal pronoun (reflexives), or the preceding direct object (verbs conjugated with **avoir**).

The ***plus-que-parfait*** *is used*:

- to describe events that occurred in the past *prior to the past events* that are the main focus of the conversation or narrative. (It is often used in the context of other verbs in the **passé composé** or **imparfait**): Nous voulions vous parler. . . Sandrine Fontenot-Chardin **avait parlé** de vous.
- to *express regret* about events that may have happened *prior to* past events that already did happen: Si seulement ils **avaient gardé** le manuscrit !

4.31 Il fut un temps Après avoir écouté l'histoire de Claire, Monsieur Gustave commence à parler. Conjuguez les verbes entre parenthèses au **plus-que-parfait**.

Vous savez, mademoiselle, ma mémoire n'est pas très bonne ces jours-ci. Je me souviens bien de mon ami américain, Henri Pierre Fontenot, et je sais qu'il était de la Nouvelle-Orléans et qu'il a eu beaucoup d'enfants avant de mourir. Je me souviens aussi du jour où j'ai acheté sa bibliothèque parce que son père (mourir) ____________________ d'une crise cardiaque. Mais, je ne me rappelle pas s'il y avait un manuscrit inédit parmi ces livres. J'ai gardé la plupart des bouquins qu'Henri Pierre m'(envoyer) ____________________. Mais, je ne sais pas. . . Si seulement j'(apprendre) ____________________ à utiliser l'ordinateur que Nicolas (vouloir) ____________________ m'acheter. Il y a mis notre inventaire.

Mon neveu Nicolas s'occupe de toutes ces affaires maintenant. Quand il avait 22 ans, il a commencé à travailler avec moi. Avant ça, je faisais tout le travail moi-même. J'(trouver) ____________________ beaucoup de clients parce que j'(choisir) ____________________ de me spécialiser en bouquins militaires. Saviez-vous qu'Henri et moi, avant de nous rencontrer, tous les deux, nous (combattre) ____________________ pendant la Seconde Guerre mondiale ? Nous avons vu des choses atroces. C'est pour cette raison que nous nous sommes entendus si bien quand nous nous sommes rencontrés. On se comprenait. Mais, vous deux, vous êtes trop jeunes pour vous souvenir de cette guerre. Vous (ne. . . pas encore / naître) ____________________ !

Enfin, pour le manuscrit, je n'en sais rien. Il fut un temps où je voulais tout faire moi-même. Puis, j'ai décidé de prendre ma retraite. Nicolas s'occupe de toutes ces affaires-là maintenant, mais il part en vacances aujourd'hui. Il va se détendre sur les plages de Tunisie pour quinze jours ! Si seulement j'(voyager) ____________________ plus souvent au temps de ma jeunesse ! Mais non, après la guerre, je suis resté près de chez moi. . .

Langue

Rappel ! Rappel ! Si vous ne vous souvenez pas des règles pour la conjugaison des verbes au **passé composé** et à l'**imparfait**, révisez l'Épisode 3 du Chapitre 2. Si vous voulez réviser l'usage de ces deux temps de verbe, consultez l'Épisode 3 du Chapitre 3.

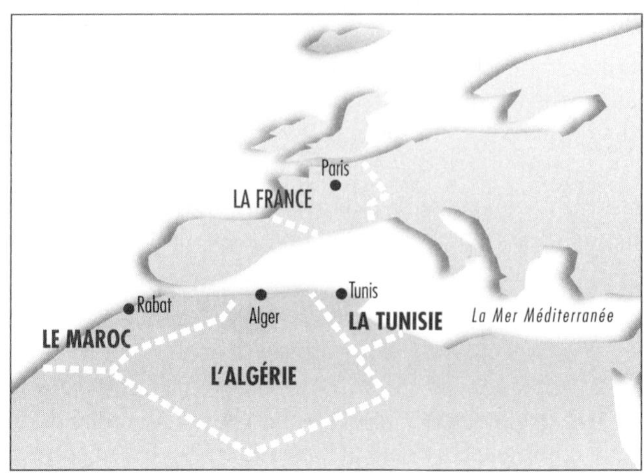

Le Maghreb

4.32 Vous en souvenez-vous bien ? Cette affaire du manuscrit volé devient de plus en plus compliquée. Faites des phrases au **plus-que-parfait** pour répondre aux questions suivantes sur l'intrigue. Utilisez les réponses suggérées, ou bien ajoutez vos propres souvenirs.

1. Au mois d'août, Claire est arrivée à l'Hôtel Le Moyne à la Nouvelle-Orléans, et avant d'y aller, qu'est-ce qu'elle avait fait ? (demander une bourse de l'université, trouver le nom de François Fontenot dans une lettre écrite par Laclos)
2. Il y a trois jours, Claire a décidé de quitter la Nouvelle-Orléans, mais avant de quitter les États-Unis, qu'est-ce qu'elle avait fait ? (rencontrer Sandrine Fontenot-Chardin, sortir avec Jean-Louis)
3. Il y a deux jours, Claire est arrivée à son hôtel à Paris, et avant d'y arriver, qu'est-ce qui s'était passé ? (prendre l'avion, perdre sa valise à l'aéroport)
4. Hier, d'après Monsieur Lateef, Nicolas Gustave était tout nerveux, et avant-hier, qu'est-ce qui s'était passé ? (deux hommes venir, parler)
5. En 1973, le père d'Henri Pierre Fontenot est mort d'une crise cardiaque, et avant sa mort, qu'est-ce qui s'était passé ? (recevoir les livres de François Fontenot en héritage, être menacé par des voleurs)

4.33 Qu'est-ce que je t'avais dit ? Claire et Jean-Louis quittent la maison de Lionel Gustave. Comme Jean-Louis avait dit, c'était le jeune Nicolas qui saurait si ce manuscrit existe toujours. Toujours en désaccord, Claire et Jean-Louis parlent de ce qu'ils avaient et n'avaient pas fait avant d'aller chez Monsieur Gustave. **Jouez une scène** où Claire et Jean-Louis se disputent et **inventez des phrases** en employant le **plus-que-parfait**.

MODÈLE : je / trouver l'adresse de Monsieur Gustave →

—J'avais trouvé l'adresse de Monsieur Gustave avant de retourner au Palais-Royal !

1. tu / ne. . . pas / réfléchir bien
2. je / suggérer de retourner chez le bouquiniste
3. je / ne. . . pas / penser à la possibilité d'acheter le manuscrit
4. tu / choisir de retourner à ton bureau
5. nous / parler à Talal Lateef

4.34 À vous Faites une interview avec un(e) camarade de classe. Répondez aux questions d'après votre expérience personnelle. Utilisez le **plus-que-parfait**.

1. Quand est-ce que tu as commencé tes études universitaires ? Qu'est-ce que tu avais fait afin de vous préparer pour les études universitaires ?
2. Qu'est-ce que tu as fait le week-end dernier ? Qu'est-ce que tu avais fait le week-end avant ?
3. À quelle heure est-ce que tu es arrivé(e) à l'université aujourd'hui ? Qu'est-ce que tu avais déjà fait avant d'y arriver ?
4. Où est-tu allé(e) la dernière fois que tu as voyagé ? Est-ce que tu avais déjà visité cet endroit ? Quels autres endroits avais-tu déjà visité ?

4.35 Désolé ! Jean-Louis accompagne Claire à son hôtel. Il se sent un peu mal à l'aise. Voici leur conversation. Mettez les verbes entre parenthèses au **passé composé**, à **l'imparfait** ou au **plus-que-parfait** selon le contexte.

JEAN-LOUIS: Est-ce que tu es fâchée contre moi ? Mais qu'est-ce que je (faire) __________________ ? On (aller) __________________ chez Monsieur Gustave, comme tu l'(suggérer) __________________ ce matin. Ce n'est pas ma faute à moi s'il (être) __________________ un peu sénile, le pauvre. Moi, je (vouloir) __________________ retourner chez le bouquiniste, mais quand nous (sortir) __________________ de la maison du vieux Gustave, il (faire) __________________ déjà nuit.

CLAIRE : Et ce n'est pas ma faute si nous (partir) __________________ du jardin du Palais-Royal si tard. Moi, je (trouver) __________________ l'adresse de Monsieur Gustave avant 1h. C'est toi qui (aller) __________________ au travail et qui m'(faire) __________________ attendre jusqu'à 3h passées. Et puis, c'est ta tante qui (prendre) __________________ une heure pour raconter son anecdote.

JEAN-LOUIS: Bon, elle (ne... pas / parler) __________________ pendant une heure, quand même ! Écoute, il faut que nous travaillions ensemble. Arrêtons de nous disputer.

CLAIRE : Tu as raison. Et l'anecdote (être) __________________ assez amusante. Bon. Demain, on repart à zéro...

Pour aller plus loin : CULTURE

ACTIVITÉ H : Connaissez-vous la célèbre chanteuse parisienne Édith Piaf ? Consultez votre cahier électronique !

4.36 J'ai des regrets En rentrant dans sa chambre, Claire ouvre la radio et écoute une vieille chanson d'Édith Piaf qui s'appelle «Je ne regrette rien». Elle commence à penser à toutes les choses qu'elle regrette d'avoir fait ou de ne pas avoir fait. Lisez les phrases en mettant les verbes au **plus-que-parfait**.

1. Si seulement j'(choisir) un autre sujet de recherche !
2. Si seulement j'(rencontrer) Jean-Louis en d'autres circonstances !
3. Si seulement mes parents m'(convaincre) d'étudier les affaires !
4. Si seulement ma sœur (venir) avec moi à Paris !
5. Si seulement Jean-Louis et moi, nous (retourner) chez le bouquiniste au lieu d'aller à la maison de Monsieur Gustave !

La chanson se termine, et Claire allume son ordinateur portable. Elle a un message provenant d'une adresse qu'elle ne reconnaît pas. . .

Un courriel énigmatique

À : Claire PLOUFFE
De : tempsperdu@nomade.fr
Date : le 3 septembre 2003
Réf : une fable

Aimez-vous les fables, Madame Plouffe ? En voici une qui pourrait vous intéresser.

Il était une fois,° une jolie jeune femme qui avait quitté sa maison à la recherche d'un trésor.° Elle voulait trouver le trésor afin de le partager avec tout le monde, tant elle était naïve et manquait d'expérience. Encore pire,° elle ne s'était pas bien préparée pour son voyage. Elle avait oublié d'apporter sa loupe° magique, celle qui lui aurait permis de voir ce qui est au fond° des cœurs des hommes. Elle ne pouvait donc pas distinguer les chevaliers des vilains. En entrant dans le bosquet° près de sa maison, elle a choisi le mauvais chemin.° Ensuite, elle a rencontré un homme au cœur impur. Peu de temps après, elle s'est perdue.° La pauvre, si seulement elle avait mis sa loupe magique dans sa grande valise verte ! Mais non ! Elle a continué de suivre ce chemin dangereux, conduite par un vilain déguisé. Savez-vous ce qui lui est arrivé ? Elle a disparu et on ne l'a jamais revue.

Abandonnez le chemin que vous avez choisi. Fuyez ! Votre trésor est ailleurs.

once upon a time; *treasure*; *even worse*; *magnifying glass*; *at the bottom of*; *woods*; *path*; *to get lost*

Après avoir lu

4.37 D'accord ou pas d'accord ? Après avoir lu la lettre ci-dessus, lisez les phrases suivantes et donnez vos opinions personnelles. Discutez-les en petits groupes.

	D'accord	Pas d'accord
1. L'auteur de ce message est un(e) ami(e) à Claire.	_______	_______
2. L'auteur du message aime la littérature.	_______	_______
3. Claire est la jeune femme de la fable.	_______	_______
4. Le manuscrit de Laclos est le trésor.	_______	_______
5. Claire suit le mauvais chemin afin de trouver le manuscrit.	_______	_______

4.38 Que pensez-vous ? Avec un partenaire, répondez aux questions suivantes. Justifiez vos réponses en citant le texte.

1. Est-ce que l'auteur du message connaît Claire Plouffe ? Comment le savez-vous ?
2. Est-ce que Claire connaît l'auteur du message ? Qui pourrait être l'auteur ?
3. Pensez-vous que cette fable soit en réalité une allégorie ? Quel est le sens allégorique de l'histoire ?
4. Comment est le caractère de la jeune femme dans la fable ? Ressemble-t-elle à Claire, à votre avis ?
5. Quels conseils est-ce que l'auteur du message donnent à Claire ? Pourquoi ?

4.39 Les regrets de Jean-Louis Pendant que Claire lit ce message troublant, Jean-Louis est chez lui. Il écoute la chanson «Caroline» du rappeur MC Solaar et il pense à sa journée. Lisez les phrases en mettant les verbes au **plus-que-parfait**.

1. Si seulement je (ne. . . pas / aller) au bureau !
2. Si seulement on (ne. . . pas / voir) ma tante à la place des Abbesses !
3. Si seulement Nicolas Gustave (ne. . . pas / partir) en vacances ce soir !
4. Si seulement Claire et moi, nous (ne. . . pas / se disputer) !
5. Si seulement ma mère m'(rappeler) la date de la fête de mon grand-père !

Pour aller plus loin : CULTURE

ACTIVITÉ 1 : Connaissez-vous des rappeurs français ? Consultez votre cahier électronique !

4.40 Préparez-vous Pensez à un événement important dans l'histoire de votre famille (un mariage, une naissance, un rite religieux, une fête importante, un anniversaire). Puis, écrivez une liste de toutes les choses que les membres de votre famille avaient faites en préparation pour cet événement. Circulez dans la classe et échangez votre liste avec celles de vos camarades de classe. Essayez de deviner de quel type d'événement il s'agit.

MODÈLE : «J'avais acheté des cadeaux. Ma mère avait aidé à décorer la maison. Mon beau-frère avait acheté des ballons bleus et des cigares. Ma tante avait tricoté des bonnets et des petits pulls bleus. Mon père nous avait conduit à l'hôpital. Ma sœur avait été enceinte avec des jumeaux depuis neuf mois !»

—C'était la naissance de tes neveux ?

À l'écrit *troisième étape*

4.41 Vos préparations avant la fête Imaginez que la réunion familiale est terminée et toute la famille est partie. Écrivez un courriel (*e-mail*) à une amie qui avait proposé de vous aider à organiser la fête. Décrivez comment était la fête et mentionnez tous les préparatifs que vous aviez faits la veille de la fête. Échangez votre message avec celui d'un de vos camarades de classe (par courriel, si vous voulez !) et offrez-lui une réponse et quelques corrections possibles. Mettez les verbes aux temps passés.

Dénouement

Activités de révision

4.42 La vie de Nicolas Gustave Voici l'emploi du temps de Nicolas Gustave le jour de son départ pour la Tunisie. Répondez aux questions sur sa journée en employant les temps passés (**passé composé**, **imparfait** ou **plus-que-parfait**).

Pour aller plus loin : CULTURE

ACTIVITÉ J : Explorez les institutions arabes à Paris. Consultez votre cahier électronique !

le 3 septembre 2003	
7h	se lever, manger le petit déjeuner, boire un café
7h30	s'habiller, regarder la télé
8h	prendre le métro jusqu'au boulevard Haussmann
9h	aller aux grands magasins, acheter un maillot de bain
10h	aller à l'Institut du monde arabe, visiter l'exposition
12h	déjeuner au restaurant de l'Institut du monde arabe
13h	rentrer à la maison
13h30	faire les valises, écouter de la musique raï
15h	téléphoner à son oncle
15h30	aller au travail, ouvrir son étalage, vendre des livres
18h	parler avec Talal Lateef, rentrer chez lui
19h	partir pour l'aéroport

1. À quelle heure est-ce que Nicolas a pris le métro pour aller au boulevard Haussmann ? Qu'est-ce qu'il avait fait déjà avant de quitter la maison ?
2. À quelle heure est-ce qu'il a déjeuné ? Qu'est-ce qu'il avait déjà fait avant ?
3. À quelle heure est-il allé au travail ? Qu'est-ce qu'il avait déjà fait avant ?
4. À quelle heure est-il parti pour l'aéroport ? Qu'est-ce qu'il avait déjà fait avant ?

Pour aller plus loin : CULTURE

ACTIVITÉ K : Voulez-vous écouter la musique du monde francophone ? Écoutez du raï, du zouk, du zydeco, du rap ou de la chanson traditionnelle. Consultez votre cahier électronique !

4.43 Votre emploi du temps Faites un emploi du temps et mettez-y toutes les activités que vous avez faites hier. Puis, échangez votre emploi du temps avec un(e) camarade de classe et posez-vous des questions à propos de ce que vous aviez fait avant de faire ces choses. Utilisez le **plus-que-parfait** autant que possible !

MODÈLE : —Hier, à midi, j'étais au gymnase.

—Est-ce que tu avais travaillé avant d'aller au gymnase ?

4.44 Les petites annonces Aidez un(e) ami(e) ou un parent à trouver l'amour ! Lisez les petites annonces (*personal ads*) suivantes. Puis, choisissez un(e) ami(e) ou un parent célibataire et écrivez une annonce pour lui/elle selon les modèles. Mettez beaucoup d'adjectifs ! Puis, circulez dans la salle de classe et lisez les annonces de vos camarades. Si vous trouvez une annonce qui pourrait intéresser votre ami(e) ou parent, posez des questions à propos du sujet !

MODÈLES :

Adorable JF, célibataire, 25 ans, musicienne. Aux yeux verts, jolie, élégante, indépendante, moderne. Très spontanée et impulsive. Cherche un homme à l'esprit ouvert, passionné, romantique et cultivé. Si vous êtes celui-là, sachez que je vous attends !

Grand, beau et brun ! Ingénieur, divorcé, 32 ans. Je suis naturel, plein d'humour, sensible, généreux, sportif, parfois timide. J'adore la nature. Si vous êtes intelligente, féminine et affectueuse, venez découvrir le bonheur paisible de la vie à la campagne.

Avant de lire *Femmes d'Alger dans leur appartement*

4.45 Vos voisins Vous écrivez un article pour un journal local sur l'idée que les Américains ne connaissent pas leurs voisins ces jours-ci. Circulez dans la salle de classe et posez des questions à vos camarades. Vous voulez trouver les réponses les plus intéressantes !

1. Connaissez-vous vos voisins ? Si non, pourquoi pas ? Si oui, comment sont-ils ?
2. Savez-vous où vos voisins sont nés et où ils ont grandi ? Savez-vous où ils avaient habité avant de devenir vos voisins ?
3. Combien d'enfants ont vos voisins ? Que font-ils dans la vie ?
4. Est-ce que vos voisins vous connaissent ? Savent-ils où vous faites vos études universitaires ?

Pour aller plus loin : CULTURE

ACTIVITÉ L : Regardez la peinture d'Eugène Delacroix, *Femmes d'Alger dans leur appartement*. Consultez votre cahier électronique !

4.46 Premières impressions **Lisez** l'extrait suivant, tiré du roman *Femmes d'Alger dans leur appartement* d'Assia Djebar, sans essayer de comprendre chaque mot. Après votre première lecture du texte, **répondez** aux questions. Ensuite, **relisez** le texte une deuxième fois, plus attentivement.

1. À qui appartient la maison voisine ? Est-ce la maison d'une grande famille ?
2. Quand se passe cette histoire ? Au présent ou au passé ?
3. Où se passe l'histoire ?
4. Quel événement a interrompu la naissance des enfants dans cette famille ?
5. Comment sont décrites les filles : plutôt traditionnelles ou modernes ? timides ou indépendantes ?

Culture

La **religion islamique** est une religion monothéiste fondée sur les principes de la charité et du respect des autres. On suit les conseils du Coran, un livre rempli de messages sacrés transmis par le dernier prophète, Mahomet. Il y a **cinq piliers** ou obligations à suivre pour être musulman pratiquant : (1) ***shehada***, c'est une profession de foi en Allah (Dieu) et en son prophète, Mahomet, (2) ***salat***, ce sont les prières du Coran qu'on fait cinq fois par jour, tourné à l'est, vers La Mecque, la ville sainte en Arabie Saoudite, (3) ***zakat***, c'est un don d'argent qu'on offre à la mosquée au profit d'autres musulmans, (4) ***sawm***, c'est faire le jeûn (*fasting*) du lever au coucher du soleil pendant le mois du Ramadan, une fête religieuse, pour se rappeler la souffrance des pauvres, (5) ***hadj***, c'est le pèlerinage à La Mecque qu'on fait une fois dans la vie, si on a les moyens, pour visiter le Kaaba, un temple sacré. Dans une communauté islamique, le ***muezzin*** est celui qui appelle les gens à la mosquée pour les prières (en chantant de la tour de la mosquée), le ***hazab*** est celui qui lit et étudie le Coran, et l'***imam*** est celui qui dirige les prières du vendredi.

lisez

Femmes d'Alger dans leur appartement

Cet extrait vient du roman d'Assia Djebar, Femmes d'Alger dans leur appartement. *Djebar est née en Algérie mais elle a habité en France. Dans cet extrait, il s'agit d'une famille qui habite une maison à Alger, la capitale d'Algérie. Selon la tradition, c'étaient les hommes qui avaient le pouvoir social, politique et religieux dans les communautés islamiques du Maghreb. Les femmes, elles, étaient traditionnellement limitées à leurs maisons (avec des cours intérieures) et au* ***hammam*** *(les bains publics). Malgré la désapprobation des musulmans conservateurs, ces rôles traditionnels ont commencé à changer pour les femmes algériennes, comme pour les femmes de l'occident, à partir des années 1960. Ici, Djebar décrit l'histoire d'une famille, et souligne le caractère des filles adultes de cette famille, pour démontrer l'évolution du statut de la femme de l'époque de la mère à la nouvelle génération de ses filles.*

■ Assia Djebar

Femmes d'Alger dans leur appartement (extrait)

Le *hazab* de la maison voisine, dans ce quartier de petites villas mal blanchies,° a dix filles. *Hazab*, c'est-à-dire lecteur du Coran à la mosquée. Cela ne l'empêche pas de rester artisan, d'aller entre les heures de prière à son échoppe de cordonnier,° lieu de rendez-vous des lettrés ès jurisdiction islamique.° C'est un vieil homme, vêtu d'une toge° blanche, chaque jour renouvelée et flottant noblement autour de son corps noueux.° Il circule maintenant entouré de la considération visible du quartier.

whitewashed
shoemaker's stall, shop
scholar of Islamic law/robe
gnarled

Plus de trente ans auparavant, au cours des émeutes° du 8 mai 1945, il avait été condamné à mort pour avoir tenté de faire sauter à la bombe l'arsenal d'une petite ville côtière.° Gracié° trois ans après, il s'était marié, était alors venu habiter la capitale, avait eu quatre filles, avait passé ensuite cinq années à la prison Barberousse (dès le début des «événements» d'Algérie, au premier soupçon° d'activité clandestine, il avait tout naturellement été arrêté).

uprisings
coastal/pardoned
suspicion

brood/poverty
concern/basket/weekly
births

Sa femme avait élevé sa première couvée° dans la misère,° mais avec le souci° primordial de remplir les couffins° hebdomadaires° de la prison. Elle avait repris le rythme des accouchements° «au lendemain de l'indépendance» (beaucoup de récits plus nobles commencent encore par cette expression oratoire. . .). À sa quarantième année et à sa douzième grossesse,° dont une fausse couche,° Allah, qu'il soit béni, lui avait enfin accordé le garçon rêvé.

pregnancy/miscarriage

L'héritier du hazab entrait dans sa sixième année. On allait ces jours prochains, célébrer la circoncision du garçon, première fête familiale.

unobtrusive

Les trois filles «d'avant l'indépendance» (la quatrième, la plus effacée,° venait d'être fiancée à un employé de banque) posaient quelques problèmes. L'aînée, vingt-quatre ans, pratiquait le judo depuis son adolescence, s'obstinait en outre à ne sortir qu'en pantalon (seule explication par ailleurs au manque persistant de demandes en mariage° sérieuses). La seconde, à vingt-deux ans, terminait à l'université une licence ès sciences naturelles° (et le père, en déambulant° au-dehors, tentait de comprendre le rapport existant entre les sciences naturelles et un cerveau° féminin mais n'osait en parler; l'âge aidant, il était devenu timide avec ses filles et souffrait davantage d'avoir à le cacher). La troisième, enfin, Sonia, vingt ans — la récitante de cette mini-chronique — occupait tous ses loisirs à des entraînements° d'athlétisme.° Elle a récemment décidé de devenir professeur d'éducation physique. «Ne vivre que sur un stade !» ajoute-t-elle avec ardeur.

marriage proposals
bachelor of science/to stroll
brain
practice, training session/
track and field

Ce même matin, Sarah entra chez le hazab, consacra un long moment à dévider° placidement les formules de politesse dans une courette° où la mère, assise, jambes écartées devant un brasero, grillait poivrons et tomates, tandis que deux de ses filles glissaient,° pieds nus dans l'eau, et se disputaient avec de petits rires.

to unwind/small courtyard
to slide

Après avoir lu

Pour aller plus loin : LITTÉRATURE

ACTIVITÉ M : Qui est Assia Djebar ? Apprenez un peu de sa vie, de ses pensées et de son œuvre. Consultez votre cahier électronique !

4.47 Avez-vous compris ? En petits groupes, discutez de vos réponses aux questions suivantes.

1. Qu'est-ce que le hazab avait fait avant de se marier ? Pourquoi est-ce qu'on l'a mis en prison pendant la guerre d'indépendance ?
2. Comment était la vie de la mère avant l'indépendance ? et après ? et aujourd'hui ?
3. Pourquoi est-ce qu'on va avoir une fête familiale cette semaine ? À votre avis, pourquoi parle-t-on du «garçon rêvé» ?
4. Comment sont les filles «d'avant l'indépendance» ? Décrivez leurs caractères. Qu'est-ce que le hazab pense de ses filles aînées ? Pourquoi dit-on qu'elles posaient des problèmes ?
5. À votre avis, quel est le rapport entre les événements politiques en Algérie et le caractère des filles ? Pensez-vous que les rôles des femmes et des hommes aux États-Unis soient influencés par les événements politiques ?

4.48 D'accord ou pas d'accord ? Après avoir lu l'extrait du roman de Djebar, lisez les phrases suivantes et donnez votre opinion. Discutez de vos réponses en petits groupes.

	D'accord	Pas d'accord
1. Le hazab est un homme important aujourd'hui.	_______	_______
2. Le hazab était un révolutionnaire.	_______	_______
3. La femme du hazab est une femme traditionnelle.	_______	_______
4. Les filles du hazab sont traditionnelles aussi.	_______	_______
5. Dans cette famille, il y a dix filles et un fils.	_______	_______

4.49 Analyse littéraire Examinez ce texte de près. Répondez aux questions suivantes et discutez de vos réponses en classe.

1. Examinons le portrait du hazab au début de l'extrait : est-il positif, négatif ou neutre ? Quels adjectifs contribuent à ce ton ? Quelle couleur est associée au hazab ? Quel en est l'effet ?
2. Regardez de près la première phrase de l'extrait. Le sujet d'une phrase est celui qui agit, qui est actif. Quel est le sujet de la phrase ? Le verbe décrit une action. Quel est le verbe et quel est le temps de verbe ? L'objet direct est celui qui accepte, passivement, l'action du verbe. Quel est l'objet direct du verbe ? Récrivez la phrase en mettant l'objet comme sujet et analysez la différence. Quel est l'effet de cette structure sur le lecteur ?
3. Dans les 2ème et 3ème paragraphes, on apprend l'histoire de la famille du hazab. Quel est l'événement qui commence cette narration chronologique ? Quel est l'événement qui est à la fin de cette narration ? Quel temps de verbe domine dans ces deux paragraphes ? Quel en est l'effet ?
4. Analysez la description des trois filles les plus âgées. Que font-elles dans la vie ? Y a-t-il un rapport thématique entre les intérêts de chaque fille ? Une image qui domine ? Quel temps de verbe domine dans cette description, le passé composé (actions terminées) ou l'imparfait (description, états, émotions, actions habituelles) ? Quel en est l'effet ?
5. Pensez à la mère, la femme du hazab. Quand on entend parler de la femme la première fois dans le 2ème paragraphe, est-elle sujet ou objet dans la phrase ? Est-elle même mentionnée ? Ensuite, dans le 3ème paragraphe, quelle image domine ? Et dans le dernier paragraphe quand on voit la femme aujourd'hui, comment est-elle décrite ? En quelle position est son corps ? Quel en est l'effet ?
6. Qui est la narratrice du récit ? Pensez-vous qu'il y ait un peu de sarcasme dans cette description de la famille du hazab ? Si oui, analysez les phrases où il y a du sarcasme. Quels éléments stylistiques contribuent à ce ton ?

Synthèses

Pour aller plus loin : CINÉMA

ACTIVITÉ N : Pour en apprendre plus sur la guerre d'indépendance en Algérie, regardez le vieux film *La Bataille d'Alger*, où on trouve une représentation réaliste de la brutalité du conflit entre le FLN et l'armée française. Consultez votre cahier électronique !

4.50 Réfléchissons à la culture Voici quelques éléments de la culture française et maghrébine que vous avez étudiés dans ce chapitre. En petits groupes, répondez aux questions et discutez de vos impressions avec vos camarades.

la famille étendue   le Maghreb   les musulmans français

1. Définissez ou décrivez chaque élément.
2. Pourquoi est-ce qu'il y a beaucoup de musulmans en France et des liens étroits aux pays du Maghreb ? Y a-t-il un phénomène historique ou social qui explique son importance ?
3. Quelle est la différence entre un arabe et un musulman ? Quelles sont les trois religions importantes qui sont pratiquées dans les pays du monde arabe ? Quels groupes ethniques trouve-t-on parmi les musulmans (pensez aux États-Unis, à l'Afrique occidentale et aux îles entre l'océan indien et l'océan pacifique) ? Est-ce qu'il est stéréotypique ou réaliste d'associer la religion musulmane à un seul groupe ethnique ?
4. En France, depuis plusieurs décennies, la natalité (*birthrate*) est en crise parmi les Français d'origine européenne, lorsque la natalité chez les Français d'origine immigrante (maghrébine, africaine, asiatique, etc.) reste plus stable. Est-ce que cela veut dire que la famille devient moins importante chez les Français d'origine européenne ou que la notion de la famille est en train de changer chez eux ? On voit la même chose aux États-Unis où la natalité des familles plus récemment immigrées est supérieure à celle des familles immigrées il y a plusieurs générations. Y a-t-il un phénomène historique ou social qui explique cette situation ?
5. Est-ce que votre impression de la culture maghrébine est différente maintenant que vous avez commencé à l'étudier ? Si oui, comment et pourquoi ? Si non, pourquoi pas ?

l'Algérie

Qu'est-ce qu'un Algérien pense du film *La Bataille d'Alger* ? Regardez la vidéo et consultez votre cahier d'activités !

4.51 À débattre Lisez les questions suivantes et discutez-les en groupes. Si possible, parlez de vos expériences personnelles relatives aux questions.

1. **La famille, disparaît-elle ?** Autrefois, la famille vivait dans un même quartier ou dans un même village, et on voyait les parents tous les jours. Aujourd'hui, les jeunes quittent la maison très tôt pour aller vivre ailleurs, les familles nucléaires déménagent loin des autres parents, on déménage partout et en général, et on n'a plus le même sens de la famille «multi-générations» qu'autrefois. À cette époque de mondialisation et de technologie, est-ce que la vie familiale est en train de disparaître ?

2. **Êtes-vous immigrant(e) ?** Aux États-Unis, on peut dire que tous les citoyens, sauf les Amérindiens, sont des descendants d'immigrants d'autres pays. Quand est-ce qu'on cesse de s'identifier comme immigrant et commence à s'identifier comme habitant d'un pays ? après une génération ? deux ? quand on a un passeport officiel ? Qu'est-ce qui mène à ce changement d'esprit ?
3. **Le bon vieux temps ?** On dit que les gens nostalgiques décrivent le passé à travers des lunettes roses ; c'est à dire, qu'on exagère le «bon» vieux temps et on oublie le mauvais. Est-ce que le bon vieux temps de vos grands-parents était vraiment bon ? Quels étaient les inconvénients de leur mode de vie ? Est-ce que le bonheur nostalgique efface les difficultés et les inconvénients de la vie d'autrefois ? Ou bien, est-ce vrai qu'on était vraiment plus heureux à cette époque ?

4.52 À l'impromptu Voici des situations interactives. Avec une ou deux autres personnes, choisissez une scène et improvisez devant la classe. Si vous ne voulez pas improviser, écrivez votre dialogue avant et puis jouez-le pour la classe.

1. Souvenirs du passé
   (a) Vous annoncez à vos grands-parents que vous allez vous marier cette année. Vous voulez une cérémonie traditionnelle. Posez-leur beaucoup de questions à propos de leurs fêtes de mariage.
   (b) Votre petit-fils ou petite-fille, qui vient d'avoir 20 ans, vous annonce ses fiançailles. Demandez-lui s'il/elle n'est pas trop jeune pour penser au mariage et partagez les regrets que vous avez de vous être marié(e) trop tôt.
   (c) Votre petit-fils ou petite-fille, qui vient d'avoir 20 ans, vous annonce ses fiançailles. Vous êtes très content(e) pour lui/elle. Racontez-lui comment vous avez fait la connaissance de votre mari/femme et les bons souvenirs qui s'y attachent.
2. Une fête de mariage
   (a) Vous assistez au mariage d'un parent éloigné. Vous êtes l'enfant de l'oncle de la mariée (*bride*). Vous rencontrez de nombreux parents éloignés et essayez de comprendre le lien de famille qui vous unit.
   (b) Vous assistez au mariage d'un parent éloigné. Vous êtes le frère de la 2ème femme du père du marié (*groom*). Essayez d'en savoir plus sur la famille de la mariée.
   (c) Vous assistez au mariage aussi, mais vous n'avez pas été invité(e) ! Vous ne connaissez ni la famille de la mariée ni la famille du marié. Essayez de convaincre les autres que vous êtes un parent éloigné et que vous les avez déjà rencontrés plusieurs fois dans le passé.
3. Une réunion familiale
   (a) Vous assistez à une réunion familiale et vous venez de voir votre cousin voler le porte-monnaie de votre tante. Confrontez-le !
   (b) Vous assistez à une réunion familiale. Votre tante vous a demandé de prendre son porte-monnaie et d'aller chercher un gâteau pour la fête. Essayez de vous expliquer auprès de votre cousin.

À l'écrit *étape finale*

4.53 Quelle fête magnifique ! Votre fête familiale était un succès. Révisez et élaborez vos travaux d'écriture de ce chapitre (À l'écrit : activités 15, 29 et 41) et rédigez une lettre formelle au membre le plus âgé de votre famille. Décrivez vos impressions de la soirée et tout ce qui s'était passé avant la fête. Utilisez le **passé composé**, l'**imparfait** ou le **plus-que-parfait**. N'oubliez pas les éléments suivants :

- Saluez
- Décrivez les parents qui sont venus pour la fête
- Donnez votre opinion de la fête
- Parlez de tout ce que vous aviez fait pour préparer la fête
- Remerciez le destinataire d'être venu(e)

Pour agir :
LE MAGHREB !
Si vous voulez bouger et faire quelque chose pour mieux connaître le Maghreb, ou pour aider les autres à mieux connaître les cultures francophones, consultez la section **Pour agir** dans votre cahier électronique ! Il y a tant de choses à faire :

- **Organisez une fête** francophone, jouez de la musique, offrez des boissons et des mets, et contribuez l'argent que vous gagnez à une organisation qui combat le racisme ou qui aide les femmes qui vivent sous l'oppression.
- **Enseignez** ce que vous savez de la musique du monde francophone à des enfants de l'école primaire.
- **Entrez en contact** avec des maghrébins ou d'autres arabes francophones qui vivent dans votre communauté ou quelque part aux États-Unis.
- **Faites une excursion** à un musée pour explorer les arts du monde arabe.
- **Cuisinez !** Préparez un vrai repas maghrébin avec vos camarades de classe.

À suivre

Claire essaie de répondre au message bizarre qu'elle a reçu, mais son message lui revient marqué «destinataire inconnu». Elle réfléchit un peu avant de téléphoner à Jean-Louis. Après tout, il est la seule personne qu'elle connaît à Paris, et malgré l'avertissement de l'inconnu qui a envoyé le message électronique, elle commence à avoir confiance en Jean-Louis. Bien sûr, quand il entend ce qui s'est passé, Jean-Louis arrive tout de suite à l'hôtel pour réconforter son amie et pour lire le message de ses propres yeux. Encore une fois, Jean-Louis se vante d'avoir eu raison. Il y a, effectivement, d'autres gens qui sont à la recherche du manuscrit et qui essaient d'intimider la jeune chercheur québécoise. Après de nombreux appels inutiles à la police, qui ne pouvait rien faire sans preuve de menace directe, Claire et Jean-Louis décident d'attendre afin de voir si cette personne reprend contact avec eux. . .

4.54 Qu'est-ce qui s'est passé ? Pensez à ce qui s'est passé dans ce chapitre. Écrivez six phrases aux temps passés pour décrire les événements que vous pensez être les plus importants. Parlez de vos idées avec vos camarades de classe.

MODÈLE : —Lionel Gustave est parti en vacances.
—Mais non ! Tu as tort ! C'est Nicolas qui est parti en vacances.

4.55 Qu'est-ce qui va se passer ? Imaginez ce qui va se passer dans le prochain chapitre. Écrivez six phrases et parlez de vos idées avec vos camarades de classe.

MODÈLE : Claire et Jean-Louis vont aller en Tunisie !
—Tu as peut-être raison.

VOCABULAIRE UTILE

La famille

aîné(e)	*oldest*
arrière-grands-parents (*m. pl.*)	*great-grandparents*
beau-fils (*m.*)	*son-in-law/stepson*
beau-frère (*m.*)	*brother-in-law*
beau-père (*m.*)	*father-in-law/stepfather*
belle-famille (*f.*)	*in-laws*
belle-fille (*f.*)	*daughter-in-law/ stepdaughter*
belle-mère (*f.*)	*mother-in-law/ stepmother*
belle-sœur (*f.*)	*sister-in-law*
cadet(te)	*youngest*
cousin(e)	*cousin*
demi-sœur (*f.*), demi-frère (*m.*)	*half-sister/brother*
femme (*f.*)	*wife*
fiancé(e)	*fiancé*
fille (*f.*)	*daughter*
filleul (*m.*)	*godson*
filleule (*f.*)	*goddaughter*
fils (*m.*)	*son*
frère (*m.*)	*brother*
grands-parents (*m. pl.*)	*grandparents*
jumeaux (*m.*), jumelles (*f.*)	*twins*
mari (*m.*)	*husband*
marié (*m.*), mariée (*f.*)	*groom/bride*
marraine (*f.*)	*godmother*
mère (*f.*)	*mother*
neveu (*m.*)	*nephew*
nièce (*f.*)	*niece*
oncle (*m.*)	*uncle*
parrain (*m.*)	*godfather*
père (*m*)	*father*
petite-fille (*f.*)	*granddaughter*
petit-fils (*m.*)	*grandson*
sœur (*f.*)	*sister*
tante (*f.*)	*aunt*

Décrire une personne

agité(e)	*agitated*
avoir la trentaine	*to be in one's 30s*
bégayer	*to stutter*
consciencieux/-euse	*conscientious*
efficace	*efficient*
énergique	*energetic*
être enrhumé(e)	*to have a cold*
faire de son mieux	*to do one's best*
fiable	*reliable*
fier/fière	*proud*
infatigable	*tireless*
nerveux/-euse	*nervous*

Divers

grève (*f.*)	*workers' strike*
quai (*m.*)	*embankment, walkway or roadway next to a river*
rater	*to miss (a day, a bus, an event, etc.)*
renseignement (*m.*)	*piece of information*
sauf	*except*
siège arrière (*m.*)	*backseat*

La vie en famille

amener	*to bring (someone)*
animal familier (*m.*)	*pet*
apparaître	*to appear*
attirer	*to attract*
bête (*f.*)	*animal*
charmant(e)	*charming*
chasse (*f.*)	*hunting*
fichu(e)	*ruined*
jeu (*m.*)	*game*
lapin (*m.*)	*rabbit*
magie (*f.*)	*magic*
messe (*f.*)	*(religious) mass*
n'importe quoi	*anything at all*
pleurer	*to cry*
ragoût (*m.*)	*stew*
se réunir	*to get together*
souvenir (*m.*)	*memory*

Chapitre 5

Les conseils d'un Français

La place des Vosges à Paris en automne.

Épisode *1* *Au café en automne*

Épisode *2* *De mauvaises nouvelles*

Épisode *3* *Un fax du patron*

Dénouement

Automne en fleurs,
hiver plein de rigueurs.
—dicton français

Culture

On dit qu'il y a autant de **journaux parisiens** que de partis politiques en France. Les journaux les plus connus sont *Libération* et *Le Monde*. Pourtant, on trouve aussi des journaux comme *France Soir*, *L'Humanité*, *Le Canard enchaîné*, *Le Figaro*, *The International Herald Tribune* (pour les anglophones) et beaucoup d'autres. Chaque journal s'engage plus ou moins avec une idéologie politico-sociale, et beaucoup de débats politiques et d'opinions diverses y sont publiés. La presse est un véhicule important pour la dissémination des nouvelles non seulement à Paris mais à travers le monde francophone. On trouve des journaux de langue française dans tous les pays francophones et même dans plusieurs pays où il n'existe qu'une minorité linguistique francophone.

À apprendre

- Comment parler des actualités et du temps
- Comment apprendre une nouvelle à quelqu'un et comment y réagir
- Comment exprimer son opinion et donner des conseils
- Comment exprimer ses souhaits et ses émotions

À lire

Malgré l'invitation renouvelée de Jean-Louis, Claire s'obstine à demeurer à l'Hôtel Quasimodo. Il a peur qu'elle soit en danger après avoir reçu ce message bizarre, mais elle ne veut pas perdre sa liberté en s'installant chez lui. Donc, ils attendent le retour de Nicolas Gustave, chacun à sa manière. Jean-Louis retourne au bureau de l'antiquaire, où il a d'autres projets à poursuivre, et Claire reprend ses recherches secondaires en consultant la collection de la Bibliothèque nationale et en lisant des livres théoriques qu'elle trouve dans les librairies du Quartier latin. Il fait exceptionnellement beau à Paris pendant ce temps-là. Ciel bleu et ensoleillé, aucune humidité, température parfaite. Alors, Claire passe ses après-midi à la terrasse d'un café, où elle lit, réfléchit et écrit tout en profitant du beau temps. . . jusqu'au moment où elle rencontre quelqu'un qui lui parle d'un article de journal assez curieux.

Épisode 1

Au café en automne

Avant de lire

5.1 Les actualités **Répondez** aux questions suivantes. **Discutez** de vos réponses avec vos camarades de classe et n'hésitez pas à poser des questions supplémentaires si vous voulez en savoir plus.

1. Pour savoir ce qui se passe dans le monde, préférez-vous lire le journal, regarder les infos à la télé, écouter la radio, consultez l'Internet ou parler à des amis ?
2. Est-ce que vous lisez le journal souvent ? de temps en temps ? rarement ? jamais ? Quel journal lisez-vous ? Où lisez-vous votre journal normalement ?
3. Quels aspects des actualités vous intéressent le plus : les nouvelles (régionales, nationales ou internationales) ? la politique ? la culture ? les sports ? les affaires ? la météo ?
4. Est-ce que vous discutez les actualités et la météo avec votre famille ou vos amis ? Où ? Quand ? Pourquoi ?
5. Pensez-vous qu'il soit important de savoir ce qui se passe dans le monde ? Pourquoi ?

Langue

Vous rappelez-vous les conjugaisons des **verbes irréguliers lire, dire, écrire** et **rire** ? Si non, mémorisez leurs conjugaisons avant de continuer !

- **lire** (*to read*) : je lis, tu lis, il/elle/on lit, nous lisons, vous lisez, ils/elles lisent (*participe passé* : lu)
- **dire** (*to say*) : je dis, tu dis, il/elle/on dit, nous disons, vous dites, ils/elles disent (*participe passé* : dit)
- **écrire** (*to write*) : j'écris, tu écris, il/elle/on écrit, nous écrivons, vous écrivez, ils/elles écrivent (*participe passé* : écrit); le verbe **décrire** est conjugué comme **écrire**.
- **rire** (*to laugh*) : je ris, tu ris, il/elle/on rit, nous rions, vous riez, ils/elles rient (*participe passé* : ri); le verbe **sourire** (*to smile*) est conjugué comme **rire**.

5.2 À la une Claire cherche toujours des nouvelles de son pays et s'arrête souvent devant les kiosques pour chercher un journal québécois. Elle y trouve un grand choix de journaux. **Regardez ces gros titres** (*headlines*) que Claire lit en s'arrêtant devant un kiosque qui vend des journaux internationaux, et **répondez** aux questions d'après vos observations. **Discutez** de vos réponses avec la classe.

Les Montréalais au Festival du rire :
rires et sourires

L'ouragan s'approche :
les Martiniquais se barricadent

Dix blessés lors d'un accident aérien au Maroc

Un tête-à-tête à l'Élysée :
les Verts parlent au Président

Une crise économique frappe la Guyane

L'UE considère la question «euro» à Strasbourg

Une exposition de folklore tahitien au musée Gauguin

1. Pour chaque gros titre, indiquez de quel pays ou région il s'agit.
2. Quels titres annoncent de mauvaises nouvelles ? Lesquels annoncent de bonnes nouvelles ?
3. Lesquels présentent des sujets : (a) de politique, (b) d'économie, (c) de culture, (d) de météorologie ?
4. Quel article vous intéresserait ? Lequel voulez-vous lire ? Pourquoi ?

Pour aller plus loin : CULTURE

ACTIVITÉ A : Voulez-vous savoir ce qui se passe dans le monde francophone ? Lisez les titres «à la une» sur Internet. Consultez votre cahier électronique !

Pour aller plus loin : LITTÉRATURE

ACTIVITÉ B : Lisez le poème «Chanson d'automne» de Paul Verlaine. Consultez votre cahier électronique !

Culture

Les **DOM-TOM**, c'est l'ensemble des territoires de la France d'outre-mer. Les DOM-TOM sont divisés, depuis 2003, en **départements d'outre-mer** (les DOM) et en **collectivités d'outre-mer** (les COM, autrefois nommés territoires d'outre-mer, d'où vient l'acronyme DOM-TOM). Pour la plupart, ce sont des anciennes colonies qui se sont intégrées au système administratif de la France au moment de la décolonisation. Tandis que les habitants des DOM-TOM ont gardé leurs propres cultures et traditions, les gens qui y vivent sont légalement des citoyens français. Dans les DOM-TOM, on trouve : **la Guadeloupe** et **la Martinique** aux Antilles, **Saint-Pierre-et-Miquelon** en Amérique du Nord, **la Guyane** en Amérique du Sud, **la Réunion** et **Mayotte** près de l'Afrique, **la Polynésie** (y compris Tahiti), **la Nouvelle-Calédonie** et **Wallis-et-Futuna** dans l'océan Pacifique. **Les Terres australes et antarctiques**, qui ne sont pas peuplées, font partie des DOM-TOM aussi. Les COM ont un peu plus d'autonomie politique que les DOM, mais dans toutes ces régions, on continue à débattre la question de l'indépendance et la praticabilité économique d'une séparation d'avec l'état français.

5.3 La météo Voici des actualités météorologiques pour la France et l'Europe. Lisez les phrases et, ensuite, **indiquez** pour chaque ville ou région **s'il fait beau** ou **s'il fait mauvais** temps aujourd'hui. En plus, identifiez le pays européen dont il s'agit. Justifiez vos réponses.

1. Un ciel chargé dans la région genevoise s'accompagne de pluies faibles ou d'averses orageuses.
2. Une journée bruxelloise généralement ensoleillée, mais la température maximale n'atteindra que 14 degrés !
3. Baignons-nous à Biarritz où la mer est calme, il fait 25 degrés et des passages nuageux laissent la place aux éclaircies matinales.
4. Avertissement aux marins à Monaco : ciel couvert et vents à rafales de l'ouest au sud-ouest qui atteindront 70 km/h entre la Corse et le continent.
5. Cet après-midi, risque de tonnerre et de foudre, un orage dans la région luxembourgeoise laissera cinq centimètres de précipitation.
6. Après la dissipation des brouillards matinaux dans la région bordelaise, le soleil brille.
7. Dans les Alpes, une rafale de neige dans les régions montagneuses où le mercure reste entre zéro et cinq degrés.

Culture

En Europe, on utilise le **système Celsius** pour calculer la température. Ce système s'emploie dans la plupart des pays du monde francophone. Pour juger de la différence entre Celsius et Fahrenheit, voici quelques points de repère approximatifs :

Celsius :	0°	5°	10°	15°	21°	27°	32°	100°
Fahrenheit :	32°	40°	50°	60°	70°	80°	90°	212°

De plus, on emploie le **système métrique** pour calculer la distance (**mètres** au lieu de «pieds», **kilomètres** au lieu de «miles»), le poids (**kilos** à la place des «livres») et le volume (en **litres**, pas en «quarts» ou «gallons»).

lisez

Au café en automne

En attendant le retour du bouquiniste à Paris, Claire a repris le rythme de vie d'un chercheur en divisant son temps entre la lecture, l'écriture et la réflexion. Au bout de 15 jours, elle a fait beaucoup de progrès dans ses études du milieu culturel dans lequel Laclos a vécu. Un après-midi, en rentrant de la Bibliothèque nationale, elle s'arrête à son café habituel sur la place Saint-André-des-Arts. Comme il fait toujours assez beau, elle s'installe dehors, à côté d'un homme qui lit le journal ***Libération****. Lunettes de soleil au visage, gilet de laine rouge boutonné jusqu'au menton, foulard de soie autour du cou, elle commande tranquillement un petit café. Souriant innocemment, elle admire les feuilles jaunes qui continuent de s'agripper faiblement aux branches des arbres. L'homme à la table voisine amorce une conversation sur le temps. . .*

Un café parisien.

GILLES LAFFONT : Quelle belle journée, n'est-ce pas ? J'adore cette saison. Le ciel est bleu comme la mer, le soleil brille et il y a une petite brise qui nous fait rougir le bout du nez.

CLAIRE : Moi aussi, j'adore l'automne. Après l'humidité et la chaleur de l'été, on est content que la température baisse légèrement chaque jour, mais ça passe si vite. Un jour, toutes les feuilles seront tombées et on se trouvera sous deux pieds de neige !

GILLES LAFFONT : Je parie que vous n'êtes pas de Paris. Ici, on a rarement des tempêtes de neige en hiver. Il fait affreusement froid, il pleut, il y a des orages et des rafales de vent et le temps est généralement maussade, mais il ne neige pas régulièrement. . . comme au Québec.

CLAIRE : Vous avez reconnu mon accent. (*Elle sourit.*)

GILLES LAFFONT : Oui et non. Enfin, nous, on ne mesure pas en pieds. Que faites-vous à Paris ?

CLAIRE : Je suis étudiante de doctorat. Je fais de la recherche littéraire.

GILLES LAFFONT : Ah, bon ? C'est intéressant. Vous travaillez sur un auteur en particulier ?

CLAIRE : Oui, Choderlos de Laclos. C'est un romancier du 18ème siècle.

GILLES LAFFONT : Non ! C'est un de mes auteurs préférés ! Vous étudiez *Les Liaisons dangereuses* ?

CLAIRE : Non, pas exactement. J'étudie ses autres écrits.

GILLES LAFFONT : Ses autres écrits ? Donc, le manuscrit que vous cherchez est un autre roman écrit par Laclos ? C'est un manuscrit inédit, alors.

CLAIRE : Quoi ? Écoutez, monsieur, je ne sais pas qui vous êtes, mais je crains que vous ne sachiez plus que vous n'en disiez. C'est vous qui m'avez envoyé ce message ?

GILLES LAFFONT : Pardonnez-moi, mademoiselle, je ne voulais pas vous faire peur. Je suis ici pour vous aider. Je m'appelle

Gilles LaFfont. Je suis inspecteur de police dans le 5ème arrondissement. Voici ma carte. (*Il lui donne une carte.*) Je suis votre cas depuis le jour du vol de votre valise à l'aéroport. On me donne systématiquement tous les dossiers de vols qui se font aux aéroports en France s'ils touchent aux habitants de notre arrondissement, et dans votre dossier, j'ai lu que vous cherchiez un manuscrit ancien. Il est important que vous sachiez que le marché de livres anciens est un commerce assez dangereux. Les manuscrits originaux se vendent normalement pour des sommes considérables. Et là où on trouve de l'argent, on trouve aussi des criminels qui veulent en profiter. Lisez les journaux, vous verrez.

CLAIRE : Franchement, monsieur, je ne crois pas qu'il soit prudent de vous parler de tout cela. Je ne vous connais pas, et je trouve votre manière de m'aborder ici si brusquement un peu déconcertante. Je suis sûre que vous comprenez.

GILLES LAFFONT : Tout à fait, mademoiselle, mais vous avez mon numéro de téléphone au bureau sur ma carte. Vous pouvez toujours m'y contacter. Et même si vous vous méfiez de moi, il faut que je vous dise ceci : Si jamais vous rencontrez un homme qui s'appelle Raphaël ou une femme qui s'appelle Julie, il est important que vous réagissiez avec prudence. Ce sont des dealers peu scrupuleux. Nous croyons qu'ils se cachent quelque part dans les DOM-TOM en ce moment, mais il est toujours possible qu'ils reviennent à Paris.

CLAIRE : Excusez-moi encore, mais je ne veux pas continuer cette conversation. (*Elle se lève.*)

GILLES LAFFONT : D'accord, d'accord, mais une dernière chose, mademoiselle. De quel message parliez-vous ?

CLAIRE : Il faut absolument que je m'en aille maintenant. Au revoir.

VOCABULAIRE

Au café

la lecture	*reading*
l'écriture (*f.*)	*writing*
la réflexion	*reflection*
au bout de	*at the end of*
sourire	*to smile*
amorcer	*to introduce (a topic of conversation)*
rougir	*to redden; to blush*
parier	*to bet*
craindre	*to fear*
dépister	*to track down*
franchement	*frankly*
aborder	*to approach*
déconcertant(e)	*disconcerting, troubling*

Le temps

une feuille	*leaf*
le ciel	*sky*
une tempête	*storm*
un orage	*thunderstorm*
une rafale de vent	*gusty wind*
maussade	*gloomy*
la neige	*snow*

Culture

Le Café Procope, établi à Paris par un Italien en 1675, se vante d'être le premier des célèbres **cafés parisiens**. À partir du 17ème siècle, les cafés sont devenus des lieux de rencontre pour les intellectuels. Des écrivains et des artistes, de Voltaire à Picasso, ont souvent fréquenté les cafés où ils pouvaient boire, manger, discuter et s'inspirer à loisir. À part le **Café Procope** (préféré par Voltaire, Rousseau, Beaumarchais), les cafés les plus connus à Paris sont le **Café des Deux-Magots** (lieu de rencontre de Verlaine, Rimbaud, Mallarmé, Picasso), le **Café de Flore** (fréquenté par Sartre, de Beauvoir, Chagall), la **Closerie des Lilas** (Hemingway, Beckett, Baudelaire) et **Lapérouse** (Maupassant, Hugo, Proust, Colette). Aujourd'hui, les clients vont aux cafés non seulement pour prendre une boisson, mais aussi pour se détendre, pour lire les journaux, pour regarder le spectacle des gens qui passent, et surtout, pour rencontrer des amis et pour discuter des actualités de vive voix.

Après avoir lu

5.4 Avez-vous compris ? Répondez aux questions suivantes. **Justifiez vos réponses** en citant le texte.

1. Quel temps fait-il normalement à Paris en hiver ? et au Québec ? et chez vous ?
2. Comment est-ce que Gilles LaFfont a trouvé Claire ? Quelle est sa profession ? Pourquoi est-ce qu'il lui parle ?
3. Quelle est la réaction de Claire ? Que pensez-vous de cette réaction ? À votre avis, a-t-elle réagi trop peureusement (*fearfully*), trop méchamment, trop naïvement ?
4. Qu'est-ce que nous avons appris de Gilles LaFfont ? Pensez-vous qu'il soit sincère en voulant avertir la jeune femme des dangers du marché des livres anciens ?

5.5 D'accord ou pas d'accord ? Indiquez si vous êtes **d'accord ou pas d'accord** avec les phrases suivantes, d'après votre compréhension du récit. **Justifiez vos opinions** en citant le texte, si possible. **Discutez** de vos réponses avec la classe.

	D'accord	Pas d'accord
1. Il fait froid à Paris en automne.	______	______
2. Claire est contente que l'été soit terminé.	______	______
3. Gilles LaFfont attendait Claire à son café habituel.	______	______
4. Gilles est un inspecteur de police qui veut aider Claire.	______	______
5. Claire a peur de parler avec cet inconnu.	______	______
6. Gilles avait envoyé le courriel menaçant à Claire.	______	______

5.6 Au café Regardez les mots de vocabulaire qui suivent. À chaque ligne, il y a un mot qui cloche avec les trois autres. **Entourez le mot qui ne va pas avec les autres** et essayez d'expliquer pourquoi. Attention ! Il y a parfois plusieurs bonnes réponses. Il faut justifier votre choix !

1. la neige	la pluie	le soleil	l'orage
2. le café	la bibliothèque	le restaurant	le kiosque
3. franchement	normalement	sincèrement	tranquillement
4. un arbre	une feuille	une branche	une fleur
5. écrire	sourire	lire	réfléchir

Pour aller plus loin : CULTURE

ACTIVITÉ C : Quel temps fait-il en France aujourd'hui ? Consultez votre cahier électronique !

Culture

En 1957, six pays ont signé un traité afin de créer la Communauté économique européenne: l'Allemagne, la Belgique, la France, l'Italie, le Luxembourg, et les Pays-Bas. En 1973, le Danemark, l'Irlande et la Grande-Bretagne se sont ajoutees aux six, et aux années quatre-vingts, on a accueilli la Grèce, l'Espagne et le Portugal. Cette «Europe des douze» a ensuite passé des accords politiques, économiques, sociaux et écologiques pour unifier l'Europe. Depuis 1992, on appelle cette organisation l'**Union Européenne**. On trouve des institutions de l'UE dans plusieurs pays francophones: à Strasbourg en France, à Bruxelles en Belgique, et à Luxembourg au Luxembourg. L'UE a un drapeau européen, un cercle de douze étoiles dorées sur un fond bleu, et une monnaie unique, l'euro, qu'on utilise dans la plupart des pays de l'UE depuis 2002. Et l'Union européenne continue à s'agrandir. En 2006, l'UE compte 25 états membres et elle est toujours en train de considérer l'addition d'autres membres.

5.7 Le courriel De retour dans sa chambre, Claire écrit un petit message au courrier électronique à sa sœur pour discuter de ce qui vient de se passer. **Remplissez les blancs** avec un mot ou une expression convenable de la liste suivante.

beau	**bouquin**	**café**	**franchement**	**préoccupés**
soleil	**sympa**	**café temps**	**vent**	**vraiment**

Chère Marie,

Salut ! Comment ça va ? Ici, cette histoire de manuscrit devient de plus en plus bizarre. Aujourd'hui, il a fait très ________________. Il y avait un peu de ________________, mais il faisait du ________________. Donc, je me suis installée dans mon ________________ préféré et j'allais lire mon ________________ quand tout d'un coup, un homme a commencé à me parler du ________________. Il avait l'air ________________. Puis il m'a dit qu'il était inspecteur de police et qu'il fallait faire attention aux criminels qui dominent le marché des livres anciens ! Bien sûr, je suis partie tout de suite. Même s'il est ________________ un inspecteur de police, c'était un peu déconcertant. Peut-être suis-je un peu trop peureuse ces jours-ci, mais ________________, j'étais choquée par sa façon de se présenter. S'il te plaît, ne dis rien de tout cela à Maman et Papa. Je ne veux pas qu'ils soient ________________ par moi. Jean-Louis connaît ce marché et il saura se procurer le manuscrit s'il existe toujours ! On verra bien la semaine prochaine. Je t'écrirai encore dans quelques jours.

Gros bisous, Claire

5.8 Un coup de téléphone À 6h du soir, comme d'habitude, Jean-Louis téléphone à Claire pour savoir si elle va bien. Choisissez un des mots ou expressions donnés entre parenthèses et **lisez le dialogue à haute voix** avec un partenaire. Quand vous voyez «? ? ?», vous pouvez imaginer votre propre expression.

CLAIRE : Allô ?
JEAN-LOUIS : Salut, Claire. C'est moi. Comment vas-tu ?
CLAIRE : (Pas mal. / Excellent. / ? ? ?). Et toi ?
JEAN-LOUIS : Oh, ça va. J'ai signé un nouveau client aujourd'hui. Il fait collection d'antiquités médiévales.

CLAIRE : Ah, bon !

JEAN-LOUIS : Je lui ai trouvé une vieille cassette (*money box*) (extraordinairement / admirablement / ? ? ?) bien préservée. Que penses-tu des antiquités médiévales ? Je les trouve intéressantes du point de vue historique, mais pas trop sur le plan esthétique. Tu les aimes ou pas ?

CLAIRE : Enfin, ça m'est égal. Je ne les déteste pas, mais ce n'est pas mon truc. En matière médiévale, je ne m'y connais guère.

JEAN-LOUIS : Ah, oui ! C'est (le 18ème siècle / la littérature) qui t'intéresse. J'ai lu un article dans *Libération* aujourd'hui qui parlait d'une hausse de ventes (de manuscrits originaux / de livres anciens) dans l'Union européenne.

CLAIRE : (Dis donc ! / Tu parles ! / Comme c'est curieux !) Raconte-moi ce qui était dans (l'article / le journal).

JEAN-LOUIS : Il paraît que les Européens cultivent une nostalgie du passé national et le commerce de livres anciens en profite. C'est (intéressant / bizarre / ? ? ?), non ?

CLAIRE : Tu n'as aucune idée. J'ai rencontré (un homme / un inspecteur de police / une personne) aujourd'hui qui m'a conseillé de lire le journal pour apprendre combien le commerce de livres anciens est devenu important.

JEAN-LOUIS : Ça alors ! (Comment était cet homme ? / Qu'est-ce que tu lui as dit ? / ? ? ?). Vas-y, raconte !

CLAIRE : Enfin, il était assez gentil, mais je ne lui ai rien dit. Je suis partie. Viens m'accompagner (au dîner / au restaurant / ? ? ?) et je te raconterai tout.

parler des actualités

News topics	Regarde(z) ce qu'il y a à la une (*front-page stories*) ! Voyons ce qui se passe dans la politique / le monde / la nation / la région. Imagine(z) ce qu'il y a du nouveau dans. . . les arts et la culture / la société / l'écologie / la technologie / les affaires / les sports / les voyages / les faits divers (*human-interest stories*) / la météo ! Est-ce que tu as lu cet article sur. . . ? / Qu'en penses-tu ? Est-ce que vous avez lu cet article ? / Qu'en pensez-vous ?
Crimes and accidents	Il y a eu un attentat (*attack*) meurtrier / un assassinat / un problème / un désastre. Une bombe a explosé. / Une personne a tiré (*fired*) un révolver. Un bâtiment a pris feu (*caught on fire*). / Il y a eu un accident sur l'autoroute. Quelqu'un a été tué (*killed*). / Dix personnes ont été blessées (*injured*). On a arrêté (*arrested*) quelqu'un. / On a interviewé des témoins (*witnesses*). Le tribunal ordonne une enquête (*investigation*). / On intente un procès (*trial*).
Politics and business	Il y a eu une manifestation (*protest*) / une grève (*strike*) / une crise / un incident. On entreprend des négotiations. / On passe un accord.

parler des actualités ***(continued)***

Politics and business	Les ouvriers (*workers*) font la grève. / Le syndicat (*union*) exige une réponse. On redoute un krach boursier (*stock-market crash*). / La bourse rebondit. Le taux de chômage (*unemployment*) s'accroît. / Le nombre de vols diminue.
Society and sports	Il y a une nouvelle exposition (*exhibit*) / un spectacle (*show*) / une pièce (*play*). Il y a eu un match / une tournée / un championnat (de foot, de boxe, etc.). L'équipe a gagné 10 à 3. / On a perdu 3 à 10.

Pour aller plus loin : CULTURE

ACTIVITÉ D : Écoutez/Regardez les actualités en direct à la radio ou à la télé ou sur Internet. C'est gratuit ! Consultez votre cahier électronique !

5.9 Vocabulaire personnel **Pensez à votre climat** et à ce qui se passe ces jours-ci. Pour chaque catégorie, **faites une liste** de cinq à dix mots importants que vous pouvez utiliser pour décrire le temps et les sujets d'actualité qui vous intéressent. Consultez un dictionnaire si nécessaire.

1. Les saisons chez vous.
2. Le temps qu'il fait en chaque saison.
3. Les sujets d'actualité dont on parle le plus souvent au niveau international.
4. Les sujets d'actualité dont on parle le plus souvent au niveau national.
5. Les sujets d'actualité dont on parle le plus souvent au niveau régional ou local.
6. Les sujets d'actualité qui vous intéressent le plus souvent.

montrer l'intérêt ou l'indifférence

To show interest	Ah, bon ? / Vraiment ? / Sans blague ? / Tu plaisantes ? Dis donc ! / Tiens, tiens ! / Tu parles ! / Pas possible ! / Ça alors ! C'est bien intéressant/formidable/bizarre/choquant ! Comme c'est curieux/passionnant/extraordinaire/incroyable ! Raconte(z)-moi tout ! Vas-y ! / Allez-y !
To show indifference	Ah, bon. / Je vois. / D'accord. / Tant pis, eh ? Ce n'est pas mon truc/affaire/genre. Cela ne me regarde pas. / Cela ne m'intéresse pas. Je n'y suis pour rien. / Je ne m'y mêle pas. / Ça m'est égal. Je ne le/la/les déteste pas, mais. . . Ça arrive ces choses-là. / Ça arrive à tout le monde. Hélas, on fait ce qu'on peut. / Il n'y a pas de solution simple. Que veux-tu ? Que voulez-vous ? C'est comme ça. Voilà.

5.10 À vous **Imaginez** que vous êtes dans les situations suivantes. **Que dites-vous ?** Êtes-vous intéressé(e) ou indifférent(e) ? Avec un(e) partenaire, écrivez un petit dialogue pour chaque situation. Jouez des scènes pour la classe.

1. Vous attendez le commencement du cours de français et un(e) camarade de classe amorce une conversation sur le temps.
2. Pendant votre trajet à l'aéroport, le chauffeur de taxi vous parle de son fils qui est au chômage.
3. Vos amis commencent à parler des fluctuations de la bourse (*stock market*).
4. Vous dînez au restaurant avec des amis qui discutent des prochaines élections au Sénégal.
5. Un inconnu que vous rencontrez au café vous parle de l'importance de conserver l'énergie.
6. Une vendeuse dans un magasin commence à critiquer les acteurs dans un film que vous avez beaucoup aimé.

décrire le temps

Seasons and climates	C'est l'automne / l'hiver / le printemps / l'été. C'est la saison pluvieuse / sèche. C'est une journée automnale / hivernale / printanière / estivale. C'est une zone équatoriale / tropicale / tempérée / polaire. C'est un climat pluvieux / sec / maritime / désertique / d'altitude / venteux. Le coucher du soleil est à 18h32. / Le lever du soleil est à 6h46. La marée basse (*low tide*) est à 10h12. / La marée haute est à 16h21.
Temperature	Aujourd'hui, on atteindra 15 degrés (Celsius). La température maximale / minimale est. . . Il fait chaud / frais / froid / un froid glacial. Il gèle. C'est une canicule (*heat wave*). / Ce sont les jours caniculaires (*dog days*). Il y a une vague de froid / un coup de froid.
Precipitation and atmosphere	Il fait beau / du soleil / mauvais / un temps variable / un temps maussade Pleuvoir : il pleut / il y a de la pluie / une averse (*downpour*) Neiger : il neige / il y a de la neige / une tempête de neige Grêler : il grêle / il y a de la grêle (*hail*) Il y a de la glace / tout est couvert de glace / les routes sont verglacées Il y a un orage / une tempête / un ouragan (*hurricane*) Voilà un grondement de tonnerre (*m.*) / un coup de foudre (*f.*) Le temps est nuageux / le ciel est couvert / il y a des nuages Il fait du brouillard / un temps brumeux / un temps de brume (*foggy*) Il y a du vent / du vent à rafales / des rafales (*gusts*) / une brise / une tornade C'est le mistral / la tramontane (*types of winds*) qui souffle.

Culture

Le **mistral** est un vent très violent qui souffle surtout en Provence, dans le sud de la France. Il tient son nom d'un poète provençal, Frédéric de Mistral. La **tramontane** est un vent très froid qui vient du nord, qui passe à travers les montagnes et qui souffle dans les régions méditérranéennes.

5.11 Le bulletin météorologique Imaginez un **bulletin météorologique** typique pour chacune des villes ou régions francophones suivantes pendant la saison indiquée. Parlez du climat, de la température, et du temps qu'il a fait hier, du temps qu'il fait aujourd'hui et du temps qu'il va faire (utilisez le futur proche : **aller** + *infinitif*) ce soir et demain.

MODÈLE : en hiver, à Baton Rouge, en Louisiane →
C'est un climat tropical. La température va atteindre 25 degrés. Hier, il a plu, mais aujourd'hui il fait du soleil et il y a du vent. Demain il va faire un peu plus chaud et le ciel va être couvert.

1. en été, à Fort-de-France, en Martinique
2. en hiver, à Québec, au Canada
3. au printemps, à Genève, en Suisse
4. pendant la saison sèche, à Bamako, au Mali
5. pendant la saison pluvieuse, à Tahiti, en Polynésie
6. dans six mois, dans votre région

la France

Rencontrez une Française ! Regardez la vidéo et consultez votre cahier d'activités !

5.12 Discutez au café Imaginez que vous êtes dans un café à Paris. Tout le monde discute des actualités et du temps. Écrivez un sujet d'actualité qui vous intéresse sur une feuille de papier. Circulez dans la classe et **essayez de commencer une conversation** avec vos camarades. Commencez en parlant du temps, et puis introduisez votre sujet. À votre tour, montrez votre intérêt ou votre indifférence pour les sujets introduits par les autres. Essayez de parler avec autant de gens que possible !

MODÈLE : Des jeunes ont saccagé (*vandalized*) une école.
—Salut ! Il fait beau aujourd'hui, n'est-ce pas ? Est-ce que tu as lu cet article sur le vandalisme. . . ?

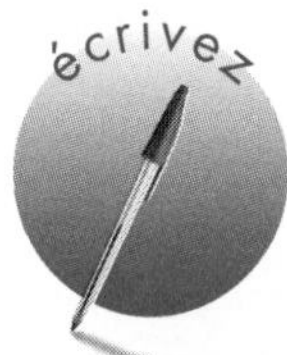

À l'écrit *première étape*

5.13 Le journal francophone Il y a un nouveau journal francophone qu'on publie pour les étudiants de français aux États-Unis. On cherche des journalistes qui peuvent relier (*to link together*) la culture américaine et le monde francophone. Imaginez que vous voulez devenir journaliste et écrire des articles pour ce journal. Choisissez la rubrique (*section*) du journal qui vous intéresse le plus : la politique, l'écologie, la société, la culture, la technologie, l'économie, les sports, les voyages. Puis, **faites une liste** de quatre ou cinq idées d'articles que vous pourriez écrire pour cette rubrique du journal. Échangez vos listes avec des camarades de classe, offrez des corrections possibles et indiquez quel article de votre partenaire vous intéresse le plus.

De mauvaises nouvelles

Épisode 2

Structures *les adverbes*

5.14 Le commerce de livres anciens Claire et Jean-Louis décident de trouver un petit restaurant dans la rue Mouffetard. Jean-Louis apporte l'article sur le commerce de livres anciens qu'il a lu dans le journal. En voici une copie. **Lisez l'article.** Ensuite, **soulignez** tous **les adverbes** dans l'article (des mots qui modifient un verbe ou un adjectif), et puis **réfléchissez à ces questions** : Quelles sont les similarités entre les adverbes en ce qui concerne la forme ? la place de l'adverbe dans la phrase ? et l'usage des adverbes ?

Le commerce de livres anciens : retour au temps perdu ou nouveau marché noir ?

Depuis le début du millenium, le marché de livres rares et anciens connaît un essor sans précédent. De plus en plus, les Français dépensent leur argent pour augmenter leurs collections de livres rares, de bouquins anciens, de premières éditions et de manuscrits originaux. Les bouquinistes parisiens sont carrément inondés par des demandes de livres ou d'éditions spécifiques, et ils vendent rapidement des bouquins sur leurs étalages que personne, depuis dix ans, n'avait probablement touchés.

Qu'est-ce qui provoque cette hausse des ventes incontestablement rapide ? D'après les économistes, ce phénomène témoigne d'un changement bien curieux de la mentalité du Français moyen suite au développement de l'Union européenne. «Tandis que le marché commun a été initié il y a déjà presque cinquante ans», dit Julien Philippe, professeur à la Sorbonne, «l'Europe en tant qu'être résolument uni n'existe vraiment que depuis les premières années du millenium. Ce n'est que récemment que les Français se voient bien intégrés à l'Europe. Évidemment, cette nouvelle passion pour les livres anciens vient d'une nostalgie pour un temps perdu.» Selon les spécialistes, c'est le passé national et l'ère pré-technologique qui nous manquent et que l'on recherche en achetant des livres anciens.

Pourtant, il existe peut-être une autre raison moins innocente pour expliquer ce phénomène. Une source anonyme qui travaille étroitement avec la police nous informe que ce marché vivifié est décidément lié aux activités clandestines d'un groupe de criminels qui veulent profiter économiquement de ce commerce mal réglé par l'état.

les adverbes

Adverbs (**les adverbes**) are used to modify verbs, adjectives, or other adverbs. They function much like English adverbs, many of which end in *-ly* (*quickly*) and are formed from adjectives (*quick*).

Formation of adverbs:

- Generally, use the *feminine form of an adjective* (**naturelle, longue,** etc.) and add the ending -**ment**: **naturellement, longuement.**
- With adjectives that end in **-i** (like **vrai**) or **-u** (like **résolu**), use the *masculine form* + **ment**: **résolument, vraiment.**
- With adjectives that end in **-ant** (like **constant**) or **-ent** (like **évident**), *drop the final* **-nt** and add the ending **-mment**: **constamment, évidemment.**
- There are some *irregular adverbs* that do not follow this pattern:

bon(ne) → **bien**	mauvais(e) → **mal**
meilleur(e) → **mieux**	petit(e) → **peu**
bref/brève → **brièvement**	gentil(le) → **gentiment**
énorme → **énormément**	précis(e) → **précisément**

- Some *common adverbs* of time, place, frequency, and quantity that do not have corresponding adjectives are:

Time:	**aujourd'hui, hier, demain, maintenant, tard, tôt**
Place:	**ici, là, partout** (*everywhere*), **quelque part** (*somewhere*)
Frequency:	**vite, déjà, enfin, souvent, toujours, jamais, quelquefois**
Quantity:	**assez, beaucoup, trop peu**

Placement of adverbs:

- Generally, with simple verb tenses, place the adverb *after the verb*: On me donne **systématiquement** tous les dossiers.
- Some adverbs of time, place, frequency, and quantity can be placed *at the beginning or end of the sentence*: **Maintenant,** on fait une enquête. On voyage **partout.**
- With adverbs that modify adjectives, place the adverb *before the adjective* to be modified: C'est une histoire **bien** intéressante.
- With compound verb tenses, usually the adverb is placed *after the auxiliary verb and before the participle*: Il a **beaucoup** dit.
- With adverbs of time and place and with long adverbs in compound verb phrases, the adverbs are placed *after the participle* or at the *end of the sentence*: J'ai lu l'article **hier**. Il a parlé **différemment** des autres.
- With negative compound verb phrases, *short adverbs follow* the **pas** or other negative term, *longer adverbs and* **peut-être** *precede* the **pas** or other negative term, while a few *adverbs follow the participle* (**longtemps, vite, aujourd'hui**): Je n'ai pas **bien** dormi. Il n'a **peut-être** pas envoyé le message. On n'est pas resté **longtemps**.

5.15 Vraiment ? Claire réagit à l'article que Jean-Louis vient de lui montrer. Remplissez les blancs avec **un adverbe** formé de l'adjectif donné.

1. Je suis (absolu) ____________________ étonnée.
2. L'article est très (petit) ____________________ rassurant.
3. L'auteur dit que les bouquinistes sont (constant) ____________________ en train de vendre des livres anciens ces jours-ci.
4. Hier, j'ignorais (complet) ____________________ l'existence de ce phénomène.
5. Penses-tu que cet article soit (bon) ____________________ recherché ?
6. (Heureux) ____________________, les économistes croient que c'est de la nostalgie et pas du crime organisé.
7. J'attends (patient) ____________________ le retour du bouquiniste, mais j'ai peur de ce qu'il va dire.
8. J'ai fait de la recherche (consciencieux) ____________________ ce matin à la bibliothèque.
9. Ce monsieur au café m'a parlé (précis) ____________________ de cet article.
10. Il a (bref) ____________________ fait allusion à cette idée d'un marché noir, mais je ne crois pas que ce soit la raison pour laquelle on vend tant de livres.

Pour aller plus loin : CULTURE

ACTIVITÉ E : Découvrez la beauté des manuscrits français anciens. Consultez votre cahier électronique !

5.16 Incontestablement Imaginez que vous êtes à Paris au même restaurant que Claire et Jean-Louis et que vous voyez leurs réactions à l'article qu'ils sont en train de lire. **Faites des phrases** en mélangeant les sujets, les verbes et les adverbes (que vous formez des adjectifs donnés) de la liste suivante.

MODÈLE : Cette jeune femme lit **attentivement**.

Cette jeune femme	lire	mauvais
Cet homme	réagir	attentif
Claire et Jean-Louis	regarder	violent
Le serveur	ne pas écouter	vif
Les autres clients	discuter	naïf
Je	dîner	tranquille
Nous	écrire	patient
	ne pas attendre	bon
	parler	gentil

5.17 Sûrement Voici quelques phrases que vous entendez en écoutant indiscrètement la discussion entre Claire et Jean-Louis au restaurant. **Ajoutez un adverbe** à chaque phrase. Vous pouvez choisir n'importe quel adverbe qui vous vient à l'esprit. Soyez imaginatif/imaginative !

MODÈLE : Mon directeur de thèse a publié son livre sur le roman épistolaire en France. →

Mon directeur de thèse a *récemment* publié son livre sur le roman épistolaire en France.

1. Nicolas n'a pas vendu le manuscrit.
2. Nous allons voir Nicolas la semaine prochaine.
3. Il a fait un voyage à Tahiti.
4. Cet article est exagéré.
5. Gilles LaFfont a parlé de cet article.

Structures *les prépositions suivies de noms géographiques*

Pour aller plus loin : CULTURE

ACTIVITÉ F : Apprenez un peu plus au sujet des DOM-TOM. Consultez votre cahier électronique !

5.18 La météo du monde francophone Après le dîner, Claire rentre à son hôtel et se couche tôt. Le matin suivant, elle se réveille et écoute les prévisions suivantes à la radio. Avec un partenaire, (1) **soulignez** toutes **les prépositions** qui précèdent les noms géographiques et (2) **répondez** à ces questions : Quelles sont les différences entre les prépositions employées avec des noms de villes, des noms d'îles, des noms de pays, des noms de continents et des noms de régions, de provinces ou d'états américains ? Pouvez-vous décrire comment fonctionnent les prépositions suivies de noms géographiques ?

EN EUROPE : Les nuages restent nombreux pendant une bonne partie de la journée de Bruxelles (en Belgique) jusqu'à Genève (en Suisse). Quelques averses en Provence et au Languedoc-Roussillon. En Corse, quelques éclaircies se développent.

EN POLYNÉSIE : De Tahiti juqu'à Bora-Bora, le soleil brille et la température reste entre 22 et 26 degrés Celsius. Quelques nuages passent de l'Australie jusqu'à la Nouvelle-Calédonie.

EN AMÉRIQUE : Au Québec, risque de neige pendant la nuit, et des températures minimales de −2 degrés de Québec jusqu'à Toronto. Aux États-Unis, à Montpelier dans le Vermont, brouillards matinaux, et à Baton-Rouge en Louisiane, un temps variable. Aux Antilles, un ciel chargé à Haïti, à la Guadeloupe et à la Martinique. En Guyane, des averses et une marée haute provoquent des inondations locales.

la France

Que dit Sophie du climat et des infos ? Regardez la vidéo et consultez votre cahier d'activités !

les prépositions suivies de noms géographiques

Although there are some exceptions, prepositions of geographical location (*les prépositions avec les noms géographiques*) follow some general rules.

To describe going *to* or being *at/in* a place:

- With *cities* and *islands*, use only the preposition **à**: Il y a du vent à Paris, à Baton-Rouge et à Haïti, à Cuba, à Québec. (exceptions: when names include a definite article—au Havre, au Caire, à la Nouvelle-Orléans, à la Martinique, à la Guadeloupe; when islands are also regions—en Corse)
- With *masculine countries* and *regions*, use **au** or **aux**: Il y a des orages au Sénégal et au Québec, et il y a des pluies aux États-Unis. (exceptions: words beginning with a vowel—en Israël, en Iran, en Afghanistan; city-states—à Monaco)
- With *masculine states and provinces*, we commonly use **dans l'état de, dans la province de,** or **dans le**: Il y a du soleil dans le Vermont. (exceptions: au Québec, au Texas, au Nouveau-Mexique)
- With *feminine continents, countries, regions,* and *states*, use **en**: Il fait beau en France et en Côte d'Ivoire en Afrique, mais il fait chaud en Louisiane et en Casamance.

To describe coming *from*, leaving *from*, or originating *from* a place:

- With *feminine continents, countries, regions, states, provinces;* and with *most cities and islands*, use only **de**: Il vient d'Afrique, de Côte d'Ivoire, de Provence, de Louisiane, de Port-au-Prince. (exceptions: cities whose names include a definite article—de la Haye, du Caire, de la Nouvelle-Orléans—and the island-DOMs—de la Martinique, de la Guadeloupe, de la Réunion)
- With *masculine countries, regions, states*, and *provinces*, use **du, de l'**, or **des**: Il vient de l'Ontario, du Canada. (exception: all countries with names beginning with vowels—d'Israël, d'Iran, d'Afghanistan)

5.19 La météo d'Afrique La météo francophone continue. Ajoutez **des prépositions** (ou **des prépositions + articles**). Si vous ne connaissez pas les noms de tous ces endroits, consultez une carte du continent africain.

__________________ Afrique : Au nord, __________________ Rabat (__________________ Maroc) jusqu' __________________ Tunis (__________________ Tunisie), la température reste élevée. __________ __________ Sénégal jusqu' __________________ Côte d'Ivoire, quelques nuages. __________________ Bénin jusqu' __________________ Congo, le vent souffle fort et les rafales d'ouest à sud-ouest atteignent 75 km/h sur la côte. __________________ Seychelles et __________________ l'île de la Réunion, quelques averses, mais __________________ Antananarivo, la capitale __________________ Madagascar, un ciel bleu et du soleil.

5.20 Où vont-ils ? Beaucoup de gens voyagent ces jours-ci. **Décrivez les voyages** des personnes suivantes et imaginez pourquoi ils voyagent.

MODÈLE : Philippe Aucoin : la Nouvelle-Orléans, Louisiane → San Francisco, Californie →

Philippe Aucoin voyage de la Nouvelle-Orléans, en Louisiane, jusqu'à San Francisco, en Californie parce qu'il assiste à un colloque (*conference*) d'hôteliers.

1. Henri Hébert : Lafayette, Louisiane, États-Unis → Montréal, Québec, Canada
2. Zachary Richard : New York, New York, États-Unis → Pointe-à-Pitre, Guadeloupe → Papeete, Tahiti, Polynésie
3. Monsieur Thuillier, le directeur des études littéraires à l'Université de Sainte-Foy : Québec, Canada, Amérique du nord → Genève, Suisse, Europe → Dakar, Sénégal, Afrique
4. Talal Lateef : Paris, France → Saint-Malo, Bretagne, France → Monte-Carlo, Monaco
5. Nicolas Gustave : Tunis, Tunisie → Ajaccio, Corse → Paris, France
6. La tante Émilie : Paris, France, Europe → Luxembourg, Luxembourg → Casablanca, Maroc, Afrique du nord

5.21 Et vous ? Avec un partenaire, **posez-vous des questions** sur les destinations suivantes. **Répondez** en donnant une raison pour laquelle vous voulez (ou ne voulez pas) y aller. Essayez d'utiliser un adverbe dans votre réponse !

MODÈLE : Tahiti, Polynésie →

—Veux-tu aller à Tahiti, en Polynésie ?

—Oui, j'aime énormément aller à la plage. *ou*

—Non, je n'aime pas vraiment le soleil.

1. Abidjan, Côte d'Ivoire, Afrique
2. Cannes, Côte d'Azur, France, Europe
3. Bamako, Mali, Afrique
4. Bruxelles, Belgique, Europe
5. Évian, Rhone-Alpes, France
6. Zermatt, Alpes, Suisse, Europe
7. Hanoi, Vietnam, Asie du sud-est
8. Fort-de-France, Martinique, Antilles

Avant d'écouter

5.22 Avant les mauvaises nouvelles En petits groupes, posez les questions suivantes et **répondez** selon vos goûts personnels.

1. Quand on vous apprend de bonnes nouvelles, quelles émotions ressentez-vous ? Et quand on vous apprend de mauvaises nouvelles ?
2. Quelles bonnes nouvelles avez-vous entendues récemment ? Quelles mauvaises nouvelles ?
3. Quand vous avez besoin d'un conseil (*advice*), à qui demandez-vous de l'aide ? Pourquoi choisissez-vous cette personne ou ces personnes ?
4. Êtes-vous généralement ouvert(e) aux conseils des autres ? reconnaissant(e) à ceux qui essaient de vous aider ? têtu(e) et rigide dans vos pensées ? méfiant(e) des conseils des autres ? Pourquoi ?
5. Quelle est votre réaction quand quelqu'un que vous ne connaissez pas bien essaie de vous donner des conseils (non demandés) ?

écoutez

De mauvaises nouvelles

Trois jours plus tard, Claire se lève et ouvre la fenêtre de sa petite chambre à l'Hôtel Quasimodo. Il semble que toutes les feuilles soient tombées des arbres pendant la nuit, que le vent qui souffle sans cesse devienne de plus en plus froid et que la couleur du ciel grisâtre ne se distingue plus de la couleur des pierres de la cathédrale de Notre-Dame. Enfin, l'automne est vraiment arrivé. Le téléphone interrompt ses réflexions. C'est Jean-Louis avec de bonnes nouvelles : Nicolas Gustave est revenu de ses vacances et rouvre son étalage de bouquiniste aujourd'hui. C'est aujourd'hui que Claire apprendra si le manuscrit de Laclos existe toujours. Se peut-il qu'elle lise le manuscrit ce soir ? Elle a hâte de savoir ce que Nicolas sait du manuscrit et se dépêche d'aller à l'étalage sans attendre Jean-Louis qui la rejoint après quelques minutes. . .

Maintenant, **écoutez le dialogue sur votre CD**. Consultez le vocabulaire et isez les notes culturelles pour mieux comprendre le dialogue, et puis répondez aux questions suivantes.

VOCABULAIRE

Apprendre des nouvelles

en chair et en os	*in the flesh (and bones)*
sous clé	*under lock and key*
une décennie	*decade*
frissonner	*to shiver*
la chair de poule	*goose bumps*
être navré(e)	*to be sorry*
il m'a fallu	*past tense of* il me faut
un entrepôt	*warehouse, storage house*
être ravi(e)	*to be delighted*
puis-je	*inversion of* je peux
de mal en pis	*from bad to worse*
qui pis est	*what's even worse*

Le climat tropical

un colon	*colonist*
le sable noir	*black sand*
le cocotier	*coconut tree*
la bougainvillée	*flower found in Polynesia, named for Bougainville*
un ouragan	*hurricane*
une inondation	*flood*
une chute de boue	*mudslide*
le paradis	*paradise, heaven*
l'enfer	*hell*

Pour aller plus loin : CULTURE

ACTIVITÉ G : Lisez des extraits du *Voyage* de Bougainville et du *Supplément au Voyage de Bougainville* de Diderot. Consultez votre cahier électronique !

Pour aller plus loin : CULTURE

ACTIVITÉ H : Lisez un extrait du *Mariage de Loti* dans lequel Pierre Loti décrit comment il a rencontré sa femme tahitienne. Consultez votre cahier électronique !

Culture

L'île de **Tahiti,** dont la capitale est la ville de Papeete, est une des nombreuses îles qui forment les deux grands archipels de la **Polynésie française** : **l'Archipel de la société** et **l'Archipel des Tuamotu**. Les Français et les Anglais, parmi eux les célèbres explorateurs Bougainville et Cooke, ont exploré les îles de l'Océanie au cours des 18ème et 19ème siècles. En 1847, suite aux combats violents, la reine Pomaré IV, reine des Tahitiens, a accepté un protectorat de la France. Son fils, le roi Pomaré V, a abdiqué en 1880 et Tahiti et ses îles voisines se sont intégrés aux Établissements français de l'Océanie (EFO), une partie de l'empire français, jusqu'après la Seconde Guerre mondiale quand la Polynésie française est devenue un Territoire d'Outre-mer de la France (TOM). Aujourd'hui, elle est une Collectivité d'Outre-mer (COM) avec beaucoup d'autonomie. De nombreux écrivains et artistes français, y compris Louis de Bougainville, Paul Gauguin et Pierre Loti, ont été attirés par la culture tahitienne qu'ils ont trouvée d'une beauté exotique incomparable. D'autres, des philosophes comme Denis Diderot et Montesquieu, n'ont jamais visité l'île mais ont été attirés par l'idée d'une culture dite «primitive». Ils ont imaginé ce pays comme une utopie où les gens peuvent vivre selon leurs passions sans les contraintes des lois ou de la religion.

Après avoir écouté

5.23 D'accord ou pas d'accord ? Après avoir écouté le dialogue entre Claire et Nicolas Gustave, lisez les phrases suivantes et **donnez votre opinion. Discutez** en petits groupes.

	D'accord	Pas d'accord
1. Claire est impatiente de savoir si le manuscrit existe.	_______	_______
2. Nicolas a de bonnes nouvelles pour Claire.	_______	_______
3. Un homme martiniquais a acheté le manuscrit de Laclos.	_______	_______
4. Nicolas veut aider Claire à racheter le manuscrit.	_______	_______
5. Le manuscrit est un roman d'amour.	_______	_______
6. Nicolas veut que Claire visite la Martinique.	_______	_______

apprendre une nouvelle à quelqu'un

Breaking news to someone

Sais-tu ce qui m'est arrivé ?
Savez-vous ce qui est arrivé à (quelqu'un) ?
Écoute(z), j'ai quelque chose à te/vous dire. . .

	J'ai des nouvelles / de bonnes nouvelles / de mauvaises nouvelles J'ai quelque chose à dire / à raconter / à avouer / à expliquer Ceci te/vous intéressera. . .
Good news	Tu ne vas pas me croire ! / C'est vraiment magnifique ! C'est fantastique / incroyable / pas possible ! Quelle chance ! / Quel bonheur ! / C'est vraiment incroyable ! Je suis impatient(e) de te/vous dire. . . J'ai hâte de te/vous dire. . . Je suis tout content(e) car (*for*). . . / On a de la chance parce que. . . Tu te rends compte ! / Vous vous rendez compte ! Mais c'est incroyable ! / Je n'arrive pas à le croire !
Bad news	C'est difficile à croire / à dire, mais. . . Il faut que je te/vous dise la vérité. Je suis vraiment désolé(e) Et ce n'est pas tout. . . Jamais deux sans trois. . . Je suis navré(e) de te/vous dire. . . C'est vraiment triste / dommage / incroyable / bouleversant Tout est perdu. / C'est fini. / On est fichu. / Quelle malchance ! Tout n'est pas perdu car. . . / Il faut voir le bon côté. . . Courage ! / Patience !. . . Comme on dit, «après la pluie, le beau temps».

5.24 J'ai des nouvelles Imaginez que vous travaillez comme concierge à l'Hôtel Quasimodo à Paris. **Qu'est-ce que vous pourriez dire** aux clients pour leur apprendre les nouvelles suivantes ? N'oubliez pas de les saluer et de vous présenter (révisez Chapitre 1, si nécessaire) avant de commencer à parler. Faites des dialogues ou jouez ces situations devant la classe.

1. On a décidé de réduire le prix des chambres à cause du mauvais temps qu'il fait ces jours-ci.
2. Le restaurant est fermé parce que le chef vient de démissionner (*to resign*).
3. Un ouragan s'approche de Paris et les clients sont priés de ne pas sortir de l'hôtel cet après-midi.
4. Il n'y a plus d'eau chaude dans les salles de bains.
5. Il y a une grève du métro, mais les autobus et les taxis circulent toujours en ville.

5.25 Ça alors ! Sur une feuille de papier, **écrivez une phrase** pour indiquer quelque chose qui s'est passé récemment dans votre vie (une nouvelle coiffure ? un examen raté ? etc.). **Circulez dans la classe** et apprenez vos nouvelles à vos camarades, sans leur montrer votre papier. Si quelqu'un réagit avec intérêt, faites-leur signer votre papier. La personne qui a reçu le plus grand nombre de signatures gagne !

MODÈLE : Hier, j'ai raté un examen de maths.

—Sais-tu ce qui m'est arrivé hier ? Je suis allé à mon cours d'algèbre, et il y avait un test. Je l'ai raté, complètement raté !

—Ce n'est pas vrai ! Je suis désolé(e) ! (signature) *ou*

—Ah bon. Ce n'est pas grave. Ça arrive à tout le monde. (pas de signature)

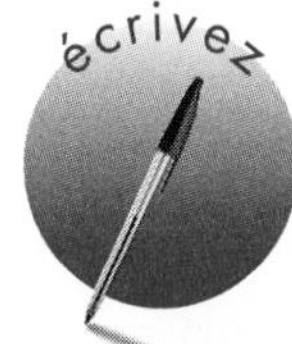

À l'écrit *deuxième étape*

5.26 Votre article de journal Imaginez que vous parlez avec une personne francophone qui habite dans votre région. Choisissez le sujet de l'article que votre camarade a préféré (de l'Activité 13), et **écrivez un dialogue** entre vous et la personne francophone dans lequel :

- vous annoncez les bonnes nouvelles que vous écrivez un article pour le journal francophone !
- vous décrivez brièvement le sujet de votre article
- vous posez des questions afin de savoir ce qu'il/elle pense de ce sujet
- vous imaginez ses réponses (enthousiastes ou indifférentes !)

Finalement, avec un partenaire, révisez vos dialogues et lisez-les à haute voix.

Un fax du patron

Structures *le subjonctif et le subjonctif passé*

5.27 L'oreille indiscrète Après avoir tout expliqué à Jean-Louis, Claire s'assied avec son ami dans un café pour réfléchir. Ils écoutent indiscrètement les conversations des gens qui parlent autour d'eux. Lisez les phrases suivantes et **indiquez** s'il s'agit (a) d'un **souhait** ou d'une **volonté** (*wish/want*), (b) d'une **nécessité**, (c) d'une **émotion**, (d) d'un **doute** ou (e) d'une **opinion**. Quels éléments structurels est-ce que toutes ces phrases ont en commun ?

1. **Il est important que** le président parle de cette situation.
2. **Tu veux qu'**on organise une manifestation pour la semaine prochaine ?
3. **Je suis triste que** nous n'ayons pas les moyens d'aider ces personnes.
4. **Il faut qu'**on apprenne tout ce qui s'est passé avant de réagir.
5. **Vous êtes fâchés que** je dise la vérité.
6. **Nous aimerions que** les gens fassent un effort pour comprendre.
7. **Penses-tu que** ce soit important ?
8. **Je doute que** nous soyons du même avis.

5.28 L'horoscope Claire a du mal à décider de ce qu'elle doit faire maintenant : aller à la Martinique toute seule, inviter Jean-Louis, ou abandonner son projet de recherche. Elle lit son horoscope en espérant y trouver un signe. Lisez son horoscope et puis **répondez aux questions** suivantes.

Pour aller plus loin : CULTURE

ACTIVITÉ 1 : Voulez-vous lire votre horoscope en français ? Consultez votre cahier électronique !

Verseau (du 20 janvier au 18 février)

Travail : *Vous avez peur que tout n'aille pas comme prévu. Il est important que vous surmontiez les obstacles qui vous attendent. Attention aux faux pas ! Votre impulsivité est votre plus grand ennemi ce mois-ci. Il est essentiel de réagir prudemment et d'être calme lors d'une prochaine réunion ou d'un prochain congrès professionnel.*

Amour : *Il semble que votre idée de l'amour ne corresponde pas du tout à celle de la personne aimée. Vous vous en fichez maintenant, mais attention, le coup de foudre qui enflamme votre cœur peut aussi vous aveugler* (to blind). *Bien que vous aimiez parler, il est douteux que vous ayez déjà parlé de vos désirs personnels. Il vaut mieux que vous en parliez maintenant. Il est important de ne pas perdre votre temps. Agissez avant qu'il ne soit trop tard.*

Santé : *Vous êtes incontestablement en bonne forme ! Il est sûr que vous vous portez bien en cette saison. Mais, il est préférable que vous ne buviez plus de boissons caféinées. Étant donné votre niveau d'énergie naturelle, un décaf vous suffit !*

1. Soulignez toutes les expressions de nécessité, de volonté, de doute, d'opinion ou d'émotion. Lesquelles sont suivies par **l'infinitif** et lesquelles par **le subjonctif** ? Pouvez-vous décrire pourquoi ?
2. Entourez tous les verbes qui sont au **subjonctif** et indiquez l'infinitif de ces verbes. Pouvez-vous décrire comment former et employer le subjonctif en analysant ces exemples ?
3. Trouvez-vous un verbe au **subjonctif passé** ? Lequel ? Comment le savez-vous ?
4. En ce qui concerne le travail, est-ce que Claire doit être impulsive ou prudente ? Pourquoi ?
5. En ce qui concerne l'amour, est-ce que Claire doit s'abandonner à ses passions ou réévaluer la situation ? Pourquoi ?
6. En ce qui concerne la santé, est-ce que Claire doit faire l'effort d'améliorer sa santé ou ne pas changer ses habitudes ? Pourquoi ?

le subjonctif

The *subjunctive* (**le subjonctif**) is a mood, rather than a verb tense. It does not describe an action in time, but rather the speaker's attitude toward, or understanding of, an action or condition. It is used to express a supposition, a contingency, or a desire. The *subjunctive* is used, therefore, after clauses that express will (**la volonté**), doubt (**le doute**), emotion (**l'émotion**), necessity (**la nécessité**), or subjective opinion (**l'opinion**). The *subjunctive* is also used after some conjunctions, superlative phrases, and relative clauses when these are used to express personal desires, uncertainty, or subjective opinion.

How do I form the subjunctive?

- The *subjunctive* is formed by adding the endings **-e, -es, -e, -ions, -iez, -ent** to the third person plural present tense stem (**ils/elles** form, drop **-ent**): que vous **surmontiez**, que vous **réagissiez**, que votre idée ne **corresponde** pas.
- The verbs **être** and **avoir** have *completely irregular* subjunctive forms:

  être → que je sois, tu sois, il/elle/on soit, nous soyons, vous soyez, ils/elles soient

  avoir → que j'aie, tu aies, il/elle/on ait, nous ayons, vous ayez, ils/elles aient
- Some irregular verbs have an *irregular subjunctive stem* but take the regular endings:

  faire → que je **fasse**
  savoir → que je **sache**
  pouvoir → que je **puisse**

- Some verbs, most of which are irregular or have spelling changes in the present tense, have *two irregular stems*: one stem for the **nous/vous** forms and one for all other forms:

acheter → que j'achète, que nous achetions	**aller** → que j'aille, que nous allions
appeler → que j'appelle, que nous appelions	**boire** → que je boive, que nous buvions
devoir → que je doive, que nous devions	**envoyer** → que j'envoie, que nous envoyions
jeter → que je jette, que nous jetions	**mourir** → que je meure, que nous mourions
payer → que je paie, que nous payions	**prendre** → que je prenne, que nous prenions
venir → que je vienne, que nous venions	**recevoir** → que je reçoive, que nous recevions
voir → que je voie, que nous voyions	**vouloir** → que je veuille, que nous voulions

- The verbs **falloir** and **pleuvoir** have *irregular* subjunctive forms:

falloir → qu'il faille	**pleuvoir** → qu'il pleuve

Langue

Voici quelques **expressions** qui sont typiquement suivies par **que** + *subjonctif* :

la volonté	**l'émotion**	**la doute**	**la nécessité**	**l'opinion**
aimer	avoir peur	douter	il faut	il est important
aimer mieux	être + *emotion*	il est douteux	il est nécessaire	il est bon
désirer	regretter	il est possible	il est essentiel	il est naturel
souhaiter	craindre	il semble		il est préférable
vouloir	c'est dommage	il se peut		il vaut mieux
suggérer	il est étonnant			penser (*neg or int*)
	il est regrettable			espérer (*neg or int*)
	il est surprenant			croire (*neg or int*)
				trouver (*neg or int*)

When do I use the subjunctive?

- When there is a sentence with *two clauses* connected by **que**, and each clause has a different subject, and the first clause shows *will, doubt, emotion, necessity, or subjective opinion*, then the verb in the second clause takes the *subjunctive*: **Vous avez peur que** tout n'**aille** pas comme prévu. **Il est préférable que** vous ne **buviez** plus de caféine.
- When there is a *conjunction* in the sentences that requires the subjunctive: **Bien que** vous **aimiez** parler. . . Agissez **avant qu'**il ne **soit** trop tard.

- When the *superlative* is followed by a *relative clause* that expresses a *subjective opinion*: C'est **le manuscrit le plus intéressant** qu'on **puisse** imaginer.
- When a *relative clause* indicates doubt or subjectivity: Je cherche un ami **qui soit** fiable.

(Note: you will review the superlative in Chapter 8 and relative clauses in Chapter 9.)

Langue

Voici quelques **conjonctions** qui sont typiquement suivies du **subjonctif** :

à moins que	bien que	jusqu'à ce que	pourvu que	quoique
avant que	de crainte que	où que	quel que	sans que
afin que	de peur que	pour que	qui que	si + *adjectif* + que

Notez qu'avec plusieurs conjonctions où il y a une expression d'incertitude (**avant que, à moins que, de crainte que, de peur que, pourvu que, sans que**), on utilise le **ne** explétif. Ce **ne** explétif n'a aucun sens dans la phrase et n'a rien à faire avec le négatif. C'est une pure formalité. Par exemple, la proposition «Avant que Claire **ne parte**» veut dire la même chose que «Avant que Claire **parte**», mais le **ne** explétif souligne l'idée que Claire n'est pas encore partie.

The subjunctive is NOT used:

- When the first clause expresses *certainty, probability, or an objective (factual) opinion*. In many cases, the use of the *subjunctive* or the *indicative* (present tense, etc.) depends on context. For example:
  - (a) **penser, espérer, croire,** and **trouver** only take the *subjunctive* in the negative or interrogative forms (with inversion only); in an affirmative statement, they do not show doubt (there is no doubt that you think it, whether it is true or not): Je pense qu'elle **a** raison. Je ne pense pas qu'elle **ait** raison. Pensez-vous qu'elle **ait** raison ?
  - (b) **douter** takes the *subjunctive* in the affirmative, but not in the negative (there is no doubt): Je doute qu'elle **sache** la réponse. Je ne doute pas qu'elle **sait** la réponse.
  - (c) **il semble que** is followed by the *subjunctive* (it seems to be so, but there is doubt), while the expression **il me semble que** is followed by the *indicative* (there's no doubt that it seems that way *to you*): Il semble qu'elle **ait** raison. Il me semble qu'elle **a** raison.
  - (d) **être sûr/certain/convaincu que** or **il est clair/évident/probable/vrai que** take the *indicative* in the affirmative and the *subjunctive* in the negative: Je suis sûr que vous **êtes** en forme. Je ne suis pas sûr que vous **soyez** en forme.
- When the *subjects are the same* in the two clauses. In these cases, the first clause is followed by **de** + *l'infinitif*: Elle a peur **de partir**. Elle a peur que **Jean-Louis ne parte**.
- When there is a conjunction that introduces objective information (like **après que, pendant que, parce que, aussitôt que, dès que**), use the indicative: **Après que** vous **finissez** vos devoirs, allez vous coucher. (but: **Bien que** vous **finissiez** vos devoirs toujours très tard . . .)

5.29 Que veux-tu ? Jean-Louis invite Claire à dîner chez lui ce soir pour continuer leur conversation, mais Claire a envie d'être seule pour réfléchir. **Conjuguez les verbes** entre parenthèses **au subjonctif**.

JEAN-LOUIS : Allez, viens chez moi ce soir. Versailles est à 20 minutes de Paris. Je veux qu'on (continuer) ________________ cette conversation et que tu me (dire) ________________ si tu veux aller à la Martinique.

CLAIRE : C'est gentil, mais avant de prendre une décision, il faut que je (réfléchir) ________________ un peu.

JEAN-LOUIS : Il est naturel que tu (vouloir) ________________ réfléchir, mais je doute que tu (avoir) ________________ vraiment envie d'être seule. Tu ne penses pas que je (pouvoir) ________________ t'aider à évaluer le pour et le contre ?

CLAIRE : Si, mais j'ai peur que tu ne (s'attendre) ________________ à une réponse immédiate, et je ne sais pas si j'en aurai une. Ceci dit, je suis contente que tu (faire) ________________ un effort de me consoler avec un repas préparé à la maison.

JEAN-LOUIS : C'est la chose la plus réconfortante que je (savoir) ________________ faire. . . à moins que tu ne (détester) ________________ pas les pâtes. C'est tout ce que j'ai à la maison.

CLAIRE : C'est parfait, mais demain serait mieux pour moi. Donne-moi ton adresse et j'y serai demain soir.

5.30 Vous prenez vos désirs pour des réalités ? Parfois, ce qu'on veut n'est pas toujours possible. **Faites correspondre** la catégorie (à gauche) avec des possibilités (à droite) selon vos propres opinions. Il est possible de redoubler vos réponses. Justifiez vos choix. Ensuite, **faites des phrases** en utilisant le subjonctif, si nécessaire.

MODÈLE : ce qu'on désire →

—Je désire que chaque étudiant dans la classe *reçoive* une bonne note en cours de français.

ce qui est nécessaire →

—Il est nécessaire que nous diminuions la pollution atmosphérique.

Catégories	**Possibilités**
1. ce qu'on désire	a. recevoir une bonne note en cours de français
2. ce qui est nécessaire	b. avoir beaucoup de bons amis
3. ce dont on a peur	c. mettre fin au chômage
4. ce qui est important	d. diminuer la pollution atmosphérique
5. ce qui est possible	e. arrêter les guerres
6. ce dont on est heureux	f. acheter une nouvelle voiture
	g. manger un bon repas
	h. avoir du temps libre
	i. trouver un poste où on est mal payé
	j. être en bonne santé
	k. ? ? ? (à vous d'ajouter d'autres possibilités)

la France

Quels conseils Sophie donne-t-elle aux touristes américains qui visitent la France ? Regardez la vidéo et consultez votre cahier d'activités !

le subjonctif passé

The *past subjunctive* (**le subjonctif passé**) is formed like the **passé composé**, except that the auxiliary verb (**être** or **avoir**) is conjugated in the *subjunctive*. The *subjunctive* auxiliary verb is followed by the past participle, and rules for agreement with the subject or object pronoun are the same as for the **passé composé**. The *past subjunctive* is used in the same circumstances as the present *subjunctive*, except it indicates that the verb in the subordinate (second) clause refers to a past action: Il **est** douteux que vous **ayez** déjà **parlé** de vos émotions. Il **était** douteux que vous **ayez** déjà **parlé** de vos émotions.

Culture

Versailles est une petite ville dans la banlieue au sud de Paris. Elle est célèbre à cause du palais de Versailles, résidence de plusieurs rois de France et des aristocrates qui faisaient partie de leurs cours. En particulier, c'est **Louis XIV**, «le roi soleil», qui a fait de Versailles sa résidence principale à partir de 1661. Les jardins et le parc, réalisés par Le Nôtre, reflètent l'opulence du règne de Louis XIV. On y trouve aussi le Hameau de Marie-Antoinette, épouse de Louis XVI, qui fut guillotinée pendant la Révolution de 1789. Le Hameau est une petite maison champêtre où la reine et ses amies jouaient aux bergères comme dans un drame pastoral. Le Palais et ses jardins accueillent de nombreux touristes chaque année.

5.31 Un moment pour réfléchir Claire rentre à son hôtel où elle a un moment pour penser aux nouvelles de Nicolas. Elle veut continuer à travailler avec Jean-Louis, mais elle n'est pas sûre s'il veut vraiment l'aider à trouver le manuscrit ou s'il l'utilise pour obtenir le manuscrit lui-même. **Conjuguez les verbes** entre parenthèses **au subjonctif passé**.

1. Avant que je (aller) ____________________ voir Nicolas, Jean-Louis m'avait téléphoné.
2. Il est étonnant qu'il m'(téléphoner) ____________________ ce matin s'il voulait garder le manuscrit pour lui-même.

3. Il est regrettable que nous (se rencontrer) ____________________ en de telles circonstances.

4. Je l'ai trouvé fort agréable, mais je suis triste qu'il m'(mentir) ____________________.

5. Il est toujours un peu surpris que cette révélation m'(choquer/tant) ____________________.

5.32 Chez Jean-Louis Le lendemain, Claire prend le RER pour aller à Versailles, dans la banlieue de Paris, où habite Jean-Louis. Quand elle arrive à son appartement, Jean-Louis est tout agité. Quelqu'un a fouillé (*rifled through*) son appartement ! Quelqu'un a forcé la porte et a jeté ses affaires partout. Lisez la conversation entre Claire et Jean-Louis et remplissez les blancs avec le **subjonctif,** l'**indicatif** ou l'**infinitif** du verbe entre parenthèses.

CLAIRE : Il faut que tu (appeler) ____________________ la police tout de suite !

JEAN-LOUIS : Mais, on ne m'a rien volé. Que veux-tu que je leur (dire) ____________________ ?

CLAIRE : Il est nécessaire d'(expliquer) ____________________ ce qui s'est passé.

JEAN-LOUIS : Mais, je suis certain que toutes mes affaires (être) ____________________ ici.

CLAIRE : Je pense que tu (devoir) ____________________ téléphoner quand même.

JEAN-LOUIS : Pourquoi ? Si bouleversant que ce (être) ____________________, il n'y a pas eu de vol. Mon voisin a entendu un bruit, et quand il est venu voir ce qui s'était passé, le voleur s'était enfui.

CLAIRE : Il est important que les policiers (savoir) ____________________ quand il y a des vols dans le quartier. Pense à tes voisins.

JEAN-LOUIS : C'est vrai, mais penses-tu que ce crime (être) ____________________ lié au manuscrit ?

CLAIRE : Je sais que tout (être) ____________________ possible... mais j'en doute.

JEAN-LOUIS : Bon, tu (avoir) ____________________ raison. Je (aller) ____________________ appeler la police. Mais, c'est dommage qu'on (ne... pas/pouvoir) ____________________ dîner ensemble comme prévu.

CLAIRE : Ce n'est pas grave. Je (pouvoir) ____________________ attendre.

JEAN-LOUIS : D'accord. Dans ce cas, voici mon bureau. Tu seras plus confortable ici. Fais comme chez toi, et après on sortira dîner ensemble et on fera un petit tour dans les jardins du palais de Versailles.

Pour aller plus loin : CULTURE

ACTIVITÉ J : Voulez-vous visiter virtuellement le château et les jardins du palais de Versailles ? Consultez votre cahier électronique !

5.33 Les conseils des policiers Les policiers arrivent pour surveiller l'appartement. Ils prennent des notes et puis ils font des remarques et donnent des conseils à Jean-Louis. **Terminez leurs phrases** en employant le **subjonctif,** le **subjonctif passé** ou l'**indicatif**.

MODÈLE : Il faut que vous. . . **changiez** vos serrures (*locks*).

1. Il est important que vous. . .
2. Il est vrai que les criminels. . .
3. Je ne doute pas que vous. . .
4. Nous voulons que. . .
5. Il est essentiel que. . .
6. Je regrette que. . .

Pendant que Claire attend dans le bureau, un fax sort de la machine devant elle. Elle ne peut pas s'empêcher de le lire. . .

Un fax du patron

À : Monsieur ROYER
De : Monsieur ROLLAND
Date : 22/09/03 18 : 46
Réf : dossier 2234

Je viens de recevoir votre fax et la copie de l'article que vous m'avez envoyée hier. Selon moi, il n'y a aucune raison de paniquer. Autant que je sache, le public est du même avis° que les économistes. Quoi que l'auteur en dise, tout le monde sait que la nostalgie est la cause principale du mouvement récent au marché de livres anciens. Voilà mon opinion.

avis: opinion

Personnellement, j'ai l'impression que tout va à merveille° en ce qui concerne votre fonction° actuelle.° De toute façon, j'ai quelques conseils à vous donner. Il y aura des risques à prendre pour atteindre° notre but. Donc, il est important que vous réfléchissiez bien avant d'agir. Il est possible que d'autres négociants° visent à° acheter ce même manuscrit. Il faut avancer prudemment. Je vous assure que vous recevrez tous les fonds° nécessaires, et davantage,° jusqu'à ce que vous réussissiez à vérifier l'authenticité du manuscrit et à me le rapporter. Tant mieux si vous arrivez à visiter quelques pays exotiques en même temps. Ceci dit, il est hors de question de revenir sans le manuscrit, mais je suis sûr que vous y arriverez. Je vous conseille de continuer sur le chemin° que vous avez déjà choisi.

Rolland

superbly
assignment/current
reach, achieve a goal
merchants/to aim for, to try to
funds/and then some
path

Après avoir lu

5.34 D'accord ou pas d'accord ? Après avoir lu le fax ci-dessus, lisez les phrases suivantes et **donnez vos opinions** personnelles. **Discutez** en petits groupes.

	D'accord	Pas d'accord
1. Monsieur Rolland est le partenaire de Jean-Louis.	______	______
2. Jean-Louis s'inquiète à cause de l'article dans le journal.	______	______
3. Monsieur Rolland est un peu paniqué aussi.	______	______
4. M. Rolland est content du travail de Jean-Louis.	______	______
5. Jean-Louis a des fonds limités pour trouver et acheter le manuscrit.	______	______

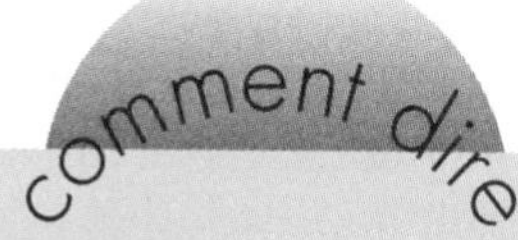

exprimer son opinion et donner des conseils

To express an opinion

À mon avis / D'après moi / Selon moi / Quant à moi / En ce qui me concerne. . .

Personnellement, je pense / crois / espère / trouve / estime que. . . (+ *indicatif*)

Il me semble que / J'ai l'impression que. . . (+ *indicatif*)

Je suis du même avis que (quelqu'un). / On est du même avis.

Autant que je sache / À ma connaissance / Sans le moindre doute. . .

Précisément / Effectivement / En effet / Au fait. . .

Quoi qu'il en dise / Quoi qu'il en soit / Malgré (*despite*) cela. . .

Au contraire / Contrairement / Voilà mon opinion / C'est mon point de vue.

To give advice

Il faut que. . . (+ *subjonctif*) / Je te/vous/lui conseille de. . . (+ *infinitif*)

Il est important / essentiel / nécessaire que. . . (+ *subjonctif*)

Pourquoi ne pas (+ *infinitif*) ? / Vous devriez. . . (+ *infinitif*)

Il est impensable de (+ *infinitif*) / Il est hors de question de (+ *infinitif*)

Tant mieux si. . . (+ *indicatif*) / Tant pis (pour lui/elle/eux) si. . . (+ *indicatif*)

5.35 Que me conseillez-vous ? Pour chaque situation suivante, **donnez votre opinion** et **puis donnez des conseils** pour résoudre le problème.

1. Votre ami(e) veut devenir médecin et travailler dans un centre dispensaire (*clinic*) pour les gens pauvres qui n'ont pas d'assurance-maladies.
2. Votre petit(e) ami(e) veut tout abandonner et faire le tour du monde en bateau l'année prochaine. . . et il/elle veut le faire tout(e) seul(e).
3. Vos voisins veulent que tous les gens du quartier fassent du recyclage, mais il y a une famille qui résiste parce que tous les membres sont trop occupés et n'ont pas le temps de séparer leurs ordures.
4. Le maire (*mayor*) de votre ville veut augmenter les impôts pour construire un nouveau parking au centre-ville.
5. Votre ami(e) dépense beaucoup d'argent en utilisant ses cartes de crédit quoiqu'il/elle soit au chômage depuis six mois.

5.36 Des conseils pour Claire et Jean-Louis ? Claire et Jean-Louis veulent la même chose : le manuscrit qui est maintenant la propriété d'un homme martiniquais. Elle veut l'étudier et lui, il doit l'acheter pour son patron. Elle a des fonds limités; lui, il a beaucoup d'argent. La situation devient de plus en plus dangereuse. Que leur conseillez-vous ? **Écrivez des conseils** sur une feuille de papier et puis échangez vos papiers avec ceux de vos camarades de classe. **Réagissez** à leurs conseils (montrez le désaccord, l'indifférence ou l'enthousiasme).

MODÈLE : —Il faut que Claire s'arrête de collaborer avec Jean-Louis ! Voilà mon opinion.

—Personnellement, je pense qu'elle devrait l'utiliser pour financier l'achat du manuscrit !

5.37 Rassurez un(e) ami(e) Avec un partenaire, **discutez** de vos problèmes personnels ou des problèmes d'actualité. Vous pouvez inventer des problèmes fictifs si vous voulez ! **Posez des questions** afin de savoir ce qui préoccupe votre partenaire, **donnez votre opinion** là-dessus, et **offrez-lui quelques suggestions ou conseils** pour résoudre ses problèmes.

MODÈLE : —Qu'est-ce qui te préoccupe ?

—C'est l'anniversaire de ma mère demain et je n'ai pas encore acheté de cadeau !

—Ah, bon ? Pourquoi ne pas l'inviter à dîner au restaurant ?

5.38 Circulez et discutez ! Est-ce qu'il y a des règles sur votre campus ou dans votre ville que vous trouvez inutiles ? Sur une feuille de papier, écrivez une phrase pour décrire la règle qui vous ennuie et pourquoi. N'y mettez pas votre nom. Ensuite, échangez vos papiers au hasard, lisez la phrase que vous recevez, et circulez dans la classe afin d'en trouver l'auteur. Quand vous aurez trouvé cette personne, **exprimez l'opinion contraire** (même si vous êtes vraiment d'accord avec la personne) et **donnez des conseils** à cette personne pour qu'il/elle puisse accepter cette règle.

MODÈLE : —Je suis fâché que les étudiants de première année soient les derniers à s'inscrire (*to register*) aux cours. Il n'y a jamais assez de place dans les cours intéressants !

—Au contraire, il est urgent que les étudiants avancés s'inscrivent en premier pour qu'ils puissent terminer leurs diplômes. Tant pis pour eux si les étudiants de première année n'aient pas accès à tous les cours.

5.39 Être heureux comme un poisson dans l'eau Que faut-il pour bien vivre et pour être heureux ? **Faites une liste** de trois choses que vous croyez être absolument indispensables pour être heureux dans la vie. **Discutez** de vos idées avec vos camarades de classe.

MODÈLE : Il est essentiel qu'on ait de la passion pour sa carrière choisie !

À l'écrit *troisième étape*

5.40 Une lettre au rédacteur du journal Le rédacteur en chef du journal francophone veut savoir vos opinions personnelles sur le sujet de votre article de journal avant de vous embaucher (*to hire*). **Écrivez-lui une lettre** dans laquelle vous exprimez vos opinions personnelles sur le sujet que vous proposez (révisez l'Activité 26). **Il faut convaincre le rédacteur** que vous êtes passionné(e) par ce sujet et que vous connaissez bien la matière. Ensuite, échangez votre lettre avec celle d'un(e) camarade de classe. Suggérez des corrections possibles et réagissez à la lettre que vous recevez en bas de page.

Dénouement

Activités de révision

5.41 Les Actu 24/24 En petits groupes, **organisez une courte émission télévisée** d'actualités mondiales. Chaque groupe doit choisir une année passée différente (par exemple : 1492, 1662, 1776, 1789, 1880, 1919, 1945, 1960, 2000) et imaginez les sujets d'actualité qu'on aurait vu à la télé, si la télé existait. Vous pouvez présenter des rubriques variées comme la politique, les sports ou n'importe quelle catégorie qui intéresserait votre public. Présentez votre émission à vos camarades de classe.

MODÈLE : —Bonjour, téléspectateurs et téléspectatrices ! Aujourd'hui, nous sommes en France et c'est l'année 1803. En politique aujourd'hui, la révolution continue à Haïti. Les révolutionnaires noirs combattent férocement contre les troupes françaises. Ils veulent établir une république indépendante. Ici en France, Napoléon Bonaparte devient de plus en plus populaire parmi les troupes françaises. Et maintenant, écoutons le rapportage culturel.

—Merci, Paul. Une mauvaise nouvelle à vous annoncer aujourd'hui. Un grand écrivain français est mort. Pierre-Ambroise Choderlos de Laclos, l'auteur du roman épistolaire *Les Liaisons dangereuses*, a été tué en Italie où il combattait pour l'armée française. Et maintenant, les prévisions météorologiques. . .

Pour aller plus loin :
LITTÉRATURE
ACTIVITÉ K : Lisez «J'accuse !», l'article dans lequel Émile Zola a donné ses opinions sur l'Affaire Dreyfus au 19ème siècle. Consultez votre cahier électronique !

5.42 Il faut que vous mettiez vos manteaux ce matin ! En petits groupes, choisissez une ville ou une région en Europe ou dans les DOM-TOM. **Recherchez** le temps qu'il fait là-bas en ce moment (sur Internet) ou imaginez le temps qu'il fait. Puis, devant la classe, **faites vos prévisions météorologiques** et donnez des conseils vestimentaires aux spectateurs.

MODÈLE : La météo pour les îles de Saint-Pierre-et-Miquelon : Aujourd'hui en Amérique du Nord, le ciel est bleu et la température va atteindre 22 degrés sur la côte. Quelques nuages en fin de journée, mais autrement une belle journée pour les marins !

5.43 La prévoyance Imaginez que vous êtes voyant(e) et que vous pouvez voir l'avenir de votre partenaire. **Posez**-lui **des questions** sur ce qu'il/elle veut accomplir dans sa vie. Ne lui dites pas ce que vous voyez dans son avenir, mais **donnez**-lui **des conseils** sur ses actions et sa vie à présent. Qu'est-ce qu'il/elle doit continuer à faire ? Que faut-il qu'il/elle change ? Quels conseils avez-vous pour cette personne ? Jouez les rôles du voyant / de la voyante et du client / de la cliente à tour.

MODÈLE : —Alors, que voulez-vous faire à l'avenir comme profession ?

—Je veux absolument devenir professeur de français.

—Ah, oui ! Alors, il faut que vous continuiez vos études de français et que vous fassiez des études à l'étranger. . .

Culture

La **Comédie française**, parfois appelée la Maison de Molière, est située rue de Richelieu près du Palais-Royal à Paris. Le théâtre était le centre de la vie culturelle et sociale à Paris au 17ème siècle. On y présentait toutes les pièces des grands auteurs classiques tels Molière, Corneille et Racine. La troupe de Molière était sous la protection du roi Louis XIV et donnait alternativement des pièces à Paris et à Versailles. On appelle cette époque «le **Grand Siècle**» à cause de la grandeur du roi, de la puissance du royaume et de l'épanouissement des arts et de la littérature pendant cette période de l'histoire française.

La Comédie française, l'ancienne Maison de Molière, à Paris.

Avant de lire *L'Avare*

5.44 Premières impressions **Lisez** l'extrait suivant, tiré de la pièce de Molière qui s'appelle *L'Avare* (*The Miser*), sans essayer de comprendre chaque mot. Après votre première lecture du texte, **répondez aux questions**. Ensuite, **relisez** le texte une deuxième fois, plus attentivement.

1. Est-ce un homme ou une femme qui parle au début ? Ce personnage, est-il jeune ou vieux ? riche ou pauvre ?
2. Comment est-il ? Calme ? Nerveux ? Fâché ? etc. ?
3. Qu'est-ce qu'il a perdu ? Quand est-ce que cela s'est passé ?
4. Où se situe l'action ? À Paris ou à la campagne ?
5. Quel est le ton de cette pièce : tragique ? mélancolique ? comique ?

lisez

L'Avare

Cette célèbre comédie de Molière, représentée pour la première fois à Paris en 1668, met en scène un personnage inoubliable : un homme avare nommé Harpagon. Dans les trois scènes qui suivent, Harpagon se rend compte du vol de la cassette qu'il a cachée dans sa maison. Le commissaire de police, son clerc et un domestique nommé Maître Jacques discutent du vol pendant qu'Harpagon devient de plus en plus irraisonnable. Le personnage d'Harpagon amuse le spectateur par son avarice exagérée, mais en même temps, il permet à Molière de critiquer cet aspect de la société bourgeoise de son temps.

■ Molière

L'Avare (extraits)

Acte IV, Scène VII : ***Harpagon criant au voleur dès le jardin***

HARPAGON : Au voleur ! au voleur ! à l'assassin ! au meurtrier ! Justice, juste ciel ! je suis perdu, je suis assassiné ; on m'a coupé la gorge° : on m'a dérobé° mon argent. Qui peut-ce être ? Qu'est-il devenu ? Où est-il ? Où se cache-t-il ? Que ferai-je pour le trouver ? Où courir ? Où ne pas courir ? N'est-il point° là ? N'est-il point ici ? Qui est-ce ? Arrête. (*À lui-même, se prenant le bras.*) Rends-moi mon argent, coquin°. . . Ah ! c'est moi ! Mon esprit est troublé, et j'ignore où je suis, qui je suis, et ce que je fais. Hélas ! mon pauvre argent ! mon pauvre argent ! mon cher ami ! on m'a privé° de toi ; et puisque tu m'es enlevé, j'ai perdu mon support, ma consolation, ma joie : tout est fini pour moi, et je n'ai plus que faire au monde. Sans toi, il m'est impossible de vivre. C'en est fait ; je n'en puis plus ; je me meurs ; je suis mort ; je suis enterré. N'y a-t-il personne qui veuille me ressusciter, en me rendant mon cher argent, ou en m'apprenant qui l'a pris ? Euh ! que dites-vous ? Ce n'est personne. Il faut, qui que ce soit qui ait fait le coup, qu'avec beaucoup de soin on ait épié° l'heure ; et l'on a choisi justement le temps que je parlais à mon traître de fils. Sortons. Je veux aller quérir° la justice, et faire donner la question à toute ma maison ; à servantes, à valets, à fils, à fille et à moi aussi. Que de gens assemblés ! Je ne jette mes regards sur personne qui ne me donne des soupçons, et tout me semble mon voleur. Hé ! de quoi est-ce qu'on parle là ? de celui qui m'a dérobé ? Quel bruit° fait-on là-haut ? Est-ce mon voleur qui y est ? De grâce, si l'on sait des nouvelles de mon voleur, je supplie° que l'on m'en dise. N'est-il point caché là parmi vous ? Ils me regardent tous, et se mettent à rire. Vous verrez° qu'ils ont part, sans doute, au vol que l'on m'a fait. Allons vite, des commissaires, des archers, des prévôts, des juges, des gênes, des potences et des bourreaux.° Je veux faire pendre° tout le monde ; et, si je ne retrouve mon argent, je me pendrai moi-même après.

throat/to steal

lesser-used equivalent of ne … pas

rascal

to deprive

to spy on, watch out for

to go fetch something, someone

noise

to beg

future tense of voir

types of law enforcers (antiquated vocabulary)/to hang

Acte V, Scène II : ***Maître Jacques*** *(servant),*
Harpagon, le Commissaire, son Clerc

MAÎTRE JACQUES : *(dans le fond du théâtre, en se retournant du côté par lequel il est entré)* : Je m'en vais revenir. Qu'on me l'égorge° tout à l'heure ; qu'on me lui fasse griller les pieds ; qu'on me le mette dans l'eau bouillante, et qu'on me le pende au plancher. — *to slit someone's throat*

HARPAGON : *(à Maître Jacques)* : Qui ? celui qui m'a dérobé ?

MAÎTRE JACQUES : Je parle d'un cochon de lait° que votre intendant me vient d'envoyer, et je veux vous l'accommoder à ma fantaisie. — *piglet*

HARPAGON : Il n'est pas question de cela ; et voilà monsieur à qui il faut parler d'autre chose.

LE COMMISSAIRE : *(à Maître Jacques)* : Ne vous épouvantez point. Je suis un homme à ne vous point scandaliser, et les choses iront dans la douceur.

MAÎTRE JACQUES : Monsieur est de votre souper ?° — *dining with you*

LE COMMISSAIRE : Il faut ici, mon cher ami, ne rien cacher à votre maître.

MAÎTRE JACQUES : Ma foi, monsieur, je montrerai tout ce que je sais faire, et je vous traiterai du mieux qu'il me sera possible.

HARPAGON : Ce n'est pas là l'affaire.

MAÎTRE JACQUES : Si je ne vous fais pas aussi bonne chère° que je voudrais, c'est la faute de monsieur notre intendant, qui m'a rogné les ailes° avec les ciseaux° de son économie. — *a feast, good meal* — *to clip one's wings/scissors*

HARPAGON : Traître ! il s'agit d'autre chose que de souper ; et je veux que tu me dises des nouvelles de l'argent qu'on m'a pris.

MAÎTRE JACQUES : On vous a pris de l'argent ?

HARPAGON : Oui, coquin ; et je m'en vais te pendre, si tu ne me le rends.

LE COMMISSAIRE : *(à Harpagon)* : Mon Dieu ! ne le maltraitez point. Je vois à sa mine° qu'il est honnête homme ; et que, sans se faire mettre en prison, il vous découvrira ce que vous voulez savoir. Oui, mon ami, si vous nous confessez la chose, il ne vous sera fait aucun mal, et vous serez récompensé comme il faut par votre maître. On lui a pris aujourd'hui son argent ; et il n'est pas que vous ne sachiez quelques nouvelles de cette affaire. — *look (on one's face)*

MAÎTRE JACQUES : *(bas, à part)* : Voici justement ce qu'il me faut pour me venger de votre intendant. Depuis qu'il est entré céans,° il est le favori ; on n'écoute que ses conseils ; et j'ai aussi sur le cœur les coups de bâton de tantôt. — *in the house*

HARPAGON : Qu'as-tu à ruminer° ? — *to ruminate*

LE COMMISSAIRE : *(à Harpagon)* : Laissez-le faire. Il se prépare à vous contenter ; et je vous ai bien dit qu'il était honnête homme.

MAÎTRE JACQUES : Monsieur, si vous voulez que je vous dise les choses, je crois que c'est monsieur votre cher intendant qui a fait le coup.

HARPAGON : Valère !

MAÎTRE JACQUES : Oui.

HARPAGON : Lui ! qui me paraît si fidèle ?

MAÎTRE JACQUES : Lui-même. Je crois que c'est lui qui vous a dérobé.

HARPAGON : Et sur quoi le crois-tu ?

MAÎTRE JACQUES : Sur quoi ?

HARPAGON : Oui.

MAÎTRE JACQUES : Je le crois. . . sur ce que je le crois.

LE COMMISSAIRE : Mais il est nécessaire de dire les indices que vous avez.

to prowl around

HARPAGON : L'as-tu vu rôder° autour du lieu où j'avais mis mon argent ?

MAÎTRE JACQUES : Oui vraiment. Où était votre argent ?

HARPAGON : Dans le jardin.

MAÎTRE JACQUES : Justement ; je l'ai vu rôder dans le jardin. Et dans quoi est-ce que cet argent était ?

box (antiquated word)

HARPAGON : Dans une cassette.°

MAÎTRE JACQUES : Voilà l'affaire. Je lui ai vue une cassette.

HARPAGON : Et cette cassette, comment est-elle faite ? Je verrai bien si c'est la mienne.

MAÎTRE JACQUES : Comment est elle faite ?

HARPAGON : Oui.

MAÎTRE JACQUES : Elle est faite. . . elle est faite comme une cassette.

LE COMMISSAIRE : Cela s'entend. Mais dépeignez-la un peu, pour voir.

MAÎTRE JACQUES : C'est une grande cassette.

HARPAGON : Celle qu'on m'a volée est petite.

MAÎTRE JACQUES : Hé ! oui, elle est petite, si on le veut prendre par là, mais je l'appelle grande pour ce qu'elle contient.

LE COMMISSAIRE : Et de quelle couleur est-elle ?

MAÎTRE JACQUES : De quelle couleur ?

LE COMMISSAIRE : Oui.

MAÎTRE JACQUES : Elle est de couleur. . . là, d'une certaine couleur. . . Ne sauriez-vous m'aider à dire ?

HARPAGON : Euh ?

MAÎTRE JACQUES : N'est-elle pas rouge ?

HARPAGON : Non, grise.

MAÎTRE JACQUES : Hé ! oui, gris-rouge ; c'est ce que je voulais dire.

from now on, hereafter
to confide in

HARPAGON : Il n'y a point de doute; c'est elle assurément. Écrivez, monsieur, écrivez sa déposition. Ciel ! à qui désormais° se fier° ! Il ne faut plus jurer de rien; et je crois après cela que je suis homme à me voler moi-même.

Après avoir lu

5.45 Avez-vous compris ? En petits groupes, **discutez** de vos réponses aux questions suivantes.

1. Dans la première scène de l'extrait, Harpagon crie hystériquement. Pourquoi ?
2. Comment Harpagon décrit-il son argent ? Pensez-vous que son argent soit plus important que ses amis et sa famille ?
3. Qui est-ce que Harpagon appelle pour trouver le criminel ? Qui est interviewé ?

4. Pourquoi est-ce que Maître Jacques implique que Valère est le voleur ? Quelles sont les preuves (*proof*) qu'il offre à Harpagon ?
5. Quel est le rôle du Commissaire dans cette enquête ? À votre avis, fait-il son travail ?
6. Imaginez le gros titre pour un article de journal sur le vol de l'argent d'Harpagon. Quelles sont les possibilités ?

Pour aller plus loin : CINÉMA

ACTIVITÉ L : Découvrez un film sur la cour à Versailles au 17ème siècle, *Tous les matins du monde*. Consultez votre cahier électronique !

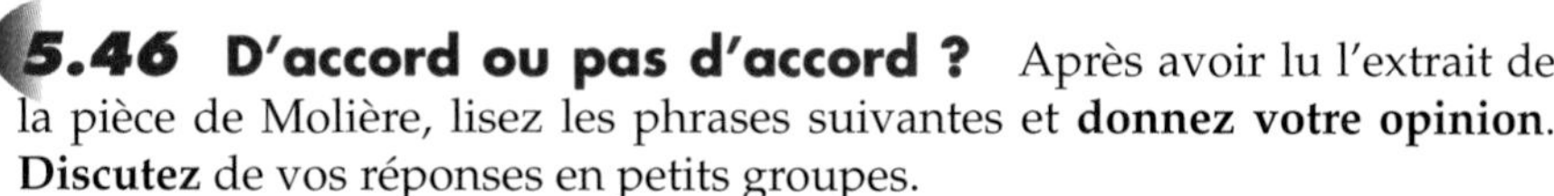

5.46 D'accord ou pas d'accord ? Après avoir lu l'extrait de la pièce de Molière, lisez les phrases suivantes et **donnez votre opinion**. **Discutez** de vos réponses en petits groupes.

	D'accord	Pas d'accord
1. Harpagon aime son argent comme si c'était une personne.	_______	_______
2. Au début, Harpagon pense que Maître Jacques a volé l'argent.	_______	_______
3. Le Commissaire réagit raisonnablement à la situation.	_______	_______
4. Maître Jacques arrive à persuader Harpagon qu'il est innocent.	_______	_______
5. Maître Jacques a vraiment vu Valère avec la cassette.	_______	_______

5.47 Analyse littéraire Examinez ce texte de près. Répondez aux questions suivantes et **discutez** de vos réponses en classe.

1. Le personnage de Harpagon est une caricature d'un bourgeois avare. Analysez l'usage de l'exaggération chez le personnage de Harpagon. Où en trouvez-vous des exemples ?
2. Ces deux scènes sont assez comiques, quoique différentes. En quoi consiste la comédie du monologue d'Harpagon ? Et, la conversation entre Harpagon et Maître Jacques, pourquoi est-elle comique ? Y a-t-il d'autres éléments structurels que l'auteur emploie systématiquement afin de rendre ces scènes comiques ?
3. Le subjonctif est employé souvent dans ces deux scènes. Analysez les verbes au subjonctif. Sont-ils concentrés dans une partie de l'extrait ou dispersés dans les deux scènes ? Quel est l'effet de l'usage du subjonctif ? Comment influence-t-il votre appréciation des personnages et du problème présenté ?
4. Regardez encore la fin de la dernière scène de l'extrait : l'interrogation de Maître Jacques. Y a-t-il un rythme ou des mots qui riment ? Quel en est l'effet ?

Synthèses

5.48 Réfléchissons à la culture Voici quelques éléments de la culture française que vous avez étudiés dans ce chapitre. En petits groupes, répondez aux questions et **discutez** de vos impressions avec vos camarades.

les cafés parisiens les DOM-TOM et l'UE le palais de Versailles

1. Définissez ou décrivez chaque élément.
2. En ce qui concerne les DOM-TOM et l'UE, comment est-ce que le rôle de la France est différent dans chacune de ces entités politiques auxquelles elle fait partie ? Comment est-ce que ces entités politiques influencent la société française d'aujourd'hui ? Est-ce que les États-Unis a des liens politiques avec d'autres pays ? Quelles en sont les similarités et les différences ?
3. La France d'aujourd'hui est une république, très fière de son indépendance et de son système démocratique. Comment explique-t-on alors l'importance du palais de Versailles ? Y a t-il des endroits historiques pré-révolutionnaires aux États-Unis qu'on cultive et qu'on visite régulièrement ? Quelles en sont les similarités et les différences ?
4. Quel est l'équivalent d'un café parisien aux États-Unis (c'est-à-dire, un lieu où les gens peuvent se reposer ou discuter) ? Quelles en sont les similarités et les différences ? Pourquoi les cafés parisiens sont-ils toujours si populaires ? Y a-t-il un phénomène historique ou social qui explique leur importance ?
5. À votre avis, est-ce que ces éléments témoignent de la richesse et de la diversité de la culture française de nos jours, ou sont-ils stéréotypiques ? Pourquoi ?

la France

Qu'est-ce que ça veut dire «être Parisienne» ? Regardez la vidéo et consultez votre cahier d'activités !

5.49 À débattre Lisez les questions suivantes et **discutez** en groupes. Si possible, parlez de vos expériences personnelles relatives aux questions.

1. **L'objectivité ou la subjectivité ?** Est-ce possible que la presse soit absolument objective en présentant les sujets d'actualités ? Même si un journaliste essaie de regarder une situation d'un point de vue objectif, il est toujours influencé par ses pensées et ses préjugés inconscients. Quels sont les dangers d'une presse qui prétend (*claims*) être objective ? Est-ce que les journalistes doivent aspirer à l'objectivité ou déclarer ouvertement leurs opinions subjectives ?
2. **Une planète en danger ?** On fait des essais nucléaires en Polynésie. La pollution en Europe augmente. Il y a des trous noirs dans l'atmosphère. La température globale augmente un peu plus chaque année.

Faut-il avoir peur pour l'avenir de la planète ? Est-ce que les actions des individus peuvent avoir un effet ? Les pays de l'ouest, sont-ils plus coupables que les autres ?

3. **Le Grand Siècle ?** Pendant le Grand Siècle, les Européens ont vu des développements très positifs en ce qui concerne les arts, la littérature, les sciences et l'économie. En même temps, c'était la période où les pays européens ont commencé à étendre leurs empires et à coloniser et à exploiter certains peuples. On peut constater que la prospérité des cultures européennes a été directement liée à l'exploitation des cultures non européennes. Est-ce que les bénéfices tirés de l'exploration mondiale ont été plus importants que les torts faits aux peuples exploités ? Est-ce que les Européens étaient motivés par l'avarice ou par la volonté d'aider des peuples dits «non civilisés» ?

5.50 À l'impromptu Voici des situations de rencontre. Avec une ou deux autres personnes, **choisissez une scène et improvisez devant la classe**. Si vous ne voulez pas improviser, écrivez votre dialogue avant et puis jouez-le pour la classe.

1. La météo
   (a) Vous assistez au mariage de votre meilleur(e) ami(e) qui se tient sur une plage à Tahiti. Vous venez d'entendre le bulletin météo qui annonce un ouragan prochain. Apprenez la nouvelle à votre ami(e) et donnez-lui des conseils.
   (b) Vous allez épouser la personne de vos rêves sur une plage à Tahiti. Tout est prêt. Le temps est idyllique. Malheureusement, votre ami(e) vous apprend une mauvaise nouvelle. Vous croyez qu'il/elle se trompe. Réagissez avec indifférence et essayez de changer le sujet de la conversation.
2. La dispute
   (a) Vous et votre époux ne sont jamais d'accord. Chaque fois que vous écoutez les informations à la télévision, vous vous disputez. Exprimez vos opinions sur la politique, le sport, l'économie, etc.
   (b) Vous êtes le psychologue que ce couple a décidé de consulter afin de sauver leur mariage. Vous devez leur montrer comment exprimer le désaccord sans se disputer. Imaginez la consultation.
3. Une mauvaise nouvelle
   (a) Vous êtes en vacances à Paris avec un(e) ami(e) francophone quand tout d'un coup, vous vous rendez compte que vous êtes dans une situation financière catastrophique. Vos cartes de crédit ne marchent plus. Votre compte bancaire est à zéro. Vous ne pourrez pas payer pour votre chambre d'hôtel, et vous avez perdu votre billet d'avion pour le voyage de retour. Apprenez ces nouvelles à la personne avec qui vous voyagez.
   (b) Vous voyagez à Paris avec un(e) ami(e) américain(e). Vous l'aimez bien, mais vous savez qu'il/elle est assez étourdi(e) (*irresponsible*). Par contre, vous êtes plus responsable. Vous avez budgétisé toutes vos dépenses, et il vous reste assez d'argent pour passer quelques jours aux casinos de Monaco avant de retourner chez vous. Réagissez aux nouvelles de votre compagnon.

À l'écrit *étape finale*

5.51 À la une du journal francophone De bonnes nouvelles ! Le rédacteur en chef a été favorablement impressionné par votre idée et a décidé de publier votre article dans son journal ! **Révisez et élaborez** vos travaux d'écriture de ce chapitre (Activités 13, 26 et 40) et **rédigez un article** pour le journal francophone. N'oubliez pas les éléments suivants :

- un gros titre et un sous-titre
- une bonne introduction
- des citations (*quotes*) de plusieurs gens que vous avez fictivement interviewés et qui donnent leurs opinions et/ou leurs conseils
- une bonne conclusion

À suivre

Claire téléphone à la Martinique, mais il n'y a pas de réponse à la maison d'André Thibodeau, le monsieur qui a acheté le manuscrit. Claire décide d'aller à la Martinique pour parler à cet homme. Quant à Jean-Louis, il insiste pour y aller lui aussi, et confirme ce que Claire a lu dans le fax de son patron. Jean-Louis doit y aller, avec ou sans elle, et doit acheter le manuscrit pour son patron. Pourtant, il promet qu'il lui laissera le temps d'étudier le manuscrit avant de le remettre à son patron. Donc, il vaut mieux qu'ils travaillent ensemble. De toute façon, elle n'a pas assez d'argent pour acheter le manuscrit elle-même et il n'est pas certain que ce monsieur veuille lui laisser lire ou copier le manuscrit sans l'acheter. Alors, ils téléphonent à l'agence de tourisme et achètent des billets d'avion. Le jour du départ, le premier octobre, les deux font leurs bagages et s'en vont à l'aéroport, mais cette fois, ensemble. . .

5.52 Qu'est-ce qui s'est passé ? Pensez à ce qui s'est passé dans ce chapitre. Écrivez six phrases aux temps passés pour **décrire les événements** que vous pensez être les plus importants. Sont-ce de bonnes nouvelles ou de mauvaises nouvelles ? Parlez de vos idées avec vos camarades de classe.

MODÈLE : —Mais c'est vraiment incroyable ! Ils ont appris à qui Nicolas Gustave avait vendu le manuscrit !

5.53 Qu'est-ce qui va se passer ? Imaginez ce qui va se passer dans le prochain chapitre. Écrivez six phrases et parlez de vos idées avec vos camarades de classe.

MODÈLE : —C'est difficile à croire, mais Claire et Jean-Louis vont se disputer !

Pour agir :
LES DOM-TOM ET L'EUROPE !

Si vous voulez bouger et faire quelque chose pour mieux connaître les DOM-TOM et l'Europe, ou pour aider les autres à mieux comprendre la Francophonie, consultez la section **Pour agir** dans votre cahier électronique ! Il y a tant de choses à faire :

- **Vendez des crêpes** sur votre campus et contribuez l'argent que vous gagnez à une organisation qui replante la forêt du parc de Versailles qui a été détruite par un ouragan en 1999.
- **Enseignez** ce que vous savez des cultures des DOM-TOM ou de l'Europe à des élèves de l'école primaire.
- **Entrez en contact** avec des francophones qui vivent dans votre communauté en faisant des interviews.
- **Publiez** un petit journal hebdomadaire sur les événements francophones dans votre région ou sur votre campus (utilisez vos articles d'actualités ou des interviews avec des gens francophones) !
- **Organisez** un colloque et invitez des professeurs dans votre université à débattre l'avenir de l'Union européenne ou des problèmes écologiques dans le monde.
- **Faites un voyage** en Europe ou dans les DOM-TOM pendant les vacances prochaines.
- **Cuisinez** ! Préparez un vrai repas français avec vos camarades de classe.

VOCABULAIRE UTILE

Au café

aborder	*to approach*
amorcer	*to introduce (a topic of conversation)*
au bout (de)	*at the end (of)*
craindre	*to fear*
déconcertant(e)	*disconcerting/troubling*
dépister	*to track down*
écriture (*f.*)	*writing*
franchement	*frankly*
lecture (*f.*)	*reading*
parier	*to bet*
réflexion (*f.*)	*reflection*
rougir	*to redden/to blush*
sourir	*to smile*

Le temps

averse (*f.*)	*downpour*
brouillard (*m.*)	*fog*
brume (*f.*)	*fog*
canicule (*f.*)	*heat wave*
ciel (*m.*)	*sky*
feuille (*f.*)	*leaf*
foudre (*f.*)	*lightning*
grêle (*f.*)	*hail*
maussade	*gloomy*
neige (*f.*)	*snow*
orage (*m.*)	*thunderstorm*
ouragan (*m.*)	*hurricane*
rafale (*f.*) de vent	*gusty wind*
tempête (*f.*)	*storm*
tonnerre (*m.*)	*thunder*

Les actualités

à la une	*front-page stories*
attentat (*m.*)	*attack*
blessé(e)	*wounded*
blesser	*to wound*
bourse (*f.*)	*stock exchange*
chômage (*m.*)	*unemployment*
enquête (*f.*)	*investigation*
exposition (*f.*)	*exhibit*
faits divers (*m.pl.*)	*human interest stories*
grève (*f.*)	*strike*
krach boursier (*m.*)	*stock-market crash*
manifestation (*f.*)	*protest*
pièce (*f.*)	*play*
prendre feu	*to catch fire*
procès (*m.*)	*trial*
s'accroître	*to increase*
spectacle (*m.*)	*show*
syndicat (*m.*)	*workers'union*
témoin (*m.*)	*witness*
tirer	*to fire (a weapon)*

Apprendre des nouvelles

chair (*f.*) de poule	*goose bumps*
de mal en pis	*from bad to worse*
décennie (*f.*)	*decade*
en chair et en os	*in the flesh (and bones)*
entrepôt (*m.*)	*warehouse, storage house*
être navré(e)	*to be sorry*
être ravi(e)	*to be delighted*
frissonner	*to shiver*
qui pis est	*what's even worse*
sous clé	*under lock and key*

Le climat tropical

bougainvillée (*f.*)	*Bougainvillea flower*
chute (*f.*) de boue	*mudslide*
cocotier (*m.*)	*coconut tree*
colon (*m.*)	*colonist*
enfer (*m.*)	*hell*
inondation (*f.*)	*flood*
ouragan (*m.*)	*hurricane*
paradis (*m.*)	*paradise, heaven*
sable noir (*m.*)	*black sand*

Interlude

Résumé de l'intrigue

chapitre *1* Claire Plouffe, une Québécoise qui prépare un doctorat en lettres françaises, arrive à la Nouvelle-Orléans à la recherche d'un manuscrit inédit. Claire pense que Pierre-Ambroise Choderlos de Laclos, le célèbre auteur des *Liaisons dangereuses*, a écrit un autre roman qu'on n'a jamais publié. Elle croit qu'un habitant de la Nouvelle-Orléans du nom de François Fontenot était en possession du manuscrit quand Laclos est mort en 1803, et elle veut trouver ses descendants. Pendant son séjour en Louisiane, Claire rencontre un touriste français, Jean-Louis Royer. Il dit qu'il travaille dans un bar à Paris, et il s'intéresse beaucoup au projet de recherche de la Québécoise.

chapitre *2* À la bibliothèque municipale de la Nouvelle-Orléans, Claire trouve le nom d'une descendante de François Fontenot, Sandrine Fontenot-Chardin. Elle rend visite à cette femme qui lui explique que sa famille avait vendu à un bouquiniste parisien un manuscrit qui passait pour être un roman inédit de Laclos. C'était en 1973, juste après la mort de son grand-père. Claire ne parle pas du bouquiniste à Jean-Louis et quitte les États-Unis sans lui dire où elle s'en va.

chapitre *3* Claire arrive à Paris, où elle revoit Jean-Louis. Jean-Louis lui avoue qu'il n'est pas un simple barman. Il travaille pour un antiquaire qui s'intéresse au manuscrit perdu de Laclos. Claire décide de collaborer avec Jean-Louis, puisqu'il cherche le même manuscrit, et elle lui parle du bouquiniste qui a acheté, il y a 30 ans, la bibliothèque privée de la famille Fontenot.

chapitre 4 Jean-Louis et Claire trouvent l'étalage du bouquiniste, Nicolas Gustave, mais il est fermé. Un homme qui travaille au kiosque d'en face leur donne l'adresse de l'oncle de Nicolas, le vieux Monsieur Lionel Gustave. C'est Lionel Gustave qui a acheté les livres de la famille Fontenot. Ils rendent visite à ce monsieur, qui ne sait rien du manuscrit et qui leur dit que son neveu vient de partir en vacances. Claire reçoit un message bizarre d'un inconnu qui essaie de lui faire peur et qui veut qu'elle quitte Paris. Elle décide néanmoins de rester.

chapitre 5 En attendant le retour à Paris du bouquiniste, Claire entreprend une recherche secondaire et Jean-Louis retourne à son bureau. Un jour, dans un café, Claire rencontre un homme qui se présente comme un inspecteur de police. Il lui parle des dangers du marché de livres anciens. Le même jour, Jean-Louis lui montre un article de journal dans lequel on parle de la corruption du marché des livres. Pourtant, ils continuent à chercher le manuscrit. Quand Nicolas Gustave retourne de ses vacances, il annonce à Claire qu'il a vendu récemment un manuscrit anonyme qui était parmi les livres achetés à la famille Fontenot. L'acheteur est un homme antillais qui habite à la Martinique. Claire et Jean-Louis décident de partir à la recherche de cet homme. . .

Chronologie des événements

1782 Pierre-Ambroise Choderlos de Laclos publie son best-seller, *Les Liaisons dangereuses,* à Paris. François Fontenot arrive à Paris pour faire des études culinaires. Ils se rencontrent et deviennent amis.

1789 La Révolution française commence. Laclos continue à écrire.

1790 François Fontenot retourne à Saint-Domingue, une colonie française aux Antilles.

1792 La Révolution haïtienne commence. François Fontenot et sa famille quittent Saint-Domingue. Ils s'installent en Louisiane, une autre colonie française. Laclos envoie un manuscrit à son ami François.

1803 Laclos meurt en France. Son manuscrit reste dans la bibliothèque privée de François Fontenot. Le manuscrit n'est jamais publié.

1804 La République d'Haïti est établie.

1806 François Fontenot ouvre un restaurant créole à la Nouvelle-Orléans.

1822 François Fontenot meurt aux États-Unis.

1941 C'est la Seconde Guerre mondiale. Henri Pierre Fontenot, un descendant de François, se fait soldat dans l'armée américaine.

1945 Henri Pierre Fontenot rencontre un bouquiniste, Lionel Gustave, à Paris.

1973 Le père d'Henri Pierre Fontenot meurt d'une crise cardiaque pendant un vol dans sa demeure. Henri Pierre Fontenot veut se débarrasser de ces livres qui n'apportent que malheur à la famille. Il vend la bibliothèque familiale à Lionel Gustave, sans lui parler du manuscrit.

2001 Claire fait des études supérieures en lettres françaises à Québec. Elle tombe sur un article qui fait référence à l'existence possible d'un manuscrit inédit de Laclos.

2002 Claire étudie la correspondance de Laclos à la Bibliothèque nationale de Paris. Elle découvre le nom de François Fontenot dans une lettre de Laclos. La lettre décrit un «paquet» envoyé à François Fontenot. Claire photocopie la lettre.

2003 Claire reprend ses recherches aidée d'une bourse de l'université. Elle va à la Nouvelle-Orléans et y rencontre Jean-Louis Royer. Là, elle rend aussi visite à Sandrine Fontenot-Chardin, la fille d'Henri Pierre Fontenot. Sandrine lui raconte l'histoire de sa famille et lui donne le nom du bouquiniste parisien. Claire va à Paris et revoit Jean-Louis Royer. Ils décident de collaborer à la recherche du manuscrit. Gilles LaFfont, un inspecteur de police, se présente à Claire et l'avertit des dangers du marché de livres anciens. Claire et Jean-Louis parlent avec Nicolas, le neveu de Lionel Gustave, qui leur donne le nom de l'homme qui vient d'acheter le manuscrit. Claire et Jean-Louis quittent la France pour trouver cet homme à la Martinique.

Personnages principaux

Claire Plouffe Québécoise. Étudiante à l'Université de Sainte-Foy au Québec, elle fait des recherches pour sa thèse de doctorat en lettres françaises. Elle cherche un manuscrit perdu écrit par un auteur français célèbre du 18ème siècle. Sa famille habite à Montréal. Elle envoie des messages régulièrement à sa sœur **Marie**.

Jean-Louis Royer Français. Il travaille à Paris pour un antiquaire, **Monsieur Rolland**, qui achète et revend des livres rares et anciens. Son appartement se trouve à Versailles, où habitent ses parents, mais sa **tante Émilie** habite à Paris. Il ne la voit pas souvent.

Sandrine Fontenot-Chardin Américaine. Une Louisianaise qui est une descendante de **François Fontenot**. François était un restaurateur qui a immigré à la Nouvelle-Orléans de Saint-Domingue (Haïti) à la fin du 18ème siècle. On pense que Laclos a donné un manuscrit inédit à son ami François Fontenot avant sa mort. Le grand-père de Sandrine est mort quand des voleurs sont entrés dans leur maison en 1973. Son père, **Henri Pierre Fontenot**, a vendu tous les livres de la famille Fontenot à un ami parisien qui était bouquiniste.

Nicolas Gustave Français. Un bouquiniste parisien qui dirige la vente des livres depuis la retraite de son oncle, **Lionel Gustave**. C'est l'oncle qui a connu Henri Pierre Fontenot lors de la Seconde Guerre mondiale et qui a acheté la bibliothèque privée de la famille Fontenot il y a 30 ans. Nicolas vient de vendre le manuscrit anonyme que cherchent Claire et Jean-Louis.

Philippe Aucoin Américain. Un hôtelier louisianais qui a présenté Claire à Jean-Louis.

P.F. Thuillier Québécois. Un professeur de littérature à l'Université de Sainte-Foy au Québec, c'est le directeur de thèse de Claire Plouffe.

François Phan Français. Un marchand d'origine vietnamienne qui tient une boutique à Paris. Il a vu le voleur de la valise de Claire à l'aéroport de Paris.

Talal Lateef Français. Un ami de Nicolas Gustave, Talal vend des journaux dans un kiosque qui fait face à l'étalage de Nicolas. Il est d'origine maghrébine.

Gilles LaFfont Français. Un inspecteur de police à Paris. Il fait une enquête sur la corruption dans le marché de livres anciens à Paris.

André Thibodeau Français. Un homme érudit qui fait collection de livres anciens. Il vient d'acheter le manuscrit du bouquiniste. Il est Martiniquais et sa résidence principale se trouve à la Martinique.

Chapitre 6

Une mésaventure martiniquaise

Une plage à la Martinique.

Épisode 1 *En allant à Schœlcher*

Épisode 2 *Le coup de téléphone*

Épisode 3 *Venez à Dakar !*

Dénouement

Ris du riz, tu pleureras
pour des lentilles.
—proverbe antillais

Culture

Christophe Colombe a «découvert» l'île de la **Martinique** en 1502, mais ce n'est qu'à partir de 1635 que les Français l'ont colonisée. Ils y ont établi des plantations de canne à sucre qui étaient très prospères. Parce que les peuples indigènes de l'île avaient été décimés, les Français ont importé des esclaves africains pour travailler les terres. Comme à Saint-Domingue, cette population noire s'est révoltée contre les Français vers la fin du 18ème siècle. Pourtant, leurs efforts de se libérer des Français n'ont pas réussi, et la Martinique est restée sous le pouvoir de la France. Cette île est un **département d'outre-mer** de la France depuis la décolonisation des Antilles en 1946, malgré plusieurs tentatives vers l'indépendance pendant la deuxième moitié du 20ème siècle. Intellectuels et activistes martiniquais, comme **Aimé Césaire**, ont favorisé l'indépendance, mais une économie affaiblie par des catastrophes écologiques (notamment plusieurs ouragans autour de 1980) ont freiné les efforts de la libération de l'île. Aujourd'hui, l'économie de la Martinique est basée sur le tourisme et, quoique l'île profite économiquement de ses liens avec la France, elle continue à avoir une identité culturelle unique.

À apprendre

- Comment parler de l'avenir
- Comment rassurer quelqu'un
- Comment interrompre quelqu'un et offrir des commentaires
- Comment faire répéter ou faire préciser

À lire

Claire et Jean-Louis arrivent à Fort-de-France, la capitale de la Martinique, et prennent un autocar pour aller au village de Schœlcher qui est à quelques minutes au nord de la capitale. Ils rencontrent une jeune activiste qui dit qu'elle les aidera à trouver la maison d'André Thibodeau. Pendant que Claire discute avec la jeune femme, Jean-Louis s'excuse et disparaît pour quelques minutes. Claire commence à douter que Jean-Louis ne veuille l'aider avec ses recherches et s'inquiète pour l'avenir. Qui pis est, Monsieur Thibodeau n'est jamais chez lui. . .

Épisode 1

En allant à Schœlcher

Avant de lire

Pour aller plus loin : CULTURE

ACTIVITÉ A : Apprenez plus sur le gouvernement et la situation politique en France. Consultez votre cahier électronique !

6.1 Vos opinions politiques Répondez aux questions suivantes. **Discutez de vos réponses** avec vos camarades de classe et n'hésitez pas à poser des questions supplémentaires si vous voulez en savoir plus.

1. Quels sont les droits humains internationaux les plus importants et les plus fondamentaux (la liberté d'expression, la liberté de religion, le droit à la propriété, le droit de vote, etc.) ? Quelles organisations internationales essaient de sauvegarder ces droits ?
2. Quels droits sont garantis aux citoyens des États-Unis par la Constitution ? Y a-t-il des droits qui sont limités ? Lesquels ? Comment ? Pourquoi ?
3. Quelles guerres d'indépendance connaissez-vous ? Quand est-ce que ces guerres ont eu lieu ? À votre avis, un peuple a-t-il droit à la souveraineté si la majorité des habitants sont d'accord ?
4. Pouvez-vous décrire les fonctions des trois parties (exécutive, judiciaire et législative) du gouvernement fédéral américain ? Quels partis politiques existent aux États-Unis ?
5. Connaissez-vous le maire de votre ville ? le gouverneur de votre état ? vos sénateurs et représentants ? le président et le vice-président des États-Unis ? Pouvez-vous nommer le président et le premier ministre de la France ?
6. Combien de chefs d'état de pays étrangers francophones pouvez-vous nommer ? Quels types de gouvernements trouve-t-on dans le monde francophone (des républiques démocratiques, des monarchies, des confédérations, etc.) ?
7. Que savez-vous des partis politiques français suivants : le RPR (Rassemblement pour la République), le PS (Parti socialiste), le PC (Parti communiste), le FN (Front national), les Verts ? Pouvez-vous décrire leurs points de vue traditionnels ?

Culture

La **République française** a été établie pour la première fois lors de la Révolution française de 1789. Pourtant, la République a été cinq fois proclamée en France ! En 1804, la Première République a été remplacée par l'empire de Napoléon Ier, dont le règne a été suivi par une restauration de la monarchie. En 1848, on a encore renversé la monarchie et on a proclamé une Deuxième République. Cette république a été renversée par l'empire de Napoléon III, mais une Troisième République a été proclamée en 1870. Pendant la Seconde Guerre mondiale, cette troisième république a été remplacée par le gouvernement de Vichy (qui a coopéré avec les Allemands). Le gouvernement de Vichy a été remplacé par une Quatrième République en 1946. En 1958, suite à la rédaction d'une nouvelle constitution, on a proclamé la Cinquième République. Aujourd'hui, il existe toujours une population minoritaire de royalistes qui espèrent la restauration d'une monarchie en France.

6.2 La Martinique ! Dans l'avion, Claire étudie sa carte touristique de la Martinique. Aidez-la à déchiffrer les symboles. Pour chaque lieu, **imaginez ce qu'on peut faire** quand on visite cet endroit.

MODÈLE : À Fort-de-France, on peut visiter des musées d'art antillais et de la vie coloniale.

1. Fort-de-France
2. Rivière-Salée
3. Sainte-Anne
4. Grand-Rivière
5. Trinité
6. Saint-Pierre

Pour aller plus loin : CULTURE

ACTIVITÉ B : Voulez-vous explorer l'île de la Martinique ? Consultez votre cahier électronique !

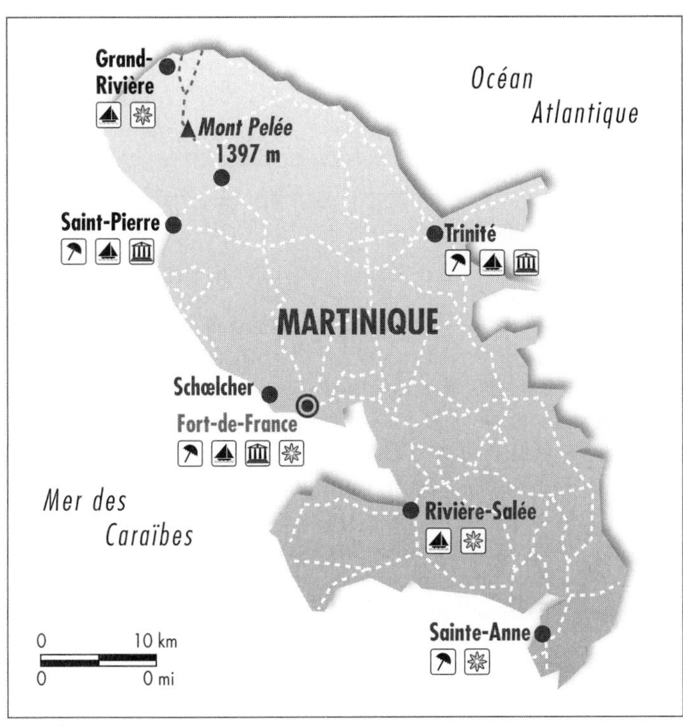

 Plage

 Bateau/Pêche/Sports nautiques

 Musée/Monument

 Jardin/Parc/Flore

Culture

Le **nom de l'île**, la Martinique, vient du mot indien **madiana,** qui veut dire «île de fleurs». Les deux groupes principaux d'indiens qui ont influencé la culture martiniquaise sont les **Arawaks** et les **Caraïbes**. **Victor Schœlcher** était un homme politique français et un antiesclavagiste actif au 19ème siècle. Il a contribué à l'abolition de l'esclavage dans l'étendue des territoires français en 1848. Ses actions en faveur de la libération des esclaves l'ont rendu célèbre aux Antilles, et la ville de Schœlcher à la Martinique est nommée en son honneur.

Une église à Fort-de-France.

lisez

En allant à Schœlcher

Claire et Jean-Louis arrivent à Fort-de-France et y passent quelques heures en attendant le prochain car pour Schœlcher. Il fait nettement plus chaud et plus beau qu'à Paris, sans aucune prévision d'ouragans. Ils se promènent près du port et dans la ville et s'arrêtent un moment au bureau de tourisme où ils réservent deux chambres dans un hôtel près de la mer. Finalement, ils trouvent la gare routière et montent dans l'autocar. Il n'y a qu'une dizaine de passagers : une famille de six personnes à l'avant, près du chauffeur, un homme assez gros en chapeau de paille qui ronfle à l'arrière, eux-mêmes au centre et une jeune femme qui leur dit bonjour et leur sourit gentiment lorsqu'elle s'assied à côté d'eux. . .

CLAIRE : Alors, quand nous arriverons à Schœlcher, nous irons directement à l'hôtel et nous téléphonerons tout de suite à Monsieur Thibodeau.

JEAN-LOUIS : Nous aurons le temps de prendre une douche et quelque chose à manger avant d'aller à la recherche de cet homme ? Je me sens un peu fatigué.

CLAIRE : Bien sûr ! Je ne propose pas d'aller le voir tout de suite, mais nous pourrions prendre rendez-vous pour demain, peut-être.

BERNADETTE : Excusez-moi, je n'ai pas pu m'empêcher d'entendre votre conversation. Est-ce que vous parlez de Monsieur Jacques Thibodeau ?

CLAIRE : Non, c'est un André Thibodeau. Vous le connaissez ?

BERNADETTE : Tout le monde le connaît. Il est le père du maire du village. C'est une famille très riche qui habite la Martinique depuis le 17ème siècle d'après ce qu'on dit d'eux. Je ne les connais pas personnellement, mais je sais qu'ils ont beaucoup de liens avec le gouvernement départemental et qu'ils ont des rapports assez intimes avec quelques ministres français.

JEAN-LOUIS : Alors, vous savez où se trouve la maison de ce monsieur ?

BERNADETTE : Oui, oui. Ils habitent une grande maison, entourée de gardes de sécurité, pas trop loin de la ville. Je trouve déplorable l'idée que les gens riches profitent de leur argent tandis que les gens pauvres qui habitent à trois pas d'eux ont du mal à nourrir leurs enfants. À cela s'ajoute le fait que la plupart des gens riches ici sont des descendants des premiers colons qui ont opprimé les ancêtres des pauvres, qui étaient leurs esclaves. Je ne dis pas cela pour vous offenser. . .

CLAIRE : Pas du tout ! Je comprends ce que vous ressentez. Nous, les Québécois, nous avons un problème comme ça aussi, mais entre anglophones et francophones. Pendant des siècles, les francophones québécois ont été systématiquement opprimés par les anglophones. Il y en a parmi nous qui cherchent la souveraineté. Nous. . .

BERNADETTE : J'ai trouvé une âme sœur ! Mais, pardon, je vous ai interrompue.

CLAIRE : J'allais dire que nous, je veux dire ceux qui sont membres du Parti québécois, nous souhaitons un nouveau référendum à l'avenir pour que le peuple francophone puisse voter pour son autonomie.

BERNADETTE : Nous aussi ! Je travaille pour un parti politique qui veut l'indépendance de la Martinique. Nous estimons que le problème économique est le plus difficile à surmonter, mais on parle de la possibilité d'une conféderation antillaise qui reliera toutes les petites îles. Si l'Europe peut se réunir, pourquoi pas les Antilles ?

CLAIRE : Tout à fait. Pour nous, le problème est différent. Personnellement, je crois que le problème le plus difficile à surmonter sera le problème de l'identité québécoise. Le peuple québécois est majoritairement francophone mais aussi multiculturel. Bien sûr, nous ne voulons pas frapper d'autres groupes ethniques d'ostracisme social. Nous voulons inclure et les francophones et les anglophones et les autochtones et les allophones et les nouveaux groupes d'immigrants dans une identité québécoise nationale. Je suis trop idéaliste, peut-être, mais je pense vraiment que tout cela est possible.

JEAN-LOUIS : Excusez-moi de vous interrompre et de changer de sujet, mais on arrive bientôt à Schœlcher. Mademoiselle, savez-vous si nous pouvons marcher jusqu'à l'Hôtel Beauséjour ?

BERNADETTE : Oui, oui. Ce n'est pas trop loin de l'arrêt en ville. Je vous montrerai le chemin et nous pourrons continuer à discuter. . .

i Langue

Voici quelques mots qui pourraient vous aider à **parler de la politique** !

- Pour parler des **gouvernements** : un pays (*country*), une république, une monarchie, une démocratie, une confédération, une union, un état, un département ou un territoire (d'outre-mer), un régime progressiste/oppressif/intolérant.
- Pour parler des **droits** : une constitution, des lois, des droits, des privilèges, un accord, un traité, la liberté, l'indépendance, l'égalité, la souveraineté, l'oppression, la discriminiation, la résistence, une guerre, un procès, un débat, gagner/perdre une élection (élire quelqu'un), un vote (voter), un référendum, équitable, légal(e), illégal(e).
- Pour parler des **gens** et des **institutions** : le chef d'état, le président, le vice-président, le premier ministre, le roi / la reine, un ministre, un sénateur, un(e) représentant(e), un gouverneur, un(e) maire, le parlement, le sénat, l'assemblée nationale, la cour, un parti politique (de droite, de gauche), un(e) citoyen(ne).

VOCABULAIRE

La politique

le maire	*mayor*
le ministre (de culture, etc.)	*minister (of culture, etc.)*
entouré(e)	*surrounded*
un pas	*step*
se sentir	*to feel*
ressentir	*to feel strongly*
opprimer, opprimé(e)	*to oppress, oppressed*
la souveraineté	*sovereignty*
estimer (que)	*to estimate, to think that*
surmonter	*to overcome*
relier	*to link together*
majoritaire(ment)	*majority (adj.), in the majority (adv.)*
un(e) autochtone	*speaker of native Indian languages in Québec*
un(e) allophone	*speaker of any language other than French, English, or native languages in Québec*

Divers

un (auto)car	*intercity bus*
nettement	*significantly*
la paille	*straw*
ronfler	*to snore*
une âme (âme sœur)	*soul (like-minded person, soulmate)*

Culture

Il existe plusieurs **mouvements pour la souveraineté**, c'est-à-dire des mouvements d'indépendance, dans le monde francophone à l'aube (*dawn*) du 21ème siècle.

- Au **Québec,** une bonne partie du peuple, surtout parmi les francophones de la région montréalaise, désirent un Québec libre du gouvernement canadien. Les questions de la langue maternelle et de l'identité culturelle y jouent un rôle très important, mais l'enjeu de l'économie est aussi un problème au cœur du débat. Aux deux derniers référendums, le peuple québécois a voté contre l'indépendance.
- À la **Martinique,** on parle de l'indépendance depuis la fin du Seconde Guerre mondiale en 1945 et la décolonisation de l'Afrique en 1960. Aujourd'hui, il existe des partis en faveur de la souveraineté à la Martinique, mais la majorité des Martiniquais acceptent la situation politique telle qu'elle est. En comparaison avec d'autres îles antillaises, l'économie de la Martinique est assez prospère, et cela rend la question de l'indépendance encore plus difficile.
- En Europe, en **Corse** (une île dans la Méditerranée) et au **Pays basque** (à la frontière entre la France et l'Espagne), des mouvements d'indépendance sont aussi populaires parmi une partie plutôt minoritaire du peuple. Dans ces deux cas, les gens revendiquent leur identité culturelle unique et veulent se gouverner eux-mêmes sans l'intervention du gouvernement français.
- En **Casamance**, une région au sud du **Sénégal** qui longe la Gambie, il existe aussi des mouvements d'indépendance où les habitants, eux aussi, revendiquent leur identité culturelle unique. Il faut noter que les mouvements souverainistes en Corse, au Pays basque et en Casamance sont affectés par des actes de violence qui remettent en question les négociations politiques.

Après avoir lu

6.3 Avez-vous compris ? Répondez aux questions suivantes. **Justifiez vos réponses** en citant le texte.

1. Pourquoi est-ce que Bernadette et Claire commencent à parler de la politique ?

2. Comment est Bernadette ? Voudriez-vous discuter de politique avec elle ? Pourquoi ou pourquoi pas ?
3. Où vont Claire et Jean-Louis ? Qu'est-ce qu'ils doivent faire quand ils arriveront à Schœlcher ? Avez-vous des conseils pour eux ?
4. Claire et Bernadette parlent des mouvements d'indépendance à la Martinique et au Québéc. Y a-t-il des similarités entre ces deux situations politiques ? Décrivez-les.

Pour aller plus loin : CULTURE

ACTIVITÉ C : Apprenez un peu plus sur le mouvement d'indépendance au Québec et sur le Parti québécois. Consultez votre cahier électronique !

6.4 D'accord ou pas d'accord ? Indiquez si vous êtes **d'accord ou pas d'accord** avec les phrases suivantes, d'après votre compréhension du récit. Justifiez vos opinions en citant le texte, si possible. Discutez de vos réponses avec la classe.

	D'accord	Pas d'accord
1. Bernadette a l'oreille indiscrète.	_______	_______
2. Bernadette a des opinions politiques assez radicales.	_______	_______
3. Claire et Bernadette s'entendent bien.	_______	_______
4. Claire veut que le Québec devienne un pays indépendant.	_______	_______
5. Jean-Louis ne s'intéresse pas à la politique.	_______	_______

6.5 Le pour et le contre Regardez la liste suivante et **indiquez si ce sont des raisons pour ou contre** l'indépendance de la Martinique. Discutez de vos opinions avec vos camarades de classe.

1. Les Martiniquais ont tous les droits accordés aux citoyens français de la métropole.
2. La France aide l'économie de la Martinique.
3. Les Martiniquais ont leur propre identité culturelle et ethnique.
4. Beaucoup de Français passent leurs vacances dans les DOM-TOM.
5. La majorité des Martiniquais sont les descendants des esclaves africains opprimés par les Français de France.
6. L'île appartenait aux peuples indigènes, les habitants originels de cette terre.
7. La société martiniquaise est multiculturelle et comprend des gens de racines africaines, arabes, chinoises, indiennes et européennes.

i Culture

Pendant **la guerre de l'Indépendance américaine**, au 18ème siècle, les Français ont aidé les révolutionnaires américains qui voulaient leur souveraineté. Le marquis de La Fayette était un des Français qui est venu au secours des Américains et qui a joué un rôle important dans leur déclaration d'indépendance. De plus, des Américains tels que Thomas Jefferson et Benjamin Franklin parlaient couramment le français et ont été influencés par les idées philosophiques françaises.

6.6 La politique Regardez les mots de vocabulaire qui suivent. Dans chaque ligne, il y a un mot qui cloche avec les trois autres. **Entourez le mot qui ne va pas avec les autres** et essayez d'expliquer pourquoi. Attention ! Il y a parfois plusieurs bonnes réponses. Il faut justifier votre choix.

1. voter	élire (*to elect*)	débattre	discuter
2. une loi	un référendum	une constitution	un droit
3. majoritaire	beaucoup	minoritaire	plusieurs
4. l'économie	la société	la culture	le gouvernement
5. radical	libéral	conservateur	apathique

la Martinique

Rencontrez un Martiniquais ! Regardez la vidéo et consultez votre cahier d'activités !

6.7 Vocabulaire personnel Pensez à votre pays et et à la situation politique d'aujourd'hui et, pour chaque catégorie, **faites une liste de cinq à dix mots importants** que vous pouvez utiliser pour décrire vos points de vue politiques. Consultez un dictionnaire si nécessaire.

1. Les élections aux États-Unis : partis politiques, postes politiques, institutions publiques.
2. Les sujets de débat politique qui vous intéressent concernant votre ville, votre région ou votre état.
3. Les sujets de débat politique qui vous intéressent au niveau national ou international.
4. Les lois et les droits les plus importants à vous.

6.8 Une âme sœur ! Bernadette accompagne ses nouveaux amis à l'hôtel et Claire l'invite à déjeuner avec eux. Pendant le repas, Jean-Louis doit se retirer et les deux jeunes femmes continuent leur conversation. Choisissez une des expressions entre parenthèses et **lisez le dialogue à haute voix** avec un partenaire. Quand vous voyez «? ? ?», vous pouvez imaginer votre propre expression.

CLAIRE : Alors, vous habitez à Schœlcher depuis longtemps ?

BERNADETTE : Oui, je suis née ici ! Toute ma famille est ici, mais je travaille à Fort-de-France dans (une agence de tourisme / un hôtel / ? ? ?). Et vous ?

CLAIRE : Moi, je suis étudiante (à l'Université de Sainte-Foy / de doctorat) en lettres françaises.

BERNADETTE : (Ça alors / Vraiment / ? ? ?) ! J'adore la littérature. Connaissez-vous des auteurs martiniquais ?

CLAIRE : (Bien sûr / Absolument / ? ? ?) ! On étudie souvent Aimé Césaire et Franz Fanon, ces chefs du mouvement de la négritude, mais mon auteur préféré est Patrick Chamoiseau parce que ses romans sont si (charmants / bien écrits / ? ? ?). . .

BERNADETTE : (À propos ! / Justement !) Chamoiseau est un des auteurs les plus populaires ici. Je suis désolée de vous interrompre, mais moi aussi j'adore les œuvres de Chamoiseau. Son

Chemin d'école me rappelle (ma jeunesse / le bon vieux temps). Mais, vous vouliez dire quelque chose. (Allez-y ! / Je vous écoute !)...

CLAIRE : J'allais dire (simplement / seulement / ? ? ?) que les auteurs martiniquais sont bien appréciés par les étudiants de lettres françaises.

BERNADETTE : Ajoutons que le public général applaudit la politique post-coloniale qu'on trouve dans ces romans... mais votre (fiancé / ami / camarade) français, apprécie-t-il notre littérature engagée ?

CLAIRE : Qui ? Jean-Louis ? Enfin, il travaille avec les livres, mais la littérature n'est pas son truc... et, pour clarifier, c'est juste un ami. Il m'aide dans mes recherches. (C'est tout. / Voilà. / ? ? ?)

BERNADETTE : (Si je puis me permettre de / Je voudrais juste) vous poser une question à ce sujet... Êtes-vous sûre qu'il vous aide de bon cœur ? Je ne le connais pas, mais il me semble un peu cachotier (*secretive*). Ça fait déjà 20 minutes qu'il est parti...

CLAIRE : (Ah bon ? / Vous avez raison. / ? ? ?) Où peut-il être ?

Littérature

La **négritude** est un mouvement littéraire mondial initié par des écrivains comme Aimé Césaire (de la Martinique), Franz Fanon (de la Martinique), Léopold Senghor (du Sénégal) et René Despestre (d'Haïti) dans les années 50 et 60. Ce mouvement a cherché à rétablir et à revaloriser l'image des noirs suite au racisme de l'ère coloniale. En même temps qu'ils critiquaient les effets sociaux et psychologiques du racisme et de la colonisation, les auteurs travaillaient à la reconnaissance de l'importance des cultures africaines et de leurs traditions populaires pour les peuples noirs. Les auteurs martiniquais d'aujourd'hui, comme Patrick Chamoiseau, Raphaël Confiant, Joseph Zobel et Édouard Glissant, reconnaissent l'importance de la négritude, mais préfèrent voir la société martiniquaise comme une société créole plutôt qu'une société noire. Leurs mouvements s'appellent **la créolité** ou **l'antillanité**, et ces auteurs représentent la société martiniquaise comme une mosaïque de cultures et ethnies diverses.

Pour aller plus loin : CULTURE

ACTIVITÉ D : Lisez un poème d'Aimé Césaire. Consultez votre cahier électronique !

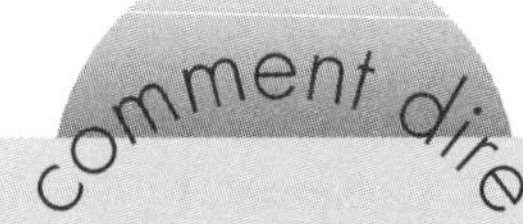

interrompre quelqu'un et ajouter quelque chose

To interrupt

À propos ! / Justement ! / Ça me rappelle un truc...
Je suis désolé(e) de vous/t' interrompre, mais...
Si je puis me permettre de dire... / Permettez, je finis ma phrase...
Je voudrais juste dire une chose à ce sujet. / Mais laisse-moi parler !
J'ai une question à te/vous poser. J'ai quelque chose à dire !
Je pourrais en placer une ? / J'arrive pas à placer un mot !
Tais-toi ! / Taisez-vous ! / Ta gueule ! (*vulgar*)

interrompre quelqu'un et ajouter quelque chose **(continued)**

To let others speak	Je vous écoute. Allez-y. Racontez ! Je vous en prie. Je t'écoute. Vas-y. Raconte ! Je t'en prie. À toi/vous de parler ! / C'est à toi/vous ! Tu voulais / Vous vouliez dire quelque chose ? Dis ce que tu as à dire. / Dites ce que vous avez à dire. Ne sois/soyez pas timide. Cela m'intéresse énormément. J'aimerais bien avoir ton/votre opinion.
To add something	Ceci dit... / De plus... / Par ailleurs... / Néanmoins... À cela s'ajoute le fait / l'idée que... / Ajoutons que... Je voulais ajouter que... / Je voulais dire que... Qui plus est... / Qui pis est... / N'oublions pas que...

i Langue

La **gueule** est un synonyme pour la bouche ou la tête. Si on a la «fine gueule», on est gourmand. Quand on dit «**ta gueule !**», cela veut dire qu'il faut fermer la bouche et arrêter de parler. Cette expression est assez vulgaire. L'expression **avoir la gueule de bois** veut dire qu'on a trop trop bu et trop fait la fête la veille et qu'on se sent un peu malade, comme si on avait une bouche en bois. La **gueule-de-loup** est un type de fleur (*snapdragon*), et il y a une bière québécoise très connue qui s'appelle **Belle Gueule**. Une **belle gueule** est une expression pour décrire un bel homme.

6.9 À vous **Imaginez** que vous êtes dans les situations suivantes. **Que dites-vous ?** Avec un partenaire, choisissez des expressions pour chaque situation.

1. Vous voulez interrompre votre professeur, qui ne cesse pas de parler de politique, pour dire que les Français ont aidé les Américains à déclarer leur indépendance de la Grande-Bretagne.
2. Vous expliquez à votre ami(e) qu'il/elle réussira ses examens seulement s'il/elle étudie tous les soirs. Ajoutez qu'il faut bien manger et faire de l'exercice aussi.
3. Votre ami(e) est timide, mais vous sentez qu'il/elle a quelque chose à vous dire à propos de votre nouvelle coiffure.
4. Vous essayez d'expliquer à vos parents l'importance de voyager à la Martinique pour les vacances de printemps, mais ils ne parlent que de l'emploi qu'ils vous ont trouvé dans un supermarché.

6.10 À propos ! Sur une feuille de papier, **écrivez une phrase** pour décrire la loi (*law*) que vous trouvez la moins efficace (*effective*) ou la moins utile (*useful*) aux États-Unis ! Puis, **circulez** dans la salle de classe et exprimez votre opinion à vos camarades. Bien sûr, les idées des autres ne vous intéressent pas trop. Interrompez les autres pour parler de votre opinion. Essayez d'exprimer votre opinion à autant de personnes que possible !

MODÈLE : —Je pense que la loi contre l'achat de l'alcool avant l'âge de 21 ans est inefficace. L'alcool est devenu une tentation au lieu d'une boisson à consommer en modération.

—Je suis désolé de t'interrompre, mais je pense que les lois concernant le recyclage sont encore moins efficaces !

6.11 L'utopie Avec un partenaire, **faites une liste** des caractéristiques d'une utopie. Parlez des gens, du gouvernement, de la société, du temps et d'autres aspects que vous trouvez importants. Ensuite, **comparez** votre liste avec celle d'un autre groupe. Interrompez-les souvent pour ajouter votre opinion, mais redonnez-leur la parole quand vous aurez terminé d'exprimer votre pensée. Soyez poli(e)s !

MODÈLE : —Dans une utopie, tous les gens ont accès à une bonne éducation et toutes les écoles sont égales.

—Excusez-moi, mais j'ai quelque chose à dire ! On doit aussi avoir de l'égalité économique, pour que tous les gens reçoivent le même salaire. Mais je vous écoute. Continuez.

Pour aller plus loin : LITTÉRATURE

ACTIVITÉ E : Lisez des citations de plusieurs auteurs francophones sur l'utopie. Consultez votre cahier électronique !

À l'écrit *première étape*

6.12 Les innovations à l'avenir Avec la technologie, les découvertes scientifiques et les nouvelles inventions, le monde change vite. **Faites une liste de quatre ou cinq innovations** qui changeront notre façon de vivre à l'avenir (*future*) et expliquez chaque innovation en une phrase. Vous pouvez parler de vraies innovations ou bien vous pouvez inventer vos propres idées innovatrices ! Ensuite, échangez votre liste avec celle d'un camarade de classe. Vérifiez que votre partenaire a bien décrit ses idées, faites des corrections possibles et ajoutez des commentaires en bas de page.

MODÈLE : L'invention des livres électroniques va changer le monde. Ça va aider l'environnment parce que nous allons utiliser moins de papier et sauver plus d'arbres.

Épisode 2

Le coup de téléphone

Un village à la Martinique.

Structures *les pronoms d'objet et les pronoms adverbiaux*

6.13 Une partie de cache-cache (*hide-and-seek*) En attendant le retour de Jean-Louis au restaurant, Claire raconte à Bernadette l'histoire du manuscrit qu'elle cherche, mais sans dire le nom de l'auteur. Regardez tous les *pronoms compléments d'objet direct* (**me, te, le/la, nous, vous, les**) et *indirects* (**me, te, lui, nous, vous, leur**) qu'elle utilise. En plus, regardez les *pronoms adverbiaux* **y** et **en**. Pour chaque pronom complément d'objet, **indiquez ce que ce pronom représente**. Pouvez-vous décrire comment fonctionnent les pronoms d'objet et les pronoms adverbiaux en analysant ces exemples ?

BERNADETTE : Votre ami **vous** aide avec votre thèse ?

CLAIRE : Enfin, oui et non. Il **m'**aide à trouver le manuscrit dont j'ai besoin. Et **le** trouver, ce n'est pas facile ! C'est comme une partie de cache-cache ! D'abord, l'auteur **l'**a donné à un homme de Saint-Domingue. Il **le lui** a donné en 1792. Puis, cet homme est allé en Louisiane. L'homme **y** a ouvert un restaurant et il a gardé le manuscrit dans sa bibliothèque. Ses descendants **l'y** ont gardé jusqu'en 1973. Puis, ils ont vendu la bibliothèque familiale. Ils **l'ont** vendue à un bouquiniste parisien. Ils ne **lui** ont pas dit que le manuscrit était parmi les livres de la bibliothèque familiale. Le bouquiniste **l'**a mis dans sa collection de livres anciens. Il **y en** avait plusieurs qui étaient très rares. Enfin, le bouquiniste **l'**a vendu récemment à un homme qui habite la Martinique. Et nous **y** sommes venus pour **le** rencontrer. Nous espérons qu'il **nous le** vendra... ou, au moins, qu'il **me** laissera le temps de **l'**étudier.

les pronoms d'objet et les pronoms adverbiaux

Pronouns (**les pronoms**) are used to replace words or phrases in order to refer to something that has already been mentioned or in order to avoid repeating it. *Object pronouns* (**les pronoms compléments d'objet**) and *adverbial pronouns* (**les pronoms adverbiaux**), which are often grouped with them, must always be used in context, so that the speaker or reader knows what is being referred to. Choose the appropriate object pronoun according to the function of the object in the sentence.

Direct object pronouns (**les pronoms compléments d'objet direct**) replace nouns that take the direct action of the verb (nouns that are not preceded by a preposition). The pronoun agrees with its noun in number and gender:

- The direct object pronouns are **me, te, le/la, nous, vous, les**.
- Example: Il a mis **le manuscrit** dans sa collection. → Il **l'**a mis dans sa collection.
- **Note:** If there is a *preceding direct object* and there is a past participle (with *passé composé, plus-que-parfait, subjonctif passé,* etc.), the past participle must agree with the object: Ils ont vendu **sa bibliothèque**. → Ils **l'**ont vendu**e**.

Indirect object pronouns (**les pronoms compléments d'objet indirect**) replace *people* introduced by a preposition (generally **à** + person):

- The indirect object pronouns are **me, te, lui, nous, vous, leur**.
- Example: Ils n'ont pas dit **au bouquiniste** que le manuscrit était parmi les livres. → Ils ne **lui** ont pas dit que le manuscrit était parmi les livres.

The *adverbial pronoun* **y** replaces nouns (objects, places, ideas, etc.) introduced by a preposition of location (**à** or any other preposition of location, such as: **chez, dans, en, sous, devant, derrière**) and does not agree in gender or number: Il a ouvert un restaurant **en Louisiane**. → Il **y** a ouvert un restaurant.

The *adverbial pronoun* **en** replaces nouns introduced by an indefinite or partitive article, an expression of quantity, or a number (**de** or **du, de la, des** or any expression of quantity, such as **trois, beaucoup, plusieurs, assez,** etc.) and does not agree in gender or number: Jean-Louis vend **des livres** à Paris. → Il **en** vend à Paris.

- **Note:** If a number or expression of quantity is present, the pronoun replaces only the noun (or **de** + *noun*), not the quantity itself: Il avait **plusieurs livres**. → Il **en** avait plusieurs.

Order of pronouns

Object pronouns and *adverbial pronouns* normally *precede the verb* to which they are attached. Sometimes more than one pronoun is used in the same sentence, though it is rare to use more than two at a time. When there is *more than one pronoun* in a sentence, the order of pronouns is as follows:

		me					
		te	**le**				
Subject + **(ne)** +		**se** +	**la** +	**lui** +	**y** + **en** +	*verb* +	**(pas)**
		nous	**les**	**leur**			
		vous					

- Example: L'auteur a donné **le manuscrit à un homme** en 1792. → Il **le lui** a donné en 1792.

Note that in a sentence with *two or more verbs*, the pronouns precede the verb to which they belong:

- Example: Je veux parler **à Monsieur Thibodeau du manuscrit.** → Je veux **lui en** parler.

With the *imperative* (commands), the placement and order of pronouns differ:

- When *pronouns* are used with the *affirmative imperative*, the pronouns follow the verb, connected by hyphens (**traits d'union**): Donnez-**lui** le manuscrit !
- When there are *multiple pronouns* in an *affirmative imperative* construction, the pronouns are placed in the following order: *Verb* **- objet direct - objet indirect - y - en !** Example: Donnez-**le-lui** !
- With the *negative imperative*, however, the pronouns *precede the verb*, as they do in declarative sentences: Ne **le lui** donnez pas !

6.14 Répétez, s'il vous plaît Bernadette essaie de comprendre l'histoire du manuscrit. Donc, elle demande à Claire de répéter chacune de ses phrases. **Récrivez les phrases suivantes** en substituant **un pronom** pour les mots en **caractères gras**. Ensuite, récrivez-les à nouveau en ajoutant d'autres pronoms possibles.

MODÈLE : Nous cherchons **un manuscrit** qui appartient à un homme martiniquais. →

—Nous *en* cherchons un qui appartient à un homme martiniquais.

—Nous *en* cherchons un qui *lui* appartient.

1. Nous cherchons un **manuscrit** qui appartient à un homme martiniquais.
2. L'auteur a offert le manuscrit **à un ami** en 1792.
3. L'ami a apporté le manuscrit **à la Nouvelle-Orléans**.
4. Il avait beaucoup **de livres rares** dans sa collection.
5. Sa famille a vendu **sa collection** à un bouquiniste parisien en 1973.
6. Le bouquiniste n'a pas pensé **au manuscrit**.
7. Il a gardé le manuscrit **dans son entrepôt** pendant des années.
8. Il vient de vendre **le manuscrit** à Monsieur Thibodeau.
9. Jean-Louis et moi voulons parler du manuscrit **à ce monsieur**.

6.15 Quelques précisions Il y a presqu'une heure que Jean-Louis a quitté la table. Bernadette et Claire continuent à parler du manuscrit, et Bernadette pose beaucoup de questions à Claire. Jouez le rôle de Claire et répondez aux questions. **Remplacez les mots en caractères gras avec des pronoms** compléments d'objet ou des pronoms adverbiaux quand vous répondez.

MODÈLE : Alors, vous avez rencontré Jean-Louis **au Québec** ? (non) →
—Non, je n'*y* ai pas rencontré Jean-Louis. Je l'ai rencontré en Louisiane.

1. Donc, le manuscrit est **à la Martinique** ? (oui)
2. Jean-Louis **vous** a dit qu'il voulait **vous** aider ? (oui)
3. Vous croyez **Jean-Louis** ? (oui)
4. Est-ce qu'il habite **chez ses parents** ? (non)
5. A-t-il beaucoup **d'argent** ? (oui)
6. Vous avez déjà téléphoné **à Monsieur Thibodeau** ? (oui)
7. Est-ce qu'il était **chez lui** ? (non)
8. Voulez-vous que je demande **à mes amis** quand les Thibodeau reviendront ? (oui)
9. Est-ce que vous restez **à l'hôtel** ce soir ? (oui)
10. Est-ce que Jean-Louis ment **aux gens** de temps en temps ? (non)
11. Est-ce que vous vous sentez à l'aise en **me** parlant ? (oui)
12. Avez-vous besoin **de mon aide** ? (oui)

6.16 Des cadeaux ! Avec un partenaire, **faites une description d'un cadeau que vous avez reçu**. Décrivez l'objet et puis précisez qui vous l'a donné, quand on vous l'a offert, pourquoi on vous l'a donné et où vous le gardez. Votre partenaire doit deviner (*to guess*) de quoi il s'agit ! Attention à l'usage des pronoms compléments d'objet et des pronoms adverbiaux !

MODÈLE : —C'est petit et carré. Ma sœur me l'a donné pour mon anniversaire. Elle me l'a donné parce qu'elle sait que j'adore la littérature française. Je le garde dans ma chambre. Je l'ai mis sur la table à côté de mon lit.
—C'est un livre en français !

Langue

Vous rappelez-vous les conjugaisons des **verbes irréguliers** suivants : **dormir, mentir** et **sentir** ? Si non, mémorisez leurs conjugaisons avant de continuer !

- **dormir** (*to sleep*) : je dors, tu dors, il/elle/on dort, nous dormons, vous dormez, ils/elles dorment (*participe passé* : dormi)
- **mentir** (*to lie, tell lies*) : je mens, tu mens, il/elle/on ment, nous mentons, vous mentez, ils/elles mentent (*participe passé* : menti)
- **sentir** (*to feel, to smell*) : je sens, tu sens, il/elle/on sent, nous sentons, vous sentez, ils/elles sentent (*participe passé* : senti) ; le verbe **ressentir** est conjugué comme sentir.

Structures *les pronoms disjoints*

6.17 Aidez-moi ! Claire commence à soupçonner que Jean-Louis lui cache quelque chose. Elle continue à discuter avec Bernadette mais devient de plus en plus impatiente. Regardez les **pronoms disjoints** dans les phrases suivantes prononcées par Claire et **indiquez de qui elle parle**. Pouvez-vous décrire comment fonctionnent les pronoms disjoints en analysant ces exemples ?

MODÈLE : Nous allons **chez lui.** →
chez Monsieur Thibodeau

1. Vous venez **avec nous**.
2. Il ne partirait pas **sans moi**.
3. Pensez-vous qu'il habite **avec elle** ?
4. Nous achèterons des fleurs **pour eux**.
5. Il habite près de **chez vous** ?
6. C'est **à lui** que je dis la vérité.

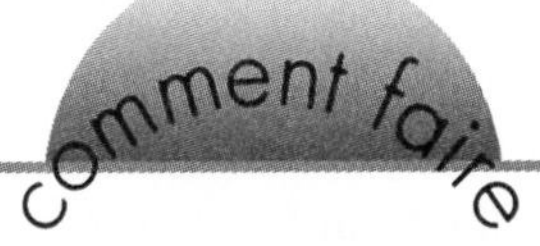

les pronoms disjoints

The *disjunctive pronouns* (les **pronoms disjoints**) are used to replace people's names or descriptions after certain prepositions (**à, de, avec, sans, pour**, etc.). The disjunctive pronouns are:

moi	nous
toi	vous
lui/elle	eux/elles

- Example: C'est **à eux** de parler ! Quant **à moi**, je me méfie **de lui.**
- **Note:** The disjunctive pronouns can also be used without a preposition as *stress pronouns* to emphasize the subject of a sentence: (**Moi** ? je me méfie de lui. **Lui**, il est parti il y a une heure !) or to emphasize a direct object (Je l'adore, **elle** !).

6.18 Claire pose des questions Claire pose des questions à Bernadette. **Remplissez les blancs** avec un **pronom disjoint**.

1. Est-ce que vous parlez de Jean-Louis ? Vous parlez de ______________, n'est-ce pas ?
2. Et vos amis, ______________, ils connaissent les Thibodeau ?

3. Les Thibodeau habitent près de la maison de tes tantes ? Je veux dire, près de chez ____________________ ?
4. Est-ce que Jean-Louis est parti pour aller chez les Thibodeau ? Il est allé chez ____________________ ?
5. Pensez-vous qu'il soit parti sans ____________________ ? Il m'a promis de m'aider !
6. ____________________, j'attends son retour. Je veux poser des questions à Jean-Louis. C'est à ____________________ que je veux parler.
7. Il m'a promis de ne plus me mentir. Donc, je veux parler avec ____________________ avant de tirer de fausses conclusions.
8. Est-ce que vous viendrez avec Jean-Louis et moi demain ? Vous ne voulez pas venir avec ____________________ ?

6.19 Des objets trouvés (*lost and found*) Sur une feuille de papier, **dessinez** (*draw*) **un objet** que vous chérissez. N'y mettez pas votre nom. Ensuite, pliez votre papier et **échangez vos «objets»** au hasard. Puis, **circulez** dans la classe et essayez de trouver le propriétaire de l'objet. Quand vous trouvez le propriétaire, échangez votre «objet» pour le sien. Ensuite, essayez de trouver le propriétaire de ce nouvel objet. Mais attention, il est possible que les gens mentent ! Posez des questions afin de vérifier que la personne est le vrai propriétaire de l'objet. Continuez jusqu'à ce que tout le monde ait retrouvé son objet !

MODÈLE : —Est-ce que cette bicyclette est à toi ?

—Non. Moi, je cherche mes boucles d'oreille.

—Ah, bon ? Je ne les ai pas. Est-ce que tu as un ordinateur ?

—Oui, j'en ai un. Comment est le tien ?

Avant d'écouter

6.20 Avant le coup de téléphone Les phrases suivantes sont très formelles, mais vous voulez avoir une conversation avec quelqu'un que vous connaissez très bien et que vous tutoyez. Transformez les phrases au registre familier.

1. C'est bien vous ? Comment allez-vous ?
2. Pardon, pouvez-vous parler moins vite ?
3. Je vous assure que tout va bien.
4. Est-ce que vous pourriez répéter ? Je ne vous ai pas entendu.
5. Qu'est-ce que vous venez de dire ?

écoutez

Le coup de téléphone

En sortant du restaurant, Bernadette voit un groupe de gens qui écoutent un conteur sur la place centrale de la ville. Elle leur demande s'ils ont vu un homme français. Ils lui disent qu'un homme a donné un coup de téléphone dans la cabine en face d'eux, et ils expliquent que cet homme a longuement parlé avec quelqu'un et qu'il était très animé pendant qu'il parlait. Claire comprend tout de suite que c'était Jean-Louis qui téléphonait. . . Mais à qui ? Et pourquoi ?

Maintenant, **écoutez le dialogue sur votre CD**. Consultez le vocabulaire et lisez les notes culturelles pour mieux comprendre le dialogue, et puis répondez aux questions suivantes.

VOCABULAIRE

Divers			
à peine	*barely*	un cadeau	*present*
un anniversaire	*birthday*	raccrocher	*to hang up*
sauf	*except*	une part	*slice*
		être ravi(e)	*to be delighted*

Culture

Un **conteur** est une personne qui raconte des histoires, des contes ou des fables pour un public assemblé. Dans les cultures africaines, le conteur, qu'on appelle un «**griot**», joue un rôle très important dans la société, non seulement parce qu'il divertit son public, mais en plus parce qu'il leur enseigne des leçons et leur raconte des nouvelles. Ils utilisent beaucoup de gestes et de chansons pour enrichir leurs contes. Cette tradition est venue aux Antilles avec les Africains et y a fleuri. Aux Antilles, quand un conteur veut commencer à raconter une histoire, il crie le mot «Cric !», et si le public veut l'entendre, ils répondent «Crac !». Ensuite, la présentation du conte est interactive et le public participe au développement de l'histoire. Dans les sociétés africaines et antillaises, il y a des griots de grande renommée qui sont très recherchés par le public à cause de leur façon de faire vivre leurs personnages et leurs contes préférés.

Après avoir écouté

6.21 Avez-vous compris ? Après avoir écouté le dialogue entre Claire et Jean-Louis, **répondez** aux questions suivantes.

1. À qui est-ce que Jean-Louis téléphone ? Pourquoi ? Pensez-vous qu'il se sente coupable (*guilty*) de ne pas être à Paris en ce moment ?
2. Pourquoi est-ce que Jean-Louis n'a pas dit à Claire qu'il devait téléphoner à sa mère ?
3. Qu'est-ce que la mère pense du travail de son fils ? Est-ce que Jean-Louis lui ment à propos de ce qu'il fait à la Martinique ?
4. Imaginez comment Claire va réagir quand elle apprend que Jean-Louis a téléphoné à sa mère.

6.22 Vrai ou faux ? D'après votre compréhension du dialogue, **dites si les phrases suivantes sont vraies ou fausses** et employez un pronom d'objet (direct ou indirect), un pronom adverbial (**y** ou **en**), ou un pronom disjoint dans votre réponse. Parfois, il faudra utiliser deux pronoms.

MODÈLE : Claire et Jean-Louis sont **à la Guadeloupe**. →
—Faux ! Ils n'*y* sont pas. Ils sont à la Martinique.
Ils déjeunent **au restaurant** avec **Bernadette.** →
—Vrai ! Ils *y* déjeunent avec *elle*.

1. Jean-Louis quitte **le restaurant** avec **Claire**.
2. Il trouve **une cabine téléphonique**.
3. Il téléphone **à son patron**.
4. Sa mère fête **son anniversaire** (*m.*).
5. Jean-Louis parle **du manuscrit à sa mère**.
6. La mère offre **de l'argent à son fils**.
7. Jean-Louis retournera **à Paris** cette semaine.
8. Il donnera **le manuscrit à son patron**.
9. Ensuite, il ira **au restaurant** avec **ses parents**.
10. Bernadette donnera **l'adresse de Monsieur Thibodeau à Claire et Jean-Louis**.

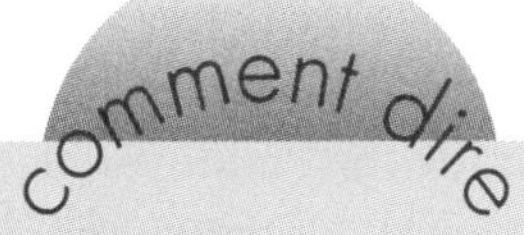

faire répéter ou faire préciser

To ask someone to repeat	Pardon ? / Comment ? / Quoi ? / Excusez-moi ? Pouvez-vous répéter, s'il vous plaît ? Qu'est-ce que vous venez de dire ? Pouvez-vous parler moins vite / plus fort ? Je n'ai pas bien compris. Je n'ai pas bien entendu. Articulez, s'il vous plaît !
To ask for more specific information	Qu'est-ce que vous voulez dire ? Je ne comprends pas ce que vous dites. Je ne comprends rien à ce que vous dites. Je n'y comprends rien ! / Je ne vois pas ce que vous voulez dire ! Mais qu'est-ce que vous racontez ? Pouvez-vous préciser ? / C'est-à-dire ?

Pour aller plus loin : CULTURE

ACTIVITÉ F : Découvrez les arts, la culture et la gastronomie de la Martinique. Consultez votre cahier électronique !

6.23 Que dites-vous ? Qu'est-ce qu'on peut dire pour se faire comprendre dans les situations suivantes ? Avec un partenaire, **décidez ce que vous pouvez dire**.

1. Vous parlez au téléphone avec votre ami(e) et vous n'entendez pas ce qu'il/elle dit.
2. Votre professeur explique comment utiliser le subjonctif (encore), mais vous ne comprenez pas ce qu'il/elle dit.
3. Vous allez à la Martinique et vous rencontrez des gens qui parlent créole. Donc, vous ne comprenez que la moitié de ce qu'ils disent.
4. Vous parlez avec une femme âgée qui parle très doucement et très vite.
5. Vous êtes une personne âgée un peu sourde (*deaf*) et vous n'entendez pas très bien ce que les jeunes gens disent.
6. Votre maire fait un discours public pour renouveller sa candidature aux prochaines élections, pourtant le microphone marche mal et on a du mal à comprendre ce qu'il dit.

la Martinique

Que pense Thierry de la politique ? Regardez la vidéo et consultez votre cahier d'activités !

6.24 Répétez ! Circulez dans la classe et **posez des questions** à vos camarades en employant les éléments suivants. Quand quelqu'un vous pose une question, demandez-lui de **répéter la question**. Ensuite, donnez une réponse en utilisant **des pronoms compléments d'objet** et/ou **des pronoms disjoints**.

MODÈLE : —Parles-tu de la politique à tes amis ?

—Pardon ? Je n'ai pas bien entendu. Peux-tu répéter la question ?

—Oui, bien sûr. Je demande si tu parles de la politique à tes amis ?

—Ah, oui ! Je leur en parle souvent !

parler de la politique à vos amis

avoir des opinions sur l'économie

promettre à vos amis de payer le dîner

acheter des journaux dans votre ville

penser à la souveraineté du Québec

donner des cadeaux à vos amis

voter aux élections presidentielles avec vos amis

mentir à votre famille de temps en temps

passer des messages à vos camarades en classe

vouloir aller à la Martinique avec votre fiancé(e)

? ? ? (à vous d'inventer d'autres questions !)

À l'écrit *deuxième étape*

6.25 La possibilité des innovations à l'avenir Vous parlez avec un(e) ami(e) de la vie à l'avenir. Révisez votre liste d'innovations qui changeront nos vies (Activité 12) et **imaginez un dialogue** où vous expliquez vos idées à un(e) ami(e) et où vous discutez de la possibilité que ces idées soient réalisées dans 20 ans. Bien sûr, votre ami(e) est très curieux(-euse) et vous interrompt souvent pour vous faire répéter une chose ou pour vous faire préciser vos idées. Finalement, avec un partenaire, révisez vos dialogues et lisez-les à haute voix.

Épisode 3

Venez à Dakar !

Structures *le futur et le futur antérieur*

6.26 Dans 20 ans. . . Imaginez comment sera votre vie dans 20 ans. Surprise ! Vous vivez dans un pays francophone ou bilingue. Vous êtes chez vous quand vous recevez cette fiche à remplir pour le recensement (*census*). **Choisissez un pays francophone que vous aimeriez habiter un jour et remplissez les blancs en imaginant votre vie dans 20 ans.**

Recensement officiel

Date : ______________________ Âge : __________

Nom et prénom : ______________________

Adresse : ______________________

Occupation : ______________________

Salaire annuel : ______________________

Célibataire, Marié(e) ou Divorcé(e) ? ______________________

Nom de l'époux/l'épouse : ______________________

Nombre d'enfants : ______________________

Noms des enfants : ______________________

Animaux familiers : ______________________

Voiture ? ______ non ______ oui, Modèle : ______________________

Passe-temps préférés : ______________________

6.27 «Demain dès l'aube» Lisez le poème suivant écrit par Victor Hugo et publié en 1856 dans un recueil intitulé *Contemplations*. Ensuite, **répondez aux questions**.

«Demain dès l'aube»

■ Victor Hugo

Demain, dès l'aube, à l'heure où blanchit la campagne,
Je **partirai**. Vois-tu, je sais que tu m'attends.
J'**irai** par la forêt, j'**irai** par la montagne.
Je ne puis demeurer° loin de toi plus longtemps. — *I can't stay*

Je **marcherai** les yeux fixés sur mes pensées,
Sans rien voir au dehors,° sans entendre aucun bruit,° — *outside/sound*
Seul, inconnu, le dos courbé,° les mains croisées, — *hunched, curved*
Triste, et le jour pour moi **sera** comme la nuit.

Je ne **regarderai** ni l'or du soir qui tombe,
Ni les voiles° au loin descendant vers Harfleur, — *sails*
Et quand j'**arriverai**, je **mettrai** sur ta tombe
Un bouquet de houx° vert et de bruyère° en fleur. — *holly plant/heather plant*

1. Où va l'homme dans le poème ? Quand ? Pourquoi ?
2. Quel est le ton du poème ? Qu'est-ce qui contribue à ce ton ?
3. La fille de Victor Hugo est morte, noyée (*drowned*) lors d'un accident de bateau, en Normandie. Pensez-vous que le poète parle à sa fille ? Justifiez votre opinion en citant le texte.
4. Examinez les verbes qui sont **au futur**. Donnez l'infinitif de chaque verbe. Lesquels sont irréguliers au futur ? Pouvez-vous décrire comment former et comment utiliser le futur ?
5. Quel est l'effet produit par l'emploi du futur dans ce poème ? Récrivez-le au passé et comparez-le avec l'original. Commencez avec : «Hier, à l'aube. . . »

Culture

Victor Hugo est un écrivain du 19ème siècle. Il a écrit plusieurs recueils de poèmes et plusieurs pièces de théâtre, parmi lesquelles *Les Misérables*. Il est reconnu comme le père du **romantisme**. Ce mouvement littéraire, souvent lié au sentiment du «mal du siècle», est caractérisé par la solitude, la nature, la passion, les rêves exotiques et une volonté de rompre avec la raison et les règles de la littérature classique. **Alphonse de Lamartine** et **Charles Baudelaire** sont d'autres poètes romantiques.

le futur et le futur antérieur

The *future tense* (**le futur**) is used to describe events that will occur at some future date. The **futur antérieur** is the future perfect tense and is used to describe events that will have occurred before some future date but are still events that lie in the future.

- The **futur** is formed by adding the appropriate endings to the *infinitive* (drop the final **-e** from **-re** verbs) or irregular future stem. The future endings are: **-ai, -as, -a, -ons, -ez, -ont**.
- Here is an example of a regular verb (**finir**) in the future tense:

je finirai	**nous finirons**
tu finiras	**vous finirez**
il/elle/on finira	**ils/elles finiront**

- Some *irregular future stems* are:

aller : **ir-**	faire : **fer-**	savoir : **saur-**
avoir : **aur-**	falloir : **faudr-**	valoir : **vaudr-**
devoir : **devr-**	pleuvoir : **pleuvr-**	venir : **viendr-**
envoyer : **enverr-**	pouvoir : **pourr-**	voir : **verr-**
être : **ser-**	recevoir : **recevr-**	vouloir : **voudr-**

- **Note:** *Slightly irregular **-er** verbs* with spelling changes, such as **acheter** or **appeler**, retain the spelling change in the future stem: j'**achèter**ai, j'**appeller**ai
- The **futur antérieur** is composed of two parts: the *future tense* of the auxiliary verb, **avoir** or **être**, plus the *past participle* of the verb you are conjugating (following the same rules for agreement as the **passé composé**):
  Example: En 2020, elle **aura reçu** son diplôme et elle **sera allée** en France.

6.28 Que ferons-nous ? Finalement, Jean-Louis retrouve Claire en ville et explique qu'il devait téléphoner à sa mère parce qu'aujourd'hui, c'est son anniversaire. Claire ne le croit pas entièrement, mais elle décide de ne pas insister. Donc, ils reprennent leur discussion à propos du manuscrit. Conjuguez les verbes entre parenthèses **au futur**.

CLAIRE : Il n'y a toujours pas de réponse chez Monsieur Thibodeau. Quand est-ce qu'il (rentrer) ____________________ chez lui ? Il est trop tard aujourd'hui, mais demain à 9h, Bernadette (aller) ____________________ chez ses tantes et elle leur (demandent) ____________________ si elles savent où il est. Tu (voir) ___________________, Bernadette nous (aider) ___________________ beaucoup.

JEAN-LOUIS : Mais, est-ce que tu (attendre) ___________________ son coup de téléphone ou est-ce que tu (aller) ___________________ chez les Thibodeau avec moi demain matin ?

CLAIRE : Nous (attendre) ___________________ son coup de téléphone, bien sûr.

JEAN-LOUIS : Mais, tu te moques de moi ? Nous avons l'adresse. Nous (partir) ___________________ demain matin sans attendre Bernadette. . .

6.29 Oui, mais. . . Claire continue à réfléchir à ce qu'ils pourraient faire demain. Conjuguez les verbes entre parenthèses **au futur antérieur**.

CLAIRE : Oui, mais si nous attendons jusqu'à 10h, Bernadette (aller) ___________________ chez ses tantes, elle leur (poser) ___________________ beaucoup de questions et elle nous (téléphoner) ___________________ avec toutes ces informations. Ensuite, nous irons chez Monsieur Thibodeau. D'accord ?

JEAN-LOUIS : Mais, peut-être que nous (rater) ___________________ l'occasion de parler avec ce monsieur avant qu'il ne sache combien nous désirons acheter ce manuscrit.

CLAIRE : Ne t'en fais pas. Tout ira bien !

6.30 Questions personnelles Répondez aux questions personnelles suivantes. **Discutez de vos réponses** avec la classe.

1. Quand est-ce que vous recevrez votre diplôme de l'université ? Nommez une chose que vous aurez déjà accomplie avant de recevoir votre diplôme.
2. Quand est-ce que vous irez en vacances ? Nommez une chose que vous aurez déjà faite avant de partir en vacances.
3. Quand est-ce que vous aurez votre prochain examen ? Qu'est-ce que vous aurez fait avant de passer cet examen ?
4. À quelle heure est-ce que vous quitterez votre résidence demain matin ? Qu'est-ce que vous aurez fait avant de quitter la maison demain ?

6.31 La vie de Claire Claire veut terminer sa thèse et devenir professeur de littérature française au Québec. Est-ce qu'elle réalisera ces objectifs ? Imaginez comment sera la vie de Claire dans 20 ans. **Écrivez six phrases** en employant **le futur** ou **le futur antérieur**. Ensuite, comparez vos idées avec celles de vos camarades de classe.

MODÈLE : Dans 20 ans, Claire sera professeur de littérature française.

la Martinique

Qu'est-ce que Thierry fera la prochaine fois qu'il visitera la Martinique ? Regardez la vidéo et consultez votre cahier d'activités !

6.32 Et vous ? Que ferez-vous le jour de votre anniversaire l'année prochaine ? **Faites une liste** de dix activités. Employez **le futur**. Comparez votre journée avec celle de vos camarades de classe.

MODÈLE : Moi, l'année prochaine, pour mon anniversaire, j'irai à Paris.

6.33 Et dans 20 ans ? En utilisant la fiche du recensement (Activité 26), **faites une interview** avec un(e) camarade de classe afin de savoir comment sera sa vie dans 20 ans. En plus, demandez-lui ce qu'il aura déjà fait avant ce moment-là. Conduisez votre interview au **futur** et au **futur antérieur**.

MODÈLE : —Où est-ce que tu habiteras dans 20 ans ?

—J'habiterai à Paris, dans le 5ème arrondissement.

—Dans quels pays est-ce que tu auras déjà habité avant de t'y installer ?

—J'aurai déjà habité aux États-Unis et en Belgique.

Venez à Dakar !

À : Claire Plouffe
De : André Thibodeau
Date : 01/10/03
Réf : che sarà sarà

Chère Mademoiselle Plouffe,

Vous ne me connaissez pas, mais je pense que vous me cherchez. J'ai des amis à Schœlcher, où se trouve ma résidence principale, qui m'ont téléphoné aujourd'hui avec la nouvelle de votre arrivée. Comme je venais de recevoir une lettre d'un bouquiniste parisien du nom de Nicolas Gustave, dans laquelle il m'expliquait qui vous êtes, je n'ai donc pas été trop surpris d'apprendre que vous étiez à la Martinique. Malheureusement, vous ne saviez pas avant de quitter Paris que j'étais chez des parents, ici au Sénégal. Pourtant, je m'intéresse énormément à votre projet de recherche et je vous invite à venir me rendre visite à Dakar où je serai jusqu'au Nouvel An.

Je sais que vous êtes étudiante et que vous n'avez pas suffisamment d'argent pour faire le tour du monde,° mais ne vous en faites pas° ! Dès que vous arriverez à Dakar, ma femme et moi nous nous occuperons de vous. Vous verrez, tout sera prêt pour vous et pour votre compagnon aussi. On préparera deux chambres dans notre maison et vous aurez des domestiques° à votre disposition, ainsi qu'une voiture et un guide au cas où vous décideriez de faire du tourisme. Rassurez-vous, mon intérêt à entendre ce que vous savez de l'histoire du manuscrit égale votre intérêt à lire le manuscrit. Je suis certain qu'on pourra régler l'affaire d'une manière convenable à nous tous. Donc, ne vous faites pas de soucis.° Venez à Dakar !

trip around the world
to be worried
household staff
to be worried

Vous trouverez mes coordonnées et des instructions pour arriver à la maison dans un document attaché à ce message. En attendant une réponse favorable, je vous prie, chère Mademoiselle, d'accepter l'expression de mes sentiments les meilleurs.

André Thibodeau

Après avoir lu

6.34 D'accord ou pas d'accord ? Après avoir lu la lettre ci-dessus, lisez les phrases suivantes et **donnez vos opinions personnelles**. Discutez en petits groupes.

	D'accord	Pas d'accord
1. Quelqu'un a averti Monsieur Thibodeau que Claire le cherchait.	_______	_______
2. Monsieur Thibodeau invite Claire, mais pas Jean-Louis, à venir chez lui à Dakar.	_______	_______
3. Monsieur Thibodeau est sympa et généreux.	_______	_______
4. Claire aura peur d'aller chez Monsieur Thibodeau.	_______	_______
5. Jean-Louis ne voudra pas accompagner Claire.	_______	_______

rassurer quelqu'un

	Formal	Informal
To reassure someone	Ne vous en faites pas !	Ne t'en fais pas !
	Ne vous faites pas de soucis !	Ne te fais pas de soucis !
	Ne vous inquiétez pas !	Ne t'inquiète pas !
	N'ayez pas peur !	N'aie pas peur !
	Vous verrez. . .	Tu verras. . .
	Rassurez-vous. Je vous assure que tout ira bien.	Rassure-toi. Je t'assure que tout ira bien.
	Vous trouverez une solution.	Tu trouveras une solution.
	Vous vous en tirerez.	Tu t'en tireras.
	Vous n'avez rien à craindre !	Tu n'as rien à craindre !

Pas de panique ! / Ça va s'arranger. / Ça s'arrangera.
Tout ira bien. / Tout ira comme prévu. / Tout ira à merveille.
Ça va se passer. / Ça se passera bien.
Ce n'est rien. / Ce n'est pas grave. / Ce n'est pas la mer à boire !

6.35 Êtes-vous sûr(e) ? Que diriez-vous dans les situations suivantes pour **rassurer les gens** ? Avec un partenaire, décidez de ce que vous pourriez leur dire.

1. Un petit garçon s'est perdu dans le centre commercial. Il ne sait pas où se trouvent ses parents.
2. Votre amie a peur d'échouer à son examen d'histoire.
3. Votre cousin se marie la semaine prochaine, mais il s'est disputé avec sa fiancée à propos du lieu où passer leur lune de miel.
4. Votre voisine part en vacances, mais elle craint un cambriolage (*break-in*) chez elle pendant son absence.
5. Vos amis hésitent entre deux possibilités : acheter une nouvelle voiture ou investir leur argent.
6. Votre premier/-ière enfant commence à l'école primaire et il/elle a peur d'y aller.

6.36 Prédire l'avenir Qu'apportera cette année ? Rassurez-vous, les astres n'ont que de bonnes nouvelles pour vous ! Avec un partenaire, à tour de rôle, **jouez la voyante** (*fortune teller*) et dites toutes les bonnes choses qui arriveront à votre partenaire cette année ! N'oubliez pas de **rassurer** votre partenaire que tout ira bien !

MODÈLE : Cette année tu rencontreras une personne qui sera très importante à votre avenir professionnel. N'aies pas peur. Tout ira à merveille !

6.37 Tout ira bien ! Vous inquiétez-vous de temps en temps ? Sur une feuille de papier, **écrivez une phrase** pour décrire ce qui vous inquiète. N'y mettez pas votre nom. Échangez vos papiers au hasard. Puis, **circulez** dans la classe et posez des questions à vos camarades de classe à propos de ce qui les inquiète. N'utilisez pas les mots de vocabulaire qui sont dans la phrase que vous avez reçue ! Quand vous aurez trouvé l'auteur de la phrase, rassurez-le que tout ira bien !

MODÈLE : —Je m'inquiète de la santé de mon chien. Il ne mange pas et n'a pas beaucoup d'énergie.

—As-tu un animal domestique ? Est-il malade ? Ne t'en fais pas. Emmène-le chez le vétérinaire. Vous trouverez bien une solution.

Pour aller plus loin : LITTÉRATURE

ACTIVITÉ G : Lisez un poème de Joachim du Bellay dans lequel il parle de l'avenir. Consultez votre cahier électronique !

À l'écrit *troisième étape*

6.38 Votre vie à l'avenir Imaginez comment sera votre vie à l'avenir avec toutes les innovations qui se réaliseront dans votre vie. **Écrivez une lettre** à un(e) camarade de classe dans laquelle vous décrivez comment sera la vie à l'avenir (révisez vos Activités 12 et 25). Rassurez-le que tout ira bien ! Échangez vos lettres (par courriel, si vous voulez !) et offrez une réponse à votre camarade de classe avec quelques corrections possibles et vos commentaires sur sa vision du monde.

Dénouement

Activités de révision

6.39 Conséquences Chaque action a ses conséquences. Imaginez les conséquences possibles pour les moments suivants. Utilisez **le futur** ou **le futur antérieur**.

1. Si Jean-Louis achète le manuscrit. . .
2. Quand Claire terminera son doctorat. . .
3. Si la Martinique devient un pays indépendant. . .
4. Quand André Thibodeau rencontrera Claire et Jean-Louis. . .
5. Si un ouragan frappe la Martinique demain. . .

6.40 Aux prochaines élections En petits groupes, pensez aux prochaines élections américaines. **Répondez aux questions** suivantes. Ensuite, discutez de vos réponses avec vos camarades de classe. Bien sûr, vous pouvez interrompre les autres personnes pour **ajouter** quelque chose, pour leur **faire préciser** leurs idées ou pour les **rassurer**.

1. Qui seront les candidats principaux ? De quels états viendront-ils ?
2. Quels seront les problèmes sociaux les plus importants pour les candidats ?
3. Quels seront les problèmes politiques les plus importants pour les candidats ?
4. Qu'est-ce qu'ils proposeront au public pour résoudre ces problèmes ?
5. Imaginez que vous êtes candidat. Quelle sera votre devise (*slogan*) ?

Avant de lire *Une enfance créole : chemin d'école*

6.41 Le premier jour de l'école Pensez à vos expériences scolaires et **répondez aux questions** personnelles suivantes.

1. Vous souvenez-vous de votre école primaire ? Comment était-elle ? Est-ce que vous êtes allé(e) à une école publique ou une école privée ? Pourquoi ?
2. Quelles matières est-ce qu'on étudie à l'école primaire ?
3. Pensez-vous qu'il existe un rapport entre l'enseignement et la politique ? Donnez un exemple.
4. Imaginez que vous envoyez vos propres enfants à l'école pour la première fois et qu'ils ont peur d'y aller. Rassurez-les et expliquez-leur ce qu'ils y feront et ce qu'ils y apprendront.

6.42 Premières impressions ? **Lisez** l'extrait suivant, qui vient du roman *Une enfance créole : chemin d'école* de Patrick Chamoiseau, sans essayer de comprendre chaque mot. Après votre première lecture du texte, **répondez** aux questions. Ensuite, **relisez** le texte une deuxième fois, plus attentivement.

1. Qui parle ? Un petit garçon ? Un homme ? Un vieillard ?
2. Quand se passe cette histoire ? Au présent ? Au passé ? À l'avenir ?
3. Où se situe l'action ?
4. Comment est le Maître de cette classe ?
5. Comment était l'expérience de l'école pour le narrateur ?

Une enfance créole : chemin d'école

Cet extrait vient du roman de Patrick Chamoiseau Une enfance créole : chemin d'école. *Dans ce roman, Chamoiseau se rappelle ses expériences à l'école à la Martinique. C'est l'histoire d'un petit garçon qui apprend peu à peu ce que cela veut dire de vivre dans une ancienne colonie française. Comme les écoles publiques du système français, y compris celles aux Antilles, visaient à apprendre aux enfants l'importance de la langue et de la culture françaises, on peut dire que l'enseignement avait un côté idéologique aussi bien qu'un côté pédagogique. Cette idéologie, issue de l'ère coloniale, avait pour but de «civiliser» les peuples non européens. En glorifiant les exploits des Français, on niait alors la valeur culturelle des sociétés non européennes vaincues. Ici, avec sarcasme, le narrateur décrit le programme scolaire de son école.*

■ Patrick Chamoiseau

Une enfance créole : chemin d'école (extrait)

On allait à l'école pour perdre de mauvaises mœurs° : mœurs d'énergumène,° mœurs nègres ou mœurs créoles — c'étaient les mêmes.

customs, morals
possessed, demonic person

Le Maître, de temps en temps, s'écriait comme Jules Monnerot : «*France toujours, France tout court !*» Ô pays de Vercingétorix, de Jeanne d'Arc, de Clémenceau, vieux foyer° de civilisation latine qui nous forgea Malherbe, Racine, Hugo. Ô grande amie du progrès qui s'honore de Pascal, de Berthelot, de Pasteur, patrie° de l'art et du goût,° douce terre des libertés de 1789, berceau° du grand et noble Schœlcher !. . . Le Maître pour lui-même s'écriait.

home
fatherland/taste
cradle

Le souffle vibrant du savoir et notre être créole semblaient en indépassable° contradiction. Le Maître devait nous affronter° mais aussi affronter le pays tout entier. Il se vivait en mission de civilisation. Un peu comme ces missionnaires enfoncés° dans des contrées sauvages. Jour après jour, de point d'eau en point d'eau, sans une once de plaisir, ces inventeurs d'âmes devaient continuer d'avancer. L'effort était terrible, hors de portée° du plus puissant° des animaux. Comme il devait, à chaque seconde parmi nous, avancer dans la fange,° chacun de ses mots, de ses gestes, chaque injonction, chaque murmure, était bardé° d'Universel. L'Universel était un bouclier,° un désinfectant, une religion, un espoir, un acte de poésie suprême. L'Universel était un ordre.

insurmountable/to confront
plunged
out of reach
strong
mud
to protect (with armor)
shield

hair *wheat* *prey* *darkness* *and then there was light* *swarming mass/to bend* *burden/summit* *taken away from*

En ce temps-là, le Gaulois aux yeux bleus, à la chevelure° blonde comme les blés,° était l'ancêtre de tout le monde. En ce temps-là, les Européens étaient les fondateurs de l'Histoire. Le monde, proie° initiale des ténèbres,° commençait avec eux. Nos îles avaient été là, dans un brouillard d'inexistence, traversée par de vagues fantômes caraïbes ou arawaks, eux-mêmes pris dans l'obscurité d'une non-histoire cannibale. Et, avec l'arrivée des colons, la lumière fut.° La Civilisation. L'Histoire. L'humanisation du grouillement° de la Terre. Ils ployaient° les épaules sous le lourd fardeau° de ce monde qu'ils élargissaient aux cimes° de la conscience. Il nous fallait produire d'opiniâtres efforts afin de ne pas les abandonner aux solitudes de cette charge. Le Maître voulait, lui aussi, porter le monde.

Christophe Colomb avait découvert l'Amérique, et aspiré au monde des millions de ces sauvages, qui durant une nuit immémoriale, soustraits° à l'humanité, l'avaient attendu.

Après avoir lu

6.43 Avez-vous compris ? En petits groupes, **discutez de vos réponses** aux questions suivantes.

1. Dans la première phrase de l'extrait, le narrateur donne la raison pour laquelle on envoyait les jeunes Martiniquais à l'école. Quelle est cette raison ? Est-ce une raison typique ? Pourquoi ou pourquoi pas ?
2. Dans le 2ème paragraphe, le Maître cite les noms des personnages historiques, des écrivains et des hommes de science français. Connaissez-vous ces gens ? Même si votre réponse est «non», pouvez-vous expliquer leur importance à la civilisation française ? et à la culture martiniquaise ?
3. Victor Schœlcher, un des personnages nommés dans le 2ème paragraphe, était un Français antiesclavagiste qui a beaucoup contribué à la fin de l'esclavage à la Martinique. Pourquoi donc est-ce que le narrateur invoque le nom de Schœlcher avec autant de sarcasme ?
4. Que veut dire l'auteur quand il dit que «le savoir» et «l'être créole» étaient en contradiction ? D'après le texte, qu'est-ce que les Français colonisateurs pensaient des habitants martiniquais ?
5. Est-ce que l'idée de «l'Universel» que le Maître présente est vraiment «universelle» ? Expliquez.
6. Qui sont les caraïbes et les arawaks ? Pourquoi est-ce que le narrateur dit qu'ils ont une «non-histoire» ?
7. En général, dans ce texte, l'auteur condamne la colonisation et le système d'éducation publique initiée par les colonisateurs. Pourquoi ? Quels ont été les effets négatifs de la colonisation sur le peuple martiniquais ?

i Culture

La Martinique n'est pas la seule **île francophone aux Antilles** ! Il y a la **Guadeloupe**, qui est aussi un département d'outre-mer de la France, et il y a les îles de **Saint-Martin**, de **Dominique** et de **Sainte-Lucie** qui ont chacune une population francophone. Bien sûr, on ne peut pas parler de francophonie antillaise sans mentionner **Haïti**.

6.44 D'accord ou pas d'accord ? Après avoir lu l'extrait du roman de Chamoiseau, lisez les phrases suivantes et **donnez votre opinion**. Discutez de vos réponses en petits groupes.

	D'accord	Pas d'accord
1. Le narrateur approuve l'idée de «civiliser» les enfants créoles.	_______	_______
2. Le Maître se croit supérieur aux enfants créoles.	_______	_______
3. Les Gaulois étaient les ancêtres du narrateur.	_______	_______
4. Avant la colonisation, l'île était déserte.	_______	_______
5. Les enfants à cette école ont appris que les valeurs culturelles créoles sont aussi importantes que les valeurs culturelles européennes.	_______	_______

6.45 Analyse littéraire Examinez ce texte de près. Répondez aux questions suivantes et **discutez de vos réponses** en classe.

1. Dans la première phrase, quel est le son qui domine ? Quelle lettre est répétée le plus souvent ? Quel est le rapport entre ce son et le ton du texte ?
2. Dans la 2ème paragraphe, où l'auteur décrit le Maître qui crie les noms de beaucoup de personnages français, quel est l'effet de la répétition de ces noms ? Qu'est-ce que cela vous rappelle ? En quoi consiste le sarcasme dans ce paragraphe ?
3. Dans ce texte, il y a plusieurs références au catholicisme. Pouvez-vous les identifier et expliquer leur fonction dans l'extrait ? Quel est l'effet de ces images religieuses ?
4. Il y a beaucoup de mots dans cet extrait qui commencent avec une lettre majuscule (*capital letter*). À part les noms de personnes, quels mots commencent avec une lettre majuscule ? Quel est l'effet de ce procédé stylistique ?
5. Quelles images sont employées pour parler du pays martiniquais ? Quel est l'effet de ces images sur le lecteur ?
6. Regardez la dernière phrase. Quel temps de verbe domine ? Quel est l'effet de l'usage de ce temps par rapport à l'idée critique du «non-histoire» des peuples non européens ?

Pour aller plus loin : CINÉMA

ACTIVITÉ H : Regardez le film *Rue cases nègres* (*Sugar Cane Alley*) où il s'agit d'un petit garçon qui grandit à la Martinique. Consultez votre cahier électronique !

6.46 Une école utopique ? Imaginez qu'on vous embauche pour établir une nouvelle école privée à la Martinique. Comment sera votre école ? Quelles matières est-ce qu'on y enseignera ? Qu'est-ce que les étudiants apprendront de leur culture et de leur histoire ? Discutez de vos idées en petits groupes.

Synthèses

6.47 Réfléchissons à la culture Voici quelques éléments de la culture martiniquaise que vous avez étudiés dans ce chapitre. En petits groupes, **répondez** aux questions et **discutez de vos impressions** avec vos camarades.

les caraïbes et les arawaks **la créolité** **l'esclavage**
le mouvement d'indépendance

1. Définissez ou décrivez chaque élément.
2. Pourquoi chaque élément est-il important à cette culture ? Y a-t-il un phénomène historique ou social qui explique son importance ?
3. À votre avis, est-ce qu'il existe un rapport entre ces quatres éléments de la culture martiniquaise ? Quel est ce rapport ?
4. Est-ce que votre impression de cette culture est différente maintenant que vous avez commencé à l'étudier ? Si oui, comment et pourquoi ? Si non, pourquoi pas ?

la Martinique

Qu'est-ce que ça veut dire «être Martiniquais» ? Regardez la vidéo et consultez votre cahier d'activités !

6.48 À débattre Lisez les questions suivantes et **discutez** en groupes. Si possible, parlez de vos expériences personnelles relatives aux questions.

1. **La souveraineté !** Discutez le pour et le contre de la souveraineté pour les Martiniquais ou pour les Québécois. Est-ce que les arguments sont les mêmes pour les deux cultures ? Pensez-vous qu'ils aient le droit de réclamer leur indépendance ? Pourquoi ou pourquoi pas ?
2. **L'éducation bilingue.** Aux États-Unis, on discute de la question des écoles bilingues. Quelques-uns pensent qu'il faut cultiver le bilinguisme pour démontrer qu'on comprend la valeur du multiculturalisme et de la diversité américaine. D'autres pensent qu'il faut apprendre aux immigrants à parler anglais pour qu'ils puissent réussir dans la culture américaine. En plus, constate-t-on, les États-Unis accueillent des immigrants de beaucoup de pays différents et leurs enfants parlent beaucoup de langues différentes. Il serait impossible d'avoir un système d'éducation multilingue pour répondre aux besoins de tous. L'éducation bilingue : un devoir, un rêve ou une impossibilité ? Que pensez-vous ?
3. **Les droits humains.** Des organisations internationales, comme le Human Rights Watch, Amnesty International et l'ONU, essaient de rassurer le monde que les droits humains sont respectés dans tous les pays du monde. Pourtant, quand on découvre que les droits humains ne sont pas respectés, est-ce que la communauté internationale a le droit d'intervenir ? Si oui, qu'est-ce qu'on devrait faire ? Comment et pourquoi ?

Culture

En 1945, à la fin de la Seconde Guerre mondiale, plusieurs états ont signé une charte pour former l'**Organisation des Nations unies**. Cette organisation vise à promouvoir la paix mondiale et à faciliter la coopération économique, sociale et culturelle entre les pays. Le siège de l'ONU est à New York, et ses deux langues officielles sont l'anglais et le français. Depuis ses origines, l'ONU et son tribunal international des crimes de guerre ont intenté des procès contre des chefs d'état et officiers militaires accusés de génocide lors de la Seconde Guerre mondiale, et plus récemment des guerres civiles au Rwanda et en Bosnie. Le désaccord entre la France et les États-Unis à l'ONU concernant la guerre en Irak a inspiré un débat international au sujet du rôle de l'ONU dans la politique mondiale du 21ème siècle.

6.49 À l'impromptu Voici des situations interactives. Avec une ou deux autres personnes, **choisissez une scène et improvisez** devant la classe. Si vous ne voulez pas improviser, écrivez votre dialogue avant et puis jouez-le pour la classe.

1. À la plage
   (a) Vous marchez sur la plage à la Martinique et vous rencontrez une personne francophone. Vous êtes content(e), idéaliste et optimiste. Vous parlez du monde avec enthousiasme. Partagez votre vision du monde dans l'avenir.
   (b) Vous marchez sur la plage à la Martinique. La beauté de la situation ne peut rien contre votre profond pessimisme en ce qui concerne le monde. Vous rencontrez une personne américaine qui parle de l'avenir du monde et qui semble avoir oublié toutes les catastrophes du passé.
2. Une élection
   (a) Cela fait une dizaine d'années que vous vivez dans un petit village de pêcheurs à la Martinique. Le village traverse une crise économique que l'on pourrait dépasser, à votre avis, si seulement un effort de développer le tourisme était lancé. Annoncez votre décision de poser votre candidature pour la mairie du village et expliquez les mesures de votre programme.
   (b) Vous êtes le maire actuel du village. Rassurez les gens du village. Vous voulez protéger leurs traditions et leur mode de vie. Si vous êtes réélu, rien ne changera au village.
   (c) Vous êtes un vieil habitant du village, plutôt conservateur. Vous aimez la tranquillité de votre village. Peu importe si on est pauvre ! C'est le bonheur qui est important. Interrompez les candidats et offrez vos commentaires.
   (d) Vous êtes propriétaire d'un restaurant dans le village. Vous vous préoccupez à cause de la situation économique et vous voulez savoir comment les candidats pourront aider les commerçants. Posez des questions aux candidats à propos de l'avenir du village.

Pour aller plus loin : CULTURE

ACTIVITÉ I : Apprenez un peu plus sur l'ONU. Consultez votre cahier électronique !

À l'écrit *étape finale*

6.50 L'avenir Comment sera votre vie à l'avenir ? Révisez et élaborez vos travaux d'écriture de ce chapitre (Activités 12, 25 et 38) et écrivez l'histoire d'**une journée typique ou bizarre** dans votre vie à l'avenir. Utilisez le **futur** et le **futur antérieur**.

À suivre

Bernadette téléphone le matin suivant comme promis, mais elle a de mauvaises nouvelles. André Thibodeau n'est pas chez lui en ce moment. Il est en Afrique, où il rend visite aux parents de sa femme qui habitent à Dakar au Sénégal. Claire la remercie, mais explique qu'elle avait déjà contacté ce monsieur et qu'il lui a dit qu'il serait ravi de la rencontrer et d'apprendre ce qu'elle sait. Bien sûr, Jean-Louis l'accompagnera. Pourtant, il faudra attendre quelques jours pour avoir un vol pour Dakar parce qu'un ouragan s'approche de l'île. . .

6.51 Qu'est-ce qui s'est passé ? Pensez à ce qui s'est passé dans ce chapitre. **Écrivez six phrases** aux temps passés pour décrire les événements que vous pensez être les plus importants. Parlez de vos idées avec vos camarades de classe.

MODÈLE : Claire a trouvé une nouvelle amie en Bernadette.

6.52 Qu'est-ce qui se passera ? Imaginez ce qui va se passer dans le prochain chapitre. **Écrivez six phrases** et parlez de vos idées avec vos camarades de classe. Utilisez **le futur** !

MODÈLE : Claire et Jean-Louis iront à Dakar !

Pour agir :
LA MARTINIQUE !

Si vous voulez bouger et faire quelque chose pour mieux connaître les Antilles, ou pour aider les autres à mieux connaître les cultures francophones, consultez la section **Pour agir** dans votre cahier électronique ! Il y a tant de choses à faire :

- **Vendez des salades de fruits exotiques antillaises** et contribuez l'argent que vous gagnez à une organisation qui aide les pauvres aux Antilles et en Afrique.
- **Enseignez** ce que vous savez de la culture de la Martinique à des enfants de l'école primaire. Lisez-leur des contes martiniquais écrits par Patrick Chamoiseau !
- **Entrez en contact** avec des francophones qui vivent dans votre communauté ou quelque part aux États-Unis.
- **Organisez un voyage** à la Martinique pour les prochaines vacances.
- **Cuisinez** ! Préparez un vrai repas antillais avec vos camarades de classe.

VOCABULAIRE UTILE

La politique

allophone (*m./f.*)	*speaker of languages other than French, English, or Indian (reg. Québec)*
autochtone (*m./f.*)	*indigenous speaker of native Indian languages (reg. Québec)*
droit (*m.*)	*right*
élire	*to elect*
entouré(e)	*surrounded*
estimer	*to estimate; to think*
loi (*f.*)	*law*
maire (*m.*)	*mayor*
majoritaire	*majority (adj.)*
majoritairement	*in the majority (adv.)*
ministre (*m.*)	*minister (of culture, of foreign affairs, etc.)*
opprimé(e)	*oppressed*
opprimer	*to oppress*
pas (*m.*)	*step*
relier	*to link together*
ressentir	*to feel strongly*
se sentir	*to feel*
souveraineté (*f.*)	*sovereignty*
surmonter	*to overcome*

Divers

à peine	*barely*
âme (*f.*)	*soul*
âme (*f.*) sœur	*soulmate; like-minded person*
anniversaire (*m.*)	*birthday*
(auto)car (*m.*)	*intercity bus*
cadeau (*m.*)	*present*
être ravi(e)	*to be delighted*
nettement	*significantly*
paille (*f.*)	*straw*
part (*f.*)	*slice*
raccrocher	*to hang up (the phone)*
ronfler	*to snore*
sauf	*except*

Chapitre 7

À la maison au Sénégal

Une maison à Dakar au Sénégal.

Épisode 1 *Bienvenue à Dakar*

Épisode 2 *La dispute*

Épisode 3 *Un courriel académique*

Dénouement

La grenouille aime l'eau,
mais pas l'eau bouillante.
—proverbe wolof

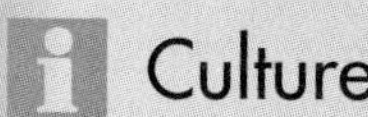

Culture

Le **baobab** est un arbre emblématique sénégalais caractérisé par un très grand tronc et des branches tortueuses. On dit que cet arbre a des pouvoirs mystiques, car autrefois on l'utilisait pour produire des médicaments naturels. Il est aussi associé aux **griots**, les conteurs africains, qui trouvaient abri dans les grands trous du tronc lorsqu'ils voyageaient de village en village. Ils y étaient aussi souvent enterrés. Aujourd'hui, le baobab rappelle les valeurs traditionnelles sénégalaises et la liaison très forte entre les peuples de cette région et la terre.

À apprendre

- Comment décrire son environnement
- Comment se plaindre et faire des reproches à quelqu'un
- Comment parler des possibilités et des regrets

À lire

Claire et Jean-Louis arrivent à l'aéroport de Dakar, la ville capitale du Sénégal, où un chauffeur les attend et les conduit à la maison d'André Thibodeau. André, un homme bon vivant et sympathique qui s'intéresse énormément à la littérature et à l'histoire, les accueille chaleureusement. Claire, ravie de trouver un homme à l'esprit littéraire, s'entend bien avec André. Jean-Louis, pourtant, aimerait mieux que la vente du manuscrit s'effectue sans délai et redoute la possibilité de ne pas réussir à convaincre cet homme de vendre le manuscrit. . .

Épisode 1

Bienvenue à Dakar

Avant de lire

7.1 Vos opinions sur votre environnement Répondez aux questions suivantes. **Discutez de vos réponses** avec vos camarades de classe et n'hésitez pas à poser des questions supplémentaires si vous voulez en savoir plus.

1. Où avez-vous grandi ? Dans une maison individuelle ou dans un appartement ? En milieu urbain, en banlieue (*suburb*) ou en milieu rural ? Quel milieu préférez-vous ? Pourquoi ?
2. Aimez-vous la nature ? Pourquoi ou pourquoi pas ? Préférez-vous la campagne, la montagne, la forêt, les parcs et jardins ou la plage et la mer ?
3. Quelles activités fait-on au grand air (*outdoors*) ? Des promenades ? Des sports ? Des pique-niques ? Du camping ? D'autres ? Lesquelles faites-vous régulièrement ?
4. Est-ce que vous faites du recyclage ? Conservez-vous l'eau et l'électricité ? Essayez-vous de minimiser la pollution que vous faites ? Souvent ? De temps en temps ? Rarement ? Comment ?
5. Pensez-vous qu'on fasse assez pour protéger l'écologie de la planète ? Pourquoi ou pourquoi pas ?

7.2 L'Afrique francophone Examinez la carte de l'Afrique dans votre livre. En petits groupes, **faites correspondre le pays** (à gauche) **avec sa description** (à droite).

Pays	Description
1. le Bénin	a. Un pays diversifié ! colonisé trois fois — par les Allemands, les Anglais et les Français. Les peuples de ce pays, qui partagent une frontière avec le Gabon et la Guinée, parlent 35 langues africaines différentes.
2. la Côte d'Ivoire	b. Une grande île à l'est du continent, ce pays est à côté des petites îles françaises faisant partie des DOM-TOM.
3. le Sénégal	c. Pour arriver à la ville légendaire de Tombouctou, les colons français ont dû traverser ce pays, en passant par sa ville capitale, Bamako.
4. le Mali	d. Une ancienne colonie belge, autrefois nommé Zaïre, ce grand pays au centre du continent se trouve à l'ouest du Rwanda et connaît aussi la violence et les problèmes politiques.

i Culture

L'Afrique occidentale (l'Afrique de l'Ouest) comprend des pays — comme le Sénégal, le Burkina Faso, le Mali, le Bénin, le Togo, la Côte d'Ivoire, le Cameroun, le Gabon et le Niger — qui sont aujourd'hui majoritairement islamiques (suite à l'influence arabe) et francophones (à cause de l'occupation française entre 1880 et 1960), quoiqu'on y trouve une grande diversité de religions, de traditions et de langues parlées. Dans tous ces pays, on trouve des sociétés multiethniques où chaque groupe ethnique a sa propre langue et ses propres traditions tribales. Les frontières culturelles entre ces groupes ne correspondent pas toujours aux frontières nationales, ce qui rend difficile parfois le gouvernement des pays au niveau national mais qui enrichit la vie culturelle et artistique dans cette partie du monde.

5. Burkina Faso
6. le Cameroun
7. Madagascar
8. la République démocratique du Congo (RDC)

e. Ancienne terre du royaume Ashanti, ce pays est situé sur la côte, entre deux pays non francophones, et sa plus grande ville, Abidjan, est souvent appelée «le Paris de l'Afrique».

f. Presque divisé en deux par la Gambie, ce pays est la terre natale du grand poète du mouvement littéraire «la négritude».

g. Antérieurement connu sous le nom de la Haute-Volta, ce petit pays au sud du Mali et du Niger se compose de deux groupes ethniques principaux dont les deux langues sont représentées dans le nom actuel du pays.

h. La capitale du vaudou africain et l'ancienne terre du royaume puissant du Dahomey, ce petit pays a été un des plus grands centres de l'exportation des esclaves de son port, nommé Ouidah, pendant 300 ans.

Pour aller plus loin : CULTURE

ACTIVITÉ A : Apprenez un peu plus sur les pays francophones d'Afrique. Consultez votre cahier électronique !

7.3 Le décor Pendant le vol en avion à Dakar, Claire lit un magazine de mode dans lequel il y a plusieurs photos de mobilier pour la maison. Pour chaque meuble, **indiquez dans quelle(s) pièce(s)** ou endroit(s) on le mettrait.

1. un fauteuil
2. des étagères
3. une table basse
4. une armoire
5. un four
6. une commode
7. un tapis
8. des rideaux
9. des chaises
10. un lit

Langue

Vous rappelez-vous les mots de vocabulaire pour décrire **une maison** ou **un appartement** ? En voici quelques-uns !

Pièces : le hall d'entrée (*foyer*), le living / le salon, la salle à manger, la cuisine, le bureau, la bibliothèque, la salle de jeux, la salle de musculation, la buanderie (*laundry room*), la chambre à coucher, la salle de bains, le garage, l'escalier (*stairs*), le couloir (*hallway*)

Meubles : un canapé, une table basse, un fauteuil, une armoire, une machine à laver, un séchoir, un évier (*large sink*), un lavabo (*small sink*), un four à micro-ondes, un four, une cuisinière, un lit, une lampe, un téléviseur, des rideaux (*curtains*), des étagères (*shelves*), un buffet, une table et des chaises, une moquette (*carpet*), un lave-vaisselle, une stéréo, un bureau, un ordinateur, un banc, une commode (*chest of drawers*), un escabeau (*stool*), un garde-manger (*cupboard for food*)

Pour aller plus loin : LITTÉRATURE

ACTIVITÉ B : Lisez un poème de Senghor. Consultez votre cahier électronique !

Culture

Le **Sénégal** est un pays habité depuis la préhistoire par plusieurs peuples africains comme les Toucouleurs, les Sérères et les Mindingues. Lors du 11ème siècle, les Arabes et les Berbères de l'Afrique du Nord ont islamisé ces peuples qui suivaient des traditions religieuses animistes. Au 12ème siècle, le royaume de Dyolof s'est établi dans cette région et a prospéré jusqu'à l'arrivée des premiers Européens, des marchands portugais, au 16ème siècle. Les Français, établis sur la côte atlantique et sur l'île de Gorée au 17ème siècle, y faisaient du commerce (d'esclaves, d'or et de produits agricoles africains). Dans les années 1880, sous le règne de Napoléon III, les Français cherchaient à élargir leur empire et ont commencé à coloniser les terres de l'Afrique de l'Ouest. Presqu'un siècle plus tard, avec l'aide de **Léopold Sédar Senghor**, homme politique et poète sénégalais, le pays est devenu une république indépendante en 1960. Senghor a été élu le premier président du pays. Il est aussi connu comme le père du mouvement littéraire «la négritude». Aujourd'hui, le Sénégal a deux langues officielles : le français et le wolof. Le pays souffre d'une économie faible, basée sur l'exportation d'arachides (*peanuts*), et de nombreux problèmes sociaux comme l'analphabétisme (*illiteracy*), la discrimination contre les femmes, le mouvement séparatiste en Casamance, le chômage et la drogue. Pourtant, on y trouve un paysage littéraire très riche et une société diversifiée qui s'ouvre à la modernité tout en protégeant ses traditions.

le Sénégal

Rencontrez une Sénégalaise ! Regardez la vidéo et consultez votre cahier d'activités !

lisez

Bienvenue à Dakar

Claire et Jean-Louis arrivent à la maison d'André Thibodeau, dans le quartier de Dakar qu'on appelle le Plateau, avec un bouquet de fleurs qu'ils ont acheté à la sortie de l'aéroport. Devant la maison où s'arrête la voiture, ils voient un homme noir distingué en chemise en batik et une belle femme habillée en boubou jaune qui achètent quelque chose à une vendeuse voilée. C'est Monsieur et Madame Thibodeau. Ils les accueillent chaleureusement. Accompagné par sa femme Aissatou, André leur montre leurs chambres à coucher avec de grands lits à quatre colonnes et de belles fenêtres entrouvertes, leurs salles de bains avec des parquets en marbre et des bidets à la française. Ce manoir semble dater de l'époque coloniale. Les Thibodeau leur donnent un petit tour de la maison et de ses environs. Il y a un beau jardin avec une jolie terrasse, beaucoup d'espaces verts et une belle vue de l'océan Atlantique. Finalement, les quatre s'assoient dans le salon lorsqu'une domestique leur apporte des boissons de citron pressé et des cacahouètes crues. . .

CLAIRE : Monsieur et Madame Thibodeau, je suis vraiment ravie d'être ici. J'avais toujours rêvé de visiter l'Afrique un jour, et vous avez la plus belle maison que j'aie jamais vue ! Quels beaux meubles !

JEAN-LOUIS : Oui, c'est très gentil de votre part de nous accueillir chez vous. Nous ne saurions exprimer notre reconnaissance.

ANDRÉ : Mais, ma femme et moi sommes très heureux de vous accueillir. C'est dommage que vous ayez perdu votre temps à la Martinique. Comme ma femme est sénégalaise et que mes ancêtres étaient sénégalais, nous partageons notre temps entre Schœlcher et Dakar.

AISSATOU : Et, où que l'on soit, on est toujours content d'accueillir des gens. Ma famille a acheté cette maison en 1968, quelques années après l'indépendance, et j'en suis très fière, ainsi que de mon pays. J'espère que vous aurez le temps de visiter un peu la ville et le pays pendant votre séjour.

ANDRÉ : Il faut toujours profiter du temps qu'on a sur cette terre pour découvrir ses beautés. Ici, on a la ville et la campagne, la mer, la forêt tropicale et le désert. La vallée du Sénégal est une vraie oasis. Mais, depuis la lettre du bouquiniste à Paris, je ne pense qu'à ce manuscrit. Les livres anciens sont une de mes passions. Pourriez-vous me dire pourquoi vous vous intéressez à ce manuscrit ?

CLAIRE : Bon, il y a quelques années, je faisais de la recherche sur Choderlos de Laclos au Québec, et j'ai trouvé un article obscur qui parlait d'un 2ème roman de Laclos qui était perdu. Cela m'a frappée, parce que j'adore *Les Liaisons dangereuses* et j'ai toujours pensé que c'était dommage que Laclos n'ait écrit qu'un seul roman dans sa vie. Puis, l'année dernière, je suis allée à Paris pour faire de la recherche sur la correspondance de Laclos, et j'ai trouvé une référence à un manuscrit que Laclos aurait envoyé à un homme nommé François Fontenot. J'ai décidé sur le coup de proposer l'étude de ce manuscrit comme sujet de thèse. J'étais très heureuse d'apprendre que mon directeur de thèse à l'Université de Sainte-Foy avait tout de suite accepté mon idée et que le département allait me donner une bourse pour m'aider avec les frais de la recherche. Et, enfin, je veux savoir si le manuscrit que vous venez d'acheter est celui que Laclos avait envoyé à François Fontenot.

ANDRÉ : Et, d'après vous, comment est-ce que ce manuscrit aurait passé de ce François Fontenot à moi ?

CLAIRE : Enfin, jusqu'à présent, je sais que François Fontenot est rentré à Saint-Domingue avec le manuscrit. Pourtant, pendant la Révolution haïtienne, sa famille a déménagé et s'est installée en Louisiane. Le manuscrit est resté dans la bibliothèque familiale des Fontenot jusqu'aux années 1970 quand la famille a vendu la bibliothèque entière à Lionel Gustave, un bouquiniste parisien. C'est son neveu, Nicolas, qui vous a vendu le manuscrit. On ne sait pas encore si c'est un vrai Laclos, mais si cela est le cas, votre manuscrit serait probablement la seule copie qui existe.

ANDRÉ : Et ce manuscrit serait plus important que la plupart des autres dans ma collection. Comme vous, mademoiselle, j'adore les bouquins. J'ai grandi en lisant les poésies de Senghor et de Césaire, et j'ai toujours apprécié la littérature française. J'aimerais beaucoup que vous examiniez ce manuscrit pour moi.

JEAN-LOUIS : Et est-ce que vous considéreriez la possibilité de nous vendre ce manuscrit ?

ANDRÉ : Je n'y avais pas pensé. Je croyais que Mademoiselle Plouffe aurait peut-être besoin d'une copie, mais je n'avais pas réfléchi à l'idée de vous vendre l'original. Je ne sais pas. . .

CLAIRE : Enfin, nous pourrions discuter de cela plus tard, quand j'aurai eu le temps d'examiner le texte. On n'est pas pressé de commencer des négociations, n'est-ce pas, Jean-Louis ?

JEAN-LOUIS : Tu as raison. Nous avons tout notre temps. Apprécions l'hospitalité de nos hôtes et la beauté de ce pays. Trinquons à leur bonheur ! Santé !

CLAIRE : Chin, chin !

VOCABULAIRE

À la maison

une colonne de lit	*bedpost*
entrouvert(e)	*half open, ajar*
un parquet	*floor*
le marbre	*marble*
un bidet	*bidet (see Centre d'Information below)*
un(e) domestique	*housekeeper, servant*
le mobilier	*furniture*
les meubles (*m. pl.*)	*furnishings*
déménager	*to move (a home or business)*
s'installer	*to settle down, move in*

Divers

les environs (*m. pl.*)	*surroundings*
une colline	*hill*
une cacahouète	*peanut*
cru(e)	*raw*
fier, fière	*proud*
la terre	*earth, land*
trinquer	*to toast*
Santé ! Chin, chin !	*To your health! Cheers!*

Après avoir lu

7.4 Avez-vous compris ? Répondez aux questions suivantes. **Justifiez vos réponses** en citant le texte.

1. Comment est la maison des Thibodeau ? À votre avis, est-ce que les maisons des familles de Claire ou de Jean-Louis ressemblent à cette maison ?
2. Décrivez la vie des Thibodeau. Où habitent-ils ? Comment est leur style de vie ? Quels sont leurs intérêts ?
3. Claire a longuement parlé de ses recherches. Pourquoi ? Quel sera le résultat de cette conversation pour elle ? et pour Jean-Louis ?
4. Pourquoi est-ce que Claire et Jean-Louis n'exigent (*demand*) pas de voir le manuscrit tout de suite ? Quand on est invité à la maison de quelqu'un qu'on ne connaît pas bien, qu'est-ce qu'on devrait faire pour être poli ?
5. Pensez-vous que Monsieur Thibodeau doive vendre le manuscrit à Jean-Louis ? Pourquoi ou pourquoi pas ?

Culture

Malgré le stéréotype qu'ont quelques Américains, l'hygiène personnelle a toujours préoccupé les Français. Ils ont souvent installé des **bidets,** des appareils sanitaires, dans les salles de bains de grandes maisons et de beaux appartements luxueux. C'était un meuble indispensable, surtout parmi les gens aisés, pendant la première moitié du 20ème siècle. Comme le lavabo, le bidet est utilisé pour la toilette intime. On peut toujours trouver des bidets dans les maisons anciennes et dans quelques hôtels, mais rarement dans la maison individuelle moderne. Pourtant, dans une maison individuelle aujourd'hui, il est très commun d'avoir un **w.-c.**, une petite pièce qui est séparée de la salle de bains ou de la douche.

7.5 D'accord ou pas d'accord ? Indiquez si vous êtes **d'accord ou pas d'accord** avec les phrases suivantes, d'après votre compréhension du récit. Justifiez vos opinions en citant le texte, si possible. Discutez de vos réponses avec la classe.

	D'accord	Pas d'accord
1. Les Thibodeau habitent une maison individuelle modeste.	_______	_______
2. Les Thibodeau aiment inviter des gens chez eux.	_______	_______
3. Claire a bien résumé l'histoire du manuscrit.	_______	_______
4. Claire veut lire le manuscrit tout de suite.	_______	_______
5. André souhaite vendre le manuscrit à Jean-Louis.	_______	_______

7.6 L'environnement Regardez les mots de vocabulaire qui suivent. Dans chaque ligne, il y a un mot qui cloche avec les trois autres. **Entourez le mot qui ne va pas** avec les autres et essayez d'expliquer pourquoi. Attention : il y a parfois plusieurs bonnes réponses. Il faut justifier votre choix !

1. déménager	s'installer	rénover une maison	décorer une maison
2. une maison	une case (*hut*)	un appartement	une péniche (*houseboat*)
3. fier	indépendant	libre	chaleureux
4. la salle de bains	la cuisine	le salon	le garage
5. une oasis	une forêt	une plage	un désert

7.7 La maison Monsieur Thibodeau montre son bureau à Claire, qui demande s'il serait possible d'utiliser son ordinateur afin d'écrire un petit mot à sa sœur. Bien sûr, il accepte et la laisse dans le bureau. **Remplissez les blancs** avec un mot de vocabulaire de la liste suivante.

colonnes	**coucher**	**jardin**	**meubles**	**oasis**
rez-de-chaussée	**salle de bains**	**urbain**		

Pour aller plus loin : CULTURE

ACTIVITÉ C : Voulez-vous explorer la ville de Dakar ? Consultez votre cahier électronique !

Langue

Pour **décrire un appartement** à vendre ou à louer, il faut indiquer où se situe l'immeuble, à quel étage se trouve l'appartement, combien de pièces ou de salles il y a, combien de **mètres carrés** (m^2) il y a, le montant du **loyer** (*rent*), si les **charges** (le coût de l'eau chaude, l'électricité, le gaz) sont comprises, si on doit signer un **bail** (un contrat d'une année) ou laisser une **caution** (de l'argent qu'on récupère si on n'endommage pas la propriété) et d'autres détails (climatisation, parking, animaux familiers permis, etc.). N'oubliez pas que le rez-de-chaussée est le niveau où on entre dans un bâtiment (de plain-pied avec le sol) ; le premier étage est au-dessus (*above*) du rez-de-chaussée ; et le sous-sol est au-dessous (*below*).

Chère Marie,

Salutations du Sénégal ! Ce pays est incroyable, et les Thibodeau sont vraiment sympa. Leur maison est énorme. Au ____________________ il y a une cuisine, une salle à manger, un grand salon, un bureau et deux chambres. Au premier étage, il y a quatre autres chambres à __________ __________. Dans la mienne, il y a un grand lit à quatre __________ __________ et une ____________________ en marbre avec un bidet ! Tous les ____________________ datent de l'époque coloniale. À l'extérieur, il y a un beau ____________________ avec une fontaine, des plantes tropicales et des oiseaux multicolores. C'est vraiment une ____________________ ! La maison est dans la ville de Dakar, mais ce quartier n'est pas vraiment un milieu ____________________. C'est plutôt comme une banlieue, avec beaucoup de grandes maisons coloniales. Et maintenant pour les nouvelles les plus importantes : Monsieur Thibodeau est en possession du manuscrit et il veut me le montrer ! Je suis l'étudiante la plus heureuse du monde ! Je t'écrirai encore bientôt !

Salut, Claire

7.8 À louer Voici des petites annonces d'appartements disponibles à Dakar. Lisez-les et décidez de quel appartement vous aimeriez louer si vous étiez à Dakar pour une année. **Discutez de votre choix** avec vos camarades de classe. (Notez: 100.000 CFA = à peu près 150 euros.)

Pour aller plus loin : CULTURE

ACTIVITÉ D : Explorez des maisons et des appartements au monde francophone. Consultez votre cahier électronique !

Bon quartier, près d'un arrêt d'autobus, 2 pièces avec beaucoup de charme au rdc, avec w.-c., douche, séjour. 250.000 CFA/mois, plus charges. Pas de bail. Propriétaires sur place.

Appt ancien rénové, 3 pièces ensoleillées, 2ème étage, balcon avec vue, au plateau, près de l'université. Pas d'animaux ! 465.000 CFA/mois, charges comprises. Bail d'une année minimum.

Nouvel immeuble à 10 étages au centre-ville, équipements modernes, ascenseur, chauffage central et climatisation. Magasins au sous-sol. Studios, 1–4 pièces, et un grand appartement-terrasse sur le toit. Plusieurs appts sont meublés. 250.000–2 millions CFA/mois, plus charges. Références.

Langue

Vous rappelez-vous le vocabulaire pour parler des **animaux** ? Révisez les mots ci-dessous ! S'il y a des animaux que vous connaissez bien qui ne sont pas sur la liste, ajoutez-les. Cherchez les mots dans le dictionnaire si nécessaire.

- **Animaux domestiques :** le chien, le chat, l'oiseau (le canari), le poisson rouge, le serpent, le furet (*ferret*), la gerbille, le hamster, la souris, le lapin, le cheval, l'âne, la vache, le cochon, le poulet, le coq, le mouton, la chèvre
- **Animaux sauvages :** l'écureuil (*squirrel*), la tortue, la grenouille, le renard (*fox*), le rat, le coyote, la mouffette (*skunk*), le raton laveur (*raccoon*), le castor (*beaver*), l'alligator, l'ours, le cerf (*deer*), le cougar (*mountain lion*), la marmotte (*groundhog*), l'orignal (*moose, reg. Québec*), le chameau, l'éléphant, le lion, le tigre, le singe, l'hyène, l'hippopotame, le phoque (*seal*), le renne (*reindeer*), le dauphin, la baleine (*whale*), le requin (*shark*), le giraffe, le loup, la chauve-souris (*bat*)
- **Oiseaux :** le corbeau (*crow*), l'hirondelle (*swallow*), le canard, l'oie (*goose*), l'aigle, le hibou (*owl*), le vautour, le pigeon, le moineau (*sparrow*), le pingouin
- **Insectes :** la fourmi, l'araignée (*spider*), le cafard (*cockroach*), la mouche (*fly*), le moustique, l'abeille (*bee*), le papillon (*butterfly*)

7.9 L'écologie Claire et Jean-Louis admirent les plantes et les arbres près de la maison des Thibodeau, et ils commencent à parler des différents climats. **Faites correspondre** le lieu (*à gauche*) avec la description des faunes et des flores qu'on y trouve (*à droite*).

Les endroits	Les descriptions
1. Tahiti	a. des bananiers, des baobabs, des singes, des éléphants, des hyènes, des lions
2. le Québec	b. des palmiers, des bougainvillées, des papillons, des oiseaux, des poissons
3. le Vietnam	c. des chênes, des pins, des pommiers, des vignes, des oies, des chèvres
4. la France	d. des érables, des sapins, des baleines, des orignaux, des phoques, des cerfs
5. la Louisiane	e. des arbres à gomme, des papayers, des singes, des moustiques
6. le Sénégal	f. des palmiers, des citronniers, des alligators, des écrevisses

Langue

Vous rappelez-vous le vocabulaire pour parler des **plantes** et des **arbres** ? Révisez les mots ci-dessous ! S'il y a des éléments que vous connaissez qui ne sont pas sur la liste, ajoutez-les. Cherchez les mots français dans le dictionnaire si nécessaire.

- **Plantes :** le buisson (*bush*), l'arbrisseau (*shrub*), la fougère (*fern*), la mousse (*moss*), le cactus, le houx (*holly*), la bruyère (*heather*), la lavande, la citrouille (*pumpkin*), le lierre (*ivy*), le sumac vénéneux (*poison ivy*), le trèfle (*clover*), la vigne (*vines*), le gui (*mistletoe*)
- **Arbres :** le baobab, le palmier, le cocotier, le bananier, le citronnier, le papayer (*papaya tree*), le pommier, le poirier, le marronnier (*chestnut*), le cerisier, l'arbre à gomme (*rubber tree*), le chêne (*oak*), l'érable, l'orme (*elm*), le platane (*plane tree*), le bouleau (*birch*), le sapin (*fir*), le pin, le cèdre
- **Fleurs :** la rose, la tulipe, le lilas, la marguerite (*daisy*), la jonquille (*daffodil*), le géranium, la bougainvillée, la pensée (*pansy*), la poinsettia, le tournesol (*sunflower*), le chèvrefeuille (*honeysuckle*), le coquelicot (*red poppy*)

7.10 La nature Regardez les personnes et les catégories suivantes. **Quelles flores (plantes) ou faunes (animaux) leur associez-vous ?**

George Washington	Mickey et Minnie	Barnum et Bailey	Nemo
Cendrillon (*Cinderella*)	Noël	Winnie the Pooh	Le Sorcier d'Oz
Lone Ranger	Indiana Jones	la plage	La Saint-Valentin (*Valentine's Day*)
un farfadet (*leprechaun*)	Old Macdonald	un safari	Shrek
Dr. Doolittle	Elmer, Bugs et Daffy	Canada	Simba et Mufasa

Pour aller plus loin : CULTURE

ACTIVITÉ E : Explorez l'écologie sénégalaise ! Consultez votre cahier électronique !

7.11 Vocabulaire personnel Pensez à votre maison et à votre environnement et, pour chaque catégorie, **faites une liste de cinq à dix mots importants** que vous pouvez utiliser. Consultez un dictionnaire si nécessaire.

1. Votre maison ou votre appartement : l'intérieur (pièces, meubles) et l'extérieur
2. Votre environnement : le climat, les eaux, la géographie
3. La flore typique de votre région : plantes, fleurs, arbres
4. La faune typique de votre région : animaux domestiques et animaux sauvages
5. Les insectes typiques de votre région

7.12 Ce n'est pas possible ! Claire et Jean-Louis continuent leur conversation mais se parlent à voix basse. Choisissez une des expressions entre parenthèses et **lisez le dialogue à haute voix** avec un partenaire. Quand vous voyez «? ? ?», vous pouvez imaginer votre propre expression.

CLAIRE : Alors, les Thibodeau sont (gentils / accueillants / ? ? ?), n'est-ce pas ?

JEAN-LOUIS : Oui, mais je ne crois pas que Monsieur Thibodeau (veuille / soit sur le point de / accepte de) nous vendre le manuscrit. Pourquoi lui as-tu parlé de Laclos ? Maintenant, il sait que le manuscrit est d'une grande valeur. Ce que c'est (insupportable / fâcheux / bête de ta part) !

CLAIRE : Écoute, je n'y vois pas de mal. Cet homme est l'homme le plus (raisonnable / honnête / amical / ? ? ?) que je connaisse. J'ai voulu lui dire la vérité. Je pense qu'il nous aidera.

JEAN-LOUIS : Il t'aidera peut-être, mais il se fiche de moi ! Ce n'est pas (juste / possible / acceptable). Tu te rends compte !

CLAIRE : (Je sais, je sais / Tant pis pour toi / On n'y peut rien) ! Mais, la situation n'est pas au pire. Il n'a pas encore refusé de le vendre.

JEAN-LOUIS : Il faut que tu (m'aides / lui parles / ? ? ?). Est-ce que tu pourrais lui expliquer (l'importance / la nécessité / ? ? ?) d'acquérir le manuscrit ? Nous pourrions lui offrir une somme d'argent assez considérable.

CLAIRE : Mais non, pas moi ! Je suis désolée d'avoir tout dit sur Laclos, mais je ne sais pas comment (négocier une vente / demander de l'argent). L'achat, c'est ton affaire.

JEAN-LOUIS : Je comprends tout à fait. (Tu as raison / C'est vrai / ? ? ?) ! C'est à moi de (négocier / parler) avec Monsieur Thibodeau.

Pour aller plus loin : LITTÉRATURE

ACTIVITÉ F : Lisez le poème «L'Albatros» où l'auteur, Charles Baudelaire, compare le poète à ce grand oiseau de mer. Consultez votre cahier électronique !

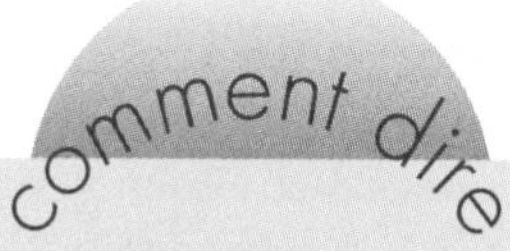

se plaindre

To complain	Ce n'est pas vrai / juste / possible / acceptable ! C'est insupportable ! Pourquoi est-ce qu'on me fait ça ? Pourquoi est-ce que tu me fais ça ? La vie ne devrait pas être comme ça ! On ne devrait pas vivre comme ça ! Je ne pourrais pas continuer comme ça ! Ça ne peut pas continuer ! J'en ai assez ! J'en ai ras-le-bol ! Ça y est ! Je n'en peux plus ! Tu te rends compte ! / Vous vous rendez compte ! Il s'en fiche ! Je m'en fiche ! On s'en fiche (de quelque chose) !
To show compassion for someone's complaints	Je comprends tout à fait ! Je sais, je sais ! Je prends pitié de toi/vous ! Ça a dû être terrible pour toi/vous ! Quel dommage ! Qu'est-ce que je peux faire pour toi/vous ? Je peux t'/vous aider ? Je suis vraiment désolé(e). Je suis navré(e).
To dismiss a complaint	Tant pis pour toi/vous ! La vie, c'est comme ça ! Je n'y vois pas de mal ! Peu importe ! Ça pourrait être pire ! On n'y peut rien ! Il n'y a pas de quoi se plaindre ! Ne te plains pas ! / Ne vous plaignez pas ! Écoute, tu exagères ! / Vous exagérez !

7.13 À vous Imaginez que vous êtes dans les situations suivantes. Que dites-vous ? Avec un partenaire, choisissez des expressions pour chaque situation et **imaginez de petits dialogues** dans lesquels vous vous plaignez à un(e) ami(e).

1. Votre petite sœur n'arrête pas de chanter la même chanson heure après heure.
2. Les autres personnes dans votre maison ne font pas de recyclage, mais vous y tenez. Pourquoi est-ce qu'elles ne peuvent pas séparer le plastique et le verre des autres déchets ?
3. Des jeunes gens parlent dans la bibliothèque pendant que vous étudiez pour un examen.
4. Vous avez préparé un pique-nique et vous arrivez à votre parc préféré, mais il y a une famille bruyante et désagréable qui s'assied à côté de vous. C'est un grand parc, pourquoi ne peuvent-ils pas s'installer plus loin ?
5. Votre professeur d'histoire est si ennuyeux que vous ne pouvez pas vous empêcher de vous endormir en classe.

Langue

Vous rappelez-vous la conjugaison du verbe **se plaindre (de)** (conjugué comme le verbe **craindre**) ? Révisez-le : je me plains, tu te plains, il/elle/on se plaint, nous nous plaignons, vous vous plaignez, ils/elles se plaignent (*participe passé* : plaint). On peut dire aussi **porter plainte contre** quelqu'un, ce qui signifie «se plaindre auprès des autorités».

7.14 Par pitié ! Sur une feuille de papier, **écrivez une phrase** pour exprimer les plaintes que vous avez à propos de votre logement ou des inconvénients de la vie en général. Puis, **circulez** dans la salle de classe et **plaignez-vous** à vos camarades. Si la personne compatit à (*sympathizes with*) votre plainte, faites-la signer votre papier. Si elle n'y compatit pas, passez à une autre personne. Essayez de vous plaindre à autant de personnes que possible ! L'étudiant avec le plus de signatures gagne !

MODÈLE : —Mon appartement est trop petit et il n'y a pas assez de fenêtres ! C'est insupportable !

—Écoute, tu exagères ! Ça pourrait être pire !

À l'écrit *première étape*

Pour aller plus loin : LITTÉRATURE

ACTIVITÉ G : Lisez le poème «Le Lac» d'Alphonse Lamartine dans lequel il décrit la nature d'une façon très émouvante. Consultez votre cahier électronique !

7.15 Une résidence secondaire Quand vous voulez vous échapper au stress de la vie quotidienne et partir pour un week-end, où allez-vous ? Préférez-vous aller à la campagne, à la montagne, dans une forêt, près d'un lac ou un fleuve ou à la mer ? Imaginez que vous avez gagné à la loterie et que vous voudriez construire une maison de campagne ou une résidence secondaire pour les week-ends et les vacances. Choisissez un endroit où vous aimeriez construire votre 2ème maison. Puis, **faites deux listes** pour décrire **la maison** (combien d'étages, combien de pièces, les meubles, etc.) et **ses environs** (la vue que vous aurez de vos fenêtres, la nature qui entoure la maison, etc.). Ensuite, échangez votre liste avec celle d'un(e) camarade de classe. Vérifiez que votre partenaire n'a rien oublié, faites des corrections possibles et ajoutez des commentaires en bas de page. Si sa maison est plus intéressante que la vôtre, plaignez-vous ! Si non, faites-lui un compliment.

La dispute

Épisode 2

Structures *les prépositions*

7.16 Dans ma chambre Claire décrit les meubles dans sa chambre pour Jean-Louis, qui a une chambre à l'autre bout du couloir. Soulignez toutes **les prépositions** dans ce paragraphe. Ensuite, **essayez de dessiner** la chambre. Pouvez-vous décrire comment fonctionnent les prépositions en analysant ces exemples ?

CLAIRE : Quelle belle chambre ! Quand on entre par la porte, on est en face d'une grande fenêtre entrouverte qui donne sur le jardin. À travers la fenêtre, à l'extérieur, on voit des arbres et des oiseaux multicolores. À l'intérieur, sous la fenêtre, il y a une table. Sur la table, il y a un vase de fleurs exotiques et quelques livres. Si on regarde à gauche, il y a une grande armoire. À côté de l'armoire, il y a une petite table de toilette. Accroché au mur au-dessus de la table, il y a un miroir oval, et sous la table, il y a une petite chaise. Si on regarde à droite, il y a un grand lit à quatre colonnes. En haut des colonnes, il y a des sculptures d'ananas, le symbole de l'hospitalité. À côté du lit, il y a une petite table avec une belle lampe en verre. Devant la lampe, il y a un petit réveil-matin. Au mur, derrière le lit, il y a un grand masque africain sculpté en bois, et sur le plancher (*floor*), au centre de la chambre, il y a un tapis qui semble être tissé à la main. C'est vraiment joli. Pourtant, j'ai remarqué une toile d'araignée au plafond (*ceiling*), dans un coin près du lit.

le Sénégal

Comment est-ce que Assata décrit sa maison ? Regardez la vidéo et consultez votre cahier d'activités !

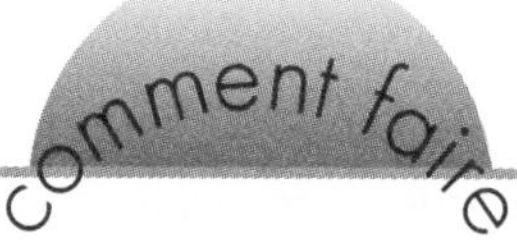

les prépositions

Prepositions (**les prépositions**) are used to indicate location or to connect various parts of a sentence. Choose the appropriate preposition according to the location or to fit the grammatical structure of the sentence.

The most common simple *prepositions* are:

à	**depuis** (*since*)	**par** (*by, for*)
après	**derrière**	**pendant** (*during, for*)
avant (*before*)	**devant** (*in front of*)	**pour**
avec	**de**	**sans**
chez	**en**	**sauf** (*except*)
contre	**entre**	**sous** (*under*)
dans	**envers** (*toward*)	**sur** (*on*)
dedans (*inside*)	**malgré** (*despite*)	

- Remember that **à** (*to, at, in, on*) and **de** (*of, from, about*) contract with definite articles **le** (**au, du**) and **les** (**aux, des**).
- Sometimes **à, de,** and **en** are used in *prepositional phrases*, such as:

à droite	**à gauche**	**à l'extérieur de**
à côté de	**au coin de**	**loin de**
à l'intérieur de	**à l'envers**	**en bas de**
au-dessus de (*above*)	**au-dessous de** (*below*)	**au centre de**
au milieu de	**à travers** (*through*)	**à l'extrémité de**
près de	**autour de** (*around*)	**hors de** (*outside of*)
en haut de	**en face de** (*across from*)	**en dehors de**
au bout de (*at the end of*)	**au fond de** (*at the bottom / heart of*)	

Modes of transportation require specific prepositions:

- Use **à** with: **à bicyclette, à cheval, à patin à roulettes, à pied, à planche à roulettes, à vélo**
- Use **en** with: **en autobus, en avion, en bateau, en métro, en moto, en taxi, en voiture, en train**
- Use **par** with: **par le train** (also **en train**)

To describe *function, content, or substance* of nouns, specific prepositions are used:

- Use **à** to describe a function, usage, or type: **une machine à laver, une tasse à café, un verre à vin, un sorbet à la vanille**
- Use **de** to describe contents or ownership: **la machine d'André, une tasse de café, un verre de vin**
- Use **en** to describe the materials used: **une fenêtre en verre, un masque en bois, une tasse en céramique**

To indicate *time*, specific prepositions are used:

- Use **à** for a specific hour: Je pars **à 2 heures**.
- Use **dans** to indicate a period of time remaining until something occurs: **Dans deux jours**, je quitte le Sénégal.
- Use **depuis** or **il y a** to indicate a period of time since something started or occurred: Je cherche ce manuscrit **depuis quatre ans**; **il y a quatre ans** que je cherche ce manuscrit.
- Use **en** with a month, season, or year: **en octobre, en automne, en 2002** (*Exception*: au printemps).

- Use **pendant** to indicate a specific length of time that an activity continued in the past: J'ai habité à Paris **pendant un an**.
- Use **en** for a duration of time taken to complete something: Elle a terminé son travail **en cinq heures**.
- Use **pour** for a duration of time planned for an activity: elle restera au Sénégal **pour une semaine**.
- Use **entre** to indicate a range of time: **Entre midi et une heure**, je fais la vaisselle.

Verbs followed by an infinitive require specific prepositions:

- Some verbs take **à**: **apprendre à, arriver à, commencer à, continuer à, demander à, dire à, s'échapper à, s'habituer à, hésiter à, manquer à, se mettre à, plaire à, renoncer à, répondre à, réussir à, servir à, téléphoner à, tenir à**
- Some verbs take **de**: **accepter de, (s')arrêter de, avoir besoin de, conseiller de, se contenter de, empêcher de, essayer de, oublier de, promettre de, refuser de, regretter de, rêver de, se souvenir de, tenter de**
- Some verbs *do not take any prepositions* when followed by infinitives: **aimer, aller, croire, désirer, devoir, écouter, espérer, faire, penser, pouvoir, préférer, regarder, savoir, souhaiter, vouloir**
- A number of verbs take either **à** or **de** or another preposition, depending on context and meaning:

parler à (*to talk to*)	**parler de** (*to talk about*)
penser à (*to think of/about*)	**penser de** (*to think about, opinion only*)
commencer à (*to begin, start*)	**commencer par** (*to start with*)
décider de (*to decide*)	**se décider à** (*to make up one's mind to*)
finir de (*to finish*)	**finir par** (*to end up*)
se servir de (*to use*)	**servir à** (*to be used to/for, to be useful for*)

7.17 Sens dessus dessous (*upside down*) Imaginez la chambre de Claire sens dessus dessous. Pour chaque préposition en caractères gras, substituez une **préposition opposée**.

1. **À droite**, il y a une armoire.
2. **Sur le haut** des colonnes, il y a des sculptures d'ananas.
3. **Sous** la table de toilette, il y a une chaise.
4. Il y a des fleurs **dans** le vase.
5. **Sous** la fenêtre, il y a une table.
6. **Devant** la lampe, il y a un réveil-matin.
7. Il y a un tapis **au centre** de la chambre.
8. **À l'extérieur**, il y a des oiseaux multicolores.
9. Il y a une toile d'araignée **près** du lit.

Pour aller plus loin : CULTURE

ACTIVITÉ H : Découvrez des plats sénégalais traditionnels comme le yassa ! Consultez votre cahier électronique !

7.18 Une sieste Jean-Louis décide de faire une petite sieste. Remplissez les blancs avec **une préposition** appropriée, si nécessaire.

JEAN-LOUIS : Je suis content que tu aimes ________________ ta chambre. Moi, j'ai besoin ________________ me reposer. Je vais faire une petite sieste ________________ une heure. Il y a un réveil-matin ________________ mon lit aussi, mais si je n'arrive pas ________________ me réveiller ________________ l'heure du dîner, réveille-moi. D'accord ? Entre temps, il faut penser ________________ comment convaincre Monsieur Thibodeau ________________ vendre le manuscrit. Après tout, on a voyagé tant d'heures ________________ avion pour venir ici. Les Thibodeau sont très gentils de nous acceuillir ________________ eux, mais on ne peut pas accepter ________________ partir sans le manuscrit. Mais, ne fais pas de négociations ________________ moi. Attends-moi, d'accord ? Et, surtout, ne dîne pas ________________ moi ! Penses-tu qu'on nous serve du yassa ?

7.19 Qu'est-ce que c'est ? Choisissez **un meuble** ou **une chose** qu'on peut voir dans votre salle de classe ou à travers la fenêtre de la salle de classe. Sans mentionner l'objet, **décrivez où il se trouve** par rapport aux choses qui l'entourent. Vos camarades de classe doivent deviner de quoi il s'agit ! Attention à l'usage des prépositions !

MODÈLE : —Cette chose est dehors, à l'extérieur de la salle. Elle est à côté de l'arbre et devant le petit mur, mais derrière le trottoir. Qu'est-ce que c'est ?

—C'est un buisson !

7.20 À l'étroit (*cramped*) Avez-vous beaucoup de meubles et d'objets dans votre chambre à coucher ? Avec un partenaire, **posez des questions** sur les meubles que l'autre personne a dans sa chambre. Dans vos **réponses**, décrivez où sont ces meubles par rapport aux autres en employant des **prépositions**.

MODÈLE : —Est-ce que tu as un sofa ?

—Oui. Il est à côté de la fenêtre.

Langue

Vous rappelez-vous l'usage et la conjugaison des verbes **manquer** et **plaire** ? Si non, mémorisez les conjugaisons suivantes et révisez l'usage des verbes avant de continuer !

- **manquer** (*to miss, to lack*) : je manque, tu manques, il/elle/on manque, nous manquons, vous manquez, ils/elles manquent (*participe passé* : manqué)
- **plaire** (*to please, to like*) : je plais, tu plais, il/elle/on plaît, nous plaisons, vous plaisez, ils/elles plaisent (*participe passé* : plu)

Ces deux verbes sont souvent utilisés avec un **pronom complément d'objet indirect**. Par exemple, si ton ami est parti, tu dis **il me manque** (littéralement, *he is lacking to me*; autrement dit, *I miss him*). Si tu aimes quelqu'un, tu dis **il me plaît** (littéralement, *he is pleasing to me*; autrement dit, *I like him*). Dans ces cas, le sujet est la chose ou la personne qui manque ou qui plaît, tandis que l'objet indirect est la personne à qui une chose ou une personne manque ou plaît.

Avant d'écouter

7.21 Avant la dispute Répondez aux questions personnelles suivantes. **Discutez de vos réponses** avec vos camarades de classe.

1. Est-ce que vous vous disputez souvent avec vos amis ou votre famille ? Pourquoi vous disputez-vous le plus souvent ?
2. Quand vous voyagez loin de chez vous, qu'est-ce qui vous manque ? Qu'est-ce qui vous plaît ?
3. Êtes-vous plutôt une personne qui se plaint beaucoup ou une personne qui accepte les choses commes elles sont ? Donnez un exemple d'un moment où vous vous êtes plaints de votre situation ou d'un moment où vous avez accepté une mauvaise situation.

écoutez

La dispute

Après sa sieste, Jean-Louis se réveille et frappe à la porte de Claire. Elle l'invite à entrer et ils commencent à discuter de leur situation. Claire comprend que son compagnon commence à s'inquiéter. Pour acquérir ce manuscrit, il est prêt à aller jusqu'au bout. D'après lui, la fin justifie les moyens. . .

Maintenant, **écoutez le dialogue sur votre CD**. Consultez le vocabulaire pour mieux comprendre le dialogue, et puis répondez aux questions suivantes.

VOCABULAIRE

Les disputes

aller jusqu'au bout	*to go the distance, all the way*
la fin justifie les moyens	*the end justifies the means*
un confort	*comfort*
un moyen	*way, means*
devoir de l'argent	*to owe money*
puissant(e)	*powerful*
au bout de; le bout	*at the end of; the end*
le but	*goal, objective*
impensable	*unthinkable*
se prendre pour	*to take oneself for, to think of oneself as*
se servir de	*to use for/as*
avoir honte de	*to be ashamed*
tu aurais dû	*you should have*

Après avoir écouté

7.22 Avez-vous compris ? En petits groupes, **répondez** aux questions suivantes.

1. Pourquoi est-ce que Jean-Louis va dans la chambre de Claire ?
2. De quoi parlent-ils au début ?
3. Pourquoi se disputent-ils ?
4. Que pensez-vous de la réaction de Claire ? Auriez-vous réagi de la même façon ?
5. À votre avis, existe-t-il des circonstances où la fin justifie les moyens ?

7.23 D'accord ou pas d'accord ? Après avoir écouté le dialogue entre Claire et Jean-Louis, lisez les phrases suivantes et **donnez votre opinion**. Discutez en petits groupes.

	D'accord	Pas d'accord
1. Jean-Louis veut le manuscrit à tout prix (*at any cost*).	_______	_______
2. Claire veut aider son ami à l'acquérir.	_______	_______
3. Leurs familles leur manquent.	_______	_______
4. Claire a un parent âgé qui a besoin d'elle.	_______	_______
5. Jean-Louis pense sérieusement à voler le manuscrit.	_______	_______

faire des reproches

To reproach someone

Vraiment ! Tu exagères ! N'exagérons pas ! Si j'avais su ! Mais quand même !
Mais non ! Mais franchement ! C'est impensable/incompréhensible !
Mais de quoi te mêles-tu ? Mais comment oses-tu (*how dare you*) !
Occupe-toi de tes affaires ! Cela ne te regarde pas !
Tu n'as pas honte ! Pour qui te prends-tu ?
Si tout le monde faisait comme toi !
Comment peux-tu dire des choses pareilles ?
Tu m'as menti. Tu aurais dû me dire la vérité / m'en parler.

7.24 Que dites-vous ? Qu'est-ce qu'on peut dire pour faire des reproches aux gens dans les situations suivantes ? Avec un partenaire, **décidez ce que vous pouvez dire**.

1. Votre ami a pris de l'argent de votre portefeuille sans demander la permission.
2. Un de vos amis arrive toujours en retard quand vous sortez ensemble.
3. Vous faites la queue pour le cinéma depuis une heure et quelqu'un qui vient d'arriver essaie de resquiller (*cut in line*).
4. Vos voisins ne font pas de recyclage.
5. Vous arrivez chez des amis et vous voyez qu'ils n'ont pas nettoyé leur appartement depuis des mois.

Langue

Dans une maison bien équipée, il faut faire des **tâches ménagères** pour que tout reste propre. On **fait la lessive** : c'est-à-dire, on lave les vêtements dans une machine à laver, et quelquefois on **repasse** les vêtements avec un fer à repasser. On **fait la vaisselle** : c'est-à-dire, on lave les assiettes et les casseroles dans un lave-vaisselle ou à la main, dans l'évier. On garde la nourriture dans un placard, un réfrigérateur ou un congélateur, et on **fait la cuisine** avec un four (électrique ou à gaz), une cuisinière (*stove*) ou bien dans un four à micro-ondes. On **fait le ménage** en passant l'aspirateur (*vacuum*), en époussetant (*dusting*), en faisant les lits et en rangeant les affaires.

7.25 Les tâches domestiques De l'escalier, Jean-Louis entend Monsieur et Madame Thibodeau qui se disputent à propos des tâches domestiques. Madame Thibodeau fait des reproches à son mari. Elle veut qu'il l'aide à la maison, mais lui, préfère faire travailler les domestiques. Avec un partenaire, **inventez un dialogue** dans lequel Madame Thibodeau reproche à son mari de ne pas faire les tâches suivantes.

MODÈLE : faire la vaisselle →

—Mais franchement ! Tu pourrais faire la vaisselle de temps en temps !

—Je fais faire la vaisselle par les domestiques.

faire la vaisselle	laver le linge
passer l'aspirateur	débarrasser (*to clean off*) la table après le dîner
cuisiner	ranger tes livres
épousseter	arroser (*to water*) les plantes
faire le lit	repasser une chemise

Pour aller plus loin : CULTURE

ACTIVITÉ 1 : Apprenez un peu plus sur les problèmes écologiques qui préoccupent les Verts. Consultez votre cahier électronique !

Langue

Savez-vous bien employer le **faire causatif** (faire + *infinitif*) ? Vous pouvez utiliser le verbe **faire** suivi d'un infinitif pour décrire une action que quelqu'un d'autre fait pour vous. Par exemple, si on dit «Aissatou prépare le dîner», cela veut dire qu'Aissatou est la cuisinière et elle cuisine elle-même. Mais, si on dit «Aissatou fait préparer le dîner», cela veut dire qu'elle demande à quelqu'un d'autre de cuisiner pour elle. On peut utiliser la préposition **par** pour indiquer qui fait le travail (Aissatou fait préparer le dîner **par** ses filles : Les filles cuisinent le repas pour leur mère). On emploie le **faire causatif** souvent en parlant des tâches domestiques. Normalement, on ne se coupe pas les cheveux, mais on **se fait couper les cheveux** par un coiffeur ; et on ne répare pas la machine à laver, mais on **fait réparer la machine à laver** par un réparateur.

7.26 Tu n'as pas honte ! Sur une feuille de papier, **écrivez une phrase** pour confesser quelque chose que vous n'auriez pas dû faire (inventez, si vous voulez !). Ensuite, **circulez** dans la salle de classe et lisez votre phrase. Vous pourriez aussi vous plaindre de votre situation. Vos camarades vont vous **faire des reproches** et **suggérer** ce que vous auriez dû faire. À la fin de l'activité, dites qui vous a donné la meilleure suggestion !

MODÈLE : —Je n'ai pas fait mes devoirs hier soir.

—Tu aurais dû aller à la bibliothèque ! Si tout le monde faisait comme toi !

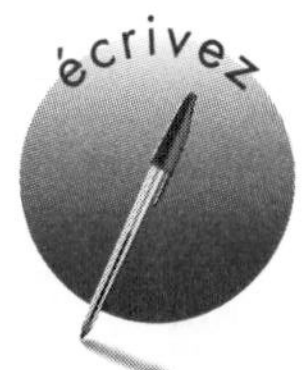

À l'écrit *deuxième étape*

7.27 Votre résidence secondaire Imaginez que vous parlez avec un(e) ami(e) de la 2ème maison que vous commencez à faire construire. Révisez vos listes des aspects de la maison et de ses environs que vous appréciez (Activité 15) et **écrivez un dialogue** dans lequel vous parlez de la maison elle-même et aussi de la région où elle se trouvera (utilisez le futur). En plus, plaignez-vous de la lenteur de la construction. Vous voulez que la maison soit prête avant les prochaines vacances ! Bien sûr, votre ami(e) pense que vous exagérez et il/elle vous fait des reproches. Finalement, avec un partenaire, révisez vos dialogues et lisez-les à haute voix.

Un courriel académique

Structures *le conditionnel et le conditionnel passé*

7.28 Si j'étais riche . . . Lisez l'extrait suivant qui vient du roman *Émile*, écrit par Jean-Jacques Rousseau et publié en Europe en 1762. Dans cet extrait, Rousseau décrit où il vivrait s'il était riche. Ensuite, **répondez aux questions**.

Émile (extrait)

■ Jean-Jacques Rousseau

Je n'**irais** pas me bâtir une ville en campagne. [. . .] Sur le penchant de quelque agréable colline (*hill*) ombragée, j'**aurais** une petite maison rustique, une maison blanche avec des contrevents (*shutters*) verts; et quoiqu'une couverture de chaume (*thatch roof*) soit en toute saison la meilleure, je **préférerais** magnifiquement, non la triste ardoise (*slate*), mais la tuile (*tile*) parce qu'elle a l'air plus propre et plus gaie que le chaume. [. . .] et que cela **me rappellerait** un peu l'heureux temps de ma jeunesse. [. . .] J'**aurais** un potager (*vegetable garden*) pour jardin, et pour parc un joli verger (*orchard*). Les fruits à la discrétion des promeneurs, ne **seraient** ni comptés ni cueillis par mon jardinier. [. . .] Or, cette petite prodigalité **serait** peu coûteuse, parce que j'**aurais choisi** mon asile dans quelque province éloignée où l'on voit peu d'argent et beaucoup de denrées (*produce*), et où règne l'abondance et la pauvreté. [. . .] Là tous les airs de la ville **seraient** oubliés, et devenus villageois du village, nous **nous trouverions** livrés à des foules d'amusements divers qui ne nous **donneraient** chaque soir que l'embarras du choix pour le lendemain. L'exercice et la vie active nous **feraient** un nouvel estomac et de nouveaux goûts. Tous nos repas **seraient** des festins où l'abondance **plairait** plus que la délicatesse.

1. Regardez tous les verbes au **conditionnel** et au **conditionnel passé** qui sont en **caractères gras**. Quel est l'infinitif de chaque verbe ?
2. Pouvez-vous décrire comment former le **conditionnel** et le **conditionnel passé** ? Pouvez-vous décrire comment employer le **conditionnel** ? et le **conditionnel passé** ?
3. Que pensez-vous de la maison rustique qu'imagine Rousseau ? Voudriez-vous habiter une maison comme celle-ci ? Pourquoi ou pourquoi pas ?

Culture

Jean-Jacques Rousseau est un écrivain du Siècle des lumières, le 18ème siècle. Né à Genève en Suisse, il s'est installé à Paris où il a écrit plusieurs discours et plusieurs romans, parmi lesquels *Émile ou De l'éducation.* Dans tous ses écrits, il critique la décadence de la société civilisée des grandes villes et fait l'éloge des bonheurs simples de la vie paysanne et de la sensibilité. Rousseau a beaucoup influencé les auteurs romantiques qui deviennent populaires au 19ème siècle. Pourtant, la philosophie de Rousseau, son dédain pour le progrès et son amour de la vie solitaire, sont critiqués par ses contemporains (comme Voltaire et Diderot) et Rousseau quitte la ville de Paris pour aller s'installer à Ermenonville où on peut, de nos jours, trouver son tombeau sur une petite île au sein de la nature qu'il admirait tant pendant sa vie.

Pour aller plus loin : CULTURE

ACTIVITÉ J : Apprenez un peu plus sur la vie de Jean-Jacques Rousseau. Consultez votre cahier électronique !

le conditionnel et le conditionnel passé

While the *future tense* expresses certainty or probability, the *conditional tense* (**le conditionnel**) expresses hypotheses or the possibility of an event occurring, if certain conditions are met. It is also used to describe future events in the context of past events, and it can be used simply to express politeness. The *past conditional* (**le conditionnel passé**) is used to describe events that would have occurred in the past, before other events could happen, or to express regret.

Formation of the *conditionnel*

The **conditionnel** is formed by adding the *imperfect tense endings* to the *future stem*. The conditional stem, therefore, is either the infinitive (drop the final **-e** from **-re** verbs) or one of the irregular future stems (review Chapter 6). The conditional endings are the same as the imperfect endings : **-ais, -ais, -ait, -ions, -iez, -aient**

- Example of **finir**: je finirais, tu finirais, il/elle/on finirait, nous finirions, vous finiriez, ils/elles finiraient

Uses of the *conditionnel*

- To express possibility: Si j'étais riche, **j'irais** à Dakar et **j'achèterais** le manuscrit. (*If I were rich, I would go to Dakar and I would buy the manuscript.*)
- In the context of the past tenses, to describe what would happen in the future: Finalement, ils sont allés à Dakar, où **ils trouveraient** le manuscrit. (*Finally, they went to Dakar, where they would find the manuscript.*)
- For politeness: Excusez-moi, est-ce que **vous pourriez** m'aider, s'il vous plaît ? (*Excuse me, could you please help me?*)

Formation of the *conditionnel passé*

The **conditionnel passé** is composed of two parts: the conditional of the *auxiliary verb*, **avoir** or **être**, plus the *past participle* of the verb you are conjugating (following the same rules for agreement as the **passé composé**).

- Example of **finir**: j'aurais fini, tu aurais fini, il/elle/on aurait fini, nous aurions fini, vous auriez fini, ils/elles auraient fini.

Uses of the *conditionnel passé*

- To describe what would have happened had certain conditions been met: Si j'avais été riche, **je serais allé(e)** à Dakar et **j'aurais acheté** le manuscrit. (*If I had been rich, I would have gone to Dakar and I would have bought the manuscript.*)
- In the context of the conditional tense, to describe what would have happened before other hypothetical actions: Ils quitteraient le Sénégal et iraient à Genève où Claire lirait le manuscrit que Jean-Louis **aurait acheté** à André. (*They would leave Senegal and would go to Geneva, where Claire would read the manuscript that Jean-Louis would have bought from André.*)
- To express regret: Il **aurait dû** dire la vérité dès le début ! (*He should have told the truth from the beginning!*)

7.29 Que ferais-je ? Jean-Louis descend pour chercher quelque chose à boire. Claire se repose sur son lit à quatre colonnes et pense à ce que Jean-Louis ferait si Monsieur Thibodeau refusait de vendre le manuscrit. Conjuguez les verbes entre parenthèses au **conditionnel**.

CLAIRE : Si Monsieur Thibodeau n'acceptait pas de vendre le manuscrit, j'(avoir) _______________ un dilemme. Je (vouloir) _______________ bien en faire une copie, et je (être) _______________ très satisfaite de cela. Pourtant, Jean-Louis ne (être) _______________ pas du tout content. Il (essayer) _______________ d'acquérir ce manuscrit par d'autres moyens. Il (faire) _______________ sans doute une grande bêtise, et les Thibodeau (se fâcher) _______________ avec lui et ils (appeler) _______________ la police. Ils (mettre) _______________ Jean-Louis en prison, et moi aussi peut-être, car ils (penser) _______________ que nous avons travaillé ensemble. Je ne (devoir) _______________ pas me taire. Ça c'est sûr.

regardez

le Sénégal

Qu'est-ce que Assata aurait fait si elle n'était pas venue aux États-Unis ? Regardez la vidéo et consultez votre cahier d'activités !

7.30 Les regrets Claire continue à réfléchir à comment la situation aurait été différente si elle n'avait pas fait la connaissance de Jean-Louis. Conjuguez les verbes entre parenthèses au **conditionnel passé**.

CLAIRE : Si je n'avais jamais rencontré Jean-Louis, je (trouver) _______________ l'adresse de Sandrine Fontenot à la bibliothèque de la Nouvelle-Orléans et je (pouvoir) _______________ aller la voir à sa maison. Je (recevoir) _______________ le nom du bouquiniste et il me (donner) _______________ le nom de Monsieur Thibodeau. Pourtant, je (ne... pas / avoir) _______________ le courage d'aller de Paris à la Martinique et en Afrique toute seule. Il est très probable que je (abandonner) _______________ ce projet de recherche et que je (retourner) _______________ au Québec. Mais qui sait ? Peut-être que je (devenir) _______________ plus courageuse et que je (chercher) _______________ le manuscrit toute seule. . .

Pour aller plus loin :
CULTURE
ACTIVITÉ K : Écoutez de la musique africaine. Consultez votre cahier électronique !

Pour aller plus loin :
LITTÉRATURE
ACTIVITÉ L : Lisez un poème de l'auteur sénégalais Birago Diop. Consultez votre cahier électronique !

7.31 Et vous ? Si vous étiez plus courageux(-euse), que feriez-vous ? Faites une liste de **cinq activités que vous feriez** cette année si vous étiez plus courageux(-euse). En plus, nommez **cinq activités que vous auriez faites** si vous aviez été moins naïf/naïve dans le passé. Comparez votre liste avec celle de vos camarades de classe.

MODÈLE : —Si j'étais plus courageux, je quitterais mon job et je deviendrais écrivain.
—Si j'avais été moins naïf dans le passé, je n'aurais jamais prêté de l'argent à mon ex !279

7.32 Et Jean-Louis ? Claire a décrit comment aurait été sa vie si elle n'avait pas rencontré Jean-Louis. Mais qu'est-ce que Jean-Louis aurait fait s'il n'avait pas rencontré Claire à la Nouvelle-Orléans ? Écrivez six phrases au **conditionnel passé**. Ensuite, comparez vos idées avec celles de vos camarades de classe.

MODÈLE : Si Jean-Louis n'avait pas rencontré Claire à la Nouvelle-Orléans, il aurait perdu son emploi chez l'antiquaire.

7.33 Questions personnelles Interviewez un(e) camarade de classe. Répondez aux questions personnelles suivantes. **Discutez de vos réponses** avec la classe.

1. Si vous pouviez choisir un pouvoir surnaturel, lequel choisiriez-vous ? Pourquoi ?
2. Quelle personne célèbre aimeriez-vous rencontrer ? Quelles questions lui poseriez-vous ?
3. Si vous étiez très riche, que feriez-vous de votre argent ? Pourquoi ?
4. Si vous étiez un animal, quel animal seriez-vous ? Pourquoi ?
5. Si vous pouviez voyager n'importe où dans le monde pendant l'été, où iriez-vous ? Pourquoi ?
6. Si vous pouviez vivre à une autre époque historique pour un mois, quelle époque choisiriez-vous ? Pourquoi ?

7.34 Que ferais-tu ? Faites une **interview** avec un camarade de classe afin de savoir ce qu'il/elle ferait pour s'amuser dans les endroits suivants. Posez des questions et répondez aux questions en utilisant le **conditionnel**.

MODÈLE : **—Que ferais-tu à Dakar ?**
—Je ferais du shopping et je visiterais les musées. Et toi ?

à Dakar	à la montagne	au Québec	en Louisiane
à la campagne	en France	à la plage	en Afrique

La prochaine fois que Claire se sert de l'ordinateur des Thibodeau pour voir si elle a reçu un message de sa sœur dans sa boîte aux lettres, elle trouve un courriel de son directeur de thèse. . .

Un courriel académique

À : Claire Plouffe
De : P.F. Thuillier
Date : 09/10/03
Réf : votre projet

Chère Mademoiselle Plouffe,

Je suis désolé de ne pas vous avoir contactée plus tôt. Comme vous le savez, je suis en congé sabbatique° cette année et je viens d'arriver en Provence où je ferai de la recherche aux Archives coloniales d'Aix-en-Provence jusqu'à Noël. J'étais à Paris la semaine dernière, et j'ai essayé de vous contacter à l'Hôtel Quasimodo, mais vous étiez déjà partie. Peut-être aviez-vous trouvé un petit appartement ? J'aurais dû vous téléphoner avant mon arrivée, mais j'étais très occupé par ma communication° pour le colloque° au Collège de France. Pourtant, j'aurais voulu vous voir afin de savoir si vous faites des progrès avec votre projet de recherche sur le manuscrit perdu de Laclos. En plus, cela aurait été bien si vous aviez pu assister au colloque. Il y avait de nombreux spécialistes de la littérature du 18ème siècle avec qui vous auriez pu discuter de votre projet.

sabbatical

scholarly paper/conference

Je serais très heureux de recevoir de vos nouvelles et de vous aider autant que° je pourrais. Écrivez-moi un petit message quand vous aurez le temps, et si jamais vous pensez venir en Provence, j'espère que vous me téléphonerez. On pourrait se donner rendez-vous pour parler de votre thèse.

as much as

Vous trouverez mes coordonnées à Aix en bas de page. En attendant de vous lire, je vous prie, chère Mademoiselle, d'accepter l'expression de mes sentiments les plus cordiaux.

P.F. Thuillier
Le Directeur de la Recherche et des Études Littéraires
L'Université de Sainte-Foy

Après avoir lu

7.35 D'accord ou pas d'accord ? Après avoir lu la lettre ci-dessus, lisez les phrases suivantes et **donnez vos opinions** personnelles. Discutez en petits groupes.

	D'accord	Pas d'accord
1. Monsieur Thuillier est en Provence maintenant.	_______	_______
2. Il était à Paris au début du mois de septembre.	_______	_______
3. Il a essayé de contacter Claire pendant son séjour à Paris.	_______	_______
4. Il regrette de ne pas avoir invité Claire au colloque.	_______	_______
5. Claire aurait aimé assister au colloque.	_______	_______
6. Claire verrait Monsieur Thuillier si elle était en Provence.	_______	_______

exprimer le regret

To express regret

Je suis sincèrement désolé(e) / navré(e) / triste de (+ *infinitif passé*)
J'aurais dû. . ./ J'aurais pu. . ./ J'aurais voulu. . . (+ *infinitif*)
Je regrette de (+ *infinitif* ou *infinitif passé*)
J'ai essayé de (+ *infinitif*) / J'aimerais bien (+ *infinitif*)
C'est dommage que / Il est triste que tu/vous (+ *subjonctif*)
Si je pouvais, je (+ *conditionnel*) / Si j'avais su, je (+ *conditionnel passé*)
Cela aurait été bien si (+ *plus-que-parfait*)
Je ne saurais vous dire combien je suis désolé(e).
Je ne pouvais pas faire autrement. C'était une situation difficile.
C'est terrible / affreux / énervant / fâcheux !
Quel dommage de vous avoir manqué ! C'est entièrement de ma faute !
Hélas ! / Mais, hélas ! / Zut ! / Flûte ! / Mais bon !

7.36 Hélas ! Que diriez-vous dans les situations suivantes pour exprimer le regret ? Avec un partenaire, **décidez de ce que vous pourriez dire**.

1. Vous avez oublié l'anniversaire de votre ami(e).
2. Vous arrivez à un restaurant chic et populaire sans avoir fait de réservations à l'avance.
3. Votre professeur vous avait invité(e) à un colloque, mais vous n'y êtes pas allé(e).

4. Vos amis vous attendent au café depuis deux heures et ils ont raté le film qu'ils allaient voir.
5. Vous êtes invité(e) à dîner chez des collègues, et vous arrivez sans cadeau pour vos hôtes.
6. Vous êtes vétérinaire et il vous faut annoncer à un client que sa vache est morte.

7.37 Ça m'énerve quand. . . Imaginez que vous êtes l'étudiant(e) parfait(e). Vous vous plaignez des mauvaises habitudes de vos camarades de classe. Sur une feuille de papier, **écrivez une phrase** pour décrire les habitudes qui vous énervent (*get on your nerves*). Ensuite, **circulez** dans la salle de classe et **plaignez-vous** à vos camarades. Si quelqu'un exprime du regret, reprochez-lui ! Si quelqu'un vous reproche vos critiques, exprimez vos regrets ! Essayez de parler à autant de personnes que possible !

MODÈLE : —Ça m'énerve quand les étudiants mangent en classe !
—Je suis désolé. J'aurais dû déjeuner avant de venir en classe. *ou*
—Tu exagères ! Pour qui te prends-tu ?

Pour aller plus loin : CINÉMA

ACTIVITÉ M : Regardez le film *Chocolat* (1988, mise en scène par Claire Denis) qui explore les regrets et les sentiments d'une jeune femme lorsqu'elle retourne au pays en Afrique où elle a grandi. Consultez votre cahier électronique !

À l'écrit *troisième étape*

7.38 Votre résidence secondaire Finalement, la construction de votre 2ème maison est terminée ! **Écrivez une lettre** à un(e) ami(e) dans laquelle vous invitez cette personne à passer un week-end dans votre nouvelle maison. Révisez les Activités 15 et 27, et décrivez comment il/elle trouverait la maison et ce que vous pourriez faire pour vous amuser dans la région (utilisez le conditionnel). Échangez votre lettre avec un(e) camarade de classe (par courriel, si vous voulez !) et offrez une réponse avec quelques corrections possibles et où vous exprimez vos regrets (vous ne pourrez pas accepter l'invitation !).

Dénouement

Activités de révision

7.39 N'importe où ! (*anywhere*) Dans chaque coin du monde, dans chaque région, on trouve un climat et une écologie particuliers. En petits groupes, **pensez à une région** spécifique et à la nature dans cette partie du monde. Puis, tour à tour, les autres groupes vont vous poser **dix questions** sur la flore et la faune afin de deviner de quelle partie du monde il s'agit ! Pourtant, vous pouvez répondre seulement avec «oui» ou «non», et chaque groupe peut poser seulement une question à son tour. Le groupe qui devine le plus grand nombre d'endroits a gagné !

MODÈLE : le Québec

—Est-ce qu'il y a des lions ?

—Non !

Il y a beaucoup de **problèmes écologiques** dans le monde aujourd'hui. Il y a des problèmes quant à la qualité et la pureté de l'air qu'on respire, causés par la **pollution**. Il y a des problèmes qui viennent de la contamination de l'eau à cause de la **pluie acide**. Il y a des **espèces d'animaux en voie de disparition** à cause des hommes qui chassent ou qui polluent. Il y a des dauphins qui meurent à cause du plastique qui nous permet de porter facilement plusieurs cannettes de coca ou à cause de filets qu'on place pour attraper les thons. Il y a le problème du **déboisement** (*deforestation*) des forêts qui détruit l'équilibre écologique pour qu'on puisse construire des maisons. Il y a des **accidents pétroliers** dans les océans qui tuent les poissons et les oiseaux. Il y a aussi des **déchets nucléaires**, des **trous dans la couche d'ozone** et **l'effet de serre** (*the greenhouse effect*) qui pourraient déstabiliser notre environnement à l'avenir.

7.40 Peut-on sauver le monde ? Pensez aux solutions possibles aux problèmes écologiques suivants. Utilisez le conditionnel. Ensuite, **discutez de vos idées** avec vos camarades de classe. Y a-t-il des choses que vous pourriez faire vous-mêmes maintenant pour éviter des désastres à l'avenir ?

MODÈLE : la sous-population de loups en Amérique du Nord →

—Les gens devraient arrêter de tuer les loups ! Nous pourrions enseigner aux enfants comment apprécier le loup. On ne devrait pas avoir peur de cet animal.

1. la disparition des phoques au Québec du nord à cause de la vente de leurs peaux (*skins*)
2. le déboisement et l'érosion à Haïti qui transforme les forêts en déserts
3. la pollution qui réduit la qualité de l'air qu'on respire à Paris
4. la déstabilisation de l'écologie marine par des accidents pétroliers
5. la mort des dauphins à cause des déchets en plastique

7.41 Vérité ou défi ? En petits groupes, jouez au jeu «Vérité ou défi ?». Demandez à un(e) camarade s'il/elle préférerait **dire la vérité** ou **oser faire quelque chose** de stupide. D'après son choix, choisissez une des questions ou un des défis des listes suivantes. Si la personne choisit un défi, il/elle doit le faire tout de suite. Si la personne choisit la vérité, il/elle doit répondre sincèrement à la question et vous avez le droit de poser des questions supplémentaires sur le même sujet !

Défis	Vérités
1. Chantez «Frère Jacques» devant la classe !	1. Avec quel acteur/actrice vous marieriez-vous ? Pourquoi ?
2. Donnez un compliment à quelqu'un !	2. À quel âge voudriez-vous prendre votre retraite ? Où habiteriez-vous après ?
3. Dessinez votre auto-portrait au tableau !	3. Quelle est votre plus grande peur ? Que feriez-vous pour ne pas l'affronter ?
4. Enlevez vos chaussures et sautez à cloche-pied (*on one foot*) !	4. Le week-end dernier, qu'avez vous fait d'ennuyeux ? Qu'auriez-vous fait autrement si vous aviez pu ?
5. Dansez devant la classe !	5. Quelle émission d'enfants aimeriez-vous regarder régulièrement à la télé ?
6. Videz votre sac et montrez tous les objets qui s'y trouvent !	6. Qu'est-ce que vous ne mangeriez riez pas, même pas pour mille euros ?

7.42 Si jamais. . . Avec un(e) partenaire, choisissez l'**invention technologique** qui vous paraît la plus utile à la société de nos jours (par exemple, l'électricité, l'ordinateur, la voiture, etc.). Maintenant, **écrivez cinq phrases** pour décrire comment nos vies auraient été différentes si on n'avait jamais inventé cette chose ! Lisez votre description à haute voix. Vos camarades vont essayer de deviner de quelle invention il s'agit !

MODÈLE : Sans cette invention, nous aurions dû garder des chevaux chez nous et les vétérinaires et les forgerons seraient devenus plus importants.

La côte sénégalaise.

Pour aller plus loin : CINÉMA

ACTIVITÉ N : Regardez le film *Faat Kiné* d'Ousmane Sembène qui raconte l'histoire d'une famille dakaroise. Consultez votre cahier électronique !

Avant de lire *Une si longue lettre*

7.43 Premières impressions Lisez l'extrait du roman *Une si longue lettre* de Miriama Bâ, sans essayer de comprendre chaque mot. Après votre première lecture du texte, **répondez aux questions**. Ensuite, relisez le texte une deuxième fois, plus attentivement.

1. Qui parle ? Une jeune femme ou une femme d'une certaine âge ?
2. Quand se passe l'histoire ? Au présent ? Au passé ? À l'avenir ?
3. Où se situe l'action ? Dans une ville ou à la campagne ?
4. Quel est le ton de l'histoire ? Triste ? Gai ? Mélancolique ? Paisible ?
5. Qu'est-ce que les personnages faisaient pour s'amuser pendant leurs séjours à l'extérieur de la ville ?

Une si longue lettre

Cet extrait vient du roman de Miriama Bâ, ***Une si longue lettre****. Dans ce roman, Bâ décrit la vie, les pensées, les plaintes, les regrets et les espoirs d'une femme sénégalaise après la mort de son mari. Dans une lettre à une amie, le personnage principal, Ramatoulaye, se souvient des beaux jours passés avec son mari, Mawdo, au début de leur mariage, avant qu'il n'ait pris une 2ème femme selon la tradition islamique. Ici, Bâ décrit avec nostalgie et admiration la beauté de son pays tout en essayant de retrouver son optimisme pour la vie. . .*

■ Miriama Bâ

Une si longue lettre (extrait)

Tandis que° la mère de Mawdo pensait à sa vengeance, nous, nous vivions : réveillons° de Noël organisés par plusieurs couples dont les frais° étaient équitablement partagés et abrités° par chaque foyer° à tour de rôle. Nous exhumions sans complexe les pas° d'antan° : biguines° ardentes, rumbas frénétiques, tangos langoureux. Nous retrouvions les battements de cœur anciens qui fortifiaient nos sentiments.

Nous sortions aussi de la ville étouffante, pour humer° l'air sain des banlieues marines.

Nous longions la corniche dakaroise, l'une des plus belles de l'Afrique de l'Ouest, véritable œuvre d'art de la nature. Des rochers arrondis ou pointus, noirs ou ocres dominaient l'Océan. De la verdure,° parfois de véritables jardins suspendus s'épanouissaient° sous le ciel clair. Nous débouchions sur la route de Ouakam qui mène également à Ngor, et plus loin à l'aérogare de Yoff. Nous reconnaissions au passage la ruelle qui mène en profondeur à la plage des Almadies.

Notre halte préférée était la plage de Ngor, située au village du même nom où de vieux pêcheurs barbus raccommodaient° les filets,° sous les bentenniers. Des enfants nus et morveux° jouaient en toute liberté, s'ils ne s'ébattaient° pas dans la mer.

Sur le sable fin, rincé par la vague° et gorgé d'eau, des pirogues,° peintes naïvement, attendaient leur tour d'être lancées sur les eaux. Dans leur coque,° luisaient° de petites flaques° bleues pleine de ciel et de soleil.

so long as
holiday midnight suppers/expenses
housed/household
steps/of the past/a type of dance
to breathe in
greenery
to open out
to mend/nets
runny-nosed
to frolic
wave/canoes
hull/to shine/puddles

Quelle affluence les jours de fête ! De nombreuses familles, assoiffées d'espace et d'air pur déambulaient.° On se dénudait sans complexe, tenté par la caresse bienfaisante de la brise iodée et la tiédeur° des rayons solaires. Des fainéants° dormaient sous les parasols déployés. Quelques gamins,° pelles et seaux° en mains, bâtissaient° et démolissaient° les châteaux de leur imagination.

to stroll
tepidness
lazy people
kids/ shovels and pails/ to build/ to demolish

Le soir, les pêcheurs revenaient de leur randonnée laborieuse. Ils avaient échappé une fois de plus, au piège° mouvant de la mer. De simples lignes noires à l'horizon, les barques° devenaient plus distinctes, les unes des autres, au fur et à mésure° de leur approche. Elles dansaient dans les creux° des vagues, puis se laissaient paresseusement drainer. Des pêcheurs descendaient gaîment voile° et matériel. Tandis que d'autres rassemblaient la moisson° frétillante,° certains tordaient° leurs habits trempés° et épongeaient° leurs fronts.

trap
boats
progressively
hollows
sail
harvest/ wriggly/ to twist/ wet clothes
to sponge off

Sous les yeux émerveillés des bambins, les poissons vivants sautillaient, tandis que s'incurvaient les longs serpents de mer. Rien n'est plus beau qu'un poisson à la sortie de l'eau, avec son œil clair et frais, ses écailles° dorées ou argentées et ses beaux reflets bleutés° !

scales/ bluish

Des mains triaient,° groupaient, divisaient. Pour la maison, nous faisions d'intéressantes provisions.

to sort

L'air marin nous incitait à la bonne humeur. Le plaisir que nous goûtions et qui fêtait tous nos sens, enivrait° sainement, aussi bien le riche que le pauvre. Notre communion, avec la nature profonde, insondable° et illimitée, désintoxiquait notre âme. Le découragement et la tristesse s'en allaient, soudainement remplacés par des sentiments de plénitude et d'épanouissement.

to intoxicate
unfathomable

Revigorés, nous reprenions le chemin de nos foyers. Comme nous avions le secret des bonheurs simples, cures bienfaisantes dans la tourmente des jours !

Te souviens-tu des pique-niques organisés à Sangalkam, dans le champ que Mawdo Bâ avait hérité de son père ? Sangalkam reste le refuge des Dakarois, qui désirent rompre° avec la frénésie° de la ville. Beaucoup de propriétés s'y côtoient donc, achetées par des jeunes qui y ont installé de véritables résidences secondaires : ces espaces verts sont propices au repos, à la méditation et au défoulement des enfants. La route de Rufisque mène à cette oasis.

to break with/ frenzy

La mère de Mawdo avait entretenu° le champ avant le mariage de son fils. Le souvenir de son mari l'avait rivée° à cette parcelle de terre où leurs mains unies et patientes avaient discipliné la végétation qui émerveillait nos yeux.

to maintain
to rivet

Toi, tu y avais ajouté la petite construction de fond : trois chambrettes simples, une salle d'eau, une cuisine. Tu avais fleuri abondamment quelques coins. Tu avais fait bâtir un poulailler,° puis un enclos pour des moutons.

hen house

Des cocotiers au feuillage entrecroisé protégeaient du soleil. Des sapotilles° fondantes° voisinaient avec des odorantes grenades.° Des mangues, lourdes à porter, faisaient ployer° des branches. Des papayes qui ressemblaient à des seins° multiformes, restaient tentantes° et inaccessibles, au sommet des troncs élancés.°

tropical trees/ melting/ pomegranates
to bend
breasts/ tempting
soaring

Feuilles vertes et feuilles bronzées, herbes nouvelles et herbes fanées° jonchaient° le sol. Sous nos pas, des fourmis reconstruisaient inlassablement leur logis.

wilted
to litter

Que l'ombre était tiède sur les lits de camp dressés. Les équipes de jeux se succédaient dans la clameur victorieuse ou les lamentations de la défaite.

to gorge oneself

to wiggle around, do a jig

Et nous nous gavions° des fruits à portée de la main ! Et nous buvions l'eau des noix de coco ! Et nous nous racontions des «histoires salées» ! Et nous nous trémoussions,° invités par les accents violents d'un phonographe ! Et l'agneau assaisonné de poivre, ail, beurre, piment, grillait sur le feu de bois.

Et nous vivions. . .

Après avoir lu

WWW

Pour aller plus loin : LITTÉRATURE

ACTIVITÉ O : Apprenez un peu plus sur les femmes écrivains de l'Afrique francophone. Consultez votre cahier électronique !

7.44 Avez-vous compris ? En petits groupes, **discutez de vos réponses** aux questions suivantes.

1. Décrivez les vies des personnes qui vont régulièrement à la plage de Ngor : les touristes, les pêcheurs, les enfants. Quelles activités font-ils ? Avez-vous l'impression que la narratrice aime aller à cette plage ? Pourquoi ?
2. Décrivez la résidence secondaire à Sangalkam. Comment est la maison ? Qu'y a-t-il à faire là-bas ? Avez-vous l'impression que la narratrice aime aller à la campagne ? Pourquoi ?
3. Faites une liste de tous les animaux et plantes mentionnés par la narratrice lorsqu'elle décrit les séjours à Sangalkam. Lesquels trouvez-vous près de chez vous ? À votre avis, est-ce que cet endroit est une «oasis» comme dit la narratrice ?
4. Pourquoi est-ce que les personnages aimaient tant la «communion avec la nature» ? Quels sont les bénéfices de ces séjours ?
5. Comparez les deux endroits décrits dans ce texte (la plage et la campagne) avec les endroits où vous passez vos vacances. Quelles sont les similarités et quelles sont les différences ? Voudriez-vous visiter Ngor ou Sangalkam ? Pourquoi ou pourquoi pas ?

le Sénégal

Comment est-ce que Assata décrit l'environnement au Sénégal ? Regardez la vidéo et consultez votre cahier d'activités !

7.45 D'accord ou pas d'accord ? Après avoir lu l'extrait du roman de Bâ, lisez les phrases suivantes et **donnez votre opinion**. Discutez de vos réponses en petits groupes.

	D'accord	Pas d'accord
1. Ramatoulaye (la narratrice) et ses amis vivaient au centre-ville de Dakar.	_______	_______
2. Ils préféraient la plage à la maison de campagne.	_______	_______
3. Ces gens sont assez riches.	_______	_______
4. Ils préparaient des festins de fruits exotiques parce qu'ils étaient végétariens.	_______	_______
5. Quand ils sortaient de la ville, c'était pour s'échapper au stress de leur vie.	_______	_______

7.46 Analyse littéraire Examinez ce texte de près. Répondez aux questions suivantes et **discutez de vos réponses** en classe.

1. Quel est le ton du texte ? Quel temps de verbe domine dans cet extrait ? Comment est-ce qu'il contribue au ton ?
2. Dans la description de la plage de Ngor, la narratrice parle de «l'affluence». En quoi consiste l'affluence de ce petit village de pêcheurs ? Examinez les adjectifs et les adverbes dans cette description, et expliquez l'importance de l'image du «poisson à la sortie de l'eau».
3. L'image de l'oasis est très important à cet extrait. Comment est-ce que cette image est présentée dans les descriptions des lieux de vacances de la narratrice ? Examinez surtout la description de l'environnement à Sangalkam.
4. Examinez l'emploi de la ponctuation, surtout les virgules (*commas*) et les points d'exclamation, dans cet extrait. Quel est l'effet de l'usage de la ponctuation ?
5. Quelle est l'importance de la dernière phrase «Et nous vivions. . . » ? Comment est-ce que la construction de cette phrase contribue à son effet sur le lecteur ?

Synthèses

7.47 Réfléchissons à la culture Pensez à la culture sénégalaise que vous avez étudiée dans ce chapitre. En petits groupes, **répondez aux questions** et **discutez** de vos impressions avec vos camarades.

1. Donnez les informations suivantes sur le Sénégal : capitale, type de gouvernement, langues parlées, groupes ethniques, religions importantes, produits économiques, situation géographique
2. Pourquoi est-ce que le français reste une langue officielle au Sénégal si les gens parlent des langues africaines comme langues maternelles ? Y a-t-il un phénomène historique ou social qui explique son importance et le fait qu'on continue à utiliser le français dans les écoles, au travail et dans le gouvernement du pays ?
3. Le baobab est un arbre très important au Sénégal, et le lion est un animal qui a beaucoup de signification pour le pays. Expliquez la signification de ces deux symboles à la culture sénégalaise. Y a-t-il des plantes ou des animaux symboliques aux États-Unis ? Lesquels ? Pourquoi est-ce qu'un pays se lie à des plantes et des animaux symboliques ? (Pensez au castor du Canada, au cèdre du Liban, au coq de la France, etc.)
4. Quels aspects de la culture sénégalaise sont différents de la vôtre ? Comment ? Pourquoi ? Est-ce que votre impression de cette culture est différente maintenant que vous avez commencé à l'étudier ? Si oui, comment et pourquoi ? Si non, pourquoi pas ?

Pour aller plus loin : CULTURE

ACTIVITÉ P : Visitez une exposition d'art africain. Consultez votre cahier électronique !

7.48 À débattre Lisez les questions suivantes et **discutez-les** en groupes. Si possible, parlez de vos expériences personnelles relatives aux questions.

1. **La pollution !** Discutez le pour et le contre de l'usage de l'essence (*gasoline*) pour les voitures, les avions, le chauffage central et le fonctionnement des usines. Pourrait-on vivre sans ces choses ? Devrait-on sacrifier les réserves naturelles pour avoir une source de pétrole ? Que pensez-vous ?
2. **L'urbanisation.** Partout dans le monde, les gens quittent les petits villages ruraux pour aller vivre dans les grands centres urbains où ils peuvent trouver des emplois et des opportunités qui n'existent pas à la campagne. Pourtant, les villes sont surpeuplées et on y trouve des problèmes de crime, de drogue et de chômage. Si on reste dans son village rural, on a des problèmes. Si on part en ville, on a des problèmes. Les banlieues sont des endroits plus favorables, mais seulement accessibles aux gens aisés. Qu'est-ce qu'une jeune personne devrait choisir : la ville ou la campagne ?
3. **La pêche à la baleine.** Les Amérindiens du Québec en Amérique du Nord font de la pêche à la baleine depuis toujours. C'est une de leurs traditions sacrées. Aujourd'hui, la pêche à la baleine est défendue par des lois qui visent à protéger ces animaux qui risquent de disparaître. Pourtant, si les Européens n'avaient jamais colonisé les terres des Amérindiens et n'avaient jamais développé l'industrie de la pêche à la baleine, ces animaux ne seraient pas en danger. Devrait-on autoriser la pêche à la baleine pour les Amérindiens ?

7.49 À l'impromptu Voici des situations interactives. Avec une ou deux autres personnes, **choisissez une scène** et **improvisez** devant la classe. Si vous ne voulez pas improviser, écrivez votre dialogue avant et puis jouez-le pour la classe.

1. Des tâches ménagères
   (a) Un(e) ami(e) vous a invité à passer quelques jours dans sa maison près de la plage au Sénégal. Malheureusement, il s'attend trop à ce que vous participiez aux tâches ménagères. Dites-lui sans trop le/la fâcher que vous êtes en vacances et que vous voulez vous reposer un peu.
   (b) Vous et votre femme/mari avez invité un(e) ami(e) à passer quelques jours dans votre maison de vacances près de la plage au Sénégal. Malheureusement, vous vous rendez compte qu'il/elle vous traite comme des domestiques. Plaignez-vous du travail ménagère à faire.
2. Un problème écologique
   (a) Vous êtes membre du parti Vert et vous vous inquiétez du progrès de la déforestation et de la pollution en Afrique de l'Ouest. Partagez vos craintes avec votre ami(e). Identifiez les causes et les solutions de ces problèmes.
   (b) Vous êtes propriétaire d'une usine qui fabrique de l'huile d'arachide au Sénégal. Vous n'aimez pas les lois écologiques qui limitent la production. Pour vous, la fin justifie les moyens. Un peu de pollution ne fait pas trop de mal si l'usine contribue à l'économie du pays.

3. La lune de miel (*honeymoon*)
   (a) Vous et votre fiancé(e) vous disputez quant à la destination de votre lune de miel. Vous aimez la nature. Vous voulez participer à un safari en Afrique. Expliquez pourquoi et essayez de convaincre votre fiancé(e) d'y aller.
   (b) Vous et votre fiancé(e) vous disputez quant à la destination de votre lune de miel. Vous voulez passer une semaine à Paris dans un hôtel luxueux avec tout le confort moderne. Expliquez pourquoi et essayez de convaincre votre fiancé(e) d'y aller.

À l'écrit *étape finale*

7.50 Maison à louer Vous voilà avec une belle maison de campagne, mais vous n'avez jamais le temps d'y aller. Donc, vous décidez de la louer pour regagner un peu de l'argent que vous avez dépensé en la faisant construire. Votre professeur de français s'intéresse à la maison pour ses vacances d'été, mais il/elle n'a jamais visité cette région. Révisez et élaborez vos travaux d'écriture de ce chapitre (Activités 15, 27 et 38) et **écrivez-lui une belle description** de votre résidence secondaire et de ses environs. En plus, expliquez pourquoi vous n'y allez pas vous-même en vous plaignant de votre emploi du temps et de ce que vous y auriez fait cet été si vous aviez eu le temps. Utilisez le conditionnel et le conditionnel passé.

À suivre

Finalement, après quelques jours de négociations, André Thibodeau accepte de vendre le manuscrit original à Jean-Louis pour une somme considérable. Le manuscrit en main, Jean-Louis et Claire partent pour la Suisse où la famille de Jean-Louis a un petit chalet au bord du Lac Léman. Pour ne pas endommager le papier ancien, Claire accepte d'attendre jusqu'à leur arrivée en Suisse avant de commencer à lire le manuscrit et passe le voyage à rêver de son avenir et de sa bonne fortune. . .

7.51 Qu'est-ce qui s'est passé ? Pensez à ce qui s'est passé dans ce chapitre. **Écrivez six phrases** aux temps passés pour décrire les événements que vous pensez être les plus importants. Parlez de vos idées avec vos camarades de classe.

MODÈLE : Claire et Jean-Louis se sont disputés ! C'est important parce que. . .

7.52 Qu'est-ce qui se passera ? Imaginez ce qui va se passer dans le prochain chapitre. **Écrivez six phrases** et parlez de vos idées avec vos camarades de classe. Employez le futur.

MODÈLE : Je pense que Jean-Louis achètera le manuscrit et quittera Dakar sans Claire !

Pour agir :
LE SÉNÉGAL !

Si vous voulez bouger et faire quelque chose pour mieux connaître le Sénégal ou pour aider les autres à mieux connaître les cultures francophones de l'Afrique, consultez la section **Pour agir** dans votre cahier électronique ! Il y a tant de choses à faire :

- **Vendez des cacahouètes** et contribuez l'argent que vous gagnez à une organisation qui aide les pauvres ou les femmes dans les pays francophones en Afrique. . . ou bien contribuez votre argent à une organisation écologique.
- **Enseignez** ce que vous savez de la culture africaine à des enfants de l'école primaire. Lisez-leur des contes africains !
- **Invitez** un chanteur ou un griot africain à donner un concert sur votre campus.
- **Entrez en contact** avec des Africains francophones qui vivent dans votre communauté ou quelque part aux États-Unis.
- **Organisez une exposition** d'art africain sur votre campus ou visitez une exposition d'art africain dans un musée près de chez vous.
- **Cuisinez !** Préparez un vrai repas africain avec vos camarades de classe.

VOCABULAIRE UTILE

À la maison

bail (*m.*)	*lease*
bureau (*m.*)	*office*
canapé (*m.*)	*couch*
case (*f.*)	*hut*
caution (*f.*)	*security deposit*
chambre (*f.*) à coucher	*bedroom*
colonne (*f.*) de lit	*bedpost*
commode (*f.*)	*dresser*
cuisine (*f.*)	*kitchen*
déménager	*to move (a home or business)*
domestique (*m./f.*)	*housekeeper, servant*
entrouvert(e)	*half open, ajar*
étagère (*m.*)	*shelf, bookcase*
évier (*m.*)	*large sink*
four (*m.*)	*oven*
four (*m.*) à micro-ondes	*microwave oven*
garage (*m.*)	*garage*
garde-manger (*f.*)	*cupboard for storing food*
hall (*m.*) d'entrée	*foyer*
lavabo (*m.*)	*small sink*
lave-vaisselle (*m.*)	*dishwasher*
loyer (*m.*)	*rent*
machine (*f.*) à laver	*washing machine*
marbre (*m.*)	*marble*
meubles (*m. pl.*)	*furnishings*
mobilier (*m.*)	*furniture*
moquette (*f.*)	*carpet*
parquet (*m.*)	*floor*
péniche (*f.*)	*houseboat*
pièce (*f.*)	*room*
rideaux (*m. pl.*)	*curtains*
salle (*f.*) à manger	*dining room*
salle (*f.*) de bains	*bathroom*
salon (*m.*)	*living room*
s'installer	*to settle down, move in*
sous-sol (*m.*)	*basement*
table basse (*f.*)	*coffee table*
téléviseur (*m.*)	*TV set*

Des tâches domestiques

épousseter	*to dust*
faire la cuisine	*to cook*
faire la lessive	*to wash clothes*
faire la vaisselle	*to do the dishes*
faire le lit	*to make the bed*
faire le ménage	*to do housework*
passer l'aspirateur	*to vacuum*

ranger les affaires	*to tidy up*
repasser	*to iron*
fer (*m.*) à repasser	*iron*

Divers

cacahouète (*f.*)	*peanut*
colline (*f.*)	*hill*
cru(e)	*raw*
environs (*m. pl.*)	*surroundings*
fier, fière	*proud*
grignoter	*to munch, to nibble*
Santé ! Chin, chin !	*To your health! Cheers!*
terre (*f.*)	*earth, land*
trinquer	*to toast*

Les animaux

abeille (*f.*)	*bee*
aigle (*m.*)	*eagle*
araignée (*f.*)	*spider*
baleine (*f.*)	*whale*
cafard (*m.*)	*cockroach*
canard (*m.*)	*duck*
castor (*m.*)	*beaver*
cerf (*m.*)	*deer*
chameau (*m.*)	*camel*
cheval (*m.*)	*horse*
chèvre (*f.*)	*goat*
cochon (*m.*)	*pig*
coq (*m.*)	*rooster*
corbeau (*m.*)	*crow*
cougar (*m.*)	*mountain lion*
dauphin (*m.*)	*dolphin*
fourmi (*f.*)	*ant*
furet (*m.*)	*ferret*
grenouille (*f.*)	*frog*
hibou (*m.*)	*owl*
hippopotame (*m.*)	*hippopotamus*
hirondelle (*f.*)	*swallow*
hyène (*m.*)	*hyena*
lapin (*m.*)	*rabbit*
marmotte (*f.*)	*groundhog*
mouche (*f.*)	*fly*
mouffette (*f.*)	*skunk*
moustique (*m.*)	*mosquito*
mouton (*m.*)	*sheep*
oie (*f.*)	*goose*
oiseau (*m.*)	*bird*
orignal (*m.*)	*moose (reg. Québec)*
ours (*m.*)	*bear*
papillon (*m.*)	*butterfly*
phoque (*m.*)	*seal*
poisson rouge (*m.*)	*goldfish*
raton laveur (*m.*)	*raccoon*
renard (*m.*)	*fox*
renne (*m.*)	*reindeer*
requin (*m.*)	*shark*
serpent (*m.*)	*snake*
singe (*m.*)	*monkey*
souris (*f.*)	*mouse*
tortue (*f.*)	*turtle*
vache (*f.*)	*cow*
vautour (*m.*)	*vulture*

Les plantes et les arbres

arbre (*m.*) à gomme	*rubber tree*
arbrisseau (*m.*)	*shrub*
bananier (*m.*)	*banana tree*
bouleau (*m.*)	*birch tree*
bruyère (*f.*)	*heather*
buisson (*m.*)	*bush*
cèdre (*m.*)	*cedar tree*
cerisier (*m.*)	*cherry tree*
chêne (*m.*)	*oak tree*
chèvrefeuille (*m.*)	*honeysuckle*
citronnier (*m.*)	*lemon tree*
citrouille (*f.*)	*pumpkin*
cocotier (*m.*)	*coconut tree*
coquelicot (*m.*)	*red poppy*
érable (*m.*)	*maple tree*
fougère (*f.*)	*fern*
houx (*m.*)	*holly*
jonquille (*f.*)	*daffodil*
lierre (*m.*)	*ivy*
marguerite (*f.*)	*daisy*
marronnier (*m.*)	*chestnut tree*
mousse (*f.*)	*moss*
orme (*m.*)	*elm tree*
palmier (*m.*)	*palm tree*
papayer (*m.*)	*papaya tree*
pensée (*f.*)	*pansy*
pin (*m.*)	*pine tree*
platane (*m.*)	*plane tree*
poirier (*m.*)	*pear tree*
pommier (*m.*)	*apple tree*
sapin (*m.*)	*fir tree*
sumac vénéneux (*m.*)	*poison ivy*
tournesol (*m.*)	*sunflower*
trèfle (*m.*)	*clover*
vigne (*f.*)	*vines*

Les disputes

aller jusqu'au bout	*to go the distance, to go all the way*
au bout de	*at the end of*
avoir honte de	*to be ashamed*
bout (*m.*)	*end*
but (*m.*)	*goal, objective*
conforts (*m. pl.*)	*comforts*
devoir de l'argent	*to owe money*
impensable	*unthinkable*
moyen (*m.*)	*way, means*
puissant(e)	*powerful*
se prendre pour	*to take oneself for, to think of oneself as*
se servir de	*to use for/as*

Chapitre 8

Un tableau suisse

Une promenade près du Lac Léman à Genève.

Épisode 1 *L'art de lire*

Épisode 2 *La visite du musée*

Épisode 3 *Une hypothèse*

Dénouement

Culture

La **Confédération helvétique**, c'est-à-dire la **Suisse**, se trouve dans les Alpes entre la France, l'Italie, l'Autriche, le Liechtenstein et l'Allemagne. Ce pays montagneux a été fondé le premier août 1291 par plusieurs communautés qui voulaient se défendre des Habsbourg, une famille autrichienne puissante. Cette confédération de communautés s'est ensuite déclarée un pays neutre. Entre 1798 et 1815, la France a occupé la Suisse, mais ce pays a regagné son indépendance et a rétabli sa neutralité politique après la chute de Napoléon 1er. Aujourd'hui composé de 26 cantons, la Suisse reste un pays neutre et indépendant, choisissant de ne pas joindre ses voisins dans l'Union européenne. À cause de sa neutralité, plusieurs organisations internationales, telles la Croix-Rouge et l'ONU, y ont leur siège. La capitale de ce pays de l'Europe centrale est la ville de Berne, quoique la ville de Zurich soit la plus grande. Il existe trois langues officielles en Suisse : le français (parlé par 19.5% de la population), l'italien (parlé par 6.6%) et l'allemand (parlé par la majorité des citoyens, 63.9%). On y parle aussi le romanche (une langue romane) et plusieurs dialectes de l'allemand et de l'italien. Les cantons francophones se trouvent à l'est du pays, entre les montagnes du Jura et le Lac Léman. Les villes francophones les plus importantes sont Genève, Neuchâtel et Lausanne.

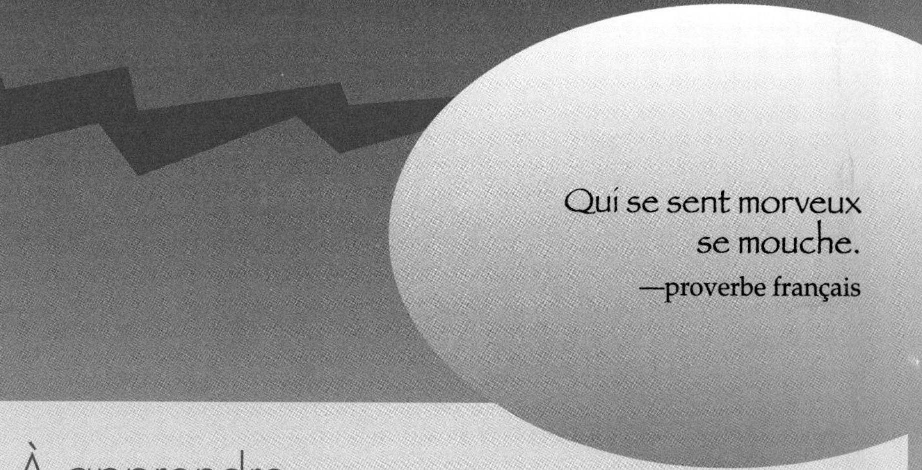

Qui se sent morveux se mouche.

—proverbe français

À apprendre

- Comment décrire, critiquer ou apprécier quelque chose
- Comment comparer deux choses
- Comment établir une hypothèse

À lire

Jean-Louis avait assuré à Claire que le petit chalet suisse de sa famille, qui se trouve dans le village de Coppet, tout près de Genève et au bord du Lac Léman, serait l'endroit le plus paisible afin d'entreprendre la lecture du manuscrit. Pourquoi pas, pensait-elle. Elle y pourrait lire le manuscrit aussi bien qu'ailleurs. Et, si Voltaire et Rousseau avaient choisi ce pays comme leur retraite littéraire au 18ème siècle, il lui servirait aussi bien. Donc, ils prennent l'avion pour Genève et s'installent dans le chalet où, finalement, Claire pourra lire le manuscrit. . .

Épisode 1

L'art de lire

Avant de lire

Langue

Pour décrire **les arts plastiques**, on peut parler de la peinture : d'un tableau (*picture*), d'une toile (*canvas*), d'un chef-d'œuvre (*masterpiece*) ou plus généralement d'une œuvre (*work*). Il y a aussi des dessins (*drawings*), des esquisses (*sketches*), des gravures (*engravings*), des mosaïques, des céramiques, des fresques, des collages ou des aquarelles (*watercolors*). Les artistes peuvent donc se spécialiser comme peintres, dessinateurs, graveurs, céramistes ou sculpteurs. Les sujets des peintures sont souvent des paysages, des portraits de gens, des scènes d'action ou bien des objets. La nature morte, par exemple, est un tableau de plusieurs objets assemblés, comme des fruits ou des outils. Quelques **grands mouvements** dans la peinture sont le symbolisme (où l'artiste représente des idées par des figures ou des objets symboliques), le réalisme (où l'artiste essaie de reproduire la réalité aussi fidèlement que possible), l'impressionnisme (où l'artiste évoque une impression ou un sentiment avec des images et des couleurs vives), l'expressionnisme (où l'artiste offre une représentation de l'angoisse et de la violence de l'esprit) et le cubisme (où l'artiste présente une abstraction de son sujet, en mettant l'accent sur le point de vue du spectateur).

8.1 Les arts Répondez aux questions suivantes. **Discutez de vos réponses** avec vos camarades de classe et n'hésitez pas à **poser des questions supplémentaires** si vous voulez en savoir plus.

1. Aimez-vous visiter les musées et les expositions d'art ? Pourquoi ou pourquoi pas ?
2. En ce qui concerne les arts plastiques, c'est-à-dire les arts qui s'intéressent à la forme, préférez-vous la peinture ? la sculpture ? le dessin ? la photographie ? autre chose ?
3. Connaissez-vous des artistes français ? Nommez-les.
4. Aimez-vous les peintures symbolistes, impressionnistes, réalistes ou abstraites ? Pourquoi ?
5. Avez-vous jamais essayé de créer une œuvre d'art ? Décrivez-la.

8.2 La Suisse Dans l'avion, Claire et Jean-Louis parlent des différences entre le Sénégal et la Suisse. Consultez les cartes de la Suisse et du Sénégal. Ensuite, indiquez si les observations suivantes sont probablement **vraies** ou peut-être **fausses**.

1. Il fait plus froid en Suisse qu'au Sénégal.
2. Il y a autant de grands lacs en Suisse qu'au Sénégal.
3. Le Sénégal a moins de montagnes que la Suisse.
4. Les cocotiers sont plus nombreux en Suisse qu'au Sénégal.
5. Le Sénégal est plus près de l'océan Atlantique que la Suisse.
6. Le fleuve, le Rhône, est aussi long que le fleuve, le Sénégal.
7. Les Suisses sont les gens les plus paisibles du monde car c'est un pays neutre.
8. La chose la plus bizarre est que les Suisses disent «huitante» et «nonante» où les Sénégalais diraient «quatre-vingts» et «quatre-vingt-dix».
9. Les montagnes suisses sont les plus belles montagnes du monde.

la Suisse

Rencontrez un Suisse ! Regardez la vidéo et consultez votre cahier d'activités !

lisez

L'art de lire

À la sortie de l'aéroport de Genève, Claire est frappée au visage par un vent froid et pénétrant descendu des sommets neigeux des montagnes, comme pour annoncer les rigueurs de l'hiver qui approche. Envahie par un vague sentiment d'appréhension qu'elle attribue à l'anxiété de pouvoir bientôt lire le roman, elle monte dans la voiture de location, le manuscrit empaqueté sous le bras, et se laisse conduire au village de Coppet. Là, sur une colline, entourée de sapins, elle trouve la petite maison champêtre. De la fenêtre de sa chambre, Claire a une belle vue du lac et des montagnes neigeuses qui se trouvent de l'autre côté. Comme il fait un peu froid, Jean-Louis fait un feu dans la cheminée. Il invite Claire à s'asseoir dans un fauteuil près du feu et à commencer sa lecture du manuscrit pendant qu'il va au supermarché et qu'il commence à préparer le dîner. Claire accepte, ouvre le manuscrit et se perd dans l'histoire d'un jeune soldat français qui est déchiré entre son amour pour une femme italienne et son devoir envers l'armée française de Napoléon Bonaparte. Le soleil se couche, le feu pétille, le vent souffle et Claire lit. Quand Jean-Louis annonce que le dîner est prêt, Claire a déjà lu une centaine de pages du manuscrit...

JEAN-LOUIS : Allez ! À table ! J'ai préparé une bonne fondue au fromage, selon une ancienne recette régionale. Si tu aimes le fromage, tu vas adorer cette fondue.

CLAIRE : Ah ! J'adore la fondue, et j'aime mieux la fondue au fromage que la fondue à la viande. Quelle heure est-il ?

JEAN-LOUIS : Neuf heures passées. Tu étais si absorbée par ta lecture, je n'ai pas voulu t'interrompre. Le manuscrit est donc aussi intéressant que tu le souhaitais ?

CLAIRE : Plus intéressant, en fait. C'est un vrai chef-d'œuvre. C'est l'histoire d'un jeune soldat français qui combat en Italie avec l'armée de Napoléon Bonaparte. Il tombe amoureux d'une jeune Italienne qu'il pense être la plus belle femme qu'il ait jamais vue. Mais, l'action se passe pendant la campagne de la plaine du Pô en 1800, et je crois que ce soldat et cette femme vont devoir être séparés. Il y a autant de violence, de passion et de volupté que dans un tableau de Delacroix ou une pièce de musique de Chopin.

JEAN-LOUIS : La campagne de la plaine du Pô ?

CLAIRE : Oui, le Pô est le fleuve le plus connu en Italie du nord, qui s'étend des Alpes jusqu'à Venise. C'est l'endroit d'où Bonaparte a lancé son invasion de l'Italie.

JEAN-LOUIS : Oui, je sais, mais pourquoi est-ce que Laclos aurait choisi cette bataille pour le cadre de son roman ?

CLAIRE : J'y réfléchissais moi-même. D'abord, l'Italie est un pays qui a inspiré beaucoup d'auteurs romantiques.

JEAN-LOUIS : Comme Madame de Staël... qui a habité ici à Coppet à la fin du 18ème siècle !

CLAIRE : Justement. Elle a écrit un roman intitulé *Corinne ou l'Italie.* Laclos était dans l'armée depuis les années 1760, mais ce n'est qu'en 1800, quand il était en Italie, qu'il a combattu pour la première fois. Alors, s'il est rentré à Paris après la campagne de la plaine du Pô, ça veut dire qu'il aurait écrit ce roman juste après cette campagne, entre 1801 et 1802, quand le souvenir des batailles était encore très vif.

Culture

L'idée d'un «**fromage suisse**» n'existe pas vraiment en Suisse. Pour les recettes régionales, les Suisses utilisent l'emmenthal ou le gruyère, les deux fromages les plus connus dans cette partie du monde. La **fondue**, dont le nom vient du verbe **fondre** (*to melt*), est un plat soit à base de fromage fondu qui se mange avec des petits morceaux de pain, soit de viande cuite dans de l'huile très chaude, soit de chocolat fondu accompagné de petits morceaux de gâteau ou de fruits. Un autre plat régional à base de fromage est la **raclette**. Pour faire une raclette, on fait fondre de petites tranches de fromage dans une machine à raclette sur des tranches de pommes de terre cuites, ou bien on racle (*scrape*) sur les pommes de terre le fromage qui fond quand on expose un grand morceau de fromage à la flamme. La raclette se sert avec du saucisson et des cornichons.

Pour aller plus loin : CULTURE

ACTIVITÉ A : Voulez-vous voir des tableaux romantiques ? Consultez votre cahier électronique !

JEAN-LOUIS : Quel âge avait-il à cette époque ?

CLAIRE : Il était assez âgé. Il est né en 1741, alors en 1801, il avait 60 ans. Tu sais, Laclos est même mort en Italie, à Tarente, quelques années plus tard quand il y est retourné avec l'armée française pour conquérir le sud.

JEAN-LOUIS : Quelle ironie que l'intrigue de son dernier roman se déroule en Italie !

CLAIRE : Hélas. . . mais il faut que je te remercie. Je suis si contente que tu me donnes le temps de lire ce manuscrit avant de le donner à ton patron. C'est vraiment sympa de ta part.

JEAN-LOUIS : Mais, c'est de l'opportunisme tout pur. Si tu vérifies l'authenticité du manuscrit en écrivant ta thèse là-dessus, la valeur du manuscrit augmentera énormément.

CLAIRE : Quand même, je tiens à te remercier. Je n'aurais jamais poursuivi ce projet si tu ne m'avais pas aidée et encouragée à chaque pas.

JEAN-LOUIS : Trinquons, alors, à la critique littéraire la plus perspicace et à l'antiquaire le plus tenace du monde francophone !

VOCABULAIRE

Les descriptions

frappé(e)	*struck, hit*	pétiller	*to crackle*
envahi(e)	*invaded*	le cadre	*setting*
empaqueté(e)	*packaged, wrapped up*	s'étendre	*to extend*
champêtre	*rustic*	combattre	*to fight, battle*
la cheminée	*fireplace*	se dérouler	*to unfold*
déchiré(e)	*torn*	perspicace	*perspicacious, shrewd*
		tenace	*tenacious, obstinate*

Culture

Le **romantisme** est un mouvement littéraire qui s'épanouit au 19ème siècle et qui a ses racines dans l'idée de la sensibilité qui caractérise la littérature de la fin du 18ème siècle. Des auteurs comme de Staël et Rousseau sont des modèles pour les écrivains romantiques comme Victor Hugo, Alexandre Dumas ou Stendhal. Mais, le romantisme comprend aussi des mouvements artistiques et musicaux. En France, des peintres comme Eugène Delacroix et Théodore Géricault traduisent l'esthétique romantique en images alors que des compositeurs comme Chopin et Berlioz la traduisent en musique.

Après avoir lu

8.3 Avez-vous compris ? Répondez aux questions suivantes. **Justifiez vos réponses** en citant le texte.

1. Que faisait Jean-Louis pendant que Claire lisait le manuscrit ?
2. Qu'est-ce que Claire pense de l'histoire qu'elle est en train de lire ? À quoi est-ce qu'elle la compare ?
3. Décrivez ce qui s'est passé en France durant la vie de Pierre-Ambroise Choderlos de Laclos. Quels événements historiques se sont passés entre sa naissance et sa mort ?
4. Qu'est-ce qui gêne (*is bothering*) Claire ? Pourquoi ?
5. Qu'est-ce qui se serait passé si Claire avait décidé que le manuscrit n'était pas de Laclos ?
6. Qu'est-ce qui se passera quand Claire et Jean-Louis retourneront à Paris ?

8.4 D'accord ou pas d'accord ? Indiquez si vous êtes **d'accord ou pas d'accord** avec les phrases suivantes, d'après votre compréhension du récit. Justifiez vos opinions en citant le texte, si possible. Discutez de vos réponses avec la classe.

	D'accord	Pas d'accord
1. Claire a déjà terminé sa lecture du manuscrit.	_______	_______
2. Jean-Louis veut faciliter son étude du manuscrit.	_______	_______
3. L'histoire du roman est intéressante.	_______	_______
4. Claire pense que ce roman est meilleur que *Les Liaisons*.	_______	_______
5. Laclos a écrit ce manuscrit.	_______	_______

Culture

Napoléon Bonaparte, ou Napoléon 1er, est né en Corse en 1769. Il a fait ses études à l'École militaire de Paris et est devenu très populaire dans les années 1790 lors de plusieurs victoires militaires en Italie et en Égypte. Ensuite, il a participé au coup d'état en 1799 où il a pris le titre de Premier consul, changeant la constitution pour rester au pouvoir pour toute sa vie. Quoiqu'il ait perdu plusieurs colonies d'outre-mer, telles la Louisiane (qu'il a vendu aux États-Unis en 1803) et Saint-Domingue (qu'il a perdu suite à la Révolution haïtienne en 1804), ayant vaincu la Suisse et l'Italie, son pouvoir en Europe s'élargissait. En 1804, il est nommé empereur des Français. Il a continué à envahir d'autres pays de l'Europe, mais sa campagne en Russie en 1812, dramatisée par Tolstoï dans son roman *Guerre et paix*, était trop coûteuse pour l'armée française. À cause de cette défaite, Napoléon a dû abdiquer et a été exilé à l'île d'Elbe. Il s'est échappé, mais a passé le reste de ses jours exilé à Sainte-Hélène, île et colonie britannique. Son tombeau est aujourd'hui aux Invalides à Paris.

8.5 Suite à la lecture Regardez les mots de vocabulaire qui suivent. Dans chaque ligne, il y a un mot qui cloche avec les trois autres. **Entourez le mot qui ne va pas** avec les autres et essayez d'expliquer pourquoi. Attention ! Il y a parfois plusieurs bonnes réponses. Il faut justifier votre choix !

1. une symphonie	un tableau	un roman	un chef-d'œuvre
2. le romantisme	le symbolisme	le réalisme	l'impressionnisme
3. peindre	sculpter	écrire	composer
4. aimer mieux	aimer autant	aimer plus	aimer trop
5. l'art	le musée	l'opéra	la bibliothèque
6. passionnant	paisible	champêtre	pittoresque

Pour aller plus loin : CULTURE

ACTIVITÉ B : Apprenez un peu plus sur la vie de Napoléon Bonaparte. Consultez votre cahier électronique !

Langue

Vous rappelez-vous les conjugaisons des **verbes irréguliers peindre, feindre** et **atteindre** ? Si non, mémorisez leurs conjugaisons avant de continuer !

- **peindre** (*to paint*) : je peins, tu peins, il/elle/on peint, nous peignons, vous peignez, ils/elles peignent (*participe passé* : peint)

Les verbes **feindre** (*to feign, pretend*) et **atteindre** (*to attain*) sont conjugués comme **peindre**, aussi bien que le verbe **dépeindre** (*to depict*).

8.6 Des œuvres célèbres Pendant le dîner, Claire et Jean-Louis discutent de l'art européen. Voici des œuvres européennes très célèbres que vous connaissez déjà probablement (si non, consultez l'Internet !). **Faites correspondre** l'œuvre (à gauche) avec sa description (à droite).

1. *la Joconde* (*Mona Lisa*) de Léonard de Vinci
2. *le Penseur* de Rodin
3. *les Nymphéas* (*Water lilies*) de Monet
4. *le Portrait de l'artiste à l'oreille coupée* de Van Gogh
5. *les Demoiselles d'Avignon* de Picasso
6. *le David* de Michel-Ange

a. Un portrait fait avec des couleurs sombres où l'angoisse du sujet est exprimée par la touche (*brushwork*) violente du peintre.
b. Une belle sculpture en marbre qui montre la force de l'homme par l'idéalisation de la forme du corps humain.
c. Un portrait fait avec des couleurs sombres où le réalisme et le détail font ressortir les sentiments ambigus du sujet.
d. Un tableau intéressant où le peintre offre une interprétation fragmentée et décomposée afin d'offrir une idée abstraite du sujet.
e. Une belle sculpture en bronze qui montre la complexité de l'esprit humain et la faillibilité de l'humanité par la posture expressive du corps.
f. C'est un tableau intéressant où le peintre évoque des sentiments en donnant une impression du sujet avec des couleurs très riches.

Culture

Marc-Aurèle Fortin et **Clarence Gagnon** sont deux **peintres québécois** qui ont souvent dépeint les paysages (*countryside*) québécois et les scènes typiques de la vie à la campagne. **Jean-Paul Lemieux** est connu pour son style moins réaliste, et ses tableaux évoquent des sentiments ambigus comme la tristesse et l'isolation qui touchent les Québécois pendant la saison hivernale. Lemieux est un des peintres les plus populaires au Québec aujourd'hui.

8.7 Vocabulaire personnel Pensez à vos goûts et à vos sensibilités artistiques et, pour chaque catégorie, **faites une liste de cinq à dix mots** importants que vous pouvez utiliser en parlant de vous-même. Consultez un dictionnaire si nécessaire.

1. Vos artistes préférés : médias, styles, mouvements, raisons pourquoi vous les aimez
2. Vos musées préférés : collections, présentation, raisons pourquoi vous les aimez
3. Vos films ou vos livres préférés : types, styles, raisons pourquoi vous les aimez
4. Ce que vous détestez dans les arts : esthétiques, couleurs, mouvements, etc.

8.8 L'art français Claire et Jean-Louis continuent à parler de l'art. Choisissez une des expressions entre parenthèses et **lisez le dialogue à haute voix** avec un partenaire. Quand vous voyez «? ? ?», vous pouvez imaginer votre propre expression.

JEAN-LOUIS : (Alors / Bon / Donc), quel est ton artiste français préféré ?

CLAIRE : J'adore les (tableaux / paysages) de Cézanne.

JEAN-LOUIS : (Ah, bon ? / Vraiment ? / Tiens, tiens !) Tu préfères Cézanne à Monet ?

CLAIRE : (Mais oui ! / Bien sûr / ? ? ?) Cézanne emploie des couleurs très vives et ses paysages me font (sourire / rêver). La façon dont il dépeint les montagnes provençales est vraiment impressionnante. Cela me rappelle (mes vacances à la campagne / ma jeunesse / ? ? ?). Il évoque des sentiments de bonheur en moi aussi bien qu'un Fortin ou un Lemieux, deux peintres québécois que j'adore.

JEAN-LOUIS : Moi, je (préfère / adore / ? ? ?) l'art surréaliste, comme les œuvres de Dalí ou de Magritte. Le surréalisme est le mouvement le plus (original / intéressant / passionnant) qui ait jamais été créé !

CLAIRE : Il est vrai que les (œuvres / tableaux / ? ? ?) surréalistes sont pleines d'imagination, mais leurs sujets n'évoquent que de la confusion.

JEAN-LOUIS : (Comment / Quoi / ? ? ?) ? Ce sont des œuvres (éblouissantes / exquises) ! Elles bouleversent l'esprit et choquent l'œil.

CLAIRE : Moi, quand je regarde une œuvre, je veux que cela me rende (heureuse / ? ? ?). Je ne veux pas être choquée. Ceci dit, j'apprécie tout à fait l'originalité du surréalisme.

Pour aller plus loin : CULTURE

ACTIVITÉ C : Appréciez-vous les œuvres d'art du 20ème siècle ? Consultez votre cahier électronique !

apprécier et critiquer

To show appreciation

Comme c'est joli / intéressant / original / différent / émouvant / fascinant.
C'est vraiment touchant / frappant / passionnant / séduisant / déroutant.
C'est plein d'imagination / d'inspiration / d'originalité.
C'est beau / admirable / charmant / éblouissant / exquis.
Qu'il/elle est bien tourné(e) / bien achevé(e) / bien joué(e) !
Regarde(z) ces couleurs / ces lignes / cette symétrie / ces formes !
La façon dont l'artiste dépeint (*nom*) est vraiment émouvante !
Cette œuvre me fait pleurer / sourire / rire / rêver !
Le sujet me rend triste / heureux / amer / mélancolique.
Cela me fait penser à ma jeunesse / à la guerre / au bon vieux temps.
Cela rappelle / évoque / représente / dépeint / symbolise / exprime. . .
C'est plus (*adjectif*) que (*nom*). / C'est le plus beau (*nom*) qui soit !

apprécier et critiquer **(continued)**

To critique C'est vraiment moche / laid / peu impressionnant / banal / décoloré.
Je trouve que ce n'est pas très joli / intéressant / original. . .
Quel horreur ! Il/Elle manque d'imagination / d'inspiration / d'originalité.
C'est mal fait / mal tourné / mal peint. . . Ceci ne m'intéresse pas.
Je ne l'aime pas trop. / Ce n'est pas mon genre.
C'est le pire imaginable ! / C'est nul / absurde / ridicule !

Culture

Le surréalisme est un mouvement artistique populaire en France. **René Magritte** est un peintre surréaliste belge très connu en France. Comme l'Espagnol **Salvador Dalí** et les autres surréalistes, ses œuvres choquent l'esprit et font penser leur public. Le style de Magritte est fondé sur la juxtaposition assez originale d'individus ou d'objets réalistes dans des contextes irréalistes. Dalí, aussi connu en France, a dépeint des objets ou des gens dans des états impossibles ou impensables, comme des montres qui fondent sur un escalier. Il y a un musée Dalí à Paris, dans le quartier de Montmartre.

8.9 À vous Imaginez que vous êtes dans les situations suivantes. Que dites-vous ? Exprimez votre appréciation ou critiquez les choses suivantes. Avec un partenaire, **jouez de petites scènes** pour chaque situation.

1. Votre ami(e) a acheté de nouveaux vêtements pour une soirée élégante. Il/Elle a l'air très sophistiqué.
2. Des gens de votre quartier ont peint leur maison de couleurs très vives : orange, rouge et jaune. Toutes les autres maisons sont grises ou blanches.
3. Votre professeur de français joue une chanson française au piano. Il/Elle ne joue pas bien, mais s'amuse beaucoup.
4. Vos amis vous achètent une copie d'un tableau de Monet pour votre salon.
5. Vous visitez un nouveau musée d'art contemporain où il y a plusieurs boîtes vides qui pendent du plafond.

8.10 Des œuvres célèbres Avec un partenaire, **choisissez une œuvre** que tout le monde connaît — une peinture ou une sculpture célèbre ou bien une œuvre d'art qui se trouve sur votre campus — et **décrivez-la** sur une feuille de papier. Ensuite, lisez votre description à vos camarades de classe. Ils devront deviner de quelle œuvre il s'agit !

MODÈLE : —C'est une sculpture d'une femme avec des ailes (*wings*), mais elle n'a pas de bras.

—Ah, c'est «La Victoire de Samothrace» ! J'adore la sculpture grecque ! Elle est vraiment exquise.

Pour aller plus loin : CULTURE

ACTIVITÉ D : Connaissez-vous bien l'art français ? Faites une visite virtuelle du musée d'Orsay. Consultez votre cahier électronique !

8.11 Au musée de la classe Sur une feuille de papier, en petits groupes, **écrivez un sujet de peinture** (par exemple, un paysage, un bol de fruits, etc.). Employez beaucoup de prépositions. Ensuite, pliez votre papier et échangez vos papiers au hasard avec les autres groupes. Sur une grande feuille de papier, une transparence, ou bien au tableau noir, **dessinez le sujet** que vous avez reçu. Utilisez votre imagination ! Ensuite, circulez dans la salle de classe et regardez tous les dessins. Faites des commentaires afin de bien montrer votre appréciation des œuvres dans ce petit «musée».

Pour aller plus loin : CULTURE

ACTIVITÉ E : Découvrez la ville de Genève. Consultez votre cahier électronique !

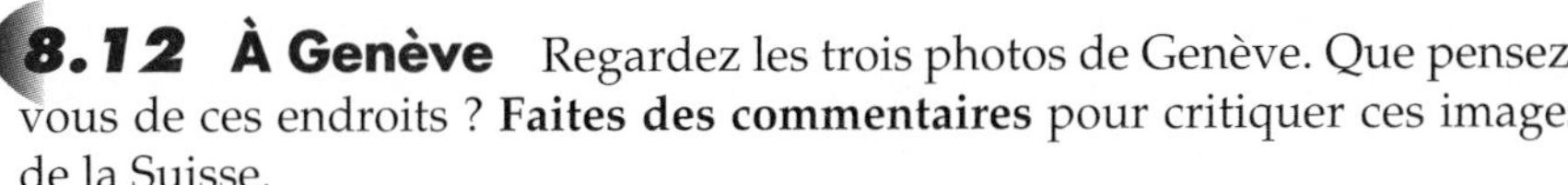

8.12 À Genève Regardez les trois photos de Genève. Que pensez-vous de ces endroits ? **Faites des commentaires** pour critiquer ces images de la Suisse.

Le jet d'eau au Lac Léman.

L'Horloge de fleurs à Genève.

Une maison genevoise.

Culture

À part la **Suisse**, il y a plusieurs autres pays qui font partie de **l'Europe francophone** et qui sont aussi des pays plurilingues. Au **Luxembourg**, un petit pays au nord-est de la France, on parle français et un dialecte allemand qui s'appelle le luxembourgeois. En **Belgique**, au nord de la France, il y a deux groupes ethniques importants, les Wallons et les Flamands. Dans la partie sud du pays, peuplée d'une majorité de gens d'origine wallonne, on parle français. Dans la partie nord du pays, peuplée d'une majorité de gens d'origine flamande, on parle hollandais. Il existe aussi des petits états indépendants où le français se parle comme **Andorre** (situé dans les Pyrenées entre la France et l'Espagne) et **Monaco** (sur la Côte d'Azur, au sud-est de la France).

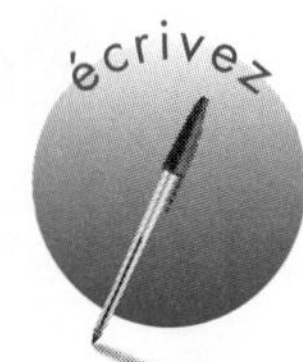

À l'écrit *première étape*

8.13 L'art du monde francophone **Choisissez une œuvre d'art** française ou francophone que vous appréciez beaucoup. Vous pourriez consulter l'Internet afin de trouver une image de votre œuvre préférée. Ensuite, **écrivez un paragraphe** pour décrire le sujet de l'œuvre (composition, couleurs, etc.) et pourquoi vous l'appréciez. Échangez votre description avec un camarade de classe et lisez la sienne avant de regarder l'image pour vérifier qu'il/elle a bien décrit le sujet. En bas de page, faites des suggestions ou des corrections possibles, et écrivez une ou deux phrases pour montrer votre appréciation de l'œuvre.

La visite du musée

Épisode 2

Structures le comparatif

8.14 Le lendemain Après avoir lu pendant toute la matinée, Claire s'arrête pour déjeuner avec Jean-Louis. Ils commencent à comparer la ville de Québec à celle de Genève. **Lisez le dialogue et**, pour chaque comparaison, **indiquez ce qu'on compare**. Pouvez-vous décrire comment fonctionne le **comparatif** en analysant ces exemples ?

CLAIRE : Il fait **plus froid** à Québec qu'à Genève.

JEAN-LOUIS : Mais en automne, Québec est une ville **moins tranquille** que la ville de Genève.

CLAIRE : Pourtant, en hiver les gens s'amusent **plus souvent** à Québec, avec le Carnaval d'hiver et tous les sports.

JEAN-LOUIS : On peut trouver des pistes de ski **plus connues** dans les Alpes. Et est-ce que la cuisine québécoise est **aussi intéressante** que la cuisine genevoise ?

CLAIRE : Nous avons **autant de plats régionaux** que les Suisses. Mais enfin, il y a **moins de sirop d'érable** en Suisse, et on trouve **plus de fromages** qu'au Québec.

JEAN-LOUIS : Ce n'est pas **si simple** que ça ! La cuisine européenne est **meilleure** que la cuisine nord-américaine.

CLAIRE : Mais non ! Les gens savent **mieux** manger en Europe, peut-être, mais la cuisine nord-américaine n'est pas **pire** que les autres.

Langue

Les mots **pire** et **pis** veulent dire, tous les deux, *worse* en anglais. Tandis que **pire** est employé le plus souvent dans les phrases comparatives et superlatives, le mot **pis** est utilisé dans plusieurs expressions. Par exemple : **tant pis** (*too bad*), **qui pis est** (*what's worse is*), **aller de mal en pis** (*to go from bad to worse*), **de pis en pis** (*worse and worse*), **en mettant les choses au pis** (*if worst comes to worst*), **au pis aller** (*at the very worst*), et **c'est un pis-aller** (*it's a last resort*).

le comparatif

The *comparative* (**le comparatif**) is used to make comparisons and can be used with nouns, adjectives, or adverbs. The forms of the comparative are:

With adjectives/adverbs	**plus... que**	**moins... que**	**aussi... que**
With nouns (quantities)	**plus de... que**	**moins de... que**	**autant de... que**

- Remember that adjectives (usually following the verb **être**) *must agree* with the first thing mentioned in the comparison, though adverbs (used with other verbs) are invariable.
- Note that **aussi** can be replaced by **si** when used with a negative: Ce n'est pas **si** simple **que** ça !

- The adjective **bon** and the adverb **bien** both have irregular forms that must be used in comparative situations where **plus** would normally be used (never say "plus bon" or "plus bien"):

bon (adj.)	**meilleur(e)(s) que**
bien (adv.)	**mieux que**

- The adjective **mauvais** has an alternative irregular form in comparative situations where **plus mauvais** can be used:

mauvais (adj.)	**plus mauvais(e)(s). . . que**
	pire que

8.15 Plus ou moins ! Faites des **phrases complètes** en combinant les éléments suivants. Utilisez un élément de chaque colonne. Ajoutez des mots ou des expressions si nécessaire.

MODÈLE : Le Louvre est moins intéressant que le musée de Genève.

la Joconde	être	plus	grand	que	le musée de Genève
le Louvre	avoir	moins	beau		*le Penseur*
notre prof	savoir	aussi	brillamment		le président des USA
Genève	peindre	autant	de peintures		le musée d'Art moderne à New York
mes dessins			intéressant		Paris
je			d'argent		toi
? ? ?			? ? ?		? ? ?

Pour aller plus loin : CULTURE

ACTIVITÉ F : Explorez les expositions aux musées suisses. Consultez votre cahier électronique !

8.16 Comparons Avec un partenaire, **comparez** les choses de la liste suivante. Une personne va apprécier une chose, et l'autre va faire une comparaison. Suivez le modèle et faites attention à l'usage du comparatif !

MODÈLE : *la Joconde* de Léonard de Vinci et le *Portrait de l'artiste à l'oreille coupée* de Van Gogh →

—*La Joconde* est un tableau très touchant !

—Mais ce tableau est moins intéressant que le *Portrait* de Van Gogh.

1. la *Joconde* de Léonard de Vinci et le *Portrait de l'artiste à l'oreille coupée* de Van Gogh
2. votre université et la Sorbonne
3. une forêt et une plage
4. Napoléon Bonaparte et Abraham Lincoln
5. la maison de Monsieur Thibodeau et l'appartement de Jean-Louis
6. la cuisine louisianaise et la cuisine suisse

Structures *le superlatif*

8.17 Après le déjeuner Claire et Jean-Louis sortent après le déjeuner pour prendre l'air et pour visiter la ville de Genève. Claire adore cette ville et ne s'arrête pas de s'exclamer avec des superlatifs. Lisez les phrases et, pour chaque exclamation superlative, **indiquez de quoi il s'agit**. Pouvez-vous décrire comment fonctionne le **superlatif** en analysant ces exemples ?

CLAIRE : Regarde la hauteur de ce jet d'eau ! C'est le jet d'eau **le plus haut** que j'aie jamais vu ! Sais-tu que les Chutes Montmorency à Québec sont les chutes d'eau **les plus hautes** d'Amérique du Nord ? C'est vrai. Et regarde cette statue des réformateurs protestants. C'est la statue **la plus sérieuse** que j'aie jamais vue. Mais regarde ces jolies petites maisons. Ce sont les maisons **les plus mignonnes** de l'Europe. Elles sont **les moins luxueuses**, peut-être, mais j'ai l'impression que les Genevois sont les Européens qui vivent avec **le moins d'ostentation**. Enfin, ils vivent **le plus simplement**. Genève est une des villes qui a **le moins de crimes**. J'adore l'horloge en fleurs. C'est **la plus belle** horloge qui soit. C'est **la meilleure** de toutes les sculptures naturelles que j'aie vues dans ma vie. Et elle marche **le mieux**. Tu vois comme elle donne l'heure exacte. Est-il vrai qu'en Suisse on compte **le plus grand nombre d'horlogers** de tous les pays du monde ? Enfin, les horlogers suisses travaillent **le plus**.

Culture

Le **protestantisme** est souvent associé à la ville de **Genève**. Au cours du 16ème siècle, des théologiens européens tels Martin Luther et Jean Calvin ont popularisé ce mouvement religieux dont le but était de simplifier la hiérarchie et le culte de la religion catholique et d'encourager la lecture et l'interprétation personnelle de la Bible. En Suisse ainsi qu'en France, cette Réforme a incité des guerres de religion et a divisé le pays. En Suisse, Genève et Berne étaient des villes protestantes tandis que Fribourg et Lucerne étaient des lieux de Contre-Réforme. Pourtant, la Confédération a réussi à maintenir son unité et sa neutralité lors des conflits. En France, Henri IV, un calviniste, a dû renoncer au protestantisme et se convertir au catholicisme pour devenir roi en 1594. Selon la légende, ce prince aurait dit que «Paris vaut bien une messe».
Après avoir pris le trône, en 1598, il a proclamé l'**Édit de Nantes** qui a autorisé le protestantisme et a mené à la paix religieuse. Cet édit a été révoqué un siècle plus tard par Louis XIV, qui a rétabli le catholicisme comme religion officielle en France.
Pour cette raison, les philosophes et les libres penseurs français ont souvent été attirés par l'Angleterre et par la Suisse, où ils trouvaient plus de tolérance.

le superlatif

The *superlative* **(le superlatif)** is used to make comparisons and can be used with verbs, nouns, adjectives, or adverbs. The forms of the comparative are:

With adjectives	**le/la/les plus** (+ *adjectif*)	**le/la/les moins** (+ *adjectif*)
With adverbs	**le plus** (+ *adverbe*)	**le moins** (+ *adverbe*)
With nouns	**le plus de** (+ *nom*)	**le moins de** (+ *nom*)
With verbs	(*verbe* +) **le plus**	(*verbe* +) **le moins**

- Note that *verbs, nouns, and adverbs* in the superlative take the *masculine singular* form, while the adjectives agree in gender and number with the noun they modify.
- The adjective **bon** and the adverb **bien** both have irregular forms that must be used in superlative situations where **plus** would normally be used (*never* say "le plus bon" or "le plus bien"):

bon (*adj.*)	**le/la/les meilleur(e)(s)**
bien (*adv.*)	**le mieux**

- The adjectives **mauvais** and **petit** have alternative irregular forms in superlative situations where **le plus mauvais/petit** can be used:

mauvais (*adj.*)	**le/la/les plus mauvais(e)(s)**	**le/la/les pire(s)**
petit (*adj.*)	**le/la/les plus petit(e)(s)**	**le/la/les moindre(s)**

- Note that the construction of a *superlative* sentence with adjectives generally conforms to one of the following structures:

With preceding *adjectives:*	*verb + superlative adj. + noun*	C'est **<u>la plus belle</u> horloge** qui soit.
With regular *adjectives:*	*verb + noun + superlative adj.*	C'est **le jet d'eau <u>le plus haut</u>** de l'Europe.

- Note that the *superlative* is often followed by **de +** *nom* to indicate what it is the superlative of: Ce sont les maisons les plus mignonnes **de l'Europe**.
- Sometimes the *superlative* is followed by **qui/que/où +** *verbe au subjonctif* to indicate a subjective opinion: C'est le jet d'eau le plus haut **que j'aie jamais vu**. C'est la plus belle horloge **qui soit**.

la Suisse

Quels artistes suisses sont les meilleurs d'après Donald ? Regardez la vidéo et consultez votre cahier d'activités !

Langue

En Suisse, comme en Belgique, les gens utilisent des **mots différents pour compter** en français. Au lieu de dire soixante-dix, on dit **septante**. Au lieu de quatre-vingts et quatre-vingt-dix, on emploie **huitante** et **nonante**. Ceci simplifie les chiffres, comme quatre-vingt-dix-neuf (99) qui est simplement **nonante-neuf**. Comment dirait-on soixante-dix-huit (78), quatre-vingt-cinq (85) et quatre-vingt-quatorze (94) en Suisse ?

8.18 Un tableau superlatif Jean-Louis aime bien la ville de Genève, mais préfère sa ville natale. Faites des **phrases superlatives** en utilisant les éléments suivants. N'oubliez pas d'ajouter des articles définis et de faire l'accord entre l'adjectif et le nom, si nécessaire.

1. Paris / ville / plus intéressant / de l'Europe
2. La tour Eiffel / monument / plus élégant / de la France
3. Le Louvre / musée / avoir / moins / tableaux impressionnistes / de Paris
4. Le musée d'Orsay / le musée / plus / bon / d'art impressionniste
5. Le TGV / train / aller / plus / vite / du monde

8.19 Le cours le plus intéressant Posez des questions à un partenaire afin de connaître ses préférences personnelles, suivant le modèle. Puis, répondez à votre tour. Employez **le superlatif** ! Attention à l'usage de l'**adjectif interrogatif** et du **pronom interrogatif** et à l'usage du **subjonctif**.

MODÈLE : cours / intéressant / suivre →

—Quel est le cours le plus intéressant que tu suives ?

—La physique est le cours le plus intéressant que je suive.

—Lequel est le moins intéressant ?

—La philosophie est le cours le moins intéressant que j'aie jamais suivi.

1. cours / intéressant / suivre
2. émissions (*TV shows*) / amusantes / regarder
3. livres / profonds / lire
4. villes / animées / visiter
5. musicien / doué (*talented*) / écouter
6. film / bon / voir

8.20 Faisons un tour de votre région ! Sans doute, il y a beaucoup d'endroits intéressants dans votre ville ou dans votre région. Imaginez que vous et votre partenaire organisez **une visite guidée** pour des touristes suisses qui viennent d'arriver dans votre région. Avec un partenaire, imaginez les endroits que vous leur montreriez. Faites des **phrases comparatives et superlatives**.

MODÈLE : —Voici le monument le plus ancien de notre ville.

—Ce n'est pas aussi ancien que l'Arc de Triomphe, mais c'est aussi intéressant.

Avant d'écouter

8.21 Avant la visite Répondez aux questions suivantes selon vos **opinions personnelles**.

1. Avez-vous un musée préféré ? Lequel ? Pourquoi ?
2. Pourquoi va-t-on au musée ? Pour le plaisir d'apprécier une œuvre d'art ? Pour apprendre quelque chose d'un lieu ou d'une époque différente ? Pour se distraire ?
3. Si quelqu'un apprécie quelque chose (une peinture, une émission télévisée, etc.) que vous détestez, quelle est votre réaction ? Dites-vous la vérité ou essayez-vous d'être poli(e) ?
4. Dans quelles circonstances peut-on s'exprimer librement ? Dans quelles circonstances vaut-il mieux être réservé(e) ?

écoutez

La visite du musée

Claire continue sa lecture du manuscrit et, au bout du 3ème jour, elle l'a presque terminé. Vu que le 18ème siècle l'intéresse tellement, elle accepte l'invitation de Jean-Louis de passer un après-midi au musée de Voltaire. Là, Claire et Jean-Louis découvrent des peintures et des sculptures du célèbre auteur, aussi bien que des objets qui lui appartenaient. Pendant leur visite, Jean-Louis pose encore quelques questions à propos du manuscrit. . .

Maintenant, **écoutez le dialogue sur votre CD**. Consultez le vocabulaire pour mieux comprendre le dialogue, et puis répondez aux questions suivantes.

VOCABULAIRE

Les descriptions

une ride	*wrinkle*	l'écriture	*writing, handwriting*
la sagesse	*wisdom*	néanmoins	*nonetheless*
en revanche	*in return, on the other hand*	une époque	*era*
quoiqu'il en soit	*be that as it may*	un scribe	*scribe*
thématique	*thematic*	transcrire	*to transcribe*
or	*now*	gaspiller	*to waste*
frappant(e)	*striking*	décevoir	*to disappoint*
		signé(e)	*signed*

Après avoir écouté

8.22 Qu'en pensez-vous ? Après avoir écouté le dialogue entre Claire et Jean-Louis, **répondez aux questions** suivantes.

1. Où sont Claire et Jean-Louis ? De quoi parlent-ils au début ?
2. Qu'est-ce qui occupe l'esprit de Claire ? Décrivez son état d'esprit.

3. Pourquoi est-ce que Claire ne peut pas vérifier que l'écriture du texte est identique aux autres textes écrits à la main par Laclos ? Pourquoi voudrait-elle faire cela ?
4. Quelle solution est-ce que Jean-Louis offre pour expliquer ce qui aurait pu se passer si les écritures n'étaient pas identiques ? Pensez-vous que ce soit une bonne explication ?
5. Pourquoi est-ce que Jean-Louis veut que Claire vérifie l'authenticité du manuscrit ? Qu'est-ce qui se passerait si elle émettait l'opinion contraire ?

Pour aller plus loin : LITTÉRATURE

ACTIVITÉ G : Qu'est-ce que c'est que la beauté ? Lisez la définition du *Dictionnaire philosophique* de Voltaire ! Consultez votre cahier électronique !

8.23 D'accord ou pas d'accord ? Après avoir écouté le dialogue entre Claire et Jean-Louis, lisez les phrases suivantes et **donnez votre opinion**. Discutez en petits groupes.

	D'accord	Pas d'accord
1. Claire et Jean-Louis aiment la même sculpture.	_______	_______
2. Ils se disputent fréquemment, mais ils aiment discuter de leurs idées ensemble.	_______	_______
3. Claire pense que le manuscrit ne ressemble pas du tout aux autres textes de Laclos.	_______	_______
4. Le manuscrit est signé par l'auteur.	_______	_______
5. Claire est absolument certaine que ce manuscrit est une œuvre de Laclos.	_______	_______

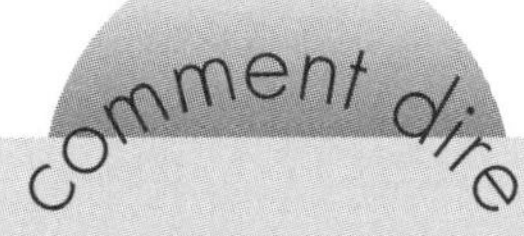

s'opposer à quelqu'un ou à quelque chose

To oppose an opinion

Or / Cependant / Néanmoins / Par ailleurs / Par contre / Quoique. . .
En revanche / Loin de là / En fait / À l'opposé de / Au lieu de. . .
Cela n'empêche pas que. . . / Quoi qu'il en soit. . .
Malgré ce que tu dis/vous dites. . . / Malgré cela. . .
Contrairement à ce que vous pensez. . . / Il n'en est pas question.
Bien au contraire ! / Mais non ! / Quelle observation !
Mais quelle idée ! / Pas du tout ! / Absolument pas !
Que dis-tu/dites-vous ? / Ai-je bien entendu ?
Tu es toqué ? (*familier*) / Tu as perdu la boule ? (*familier*)

8.24 Que dites-vous ? Qu'est-ce qu'on peut dire pour s'opposer aux opinions des autres dans les situations suivantes ? Avec un partenaire, décidez ce que vous pouvez dire et **imaginez de petits dialogues**.

1. Votre ami(e) pense que la peinture impressionniste est banale. Vous n'êtes pas d'accord.
2. Un vieil homme vous dit que tous les jeunes sont impolis. Vous n'êtes pas d'accord.
3. Vos amis adorent la musique zydeco. Vous préférez la musique classique.
4. La présidente de votre université veut éliminer le programme d'études françaises parce qu'elle ne pense pas que le français soit une langue mondiale. Certainement, vous n'êtes pas d'accord.
5. Votre fiancé(e) dit que les films de science-fiction sont les films les plus amusants. Vous préférez les comédies romantiques.

Pour aller plus loin : CINÉMA

ACTIVITÉ H : Regardez le film *Camille Claudel* qui met en scène le rapport passionné entre le sculpteur Auguste Rodin et son apprentie, Camille Claudel. Consultez votre cahier électronique !

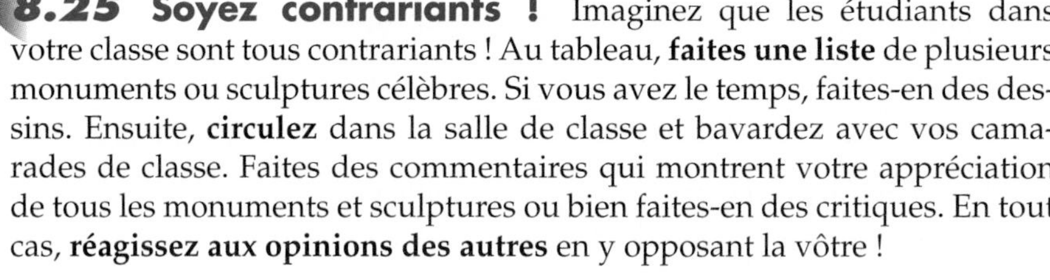

8.25 Soyez contrariants ! Imaginez que les étudiants dans votre classe sont tous contrariants ! Au tableau, **faites une liste** de plusieurs monuments ou sculptures célèbres. Si vous avez le temps, faites-en des dessins. Ensuite, **circulez** dans la salle de classe et bavardez avec vos camarades de classe. Faites des commentaires qui montrent votre appréciation de tous les monuments et sculptures ou bien faites-en des critiques. En tout cas, **réagissez aux opinions des autres** en y opposant la vôtre !

MODÈLE : La tour Eiffel

—Qu'elle est belle ! C'est le monument le plus connu du monde !

—C'est un monument bien connu, mais malgré ce que tu dis, ce n'est pas du tout beau. Il manque d'inspiration.

À l'écrit *deuxième étape*

8.26 L'art du monde francophone Imaginez que vous êtes au musée avec un(e) ami(e) et que vous lui montrez votre œuvre préférée. Dites-lui pourquoi vous appréciez cette œuvre. Votre ami(e), qui n'aime pas ce genre d'art, s'oppose à vos vues. Il/Elle compare l'œuvre à une autre qu'il/elle trouve supérieure. **Inventez un dialogue** où vous discutez de vos opinions sur l'art. Finalement, avec un partenaire, révisez vos dialogues et lisez-les à haute voix.

Une hypothèse

Structures *les phrases de condition*

8.27 Si seulement. . . Voici quelques citations d'auteurs du 18ème siècle qui ont vécu en Suisse. Pour chaque citation, **indiquez le temps des verbes** en **caractères gras**. Pouvez-vous décrire comment choisir le temps des verbes quand on construit une phrase où il y a une proposition qui commence par «Si. . . » ?

> «Je m'aperçois que je n'ai parlé que des femmes infidèles riches ou pauvres; j'aurais la même chose à dire des maris. **S'ils ne sont pas** riches, **ils donnent** à une maîtresse le nécessaire de leurs femmes; **s'ils sont** riches, **ce n'est** que du superflu, et **ils leur laissent** mille amusements, mille ressources, mille consolations. Pour laisser épouser à ma fille un homme sans fortune, je veux qu'ils s'aiment passionnément : **s'il est** question d'un grand seigneur fort riche, **j'y regarderai** peut-être d'un peu moins près.»
>
> —Madame de Charrière, *Caliste ou Lettres écrites de Lausanne*

> «Tous les événements sont enchaînés dans le meilleur des mondes possibles : car enfin **si vous n'aviez pas été chassé** d'un beau château à coups de pied dans le derrière pour l'amour de mademoiselle Cunégonde, **si vous n'aviez pas été mis** à l'Inquisition, **si vous n'aviez pas couru** l'Amérique à pied, **si vous n'aviez pas donné** un bon coup d'épée au baron, **si vous n'aviez pas perdu** tous vos moutons du bon pays d'Eldorado, **vous ne mangeriez pas** ici des cédrats confits et des pistaches. Cela est bien dit, répondit Candide, mais il faut cultiver notre jardin.»
>
> —Voltaire, *Candide ou l'Optimisme*

> «Il semble que, quand on nous eût formés exprès pour nous unir, on n'aurait pu réussir mieux. **S'il avait** le cœur aussi tendre que moi, **il serait** impossible que tant de sensibilité de part et d'autre ne se heurtât quelquefois, et qu'il n'en résultât que des querelles. **Si j'étais** aussi tranquille que lui, trop de froideur **régnerait** entre nous et **rendrait** la société moins agréable et moins douce. **S'il ne m'aimait** point, **nous vivrions** mal ensemble . . . »
>
> —Rousseau, *Julie ou la Nouvelle Héloïse*

Culture

Plusieurs **auteurs du Siècle des lumières** ont vécu en Suisse pour des raisons politiques ou philosophiques. Vers la fin de sa vie, **Voltaire** a habité à Ferney, tout près de Genève et loin de la corruption de la cour à Versailles. Jean-Jacques **Rousseau** est né à Genève et s'est souvent enfui en Suisse quand il ne pouvait pas tolérer la vie parisienne. Germaine **de Staël**, exilée par Napoléon Bonaparte à cause de son salon littéraire qui réunissait des intellectuels qui critiquaient la situation politique, s'est installée à Coppet, tout près de Genève. Isabelle **de Charrière** s'est installée à Colombier, près de Neuchâtel, après son mariage.

les phrases de condition

Si-*clauses*, or *conditional sentences* (**les phrases de condition**), are used to describe cause and effect, or the consequences of certain conditions in hypothetical situations. They can also be used to state a general rule or trend. Sentences with **si** require special attention to the sequence of verb tenses. With few exceptions (such as in the Voltaire quote above), the sequence of tenses is as follows:

si + *présent*	→	*présent* ou *futur* ou *impératif*
si + *imparfait*	→	*conditionnel*
si + *plus-que-parfait*	→	*conditionnel passé*

Langue

Rappel ! Rappel ! Si vous ne vous souvenez pas des règles pour la conjugaison des verbes à l'**imparfait** ou au **plus-que-parfait**, révisez les Chapitres 2 et 4. Si vous voulez réviser la conjugaison du **futur**, du **conditionnel** et du **conditionnel passé**, relisez les Chapitres 6 et 7.

Some examples:

- si + *présent* → *présent* ou *futur* ou *impératif*:

  Si je gagne au loto, **j'irai** en Suisse. (*If I win, I will go . . .*)

  Si je suis fatigué, **je me couche**. (*If I'm tired, I go to bed.*)

  Si vous êtes pauvres, **jouez** à la loterie ! (*If you are poor, play the lottery!*)

- si + *imparfait* → *conditionnel*:

  Si je gagnais au loto, **j'irais** en Suisse. (*If I won, I would go . . .*)

- si + *plus-que-parfait* → *conditionnel passé*:

  Si j'avais gagné au loto, **je serais allé(e)** en Suisse. (*If I had won, I would have gone . . .*)

8.28 Probabilités Claire et Jean-Louis rentrent au chalet et continuent à discuter du manuscrit et de la vie de Laclos. **Conjuguez les verbes** entre parenthèses **au présent** ou **au futur**.

JEAN-LOUIS : Si tu dis que c'est un roman de Laclos, tout le monde te (croire) ______________. Si la communauté littéraire accepte cette notion, nous (revendre) ______________ ce texte pour une fortune.

CLAIRE :	Comment ? Si tu (revendre) _________________ le manuscrit, à qui appartiendra-t-il ? J'espère que tu sauras choisir un bon acheteur.
JEAN-LOUIS :	Mais, si nous te donnons une photocopie du manuscrit, tu l'(avoir) _________________ pour toujours. Et, si tu (être) _________________ la première personne à publier un article sur ce manuscrit, tu seras célèbre !

regardez

la Suisse

Qu'est-ce que Donald ferait s'il allait visiter la Suisse cette année ? Regardez la vidéo et consultez votre cahier d'activités !

8.29 Possibilités La conversation continue. **Conjuguez les verbes** entre parenthèses à l'**imparfait** ou au **conditionnel**.

CLAIRE :	Si je parlais à ton patron, est-ce qu'il (envisager) _________________ de faire un don du manuscrit à la Bibliothèque nationale ?
JEAN-LOUIS :	Si nous (proposer) _________________ cela à mon patron, il éclaterait de rire ! Il ne (dépenser) _________________ pas tant d'argent pour acquérir le manuscrit s'il ne pensait pas pouvoir en tirer un bon profit. Le marché de livres anciens, c'est comme un jeu. On doit hasarder un peu, et si jamais on tombait sur un trésor, on ne le (garder) _________________ pas... on le (vendre) _________________ pour en acheter d'autres encore plus précieux.

8.30 Impossibilités Et elle continue. **Conjuguez les verbes** entre parenthèses au **plus-que-parfait** ou au **passé du conditionnel**.

CLAIRE :	Si je n'avais pas déjà dépensé presque toute ma bourse, je (acheter) _________________ le manuscrit moi-même.
JEAN-LOUIS :	Toi ? Mais, tu as perdu la tête ? Même si tu (garder) _________________ tout ton argent, cela (ne... pas / être) _________________ assez pour acheter ce manuscrit ! Je ne t'ai pas dit ce que j'ai payé à Monsieur Thibodeau ? Enfin, disons qu'il (ne... pas / vendre) _________________ le manuscrit si je (ne... pas / lui offrir) _________________ une somme considérable.

8.31 L'authenticité Et elle continue. **Conjuguez les verbes** entre parenthèses à un temps qui convient.

JEAN-LOUIS : Si tu trouves que l'écriture du manuscrit est différente de celle des lettres de Laclos, est-ce que tu (vérifier) ____________ quand-même l'authenticité du manuscrit ?

CLAIRE : Je pense qu'elle sera identique. Pourtant, je pourrais demander à mon directeur de thèse, si je n'(arriver) ____________ pas à en tirer une conclusion définitive. Mais, si tu avais raison, il (être) ____________ bien possible que Laclos ait engagé un scribe. Si Laclos avait été en Italie en 1800, il (retourner) ____________ en France l'année suivante et il (avoir) ____________ 60 ans. S'il (vouloir) ____________ faire copier rapidement son brouillon (*rough draft*), il aurait pu très facilement engager un scribe.

JEAN-LOUIS : Mais, si tu demandes l'aide de ton professeur, est-ce qu'il t'(aider) ____________ ?

CLAIRE : Bien sûr ! Il me dit toujours, «Si jamais vous avez des difficultés, (contacter) ____________ -moi !» Il est très sympa. Il y a beaucoup de professeurs qui (ne... pas / aider) ____________ leurs étudiants s'ils étaient en congé sabbatique, mais le mien n'est pas comme ça.

8.32 Que pensez-vous ? Faites une interview avec un(e) camarade de classe. **Répondez aux questions** en utilisant pour chaque verbe le temps qui convient.

1. Que porteriez-vous demain s'il pleuvait ? si on vous invitait à une soirée élégante ?
2. Si vous n'étiez pas allé(e) à l'université, qu'auriez-vous fait dans la vie ?
3. Si vous aviez le choix entre la Suisse, le Sénégal, la Martinique et la France, où passeriez-vous une année ?
4. Où iriez-vous si vous alliez en Europe pour les prochaines vacances ?
5. Si Claire Plouffe était venue à votre université pour faire de la recherche avant d'aller à la Nouvelle-Orléans, qu'est-ce qu'elle y aurait trouvé ?
6. Si vous rencontriez Claire et Jean-Louis au musée, que leur diriez-vous ?

8.33 À condition que. . . Avec un partenaire, **posez des questions** hypothétiques et **répondez** à votre tour en disant sous quelles conditions vous feriez chaque chose suggérée. Utilisez, pour chaque verbe, le temps qui convient.

MODÈLE : peindre un autoportrait →

—Peindrais-tu ton autoportrait ?

—Je peindrais mon autoportrait si j'avais du talent.

1. acheter une nouvelle voiture
2. chanter à l'Opéra de Paris
3. aller en Louisiane
4. quitter l'université
5. commencer une conversation avec un inconnu
6. visiter un musée
7. danser dans la rue
8. se raser la tête

Claire va dans le bureau pour terminer sa lecture du manuscrit, mais d'abord, elle branche son ordinateur portable. Elle trouve un message de Gilles LaFfont, l'inspecteur de police à Paris. . .

Une hypothèse

À : Claire PLOUFFE
De : Gilles LAFFONT
Date : le 18 octobre 2003
Réf : une hypothèse

Chère Madame Plouffe,

J'espère que vous vous souvenez de moi. Vous vous rappelez peut-être notre rencontre au café à Paris il y a un mois ? Je suis l'inspecteur de police qui vous a averti du danger du marché des livres anciens. Évidemment, vous n'avez pas écouté mes conseils. Mes sources me disent que vous êtes actuellement en Suisse et que le manuscrit est en votre possession. Je continue à mener mon enquête° sur le marché des livres anciens en France, et je vous écris afin de vous tenir au courant des derniers développements de l'affaire et de vous avertir encore une fois du danger que vous courez.

Peut-être connaissiez-vous le bouquiniste Nicolas Gustave ? Enfin, ils ont trouvé son corps° il y a huit jours sous un pont de la Seine. Apparemment, il a été empoisonné.° Il se peut que ce meurtre° soit lié° au commerce des livres, car l'empoisonnement n'est pas le modus operandi le plus commun chez les petits voleurs. Par hypothèse, si Gustave s'était mêlé° à ces hommes dont je vous ai parlé lors de notre première rencontre et s'il les avait trahis° d'une manière ou d'une autre, ces hommes ou leurs associés auraient pu le tuer afin de le faire taire.° On ne sait pas encore exactement ce qui s'est passé, mais admettons-le comme hypothèse. Je vous répète qu'il existe des dealers peu scrupuleux qui essaient

enquête°: investigation
corps°: body
empoisonné°: poisoned
meurtre°/lié°: murder/to link
mêlé°: to get mixed up with
trahis°: to betray
taire°: shut up

de profiter de la naïveté des acheteurs étrangers. Ce ne sont que des brutes° qui s'habillent en costume et qui sourient poliment pendant qu'ils trichent et volent. Je n'essaie pas de vous faire peur, mais je veux que vous sachiez combien cette situation est dangereuse pour des jeunes chercheurs tels que vous.

thugs

Je vous assure que je ne pense qu'à votre sécurité et que je voudrais vous aider. En espérant que vous êtes tombée sur° le bon manuscrit, que rien de mauvais ne vous arrivera, et en attendant d'entendre de vos nouvelles, je vous prie, chère madame, d'accepter l'expression de mes sentiments les meilleurs.

to come across

Gilles LaFfont

Langue

Il existe plusieurs expressions en français **pour dire pourquoi** quelque chose se passe. La plus commune est la conjonction **parce que** + subject/verb (*because*), mais il y a aussi le mot **car** + subject/verb (*for*) qu'on utilise plutôt pour faire une observation ou pour établir un rapport entre deux événements que pour indiquer la raison pour laquelle un événement s'est passé. L'expression **à cause de** + noun (*because of, due to*) est employé, effectivement, pour indiquer la cause d'un événement quand la cause n'est pas une action mais une raison ou un état. Notez que cette expression a une connotation négative lorsque **grâce à** + noun (*thanks to*) a une connotation plutôt positive. Par exemple : «Gilles écrit à Claire **parce qu'il** est inquiet, mais il écrit aussi **à cause du** meurtre, **car** Claire avait rencontré Gustave à Paris. C'est **grâce à** Gustave qu'elle a pu trouver le manuscrit au Sénégal.»

Après avoir lu

8.34 Avez-vous compris ? Avec un partenaire, **répondez aux questions** suivantes. Justifiez vos réponses en citant le texte.

1. Comment est-ce que l'auteur du message connaît Claire Plouffe ? Décrivez leur première rencontre au café (utilisez des verbes au passé).
2. Qu'est-ce que Gilles LaFfont annonce ? Quelle est son hypothèse ?
3. Qu'est-ce que Gilles sait des activités de Claire ? Comment le sait-il ?
4. Pourquoi est-ce que Gilles écrit à Claire ? Pensez-vous qu'il soit vraiment préoccupé de la sécurité de Claire ? Est-ce qu'il veut quelque chose d'autre ?

8.35 D'accord ou pas d'accord ? Après avoir lu la lettre ci-dessus, lisez les phrases suivantes et donnez vos **opinions personnelles**. Discutez-en en petits groupes.

	D'accord	Pas d'accord
1. Claire connaît l'auteur de ce message.	_______	_______
2. Il croit que le meurtre de Gustave est lié au marché de livres.	_______	_______
3. Ces criminels sont des gens peu sophistiqués.	_______	_______
4. Gilles LaFfont se fait du souci (*is worried*) à propos de Claire.	_______	_______
5. Claire devrait répondre à ce message.	_______	_______

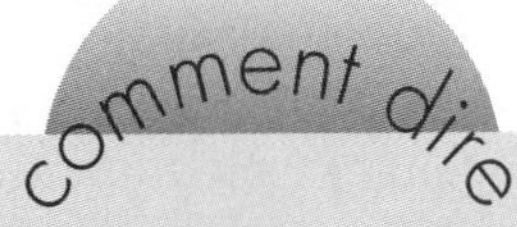

établir une hypothèse

To hypothesize Admettons comme hypothèse / Par hypothèse / Hypothétiquement. . .
Dans la limite du possible. . . / Dans la mesure du possible. . . / Si c'est possible. . .
Avez-vous envisagé la possibilité que. . . ? / En envisageant toute éventualité. . .
Il est possible que / Il se peut que / Supposons que . . . (+ *subjonctif*)
À supposer que. . . / Imaginons que. . . (+ *subjonctif*)
Peut-être (+ *inversion*) / Peut-être que (+ *subjonctif*)
Disons que. . . / Estimons que. . . / Si je devais choisir. . .
C'est pure conjecture, mais. . . / À vue de nez. . .
Tâchons de deviner. . . / Hasardons une conjecture. . .

8.36 Que dites-vous ? Avec un partenaire, **faites des hypothèses** pour chacune des situations suivantes. Comparez vos idées.

1. Quelqu'un a volé le tee-shirt de votre ami(e). Vous pensez que la femme de ménage l'a utilisé pour épousseter l'appartement.
2. Deux vieilles dames vous demandent s'il va neiger à la Martinique cet hiver.
3. Des petits enfants français veulent savoir si le Père Noël (*Santa Claus*) existe et comment il pourra entrer dans leur appartement cette année parce qu'il n'y a pas de cheminée.
4. Votre ami(e) croit que des extraterrestres vivent parmi les êtres humains.
5. Vous avez fait vos devoirs, mais quand vous arrivez en classe, ils ne sont pas dans votre cahier.

8.37 Qui est le criminel ? Sur une feuille de papier, **écrivez le nom d'une chose** que vous n'aimeriez pas perdre. Maintenant, imaginez que vous ne pouvez pas trouver cette chose ! Quelqu'un l'a peut-être volée ? Peut-être l'avez-vous laissée quelque part ? **Circulez** dans la salle de classe et demandez à vos camarades de **faire des hypothèses**. Si vous acceptez leur hypothèse comme possible, écrivez leur nom sur votre papier et passez au prochain étudiant. Si leur hypothèse est peu probable, passez sans écrire leur nom. À la fin du jeu, choisissez le nom de la personne qui a donné la meilleure hypothèse. L'étudiant le plus souvent choisi gagne !

MODÈLE : —J'ai perdu mon téléphone portable ! Sais-tu où il pourrait être ?

—Ton téléphone ? C'est pure conjecture, mais as-tu envisagé la possibilité d'avoir laissé ton téléphone dans ta voiture ?

Pour aller plus loin : CULTURE

ACTIVITÉ 1 : Explorez les arts africains et antillais. Consultez votre cahier électronique !

8.38 Point d'interrogation ? Le/La président(e) de votre université propose d'élever une statue géante d'un point d'interrogation (?) orange au milieu de votre campus. La sculpture représentera l'esprit critique qui règne sur votre campus. En petits groupes, **discutez de vos opinions** sur cette proposition. Critiquez l'œuvre et opposez-la aux autres sculptures sur le campus. Si la plupart des étudiants sont contre cette idée, le/la président(e) y mettra une autre sculpture. **Faites des hypothèses** sur le type de statue qui représenterait le mieux l'esprit de votre université.

MODÈLE : —Que pensez-vous de cette nouvelle sculpture ? Je la trouve complètement ridicule !

—Mais non ! C'est une idée très originale ! Cette statue serait plus intéressante que le portrait du premier président de l'université. Quoiqu'il en soit, je n'aime pas trop la couleur orange.

À l'écrit *troisième étape*

8.39 L'art du monde francophone Imaginez que vous avez un vieil oncle très riche qui veut vous offrir un cadeau extraordinaire pour votre prochain anniversaire. Pourtant, la dernière fois qu'il vous a invité(e) chez lui, vous n'y êtes pas allé(e) parce que vos amis vous avaient invité(e) à une fête. **Écrivez-lui une lettre** dans laquelle vous décrivez votre œuvre d'art préférée. Dites pourquoi vous l'aimez, comparez-la à d'autres œuvres. En plus, demandez-lui pardon de ne pas être allé(e) chez lui la dernière fois et expliquez ce que vous feriez si vous pouviez revivre ce moment. Échangez votre lettre avec celle d'un(e) de vos camarades de classe (par courriel, si vous voulez !) et offrez-lui une réponse et quelques corrections possibles.

Dénouement

Activités de révision

8.40 Une soirée amusante En groupes de trois personnes, imaginez que vous êtes à une soirée en Suisse où l'on discute de la ville de Genève et de son histoire. Choisissez l'un des rôles suivants et **jouez une scène** pour la classe.

PERSONNE 1 : Vous ne parlez qu'en **superlatifs** !
PERSONNE 2 : Vous **contredites** tout le monde !
PERSONNE 3 : Vous ne vous arrêtez pas de faire des **hypothèses** ! Toutes vos phrases commencent par «Si . . . » !

MODÈLE : **—La ville de Genève est la ville la plus pittoresque du monde !**

—Mais non ! Au contraire, c'est la moins belle ville de l'Europe !

—Si elle avait une histoire plus ancienne, elle serait aussi intéressante que Paris.

8.41 Un tour du campus Avec un partenaire, choisissez une sculpture, une peinture, une fontaine, un jardin, une cour, une salle ou un bâtiment intéressants sur votre campus. **Faites la description détaillée de cette œuvre** ou de cet espace architectural. Ensuite, avec la classe, faites le tour du campus à pied et quand vous passez près de votre objet ou espace, lisez votre description. Les autres vont critiquer l'œuvre en la comparant aux autres !

Pour aller plus loin : CULTURE
ACTIVITÉ J : Apprenez un peu au sujet de l'architecture. Consultez votre cahier électronique !

8.42 Devinez l'objet Avec un partenaire, choisissez un objet qu'on utilise tous les jours. Utilisez le **comparatif** et le **superlatif** pour décrire cet objet en moins de **cinq phrases**. Les autres groupes vont essayer de deviner de quel objet il s'agit.

MODÈLE : un téléviseur

—Il est plus grand qu'un four à micro-ondes. Regarder cette chose est aussi amusant qu'aller au cinéma. C'est un objet moins interactif qu'un ordinateur. C'est l'invention la moins pratique pour la maison, mais la plus aimée par les enfants !

—C'est un téléviseur !

8.43 Devinez la personne Avec un partenaire, **choisissez une personne célèbre** (vivante, fictive ou historique). Utilisez des **hypothèses** pour décrire cette personne. Écrivez au moins **trois phrases**. Les autres groupes vont essayer de deviner de quelle personne il s'agit.

MODÈLE : —Si elle avait été plus perspicace, elle aurait su que son ami n'était pas un barman. Si elle avait choisi un autre sujet de thèse, elle n'aurait pas voyagé autour du monde. Si elle termine sa thèse sur le manuscrit Laclos, elle deviendra un professeur célèbre.

—**C'est Claire Plouffe !**

Avant de lire *Corinne ou l'Italie*

Pour aller plus loin : CULTURE

ACTIVITÉ K : Explorez les collections, les heures d'ouverture et les tarifs des musées parisiens. Consultez votre cahier électronique !

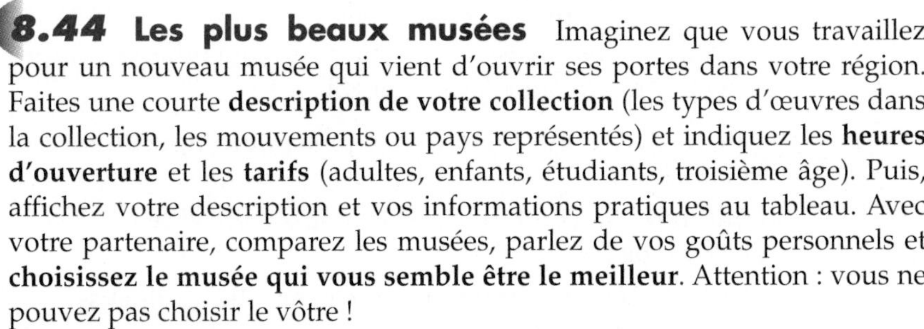

8.44 Les plus beaux musées Imaginez que vous travaillez pour un nouveau musée qui vient d'ouvrir ses portes dans votre région. Faites une courte **description de votre collection** (les types d'œuvres dans la collection, les mouvements ou pays représentés) et indiquez les **heures d'ouverture** et les **tarifs** (adultes, enfants, étudiants, troisième âge). Puis, affichez votre description et vos informations pratiques au tableau. Avec votre partenaire, comparez les musées, parlez de vos goûts personnels et **choisissez le musée qui vous semble être le meilleur**. Attention : vous ne pouvez pas choisir le vôtre !

8.45 Premières impressions Lisez l'extrait tiré du roman *Corinne ou l'Italie* de Germaine de Staël, sans essayer de comprendre chaque mot. Après votre première lecture du texte, **répondez aux questions**. Ensuite, relisez le texte une deuxième fois, plus attentivement.

1. Quel est le rapport entre Corinne et Oswald ? Sont-ils amis, amants, époux, cousins ou frère et sœur ?
2. Quand se passe cette histoire ? Au présent ou au passé ?
3. Où se passe l'histoire ?
4. Qu'est-ce que Corinne propose à Oswald ?
5. Quelle est leur réaction à ce qu'ils voient ? Sont-ils ennuyés, indifférents, intéressés ou passionnés par ce qu'ils voient ?

lisez

Corinne ou l'Italie

Cet extrait est tiré du roman de Germaine de Staël, Corinne ou l'Italie. *Dans ce roman, écrit à l'aube du romantisme, de Staël nous présente une poète italienne du nom de Corinne qui représente la femme indépendante du nouveau siècle. Corinne rencontre à Rome un Anglais nommé Oswald Nelvil. Cet étranger tombe éperdument amoureux de Corinne, mais souffre d'un malaise. Et cet étranger ne connaît pas encore assez bien cette femme qui a des secrets qu'elle ne veut pas révéler par peur de gâcher leur amour naissant. La faiblesse mélancolique d'Oswald et la passion calme et déterminée de Corinne sont mises en relief lors d'une visite au musée du Vatican. . .*

■ Germaine de Staël

Corinne ou l'Italie (extrait)

Pendant les jours qui suivirent la maladie d'Oswald, Corinne évita soigneusement° ce qui pouvait amener une explication entre eux. Elle voulait rendre la vie de son ami aussi douce qu'il était possible ; mais elle ne voulait point lui confier° encore son histoire. Tout ce qu'elle avait remarqué dans leurs entretiens ne l'avait que trop convaincue de l'impression qu'il recevrait en apprenant, et ce qu'elle était, et ce qu'elle avait sacrifié ; et rien ne lui faisait plus de peur que cette impression qui pouvait le détacher d'elle.

carefully

to confide

Revenant donc à l'aimable adresse dont elle avait coutume de se servir pour empêcher Oswald de se livrer° à ses inquiétudes° passionnées, elle voulut intéresser de nouveau son esprit et son imagination par les merveilles° des beaux-arts° qu'il n'avait point encore vus, et retarder ainsi l'instant où le sort devait s'éclaircir et se décider. Une telle situation serait insupportable dans tout autre sentiment que l'amour ; mais il donne des heures si douces ; il répand un tel charme sur chaque minute, que bien qu'il ait besoin d'un avenir indéfini, il s'enivre du présent, et reçoit un jour comme un siècle de bonheur ou de peine, tant ce jour est rempli par une multitude d'émotions et d'idées ! Ah ! sans doute, c'est par l'amour que l'éternité peut être comprise; il confond toutes les notions du temps ; il efface les idées de commencement et de fin ; on croit avoir toujours aimé l'objet qu'on aime, tant il est difficile de concevoir qu'on ait pu vivre sans lui. Plus la séparation est affreuse,° moins elle paraît vraisemblable° ; elle devient, comme la mort, une crainte dont on parle plus qu'on n'y croit, un avenir qui semble impossible, alors même qu'on le sait inévitable.

to give in to/worries

marvels/fine arts

horrible/realistic

Corinne, parmi ses innocentes ruses pour varier les amusements d'Oswald, avait encore réservé les statues et les tableaux. Un jour donc, lorsque lord Nelvil fut rétabli, elle lui proposa d'aller voir ensemble ce que la sculpture et la peinture offraient à Rome de plus beau. — Il est honteux, lui dit-elle en souriant, que vous ne connaissiez ni nos statues, ni nos tableaux, et demain il faut commencer le tour des musées et des galeries. — Vous le voulez, répondit lord Nelvil, j'y consens. Mais en vérité, Corinne, vous n'avez pas besoin de ces ressources étrangères pour me fixer auprès° de vous ; c'est, au contraire, un sacrifice que je vous fais, quand je détourne mes regards de vous pour quelque objet que ce puisse être. [. . .]

next to

Ils allèrent d'abord au musée du Vatican, ce palais des statues où l'on voit la figure humaine divinisée° par le paganisme, comme les sentiments de l'âme° le sont maintenant par le christianisme. Corinne fit remarquer à lord Nelvil ces salles silencieuses où sont rassemblées les images des Dieux et des héros, où la plus parfaite beauté, dans un repos éternel, semble jouir° d'elle-même. En contemplant ces traits et ces formes admirables, il se révèle je ne sais quel dessein de la divinité sur l'homme, exprimé par la noble figure dont elle a daigné° lui faire don.° L'âme s'élève par cette contemplation à des espérances pleines d'enthousiasme et de vertu ; car la beauté est une dans l'univers, et, sous quelque forme qu'elle se présente, elle excite toujours une émotion religieuse dans le cœur de l'homme. Quelle poésie que ces visages où la plus sublime expression est pour jamais fixée, où les plus grandes pensées sont revêtues° d'une image si digne° d'elles !

made god-like

soul

to enjoy

to deign/make a donation

to clothe/worthy

Quelquefois un sculpteur ancien ne faisait qu'une statue dans sa vie, elle était toute son histoire. Il la perfectionnait chaque jour : s'il aimait, s'il était aimé, s'il recevait par la nature ou par les beaux-arts une impression nouvelle, il embellissait° les traits de son héros par ses souvenirs et par ses affections. Il savait ainsi traduire aux regards tous les sentiments de son

to embellish

âme. La douleur dans nos temps modernes, au milieu de notre état social si froid et si oppressif, est ce qu'il y a de plus noble dans l'homme ; et, de nos jours, qui n'aurait pas souffert, n'aurait jamais senti ni pensé. Mais il y avait dans l'antiquité quelque chose de plus noble que la douleur, c'était le calme héroïque, c'était le sentiment de sa force qui pouvait se développer au milieu d'institutions franches et libres. Les plus belles statues des Grecs n'ont presque jamais indiqué que le repos. Le Laocoon et la Niobé° sont les seules qui peignent des douleurs violentes ; mais c'est la vengeance° du ciel° qu'elles rappellent toutes les deux, et non les passions nées dans le cœur humain. L'être moral avait une organisation si saine° chez les anciens, l'air circulait si librement dans leur large poitrine et l'ordre politique était si bien en harmonie avec les facultés,° qu'il n'existait presque jamais, comme de notre temps, des âmes mal à l'aise° : cet état fait découvrir beaucoup d'idées fines, mais ne fournit point aux arts, et particulièrement à la sculpture, les simples affections, les éléments primitifs des sentiments qui peuvent seuls s'exprimer° par le marbre éternel.

figures from Greek mythology
revenge
the gods
healthy
faculties, senses
ill at ease
to exrpress oneself (in this case, passive voice: to be expressed)

Après avoir lu

Pour aller plus loin : LITTÉRATURE

ACTIVITÉ L : Qui est Germaine de Staël ? Apprenez un peu sur sa vie, ses pensées et son œuvre. Consultez votre cahier électronique !

8.46 Avez-vous compris ? En petits groupes, **discutez de vos réponses** aux questions suivantes.

1. **1er paragraphe :** Pourquoi est-ce que Corinne veut rendre aussi douce que possible la vie d'Oswald ? Pourquoi est-ce qu'elle veut éviter de discuter son passé avec lui ? À votre avis, qu'est-ce qu'elle cache ?
2. **2ème paragraphe :** Qu'est-ce que Corinne veut faire pour «retarder» leur rupture inévitable ? Comment est-ce qu'elle décrit l'amour ? Quel est le rapport entre l'amour et le temps ? D'après le narrateur, est-ce que le temps passe plus vite ou est-ce que le temps semble s'arrêter quand on est avec la personne aimée ? Êtes-vous d'accord avec cette idée ?
3. **3ème paragraphe :** Quelle est la «ruse» de Corinne ? Quel compliment est-ce qu'Oswald fait à Corinne en acceptant sa proposition ?
4. **4ème paragraphe :** Quels types de sculptures trouvent-ils au musée du Vatican ? Comment est-ce qu'ils les admirent ou les critiquent ? Connaissez-vous des sculptures grecques ou romaines célèbres ? Pensez-vous que la description donnée soit une bonne description ?
5. **5ème paragraphe :** Quel est le rapport entre le sculpteur ancien et sa sculpture ? D'après le narrateur, y a-t-il plus de douleur dans les vies des anciens que dans les vies des gens «modernes» de son époque ? Le sentiment du malaise est un thème très répandu chez les auteurs, musiciens et artistes romantiques. Pensez-vous que ce thème soit important dans cet extrait ? Pourquoi ?

8.47 D'accord ou pas d'accord ? Après avoir lu l'extrait du roman de Germaine de Staël, lisez les phrases suivantes et **donnez votre opinion**. Discutez de vos réponses en petits groupes.

	D'accord	Pas d'accord
1. Oswald est un homme très fort et très énergique.	_______	_______
2. Corinne aime Oswald.	_______	_______
3. Oswald n'a pas envie de visiter les musées avec Corinne.	_______	_______
4. Les sculptures grecques sont généralement belles et nobles.	_______	_______
5. L'homme «moderne» et l'homme ancien se ressemblent.	_______	_______

8.48 Analyse littéraire Examinez ce texte de près. Répondez aux questions suivantes et **discutez de vos réponses** en classe.

1. Au début de l'extrait, le narrateur explique que Corinne n'a pas envie de parler de son passé et qu'elle veut le distraire avec les beaux-arts, vivre dans le moment. Quel temps de verbe domine dans le deuxième paragraphe où ceci est expliqué ? Quel est le rapport entre le temps de verbe et le message communiqué (c'est-à-dire, la forme et le fond) ?
2. Dans la description du musée du Vatican, le pronom relatif «où» est employé plusieurs fois. Analysez l'usage de cette structure. Quel en est l'effet dans ce paragraphe ?
3. Dans le dernier paragraphe, où le narrateur parle de la beauté des statues grecques, le mot «si» (*if, so*) se répète souvent, et le son de la lettre **s** semble dominer. Lisez le texte à haute voix et dites si vous êtes d'accord avec cette observation. Ensuite analysez l'effet de l'usage du mot «si» et du son **s**. Quel est le rapport entre ce son et le ton / le sens de ce paragraphe ?
4. Y a-t-il d'autres éléments structurels (ponctuation, mots ou sons répétés, phrases longues ou courtes, contrastes, métaphores, etc.) que l'auteur emploie systématiquement ? Si oui, quels sont les effets de l'emploi de ces éléments ?

Synthèses

8.49 Réfléchissons à la culture Voici quelques éléments de la culture suisse que vous avez étudiés dans ce chapitre. En petits groupes, répondez aux questions et **discutez de vos impressions** avec vos camarades.

la fondue	la neutralité politique	le protestantisme

1. Définissez ou décrivez chaque élément.
2. Pourquoi chaque élément est-il important à cette culture ? Y a-t-il un phénomène historique ou social qui explique son importance ?
3. À votre avis, est-ce que ces éléments témoignent de la richesse et de la diversité de la culture suisse de nos jours, ou sont-ils stéréotypiques ? Pourquoi ?
4. Est-ce que votre impression de cette culture est différente maintenant que vous avez commencé à l'étudier ? Si oui, comment et pourquoi ? Si non, pourquoi pas ?

la Suisse

Pour Donald, qu'est-ce que ça veut dire «être Suisse» ? Regardez la vidéo et consultez votre cahier d'activités !

Pour aller plus loin : CULTURE

ACTIVITÉ M : Apprenez un peu plus sur la cuisine dans les pays de l'Europe francophone (la Suisse, la Belgique, le Luxembourg). Consultez votre cahier électronique !

8.50 À débattre Lisez les questions suivantes et **discutez-les** en groupes. Si possible, parlez de vos expériences personnelles relatives aux questions.

1. **L'art !** Aujourd'hui, l'art n'est plus limité à la peinture et la sculpture. Il y a des formes d'art moins traditionnelles comme les graffiti sur les murs dans les espaces urbains ou des objets quotidiens ou même des déchets qu'on met dans les expositions aux musées d'art moderne. Pensez-vous que les graffiti et les déchets soient de l'art ? Doit-on définir plus strictement ce qu'est une œuvre d'art ?

2. **Un pays neutre ?** On pense que la neutralité est généralement une bonne chose, mais est-ce que la neutralité peut être une mauvaise chose aussi ? En Suisse, par exemple, on a établi des lois qui protègent l'anonymité des clients qui mettent leur argent dans les banques. Un client peut y garder son argent sans donner son nom ou son adresse à la banque. Ce système est intéressant surtout pour les riches étrangers qui ne veulent pas payer d'impôts dans leur propres pays, mais il intéresse aussi les trafiquants de drogues et les organisations criminelles internationales qui veulent cacher leurs affaires aux représentants de la loi dans leurs pays d'origine. En admettant comme hypothèse que la vente des drogues et les activités terroristes globales diminueraient si les Suisses avaient des lois plus strictes en ce qui concerne l'usage des banques, pensez-vous que la Suisse ait tort de rester «neutre» dans ce cas ? Ou croyez-vous qu'ils aient raison de protéger le droit de chacun de mener une vie privée et de placer son argent ?

3. **La civilisation ou la vie primitive ?** Une des idées de Jean-Jacques Rousseau, célèbre écrivain suisse, était l'idée que plus une société devient «civilisée», plus elle devient décadente. Il admirait la vie simple et heureuse des paysans à la campagne et critiquait souvent l'excès et le manque de moralité qu'on trouvait dans les grandes villes. Êtes-vous d'accord avec Rousseau que la civilisation mène à la décadence ? Ou pensez-vous que les bénéfices de la civilisation (le développement des arts, des sciences et de la technologie) soient plus importants que ses aspects négatifs ?

Pour agir :
LA SUISSE !

Si vous voulez bouger et faire quelque chose pour mieux connaître la Suisse, ou pour aider les autres à mieux connaître les arts des pays francophones, consultez la section **Pour agir** dans votre cahier électronique ! Il y a tant de choses à faire :

- **Organisez une exposition d'art**, ou bien **faites des dessins et faites imprimer des cartes de vœux** que vous pouvez vendre, et contribuez l'argent que vous gagnez à une organisation qui aide les artistes au monde francophone ou qui restaure des peintures européennes.
- **Enseignez** ce que vous savez des arts du monde francophone à des enfants de l'école primaire.
- **Entrez en contact** avec des Suisses ou d'autres Européens francophones qui vivent dans votre communauté ou quelque part aux États-Unis.
- **Faites une excursion** à un musée pour explorer les arts du monde francophone.
- **Cuisinez !** Préparez une vraie fondue suisse avec vos camarades de classe.

8.51 À l'impromptu Voici des situations interactives. Avec une ou deux autres personnes, choisissez une scène et **improvisez devant la classe**. Si vous ne voulez pas improviser, écrivez votre dialogue avant et puis jouez-le pour la classe.

1. Qu'est-ce que c'est que l'art ?
   (a) Vous accompagnez les parents de votre fiancé(e) qui arrivent de Suisse pour passer quelques jours avec vous à la Nouvelle-Orléans. Vous avez choisi de leur faire visiter le musée du Mardi gras et de leur présenter les masques, objets importants dans la culture de la Louisiane. Essayez de prouver à vos beaux-parents, qui sont plutôt conservateurs, que ces objets ont une valeur artistique.
   (b) et (c) Jouez le rôle des beaux-parents qui ne sont pas du tout convaincus de la beauté de ces masques. Comparez-les à des tableaux européens plus classiques que vous appréciez davantage. Essayez cependant de ne pas blesser la sensibilité de votre beau-fils ou belle-fille !
2. Les vacances
   (a) Vous voulez passer vos vacances de printemps dans une île ensoleillée comme la Martinique ou la Guadeloupe ou même Tahiti. Essayez de convaincre vos amis québécois qui, eux, voudraient aller faire du ski. Comparez la plage à la montagne et exprimez votre enthousiasme pour les vacances à la plage en utilisant de nombreuses expressions superlatives.
   (b) Vous êtes un(e) étudiant(e) québécois(e) qui a décidé de rester au Québec pour les vacances de printemps. Votre budget-vacances est limité. Essayez de dissuader votre ami d'aller à une île tropicale en imaginant tout ce qui pourrait mal se passer.

À l'écrit *étape finale*

8.52 L'art du monde francophone Un magazine francophone cherche à publier des critiques d'œuvres d'art du monde francophone. Révisez et élaborez vos travaux d'écriture de ce chapitre (Activités 13, 26 et 39) et rédigez **un article critique** au sujet de votre œuvre d'art préférée. Décrivez l'œuvre et l'artiste, et comparez-la à d'autres œuvres de la même période ou du même mouvement artistique. Utilisez le **comparatif** et le **superlatif** et les temps de verbes qui conviennent. N'oubliez pas les éléments suivants :

- une introduction
- une description de l'œuvre
- une description de l'artiste
- une comparaison à d'autres œuvres
- une conclusion

À suivre

«Mais non ! Il y a quelque chose qui ne va pas», a pensé Claire en terminant sa lecture du manuscrit. Il y avait quelque chose d'abérrant, de gênant, de troublant dans le dernier chapitre du manuscrit. D'abord, elle n'arrivait pas à identifier d'où venait son angoisse, mais en relisant ce dernier chapitre, elle l'a trouvé. À l'avant-dernière page, il était là. Un terrible anachronisme. Une référence très brève dans une conversation entre deux soldats à la perte de Saint-Domingue aux Antilles et à l'établissement d'une nouvelle république nommée Haïti. C'était en 1804 que la République haïtienne avait été établie mais Laclos était mort en Italie en 1803. Le manuscrit ne pouvait donc pas avoir été écrit par Laclos. . .

8.53 Qu'est-ce qui s'est passé ? Pensez à ce qui s'est passé dans ce chapitre. **Écrivez six phrases au temps passé** pour décrire les événements que vous pensez être les plus importants. Parlez de vos idées avec vos camarades de classe.

MODÈLE : Claire a finalement lu le manuscrit !

8.54 Qu'est-ce qui se passera ? Imaginez ce qui va se passer dans le prochain chapitre. **Écrivez six phrases** et parlez de vos idées avec vos camarades de classe. Utilisez le futur.

MODÈLE : Claire ne dira rien à Jean-Louis à propos de l'anachronisme !

VOCABULAIRE UTILE

Les arts

aquarelle (*f.*)	*watercolor*
chef-d'œuvre (*m.*)	*masterpiece*
dessin (*m.*)	*drawing*
esquisse (*f.*)	*sketch*
gravure (*f.*)	*engraving*
nature morte (*f.*)	*still-life painting*
œuvre (*f.*)	*work (of art)*
tableau (*m.*)	*picture*

Les descriptions

cadre (*m.*)	*setting*
champêtre	*rustic*
cheminée (*f.*)	*fireplace*
combattre	*to fight, battle*
déchiré(e)	*torn*
décevoir	*to disappoint*
écriture	*writing, handwriting*
empaqueté(e)	*packaged, wrapped up*
en revanche	*in return, on the other hand*
envahi(e)	*invaded*
époque (*f.*)	*era*
frappant(e)	*striking*
frappé(e)	*struck, hit*
gaspiller	*to waste*
néanmoins	*nonetheless or now*
perspicace	*perspicacious, shrewd*
pétiller	*to crackle*
quoiqu'il en soit	*be that as it may*
ride (*f.*)	*wrinkle*
sagesse (*f.*)	*wisdom*
se dérouler	*to unfold*
s'étendre	*to extend*
signé(e)	*signed*
tenace	*tenacious, obstinate*
thématique	*thematic*
transcrire	*to transcribe*

Chapitre 9

Une affaire provençale

Une petite rue à Châteauneuf-du-Pape, en Provence.

Épisode 1 *L'anachronisme*

Épisode 2 *L'explication*

Épisode 3 *«Le devoir m'appelle»*

Dénouement

Culture

La **Provence** est une région au sud-est de la France qui comprend plusieurs départements comme le Gard, le Vaucluse, les Bouches du Rhône, etc. Cette région variée, près de la frontière italienne, a été développée par les Romains sous Jules César. La ville d'Avignon, avec son grandiose palais des Papes, était le siège de l'église catholique de 1309 à 1377. La région a été réunie à la France en 1487 sous Charles VIII. On y parlait **provençal**, une langue occitane qui est encore parlée aujourd'hui par une minorité de la population. La célèbre Côte d'Azur (*Riviera*) se trouve en Provence aussi, mais ses plages et villes touristiques (Nice, Antibes, Cannes, Saint-Tropez) se distinguent très fort des petites villes et villages pittoresques de l'intérieur de la région. À part Marseille, ville plus moderne, les villes provençales comme Nîmes, Arles, Avignon et Aix-en-Provence sont caractérisées par leurs petites rues pavées (*cobbled streets*), leurs places charmantes, leurs marchés en plein air et leurs ruines romaines. À la campagne, on trouve des champs de lavande, des vignobles et des villages construits aux sommets de montagnes rocheuses.

Quand on parle du loup,
on en voit la queue.
—expression française

À apprendre

- Comment parler des affaires et de la vie moderne
- Comment diminuer ou accentuer l'importance d'un fait
- Comment s'expliquer et exprimer une obligation

À lire

Dans le dernier chapitre du manuscrit, deux soldats français discutent de la perte de l'île de Saint-Domingue et l'établissement de la République d'Haïti. Ces événements se sont passés en 1804, une année après la mort de Laclos. Ayant découvert cet anachronisme, Claire doit admettre à Jean-Louis que ce texte qu'ils ont cherché jusqu'au bout du monde ne peut pas avoir été écrit par Laclos. Que faire maintenant ? Jean-Louis décide de retourner à Paris afin d'expliquer ce qui se passe à son patron. Claire, elle, prend le TGV en direction de la Provence où elle espère consulter son directeur de thèse, le Professeur Thuillier. Dans le train, elle rencontre une femme qui lui parle, par coïncidence, du marché des livres anciens, et quand elle arrive en Provence, elle est surprise de rencontrer la personne dont elle vient de parler. . .

Épisode 1

L'anachronisme

Avant de lire

9.1 Vos opinions sur les affaires et la vie moderne Répondez aux questions suivantes. Discutez de vos réponses avec vos camarades de classe et n'hésitez pas à poser des questions supplémentaires si vous voulez en savoir plus.

1. Avez-vous jamais travaillé pour une grande entreprise ? Si oui, quelles étaient vos responsabilités ? Si non, connaissez-vous quelqu'un qui travaille dans les affaires ? Si oui, pour quelle compagnie ?
2. Pouvez-vous décrire ce que font les hommes et femmes d'affaires qui travaillent pour des compagnies internationales ou de grandes sociétés (*corporations*) ? Quelles activités quotidiennes font-ils ? Quels sont leurs buts (*goals*) ?
3. À votre avis, une connaissance de la technologie est-elle nécessaire afin de survivre dans notre société moderne ? Quels appareils technologiques utilisez-vous le plus souvent : la télé, l'ordinateur, le téléphone portable, la voiture. . . ?
4. Quels sont les avantages de la technologie ? et ses inconvénients (*disadvantages*) ?
5. Pensez-vous que le commerce soit important à l'économie de votre pays ? Est-il important à votre bonheur personnel ? Pourquoi ou pourquoi pas ?
6. Quel est votre conte de fées (*fairy tale*) préféré ? Quelle leçon est-ce qu'il enseigne ? Est-ce que cette leçon est encore valable aujourd'hui ?

i Langue

La France est souvent divisée en deux parties : Paris et la province. **La province**, c'est tout ce qui n'est pas la région urbaine parisienne; c'est-à-dire, toutes les régions en province. Il ne faut pas confondre la province avec **la Provence**, une région au sud-est du pays. Bien sûr, la Provence est en province, mais elle n'est pas la seule région en province !

9.2 En province Souvent les régions en province souffrent du fait que l'économie française se concentre dans la région parisienne. Pourtant, chaque région a des produits régionaux qu'elle vend à l'intérieur du pays et sur le marché mondial. En voici quelques-uns des plus connus : en petits groupes, **faites correspondre la région** (à gauche) **avec les produits traditionnels qu'elle vend** (à droite). Utilisez une carte de la France afin de vous aider à deviner de quelle région il s'agit.

Région	Produits traditionnels
1. Provence	a. la moutarde dijonnaise et le vin rouge
2. Bretagne/Normandie	b. les textiles colorés, les parfums et le vin des Côtes-du-Rhône
3. Champagne-Ardenne	c. le vin rouge de Bordeaux
4. Aquitaine	d. la bière, la choucroute et la quiche lorraine
5. Bourgogne	e. le vin blanc pétillant et le foie gras
6. Alsace-Lorraine	f. le cidre, la tarte aux pommes, les huîtres, les crêpes

la Provence

Rencontrez une Française qui vient du sud de la France ! Regardez la vidéo et consultez votre cahier d'activités !

Langue

Pour **parler des affaires**, au lieu d'utiliser le terme «compagnie», on peut parler d'une **société**, d'une **maison de commerce** ou d'une **entreprise**. Les grandes sociétés ont souvent des **succursales** (*branches*) ou des **filiales** (*subsidiaries*) dans plusieurs villes et un **siège** (*headquarters*) dans une ville principale. Les personnes qui travaillent pour une société sont des **hommes et femmes d'affaires**, ou plus précisément des **administrateurs**, des **cadres** (*executives*) ou des **directeurs**. Le chef de la société est le **PDG** ou président-directeur général. Il y a aussi des **gérants** (*managers*), des **vendeurs** (*salespeople*), des **comptables** (*accountants*), des **techniciens**, des **secrétaires** et des **assistants** qui travaillent dans un **bureau** (*office*). Normalement, les sociétés vendent au public des services ou des produits. Il y a beaucoup de **concurrence** (*competition*), donc la **gestion** (*management*), le **marketing** de leur **marque** (*brand*) et la **publicité** sont importants. Si une **SA**, ou **société anonyme** (*public corporation*), réalise de gros **bénéfices** (*profits*), des individus peuvent investir dans la société en achetant des **actions** (*shares of stock*) à la **bourse** (*stock exchange*). Mais si la société perd trop d'argent à cause d'une **grève** (*strike*) des travailleurs, des **créances gelées** (*frozen assets*) suite à un **procès** (*trial*) ou simplement à cause d'une concurrence croissante, elle risque de **faire faillite** (*to go bankrupt*) et de laisser tous ses employés au **chômage**.

9.3 Passif ou actif ? Avant de parler avec Jean-Louis, Claire essaie de réviser les faits. Pour chaque phrase, **indiquez** si l'action est décrite d'une façon **active** (le sujet fait l'action) ou **passive** (l'action est fait au sujet).

1. Le manuscrit de Laclos **a été donné** à la famille de Sandrine Fontenot.
2. La famille Fontenot **a vendu** le manuscrit à Lionel Gustave.
3. Le manuscrit **a été vendu** à Monsieur Thibodeau par Nicolas Gustave.
4. Les policiers **ont trouvé** le corps de Nicolas Gustave la semaine dernière.
5. Nicolas **avait été empoisonné** par des criminels.
6. Jean-Louis **a acheté** le manuscrit à Monsieur Thibodeau au Sénégal.
7. Je **viens de trouver** un anachronisme dans le dernier chapitre du manuscrit.
8. Ce manuscrit n'**est** pas de Laclos.

Pour aller plus loin : CULTURE

ACTIVITÉ A : Apprenez un peu plus au sujet du français des affaires. Consultez votre cahier électronique !

Pour aller plus loin : CULTURE

ACTIVITÉ B : Voulez-vous explorer les régions de la France ? Consultez votre cahier électronique !

L'anachronisme

Et voilà. L'anachronisme montre indisputablement que le manuscrit qu'ils ont acheté à Monsieur Thibodeau n'est pas de Choderlos de Laclos. Quand Claire descend à la cuisine du chalet le matin après avoir terminé sa lecture du manuscrit, son visage révèle sa déception. Quand elle explique à Jean-Louis ce qu'elle a trouvé, il est stupéfait. Bouche bée, il reste immobile pendant plusieurs moments à réfléchir à ce que cela veut dire avant de répondre. . .

CLAIRE : Tu entends ce que je te dis ? Ce manuscrit n'est pas de la main de Laclos.

JEAN-LOUIS : Mais, ce n'est pas possible ! Tu dois te tromper.

CLAIRE : Non. À la mort de Laclos, les troupes françaises n'avaient pas encore perdu Saint-Domingue et une République haïtienne n'était pas encore concevable. Je ne sais pas qui est l'auteur de ce texte, mais ce n'est pas l'auteur des *Liaisons dangereuses*.

JEAN-LOUIS : Mais qu'est-ce que je vais dire à Jules ?

CLAIRE : À qui ?

JEAN-LOUIS : À mon patron, Jules Raphaël Rolland. C'est l'antiquaire qui a fourni l'argent pour l'achat du manuscrit. Oh là là là là là là ! Je suis fichu !

CLAIRE : Ce n'est pas si grave que ça, quand même. Ce Monsieur Rolland. . . Jules Raphaël, tu as dit ? . . . enfin, c'est un homme d'affaires calé, n'est-ce pas ? Il a sûrement calculé les risques d'un tel investissement ?

JEAN-LOUIS : Nous étions sûrs de gagner le gros lot avec ce manuscrit. On allait le revendre à un client allemand qui fait collection de manuscrits inédits de la fin du 18ème siècle. Tout le monde comprend la nature aléatoire de ce commerce, mais Monsieur Rolland est un homme très fier qui a créé une grosse entreprise à partir d'une petite maison. Il en est PDG, tu sais, et il n'aime pas quand son argent est mal placé. Ce n'est pas une organisation à but non lucratif ! Il avait d'autres employés plus rompus aux affaires que moi, mais je l'ai convaincu que j'étais prêt à devenir acheteur et à négocier des transactions importantes. Avant, je n'étais qu'un assistant au gérant de la service de ventes. Et j'ai tout gâché ! Maintenant, j'aurai de la chance s'il ne me renvoie pas sur-le-champ.

CLAIRE : Tu exagères, j'en suis sûre. Ce n'est pas de ta faute que le manuscrit n'est pas de Laclos. Tu ne perdras pas ton boulot. Mais qu'est-ce que je vais faire, moi ? Voilà un semestre passé, une bourse gaspillée et un sujet de thèse qui est lettre morte. Je vais devoir recommencer à zéro.

JEAN-LOUIS : Zut ! Tu as raison. Je n'avais pas pensé à ta situation. Enfin, moi, je dois retourner à Paris aussitôt que possible pour apprendre la nouvelle à Monsieur Rolland.

Mais, toi, tu n'es pas obligée de venir avec moi. Il faut que tu t'occupes de tes propres affaires. Vas-tu au Québec ? Que vas-tu faire ?

CLAIRE : Je devrai me décider sur un nouveau sujet de thèse, et vite. J'irai en Provence où travaille mon directeur de thèse et je vais lui parler. Après cela, qui sait !

JEAN-LOUIS : Bon. Je vais faire mes valises. Alors, nous irons à la gare de Genève ensemble. . . disons dans une demi-heure ? Tu prends le TGV, n'est-ce pas ?

CLAIRE : Oui, si possible. . . Je vais juste faire quelques appels, en PCV bien sûr, et puis je serai prête à partir moi aussi. Mais, Jean-Louis. . . après ?

JEAN-LOUIS : Ne t'inquiète pas. On se parlera.

VOCABULAIRE

Les affaires

un(e) patron(ne)	*boss*
fournir	*to furnish, supply*
un investissement	*investment*
le gros lot	*jackpot*
aléatoire	*risky, uncertain*
à but non lucratif	*nonprofit (organization)*
rompu(e) aux affaires	*experienced in business*
une entreprise	*company, business*
une maison	*company, business*
placer (de l'argent)	*to invest (money)*
le PDG (président directeur-général)	CEO
le/la gérant(e)	*manager*
le service de ventes	*sales division*
renvoyer	*to fire (an employee)*
sur-le-champ	*immediately*
un boulot	*job (slang)*

Divers

stupéfait(e)	*stunned*
bouche bée	*open-mouthed*
vouloir dire	*to mean*
lettre morte	*worthless; a dead issue*
s'éloigner	*to distance oneself*
être fichu(e)	*to be done for, to have had it*
grave	*serious*
calé(e)	*smart, clever (slang)*
tel(le)	*such*
le TGV (train de grande vitesse)	*high-speed express train*
un appel PCV (payable chez vous)	*collect call*

Après avoir lu

9.4 Avez-vous compris ? Répondez aux questions suivantes. **Justifiez vos réponses** en citant le texte.

1. Pourquoi est-ce que Claire déclare que le manuscrit n'est pas de Laclos ?
2. Quelle est la réaction de Jean-Louis ? Est-ce une réaction normale ?
3. Où vont Claire et Jean-Louis ? Pourquoi est-ce qu'ils doivent se séparer ? Que pouvez-vous leur conseiller ?
4. Que pensez-vous de l'entreprise pour laquelle Jean-Louis travaille ? Imaginez et décrivez comment elle fonctionne. Quels postes pourrait-on y avoir ?
5. Voudriez-vous travailler dans cette entreprise ? Pourquoi ou pourquoi pas ?

Pour aller plus loin : CULTURE

ACTIVITÉ C : Voulez-vous explorer le marché des livres anciens et d'antiquaires à Paris ? Consultez votre cahier électronique !

9.5 D'accord ou pas d'accord ? Indiquez si vous êtes d'accord ou pas d'accord avec les phrases suivantes, d'après votre compréhension du récit. Justifiez vos opinions en citant le texte, si possible. Discutez de vos réponses avec la classe.

	D'accord	Pas d'accord
1. Jean-Louis est surpris d'apprendre la nouvelle de l'anachronisme.	_______	_______
2. Monsieur Rolland a une petite entreprise modeste.	_______	_______
3. En affaires, on prend toujours des risques.	_______	_______
4. Claire veut retourner à Paris avec Jean-Louis.	_______	_______
5. Jean-Louis espère revoir Claire un jour.	_______	_______

9.6 Les affaires Regardez les mots de vocabulaire qui suivent. Dans chaque ligne, il y a un mot qui cloche avec les trois autres. **Entourez le mot qui ne va pas** avec les autres et essayez d'expliquer pourquoi. Attention : il y a parfois plusieurs bonnes réponses. Il faut justifier votre choix !

1. les affaires	le commerce	le marché	l'investissement
2. investir	acheter	vendre	placer son argent
3. une entreprise	une maison	un bureau	une société
4. fichu	rompu	calé	intelligent
5. le patron	l'employée	le gérant	l'assistant

9.7 Qui paie ses dettes s'enrichit ! Voici plusieurs entreprises qui s'occupent d'argent. Avec un partenaire, essayez de **décrire ce que font les gens qui travaillent** pour chaque entreprise et **comment l'entreprise gagne son argent**.

MODÈLE : un café →

—Il y a le propriétaire ou le manager qui engage les employés et qui s'occupent de l'argent. En plus, le manager commande (*orders*) les produits, comme le café, les tasses en papier, etc. Puis il y a des caissiers et des serveurs qui vendent et servent des boissons et qui nettoient le café. Le café gagne de l'argent parce qu'on vend une tasse de café pour plus d'argent qu'on paie pour les produits et la main-d'œuvre (*labor*).

une banque	la bourse (*stock market*)
un grand magasin	une maison d'édition (*publisher*)
une agence de tourisme	une agence immobilière (*real-estate agency*)
une crèche (*day care center*)	un atelier de réparations (*repair shop*)

Culture

En France, on utilise beaucoup de **sigles** (abréviations) pour parler des aspects de la vie moderne. Vous connaissez déjà quelques sigles pour les partis politiques (RPR, PS, UDF, PCF, FN), mais connaissez-vous tous les sigles suivants ? Y a-t-il des sigles équivalents en anglais ?

- **en affaires :** PDG (président-directeur général), PNB (produit national brut), BNP (Banque Nationale de Paris), DAB (distributeur automatique de billets), TTC (toutes taxes comprises), SMIC (salaire minimum interprofessionnel de croissance, *minimum wage*), SA (société anonyme), TVA (taxe à valeur ajoutée)
- **en politique :** RF (République française), UE (Union européenne), ONG (organisation non gouvernementale), ONU (Organisation des Nations unies), OTAN (Organisation du traité de l'Atlantique Nord)
- **à la poste :** PTT (Poste, Télécommunications et Télédiffusion), a/s (aux soins de), BP (boîte postale)
- **en télécommunications :** FAI (fournisseur d'accès à l'Internet), PCV (payable chez vous, *collect call*), TF1 (Télé France 1), AFP (Agence France-Presse), RFI (Radio France International)
- **en transports :** TGV (train à grande vitesse), SNCF (Société nationale des chemins de fer), RER (Réseau express régional), RATP (Régie autonome des transports parisiens)
- **divers :** BCBG (bon chic bon genre), RSVP (répondez, s'il vous plaît), QI (quotient d'intelligence), QG (quartier général), RdC (rez-de-chaussée), HLM (habitation à loyer modéré), SDF (sans domicile fixe, *homeless*), OVNI (objet volant non identifié), SPA (Société protectrice des animaux), W.-C. (toilettes, *water closet*), EDF (Électricité de France), GDF (Gaz de France)

Voulez-vous montrer votre familiarité avec les sigles qu'on utilise en conversation en France ? Écrivez deux ou trois phrases dans lesquelles vous employez autant de sigles que possible ! Par exemple: «Hier, j'ai pris le TGV de Paris au QG de l'ONU à Genève où j'ai rencontré le PDG de la BNP parce que je travaille pour RFI et je fais un reportage sur le SMIC et l'UE.»

9.8 Vocabulaire personnel Pensez à vos emplois, à vos ambitions professionnelles et à l'économie de votre région et, pour chaque catégorie, faites une liste de cinq à dix mots importants que vous pouvez utiliser en parlant de vous-même. Consultez un dictionnaire si nécessaire.

1. Vos emplois passés : postes, responsabilités, avantages, inconvénients
2. Les professions qui vous intéressent le plus : postes, responsabilités, avantages, inconvénients
3. Les professions qui vous intéressent le moins : postes, responsabilités, avantages, inconvénients
4. Les emplois ou professions de vos amis et de vos parents
5. Les compagnies ou les industries les plus importantes dans votre ville ou votre région et les emplois qu'on peut y avoir

Pour aller plus loin : CULTURE

ACTIVITÉ D : Cherchez des renseignements sur le Festival du film à Cannes. Consultez votre cahier électronique !

Langue

La **litote** est souvent employée en conversation ou dans la littérature. Employer une litote, c'est essayer de diminuer l'importance de quelque chose pour faire entendre que c'est vraiment une chose très importante. Par exemple, on dit souvent «pas mal» pour dire qu'on va assez bien. Ou, une personne pourrait dire «je ne le déteste pas» pour signifier qu'elle l'aime. Donc, si on emploie une litote, on diminue l'importance d'une chose afin de l'accentuer. Dans la tragédie classique *Phèdre* (1677) de Jean Racine, le personnage principal est amoureuse du fils de son mari. En avouant sa passion, Phèdre emploie une litote. Elle lui dit : «Va, je ne te hais point».

9.9 Ne quittez pas ! Claire ferme la porte de sa chambre pour faire ses appels. D'abord, elle téléphone à l'hôtel de Monsieur Thuillier, son directeur de thèse, mais il n'y est pas. Elle lui laisse un message disant qu'elle arrive le soir-même à Aix-en-Provence. Ensuite, elle retire de son portefeuille la carte d'affaires du détective parisien, Gilles LaFfont. Elle doit lui parler. Donc, elle compose le numéro, et une femme répond au téléphone. Choisissez une des expressions entre parenthèses et **lisez le dialogue à haute voix** avec un partenaire. Quand vous voyez «? ? ?», vous imaginez votre propre expression.

LA SECRÉTAIRE : Allô ? Oui ?
CLAIRE : Bonjour, madame. Est-ce bien le bureau de l'inspecteur LaFfont, Gilles LaFfont ?
LA SECRÉTAIRE : Oui, mademoiselle. Vous ne vous êtes pas trompée de numéro. Voulez-vous que je vous le passe ?
CLAIRE : (Oui, merci / S'il vous plaît, madame / ? ? ?).
LA SECRÉTAIRE : C'est de la part de qui ?
CLAIRE : Je m'appelle Claire Plouffe. (Je l'ai rencontré à Paris. / Il vient de m'envoyer un e-mail. / ? ? ?)
LA SECRÉTAIRE : (Un instant / Un moment / Une minute). Ne quittez pas. . . [*quelques secondes passent*] . . . (Excusez-moi / Zut alors / Quelle bêtise) ! Je suis (désolée / navrée), mais Monsieur est parti. J'aurais dû le savoir ! Et maintenant, je vous ai fait attendre pour rien. Ce n'est pas (gentil / très professionnel / ? ? ?) de faire attendre des clients.
CLAIRE : (Ce n'est pas grave / Cela ne fait rien / Ne vous inquiétez pas), madame. (Je rappellerai plus tard. / Je lui enverrai un e-mail. / ? ? ?)
LA SECRÉTAIRE : Vous ne voulez pas laisser de message ?
CLAIRE : Non, merci. (Au revoir / À bientôt / ? ? ?), madame.

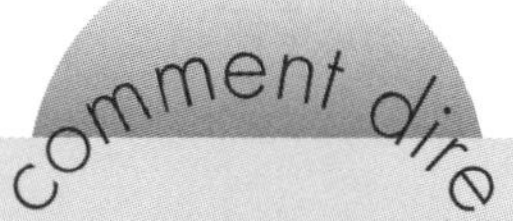

diminuer ou accentuer l'importance d'un fait

To downplay
Ce n'est pas grave / grand-chose / la fin du monde !
Ce n'est rien (du tout) ! / Ce n'est pas la mer à boire !
Il n'y a pas de mal ! / Ne vous en faites pas !
C'est une bagatelle / un petit rien / sans importance.
Peu importe. / Cela importe peu. / Cela ne fait rien. / Ce n'est rien.
Ne t'inquiète pas. / Ne vous inquiétez pas.

To emphasize
Zut ! / Zut, alors ! / Bon sang ! / Bonté divine !
Oh là là ! / Oh là là là là là là ! / Oh la vache !
C'est incroyable / super / inimaginable / urgent !
Ce n'est pas amusant / rigolo / une blague / vrai / possible !
Quel scandale ! / Quelle bêtise ! / Quelle horreur ! / Quelle catastrophe !
C'est vraiment quelque chose ! / Ça, c'est déjà quelque chose !
J'en crois pas mes oreilles ! / Mais c'est impossible !

9.10 À vous Avec un partenaire, imaginez que vous êtes dans les situations suivantes. Une personne veut **diminuer l'importance** du fait et l'autre veut l'**accentuer**. Que dites-vous ? Choisissez des expressions diverses pour chaque situation.

1. Votre ami(e) veut encore vous emprunter (*to borrow*) de l'argent.
2. Une vieille femme à la gare de Genève se plaint parce que son train est en retard.
3. Votre patron annonce qu'il doit renvoyer tous les employés de votre bureau parce que vous n'êtes pas assez rompus en affaires.
4. Vous devez terminer une lettre d'affaires avant la fin de la journée, mais votre ordinateur est tombé en panne (*broken down*).
5. Vos collègues vont passer un week-end à une réunion d'affaires dans un grand hôtel de luxe à Cannes, pendant le Festival du film, mais vous n'êtes pas invité(e).

9.11 À vendre ! Sur une feuille de papier, **écrivez une phrase** pour décrire un produit (réel ou imaginaire) que vous voulez vendre à vos camarades de classe. Ensuite, pliez votre papier et échangez-le au hasard avec un(e) autre étudiant(e). Puis, **circulez** dans la salle de classe et essayez de **vendre le produit** que vous avez reçu. Bien sûr, il faut accentuer son importance. Si une personne accepte de l'acheter, faites-lui signer votre papier ; si l'étudiant(e) refuse, diminuez l'importance de la vente et passez à quelqu'un d'autre. Essayez de vendre votre produit à autant de personnes que possible !

MODÈLE : —C'est du papier d'emballage (*wrapping paper*) pour des cadeaux, mais c'est un tissu (*cloth*) coloré lavable qu'on peut utiliser encore et encore. C'est pratique, peu coûteux, et c'est bon pour l'environnement. Voulez-vous l'acheter ?

9.12 Une réunion d'affaires En petits groupes, **faites une liste de produits ou de services** que vous voulez vendre au public tout en justifiant leur intérêt. Ensuite, **préparez une présentation** pour la classe en imaginant que vos camarades sont des investisseurs qui vous donneront de l'argent afin de développer votre entreprise. À votre tour, écoutez les présentations des autres. Posez des questions tout en exagérant ou en diminuant l'importance des faits.

Pour aller plus loin : CULTURE

ACTIVITÉ E : Connaissez-vous les grandes marques françaises ? Consultez votre cahier électronique !

À l'écrit *première étape*

9.13 Un conte de fées moderne Choisissez un conte de fées que vous aimeriez adapter au 21ème siècle. Faites **une liste des personnages** et **des objets** importants dans l'histoire et décrivez brièvement leurs caractéristiques et fonctions dans le conte original. En plus, indiquez **ce que vous changeriez** pour rendre le conte plus moderne. Ensuite, échangez votre liste avec celle d'un camarade de classe. Vérifiez que votre partenaire s'est bien exprimé, faites des corrections possibles et ajoutez vos commentaires en bas de page.

Épisode 2

L'explication

Structures *les pronoms relatifs*

Pour aller plus loin : LITTÉRATURE

ACTIVITÉ F : Connaissez-vous des titres de contes de fées français ? Consultez votre cahier électronique !

9.14 Le Petit Chaperon rouge (*Little Red Riding Hood*) En attendant leurs trains dans la gare de Genève, Claire et Jean-Louis s'assoient dans la salle d'attente. Là, ils entendent un homme qui raconte une histoire à sa fille. C'est une version moderne de l'histoire du Petit Chaperon rouge. Lisez-la et comparez-la avec la version traditionnelle que vous connaissez. Ensuite, **examinez les pronoms relatifs**, qui sont en **caractères gras**, et répondez aux questions qui suivent.

Il était une fois une jeune fille **qui** portait toujours un manteau rouge. Le manteau **qu'**elle portait avait un chaperon. C'est la raison **pour laquelle** on l'appelait le Petit Chaperon rouge. Elle aimait aller chez sa grand-mère **qui** habitait de l'autre côté d'un bois. C'était le bois **où** habitait un méchant loup. Mais, elle voulait voir sa grand-mère et lui apporter les provisions **dont** elle avait besoin.

Le jour **où** elle a traversé le bois pour aller chez sa grand-mère, il faisait froid. Elle portait deux sacs en plastique **dans lesquels** elle avait mis les provisions. Tout d'un coup, le loup **dont** tout le monde parlait est sorti du bois. «Où vas-tu avec ces provisions ?» a-t-il demandé à la jeune fille **qui** souriait. «Je vais à la maison **qui** est de l'autre côté du bois», a-t-elle répondu. Et, regardant le loup **qui** était très mince et affamé, elle a ajouté : «Viens avec moi et ma grand-mère te donnera le dîner **dont** tu rêves».

Cet acte de charité inattendu a touché le cœur du loup. Il a accompagné la jeune fille à la maison **dont** elle lui avait parlé. Là, la grand-mère a préparé le festin **que** la fille avait promis au loup. Ils ont tous bien mangé. La jeune fille a dit au loup, «Quels grands yeux vous avez ! Quelle grande bouche vous avez !» Le loup, content du repas et de ses nouvelles amies, a répondu, «C'est la bouche **avec laquelle** j'ai bien mangé ce soir. Le repas **que** vous avez préparé était délicieux ! Et, ce sont les yeux **avec lesquels** je regarde mes nouvelles amies !». Après le dîner, il a promis à la jeune fille de la protéger quand elle traverserait le bois, et il est reparti au fond du bois **d'où** il était venu.

1. Le pronom relatif **qui** est suivi de quoi ?
   (a) un sujet (b) un verbe (c) une préposition
2. Le pronom relatif **que** est suivi de quoi ?
   (a) un sujet (b) un verbe (c) une préposition
3. Le pronom relatif **où** est employé pour indiquer un endroit où (*a place where*) quelque chose se passe et aussi pour indiquer. . . ?
   (a) une chose (*what*) (b) une personne (*who*) (c) un moment (*when*)

4. Les verbes qui suivent le pronom relatif **dont** sont des verbes qui sont normalement suivis de quelle préposition ?
   (a) à (b) de (c) avec
5. Le pronom relatif **lequel** est toujours précédé par quoi ?
   (a) un sujet (b) un verbe (c) une préposition
6. Il faut faire l'accord entre le pronom relatif **lequel** et. . . ?
   (a) le nom qui précède (b) le nom qui suit (c) le sujet du verbe

Pour aller plus loin : LITTÉRATURE

ACTIVITÉ G : Lisez le poème «La mort du loup» d'Alfred de Vigny. Consultez votre cahier électronique !

Le loup est un animal folklorique présent dans beaucoup de contes et proverbes français, comme les proverbes : «Quand on parle du loup on en voit la queue», «Il faut hurler avec les loups» (il faut faire comme les autres) ou «Les loups ne se mangent pas entre eux» (les amis se protègent). Le loup est un animal parfois méchant, toujours affamé et souvent nocturne qui vit en liberté dans la forêt. On est fasciné par ce côté sauvage du loup dont on parle toujours dans la langue quotidienne. Il y a toute une mythologie du **loup-garou**, l'homme-loup qui sort pendant la pleine lune. À l'heure du coucher du soleil, on est **entre chien et loup** (c'est-à-dire entre la journée et la nuit). Si on est très connu dans la société, on est **connu comme le loup blanc**. Si on marche sans faire de bruit, comme pour surprendre quelqu'un, on marche **à pas de loup**. Y a-t-il des expressions en anglais où on parle du loup ?

les pronoms relatifs

Relative pronouns (les **pronoms relatifs**) are used to join two clauses together and to avoid repetition. Choose the appropriate relative pronoun according to the verb phrase in the second clause.

With verbs that *do not take prepositions* before a noun:	**qui, que, où**
With verbs that are followed by the *preposition* **de** before a noun:	**dont**
With verbs that take *other prepositions* (other than **de**) before a noun:	(*preposition* +) **qui** (*preposition* +) **lequel**

The *relative pronoun* **qui** (*who, that*) is usually followed by a conjugated verb and functions as a subject of the relative clause.

- Example: Il était une fois une jeune fille. La jeune fille portait toujours un manteau rouge. : Il était une fois une jeune fille **qui** portait toujours un manteau rouge.
- **Note:** Never drop the **i** to contract **qui** with a verb beginning with a vowel or silent **h**.

- **Note: Qui** can also be the object of a preposition (other than **de**), in which case it is followed by a subject and verb (*preposition* + **qui** + *subject* + *verb*) and can only refer to people. → C'est la fille **avec qui** le loup a dîné.

The *relative pronoun* **que** (*that, which*) is usually followed by a subject and verb. **Que** often follows the direct object of the verb in the relative clause.

- Example: La jeune fille portait un manteau. Le manteau avait un chaperon. → Le manteau **qu'**elle portait avait un chaperon.
- **Note:** Always drop the **e** to contract **que** with a subject beginning with a vowel or silent **h**.
- **Note:** Always make the past participle agree with the preceding direct object if the second verb is in the passé composé. → C'est la forêt **qu'**elle a traversé**e**.

The *relative pronoun* **où** (*where, when*) is usually followed by a subject and verb. **Où** also often follows a direct object of the verb in the relative clause, but is used only to indicate place or time.

- Example: C'était un bois. Le loup habitait dans le bois. → C'était le bois **où** habitait un méchant loup.
- **Note:** When used to indicate a place, **où** is interchangeable with a *preposition* + **lequel**. → C'était le bois **dans lequel** habitait un méchant loup.

The *relative pronoun* **dont** (*about/of which, that*) is usually followed by a subject and verb. **Dont** is used exclusively with verbs that take the preposition **de**.

- Example: Elle voulait lui apporter des provisions. Sa grand-mère avait besoin de provisions. → Elle voulait apporter les provisions **dont** sa grand-mère avait besoin.
- **Note:** Remember that a number of French verbs require the preposition **de**, although it is sometimes not evident in the English translation. (*She wanted to bring the groceries that her grandmother needed.*)

The *relative pronouns* **qui** and **lequel** (*whom, which*), which function as objects of any *preposition other than* **de** (**à, avec, sur, dans, chez**, etc.), are usually followed by a subject and verb. Use **qui** when referring to people (**à qui** = *to/about whom*) and use the appropriate form of **lequel** when referring to other nouns (**auquel** = *to/about which*).

- Example: J'ai une bouche. J'ai bien mangé avec cette bouche ce soir. → C'est la bouche **avec laquelle** j'ai bien mangé ce soir.
- Remember that **lequel** has four forms (**lequel, laquelle, lesquels, lesquelles**) and must agree in number and gender with the noun in the first clause; also remember that the preposition **à** contracts with **lequel** in the masculine and plural forms (**auquel, auxquels, auxquelles**).
- **Note:** Sometimes **lequel** can also be used when referring to people. → C'est la fille avec **laquelle** le loup a dîné.

Langue

Vous rappelez-vous quels verbes ont besoin d'une préposition avant un nom ? Voici **quelques verbes** fréquemment utilisés qui sont suivis d'une préposition. Révisez-les avant de continuer !

- *Verbes qui ne sont pas suivis d'une préposition* : aimer, apprendre, attendre, chercher, comprendre, écouter, essayer, étudier, parler (une langue), payer, prendre, recevoir, savoir, visiter, voir
- *Verbes qui sont suivis de la préposition* **de** : avoir besoin de, avoir envie de, avoir peur de, parler de (quelqu'un ou quelque chose), rêver de, s'agir de, s'inquiéter de, se souvenir de
- *Verbes qui sont suivis de la préposition* **à** : dire à, écrire à, parler à (quelqu'un), penser à, permettre à, réfléchir à, rendre visite à, s'intéresser à, téléphoner à

Notez que le verbe **parler** peut être suivi de **à**, de **de** ou de rien. Tout dépend du contexte : Claire parle à Jean-Louis ; elle parle du manuscrit ; elle parle beaucoup !

9.15 Un message important Claire et Jean-Louis se disent au revoir à la gare sans cérémonie, et Claire monte dans le TGV où elle trouve son siège. Elle décide d'écrire un e-mail à Gilles LaFfont qu'elle enverra quand elle arrivera à son hôtel en Provence. Lisez le message et **remplissez les blancs** avec le pronom relatif **qui**, **que** ou **où**.

À : Gilles LaFfont
De : Claire Plouffe
Date : 20/10/03
Ref : renseignements

Cher Inspecteur LaFfont :

J'ai essayé de vous téléphoner ce matin, mais vous n'étiez pas au bureau. Mon ami et moi avons acheté le manuscrit ________________ nous cherchions, celui ________________ je croyais être écrit par Choderlos de Laclos. Pourtant, le manuscrit ________________ je viens de lire n'est pas de Laclos. Un anachronisme ________________ se trouve dans le dernier chapitre en est la preuve. Deux personnages parlent d'une bataille ________________ a eu lieu après la mort de Laclos. Donc, l'homme ________________ m'a aidé à trouver le manuscrit est rentré aujourd'hui à Paris, la ville ________________ il demeure. Quant à moi, je me dirige vers Aix-en-Provence ________________ j'espère consulter mon directeur de thèse. Évidemment, le sujet de thèse ________________ j'ai choisi s'est révélé être une perte de temps ! Hélas, la chose ________________ je voulais vous dire c'est le nom du patron de mon ami. Vous m'avez dit une fois de me méfier de quelqu'un ________________ s'appelle Julie ou de quelqu'un ________________ s'appelle Raphaël. Enfin, le nom de l'antiquaire parisien ________________ a fourni l'argent pour l'achat du manuscrit, est Jules Raphaël Rolland. Je ne sais pas si c'est une coïncidence ou non, mais voilà ce ________________ j'ai appris ce matin. Je ne pense pas être en danger moi-même, mais je m'inquiète un peu pour mon ami. Je dormirai mieux le jour ________________ vous arrêterez la personne ________________ a tué le bouquiniste. . .

9.16 Une rencontre Claire est interrompue par une femme qui s'assoit à côté d'elle et qui commence à lui parler. **Remplissez les blancs** avec le pronom relatif **dont** ou avec la forme appropriée de **lequel**.

LA FEMME : Excusez-moi, madame. Est-ce que cette place est libre ?

CLAIRE : Oui, oui. Je vous en prie.

LA FEMME : J'aime votre ordinateur. C'est l'ordinateur ____________ j'ai besoin. Je suis vendeuse dans une parfumerie en Provence, et je voyage souvent à Paris. Pourtant, la parfumerie pour ____________ je vends du parfum est assez petite, et les collègues avec ____________ je travaille sont assez traditionnels. Ils n'utilisent pas les ordinateurs. La compagnie ____________ je parle est à Grasse. Connaissez-vous cette ville ?

CLAIRE : Oui, j'ai entendu dire que c'est la ville dans ____________ se trouvent de nombreuses parfumeries.

LA FEMME : C'est exact. Vous êtes touriste ? Tenez, je peux vous donner un guide touristique gratuit, sur ____________ j'ai travaillé l'année dernière, qui parle de tous les sites importants de la région.

Culture

La ville de **Grasse**, en Provence, est très connue pour ses parfumeries. Dans cette région, on trouve beaucoup de fleurs qu'on utilise pour fabriquer des huiles et des essences pour les parfums. Les champs de lavande sont abondants dans cette région. Grasse est le village natal de Jean-Honoré Fragonard, célèbre peintre du 18ème siècle qui a fait plusieurs tableaux fantaisistes dans le style rococo. La parfumerie Fragonard est une des plus importantes de la région.

Le Pont du Gard, un acqueduc romain, en Provence.

9.17 Les sites touristiques provençaux Claire regarde les photos dans le guide et écoute la femme qui décrit les sites historiques provençaux. **Combinez les phrases** en employant des pronoms relatifs. Choisissez le pronom qui convient.

MODÈLE : Voilà la Maison carrée. J'ai visité la Maison carrée l'été dernier. →

Voilà la Maison carrée *que* j'ai visitée l'été dernier.

1. Voilà la Camargue. Des chevaux et taureaux sauvages habitent la Camargue.
2. C'est le palais des Papes. Ce palais est situé à Avignon.
3. Voici le fleuve du Gard. Les gens se baignent dans le Gard en été.
4. Ce sont des champs de lavande à Grasse. J'ai parlé de ces champs tout à l'heure.
5. Vincent Van Gogh a habité à Arles. Il y a peint de nombreuses toiles.
6. Ce sont les Arènes de Nîmes. Vous pouvez assister à une corrida aux Arènes ce week-end.

Pour aller plus loin : CULTURE

ACTIVITÉ H : Explorez la Provence. Consultez votre cahier électronique !

la Provence

De quels produits régionaux parle Catherine ? Comment décrit-elle la Provence ? Regardez la vidéo et consultez votre cahier d'activités !

Culture

On trouve beaucoup de **ruines romaines** en **Provence**, une région conquise par Jules César. Les Romains ont construit des temples, comme la Maison carrée à Nîmes, et des arènes, comme celles à Nîmes ou à Arles, où on organise des **corridas** (*bullfights*) traditionnelles. Un des chefs-d'œuvre des Romains, pourtant, est l'aqueduc du Pont du Gard qui conduit de l'eau courante d'un côté du fleuve (le Gard) à l'autre. En Camargue, une région en Provence sur la côte de la Méditerranée, on trouve beaucoup de marécages et de parcs naturels. On peut y voir des chevaux et des taureaux sauvages. Les **taureaux** sont importants à la culture provençale. À part les spectacles de corridas organisés aux arènes, on peut trouver des jeux de «taureau-piscine» dans les petits villages pendant les fêtes. Pour gagner à ce jeu, une personne doit retirer une décoration des cornes du taureau. Au centre de la cour, on met une petite piscine. Si le taureau commence à poursuivre le joueur, il peut sauter dans l'eau de la piscine afin de se sauver !

Un spectacle de corrida aux Arènes de Nîmes, en Provence.

9.18 Qu'est-ce que c'est ? Avec un partenaire, posez des questions à propos des objets suivants. Décrivez l'objet en employant un pronom relatif. Offrez autant de descriptions que possible.

MODÈLE : —Qu'est-ce que c'est qu'un bureau ?

—C'est une salle *où* on a des rendez-vous d'affaires.

—C'est aussi un meuble *sur lequel* on écrit des lettres.

1. un bureau (une salle, un meuble)
2. un ordinateur (une machine)
3. un tableau (une chose)
4. des arènes (un endroit, une structure)
5. le parfum (un liquide)
6. des taureaux (des animaux)

Structures *les pronoms relatifs indéfinis*

Pour aller plus loin : LITTÉRATURE

ACTIVITÉ 1 : Lisez quelques maximes de François de La Rochefoucauld. Consultez votre cahier électronique !

9.19 Ce qui se passe aujourd'hui Quand Claire finit de regarder le guide touristique, la femme assise à côté d'elle dans le TGV lui offre son journal dans lequel il y a un article intéressant. Regardez tous les pronoms relatifs indéfinis : **ce qui, ce que, ce dont** ou **ce à quoi**. Quelles sont les similarités entre les **pronoms relatifs** (**qui, que, dont, à qui/lequel**) et les **pronoms relatifs indéfinis** qu'on trouve dans ce dialogue ? Pouvez-vous décrire comment employer les pronoms relatifs indéfinis ?

LA FEMME : Voudriez-vous lire le journal ? C'est un journal parisien que j'ai acheté avant de quitter la gare ce matin. Il y a un article intéressant sur l'économie. C'est **ce à quoi** tout le monde pense ces jours-ci avec le chômage et tout ça.

CLAIRE : **Ce qui** m'intéresse n'est pas l'économie, mais la littérature.

LA FEMME : Ah, alors, **ce dont** vous avez besoin, c'est d'une revue littéraire. C'est **ce que** j'achète chaque semaine moi. Tenez, voici une copie du dernier numéro. Vous pouvez la garder. Comme dit La Rochefoucauld, «C'est une grande folie de vouloir être sage tout seul !»

CLAIRE : Merci beaucoup. C'est très gentil.

les pronoms relatifs indéfinis

The *indefinite relative pronouns* (**les pronoms relatifs indéfinis**) are used in context, when there is no definite phrase or antecedent clause in the sentence. The *indefinite relative pronouns* are: **ce qui** (*that which*), **ce que** (*that which*), **ce dont** (*that of/about which*), and **ce à quoi** (*that of/about which*).

- The choice of pronoun depends on whether the pronoun is a subject (**ce qui** + *verb*), a direct object (**ce que** + *subject* + *verb*), or an object of the preposition **à** or **de** (**ce à quoi / ce dont** + *subject* + *verb*).
- Some examples of *indefinite relative pronouns* are:

Quelque chose m'embête. Le voilà.	→	Voilà **ce qui** m'embête.
Je veux dire *quelque chose*. Vous voyez ?	→	Vous voyez **ce que** je veux dire ?
Vous avez parlé *de quelque chose*. C'est ça.	→	C'est **ce dont** vous avez parlé.
Je pensais *à quelque chose*. Vous le savez.	→	Vous savez **ce à quoi** je pensais.

9.20 Quelle coïncidence ! Claire commence à feuilleter (*to leaf through*) la revue littéraire et trouve un article éditorial intéressant. **Remplissez les blancs** avec un pronom relatif indéfini.

CLAIRE : Quelle coïncidence ! Il y a un article sur le marché des livres anciens. J'écrivais un message à ce sujet quand vous vous êtes assise. Comme c'est bizarre.

LA FEMME : Mais, ______________ vous ignorez peut-être, madame, c'est que ce marché est très respecté en France. Les livres font partie de notre patrimoine national.

CLAIRE : Vous avez raison. C'est ______________ je me disais. Mais, quand même, c'est bizarre. C'est exactement ______________ s'intéresse le destinataire du message que je viens d'écrire. Il est. . .

LA FEMME : Oh, regardez ! On est presque arrivé à Avignon où je vais descendre. Vous descendez aussi ?

CLAIRE : Oui, je dois changer de trains pour aller à Aix-en-Provence. Savez-vous ______________ me gêne un peu ? Il y a un train qui part à 16 heures vingt, mais je crains de le rater à cause de tous ces bagages. C'est ______________ j'ai peur.

LA FEMME : Ne vous inquiétez pas. La gare d'Avignon est assez petite. Tout ____________________ vous avez à faire, c'est de descendre, d'attendre cinq minutes le prochain train, et de remonter. C'est facile. Bon voyage, madame, et bon séjour en Provence !

9.21 C'est quoi ? Sur une feuille de papier, **écrivez un nom** (un objet, une personne ou un endroit). Pliez votre papier et échangez vos papiers au hasard avec vos camarades de classe. Puis, **circulez** dans la classe et essayez de **trouver l'auteur** du papier que vous avez reçu. Attention ! Vous ne pouvez pas révéler le mot qui est sur le papier. Vous devez le décrire en employant des pronoms relatifs !

MODÈLE : un livre

—C'est *ce qu'***on utilise pour étudier. C'est un objet** *qui* **se trouve en bibliothèque.**

9.22 C'est quoi encore ? En petits groupes, **écrivez trois ou quatre phrases** pour décrire un nom (un objet, une personne, un endroit). Ensuite, **lisez votre description à haute voix**. Les autres groupes vont essayer de deviner le nom dont il s'agit. Attention à l'usage des **pronoms relatifs**.

MODÈLE : la lavande →

—**C'est une plante qu'on trouve en Provence. C'est une plante qui est de couleur violette et qui sent très bon. C'est ce qu'on met dans les sachets.**

Avant d'écouter

9.23 Avant l'explication Voici quelques conversations animées que Claire entend en descendant du TGV. Imaginez pourquoi ces gens s'expliquent. Qu'est-ce qu'ils ont fait ? **Discutez de vos idées** avec vos camarades de classe.

1. «Chérie, ne te fâche pas ! Je vais tout t'expliquer. Le train était en retard. . . »
2. «Écoutez, ce que j'avais l'intention de faire, c'était de vous aider avec vos bagages, monsieur. Je ne suis pas un voleur, moi !»
3. «Pas de panique ! Je vais vous arranger ça ! Oh là là, quelle grande tâche ! Je vais vous acheter une nouvelle chemise. C'est promis !»
4. «Mais, maman, j'ai déjà dépensé l'argent que tu m'avais donné ce matin ! J'avais besoin de quelques bonbons !»

écoutez

L'explication

Claire descend à la gare d'Avignon et attend le prochain train sur le quai. Il fait assez froid et il y a un vent terrible. C'est peut-être le Mistral, pense-t-elle en mettant ses gants et son chapeau de laine. Tout d'un coup, elle entend une voix d'homme. Qui est-ce ? Enfin, quand on parle du loup. . .

Maintenant, **écoutez le dialogue sur votre CD**. Consultez le vocabulaire et lisez les notes culturelles pour mieux comprendre le dialogue, et puis répondez aux questions suivantes.

VOCABULAIRE

Décrire les circonstances

en partie	*partially, in part*
une enquête	*inquiry, investigation*
un reporter	*reporter*
mettre en lumière	*to bring to light, to expose*
gâcher	*to spoil, to ruin*
prétendu(e)	*so-called*
un parafe	*initials*
contrefait (contrefaire)	*forged (to forge)*
la contrefaçon	*forgery*
se déguiser	*to disguise oneself*
un(e) associé(e)	*associate*
la fontaine de jouvence	*fountain of youth*

Culture

Frédéric Mistral était un poète provençal qui a gagné le Prix Nobel en 1904. En son honneur, on a donné le nom de **Mistral** au vent qui souffle très fort en Provence. Mistral a écrit ses poèmes en **provençal**, une variante de la langue occitane qu'on appelle aussi la langue d'oc. Au Moyen Âge, la France était divisée en deux zones linguistiques. Ceux qui parlaient la **langue d'oc** vivaient au sud et ceux qui parlaient la **langue d'oïl** habitaient au nord. «Oc» et «oïl» étaient leurs deux façons de dire «oui». Au cours des siècles, on a supprimé l'enseignement et l'usage des langues et dialectes régionaux (le provençal en Provence, le breton en Bretagne, l'alsacien en Alsace), et on a promu l'usage d'un français standard.

Craignant la perte de leurs cultures régionales et valeurs traditionnelles face à la modernisation et à la **mondialisation** (*globalization*) qui ont marqué les dernières décennies du 20ème siècle, les Français de plusieurs régions ont tenté de ranimer l'intérêt du public pour les langues et les traditions régionales qui commençaient à disparaître. Cet esprit du **régionalisme** a touché la Provence et beaucoup d'autres régions, comme la Bretagne et l'Alsace, où on trouve aujourd'hui des gens qui parlent le dialecte ou la langue régionale et des enseignes (*signs*) publiques et privées en français et en dialecte ou langue régionale.

Pour aller plus loin : CULTURE

ACTIVITÉ J : Lisez un article sur le régionalisme. Consultez votre cahier électronique !

Après avoir ecouté

9.24 Avez-vous compris ? En petits groupes, **répondez** aux questions suivantes.

1. Pourquoi est-ce que Gilles est à la gare d'Avignon ? À propos de quoi a-t-il menti ?
2. Quelle est la réaction de Claire ? Est-ce que vous réagiriez de la même façon ?
3. Quel est le problème avec le marché des livres anciens que Gilles étudie ? Pourquoi est-ce qu'il s'intéresse à ce sujet ?
4. Depuis quand est-ce que Gilles suit Claire ? Pourquoi ? Comment est-ce qu'il a réussi à la suivre sans qu'elle ne le sache ?
5. Pensez-vous que Jean-Louis soit un criminel ? Pourquoi ou pourquoi pas ?

9.25 D'accord ou pas d'accord ? Après avoir écouté le dialogue à la gare d'Avignon, lisez les phrases suivantes et donnez votre opinion. Discutez en petits groupes.

	D'accord	Pas d'accord
1. C'est une coïncidence que Claire rencontre Gilles à la gare d'Avignon.	______	______
2. Gilles a menti à Claire.	______	______
3. Claire s'est fâchée d'entendre l'explication de Gilles.	______	______
4. Gilles est un beau jeune homme blond.	______	______
5. Claire va continuer à aider Gilles dans son enquête.	______	______

s'expliquer

To begin an explanation	Il faut que je m'explique. / Attendez que je m'explique. Patience ! / Du calme ! / Pas de panique ! / Ne paniquez pas ! Vous verrez. / Tout sera clair. / Laissez-moi parler. Laissez-moi vous expliquer. / Je vous dois une explication. Vous allez comprendre pourquoi j'ai agi ainsi. Ce que je vais dire va vous choquer, mais. . .
To explain one's actions	Il fallait / J'ai dû / J'ai voulu (faire quelque chose) parce que. . . Voici / Voilà ce que j'ai fait. . . Ce que j'avais envie / l'intention de faire, c'était de. . . Ce que j'ai décidé de faire, c'était de. . . Je n'avais pas l'intention de vous blesser / impliquer / mettre en danger. Ce qui m'embête, c'est. . . / Ce qui me gêne, c'est. . . J'étais bouleversé(e) / choqué(e) / fâché(e) parce que. . .

Pour aller plus loin : CULTURE

ACTIVITÉ K : Explorez la ville d'Avignon et les sites touristiques provençaux. Consultez votre cahier électronique !

Pour aller plus loin : CINÉMA

ACTIVITÉ L : Regardez les films *Jean de Florette* et *Manon de la Source*, où l'action se déroule en Provence. Consultez votre cahier électronique !

9.26 Que dites-vous ? Qu'est-ce qu'on peut dire pour s'expliquer dans les situations suivantes ? Avec un partenaire, **décidez de ce que vous pouvez dire**.

1. Vous vous asseyez dans le bureau de votre patron pour téléphoner à votre fiancé(e) quand le patron revient brusquement et vous y trouve.
2. Vous n'avez pas fait vos devoirs pour la classe d'histoire aujourd'hui et votre professeur veut savoir pourquoi.
3. Vous êtes en Provence et vous quittez un café sans payer l'addition. Vous avez oublié ! Bien sûr, le patron vous poursuit et veut savoir ce qui s'est passé.
4. Vos amis veulent savoir pourquoi vous ne voulez pas voyager à Saint-Tropez avec eux ce printemps. Vous aviez accepté d'y aller il y a trois mois, mais vous avez changé d'avis !

9.27 Expliquez-vous ! Sur une feuille de papier, **écrivez une phrase** pour décrire une faute que les gens commettent souvent dans notre monde moderne. Ensuite, pliez vos papiers et échangez-les au hasard. Lisez la faute que vous recevez et **circulez** dans la salle de classe en vous expliquant. Vos camarades vont comprendre ou critiquer votre conduite ! Si quelqu'un comprend ce dont il s'agit, faites-lui signer votre papier. Celui avec le plus grand nombre de signatures aura gagné !

MODÈLE : —Excusez-moi d'avoir répondu à mon téléphone portable en classe. Vous allez comprendre pourquoi j'ai agi ainsi. Ma sœur est enceinte et elle va avoir le bébé cet après-midi !

—Ah, bon ? Je comprends tout à fait. Félicitations ! (signature) *ou*

—Mais non ! Ça ne va pas ! Tu aurais dû quitter la salle de classe. (pas de signature)

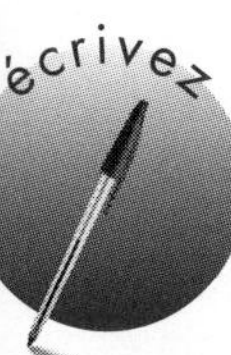

À l'écrit *deuxième étape*

9.28 Un conte de fées moderne Vous voulez vendre votre conte de fées moderne à Canal+, une maison de production cinématographique en France. Révisez votre liste des personnages et des objets du conte (Activité 13) et **imaginez un dialogue** où vous expliquez vos idées au PDG de la compagnie pour rendre le conte plus moderne. Bien sûr, le PDG essaie de diminuer l'importance de vos idées (afin de vous payer moins). Finalement, avec un partenaire, révisez vos dialogues et lisez-les à haute voix.

Épisode 3

«Le devoir m'appelle»

Structures *la voix passive et la voix active*

9.29 Un scénario Claire et Gilles vont au restaurant. Ils discutent comment et pourquoi on vendrait des livres contrefaits. Lisez les propositions suivantes. Dans chaque phrase, dites si le sujet du verbe, qui est en **caractères gras,** est un sujet **actif** (qui fait l'action du verbe) ou un sujet **passif** (qui reçoit l'action du verbe). Pouvez-vous décrire comment fonctionne la voix passive en analysant ces exemples ?

GILLES : Voici le scénario. **Les manuscrits** sont produits par des contrefacteurs. **Ces contrefacteurs** donnent les manuscrits à votre ami Jean-Louis Royer. **Royer** place chaque manuscrit chez un bouquiniste. **Un collectionneur** est identifié par le bouquiniste. **Le manuscrit** est acheté par le collectionneur. **Royer, le bouquiniste et les contrefacteurs** partagent l'argent. **Tout le monde** est bien payé pour son rôle dans l'affaire.

CLAIRE : Et moi, alors ?

GILLES : Bonne question. Cette fois, **le manuscrit** fait du bruit dans le monde académique. **Une étudiante québécoise** commence à s'y intéresser. **Le patron de Royer** désire acquérir le manuscrit. **Royer** est chargé d'acheter le manuscrit au collectionneur et de collaborer avec vous afin de l'authentifier. **Il** fait son travail parce qu'**il** a peur que **son patron** découvre son jeu illégal. **Ce patron** est craint de tous ses employés.

CLAIRE : Alors, **j**'ai été dupée par ce mec (*guy*) ! Mais **il** était si gentil ! Pourquoi est-ce qu'**il** m'a fait ça ? De toute façon, **je** ne vais pas authentifier ce manuscrit. **Monsieur Rolland**, le patron, va tout découvrir.

GILLES : Surtout après la publication de mon article. . .

la voix passive et la voix active

The *passive voice* (**la voix passive**) describes how events happened to someone or something, making the subject of the verb a recipient of the action of the verb rather than an active agent. In French, only verbs that take direct objects can be constructed in the *passive voice*, as the *direct object* becomes the subject of the verb. There are some constructions, therefore, that are common in English but cannot exist in French. Below you will find ways to deal with such situations by avoiding the passive construction in French.

Formation of the passive voice

The **voix passive** is composed of two parts: the verb **être**, conjugated according to the tense desired, plus the *past participle* of the passive verb.

	Actif	*Passif*
présent	Royer vend le manuscrit.	Le manuscrit **est vendu** par Royer.
passé composé	Royer a vendu le manuscrit.	Le manuscrit **a été vendu** par Royer.
imparfait	Royer vendait le manuscrit.	Le manuscrit **était vendu** par Royer.
futur proche	Royer va vendre le manuscrit.	Le manuscrit **va être vendu** par Royer.
futur	Royer vendra le manuscrit.	Le manuscrit **sera vendu** par Royer.
futur antérieur	Royer aura vendu le manuscrit.	Le manuscrit **aura été vendu** par Royer.
conditionnel	Royer vendrait le manuscrit.	Le manuscrit **serait vendu** par Royer.
subjonctif	Il faut que Royer vende le manuscrit.	Il faut que le manuscrit **soit vendu** par Royer.

- Remember that the *past participle*, which acts like an adjective in a passive construction, must always agree in number and gender with the subject of the verb: **les manuscrits** sont produit**s.**
- Use the *preposition* **par** to indicate the agent of an action: Les manuscrits sont produits **par** des contrefacteurs.
- Use the *preposition* **de** to indicate the agent of a state or emotion: Ce patron est craint **de** tous ses employés.
- In a *negative* construction, place the **ne. . . pas** (or other negative expression) around the verb **être**, following the same rules as you normally would for each tense: Les manuscrits **ne** sont **pas** produits par des contrefacteurs.

Uses of the passive voice

The *passive voice* is used much less frequently in French than in American English and often sounds awkward to native speakers. You should usually try to avoid the *passive voice* in written French unless you intend to make your subject a passive one. Here are some ways to turn a passive construction into an *active* one:

- Turn *the agent* of the verb (indicated by **par** or **de**) into the subject:

  Les manuscrits *sont produits par des contrefacteurs.* →
  Des contrefacteurs produisent les manuscrits.

  Ce patron *est craint de tous ses employées.* →
  Tous les employées craignent ce patron.

- Use the *general subject* **on**:

  Royer *est chargé* d'acheter le manuscrit. →
  On charge Royer d'acheter le manuscrit.

- Use a *reflexive verb*:

  Les manuscrits *sont vendus* facilement par les bouquinistes. →
  Les manuscrits **se vendent** facilement chez les bouquinistes.

Pour aller plus loin : LITTÉRATURE

ACTIVITÉ M : Lisez la fable «Le Chien et le Loup» de Jean de La Fontaine. Consultez votre cahier électronique !

9.30 Le loup et le chien

Gilles essaie de rassurer Claire et d'expliquer pourquoi son ami aurait fait ce crime s'il avait déjà un bon emploi chez Monsieur Rolland. Il lui raconte la fable du loup et du chien. **Récrivez** les phrases passives **à la voix active.** Ensuite, discutez et expliquez la morale de la fable.

MODÈLE : Le chien **est regardé** par le loup. →
Le loup regarde le chien.

1. Le chien, qui était gros, **a été bien nourri** par son maître.
2. Le loup, qui était mince, **n'a pas été nourri**.
3. Un jour, le chien **est vu** par le loup.
4. Une question **est posée** au chien par le loup : «Pourquoi est-ce que tu es si robuste et si content ?»
5. La situation **est expliquée** au loup par le chien.
6. Le chien **est caressé** par le maître, et il **est aimé** de toute la famille.
7. Tous les jours, des os (*bones*) **sont donnés** au chien par le maître.
8. Le loup **est invité** par le chien à vivre avec lui dans la maison du maître.
9. Le collier qui attache le chien à la maison **est vu** par le loup.
10. Une autre question **est posée** par le loup : «Qu'est-ce là ?»
11. Une explication **est donnée** par le chien.
12. La vie du chien **est contrôlée** par le maître.
13. L'offre de rester à la maison **est rejetée** par le loup.
14. La liberté **sera toujours aimée** du loup.
15. Le chien **sera toujours attaché** à la maison.
16. La forêt **sera toujours habitée** par le loup.

9.31 L'article de Gilles

Gilles explique qu'il va essayer d'écrire un article de fond qui exposera les contrefacteurs. Dans les articles d'actualité, il faut parfois employer la voix passive. Gilles ouvre son cahier où il a déjà commencé à écrire quelques notes pour son article. **Formez des phrases** en mettant les verbes **à la voix passive** selon le temps de verbe indiqué.

1. (*présent*) Le public français / impressionner / par les ventes du marché des livres anciens
2. (*passé*) Un bouquiniste / tuer / il y a deux semaines
3. (*présent*) Les assassins / ne. . . pas, connaître / de la police
4. (*passé*) Des livres contrefaits / vendre / par plusieurs bouquinistes
5. (*futur*) Un lien / établir / entre le meurtre et la contrefaçon
6. (*conditionnel*) La maison de l'antiquaire Rolland / mettre / au centre de la controverse par un employé infidèle
7. (*passé*) L'employé / payer / pour son rôle dans la vente des manuscrits contrefaits
8. (*subjonctif*) Il est nécessaire que cette affaire / résoudre / par la police

9.32 Les dates et les lieux Gilles doit partir pour Paris, mais il donne à Claire une copie de ses notes sur l'affaire du faux manuscrit de Laclos. Il lui demande de les lire et de le contacter si elle pense à d'autres événements importants. **Faites des phrases, passives** ou **actives** selon votre goût, pour décrire ce qui s'est passé à chaque moment suivant. Vous pouvez parler des événements indiqués entre parenthèses ou ajouter d'autres événements dont vous vous souvenez !

1. août 2003 à la Nouvelle-Orléans (la rencontre de Claire et Jean-Louis)
2. septembre 2003 à Paris (la vente du manuscrit à Monsieur Thibodeau)
3. octobre 2003 à Dakar (l'achat du manuscrit)
4. octobre 2003 en Suisse (la lecture du manuscrit, la découverte de l'anachronisme)
5. novembre 2003 à Paris (la publication de l'article de Gilles)

9.33 Le malchanceux Imaginez une personne très malchanceuse à qui il arrive toujours de malheureuses aventures. **Faites une liste de dix événements** qui lui arrivent et comparez-la avec celles de vos camarades de classe.

MODÈLE : Ses croissants sont dévorés par son chien.
Son ordinateur est cassé par son secrétaire.

Claire et Gilles se séparent à la gare après leur dîner ensemble, et Claire prend le train à Aix-en-Provence où elle s'installe dans son hôtel. Il est tard, et il n'y a pas de messages pour elle à la réception. Le lendemain matin, elle se lève et essaie encore de contacter le Professeur Thuillier, mais sans succès. Le soir, elle branche son ordinateur portable et trouve le message suivant. . .

«Le devoir m'appelle»

```
   À :  Claire Plouffe
  De :  P.F. Thuillier
Date :  21/10/03
 Réf :  le devoir m'appelle
```

Chère Mademoiselle Plouffe,

Je viens de rentrer à mon hôtel où la réceptionniste m'a donné les messages que vous m'aviez laissés. J'ai été absent pendant toute la journée, et, malheureusement, je dois partir demain matin de très bonne heure.° Pas moyen de faire autrement.° Une affaire administrative me fait rentrer à

early
there's no way out of it

duty calls Québec. Le devoir m'appelle.° On n'aura donc pas le temps de se voir cette semaine. C'est dommage que vous soyez venue à Aix-en-Provence le jour où je dois partir pour Québec, mais je vous conseille de rester ici encore quelque temps et de profiter des sources historiques aux Archives coloniales.

J'ai compris, d'après ce que vous m'aviez dit dans votre dernier message, que vous aviez réussi à retrouver le manuscrit perdu de Laclos et que vous croyiez y avoir trouvé un anachronisme. Êtes-vous sûre de ne pas vous tromper° ? N'est-il pas possible que Laclos ait prévu,° par une coïncidence bizarre, un événement° historique inévitable et imminent ? Si j'étais à votre place, je relirais le texte et je me renseignerais° mieux sur l'événement en question. N'abandonnez pas votre projet maintenant. N'oubliez pas que dans la fiction, tout est possible !

to be mistaken
to foresee, anticipate
event
to inform oneself

Encore une fois, je suis désolé de ne pouvoir vous rencontrer afin de discuter plus longuement de votre situation. Soyez sans crainte,° mademoiselle, je vous assure que nous nous verrons cet hiver. J'imagine que vous rentrerez au Québec pour les fêtes de Noël,° et je m'engage à passer un après-midi avec vous. Et, je serai toujours heureux de répondre à vos demandes de renseignements électroniquement. Vive la technologie !

fear
Christmas holidays

En espérant que vous continuerez à faire des progrès dans vos recherches, et en attendant de vous lire, je vous prie d'accepter l'expression de mes sentiments les plus cordiaux.

P.F. Thuillier
Directeur de la Recherche et des Études Littéraires
L'Université de Sainte-Foy

Après avoir lu

9.34 D'accord ou pas d'accord ? Après avoir lu le message ci-dessus, lisez les phrases suivantes et **donnez vos opinions personnelles**. Discutez en petits groupes.

	D'accord	Pas d'accord
1. Professeur Thuillier est obligé de rentrer à Québec.	_______	_______
2. Il espère voir Claire le lendemain matin avant son départ.	_______	_______
3. Il lui conseille d'abandonner son sujet de thèse.	_______	_______
4. Laclos est peut-être l'auteur du manuscrit.	_______	_______
5. Claire va rester à Aix-en-Provence et continuer ses recherches.	_______	_______

exprimer une obligation

Making a promise
Je vous le promets. / Je promets de (faire quelque chose).
Je m'engage à (faire quelque chose). / Je vous assure que je le ferai.
Je le ferai. / Je n'oublierai pas. / Je serai là.
Vous pouvez compter sur moi. C'est promis.
Je vous le jure. / Je vous donne ma parole.
Soyez sans crainte. / Je tiens à le faire sans délai.

Expressing obligation
Il faut que je... / Je dois absolument... / Je suis obligé(e) de...
J'ai promis de... / Je suis tenu(e) de... / Je ferai tout ce qu'il faudra...
Je suis dans l'incapacité de... / Je ne peux pas me dégager de mes obligations.
Impossible de lui refuser ce service. / Pas moyen de faire autrement.
Le devoir m'appelle. / C'est obligatoire. / Impossible d'annuler.
Je suis votre obligé(e). / Je vous suis reconnaissant(e).

Langue

Vous rappelez-vous l'usage du verbe irrégulier **devoir** ?

- **devoir** + *objet direct* = une dette à payer (*to owe*) : Je dois dix euros à mon frère.
- **devoir** + *infinitif* = une obligation ou une nécessité (*to have to*) : Tu dois partir ce soir. Il a dû partir ce matin.
- **devoir** + *infinitif* = une probabilité (*must be, probably*) : Il doit être fou ! Tu as dû te tromper !
- **devoir** + *infinitif* = une intention ou une hypothèse (*to be supposed to*) : L'article doit paraître dimanche. Il devait parler avec son patron.

9.35 Situations Que diriez-vous dans les situations suivantes pour exprimer votre obligation auprès des gens suivants ? Avec un partenaire, **décidez de ce que vous pourriez dire**.

1. Votre tante vous avait présenté à son patron, et à cause de cela vous avez reçu une offre d'emploi dans l'entreprise.
2. Vos amis vous invitent à dîner parce que vous avez oublié votre portefeuille.
3. Votre patron vous donnera une promotion si vous acceptez de travailler le week-end.
4. Vos parents vous demandent de les aider à peindre leur maison, et vous acceptez même si vous préféreriez sortir avec vos copains.
5. Votre fiancé(e) n'aime pas votre chien et ne veut pas être obligé(e) de le promener.
6. Vos voisins ont surveillé votre maison pendant votre voyage en Provence, et vous avez promis de leur préparer un vrai repas provençal à votre retour !

Culture

La **cuisine provençale** est caractérisée d'une influence italienne et du grand nombre de produits frais qu'on peut trouver dans cette région ensoleillée. Viandes et légumes peuvent être cuits **à la provençale**, c'est-à-dire avec de l'ail, des olives, des tomates, de l'huile d'olive et des herbes de Provence. Les plats spécialisés de cette région sont **la bouillabaisse** (une soupe aux fruits de mer), **la ratatouille** (un râgout de tomates et d'aubergines), **la pissaladière** (une pizza sans tomates et sans fromage faite avec des oignons caramélisés, des olives et des anchois) et **la salade niçoise** (une salade composée entre autres d'anchois et d'œufs durs).

Pour aller plus loin : CULTURE

ACTIVITÉ N : Apprenez un peu plus sur la cuisine provençale. Consultez votre cahier électronique !

la Provence

Qu'est-ce que Catherine pense de la diversité régionale en France ? Regardez la vidéo et consultez votre cahier d'activités !

9.36 Promesses et obligations Souvent, dans les contes de fées, il y a des personnages qui font des promesses ou qui sont obligés de faire quelque chose. En petits groupes, **pensez à quatre personnages féeriques** connus qui font des promesses ou qui ont des obligations à tenir. Écrivez leurs promesses ou obligations sur une feuille de papier, sans nommer le personnage. Ensuite, échangez votre papier avec celui d'un autre groupe et **essayez de deviner les noms des personnages** !

MODÈLE : —C'est une jeune fille qui s'engage à apporter des provisions chez sa grand-mère. Elle doit traverser la forêt toute seule.
—C'est le Petit Chaperon rouge !

9.37 Les contes de fées mélangés Avez-vous un personnage préféré (bon ou méchant) de contes de fée, de films de dessins animés ou de bandes dessinées de super-héros ? Sur une feuille de papier, **écrivez le nom** de ce personnage féerique et une phrase pour décrire **son rôle** dans le conte. N'y mettez pas votre nom. Pliez et échangez vos papiers au hasard. Puis, **circulez** dans la classe en jouant le rôle du personnage que vous avez reçu. Les autres vont essayer de deviner qui vous êtes. Faites signer votre papier par chaque personne qui devine bien. La personne qui a reçu le plus grand nombre de signatures gagne !

MODÈLE : Vous écrivez : La Bête (de *La Belle et la Bête*) — Il est méchant et maladroit. Il crie beaucoup et a de mauvaises manières. Mais à la fin, il redevient un prince.

Pour aller plus loin : CULTURE

ACTIVITÉ O : Voulez-vous savoir comment écrire une lettre d'affaires ou un curriculum vitae en français ? Consultez votre cahier électronique !

9.38 Des héros modernes En petits groupes, imaginez un héros ou une héroïne moderne dont l'histoire pourrait servir à enseigner aux enfants d'aujourd'hui le fonctionnement du capitalisme et des affaires. **Décrivez votre héros ou héroïne** du monde des affaires (faites le portrait physique et moral) et **faites une liste de ses obligations**. Comparez votre personnage avec ceux de vos camarades de classe.

À l'écrit *troisième étape*

9.39 Un conte de fées moderne Le PDG de Canal+ s'intéresse à votre idée de faire un film adapté d'un conte de fées moderne. **Écrivez une lettre** au PDG dans laquelle vous redécrivez votre idée pour un conte de fées moderne (révisez vos Activités 13 et 28). N'oubliez pas de préciser quand le manuscrit sera terminé, quand et où le film sera tourné (*filmed*) et le type de publicité qui sera diffusée. Échangez vos lettres (par courriel, si vous voulez !) et offrez une réponse à votre camarade de classe avec quelques corrections possibles et vos commentaires sur son projet.

Dénouement

Activités de révision

9.40 À vous de parler **Pensez à une réponse** à chaque question suivante. En petits groupes, partagez vos réponses avec les autres et expliquez pourquoi. Ensuite, **imaginez quatre à six autres catégories**. Échangez vos catégories avec un autre groupe et parlez-en de la même façon ! Attention à l'usage des **pronoms relatifs**.

1. Quel est l'endroit où vous aimez vous reposer quand vous êtes stressé(e)?
2. Qui est le professeur avec qui vous aimeriez dîner?
3. Quel est le moment de la journée que vous aimez le plus?
4. Comment serait le voyage dont vous rêvez?
5. Qui est l'acteur ou l'actrice que vous aimeriez rencontrer?

9.41 Devinez qui c'est ! En petits groupes, **pensez à une personne** que tout le monde connaît. Écrivez quelques phrases pour **décrire la vie** de cette personne, et utilisez **la voix passive** dans chaque description ! Mettez vos phrases au tableau. Les autres groupes vont essayer de deviner la personne. Ils peuvent poser des questions supplémentaires !

MODÈLE : —Il a été nommé un des hommes les plus riches du monde. Il est chef d'une entreprise de technologie. Il a été accusé d'avoir restreint la concurrence.

—C'est Bill Gates !

Avant de lire *Lettres de mon moulin*

9.42 Vivre libre ! Imaginez comment seraient vos vies si vous n'aviez pas les contraintes des factures (*bills*) à payer ou du travail à faire. Tout est gratuit (*free*), tout le monde reçoit ce dont il a besoin pour vivre confortablement, et tout le monde est libre de faire ce qu'il/elle veut. Comment serait votre vie ? Que feriez-vous de votre temps ? Quels seraient les inconvénients de ce système ? **Discutez de vos idées** en petits groupes. Attention à l'usage de la **voix passive** et des **pronoms relatifs**.

Le moulin de Daudet à Fontvieille, en Provence.

9.43 Premières impressions Lisez le conte «La Chèvre de M. Seguin», tiré des *Lettres de mon moulin* d'Alphonse Daudet, sans essayer de comprendre chaque mot. Après votre première lecture du texte, **répondez** aux questions. Ensuite, relisez le texte une deuxième fois, plus attentivement.

1. Qui parle ? Un petit garçon ? Un homme ? Un vieillard ?
2. À qui parle le narrateur ? Quelle est la profession du destinataire du conte ?
3. À quelle période se passe cette histoire ? Au présent ? Au passé ? À l'avenir ?
4. Où se passe l'histoire ?
5. Que veut la chèvre de Monsieur Seguin ? Que veut Monsieur Seguin ?
6. Que devient la chèvre à la fin de l'histoire ?

lisez

Lettres de mon moulin : «La Chèvre de M. Seguin»

Ce conte vient du recueil d'Alphonse Daudet, Lettres de mon moulin. *Dans ce recueil de contes provençaux, écrit en Provence au 19ème siècle, Daudet cherche dans le folklore de la région des histoires simples et touchantes qu'il raconte pour son public «moderne» — le public sophistiqué de la métropole parisienne. Dans ce conte capricieux, Daudet écrit à un poète imaginaire à Paris afin de le persuader des dangers de la vie bohème de l'auteur indépendant. En même temps, il dépeint avec compassion le conflit essentiel de l'homme moderne : vendre sa liberté pour un peu de sécurité économique ou sacrifier sa tranquillité d'esprit pour être indépendant et réaliser ses rêves. Autrement dit, peut-on vivre libre dans une société capitaliste où il faut de l'argent pour bien vivre ? Ce conte nous présente ce dilemme en toute sa complexité psychologique et se termine avec ambiguïté. Veut-il nous persuader qu'il ne faut pas poursuivre la vie dont nous rêvons, ou veut-il simplement nous rappeler les dangers d'une telle décision ?*

■ **Alphonse Daudet**

«La Chèvre de M. Seguin»

columnist
audacity
clothes with holes/pants

Tu seras bien toujours le même, mon pauvre Gringoire ! Comment ! on t'offre une place de chroniqueur° dans un bon journal de Paris et tu as l'aplomb° de refuser. . . Mais regarde-toi, malheureux garçon ! Regarde ce pourpoint° troué, ces chausses° en déroute, cette face maigre qui crie la faim. Voilà pourtant où t'a conduit ta passion des belles rimes ! Voilà ce que t'ont valu dix ans de loyaux services dans les pages du sire Apollo. . . Est-ce que tu n'as pas honte, à la fin ?

unit of money/meal/a good restaurant
feather pen/bar
as you please

Fais-toi donc chroniqueur, imbécile ! fais-toi chroniqueur ! Tu gagneras de beaux écus° à la rose, tu auras ton couvert° chez Brébant,° et tu pourras te montrer les jours de première avec une plume° neuve à ta barrette°. . .

Non ? Tu ne veux pas ? Tu prétends rester libre à ta guise° jusqu'au bout. . . Eh bien, écoute un peu l'histoire de *La Chèvre de M. Seguin*. Tu verras ce que l'on gagne à vouloir vivre libre.

M. Seguin n'avait jamais eu de bonheur avec ses chèvres.

Il les perdait toutes de la même façon; un beau matin, elles cassaient° leur corde, s'en allaient dans la montagne, et là-haut le loup les mangeait. Ni les caresses de leur maître, ni la peur du loup, rien ne les retenait.° C'étaient, paraît-il, des chèvres indépendantes, voulant à tout prix° le grand air et la liberté.

to break
to hold back
at any cost

Le brave° M. Seguin, qui ne comprenait rien au caractère de ses bêtes, était consterné.° Il disait : «C'est fini ; les chèvres s'ennuient chez moi, je n'en garderai pas une.»

good
dismayed

Cependant, il ne se découragea pas, et, après avoir perdu six chèvres de la même manière, il en acheta une septième ; seulement, cette fois, il eut soin de la prendre toute jeune, pour qu'elle s'habituât mieux à demeurer chez lui.

Ah ! Gringoire, qu'elle était jolie la petite chèvre de M. Seguin ! qu'elle était jolie avec ses yeux doux, sa barbiche° de sous-officier, ses sabots° noirs et luisants, ses cornes zébrées et ses longs poils° blancs qui lui faisaient une houppelande° ! C'était presque aussi charmant que le cabri° d'Esméralda — tu te rappelles, Gringoire ? — et puis, docile, caressante, se laissant traire sans bouger, sans mettre son pied dans l'écuelle.° Un amour de petite chèvre. . .

goatee/ hoofs
hair
greatcoat/kid, baby goat
bowl

M. Seguin avait derrière sa maison un clos entouré d'aubépines.° C'est là qu'il mit la nouvelle pensionnaire. Il l'attacha à un pieu° au plus bel endroit du pré,° en ayant soin de lui laisser beaucoup de corde, et de temps en temps il venait voir si elle était bien. La chèvre se trouvait très heureuse et broutait° l'herbe de si bon cœur que M. Seguin était ravi. «Enfin, pensait le pauvre homme, en voilà une qui ne s'ennuiera pas chez moi !»

hawthorns
stake
meadow
to graze

M. Seguin se trompait, sa chèvre s'ennuya.

Un jour, elle se dit en regardant la montagne : «Comme on doit être bien là-haut ! Quel plaisir de gambader° dans la bruyère, sans cette maudite longe qui vous écorche° le cou !. . . C'est bon pour l'âne ou le bœuf de brouter dans un clos !. . . Les chèvres, il leur faut du large.»

to gambol, bound
to chafe

À partir de ce moment, l'herbe du clos lui parut fade. L'ennui lui vint. Elle maigrit, son lait se fit rare. C'était pitié de la voir tirer tout le jour sur sa longe, la tête tournée du côté de la montagne, la narine ouverte, en faisant *Mé !*. . . tristement.

M. Seguin s'apercevait bien que sa chèvre avait quelque chose, mais il ne savait pas ce que c'était. . .

Un matin, comme il achevait de la traire,° la chèvre se retourna et lui dit dans son patois° : «Écoutez, monsieur Seguin, je me languis° chez vous, laissez-moi aller dans la montagne.

to milk
jargon, lingo/ to languish

—Ah ! mon Dieu !. . . Elle aussi !» cria M. Seguin stupéfait, et du coup il laissa tomber son écuelle; puis, s'asseyant dans l'herbe à côté de sa chèvre : «Comment, Blanquette, tu veux me quitter !» Et Blanquette répondit : «Oui, monsieur Seguin.»

—Est-ce que l'herbe te manque ici ?

—Oh ! non, monsieur Seguin.

—Tu es peut-être attachée de trop court. Veux-tu que j'allonge la corde ?

—Ce n'est pas la peine, monsieur Seguin.

—Alors, qu'est-ce qu'il te faut ? qu'est-ce que tu veux ?

—Je veux aller dans la montagne, monsieur Seguin.

—Mais, malheureuse, tu ne sais pas qu'il y a le loup dans la montagne. . . Que feras-tu quand il viendra ?

—Je lui donnerai des coups de corne, monsieur Seguin.

—Le loup se moque bien de tes cornes. Il m'a mangé des biques autrement encornées que toi. . . Tu sais bien, la pauvre vieille Renaude qui était ici l'an dernier ? une maîtresse chèvre, forte et méchante comme un bouc.° Elle s'est battue avec le loup toute la nuit. . . puis, le matin, le loup l'a mangée.

—Pécaïre° ! Pauvre Renaude !. . . Ça ne fait rien, monsieur Seguin, laissez-moi aller dans la montagne !

—Bonté divine !. . . dit M. Seguin ; mais qu'est-ce qu'on leur fait donc à mes chèvres ? Encore une que le loup va me manger. . . Eh bien, non. . . je te sauverai malgré toi, coquine° ! et de peur que tu ne rompes ta corde, je vais t'enfermer dans l'étable°, et tu y resteras toujours.»

Là-dessus, M. Seguin emporte la chèvre dans une étable toute noire, dont il ferma la porte à double tour.° Malheureusement, il avait oublié la fenêtre, et à peine eut-il le dos tourné, que la petite s'en alla. . .

Tu ris, Gringoire ? Parbleu ! je crois bien ; tu es du parti des chèvres, toi, contre ce bon M. Seguin. . . Nous allons voir si tu riras tout à l'heure.

Quand la chèvre blanche arriva dans la montagne, ce fut un ravissement général. Jamais les vieux sapins n'avaient rien vu d'aussi joli. On la reçut comme une petite reine.° Les châtaigniers° se baissaient jusqu'à terre pour la caresser du bout de leurs branches. Les genêts° d'or s'ouvraient sur son passage, et sentaient bon tant qu'ils pouvaient. Toute la montagne lui fit fête.

Tu penses, Gringoire, si notre chèvre était heureuse ! Plus de corde, plus de pieu. . . rien qui l'empechât de gambader, de brouter à sa guise. . . C'est là qu'il y en avait de l'herbe ! jusque par-dessus les cornes, mon cher !. . . Et quelle herbe ! Savoureuse, fine, dentelée,° faite de mille plantes. . . C'était bien autre chose que le gazon du clos. Et les fleurs donc !. . . De grandes campanules° bleues, des digitales° de pourpre à longs calices,° toute une forêt de fleurs sauvages débordants de sucs capiteux° !. . .

La chèvre blanche, à moitié saoule,° se vautrait° là-dedans les jambes en l'air et roulait le long des talus,° pêle-mêle avec les feuilles tombées et les châtaignes. . . Puis, tout à coup, elle se redressait d'un bond sur ses pattes.° Hop ! la voilà partie, la tête en avant, à travers les maquis° et les buissières, tantôt sur un pic,° tantôt au fond d'un ravin, là-haut, en bas partout. . . On aurait dit qu'il y avait dix chèvres de M. Seguin dans la montagne.

C'est qu'elle n'avait peur de rien, la Blanquette. Elle franchissait° d'un saut de grands torrents qui l'éclaboussaient° au passage de poussière humide et d'écume. Alors, toute ruisselante,° elle allait s'étendre sur quelque roche plate et se faisait sécher par le soleil. . . Une fois, s'avançant au bord d'un plateau, une fleur de cytise° aux dents, elle aperçut en bas, tout en bas dans la plaine, la maison de M. Seguin avec le clos derrière. Cela la fit rire aux larmes. «Que c'est petit ! dit-elle ; comment ai-je pu tenir là-dedans ?»

Pauvrette ! de se voir si haut perchée, elle se croyait au moins aussi grande que le monde. . .

En somme, ce fut une bonne journée pour la chèvre de M. Seguin. Vers le milieu du jour, en courant de droite et de gauche, elle tomba dans une troupe de chamois° en train de croquer° une lambrusque° à belles dents. Notre petite coureuse en robe blanche fit sensation. On lui donna la meilleure place à la lambrusque, et tous ces messieurs furent très galants. . . Il paraît même — ceci doit rester entre nous, Gringoire — qu'un jeune chamois à pelage° noir eut la bonne fortune de plaire à Blanquette. Les deux amoureux s'égarèrent° parmi le bois une heure ou deux, et si tu veux savoir ce qu'ils dirent, va le demander aux sources bavardes qui courent invisibles dans la mousse.°

goat · *too bad* · *scoundrel* · *stable* · *two turns* · *queen/chestnut tree* · *broom* · *lacy* · *types of flowers* · *heady sap* · *drunk/ to wallow* · *slopes* · *paws* · *bush* · *peak* · *to cross* · *to splash* · *dripping* · *type of flower* · *type of deer/to munch on/ wild vine* · *animal coat* · *to wander off* · *moss*

Tout à coup le vent fraîchit. La montagne devint violette ; c'était le soir... «Déjà !» dit la petite chèvre, et elle s'arrêta fort étonnée.

En bas, les champs étaient noyés de brume.° Le clos de M. Seguin disparaissait dans le brouillard, et de la maisonnette on ne voyait plus que le toit avec un peu de fumée. Elle écouta les clochettes d'un troupeau° qu'on ramenait, et se sentit l'âme toute triste... Un gerfaut,° qui rentrait, la frôla° de ses ailes en passant. Elle tressaillit°... puis ce fut un hurlement° dans la montagne : «Hou ! hou !»

drowned in fog
herd
falcon/ to graze
to quiver/howl

Elle pensa au loup, de tout le jour la folle n'y avait pas pensé... Au même moment une trompe sonna bien loin dans la vallée. C'était ce bon M. Seguin qui tentait un dernier effort.

«Hou ! hou !... faisait le loup.

—Reviens ! reviens !... criait la trompe.

Blanquette eut envie de revenir ; mais en se rappelant le pieu, la corde, la haie° du clos, elle pensa que maintenant elle ne pouvait plus se faire à cette vie, et qu'il valait mieux rester.

hedge

La trompe ne sonnait plus...

La chèvre entendit derrière elle un bruit de feuilles. Elle se retourna et vit dans l'ombre deux oreilles courtes, toutes droites, avec deux yeux qui reluisaient°... C'était le loup.

to gleam

Enorme, immobile, assis sur son train de derrière, il était là regardant la petite chèvre blanche et la dégustant° par avance. Comme il savait bien qu'il la mangerait, le loup ne se pressait pas ; seulement, quand elle se retourna, il se mit à rire méchamment. «Ha ! ha ! la petite chèvre de M. Seguin» ; et il passa sa grosse langue rouge sur ses babines d'amadou.°

to taste
cajoling mouth, chops

Blanquette se sentit perdue... Un moment, en se rappelant l'histoire de la vieille Renaude, qui s'était battue toute la nuit pour être mangée le matin, elle se dit qu'il vaudrait peut-être mieux se laisser manger tout de suite ; puis, s'étant ravisée,° elle tomba en garde, la tête basse et la corne en avant, comme une brave chèvre de M. Seguin qu'elle était... Non pas qu'elle eût l'espoir de tuer le loup — les chèvres ne tuent pas le loup — mais seulement pour voir si elle pourrait tenir aussi longtemps que la Renaude...

to change one's mind

Alors le monstre s'avança, et les petites cornes entrèrent en danse.

Ah ! la brave petite chevrette, comme elle y allait de bon cœur ! Plus de dix fois, je ne mens pas, Gringoire, elle força le loup à reculer° pour reprendre haleine.° Pendant ces trêves° d'une minute, la gourmande cueillait° en hâte encore un brin° de sa chère herbe ; puis elle retournait au combat, la bouche pleine... Cela dura toute la nuit. De temps en temps la chèvre de M. Seguin regardait les étoiles danser dans le ciel clair, et elle se disait : «Oh ! pourvu que je tienne jusqu'à l'aube... »

to pull back
to get your breath back/truce, respite
gather, cut down/blade of grass

L'une après l'autre, les étoiles s'éteignirent. Blanquette redoubla de coups de cornes, le loup de coups de dents... Une lueur° pâle parut dans l'horizon... Le chant du coq enroué° monta d'une métairie.°

glimmer, flash
hoarse/farm

«Enfin !» dit la pauvre bête, qui n'attendait plus que le jour pour mourir ; et elle s'allongea par terre dans sa belle fourrure° blanche toute tachée de sang°...

fur
bloodstained

Alors le loup se jeta sur la petite chèvre et la mangea.

Adieu, Gringoire ! L'histoire que tu as entendue n'est pas un conte de mon invention. Si jamais tu viens en Provence, nos ménagères° te parleront souvent de *la cabro de moussu Seguin, que se battègue touto la neui emé lou loup, e piei lou matin lou loup la mangé.*

housewives

Tu m'entends bien, Gringoire : *E piei lou matin lou loup la mangé.*

Après avoir lu

Pour aller plus loin : CULTURE

ACTIVITÉ P : Apprenez un peu plus sur la vie et l'œuvre d'Alphonse Daudet. Consultez votre cahier électronique !

9.44 Avez-vous compris ? En petits groupes, **discutez de vos réponses** aux questions suivantes.

1. Qui sont les trois personnages principaux de cette histoire ? Décrivez le caractère de chaque personnage.
2. Pourquoi est-ce que Blanquette décide de s'échapper vers la montagne ? À votre avis, est-ce que c'était une bonne décision ou une mauvaise décision ? Pourquoi ?
3. Est-ce que le personnage du loup est stéréotypique dans ce conte ? Pourquoi ou pourquoi pas ? Comparez-le à d'autres loups fictifs dans les contes populaires que vous connaissez.
4. Quelle est la morale du conte ? Que pensez-vous de cette morale ? Est-ce que la morale aurait été différente si Blanquette avait survécu à la fin ? Comment ?
5. À la fin du conte, le narrateur écrit une phrase en langue provençale. Pouvez-vous traduire cette phrase en français ?

9.45 D'accord ou pas d'accord ? Après avoir lu le conte de Daudet, lisez les phrases suivantes et **donnez votre opinion**. Discutez de vos réponses en petits groupes.

	D'accord	Pas d'accord
1. Le narrateur parle à quelqu'un qu'il ne connaît pas bien.	_______	_______
2. Toutes les chèvres de M. Seguin se sont échappées de la ferme.	_______	_______
3. La nouvelle chèvre est assez contente chez M. Seguin.	_______	_______
4. La chèvre voulait tuer le loup.	_______	_______
5. Blanquette était une chèvre très courageuse.	_______	_______

9.46 Analyse littéraire Examinez ce texte de près. Répondez aux questions suivantes et **discutez de vos réponses** en classe.

1. Quel est le ton du début du texte où le narrateur parle à son ami-poète «Gringoire» ? Qu'est-ce qui contribue à ce ton (le vocabulaire, le style d'écriture, la forme du texte, les temps de verbe, la ponctuation) ?
2. Il y a beaucoup de description dans ce conte, surtout quand le narrateur raconte les activités de Blanquette après sa fuite. Qu'est-ce que l'auteur décrit ? À quoi sert cette description ? Quelle est l'effet sur le lecteur ?
3. Quel temps domine dans le récit du conte de la chèvre de M. Seguin ? Quel est l'effet de l'usage de ce temps (un sens d'urgence, la nostalgie, la possibilité ou l'impossibilité, la certitude ou l'incertitude, l'orgueil, etc.) ? Y a-t-il un moment où le temps de verbe change dramatiquement ? Quand ? Quel en est l'effet ?
4. Pourquoi est-ce que l'auteur écrit la dernière phrase en provençal et pas en français ? Quel est l'effet de répéter la dernière partie de la phrase à la fin du conte ?

Synthèses

Réfléchissons à la culture

Voici quelques éléments de la culture provençale que vous avez étudiés dans ce chapitre. En petits groupes, **répondez** aux questions et **discutez de vos impressions** avec vos camarades.

la langue provençale   la mondialisation   les produits régionaux

1. Définissez ou décrivez chaque élément.
2. Pourquoi la langue provençale est-elle toujours importante à cette culture ? Y a-t-il un phénomène historique ou social qui explique sa renaissance récente ? Comparez-la aux langues, dialectes et accents différents qu'on trouve aux États-Unis. Y a-t-il un mouvement de protéger et enseigner l'anglais tel qu'il est parlé dans le sud des États-Unis ? Pourquoi ou pourquoi pas ?
3. Quel est le rapport entre ces trois éléments de la culture provençale ? Les petits villages sont-ils vraiment touchés par les tendances économiques mondiales ?
4. En ce qui concerne les produits régionaux, en général, est-ce qu'ils sont populaires parce qu'ils sont les meilleurs produits, ou y a-t-il une raison géographique, historique ou sociale qui explique leur popularité ?

la Provence

Pour Catherine, qu'est-ce que ça veut dire «être Française» ? Regardez la vidéo et consultez votre cahier d'activités !

9.48 À débattre Lisez les questions suivantes et **discutez** en groupes. Si possible, parlez de vos expériences personnelles relatives aux questions.

1. **Entre chien et loup.** Jean Cocteau, un auteur et cinématographe français, a écrit une fois une lettre dans laquelle il préconise (*advocates*) un équilibre entre la sécurité et la liberté. Il termine la lettre en disant : «Mon conseil à la jeunesse est de vivre entre chien et loup». Que pensez-vous de son conseil ? Ne devrait-on pas prendre des risques afin de réaliser ses rêves ? Ne pourrait-on pas vivre en liberté totale ? Que pensez-vous ?
2. **Le régionalisme contre la mondialisation.** En Europe, à l'aube de l'expansion de l'Union européenne, on est très conscient de l'importance de la mondialisation, du marché économique global, au succès de son pays. Pourtant, il y a un contre-courant de cette pensée. On dit qu'en devenant esclaves de l'économie mondiale, un peuple perdra son caractère individuel et ses traditions culturelles uniques. Les petits commerçants, les artisans et les fermiers perdront leurs clients locaux à de grandes entreprises multinationales. Dans les régions où il n'y a pas de grand centre urbain ou de développement industriel, le mode de vie traditionnel disparaîtra. Qu'en pensez-vous ?

Pour aller plus loin : CINÉMA

ACTIVITÉ Q : Regardez un des films basés sur les romans de l'auteur provençal Marcel Pagnol : *La Gloire de mon père* ou *Le Château de ma mère*. Consultez votre cahier électronique !

Pour agir :
LA PROVENCE !

Si vous voulez bouger et faire quelque chose pour mieux connaître la Provence, ou pour aider les autres à mieux connaître les cultures francophones, consultez la section **Pour agir** dans votre cahier électronique ! Il y a tant de choses à faire :

- **Vendez des sachets de lavande** et contribuez l'argent que vous gagnez à une organisation qui aide les jeunes en Provence.
- **Enseignez** ce que vous savez de la culture provençale à des enfants de l'école primaire. Lisez-leur des contes de fées français.
- **Entrez en contact** avec des francophones qui vivent dans votre communauté ou quelque part aux États-Unis.
- **Organisez un voyage** en Provence pour les prochaines vacances.
- **Cuisinez** ! Préparez un vrai repas provençal avec vos camarades de classe.

3. **Des contes didactiques.** Les versions originales de beaucoup de contes populaires européens sont très violentes et parfois très sombres. Dans la version originale du «Petit Chaperon rouge», par exemple, la petite fille meurt violemment, mangée par le loup. Aujourd'hui, on ne veut pas faire peur aux enfants ou enseigner la violence, donc on invente de nouveaux contes plus polis et moins choquants. Est-ce vraiment une mauvaise chose de raconter un conte qui fait peur ? Est-ce que les contes doivent enseigner une leçon morale ou est-ce qu'ils peuvent simplement être amusants et intéressants ? Est-ce une hypocrisie d'éliminer la violence des contes quand les enfants peuvent voir des scènes violentes à la télé ? Qu'en pensez-vous ?

9.49 À l'impromptu Voici des situations interactives. Avec une ou deux autres personnes, **choisissez une scène** et **improvisez** devant la classe. Si vous ne voulez pas improviser, écrivez votre dialogue avant et puis jouez-le pour la classe.

1. Des produits de Provence
   (a) Vous êtes PDG d'une petite entreprise américaine qui vend des produits provençaux en Amérique du Nord. Vous avez de bonnes nouvelles à partager avec vos collègues français : Ces produits se vendent bien et vous réalisez de gros bénéfices ! Expliquez pourquoi.
   (b) Vous êtes agriculteur en Provence où vous cultivez de la lavande (*lavender*). Vous voulez en vendre au PDG. Exagérez l'importance du marché international et essayez de vendre votre produit au PDG.
   (c) Vous êtes gérant(e) d'une usine en Provence qui fabrique des tissus (*fabric*) provençaux traditionnels. Vous préféreriez vendre vos produits en Provence et contribuer à l'économie régionale. Diminuez l'importance de l'exportation à l'étranger.
2. À la boutique
   (a) Vous travaillez comme caissier/caissière dans une petite boutique en Provence. Vous travaillez souvent seul(e), il n'y a pas beaucoup de clients, et vous vous ennuyez. Un jour, vous décidez de fermer la boutique une heure plus tôt que d'habitude parce que vous avez rendez-vous avec un(e) ami(e). Le/La propriétaire s'est fâché(e) quand il/elle apprend ce que vous avez fait. Expliquez-vous et promettez de ne plus faire de choses pareilles !
   (b) Vous êtes propriétaire d'une petite boutique en Provence. Vous vous rendez compte que votre employé(e) a l'habitude de fermer la boutique avant l'heure de la fermature. Demandez à l'employé(e) de s'expliquer et accentuez la gravité (*seriousness*) de son erreur. Ensuite, décidez si vous voulez renvoyer (*to fire*) l'employé(e).

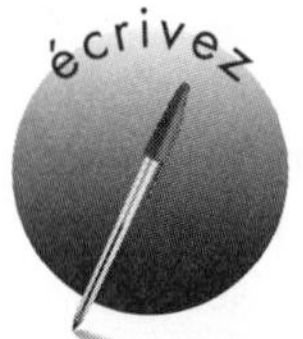

À l'écrit *étape finale*

9.50 Un conte de fées moderne Le PDG a accepté votre idée ! Maintenant, il faut écrire votre conte ! Révisez et élaborez vos travaux d'écriture de ce chapitre (Activités 13, 28 et 39) et **écrivez votre conte de fées moderne**. Attention à l'usage des pronoms relatifs et de la voix passive.

À suivre

Suivant les conseils de son directeur de thèse, Claire décide de passer quelque temps aux Archives coloniales mais ne trouve rien de nouveau en ce qui concerne Laclos et la Révolution haïtienne. Chaque jour, elle achète le journal et cherche l'article de Gilles sur la corruption dans le marché des livres anciens, mais on ne l'a pas encore publié. Elle essaie aussi de téléphoner à l'appartement de Jean-Louis à Paris, mais la ligne est toujours en panne. Après quelques semaines, ne faisant pas de progrès et presque sans argent, elle décide de quitter le soleil du sud de la France et de rentrer chez elle au Québec. . .

9.51 Qu'est-ce qui s'est passé ? Pensez à ce qui s'est passé dans ce chapitre. **Écrivez six phrases aux temps passés** pour décrire les événements que vous pensez être les plus importants. Parlez de vos idées avec vos camarades de classe.

MODÈLE : Gilles a révélé sa vraie identité.

9.52 Qu'est-ce qui se passera ? Imaginez ce qui va se passer dans le dernier chapitre ! **Écrivez six phrases** et parlez de vos idées avec vos camarades de classe. Utilisez **le futur**.

MODÈLE : Claire retournera au Québec.

VOCABULAIRE UTILE

Les affaires	
à but non lucratif	*nonprofit (organization)*
actions (*f.*)	*shares of stock*
aléatoire	*risky, uncertain*
bénéfices (*f. pl.*)	*profits*
boulot (*m.*)	*job (slang)*
bourse (*f.*)	*stock exchange*
cadre (*m.*)	*executive*
chômage (*m.*)	*unemployment*
comptable (*m./f.*)	*accountant*
concurrence (*f.*)	*competition*
créances gelées (*f. pl.*)	*frozen assets*
entreprise (*f.*)	*company, business*
faire faillite	*to go bankrupt*
filiale (*f.*)	*subsidiary*
fournir	*to furnish, supply*
gérant(e) (*m./f.*)	*manager*
gestion (*f.*)	*management*
grève (*f.*)	*workers' strike*
gros lot (*m.*)	*jackpot*
inconvénients	*disadvantages*
investir	*to invest*
investissement (*m.*)	*investment*
maison (*f.*)	*company, firm*
marketing (*m.*)	*marketing*
marque (*f.*)	*brand*
patron(ne) (*m./f.*)	*boss*
le PDG (*m.*)	*CEO*
placer (de l'argent)	*to invest (money)*
procès (*m.*)	*trial*
publicité (*f.*)	*advertising*
renvoyer	*to fire (an employee)*
rompu(e) aux affaires	*experienced in business*
secrétaire (*m./f.*)	*secretary*
service (*f.*) de ventes	*sales division*
siège (*m.*)	*headquarters*
société (*f.*)	*company, firm*
société anonyme (*f.*)	*public corporation*
succursale (*f.*)	*branch office*
sur-le-champ	*immediately*
technicien(ne) (*m./f.*)	*technician*
vendeur(-euse) (*m./f.*)	*salesperson*
Divers	
bouche bée	*open-mouthed*
calé(e)	*smart, clever (slang)*
être fichu(e)	*to be done for, to have had it*
grave	*serious*
lettre morte (*f.*)	*worthless; a dead issue*
un appel PCV (payable chez vous)	*collect call*
s'éloigner	*to distance oneself*
stupéfait(e)	*stunned*
tel(le)	*such*
le TGV (train de grande vitesse)	*high-speed train*
vouloir dire	*to mean*
Décrire les circonstances	
associé(e) (*m./f.*)	*associate*
contrefaçon (*f.*)	*forgery*
contrefaire	*to forge*
en partie	*partially, in part*
enquête (*f.*)	*inquiry, investigation*
fontaine (*f.*) de jouvence	*fountain of youth*
gâcher	*to spoil, to ruin*
mettre en lumière	*to bring to light, to expose*
parafe (*m.*)	*initials*
prétendu(e)	*so-called*
reporter (*m.*)	*reporter*
se déguiser	*to disguise oneself*

Chapitre 10

De retour au Québec

À la Terrace Dufferin, devant le Château Frontenac à Québec.

Épisode *1* *«Je me souviens»*

Épisode *2* *Le choc*

Épisode *3* *En fin de compte*

Dénouement

L'arbre tombe toujours du côté où il penche.
—proverbe québécois

À apprendre

- Comment parler de la santé et exprimer ses émotions
- Comment rapporter une conversation
- Comment conclure une histoire

À lire

En descendant de l'avion à Montréal, Claire regarde la terre blanche de neige et entend l'accent familier de ses compatriotes. Elle est, enfin, de retour chez elle. Sa sœur, Marie, et ses parents l'attendent à l'aéroport et ils rentrent ensemble à la maison. La mère de Claire, qui s'inquiète toujours de la santé de sa famille, prépare un copieux repas, et la famille écoute Claire raconter tout ce qui s'est passé pendant son voyage. La jeune chercheuse a toujours des doutes et des questions. Comment est-ce que Jean-Louis a pu lui mentir ? Que savait-il du meurtre du bouquiniste ? Ira-t-il en prison ? Le manuscrit, était-il un faux ou un vrai Laclos ? Le reporter Gilles LaFfont, qui téléphone avec des nouvelles de Paris, va lui procurer les réponses qu'elle attendait tout en donnant naissance à d'autres questions. . .

i Culture

Le **Québec** est la plus grande province du Canada. **Jacques Cartier**, un explorateur français, a été le premier Français à parcourir, en 1534, cette région peuplée d'Amérindiens. Les Français ont nommé ce pays la Nouvelle France. En 1608, **Samuel de Champlain** a fondé la ville de Québec, qui est aujourd'hui la capitale de la province, et en 1643, Paul de Chomedey a établi la colonie de Ville-Marie, qui deviendrait la ville de Montréal. L'expansion française a continué jusqu'en 1759, date à laquelle les troupes françaises perdent une bataille importante contre les envahisseurs anglais sur les **Plaines d'Abraham**. À partir de cette date, le Québec devient la possession des Anglais et une province du Canada.

Épisode 1

«Je me souviens»

Avant de lire

10.1 Vos opinions sur la santé Répondez aux questions suivantes. **Discutez de vos réponses** avec vos camarades de classe et n'hésitez pas à poser des questions supplémentaires si vous voulez en savoir plus.

1. Pensez-vous que la santé soit importante dans la vie ? Pourquoi ou pourquoi pas ? Y a-t-il d'autres aspects de la vie qui sont plus ou aussi importants ? Lesquels ?
2. D'après vous, que faut-il faire pour être en bonne santé ? Faire du sport ou de l'exercice ? Manger bien ? Être heureux ? Dormir assez ?
3. Allez-vous régulièrement chez le médecin et le dentiste ou y allez-vous seulement quand vous êtes malade ? Quelles sont les raisons pour lesquelles les gens évitent d'aller chez le médecin ou le dentiste ?
4. Faites-vous du sport régulièrement ? Combien de fois par semaine ? Pendant combien de temps ?
5. Aimez-vous participer à des compétitions sportives ? Pourquoi ou pourquoi pas ?

i Langue

Quand on parle du Québec, il faut faire attention aux prépositions qu'on emploie pour distinguer entre la ville de Québec et la province du Québec. Pour **parler de la ville**, il faut préciser qu'on va **à** Québec ou qu'on vient **de** Québec. Pour **parler de la province**, on dit qu'on va **au** Québec ou on vient **du** Québec (*préposition + article défini*).

10.2 Les sports au Québec Les sports d'hiver et d'été sont très populaires au Québec, où la topographie variée permet toutes sortes d'activités sportives. En voici quelques-unes des plus connues. En petits groupes, faites correspondre le nom d'un sport (*à gauche*) avec la description d'une activité sportive au Québec (*à droite*). Utilisez la carte du Québec afin de trouver les villes et régions dont il s'agit.

Sports	Activités sportives au Québec
1. le ski	a. À Sainte-Anne, près du grand canyon et de la chute d'eau (*waterfall*), il y a des gens qui marchent sur les pistes (*trails*) à travers les bois et autour du canyon.
2. le kayak	b. Dans les rues de Montréal, en été, des gens font le tour de l'île sur un truc en métal avec deux roues qu'on peut faire avancer en poussant sur des pédales avec les pieds.
3. la planche à voile	c. À Baie-Sainte-Catherine, sur le fleuve Saint-Laurent et près de l'estuaire Saguenay, des gens regardent les baleines de près, assis sur de petits bateaux étroits et tenant des pagaies (*paddles*) qu'on met dans l'eau pour avancer.
4. le hockey sur glace	d. À Magog, sur le lac Memphrémagog, des gens balancent sur de grands morceaux de bois et tiennent des perches, qui guident des morceaux de tissu dans le vent.

5. les randonnées — e. À Mont-Tremblant, dans les Laurentides, les gens mettent beaucoup de vêtements chauds et glissent du haut d'une montagne jusqu'en bas sur deux longs morceaux de bois.

6. le vélo — f. Au centre Molson, au centre-ville de Montréal, une foule regarde des gens qui glissent sur une surface d'eau gelée et utilisent des morceaux de bois pour projeter un petit palet noir dans un filet (*net*).

Langue

Connaissez-vous **les sports** suivants ? Lesquels avez-vous déjà essayés ? Lesquels voudriez-vous essayer ? Y a-t-il d'autres sports que vous aimez faire qui ne sont pas sur la liste ?

- **Sports d'hiver :** le ski, le ski de fond (*cross-country skiing*), le patinage (*skating*), le hockey sur glace, le toboggan, l'escalade de glace (*ice climbing*), la raquette de neige (*snowshoeing*), la planche de neige (*snowboarding*)
- **Autres sports :** les randonnées, le jogging, le vélo (le cyclisme), le VTT (vélo tout-terrain), le golf, le tennis, le foot, la natation, le surfing, la planche à voile (*windsurfing*), le ski nautique, le kayak, le canoë (le canot, au Québec), le football américain, la marche, l'équitation (*horseback riding*), le basket, le base-ball, le patin en ligne (*in-line skating*)

Notez qu'en français, on emploie souvent le verbe **faire** avec les sports (faire du vélo, faire du ski, faire du cheval). Pourtant, avec des sports d'équipe et avec quelques sports où il y a des compétitions, on utilise le verbe **jouer** (jouer au golf, jouer au foot).

Pour aller plus loin : CULTURE

ACTIVITÉ A : Apprenez plus au sujet des sports au Québec. Consultez votre cahier électronique !

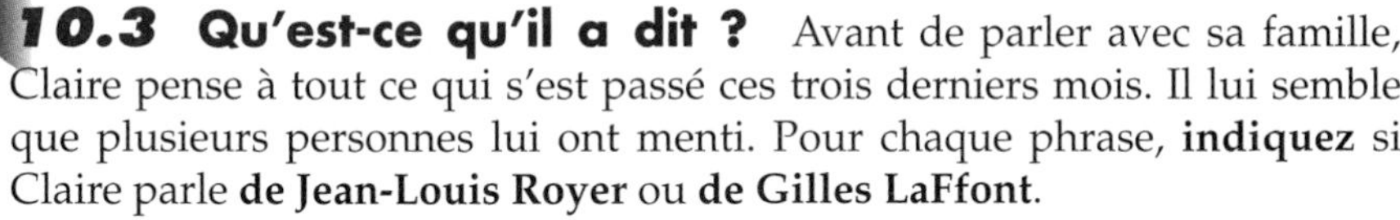

10.3 Qu'est-ce qu'il a dit ? Avant de parler avec sa famille, Claire pense à tout ce qui s'est passé ces trois derniers mois. Il lui semble que plusieurs personnes lui ont menti. Pour chaque phrase, **indiquez** si Claire parle **de Jean-Louis Royer** ou **de Gilles LaFfont**.

1. Au début, il a dit qu'il avait travaillé comme barman, mais plus tard il a avoué qu'il travaillait pour un antiquaire.
2. Il répétait tout le temps que le marché des livres anciens était un commerce dangereux.
3. Il m'a dit au début qu'il était détective de police.
4. Un jour, il a annoncé qu'il publierait un article sur l'affaire du faux manuscrit.
5. Il a affirmé que son patron revendrait le manuscrit à un collectionneur.
6. Il a dit qu'il était surpris d'apprendre que le manuscrit n'était pas de Laclos.

le Québec

Rencontrez un Québécois ! Regardez la vidéo et consultez votre cahier d'activités !

Pour aller plus loin : CULTURE

ACTIVITÉ B : Voulez-vous explorer la ville de Montréal ? Consultez votre cahier électronique !

lisez

«Je me souviens»

Rentrée chez ses parents à Montréal, Claire se sent finalement chez elle. Après avoir mangé une bonne tourtière que sa mère a préparée pour fêter son retour au Québec, Claire et sa famille s'assoient autour de la cheminée avec leurs cafés. Lorsque la neige tombe dehors, Claire commence à parler de ses aventures. Marie essaie de comprendre ce que sa sœur a éprouvé, et elle a beaucoup de questions. Claire pense aux événements, et elle devient émue. Plus elle parle de ses souvenirs, plus elle a mal à la tête et mal à la gorge.

CLAIRE : Rien n'était comme je l'avais imaginé avant mon départ. Deux ans auparavant, à l'université de Sainte-Foy, j'avais lu cet article que mon professeur m'avait suggéré. Il se trouvait dans une revue littéraire où on mentionnait un manuscrit perdu de Laclos. L'année d'après, quand j'ai trouvé à la Bibliothèque nationale de Paris une lettre de Laclos à un certain François Fontenot, dans laquelle il décrit un paquet envoyé à ce dernier, j'ai cru avoir résolu le mystère. Enfin, je me suis dit que j'irais à la Nouvelle-Orléans au mois d'août, que j'y trouverais le manuscrit, que je l'étudierais et que je rentrerais à Québec en septembre pour écrire ma thèse.

MARIE : Nous t'avons averti que la Nouvelle-Orléans serait un endroit dangereux.

CLAIRE : Mais, cette ville n'était pas plus dangereuse qu'une autre. Mon hôtelier, Philippe Aucoin, était très sympa, et Sandrine Fontenot-Chardin était charmante. C'est elle qui m'a raconté l'histoire du manuscrit hérité de son ancêtre François Fontenot. Il est vrai, pourtant, qu'elle m'a dit de me méfier des inconnus, et je ne l'ai pas fait.

MARIE : Tu parles de Jean-Louis ?

CLAIRE : Oui. . . au début, j'ai pensé qu'il voulait sortir avec moi. Mais je crois maintenant qu'il est venu à la Nouvelle-Orléans exprès pour me rencontrer. Il voulait se servir de moi pour authentifier le manuscrit contrefait. Et il m'a menti plusieurs fois. Il m'a dit qu'il était barman, et puis plus tard, à Paris, il m'a avoué qu'il travaillait pour un antiquaire. J'aurais dû comprendre qui il était ! (*Elle éternue et se mouche.*)

MARIE : À tes souhaits. Tu vas bien ? Tu as l'air un peu pâle.

CLAIRE : Ça va. C'est que je suis à bout de nerfs. Comment Jean-Louis a-t-il pu me mentir autant ? Quelle idiote ! Comme j'ai pu être naïve ! Savait-il depuis le début que j'irais chez le bouquiniste Gustave à Paris et que ce bouquiniste nous enverrait chez Monsieur Thibodeau ? Mais comment est-ce possible ? Je suis sûre que

Sandrine m'a dit la vérité à propos du manuscrit. Je n'arrive pas à saisir comment Jean-Louis aurait tout organisé comme cela. Quand nous étions en Suisse, dans son chalet, il avait l'air si sincère. J'ai vraiment cru qu'il voulait m'aider avec ma thèse et qu'il s'intéressait à la littérature. Est-ce possible qu'il ait collaboré avec Nicolas Gustave et des contrefacteurs, qu'il ait trahi son patron, qu'il ait payé Sandrine pour mentir ? Et maintenant le pauvre Nicolas Gustave est mort. Est-ce que Jean-Louis a commandité ce meurtre ? Ira-t-il en prison ? Ah ! l'angoisse. . .

MARIE : Mais, comment as-tu deviné finalement que Jean-Louis avait tout manigancé ?

CLAIRE : En discutant avec Gilles LaFfont, le reporter dont je t'ai parlé. Il a un informateur qui lui a dit qu'un vendeur de livres anciens collaborait avec des bouquinistes et des contrefacteurs. Pourtant, Gilles, lui aussi, m'a menti. Il a prétendu au début qu'il était détective de police.

MARIE : Et tu es absolument sûre que le manuscrit que Jean-Louis a acheté à Monsieur Thibodeau à Dakar était un faux ?

CLAIRE : Je ne suis sûre de rien. Quand j'ai découvert l'anachronisme, et que je l'ai révélé à Jean-Louis, nous étions assez certains que ce n'était pas un roman de Laclos. Et pourtant, mon directeur de thèse, le Professeur Thuillier, m'a dit qu'un anachronisme ne prouve rien. Alors, que penser maintenant ?

MARIE : Je ne sais pas, mais j'ai une question. Comment Jean-Louis a-t-il pu savoir que tu cherchais le manuscrit perdu de Laclos en Louisiane en août ? L'article que tu as lu sur le manuscrit a été publié il y a trois ans. Il t'a fallu une année pour trouver le nom de François Fontenot, et tu es partie pour la Nouvelle-Orléans une année après cela. C'est vraiment trop. Je crois que ta rencontre avec Jean-Louis a dû être une vraie coïncidence.

CLAIRE : Belle coïncidence ! Alors, je suis naïve et malchanceuse. (*Elle renifle.*) Écoute, tu as raison. Ça ne va pas très fort. Je suis un peu déprimée et un peu enrhumée aussi, je crois. Je vais me coucher et essayer d'oublier tout cela. Si je me sens mieux demain, nous pourrons aller faire du ski. Cela me fait toujours du bien.

Que ce soit à cause de la fatigue du voyage, du stress de sa thèse ou d'un petit rhume, Claire ne le sait pas, mais elle est tombée malade. Se sentant un peu fiévreuse à la fin de la conversation, elle décide de prendre quelques comprimés et de se mettre au lit. . .

VOCABULAIRE

Décrire son état		un rhume	*cold*
ému(e)	*emotional; moved; upset*	fiévreux(-euse)	*feverish*
mal à la gorge	*sore throat*	un comprimé	*tablet, lozenge*
éternuer	*to sneeze*		
se moucher	*to blow one's nose*	**Divers**	
à tes souhaits	*in American, "Bless you!"*	la tourtière	*meat pie (reg. Québec)*
être à bout de nerfs	*to have frazzled nerves*	exprès	*on purpose*
renifler	*to sniffle*	saisir	*to grasp, understand*
déprimé(e)	*depressed*	trahir	*to betray*
enrhumé(e)	*sick with a cold*	manigancer	*to plot*
faire du bien (à quelqu'un)	*to do good; to make (someone) feel better*	jurer	*to swear*
tomber malade	*to get sick*	prétendre que	*to claim that*

Après avoir lu

10.4 Avez-vous compris ? Répondez aux questions suivantes. **Justifiez vos réponses** en citant le texte.

1. Pourquoi est-ce que Claire est allée à la Nouvelle-Orléans en août ? À votre avis, est-ce que la rencontre de Jean-Louis et Claire était une coïncidence ? Pourquoi ou pourquoi pas ?
2. Est-ce que l'histoire que Sandrine a racontée à Claire à propos du manuscrit était la vérité ou est-ce que Jean-Louis l'a payée pour qu'elle l'invente ? Qu'en pense Claire ? Qu'en pensez-vous ?
3. Jean-Louis et Gilles LaFfont, tous les deux, ont menti à Claire. Pourquoi est-ce que chacun a menti ? Quelles étaient leurs motivations ?
4. Décrivez l'état physique et émotif de Claire. Est-ce une réaction normale au stress ? Devrait-elle aller chez le médecin ? Pourquoi ou pourquoi pas ?

10.5 D'accord ou pas d'accord ? Indiquez si vous êtes **d'accord ou pas d'accord** avec les phrases suivantes, d'après votre compréhension du récit. Justifiez vos opinions en citant le texte, si possible. Discutez de vos réponses avec la classe.

	D'accord	Pas d'accord
1. Claire est heureuse et en bonne santé.	_______	_______
2. Elle comprend pourquoi Jean-Louis lui a menti.	_______	_______
3. Jean-Louis a commandité le meurtre de Nicolas Gustave.	_______	_______
4. Le manuscrit était un faux.	_______	_______
5. La rencontre de Claire et Jean-Louis à la Nouvelle-Orléans était une vraie coïncidence.	_______	_______

Langue

Connaissez-vous les maux, les états, les symptômes et les remèdes suivants ?

- **Maux typiques** avoir un rhume / être enrhumé(e), avoir la grippe (*flu*) / être grippé(e), avoir des allergies / être allergique (à quelque chose), avoir une bronchite (*bronchitis*), avoir mal au cœur (*nausea*), être atteint(e) (*to suffer*) d'arthrite / de rhumatisme (*rheumatoid arthritis*), avoir une carie dentaire (*cavity in a tooth*), avoir la gueule de bois (*hangover*), avoir une infection, avoir un coup de soleil (*sunburn*), avoir une migraine
- **Maux sérieux** avoir un cancer, une crise cardiaque, une maladie du cœur (*heart disease*), une attaque d'apoplexie (*stroke*), une pneumonie, le SIDA (*AIDS*)
- **États physiques** être en forme, être en bonne santé, être enceinte (*pregnant*), être fumeur/fumeuse, avoir le bras cassé, se casser le bras (la jambe, le doigt, etc.), se fouler la cheville / le poignet (*to sprain one's ankle/wrist*), être contagieux (*contagious*)
- **Symptômes** avoir mal à la tête (à l'oreille, à l'estomac, à la gorge, aux dents, etc.), éternuer, renifler, avoir le nez qui coule, avoir la toux, tousser, frissonner (*to shiver*), avoir de la fièvre, se sentir froid (chaud, mal à l'aise, bizarre, etc.), avoir des crampes / des courbatures (aux muscles), avoir la nausée, avoir une inflammation, ne pas avoir d'appétit, avoir le vertige (*to be dizzy*), être paralysé(e), être fatigué(e), avoir une démangeaison (*to have an itch / be itchy*), avoir du mal à respirer (parler, bouger, marcher, etc.)
- **Remèdes** un comprimé, une aspirine, un sirop, un médicament, une crème, des vitamines, du repos, de l'activité physique, des liquides (de la soupe au poulet, du jus d'orange), un plâtre (*cast*), des béquilles (*crutches*), l'hospitalisation

10.6 La santé Regardez les mots de vocabulaire qui suivent. Dans chaque ligne, il y a un mot qui cloche avec les trois autres. **Entourez le mot qui ne va pas** avec les autres et essayez d'expliquer pourquoi. Attention ! Il y a parfois plusieurs bonnes réponses. Il faut justifier votre choix !

1. déprimé	enrhumé	pâle	fiévreux
2. renifler	éternuer	se moucher	tousser
3. sportive	active	en forme	enceinte
4. dormir	se mettre au lit	se reposer	se coucher
5. un médecin	un dentiste	un chirurgien	un pédiatre (*pediatrician*)

Une vieille pharmacie à Québec.

Culture

La province de Québec, la plus grande des dix provinces et trois territoires canadiens, est trois fois la taille de la France. Dans cette grande région, on trouve onze nations **autochtones** (c'est-à-dire des peuples amérindiens). Parmi eux sont les Hurons, les Iroquois et les Inuits. Depuis l'arrivée des Français au 16ème siècle, ces peuples autochtones partageaient avec les Européens leurs connaissances de la terre et des eaux. En échange, les Européens faisaient du commerce avec les autochtones. Les **industries principales** à cette époque étaient la pêche, la pêche à la baleine et la traite de la fourrure de castor. De ce point de vue, les échanges entre les autochtones et les colonisateurs français étaient mutuellement profitables. Pourtant, les Européens ont aussi amenés avec eux des **maladies infectieuses** qui ont tué une grande partie de la population indigène. Au 19ème siècle, les autochtones ont été poussés plus au nord de la province ou bien sur des réserves, lorsque les Français ont voulu développer le commerce du bois, commerce qui dépendait du fleuve Saint-Laurent et qui a entraîné le développement des villes dans le sud de la province.

Pour aller plus loin : LITTÉRATURE

ACTIVITÉ C : Lisez un extrait du *Malade imaginaire* de Molière. Consultez votre cahier électronique !

10.7 Des symptômes Beaucoup des amis de Marie sont malades en ce moment. Elle décrit leurs symptômes. Avec un partenaire, **essayez de deviner** la maladie typique ou l'état physique de ses amis, et ensuite suggérez un remède.

1. Paul m'a dit qu'il était tombé en faisant du ski hier et qu'il s'était fait mal à la cheville.
2. Aurélie m'a avoué qu'elle avait la nausée chaque matin et qu'elle se sentait un peu bizarre.
3. Benoît et Georges me disent toujours qu'ils ont mal à la tête, qu'ils ont la nausée et qu'ils sont fatigués le matin après un grand match de hockey.
4. Grand-mère me dit qu'elle a mal aux mains et aux genoux quand il pleut.
5. Sophie m'a dit ce matin qu'elle avait toussé et reniflé toute la nuit, mais qu'autrement elle se sentait bien.
6. Louis-Philippe explique qu'il frissonne, qu'il n'a pas d'appétit et qu'il a de la fièvre.

10.8 Des maladies En petits groupes, imaginez les symptômes qu'on pourrait avoir si on avait les maladies suivantes.

1. une allergie aux chats
2. un rhume
3. l'arthrite
4. une carie dentaire
5. une bronchite
6. une migraine

10.9 Allô ? Claire ne va pas directement au lit. Il y a quelque chose qui la gêne. Elle veut poser une question à Sandrine Fontenot-Chardin et elle ne veut pas attendre. Donc, elle lui téléphone. Choisissez une des expressions entre parenthèses et **lisez le dialogue à haute voix** avec un partenaire. Quand vous voyez «? ? ?», vous pouvez imaginer votre propre expression.

SANDRINE : Allô ?

CLAIRE : Madame Fontenot-Chardin ? Excusez-moi de (vous téléphoner / vous déranger) si tard. C'est Claire Plouffe, l'étudiante qui est venue vous voir en août. Vous allez bien ?

SANDRINE : Mademoiselle Plouffe ! Quelle (bonheur / surprise) ! Je suis si (contente / heureuse / ? ? ?) d'entendre votre voix. Je pense souvent à vous. Ici, tout va à merveille. Je suis en pleine forme. Et vous ? (Tout va bien / Ça ne va pas / ? ? ?) ?

CLAIRE : Enfin, ça ne marche pas très fort en ce moment. (*Elle se mouche.*) Excusez-moi. J'ai un petit rhume, et. . . enfin. . . Ça pourrait aller mieux. (*Elle renifle.*)

SANDRINE : Oh, mais ! Vous pleurez ? (Qu'est-ce qui se passe ? / Qu'avez-vous ?)

CLAIRE : Je ne sais pas ce que j'ai. . . J'ai peur. Je suis (triste / angoissée / ? ? ?). J'ai des frissons. J'aurai peut-être besoin de (tranquillisants / médicaments / être hospitalisée) à cause de ce maudit manuscrit.

SANDRINE : Vous exagérez, j'en suis sûre. Dites-moi ce qui ne va pas. N'avez-vous pas réussi à trouver le manuscrit de Laclos (en France / à Paris / chez le bouquiniste) ?

CLAIRE : Si, je l'ai trouvé à Dakar, mais on croit que c'est (un faux / une contrefaçon). J'ai rencontré un reporter de Paris qui m'a dit que le manuscrit avait été contrefait et que l'homme qui m'avait aidé à le trouver était un grand criminel.

SANDRINE : (C'est incroyable ! / Oh là là ! / ? ? ?) Alors, ce n'était pas le manuscrit que mon grand-père avait vendu à Monsieur Gustave ?

CLAIRE : (Alors / Eh bien / ? ? ?), est-ce que l'histoire que vous m'avez racontée est vraie ?

SANDRINE : (Bien sûr / Certainement / ? ? ?), mais je ne vous ai raconté que ce que mes parents et mes grands-parents m'ont toujours dit. Je n'ai jamais vu le manuscrit de mes propres yeux.

CLAIRE : Et vous n'avez jamais parlé avec un Jean-Louis Royer ? Il ne vous a pas demandé (de mentir / d'inventer cette histoire) ?

SANDRINE : (Bien sûr que non ! / Absolument pas ! / ? ? ?)

CLAIRE : J'en étais sûre, mais je devais quand même vous poser la question. Merci beaucoup, Madame.

exprimer les émotions (le bonheur et la tristesse)

To express happiness	Quel bonheur ! / Quelle joie ! / Quel honneur ! / Quelle surprise ! Je suis si heureux(-euse) / content(e) / surpris(e) / ravi(e) que. . . (+ *subjonctif*) Je suis ravi(e) d'entendre ces nouvelles. / J'en suis ravi(e). Je me sens bien. / Je suis en forme. / Je suis en pleine forme. Ça va bien / très bien / parfaitement bien / super-bien. La vie est belle ! / Tout va à merveille ! / Le moral remonte. Ça marche très fort. / Ça ne va pas mal du tout !
To express sadness	Je suis triste / angoissé(e) / déprimé(e) / troublé(e) / malade. Je suis triste que. . . (+ *subjonctif*) / J'ai peur que. . . (+ **ne** + *subjonctif*) C'est la déprime totale. / J'ai le cafard (*the blues*). Ça ne va pas du tout. / Ça va mal ! / Ça pourrait aller mieux. Ça ne marche pas très fort. / Je ne sais pas ce que j'ai. Je pleure. / Je panique. / Je perds la tête. / J'ai peur de tout. J'en ai assez. / J'en ai marre. / Rien ne va.

Culture

Les **jeux Olympiques** sont des compétitions sportives internationales qui, chez les Grecs, se célébraient tous les quatre ans. Un Parisien, **Pierre de Coubertin**, a rénové les jeux Olympiques en 1893. Aujourd'hui, le Comité international des jeux Olympiques organise les jeux tous les deux ans partout dans le monde. Les deux langues officielles des jeux Olympiques sont l'anglais et le français. Le Stade Olympique à Montréal, construit pour les jeux de 1976, se trouve sur l'avenue Pierre-de-Coubertin et offre une vue spectaculaire de la ville et des montagnes au nord.

Pour aller plus loin : CULTURE
ACTIVITÉ D : Apprenez un peu plus sur les jeux Olympiques. Consultez votre cahier électronique !

Langue

Vous rappelez-vous la conjugaison des verbes **naître** et **mourir** ?

- **naître :** je nais, tu nais, il/elle/on naît, nous naissons, vous naissez, ils/elles naissent ; la plupart du temps utilisé au *passé composé* : je suis né(e)
- **mourir :** je meurs, tu meurs, il/elle/on meurt, nous mourons, vous mourez, ils/elle meurent ; souvent utilisé au *passé composé* : il est mort, elle est morte

Notez les synonymes et autres verbes associés à ceux-ci. Pour parler de la naissance, on peut dire : donner naissance à un bébé, accoucher (*to give birth*) ou arriver au monde. L'expression «être décédé(e)» est un synonyme de l'expression «être mort(e)».

10.10 À vous Avec un partenaire, imaginez que vous êtes dans les situations suivantes. Êtes-vous heureux/heureuse ou triste ? **Choisissez des expressions d'émotion diverses** pour chaque situation.

1. Vous alliez faire du kayak avec votre ami, mais il n'arrête pas de pleuvoir.
2. Des amis vous invitent à passer le week-end avec eux à une station de ski dans les Laurentides.
3. Votre boa (*snake*) est mort, et vous êtes inconsolable.
4. Votre patron doit renvoyer dix employés à cause de la crise économique. Vous êtes un(e) de ces employé(e)s !
5. Votre meilleure amie vient d'accoucher : Ce sont des jumeaux !
6. Votre ami vient de gagner la médaille d'or aux jeux Olympiques !

10.11 Comment allez-vous ? Avec un partenaire, ou en petits groupes, regardez les événements suivants. À votre tour, choisissez au hasard un des événements et **décrivez les émotions que vous ressentiriez** à ce moment-là. Les autres vont essayer de deviner quel événement vous avez choisi.

après avoir fait du sport	le jour où vous attrapez un rhume	quand vous avez mal à la tête
après un bon concert	le mariage de votre ami	quand vous avez une bronchite
la naissance de votre enfant	lundi matin	quand vous avez une carie
le début d'un voyage	quand il fait beau	quand vous recevez une promotion
le jour où votre chien est mort	quand il pleut	un accident de ski
le jour où votre fiancé(e) vous quitte	quand vos allergies sont au pire	votre anniversaire

10.12 Vocabulaire personnel Pensez à votre santé et aux sports que vous aimez et, pour chaque catégorie, **faites une liste de cinq à dix mots importants** que vous pouvez utiliser en parlant de vous-même. Consultez un dictionnaire si nécessaire.

1. Vos sports préférés : ceux que vous faites régulièrement, ceux que vous regardez, ceux que vous voulez essayer de faire un jour, ceux que vous détestez
2. Les sports les plus populaires et les moins populaires dans votre région
3. Les maux auxquels vous souffrez souvent et auxquels souffrent vos amis ou vos parents
4. Ce que vous faites pour vous occuper de votre santé
5. Ce que vous devriez faire pour mieux vous occuper de votre santé

Pour aller plus loin : CULTURE

ACTIVITÉ E : Écoutez de la musique québécoise. Elle remonte le moral ! Consultez votre cahier électronique !

À l'écrit *première étape*

10.13 À votre santé ! Choisissez un des personnages du texte (mais pas Claire !). **Décrivez brièvement la santé de ce personnage** (physique et psychique, sports pratiqués, maladies, préférences alimentaires, mauvaises habitudes) en imaginant la vie de cette personne. Inventez tout ce que vous ne savez pas de cette personne. Ensuite, faites la même chose pour décrire votre santé et vos habitudes. Échangez vos descriptions avec celles d'un(e) camarade de classe. Vérifiez que votre partenaire a bien décrit ses idées, faites des corrections possibles et réagissez à ce que vous lisez en ajoutant des commentaires en bas de page.

Épisode 2

Le choc

Structures *les adjectifs et pronoms indéfinis*

10.14 Chacun pour soi ! Le lendemain matin, Claire se lève et rencontre sa mère dans la cuisine. Celle-ci essaie de soulager sa fille en répétant quelques proverbes et expressions françaises. Regardez les mots en **caractères gras** et indiquez si ces mots sont des **adjectifs indéfinis** ou des **pronoms indéfinis**. Quelles sont les différences que vous remarquez ? Pouvez-vous décrire comment employer les adjectifs et les pronoms indéfinis en analysant ces exemples ?

Chacun à son goût, dit la vieille dame en embrassant sa vache !
Chacun sait ce qui bout dans sa marmite.
Chaque chaudron trouve son couvercle.
À **chaque** cour son traître.
Tout est bien qui finit bien.
Toute vérité n'est pas bonne à dire.
Tout le monde sait être sage après le coup.
Dans **toutes** les entreprises, il y a un moment difficile.
Tout vient à point à qui sait attendre.

Culture

Fiers de leur langue et de leurs traditions, mais souffrant de leur statut minoritaire au cours de deux siècles (de la défaite sur les Plaines d'Abraham au 18ème siècle jusqu'aux bouleversements du 20ème siècle), les Québécois francophones voient une renaissance culturelle et une nouvelle activité politique dans les années 1960. On appelle cette renaissance, qui a mené au mouvement indépendantiste, la **Révolution tranquille**. Les séparatistes québécois, pourtant, ont été battus par les fédéralistes (ceux qui veulent que le Québec reste une province du Canada) aux référendums de 1980 et de 1995. Aujourd'hui, la question de l'indépendance de la province reste d'actualité.

regardez

le Québec

Apprenez des expressions québécoises ! Regardez la vidéo et consultez votre cahier d'activités !

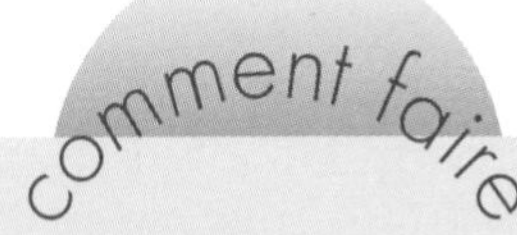

comment faire

les adjectifs et pronoms indéfinis

Indefinite adjectives and pronouns (**les adjectifs et pronoms indéfinis**) are used to indicate a subject or describe a person or thing that is unspecified. There are a number of common indefinite adjectives and pronouns, including:

	Adjectives	*Pronouns*
each; each one	chaque	chacun(e)
any; any one	n'importe quel	n'importe lequel (laquelle, etc.)
several	plusieurs	plusieurs
every, all; everything, all	tout(e), tous/toutes	tout(e), tous/toutes
some; someone, a few, something	quelque(s)	quelqu'un, quelques-un(e)s, quelque chose

The *indefinite adjectives* must agree with the noun they modify. Note, however, that there are invariable indefinite adjectives, such as **chaque** (always used in the singular) and **plusieurs** (always used in the plural).

- Examples: **Chaque** chaudron trouve son couvercle. **Toute** vérité n'est pas bonne à dire.
- **Note** that the final **s** of **tous** is *not* pronounced when it is an adjective: Elle fait du ski tous les jours.
- **Note** that the negative expression **ne... aucun(e)** (*not any*) can also function as an *indefinite adjective*: Il n'y a aucune compétition sportive à la télé.

The *indefinite pronouns* agree with the nouns they replace. However, when the noun being replaced is not specified, the masculine singular is used.

- Examples: **Tout** est bien qui finit bien. **Chacun** sait ce qui bout dans sa marmite.
- **Note** that the final **s** of **tous** is pronounced when it is a pronoun: Tous sont arrivés à la fois.
- **Note** that the pronoun **tout** is often followed by the *indefinite relative pronouns* **ce qui**, **ce que**, or **ce dont**: Tout ce qui brille n'est pas or.
- **Note** that the expression **n'importe** can be used in several other ways: **n'importe comment** (*anyway*), **n'importe où** (*anywhere*), **n'importe quand** (*anytime*), **n'importe qui** (*anybody*), **n'importe quoi** (*anything*), **n'importe lequel** (*anyone*)
- **Note** that the negative expressions **ne... rien** and **ne... personne** can function as *indefinite pronouns*: Rien ne m'intéresse. Personne ne me connaît.

10.15 Toute fâchée ! Claire essaie d'écrire un message à Jean-Louis, mais décide finalement de ne pas l'envoyer. Lisez le message et **remplissez les blancs** avec un des **adjectifs indéfinis** suivants : **chaque, n'importe quel, plusieurs, tout** ou **quelque**. Utilisez chaque adjectif une fois. N'oubliez pas de faire l'accord.

Cher Jean-Louis :

Salut, traitre. ____________________ fois que je pense à ce qui s'est passé, je deviens de plus en plus en colère. Il y avait ____________________ signes que tu en savais plus que tu ne voulais avouer. Il y avait aussi ____________________ coïncidences bizarres, comme notre rencontre à la Nouvelle-Orléans. Et quelle chance pour toi que je ne cherchais pas ____________________ manuscrit ancien, mais que je cherchais le manuscrit que tu avais contrefait ! Mais comment as-tu pu organiser ____________________ cela ? Comment as-tu pu agir ainsi envers moi ?

Le mot **tout** peut aussi fonctionner **comme adverbe**. C'est-à-dire qu'il modifie un verbe, un adjectif ou un autre adverbe. Comme tous les adverbes, il est invariable, sauf devant un adjectif féminin qui commence par une consonne ! Exemple : Claire est **tout** émue. Ses parents sont **tout** contents de la voir. *Mais* : Sa sœur est **toute** contente de la voir aussi.

10.16 N'importe quoi Claire est interrompue par sa sœur. **Remplissez les blancs** avec un des **pronoms indéfinis** suivants : **chacun, n'importe lequel, plusieurs, tout** ou **quelque chose**. Utilisez chaque pronom une fois. N'oubliez pas de faire l'accord.

MARIE : Tu te sens mieux aujourd'hui ? À quelle station de ski veux-tu aller ? À Mont-Tremblant ?

CLAIRE : ____________________ ! Ça m'est égal. À vrai dire, je ne suis pas d'humeur à faire du ski aujourd'hui. As-tu ____________________ à lire ? Un roman, par exemple. Je veux me distraire.

Pour aller plus loin : CULTURE

ACTIVITÉ F : Apprenez un peu plus sur la littérature québécoise. Consultez votre cahier électronique !

MARIE : Quel type de roman veux-tu ? Dans cette maison, ________________ lit un genre différent. Veux-tu un roman policier ? Il y en a ________________ dans ma chambre.

CLAIRE : Ah, non ! Pas ça ! Ma vie est un roman policier ! ________________ ce que je veux c'est d'oublier le passé.

MARIE : Vraiment ? Tu ne veux pas savoir ce qui se passera quand l'article de Gilles LaFfont sera publié ?

CLAIRE : Oui et non. Je sais déjà le résultat.

10.17 Et tout tout ! Avec un partenaire, inventez vos propres proverbes ! Utilisez les proverbes de l'Activité 14 comme exemples. **Faites trois phrases** en employant les **adjectifs et pronoms indéfinis**. Ensuite, lisez vos proverbes à vos camarades et expliquez leur sens. Votez pour le meilleur proverbe !

MODÈLE : ***Chacun* sait ce qui est dans son frigo.**
***Tout* ce qui est mouillé n'est pas eau.**

Avant d'écouter

10.18 Avant le choc Voici quelques événements choquants dont parlent les parents de Claire. Imaginez pourquoi on trouve ces choses choquantes. **Discutez de vos idées** avec vos camarades de classe.

1. «Monsieur Côté est rentré à deux heures du matin le week-end dernier !»
2. «Solange n'a jamais reçu son diplôme universitaire !»
3. «La police a arrêté le fils de Benoît devant le magasin.»
4. «Camille Rouget sert des produits congelés.»

écoutez

Le choc

Deux jours plus tard, le téléphone sonne chez la famille Plouffe à Montréal. On appelle Claire. C'est Gilles LaFfont qui téléphone de Paris avec des nouvelles. Il admet qu'il a eu tort. . .

Maintenant, **écoutez le dialogue sur votre CD**. Consultez le vocabulaire pour mieux comprendre le dialogue, et puis répondez aux questions suivantes.

VOCABULAIRE

Décrire les circonstances

faux, (fausse)	*wrong; fake*
ébruiter	*to leak (news, information)*
une trouvaille	*find*
soupçonner	*to suspect*
un amateur de livres	*book lover*
quelle horreur !	*how horrible!*
affreux(-euse)	*atrocious*
de bon cœur	*with sincerity, sincerely*
être abasourdi(e)	*to be flabbergasted*
tout s'explique !	*everything makes sense!*
une bêtise	*mistake, gaffe*
un procès	*trial*

Après avoir écouté

10.19 Avez-vous compris ? Après avoir écouté le dialogue, **répondez aux questions** suivantes.

1. Pourquoi est-ce que Gilles dit que Monsieur Rolland est coupable (*guilty*) ? Qu'est-ce qu'il a fait ?
2. Quel a été le rôle de Jean-Louis dans l'affaire du faux manuscrit de Laclos ? Quel a été le rôle de Nicolas Gustave ? Et le rôle du professeur Thuillier ? Et le rôle de Claire ?
3. Qu'est-ce qui se serait passé si Nicolas n'avait pas vendu le manuscrit avant l'arrivée de Jean-Louis et Claire ? Et si Claire n'avait pas trouvé l'anachronisme, comment se serait terminée l'histoire ? (Attention à l'usage du conditionnel passé !)
4. Pourquoi est-ce que Gilles et Jean-Louis essaient de protéger l'anonymité de Claire ?
5. Que pensez-vous de ce que Gilles raconte à Claire ? Êtes-vous choqué(e) ? Pourquoi ou pourquoi pas ?

Culture

La seule langue officielle du Québec est le français. La **Loi 101**, qui date de 1977, établit le français comme langue officielle. Pourtant, le Canada a deux langues officielles : l'anglais et le français. Quoique le Québec ait le plus grand nombre de francophones parmi toutes les provinces canadiennes, on trouve une présence francophone importante dans d'autres provinces, notamment en Ontario et au Nouveau-Brunswick. Les services sociaux sont offerts en anglais et en français partout au Canada afin de ne jamais manquer aux besoins des deux groupes linguistiques.

Pour aller plus loin : CULTURE

ACTIVITÉ G : Apprenez un peu plus sur les traditions québécoises en visitant le site du musée de la Civilisation à Québec. Consultez votre cahier électronique !

10.20 D'accord ou pas d'accord ? Après avoir écouté le dialogue, lisez les phrases suivantes et donnez votre opinion. Discutez en petits groupes.

	D'accord	Pas d'accord
1. Jean-Louis est coupable (*guilty*).	______	______
2. Monsieur Rolland est innocent.	______	______
3. Claire est choquée quand elle entend les nouvelles.	______	______
4. Gilles dit que Claire a été la dupe de son professeur.	______	______
5. Claire va continuer à travailler avec Thuillier.	______	______

exprimer les émotions (le choc, la peur et la colère)

To express shock	Mais non ! / Ce n'est pas vrai ! / Ce n'est pas possible ! / Je n'arrive pas à le croire ! Je suis complètement surpris(e) / choqué(e) / abasourdi(e) ! C'est impossible / incroyable / sans précédent / historique ! Quel choc ! / Quelle surprise ! / Quel cauchemar (*nightmare*) ! Je ne sais pas. . . quoi dire / quoi faire / qui appeler / où aller !
To express fear	J'ai peur ! Je panique ! J'ai le trac ! J'ai la trouille ! (*familier*) J'ai peur que (+ *subjonctif*) / J'ai peur de (+ *infinitif*) / J'ai horreur de (+ *infinitif*) Ça m'inquiète vraiment ! / C'est épouvantable ! / C'est aberrant ! Tu me fais peur ! / Quelle angoisse !
To express anger	Je suis fâché(e) / en colère / troublé(e) / hors de moi (*beside myself*) ! Je suis fâché(e) que (+ *subjonctif*) / Je suis fâché(e) contre. . . Je me suis mis(e) en colère quand. . . / Cela m'agace ! Non, non et non ! / Je n'en peux plus ! / C'est fini ! / J'en ai assez !

Langue

Vous rappelez-vous comment former et employer le **subjonctif** ? Révisez l'explication suivante et consultez le Chapitre 5 pour en savoir plus. Le subjonctif est employé dans les phrases où il y a une proposition qui exprime **la volonté**, **le doute**, **l'émotion**, **la nécessité** ou **l'opinion**. Le subjonctif est aussi employé après quelques conjonctions, le superlatif et des propositions qui expriment des désirs personnels, l'incertitude ou l'opinion subjective.

Comment former le subjonctif ?

- On ajoute les terminaisons **-e, -es, -e, -ions, -iez, -ent** au radical qu'on compose de la troisième personne plurielle (la forme **ils/elles**, sans **-ent**) : que vous **surmontiez**, que vous **réagissiez**, que votre idée ne **corresponde** pas.
- Les verbes **être** et **avoir** sont irréguliers :
  être → que je sois, tu sois, il/elle/on soit, nous soyons, vous soyez, ils/elles soient
  avoir → que j'aie, tu aies, il/elle/on ait, nous ayons, vous ayez, ils/elles aient
- Plusieurs verbes ont un radical irrégulier mais on emploie les terminaisons régulières :
  faire → que je **fasse** **pouvoir** → que je **puisse** **savoir** → que je **sache**
- D'autres verbes ont deux radicaux irréguliers : un radical pour les formes **nous/vous** et un autre pour les autres formes :
  acheter → que j'achète, que nous achetions
  appeler → que j'appelle, que nous appelions
  devoir → que je doive, que nous devions
  jeter → que je jette, que nous jetions
  payer → que je paie, que nous payions
  venir → que je vienne, que nous venions
  voir → que je voie, que nous voyions
  aller → que j'aille, que nous allions
  boire → que je boive, que nous buvions
  envoyer → que j'envoie, que nous envoyions
  mourir → que je meure, que nous mourions
  prendre → que je prenne, que nous prenions
  recevoir → que je reçoive, que nous recevions
  vouloir → que je veuille, que nous voulions
- Les verbes **falloir** and **pleuvoir** sont irréguliers aussi :
  falloir → qu'il faille
  pleuvoir → qu'il pleuve

Quand utiliser le subjonctif ?

- Quand il y a *deux propositions* liées par **que**, avec deux sujets différents, et la première proposition exprime **la volonté, le doute, l'émotion, la nécessité ou l'opinion**. Dans ces cas, le verbe dans la deuxième proposition (la proposition subordonnée) est au subjonctif : **Vous avez peur que** tout n'**aille** pas comme prévu. **Il est préférable que** vous ne **buviez** plus de caféine.
- Quand il y a *une conjonction* qui est obligatoirement suivie du subjonctif : **Bien que** vous **aimiez** parler. . . Agissez **avant qu'**il ne **soit** trop tard.
- Quand *le superlatif* exprime une opinion subjective : C'est **le manuscrit le plus intéressant** qu'on **puisse** imaginer.
- Dans n'importe quelle *phrase relative* où le doute ou la subjectivité est exprimée : Je cherche un ami **qui soit** fiable.

10.21 Que dites-vous ? Qu'est-ce qu'on peut dire pour s'exprimer dans les situations suivantes ? Avec un partenaire, **indiquez vos réactions**. Utilisez le **subjonctif** si possible !

1. Quelqu'un a volé la voiture de votre voisin(e) !
2. Votre professeur de français démissionne suite à un scandale : Il/Elle est accusé(e) d'avoir accepté de l'argent en échange de bonnes notes.
3. Un ami québécois téléphone pour vous inviter à faire de l'escalade de glace avec lui cet hiver. C'est un sport assez dangereux et vous en avez peur.
4. Votre fiancé(e) annonce qu'il/elle ne vous aime plus !
5. Vous vous sentez malade, et vous craignez d'aller chez le médecin.
6. Vous venez d'aller chez le médecin. La visite a duré dix minutes. Il vous a dit que vous êtes en bonne forme. Ensuite, vous devez lui verser une somme d'argent considérable !

Pour aller plus loin : CINÉMA

ACTIVITÉ H : Regardez le film québécois *Bonheur d'occasion*, basé sur le roman du même nom de Gabrielle Roy. Consultez votre cahier électronique !

10.22 Exprimez-vous ! Sur une feuille de papier, **écrivez une phrase** pour décrire un événement choquant ou bizarre (réel ou imaginaire). Ensuite, pliez vos papiers et échangez-les au hasard. Lisez le papier que vous recevez et **circulez** dans la salle de classe en décrivant ce qui s'est passé et en exprimant vos émotions. Vos camarades vont réagir en exprimant leurs émotions. Essayez de parler avec autant de personnes que possible !

MODÈLE : —Les scientifiques ont fait pousser une oreille humaine sur le dos d'une souris.

—Je n'arrive pas à le croire ! C'est aberrant !

À l'écrit *deuxième étape*

10.23 À votre santé ! Vous décidez de téléphoner au personnage que vous avez décrit et de lui parler de la santé et de vos sentiments. Révisez vos descriptions de votre santé et de la santé du personnage que vous avez choisi, et **imaginez un dialogue** entre vous et cette personne. Parlez de votre santé, des maladies que vous avez, des sports que vous faites, et donnez-lui des conseils pour se maintenir en forme et en bonne santé. Bien sûr, vous voulez exprimer vos émotions aussi. Finalement, avec un partenaire, révisez vos dialogues et lisez-les à haute voix.

Épisode 3

En fin de compte

Structures *le discours indirect*

Une enseigne historique à la Place Royale à Québec.

10.24 Qu'est-ce qu'il a dit ? Au moment où Claire raccroche le téléphone, Marie veut tout savoir. Lisez la conversation suivante dans laquelle Claire raconte ce que Gilles lui a dit. Claire va employer le discours indirect pour rapporter les paroles que Gilles lui a dites au téléphone. Dans chaque **phrase originale**, **soulignez le verbe** et **indiquez le temps** utilisé. Dans chaque **phrase de la conversation** où Claire utilise le discours indirect, **soulignez le verbe** subordonné (de la phrase répétée) et **indiquez le temps** utilisé. Ensuite comparez-les ! Pouvez-vous décrire comment fonctionne le discours indirect en analysant ces exemples ?

Les phrases originales : On publie mon article aujourd'hui. Le manuscrit était contrefait. Monsieur Rolland était le cerveau de ce crime. Rolland a tué le bouquiniste parisien. Ne vous inquiétez pas ! Jean-Louis ne savait rien de la contrefaçon des livres. Il aidera les avocats lors du procès contre Rolland. Le professeur Thuillier était le partenaire de Rolland et il a préparé le faux manuscrit !

Le rapportage du dialogue :

CLAIRE : Gilles m'a dit qu'on publiait son article aujourd'hui.
MARIE : Ah bon ?
CLAIRE : Il a affirmé que le manuscrit était contrefait, et il a expliqué que Monsieur Rolland était le cerveau de ce crime. Il a ajouté que Rolland avait tué le bouquiniste parisien.
MARIE : Ça alors !
CLAIRE : Il m'a dit de ne pas m'inquiéter. Il a constaté que Jean-Louis ne savait rien de la contrefaçon des livres et qu'il aiderait les avocats lors du procès contre Rolland.
MARIE : Dis donc !
CLAIRE : Ce n'est pas tout ! Il m'a juré que le professeur Thuillier était le partenaire de Rolland et qu'il avait préparé le faux manuscrit !

le discours indirect

Indirect discourse (**le discours indirect**) is used to relate a conversation to someone. Indirect discourse is very common in spoken French, and the changes in tense sequences in French correspond to the changes one would make in English.

Indirect discourse: present or future

If the verb in the *introductory clause* (usually **dire**) is in the *present or future tense,* there is *no change* to the tense of the verb in the subordinate clause (the sentence being repeated):

Direct	*Indirect* (introductory verb in present/future tense)
«On **publie** mon article.»	Gilles dit qu'on **publie** son article.
«Rolland **a tué** le bouquiniste.»	Il annoncera que Rolland **a tué** le bouquiniste.

Indirect discourse: past tense

If the verb in the *introductory clause* is in a *past tense* (*passé composé, imparfait, plus-que-parfait*), as it often is when relating a prior conversation, some subordinate verbs change tenses and some remain the same:

- There is *no change* to the tense of *the subordinate verb* if the original utterance was in the imperfect, pluperfect, conditional, or past conditional:

Direct	*Indirect* (introductory verb in past tense)
«Le manuscrit **était** contrefait.»	Il a affirmé que le manuscrit **était** contrefait.
«Jean-Louis **n'avait rien fait.**»	Il avait dit que Jean-Louis **n'avait rien fait.**
«Les journalistes **parleraient** de lui.»	Il disait que les journalistes **parleraient** de lui.
«On **aurait interviewé** Jean-Louis.»	Il a dit qu'on **aurait interviewé** Jean-Louis.

- There are *changes* to the tense of the *subordinate verb* if the original utterance was in the present, future, future perfect, or passé composé:

Direct		***Indirect*** (introductory verb in past tense)
présent	→	*imparfait*
«On **publie** mon article.»		Il a dit qu'on **publiait** son article.
passé composé	→	*plus-que-parfait*
«Rolland **a tué** le bouquiniste.»		Il a dit que Rolland **avait tué** le bouquiniste.
futur	→	*conditionnel*
«Jean-Louis **aidera** les avocats.»		Il a dit que Jean-Louis **aiderait** les avocats.
futur antérieur	→	*conditionnel passé*
«Tout le monde **aura lu** mon article.»		Il disait que tout le monde **aurait lu** son article.

Indirect discourse: commands or questions

Use the *conjunction* **que** to link the introductory and subordinate clauses in most instances. Except:

- When relating a command, use the *conjunction* **de** and put the subordinate verb in the *infinitive*:

Direct	***Indirect***
impératif	*infinitif*
«Ne **vous inquiétez** pas !»	Il m'avait dit **de** ne pas **m'inquiéter**.

- When relating a yes/no question, use the *conjunction* **si**, following the sequence of tenses above:

Direct	***Indirect***
«Tu as **lu** mon article ?»	Il demande **si** j'ai **lu** son article. Il a demandé **si** j'avais **lu** son article.

- When relating an information question, use the *relative pronouns* **ce qui** (who?) and **ce que** (what?) or the appropriate interrogative expression, following the sequence of tenses above:

Direct	***Indirect***
«**Qu'est-ce qui** se passe ?»	Il a demandé **ce qui** se passait.
«**Qu'est-ce que** tu as fait ?»	Il a demandé **ce que** j'avais fait.
«**Pourquoi** a-t-il peur ?»	Il a demandé **pourquoi** il avait peur.
«**Où** habiterez-vous ?»	Il a demandé **où** j'habiterais.

Note: In written French, you can avoid indirect discourse by using quotation marks: Gilles a dit: «On publie mon article aujourd'hui».

10.25 Répétez, s'il vous plaît Tout d'un coup, Claire se sent mieux. Les nouvelles de Gilles l'ont ranimée. La mère de Claire veut savoir ce que Claire a appris. Jouez le rôle de Claire, et utilisez le **discours indirect** pour **rapporter les phrases suivantes** que Gilles a prononcées pendant leur conversation téléphonique. Variez les verbes afin de ne pas répéter le verbe **dire** chaque fois !

MODÈLE : «J'ai eu tort.» →
Gilles m'a dit qu'il avait eu tort.

1. «J'ai évité de mentionner votre nom.»
2. «Jean-Louis est innocent.»
3. «Le professeur Thuillier avait fabriqué le manuscrit.»

4. «Thuillier a averti Rolland que je commençais mes recherches.»
5. «On a arrêté Monsieur Thuillier en Belgique.»
6. «André Thibodeau était un vrai amateur de livres anciens.»
7. «Jean-Louis sera libéré après le procès.»
8. «Je vous dis la vérité.»
9. «Thuillier ne retournera pas à l'université.»
10. «L'université aura renvoyé Thuillier avant son retour au Québec.»
11. «Il faudra vous trouver un nouveau directeur de thèse.»
12. «On n'est jamais sûr de rien.»

le Québec

Qu'est-ce que Sinbad dit à propos de la culture québécoise ? Regardez la vidéo et consultez votre cahier d'activités !

10.26 Quelles questions ? Marie, qui écoutait pendant que Claire parlait au téléphone, a entendu toutes les questions que Claire a posées à Gilles. Elle veut savoir les réponses exactes que Gilles lui a données, mais Claire ne se souvient pas de toutes ses questions. Donc, Marie répète toutes les questions que Claire a posées. En jouant le rôle de Marie, employez **le discours indirect** pour **rapporter les questions** suivantes.

MODÈLE : «Le manuscrit que j'ai lu était contrefait ?» →
Tu lui as demandé si le manuscrit que tu avais lu était contrefait.

1. «Rolland a tué Nicolas Gustave ?»
2. «Qu'est-ce que Jean-Louis savait de ce crime ?»
3. «Jean-Louis est-il innocent ?»
4. «Notre rencontre, était-elle une vraie coïncidence ?»
5. «Qu'est-ce qui se passera ?»

10.27 Devinez les citations ! Claire branche son ordinateur portable et trouve l'article de Gilles sur Internet. En voici quelques phrases dans lesquelles Gilles a employé le discours indirect. Imaginez les citations originales !

MODÈLE : Un informateur a dit que plusieurs bouquinistes vendaient des livres contrefaits. →
«Plusieurs bouquinistes vendent des livres contrefaits.»

1. Un employé de la maison Rolland a affirmé que le manuscrit était faux.
2. On lui a demandé depuis combien de temps il travaillait pour Rolland.
3. L'employé a affirmé qu'il avait acheté le manuscrit à Dakar avec l'argent de Rolland.
4. Une étudiante de doctorat lui a révélé qu'un anachronisme existait dans le texte.
5. Rolland a dit qu'il consulterait ses avocats avant de répondre aux accusations.
6. Rolland a conseillé au public d'attendre les résulats du procès avant de le condamner.
7. Thuillier a promis qu'il n'enseignerait plus la littérature si on le libérait.

Langue

Pour **rapporter une conversation**, il y a beaucoup de verbes qu'on peut employer. On n'est pas limité au verbe **dire** ! On peut substituer un des verbes suivants : affirmer que, ajouter que, annoncer que, apprendre à quelqu'un que, assurer que, avertir quelqu'un que, avouer que, communiquer que, confirmer que, constater que, convaincre quelqu'un que, crier à quelqu'un que, déclarer que, démontrer que, s'exclamer que, indiquer que, insister que, juger que, jurer que, mentionner que, montrer que, prétendre que (*to claim that*), promettre que, prouver que, répondre que, révéler que.

Pour aller plus loin : CULTURE

ACTIVITÉ 1 : Explorez le Festival de la Santé à Montréal. Consultez votre cahier électronique !

10.28 Qu'est-ce que je vous ai dit ? Pensez à ce que vos professeurs vous ont dit dans le passé : leurs conseils, leurs blagues, leurs anecdotes. Avec un partenaire, **faites une liste de trois ou quatre choses** que vos professeurs vous ont dites. Utilisez le **discours indirect**. Ensuite, comparez votre liste avec celles de vos camarades.

Pour aller plus loin : CULTURE

ACTIVITÉ J :

Connaissez-vous des athlètes canadiens ? Consultez votre cahier électronique !

10.29 Écoutez et faites circuler ! *(Listen and pass it on)* Placez vos chaises en cercle. **Pensez à une question** au sujet des sports ou de la santé, et posez-la à la personne à votre droite. Ensuite, **rapportez la réponse de cette personne à la personne à votre gauche**. Cette personne répétera la phrase dans l'oreille de la personne à sa gauche et ainsi de suite. Continuez jusqu'à ce que vous entendez votre réponse de la personne à votre droite ! Est-ce exactement ce que vous avez dit ?

MODÈLE : (*à droite*) — Marie, as-tu déjà fait du ski ?
(*Marie répond*) — Oui, j'ai fait du ski l'hiver dernier.
(*à gauche*) — Marie a dit qu'elle avait fait du ski l'hiver dernier.

Un jour, Claire reçoit une lettre écrite à la main, envoyée de Paris. . .

En fin de compte

Paris, le 5 décembre 2003

Ma chère Claire,

Je ne sais pas comment commencer cette lettre. J'éprouve° de si nombreuses émotions à la fois° : de la tristesse, de la colère, de la honte, de l'angoisse. Enfin, j'imagine que le reporter qui a exposé l'affaire du faux manuscrit t'a déjà tout expliqué. Il faut que je te dise que je suis complètement innocent dans cette affaire. J'ignorais° ce que mon patron faisait. Je voulais l'impressionner et atteindre mon but, celui d'acquérir et d'authentifier le manuscrit, mais je ne savais pas que ce manuscrit était contrefait. Je ne l'aurais jamais poursuivi si je l'avais su, et je ne t'aurais jamais impliquée dans cette affaire. J'ai vraiment voulu t'aider avec ta thèse. Tout ce que j'ai fait au cours° des mois que nous avons passés ensemble, je l'ai fait de bon cœur.° Il est important que tu comprennes cela. Je suis vraiment désolé. Je n'ai jamais eu l'intention de te mettre dans une situation aussi difficile.

En fin de compte,° j'ai été la dupe de mon patron. Je me sens entièrement responsable des ennuis que je t'ai causés. J'aurais dû deviner° que ce que mon patron faisait était illégal. Avant mon départ pour la Nouvelle-Orléans en août, il m'avait

to feel · *at once* · *to not know, be ignorant of* · *throughout, during* · *sincerely* · *all said and done* · *to guess*

parlé de l'importance de la discrétion et il m'avait défendu de contacter la police. C'est pour cette raison que je n'ai pas voulu téléphoner à la police quand on a cambriolé° mon appartement à Versailles. Ce que j'étais aveugle° ! Mais après tout cela, j'ai appris une bonne leçon. En un mot, dans le monde des affaires, c'est chacun pour soi. Il faut toujours écouter son instinct, poser des questions difficiles et faire ce qu'on pense être juste.

to burglarize
blind

Encore une fois, je suis navré que tu aies été la victime de cette affaire, et j'espère que tu me pardonneras un jour. Je me permets de te souhaiter mes meilleurs en cette fin d'année. Écris-moi, si tu le veux. Je serai toujours heureux d'avoir de tes nouvelles.

Bien à toi,
Jean-Louis

Après avoir lu

10.30 Avez-vous compris ? Après avoir lu la lettre ci-dessus, lisez les questions suivantes et **donnez vos opinions personnelles**. Discutez en petits groupes.

1. Pourquoi est-ce que Jean-Louis écrit à Claire ? Quel est son état d'esprit ?
2. Comment explique-t-il sa naïveté ou son manque de perspicacité en ce qui concerne les affaires de son patron ?
3. Quelles leçons Jean-Louis a-t-il apprises ? Êtes-vous d'accord avec ses conclusions ?
4. Jean-Louis vous paraît-il sincère ? Est-ce que vous lui pardonneriez ?
5. Imaginez la réaction de Claire lorsqu'elle lit cette lettre. Écrira-t-elle une réponse ? Quel en sera le ton ?

10.31 D'accord ou pas d'accord ? Après avoir lu le message ci-dessus, lisez les phrases suivantes et donnez vos opinions personnelles. Discutez en petits groupes.

	D'accord	Pas d'accord
1. Jean-Louis est vraiment désolé.	_______	_______
2. Il savait que son patron faisait des choses illégales.	_______	_______
3. Il écrit à Claire parce qu'il se sent coupable.	_______	_______
4. Claire a été la seule victime dans cette affaire.	_______	_______
5. Claire enverra une réponse à Jean-Louis.	_______	_______

conclure une histoire

To conclude En conclusion / En fin de compte / En somme / En un mot / En bref. . .
Pour conclure / Finalement / Tout compte fait / Après tout / Ils ont fini par. . .
Au fond / Enfin / En guise de conclusion (*by way of conclusion*). . .
J'ai tout dit ! / Et voilà ! / Voilà l'affaire ! / C'est tout ! / Tout est bien qui finit bien !
Ils vécurent heureux et eurent beaucoup d'enfants. Fin !

10.32 Situations Que diriez-vous dans les situations suivantes pour conclure l'histoire ? Avec un partenaire, **décidez de ce que vous pourriez dire**.

1. Vous venez d'expliquer à votre ami(e) pourquoi vous êtes en retard à votre rendez-vous.
2. Vos amis voulaient savoir comment vous avez rencontré votre meilleur(e) ami(e). Vous achevez l'histoire.
3. Vous terminez un conte de fées que vous avez inventé pour votre neveu/nièce.
4. Vous venez d'expliquer à votre fiancé(e) comment vous avez rencontré quelqu'un au cours d'un voyage au Québec.
5. Dans votre classe de français, vous terminez une présentation orale au sujet de l'histoire du Québec.

10.33 Achevons ! Vous ennuyez-vous rapidement quand les autres parlent de leurs émotions ? En petits groupes, pensez à une histoire émouvante que vous n'avez pas envie d'entendre. **Écrivez le début de votre histoire** au tableau. Ensuite, lisez les débuts des histoires des autres groupes et **écrivez une conclusion** rapide à chaque histoire ! Comparez vos conclusions avec celles de vos camarades.

À l'écrit *troisième étape*

10.34 À votre santé Écrivez une lettre à Claire dans laquelle vous rapportez tout ce que l'autre personne vous a dit de sa santé et tout ce qu'il/elle vous a conseillé de faire (révisez vos Activités 13 et 23). N'oubliez pas d'exprimer vos sentiments sur ce qui se passe dans la vie de Claire en ce moment. Faites attention à l'usage du **discours indirect** et à votre façon de **conclure la lettre**. Échangez vos lettres (par courriel, si vous voulez !) et offrez une courte réponse à votre camarade de classe en jouant le rôle de Claire.

Dénouement

Activités de révision

10.35 Belle opinion ! Sur une feuille de papier, **écrivez une opinion** au sujet des sports ou de la santé des gens qui habitent en Amérique du Nord (aux États-Unis, au Canada, au Mexique). Cette fois, mettez-y votre nom ! Pliez vos papiers et échangez-les au hasard. Ensuite, **circulez** parmi vos camarades et rapportez l'opinion de l'auteur. Exprimez vos émotions en ce qui concerne cette opinion (le bonheur, la tristesse, la surprise, le peur, la colère). Attention à l'usage du **discours indirect** en rapportant l'opinion de l'auteur et à l'usage du **subjonctif** en exprimant vos émotions !

MODÈLE : «Je pense que les Américains sont trop stressés parce qu'ils sont trop préoccupés par l'argent.»

Élisabeth pense que les Américains sont trop stressés parce qu'ils sont trop préoccupés par l'argent. J'ai peur qu'elle ait raison !

Pour aller plus loin : CULTURE

ACTIVITACTIVITÉ K : Voulez-vous apprendre à jouer aux boules ? C'est un jeu français amusant ! Consultez votre cahier électronique !

10.36 Une charade ! Divisez la classe en équipes (quatre ou cinq équipes). Choisissez une personne de la première équipe qui se présente devant la classe. Le professeur lui indique un sport ou une maladie de la liste de vocabulaire de ce chapitre. **L'étudiant(e) aura une minute pour faire comprendre à son équipe le mot de vocabulaire** en question, mais **sans parler** ! Il faut faire des gestes ou de la pantomime. Si son équipe devine le mot, elle reçoit un point et on passe à la prochaine équipe. Si son équipe n'arrive pas à deviner le mot, les autres équipes peuvent tenter une réponse. L'équipe qui devine le mot gagne un point. L'équipe avec le plus grand nombre de points à la fin gagne !

Avant de lire *Les Aurores montréales*

10.37 Premières impressions Lisez l'extrait suivant, qui vient d'une nouvelle du recueil *Les Aurores montréales* de Monique Proulx, sans essayer de comprendre chaque mot. Après votre première lecture du texte, **répondez** aux questions suivantes. Ensuite, **relisez** le texte une deuxième fois, plus attentivement.

1. Quel est le rapport entre Martine et Fabienne ? Amies ? Cousines ? Sœurs ? Mère et fille ?
2. Où se passe cette histoire ? En ville ? À la campagne ?
3. Quand se déroule cette histoire ? Au présent ? Au passé ? À l'avenir ?
4. Décrivez les émotions de Martine lors de la visite de Fabienne : Est-elle contente ? fâchée ? ennuyée ? angoissée ? Ou ressent-elle plusieurs émotions à la fois ?
5. Quelles émotions éprouve-t-elle à la fin de l'extrait ?

La ville de Montréal vue du plateau au sommet du Mont Royal.

lisez

Les Aurores montréales

Cette nouvelle vient du recueil de Monique Proulx intitulé Les Aurores montréales. *En choisissant ce titre, Proulx joue sur l'expression «aurore boréale» — phénomène lumineux observable dans les cieux dans les régions du nord — et le nom de la ville de Montréal, la plus grande ville de la province du Québec. Dans ce recueil, publié au Québec en 1996, Proulx nous offre une pluralité de perspectives sur la vie humaine à travers les histoires de plusieurs habitants de la ville de Montréal. Dans la nouvelle «Le futile et l'essentiel», d'où est tiré l'extrait suivant, une mère arrive de la campagne pour passer quelques jours chez sa fille, une jeune femme qui habite à Montréal. La visite soulève toutes sortes d'émotions de la part de la jeune femme qui, depuis quelques années, cherche à oublier le passé et à vivre indépendamment. . .*

■ Monique Proulx

Les Aurores montréales (extrait)

Échoué° devant la gare comme une baleine anthropophage,° l'autobus avait commencé à se délester° de ses intérieurs : de petits êtres fripés° émergeaient de l'air conditionné en clignotant des yeux, parmi lesquels Martine reconnut instantanément Fabienne, le chapeau de guingois° sur la tête. Le chapeau ondoya° jusqu'à la soute à bagages,° parut engager là quelque rixe° sanglante avec des têtes nues,° puis resurgit triomphant de la mêlée avec, en guise de butin,° deux valises corpulentes. Le visage de Fabienne, d'abord flou,° devint quelque chose de très anxieux qui s'avançait rapidement vers Martine, en essayant de sourire.

run aground/man-eating
to unburden oneself/tired
lopsided
to undulate/luggage compartment
scuffle/uncovered
spoils
soft

—J'ai faim, clama de loin Fabienne, bien avant qu'elles se touchent. Le voyage a été horrible, des enfants mal élevés m'ont crié trois heures dans les oreilles, ma voisine puait° la sueur, j'aurais dû prendre le train, quelle chaleur, quel monde, j'ai très faim, où on va ?. . .

to stink

—Bonjour, maman.

Elles s'étreignirent° maladroitement. Fabienne sentait° l'eau de Cologne bon marché et la confiture, la naphtaline° des armoires et le gazon° fraîchement tondu° du petit bungalow de Val-Bélair. Martine fut envahie aussitôt par des relents° fantômes qui la secouèrent.° Une touffeur° de marécage sourdait° de la rivière Jacques-Cartier en crue° tandis que les vêtements humides trépidaient° sur la corde à linge, son père allumait une pipe sur la galerie et tout à coup c'était l'été crissant° de foin,° de cigales et de tabac sucré, «tu fumes trop, disait Fabienne, tu fumes trop, c'est dangereux.»

to embrace/to smell
mothballs/lawn
to mow
musty smells/to shake up/suffocating heat
springing up/rising
to vibrate
squeaking/hay

Martine s'empara° des corpulentes valises et elles se mirent° à louvoyer° vers la sortie. Fabienne déambulait° de côté tel un crabe, le regard sollicité par mille monstruosités citadines° («Mon Dieu ! La fille a les cheveux roses. . . Ma parole, ce type se promène quasiment° TOUT NU !. . . As-tu vu, c'est tous des nègres, les chauffeurs de taxi. . . »). Mais ce n'est qu'à bord de la voiture, alors qu'elles remontaient la rue Berri dans la fièvre assassine des fins de journée, plongées soudain au cœur de la faune cavalant° chacun pour soi vers sa tanière,° que Martine retrouva intégralement sa mère, moulin à débiter du vide,° incroyable déversoir° de puérilités° diverses. «Ton frère s'est acheté une tondeuse° à propulsion avec une manette° intégrée qui verse de l'insecticide, la petite Agnès s'est fait couper les cheveux comme Madonna c'est un amour, Madame Cayouette tu te rappelles la voisine d'en face avec une tache de vin° sur la joue ? m'a dit l'autre jour que Madame Bigras — la nouvelle voisine d'en arrière qui a un petit chien bâtard insupportable — prétend que je jette mes feuilles mortes dans sa cour, est-ce assez insultant ?»

to take hold of/began to
to tack/to saunter
city (adj)
almost
running away/ den, hovel
rumor mill of emptiness/safety-valve/ childishness/mower
handle
birthmark

Martine, prise de vertige, luttait désespérément pour ne pas couler° : peut-être pouvait-on mourir d'une surdose° d'insignifiances, ou, à tout le moins, en rester diminuée pour la vie, et luttait pour recréer le silence intérieur tandis que toutes sortes d'animalcules criards° — petite Agnès Madonna à propulsion insecticide tache de vin de petit chien bâtard sur feuilles mortes — s'infiltraient en ricanant° dans ses oreilles. Elle risqua un coup d'œil vers sa mère : le visage de Fabienne, anémié° par l'âge et les diètes successives, était tendu° avec avidité vers la rue Saint-Denis, mais son regard demeurait replié en dedans, au creux° des vaguelettes clapotantes° qui lui tenaient lieu d'univers.

to run, slip away
overdose
minuscule nagging insects
to sneer
made anemic
to stretch
hollow
choppy little waves

Sitôt franchie la porte de l'appartement de Martine, Fabienne manifesta un désarroi° infini. Elle était venue à Montréal deux ans auparavant, alors que le coquet six pièces de sa fille empruntait toutes les apparences de la normalité. Maintenant, elle se retrouvait dans un désert immense et blanc, ANORMALEMENT immense et blanc, et elle cherchait des yeux les cloisons,° les portes, les meubles, toutes ces choses familières qui proclament clairement l'individu civilisé.

disarray
partitions

—Où est Simon ? finit-elle par lâcher,° d'un ton effaré qui suggérait : où diable sont passés les murs et le seul être raisonnable de cet endroit ?. . .

to release

—Voyons, maman.

Simon s'était volatilisé° depuis deux ans, en même temps que les murs et la pesanteur° ancienne de l'existence, et Fabienne avait été la première à l'apprendre et à l'oublier aussitôt. Martine n'eut pas l'énergie de lui reprocher sa bévue.° Elle pressentait° que cette semaine serait infernale, elle l'avait pressenti avant même de s'abandonner à cette masochiste invitation, et maintenant sa mère se tenait devant elle, flanquée de son absurde éternel petit chapeau et de ses valises de provinciale, silencieuse pour un moment infinitésimal, et la certitude s'installait : la semaine, oui, serait infernale.

to fade away
weight, heaviness
blunder/to sense, foreshadow

to get up the courage Avec une audace de petite fille, Fabienne s'enhardit° à pénétrer plus avant dans le loft, amusée par le claquement martial que produisaient ses talons sur le plancher de cette cathédrale vide. Elle ouvrit avec empressement la porte qui menait aux toilettes — enfin ! quelque chose d'un peu conventionnel ! — puis une autre porte, qui ouvrait sur une petite pièce sans fenêtre, munie d'un seul futon, baignée par un éclairage bleuâtre.

—C'est ma chambre ? s'enquit-elle avec terreur.

—Non, dit Martine. C'est mon. . . mon coin de méditation. De réflexion, corrigea-t-elle, devant le regard ahuri° de Fabienne. *disconcerted*

Après, il fallut manger de toute urgence, car l'estomac de Fabienne exigeait de la ponctualité dans l'ingurgitation des nourritures. Sa mère aurait préféré se bâfrer° parmi le monde, au sein de la foule huppée° si possible, mais Martine avait confectionné un couscous aux légumes que Fabienne, amante enragée de protéines animales, dévora avec désolation. *to stuff oneself/high-class*

Après, toute la soirée se tenait encore devant elles, inentamée,° stagnante, attendant lugubrement de passer, et ce n'était que la première. Fabienne fut saisie d'une recrudescence de volubilité° : les inepties° de la tribu abominable, là-bas, connurent de nouveau leur heure de gloire. En proie à une lâche résignation, Martine écoutait vraiment par moments, sidérée° une fois de plus par l'éloignement galactique de ces êtres tiédasses,° ses frères, ses sœurs, agglutinés° à des semblablement tarés,° qui vivaient dans la détestation inquiète de tout ce qui émergeait de Val-Bélair. Fabienne était la plus récupérable, mais elle traînait° tant de choses lourdes avec elle, tant de fardeaux° auxquels Martine tentait depuis toujours d'échapper. Et elle ne s'informait jamais de Martine, jamais sincèrement, comme horrifiée par l'étrange vie que menait sa cadette. Martine se laissait sombrer dans une hargne° marécageuse lorsque Fabienne, d'elle-même, interrompit soudain le déluge pour bondir vers la plus volumineuse de ses valises.

unbroached · *new outbreak of talkiness/ineptitudes* · *flabbergasted/tepid* · *bound to/degenerate* · *to drag* · *burdens* · *bad temper*

—C'est vrai ! J'oubliais !. . . Je t'ai apporté des petites choses. . .

Et elle sortit des entrailles de sa valise de provinciale des confitures de framboises et de prunes, des poires à l'alcool, du vinaigre de mûres sauvages, des marinades fruitées, des pains de ménage, du vin de gadelle,° des noisettes, du sucre d'érable, des brioches, une catalogne° tissée° à la main, deux chandails,° des gants et un passe-montagne° assortis en laine rouge sur lesquels voletaient° des bernaches° noires. Et ce qui luisait° dans ses yeux, tandis qu'elle étalait fièrement ses trésors, était de l'authentique amour maternel, qui ne s'achète ni ne se feint, qui laisse un trou° vertigineux quand il vient à manquer, devant lequel il n'y a rien d'autre à faire que fondre° d'émotion.

red currant · *wool rug/to weave* · *sweaters/balaclava (a hat that covers ears)* · *to flutter/barnacles/to glow* · *hole* · *to melt*

Pour aller plus loin : CULTURE

ACTIVITÉ L : Apprenez un peu plus sur la vie et l'œuvre de Monique Proulx. Consultez votre cahier électronique !

Après avoir lu

10.38 Avez-vous compris ? En petits groupes, **discutez de vos réponses** aux questions suivantes.

1. Décrivez le ton de cet extrait et la gamme d'émotions que ressent Martine à cause de l'arrivée de sa mère à Montréal. Justifiez vos impressions en citant le texte.
2. Est-ce que les émotions de Martine sont typiques pour une femme qui reçoit sa mère chez elle ? Pourquoi ou pourquoi pas ?

3. Imaginez le passé de Martine : Pourquoi a-t-elle quitté Val-Bélair pour aller vivre en ville ? Avec qui vivait-elle ? Quelle était sa réaction dans les débuts ? De quelle façon sa vie a-t-elle changé ?
4. Que savez-vous de la vie de Fabienne à Val-Bélair ? Qu'est-ce que Fabienne disait à son mari lorsqu'il fumait sa pipe ? Qu'est-ce que la voisine, Madame Cayouette, a dit que Madame Bigras avait dit de Fabienne ?
5. Quels cadeaux est-ce que Fabienne a apportés ? Est-ce que ce sont des cadeaux que vous recevriez d'un membre de votre famille lors d'une visite ?
6. À la fin de l'extrait, Martine est émue : est-ce à cause des cadeaux ou est-ce autre chose ? Expliquez.

10.39 D'accord ou pas d'accord ? Après avoir lu l'extrait de la nouvelle de Proulx, lisez les phrases suivantes et **donnez votre opinion**. Discutez de vos réponses en petits groupes.

	D'accord	Pas d'accord
1. Fabienne a pris l'avion pour aller à Montréal.	_______	_______
2. Martine est contente de voir Fabienne au début.	_______	_______
3. Fabienne est une femme réservée et timide.	_______	_______
4. Martine s'intéresse à ce qui se passe à Val-Bélair où habitent Fabienne et son frère.	_______	_______
5. En fin de compte, Martine est touchée par l'amour de Fabienne.	_______	_______

10.40 Analyse littéraire Examinez ce texte de près. Répondez aux questions suivantes et **discutez de vos réponses** en classe.

1. Quel est le ton du texte ? Qu'est-ce qui contribue à ce ton ? Le vocabulaire ? Le style d'écriture ? La forme du texte ? Les verbes ? La ponctuation ? Le choix de vocabulaire ?
2. Y a-t-il des images ou des couleurs qui dominent dans ce texte ? Comment est-ce que ces images ont influencé votre lecture du texte ?
3. Quel temps domine dans ce texte (le présent, le passé, le futur, etc.) ? Quel est l'effet de l'usage de ce temps ? Un sens d'urgence ? Une distance impersonnelle ? La nostalgie ? La possibilité ? La certitude ou l'incertitude ? L'orgueil ? Autre chose ? Y a-t-il un moment où le temps change ? Quel en est l'effet ?
4. Y a-t-il d'autres éléments structurels (ponctuation, mots ou sons répétés, phrases longues ou courtes, contrastes, métaphores, etc.) que l'auteur emploie systématiquement ? Si oui, quels sont les effets de l'emploi de ces éléments ?

Synthèses

10.41 Réfléchissons à la culture Voici quelques éléments de la culture québécoise que vous avez étudiés dans ce chapitre. En petits groupes, **répondez** aux questions et **discutez de vos impressions** avec vos camarades.

les autochtones **les sports d'hiver** **la Loi 101**

1. Définissez ou décrivez chaque élément.
2. Pourquoi chaque élément est-il important à cette culture ? Y a-t-il un phénomène historique, géographique ou social qui explique son importance ?
3. À votre avis, est-ce que ces éléments témoignent de la richesse et de la diversité et de la complexité de la culture québécoise de nos jours, ou sont-ils stéréotypiques ? Pourquoi ?
4. Est-ce que votre impression de cette culture est différente maintenant que vous avez commencé à l'étudier ? Si oui, comment et pourquoi ? Si non, pourquoi pas ?

le Québec

Pour Sinbad, qu'est-ce que ça veut dire «être Québécois» ? Regardez la vidéo et consultez votre cahier d'activités !

10.42 À débattre Lisez les questions suivantes et **discutez** en groupes. Si possible, parlez de vos expériences personnelles relatives aux questions.

1. **Les effets psychologiques ?** Une des raisons pour lesquelles beaucoup de Québécois francophones revendiquent leur souveraineté est le souvenir de la discrimination qu'ils ont subie de la part des colonisateurs anglais. On peut constater que les effets psychologiques de la colonisation ont été plus importants que les effets économiques ou sociaux. Pensez-vous que les effets psychologiques jouent un rôle important dans le débat de la souveraineté ? Pourquoi ou pourquoi pas ?
2. **Le rapport esprit-corps !** Existe-t-il un rapport entre la santé physique et l'état d'esprit (*mind*) ? Les médecins de l'Europe et de l'Amérique du Nord, pour la plupart, guérissent les malades avec des médicaments ou des traitements qui s'adressent au corps. Pourtant, dans beaucoup de cultures, on croit que ces maladies peuvent être soignées, ou mieux évitées, en traitant l'esprit. Qu'en pensez-vous ? Et, si vous pensez qu'un rapport existe entre l'esprit et le corps, est-ce que les frais des massages et de la méditation devraient être payés par les compagnies d'assurance médicale ? Pourquoi ou pourquoi pas ?
3. **Fumeur ou non-fumeur ?** Le grand débat continue ! Dans beaucoup de bâtiments et restaurants, on n'a plus le droit de fumer. On dit que la fumée est nocive (*harmful*) pour ceux qui la respirent. Pourtant, les

cigarettes ne sont pas illégales. Les fumeurs ont-ils le droit de fumer où ils veulent ? Même si vous êtes non-fumeur, pensez-vous que les règles contre les fumeurs soient arbitraires ? Il y a beaucoup d'autres choses qui nuisent plus sérieusement à la santé publique. Alors, pourquoi limiter particulièrement l'usage du tabac ?

10.43 À l'impromptu Voici des situations interactives. Avec une ou deux autres personnes, **choisissez une scène et improvisez devant la classe**. Si vous ne voulez pas improviser, écrivez votre dialogue avant et puis jouez-le pour la classe.

1. À Mont-Tremblant
   (a) Vous êtes en vacances au Québec. Vous venez d'arriver à Mont-Tremblant pour faire du ski avec des amis mais vous n'avez plus envie de monter au sommet de la montagne. Essayez d'expliquer à vos amis que pour la première fois de votre vie, vous souffrez du vertige (*fear of heights*) ! Revenez sur le sujet jusqu'à ce que vous soyez entendu(e).
   (b) Vous êtes à Mont-Tremblant pour skier avec des amis. Un(e) de vos amis dit qu'il/elle souffre du vertige. Vous pensez qu'il/elle exagère un peu. Vous ne voulez pas passer la journée à parler dans votre chambre d'hôtel. Essayez de mettre fin à cette conversation.
   (c) Vous aussi vous êtes à Mont-Tremblant pour skier avec des amis. Un(e) de vos amis souffre du vertige. Donnez-lui des conseils en suggérant de nombreux remèdes contre le vertige (massages, jacuzzi, sauna, méditation, etc.).
2. Aux jeux Olympiques
   (a) Vous assistez aux jeux Olympiques d'hiver. Votre ami(e) qui connaît un juge canadien vous invite à une réception afin de rencontrer les athlètes canadiens. Quelques-uns d'entre eux sont légèrement blessés et vous font part de ce qui leur est arrivé et des blessures qu'ils ont endurées.
   (b) Vous êtes skieur/skieuse et vous vous êtes blessé(e) au genou. Parlez de l'incident et dites ce que vous ont conseillé les médecins afin de vous rétablir au plus tôt. Avouez aussi que vous êtes arrivé à la 18ème place.
   (c) Vous êtes patineur/patineuse de glace. Cela fait une semaine que vous avez mal au cœur. Parlez de vos symptômes et des remèdes suggérés par les médecins. Annoncez que vous avez gagné la médaille d'argent dans votre compétition de patinage artistique.

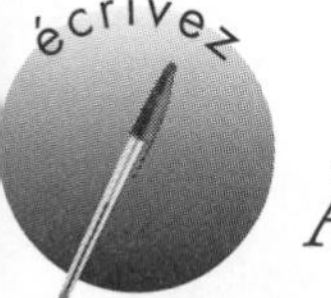

À l'écrit *étape finale*

10.44 À votre santé ! Tout est bien qui finit bien ! Vous venez d'écrire une lettre à Claire. Quelle sera sa réaction ? Comment est-ce que l'histoire se conclut ? Révisez et élaborez vos travaux d'écriture de ce chapitre (Activités 13, 23 et 34) et **écrivez une conclusion narrative à l'histoire du faux manuscrit de Laclos**.

Pour agir :
LE QUÉBEC !

Si vous voulez bouger et faire quelque chose pour mieux connaître le Québec, ou pour aider les autres à mieux connaître les cultures francophones, consultez la section **Pour agir** dans votre cahier électronique ! Il y a tant de choses à faire :

- **Vendez du sirop d'érable** et contribuez l'argent que vous gagnez à une organisation à but non lucratif au Québec.
- **Entrez en contact** avec des québécois francophones.
- **Organisez des jeux francophones** sur votre campus et contribuez l'argent à une organisation à but non lucratif !
- **Voyagez au Québec ou suivez des cours d'été** à l'Université Laval à Québec.

VOCABULAIRE UTILE

Les sports

canoë (*m.*) — *canoe*
canot (*m.*) — *canoe (reg. Québec)*
cyclisme (*m.*) — *cycling*
équitation (*f.*) — *horseback riding*
escalade (*f.*) de glace — *ice climbing*
filet (*m.*) — *net*
hockey (*m.*) sur glace — *ice hockey*
marche (*f.*) — *walking*
natation (*f.*) — *swimming*
pagaies (*f. pl.*) — *paddles*
patin (*m.*) en ligne — *in-line skating*
patinage (*m.*) — *skating*
piste (*f.*) — *trail*
planche (*f.*) à voile — *windsurfing*
planche (*f.*) de neige — *snowboarding*
randonnée (*f.*) — *hiking*
raquette (*f.*) de neige — *snowshoeing*
ski (*m.*) de fond — *cross-country skiing*
ski (*m.*) nautique — *waterskiing*
toboggan (*m.*) — *sledding*
vélo (*m.*) — *biking*
VTT (vélo tout-terrain) (*m.*) — *mountain bike*

Décrire son état

à tes souhaits — *in America, "Bless you!"*
déprimé(e) — *depressed*
ému(e) — *emotional, moved*
enrhumé(e) — *sick with a cold*
être à bout de nerfs — *to have frazzled nerves*
faire du bien à qqn — *to do good, to make someone feel better*
fiévreux(-euse) — *feverish*
mal (*m.*) à la gorge — *sore throat*
rhume (*m.*) — *cold (illness)*
se moucher — *to blow one's nose*
tomber malade — *to get sick*

Divers

exprès — *on purpose*
jurer — *to swear*
manigancer — *to plot*
prétendre que — *to claim that*
saisir — *to grasp, understand*
tourtière (*f.*) — *meat pie (reg. Québec)*
trahir — *to betray*

La santé

aspirine (*f.*) — *aspirin*
attaque (*f.*) d'apoplexie — *stroke*
avoir une bronchite — *to have bronchitis*
béquilles (*f. pl.*) — *crutches*
carie (*f.*) dentaire — *cavity (in a tooth)*
comprimé (*m.*) — *tablet, lozenge*
contagieux(-euse) — *contagious*
coup (*m.*) de soleil — *sunburn*
courbature (*f.*) — *muscle aches*
crise (*f.*) cardiaque — *heart attack*
démangeaison (*f.*) — *itch*
enceinte — *pregnant*
éternuer — *to sneeze*
être allergique — *to be allergic to something*
être atteint(e) de l'arthrite — *to have arthritis*
  de rhumatisme — *rheumatoid arthritis*
être en forme — *to be in shape*
être enrhumé(e) — *to have a cold*
gueule (*f.*) de bois — *hangover (slang)*
être grippé(e) — *to have the flu*
fièvre (*f.*) — *fever*
frissonner — *to shiver*
grippe (*f.*) — *flu*
mal (*m.*) au cœur — *heartburn*
maladie (*f.*) du cœur — *heart disease*
médicament (*m.*) — *medicine*
nausée (*f.*) — *nausea*
plâtre (*m.*) — *cast*
pneumonie (*f.*) — *pneumonia*
poignet (*m.*) — *wrist*
renifler — *to sniffle*
repos (*m.*) — *rest*
se casser le bras — *to break one's leg*
se fouler la cheville — *to sprain one's ankle*
SIDA (*m.*) — *AIDS*
sirop (*m.*) — *cough syrup*
tousser — *to cough*
toux (*f.*) — *cough*
vertige (*m.*) — *vertigo, dizziness*

Décrire les circonstances

affreux(-euse) — *atrocious*
bêtise (*f.*) — *mistake, gaffe*
de bon cœur — *with sincerity, sincerely*
ébruiter — *to leak (news, information)*
être abasourdi(e) — *to be flabbergasted*
faux, fausse — *wrong; fake*
soupçonner — *to suspect*
tout s'explique ! — *everything makes sense !*
trouvaille (*f.*) — *a find*

Conjugaisons de verbes

Verbes réguliers en -er

Modèle: **travailler** (*to work*)

Présent	*je travaille, tu travailles, il/elle/on travaille, nous travaillons, vous travaillez, ils/elles travaillent*
Impératif	*travaille, travaillons, travaillez*
Passé composé	*j'ai travaillé, tu as travaillé, il/elle/on a travaillé, nous avons travaillé, vous avez travaillé, ils/elles ont travaillé*
Imparfait	*je travaillais, tu travaillais, il/elle/on travaillait, nous travaillions, vous travailliez, ils/elles travaillaient*
Plus-que-parfait	*j'avais travaillé, tu avais travaillé, il/elle/on avait travaillé, nous avions travaillé, vous aviez travaillé, ils/elles avaient travaillé*
Passé simple	*je travaillai, tu travaillas, il/elle/on travailla, nous travaillâmes, vous travaillâtes, ils/elles travaillèrent*
Subjonctif	*je travaille, tu travailles, il/elle/on travaille, nous travaillions, vous travailliez, ils/elles travaillent*
Subjonctif passé	*j'aie travaillé, tu aies travaillé, il/elle/on ait travaillé, nous ayons travaillé, vous ayez travaillé, ils/elles aient travaillé*
Futur	*je travaillerai, tu travailleras, il/elle/on travaillera, nous travaillerons, vous travaillerez, ils/elles travailleront*
Futur antérieur	*j'aurai travaillé, tu auras travaillé, il/elle/on aura travaillé, nous aurons travaillé, vous aurez travaillé, ils/elles auront travaillé*
Conditionnel	*je travaillerais, tu travaillerais, il/elle/on travaillerait, nous travaillerions, vous travailleriez, ils/elles travailleraient*
Conditionnel passé	*j'aurais travaillé, tu aurais travaillé, il/elle/on aurait travaillé, nous aurions travaillé, vous auriez travaillé, ils/elles auraient travaillé*

Quelques autres ***verbes réguliers en -er****: adorer, aimer, apprécier, arriver, chanter, danser, détester, discuter, donner* (to give), *écouter, gérer* (to manage), *s'intéresser à* (to be interested in), *jouer, louer* (to rent), *marcher* (to walk, to function), *parler, penser, préparer, rester* (to stay), *s'habiller* (to get dressed), *se brosser, se coiffer* (to do one's hair), *se contenter de* (to be happy with), *se coucher, se parler, se raser, se reposer* (to relax, to rest), *se réveiller* (to wake up), *se téléphoner, sembler* (to seem), *téléphoner, visiter* (to visit a place), *etc.*

Verbes réguliers en -ir

Modèle: **finir** (*to finish*)

Présent	*je finis, tu finis, il/elle/on finit, nous finissons, vous finissez, ils/elles finissent*
Impératif	*finis, finissons, finissez*
Passé composé	*j'ai fini, tu as fini, il/elle/on a fini, nous avons fini, vous avez fini, ils/elles ont fini*
Imparfait	*je finissais, tu finissais, il/elle/on finissait, nous finissions, vous finissiez, ils/elles finissaient*
Plus-que-parfait	*j'avais fini, tu avais fini, il/elle/on avait fini, nous avions fini, vous aviez fini, ils/elles avaient fini*
Passé simple	*je finis, tu finis, il/elle/on finit, nous finîmes, vous finîtes, ils/elles finirent*
Subjonctif	*je finisse, tu finisses, il/elle/on finisse, nous finissions, vous finissiez, ils/elles finissent*
Subjonctif passé	*j'aie fini, tu aies fini, il/elle/on ait fini, nous ayons fini, vous ayez fini, ils/elles aient fini*
Futur	*je finirai, tu finiras, il/elle/on finira, nous finirons, vous finirez, ils/elles finiront*
Futur antérieur	*j'aurai fini, tu auras fini, il/elle/on aura fini, nous aurons fini, vous aurez fini, ils/elles auront fini*
Conditionnel	*je finirais, tu finirais, il/elle/on finirait, nous finirions, vous finiriez, ils/elles finiraient*
Conditionnel passé	*j'aurais fini, tu aurais fini, il/elle/on aurait fini, nous aurions fini, vous auriez fini, ils/elles auraient fini*

Quelques autres ***verbes réguliers en -ir****: aboutir* (to complete), *accomplir* (to accomplish), *choisir, fleurir* (to flourish), *grandir* (to grow up), *grossir, maigrir* (to lose weight), *maudire* (to curse), *obéir* (to obey), *réfléchir* (to think, reflect), *réjouir* (to rejoice), *réussir* (to succeed, pass a test), *rougir* (to blush), *se réunir* (to get together), *vieillir, etc.*

Verbes réguliers en -re

Modèle: **vendre** (*to sell*)

Présent	*je vends, tu vends, il/elle/on vend, nous vendons, vous vendez, ils/elles vendent*
Impératif	*vends, vendons, vendez*
Passé composé	*j'ai vendu, tu as vendu, il/elle/on a vendu, nous avons vendu, vous avez vendu, ils/elles ont vendu*
Imparfait	*je vendais, tu vendais, il/elle/on vendait, nous vendions, vous vendiez, ils/elles vendaient*
Plus-que-parfait	*j'avais vendu, tu avais vendu, il/elle/on avait vendu, nous avions vendu, vous aviez vendu, ils/elles avaient vendu*
Passé simple	*je vendis, tu vendis, il/elle/on vendit, nous vendîmes, vous vendîtes, ils/elles vendirent*
Subjonctif	*je vende, tu vendes, il/elle/on vende, nous vendions, vous vendiez, ils/elles vendent*
Subjonctif passé	*j'aie vendu, tu aies vendu, il/elle/on ait vendu, nous ayons vendu, vous ayez vendu, ils/elles aient vendu*
Futur	*je vendrai, tu vendras, il/elle/on vendra, nous vendrons, vous vendrez, ils/elles vendront*
Futur antérieur	*j'aurai vendu, tu auras vendu, il/elle/on aura vendu, nous aurons vendu, vous aurez vendu, ils/elles auront vendu*
Conditionnel	*je vendrais, tu vendrais, il/elle/on vendrait, nous vendrions, vous vendriez, ils/elles vendraient*
Conditionnel passé	*j'aurais vendu, tu aurais vendu, il/elle/on aurait vendu, nous aurions vendu, vous auriez vendu, ils/elles auraient vendu*

Quelques autres ***verbes réguliers en -re****: défendre, descendre, entendre* (to hear), *fondre* (to melt), *pendre* (to hang), *perdre* (to lose), *rendre* (to give back), *rendre visite à* (to pay a visit to someone), *répondre, se détendre* (to relax), *s'entendre* (to get along), *se rendre compte* (to realize), *etc.*

Verbes pronominaux

Modèle: **se coucher** (*to go to bed*)

Présent	*je me couche, tu te couches, il/elle/on se couche, nous nous couchons, vous vous couchez, ils/elles se couchent*
Impératif	*couche-toi, couchons-nous, couchez-vous*
Passé composé	*je me suis couché(e), tu t'es couché(e), il/elle/on s'est couché(e), nous nous sommes couché(e)s, vous vous êtes couché(e)(s), ils/elles se sont couché(e)s*
Imparfait	*je me couchais, tu te couchais, il/elle/on se couchait, nous nous couchions, vous vous couchiez, ils/elles se couchaient*
Plus-que-parfait	*je m'étais couché(e), tu t'étais couché(e), il/elle/on s'était couché(e), nous nous étions couché(e)s, vous vous étiez couché(e)(s), ils/elles s'étaient couché(e)s*
Passé simple	*je me couchai, tu te couchas, il/elle/on se coucha, nous nous couchâmes, vous vous couchâtes, ils/elles se couchèrent*
Subjonctif	*je me couche, tu te couches, il/elle/on se couche, nous nous couchions, vous vous couchiez, ils/elles se couchent*
Subjonctif passé	*je me sois couché(e), tu te sois couché(e), il/elle/on se soit couché(e), nous nous soyons couché(e)s, vous vous soyez couché(e)(s), ils/elles se soient couché(e)s*
Futur	*je me coucherai, tu te coucheras, il/elle/on se couchera, nous nous coucherons, vous vous coucherez, ils/elles se coucheront*
Futur antérieur	*je me serai couché(e), tu te seras couché(e), il/elle/on se sera couché(e), nous nous serons couché(e)s, vous vous serez couché(e)(s), ils/elles se seront couché(e)s*
Conditionnel	*je me coucherais, tu te coucherais, il/elle/on se coucherait, nous nous coucherions, vous vous coucheriez, ils/elles se coucheraient*
Conditionnel passé	*je me serais couché(e), tu te serais couché(e), il/elle/on se serait couché(e), nous nous serions couché(e)s, vous vous seriez couché(e)(s), ils/elles se seraient couché(e)s*

*Autres **verbes pronominaux**: les verbes pronominaux peuvent être verbes réguliers en **-er**, **-ir** ou **-re** (consultez les listes ci-dessus), ou bien des verbes irréguliers (consultez la liste ci-dessous).*

Verbes irréguliers

aller (*to go*)

Présent	*je vais, tu vas, il/elle/on va, nous allons, vous allez, ils/elles vont*
Impératif	*va, allons, allez*
Passé composé	*je suis allé(e), tu es allé(e), il/elle/on est allé(e), nous sommes allé(e)s, vous êtes allé(e)(s), ils/elles sont allé(e)s*
Imparfait	*j'allais, tu allais, il/elle/on allait, nous allions, vous alliez, ils/elles allaient*
Passé simple	*j'allai, tu allas, il/elle/on alla, nous allâmes, vous allâtes, ils/elles allèrent*
Subjonctif	*je aille, tu ailles, il/elle/on aille, nous allions, vous alliez, ils/elles aillent*
Futur	*j'irai, tu iras, il/elle/on ira, nous irons, vous irez, ils/elles iront*
Conditionnel	*j'irais, tu irais, il/elle/on irait, nous irions, vous iriez, ils/elles iraient*

Verbes irréguliers

appeler (*to call*)

Présent	*j'appelle, tu appelles, il/elle/on appelle, nous appelons, vous appelez, ils/elles appellent*
Impératif	*apelle, appelons, appelez*
Passé composé	*j'ai appelé, tu as appelé, il/elle/on a appelé, nous avons appelé, vous avez appelé, ils/elles ont appelé*
Imparfait	*j'appelais, tu appelais, il/elle/on appelait, nous appelions, vous appeliez, ils/elles appelaient*
Passé simple	*j'appelai, tu appelas, il/elle/on appela, nous appelâmes, vous appelâtes, ils/elles appelèrent*
Subjonctif	*j'appelle, tu appelles, il/elle/on appelle, nous appelions, vous appeliez, ils/elles appellent*
Futur	*j'appellerai, tu appelleras, il/elle/on appellera, nous appellerons, vous appellerez, ils/elles appelleront*
Conditionnel	*j'appellerais, tu appellerais, il/elle/on appellerait, nous appellerions, vous appelleriez, ils/elles appelleraient*

Autres verbes comme **appeler**: *jeter* (to throw), *rejeter* (to reject), *s'appeler* (to call oneself, be named), *se rappeler* (to remember)

s'asseoir (*to sit down*)

Présent	*je m'assoie (m'assieds), tu t'assoies (t'assieds), il/elle/on s'assoit (s'assied), nous nous asseyons, vous vous asseyez, ils/elles s'assoient (s'asseyent)*
Impératif	*assieds-toi, asseyons-nous, asseyez-vous*
Passé composé	*je me suis assis(e), tu t'es assis(e), il/elle/on s'est assis(e), nous nous sommes assis(e)s, vous vous êtes assis(e)(s), ils/elles se sont assis(e)s*
Imparfait	*je m'asseyais, tu t'asseyais, il/elle/on s'asseyait, nous nous asseyions, vous vous asseyiez, ils/elles s'asseyaient*
Passé simple	*je m'assis, tu t'assis, il/elle/on s'assit, nous nous assîmes, vous vous assîtes, ils/elles assirent*
Subjonctif	*je m'assoie (m'asseye), tu t'assoies (t'asseyes), il/elle/on s'assoie (s'asseye), nous nous asseyions, vous vous asseyiez, ils/elles s'assoient (s'asseyent)*
Futur	*je m'assiérai, tu t'assiéras, il/elle/on s'assiéra, nous nous assiérons, vous vous assiérez, ils/elles s'assiéront*
Conditionnel	*je m'assiérais, tu t'assiérais, il/elle/on s'assiérait, nous nous assiérions, vous vous assiériez, ils/elles s'assiéraient*

Note: ***s'asseoir*** *has two alternative present tense forms; the alternates are given in parentheses.*

avoir (*to have*)

Présent	*j'ai, tu as, il/elle/on a, nous avons, vous avez, ils/elles ont*
Impératif	*aie, ayons, ayez*
Passé composé	*j'ai eu, tu as eu, il/elle/on a eu, nous avons eu, vous avez eu, ils/elles ont eu*
Imparfait	*j'avais, tu avais, il/elle/on avait, nous avions, vous aviez, ils/elles avaient*
Passé simple	*j'eus, tu eus, il/elle/on eut, nous eûmes, vous eûtes, ils/elles eurent*
Subjonctif	*j'aie, tu aies, il/elle/on ait, nous ayons, vous ayez, ils/elles aient*
Futur	*j'aurai, tu auras, il/elle/on aura, nous aurons, vous aurez, ils/elles auront*
Conditionnel	*j'aurais, tu aurais, il/elle/on aurait, nous aurions, vous auriez, ils/elles auraient*

boire (*to drink*)	
Présent	*je bois, tu bois, il/elle/on boit, nous buvons, vous buvez, ils/elles boivent*
Impératif	*bois, buvons, buvez*
Passé composé	*j'ai bu, tu as bu, il/elle/on a bu, nous avons bu, vous avez bu, ils/elles ont bu*
Imparfait	*je buvais, tu buvais, il/elle/on buvait, nous buvions, vous buviez, ils/elles buvaient*
Passé simple	*je bus, tu bus, il/elle/on but, nous bûmes, vous bûtes, ils/elles burent*
Subjonctif	*je boive, tu boives, il/elle/on boive, nous buvions, vous buviez, ils/elles boivent*
Futur	*je boirai, tu boiras, il/elle/on boira, nous boirons, vous boirez, ils/elles boiront*
Conditionnel	*je boirais, tu boirais, il/elle/on boirait, nous boirions, vous boiriez, ils/elles boiraient*

commencer (*to begin*)	
Présent	*je commence, tu commences, il/elle/on commence, nous commençons, vous commencez, ils/elles commencent*
Impératif	*commence, commençons, commencez*
Passé composé	*j'ai commencé, tu as commencé, il/elle/on a commencé, nous avons commencé, vous avez commencé, ils/elles ont commencé*
Imparfait	*je commençais, tu commençais, il/elle/on commençait, nous commencions, vous commenciez, ils/elles commençaient*
Passé simple	*je commençai, tu commenças, il/elle/on commença, nous commençâmes, vous commençâtes, ils/elles commencèrent*
Subjonctif	*je commence, tu commences, il/elle/on commence, nous commencions, vous commenciez, ils/elles commencent*
Futur	*je commencerai, tu commenceras, il/elle/on commencera, nous commencerons, vous commencerez, ils/elles commenceront*
Conditionnel	*je commencerais, tu commencerais, il/elle/on commencerait, nous commencerions, vous commenceriez, ils/elles commenceraient*

Autres verbes comme ***commencer****: avancer* (to advance), *balancer* (to balance), *placer* (to place), *remplacer* (to replace)

conduire (*to drive*)	
Présent	*je conduis, tu conduis, il/elle/on conduit, nous conduisons, vous conduisez, ils/elles conduisent*
Impératif	*conduis, conduisons, conduisez*
Passé composé	*j'ai conduit, tu as conduit, il/elle/on a conduit, nous avons conduit, vous avez conduit, ils/elles ont conduit*
Imparfait	*je conduisais, tu conduisais, il/elle/on conduisait, nous conduisions, vous conduisiez, ils/elles conduisaient*
Passé simple	*je conduisis, tu conduisis, il/elle/on conduisit, nous conduisîmes, vous conduisîtes, ils/elles conduisirent*
Subjonctif	*je conduise, tu conduises, il/elle/on conduise, nous conduisions, vous conduisiez, ils/elles conduisent*
Futur	*je conduirai, tu conduiras, il/elle/on conduira, nous conduirons, vous conduirez, ils/elles conduiront*
Conditionnel	*je conduirais, tu conduirais, il/elle/on conduirait, nous conduirions, vous conduiriez, ils/elles conduiraient*

Autres verbes comme ***conduire****: construire* (to construct), *cuire* (to cook), *nuire* (to do harm)

Verbes irréguliers

connaître (*to know*)

Présent	*je connais, tu connais, il/elle/on connaît, nous connaissons, vous connaissez, ils/elles connaissent*
Impératif	*connais, connaissons, connaissez*
Passé composé	*j'ai connu, tu as connu, il/elle/on a connu, nous avons connu, vous avez connu, ils/elles ont connu*
Imparfait	*je connaissais, tu connaissais, il/elle/on connaissait, nous connaissions, vous connaissiez, ils/elles connaissaient*
Passé simple	*je connus, tu connus, il/elle/on connut, nous connûmes, vous connûtes, ils/elles connurent*
Subjonctif	*je connaisse, tu connaisses, il/elle/on connaisse, nous connaissions, vous connaissiez, ils/elles connaissent*
Futur	*je connaîtrai, tu connaîtras, il/elle/on connaîtra, nous connaîtrons, vous connaîtrez, ils/elles connaîtront*
Conditionnel	*je connaîtrais, tu connaîtrais, il/elle/on connaîtrait, nous connaîtrions, vous connaîtriez, ils/elles connaîtraient*

Autres verbes comme ***connaître****: apparaître* (to appear), *disparaître* (to disappear), *paraître* (to appear, be published), *se connaître* (to know each other)

courir (*to run*)

Présent	*je cours, tu cours, il/elle/on court, nous courons, vous courez, ils/elles courent*
Impératif	*cours, courons, courez*
Passé composé	*j'ai couru, tu as couru, il/elle/on a couru, nous avons couru, vous avez couru, ils/elles ont couru*
Imparfait	*je courais, tu courais, il/elle/on courait, nous courions, vous couriez, ils/elles couraient*
Passé simple	*je courus, tu courus, il/elle/on courut, nous courûmes, vous courûtes, ils/elles coururent*
Subjonctif	*je coure, tu coures, il/elle/on coure, nous courions, vous couriez, ils/elles courent*
Futur	*je courrai, tu courras, il/elle/on courra, nous courrons, vous courrez, ils/elles courront*
Conditionnel	*je courrais, tu courrais, il/elle/on courrait, nous courrions, vous courriez, ils/elles courraient*

Autres verbes comme ***courir****: parcourir* (to travel or skim through), *secourir* (to help)

craindre (*to fear*)

Présent	*je crains, tu crains, il/elle/on craint, nous craignons, vous craignez, ils/elles craignent*
Impératif	*crains, craignons, craignez*
Passé composé	*j'ai craint, tu as craint, il/elle/on a craint, nous avons craint, vous avez craint, ils/elles ont craint*
Imparfait	*je craignais, tu craignais, il/elle/on craignait, nous craignions, vous craigniez, ils/elles craignaient*
Passé simple	*je craignis, tu craignis, il/elle/on craignit, nous craignîmes, vous craignîtes, ils/elles craignirent*
Subjonctif	*je craigne, tu craignes, il/elle craigne, nous craignions, vous craigniez, ils/elles craignent*
Futur	*je craindrai, tu craindras, il/elle/on craindra, nous craindrons, vous craindrez, ils/elles craindront*
Conditionnel	*je craindrais, tu craindrais, il/elle/on craindrait, nous craindrions, vous craindriez, ils/elles craindraient*

Autres verbes comme ***craindre****: contraindre* (to constrain, compel), *plaindre* (to pity, feel sorry for someone)

croire (*to believe*)

Présent	*je crois, tu crois, il/elle/on croit, nous croyons, vous croyez, ils/elles croient*
Impératif	*crois, croyons, croyez*
Passé composé	*j'ai cru, tu as cru, il/elle/on a cru, nous avons cru, vous avez cru, ils/elles ont cru*
Imparfait	*je croyais, tu croyais, il/elle/on croyait, nous croyions, vous croyiez, ils/elles croyaient*
Passé simple	*je crus, tu crus, il/elle crut, nous crûmes, vous crûtes, ils/elles crurent*
Subjonctif	*je croie, tu croies, il/elle/on croie, nous croyions, vous croyiez, ils croient*
Futur	*je croirai, tu croiras, il/elle/on croira, nous croirons, vous croirez, ils/elles croiront*
Conditionnel	*je croirais, tu croirais, il/elle/on croirait, nous croirions, vous croiriez, ils/elles croiraient*

devoir (*to have to, must*)

Présent	*je dois, tu dois, il/elle/on doit, nous devons, vous devez, ils/elles doivent*
Impératif	*dois, devons, devez*
Passé composé	*j'ai dû, tu as dû, il/elle/on a dû, nous avons dû, vous avez dû, ils/elles ont dû*
Imparfait	*je devais, tu devais, il/elle/on devait, nous devions, vous deviez, ils/elles devaient*
Passé simple	*je dus, tu dus, il/elle/on dut, nous dûmes, vous dûtes, ils/elles durent*
Subjonctif	*je doive, tu doives, il/elle/on doive, nous devions, vous deviez, ils/elles doivent*
Futur	*je devrai, tu devras, il/elle/on devra, nous devrons, vous devrez, ils/elles devront*
Conditionnel	*je devrais, tu devrais, il/elle/on devrait, nous devrions, vous devriez, ils/elles devraient*

dire (*to say, tell*)

Présent	*je dis, tu dis, il/elle/on dit, nous disons, vous dites, ils/elles disent*
Impératif	*dis, disons, dites*
Passé composé	*j'ai dit, tu as dit, il/elle/on a dit, nous avons dit, vous avez dit, ils/elles ont dit*
Imparfait	*je disais, tu disais, il/elle/on disait, nous disions, vous disiez, ils/elles disaient*
Passé simple	*je dis, tu dis, il/elle/on dit, nous dîmes, vous dîtes, ils/elles dirent*
Subjonctif	*je dise, tu dises, il/elle/on dise, nous disions, vous disiez, ils/elles disent*
Futur	*je dirai, tu diras, il/elle/on dira, nous dirons, vous direz, ils/elles diront*
Conditionnel	*je dirais, tu dirais, il/elle/on dirait, nous dirions, vous diriez, ils/elles diraient*

écrire (*to write*)

Présent	*j'écris, tu écris, il/elle/on écrit, nous écrivons, vous écrivez, ils/elles écrivent*
Impératif	*écris, écrivons, écrivez*
Passé composé	*j'ai écrit, tu as écrit, il/elle/on a écrit, nous avons écrit, vous avez écrit, ils/elles ont écrit*
Imparfait	*j'écrivais, tu écrivais, il/elle/on écrivait, nous écrivions, vous écriviez, ils/elles écrivaient*
Passé simple	*j'écrivis, tu écrivis, il/elle/on écrivit, nous écrivîmes, vous écrivîtes, ils écrivirent*
Subjonctif	*j'écrive, tu écrives, il/elle/on écrive, nous écrivions, vous écriviez, ils/elles écrivent*
Futur	*j'écrirai, tu écriras, il/elle/on écrira, nous écrirons, vous écrirez, ils/elles écriront*
Conditionnel	*j'écrirais, tu écrirais, il/elle/on écrirait, nous écririons, vous écririez, ils/elles écriraient*

Autres verbes comme ***écrire:*** *décrire* (to describe), *récrire* (to rewrite), *s'inscrire* (to register, sign up), *souscrire* (to subscribe)

essayer (*to try*)

Présent	*j'essaie, tu essaies, il/elle/on essaie, nous essayons, vous essayez, ils/elles essaient*
Impératif	*essaie, essayons, essayez*
Passé composé	*j'ai essayé, tu as essayé, il/elle/on a essayé, nous avons essayé, vous avez essayé, ils/elles ont essayé*
Imparfait	*j'essayais, tu essayais, il/elle/on essayait, nous essayions, vous essayiez, ils/elles essayaient*
Passé simple	*j'essayai, tu essayas, il/elle/on essaya, nous essayâmes, vous essayâtes, ils/elles essayèrent*
Subjonctif	*j'essaie, tu essaies, il/elle/on essaie, nous essayions, vous essayiez, ils/elles essaient*
Futur	*j'essaierai, tu essaieras, il/elle/on essaiera, nous essaierons, vous essaierez, ils/elles essaieront*
Conditionnel	*j'essaierais, tu essaierais, il/elle/on essaierait, nous essaierions, vous essaieriez, ils/elles essaieraient*

Autres verbes comme ***essayer:*** *envoyer* (to send), *nettoyer* (to clean), *renvoyer* (to fire an employee), *payer, s'ennuyer* (*to get bored*)
Note: verbs ending in -ayer may alternatively keep the *y* instead of *i* before an *e*, but verbs ending in -oyer must change the *y* to an *i* before an *e*.

Verbes irréguliers

être (*to be*)

Présent	*je suis, tu es, il/elle/on est, nous sommes, vous êtes, ils/elles sont*
Impératif	*sois, soyons, soyez*
Passé composé	*j'ai été, tu as été, il/elle/on a été, nous avons été, vous avez été, ils/elles ont été*
Imparfait	*j'étais, tu étais, il/elle/on était, nous étions, vous étiez, ils/elles étaient*
Passé simple	*je fus, tu fus, il/elle/on fut, nous fûmes, vous fûtes, ils/elles furent*
Subjonctif	*je sois, tu sois, il/elle/on soit, nous soyons, vous soyez, ils/elles soient*
Futur	*je serai, tu seras, il/elle/on sera, nous serons, vous serez, ils/elles seront*
Conditionnel	*je serais, tu serais, il/elle/on serait, nous serions, vous seriez, ils/elles seraient*

faire (*to do, make*)

Présent	*je fais, tu fais, il/elle/on fait, nous faisons, vous faites, ils/elles font*
Impératif	*fais, faisons, faites*
Passé composé	*j'ai fait, tu as fait, il/elle/on a fait, nous avons fait, vous avez fait, ils/elles ont fait*
Imparfait	*je faisais, tu faisais, il/elle/on faisait, nous faisions, vous faisiez, ils/elles faisaient*
Passé simple	*je fis, tu fis, il/elle/on fit, nous fîmes, vous fîtes, ils/elles firent*
Subjonctif	*je fasse, tu fasses, il/elle/on fasse, nous fassions, vous fassiez, ils/elles fassent*
Futur	*je ferai, tu feras, il/elle/on fera, nous ferons, vous ferez, ils/elles feront*
Conditionnel	*je ferais, tu ferais, il/elle/on ferait, nous ferions, vous feriez, ils/elles feraient*

Autres verbes comme ***faire****:* *défaire* (to undo/remove), *refaire* (to redo), *satisfaire* (to satisfy)

falloir (*to be necessary*)

Présent	*il faut*	***Passé composé***	*il a fallu*	***Passé simple***	*il fallut*	***Futur***	*il faudra*
Impératif	*(not usable)*	***Imparfait***	*il fallait*	***Subjonctif***	*il faille*	***Conditionnel***	*il faudrait*

fuir (*to flee*)

Présent	*je fuis, tu fuis, il/elle/on fuit, nous fuyons, vous fuyez, ils/elles fuient*
Impératif	*fuis, fuyons, fuyez*
Passé composé	*j'ai fui, tu as fui, il/elle/on a fui, nous avons fui, vous avez fui, ils/elles ont fui*
Imparfait	*je fuyais, tu fuyais, il/elle fuyait, nous fuyions, vous fuyiez, ils/elles fuyaient*
Passé simple	*je fuis, tu fuis, il/elle/on fuit, nous fuîmes, vous fuîtes, ils/elles fuirent*
Subjonctif	*je fuie, tu fuies, il/elle/on fuie, nous fuyions, vous fuyiez, ils/elles fuient*
Futur	*je fuirai, tu fuiras, il/elle/on fuira, nous fuirons, vous fuirez, ils/elles fuiront*
Conditionnel	*je fuirais, tu fuirais, il/elle/on fuirait, nous fuirions, vous fuiriez, ils/elles fuiraient*

interdire (*to forbid*)

Présent	*j'interdis, tu interdis, il/elle/on interdit, nous interdisons, vous interdisez, ils/elles interdisent*
Impératif	*interdis, interdisons, interdisez*
Passé composé	*j'ai interdit, tu as interdit, il/elle/on a interdit, nous avons interdit, vous avez interdit, ils/elles ont interdit*
Imparfait	*j'interdisais, tu interdisais, il/elle/on interdisait, nous interdisions, vous interdisiez, ils/elles interdisaient*
Passé simple	*j'interdis, tu interdis, il/elle/on interdit, nous interdîmes, vous interdîtes, ils/elles interdirent*
Subjonctif	*j'interdise, tu interdises, il/elle/on interdise, nous interdisions, vous interdisiez, ils/elles interdisent*
Futur	*j'interdirai, tu interdiras, il/elle/on interdira, nous interdirons, vous interdirez, ils/elles interdiront*
Conditionnel	*j'interdirais, tu interdirais, il/elle/on interdirait, nous interdirions, vous interdiriez, ils/elles interdiraient*

Autres verbes comme ***interdire****:* *contredire* (to contradict), *médire* (to bad-mouth), *prédire* (to predict)

lever (*to lift*)

Présent	*je lève, tu lèves, il/elle/on lève, nous levons, vous levez, ils/elles lèvent*
Impératif	*lève, levons, levez*
Passé composé	*j'ai levé, tu as levé, il/elle/on a levé, nous avons levé, vous avez levé, ils/elles ont levé*
Imparfait	*je levais, tu levais, il/elle/on levait, nous levions, vous leviez, ils/elles levaient*
Passé simple	*je levai, tu levas, il/elle/on leva, nous levâmes, vous levâtes, ils/elles levèrent*
Subjonctif	*je lève, tu lèves, il/elle/on lève, nous levions, vous leviez, ils/elles lèvent*
Futur	*je lèverai, tu lèveras, il/elle/on lèvera, nous lèverons, vous lèverez, ils/elles lèveront*
Conditionnel	*je lèverais, tu lèverais, il/elle/on lèverait, nous lèverions, vous lèveriez, ils/elles lèveraient*

Autres verbes comme ***lever****: acheter, amener* (to bring somewhere), *élever* (to raise), *emmener* (to take somewhere), *mener* (to conduct, run), *se lever* (to get up)

lire (*to read*)

Présent	*je lis, tu lis, il/elle/on lit, nous lisons, vous lisez, ils/elles lisent*
Impératif	*lis, lisons, lisez*
Passé composé	*j'ai lu, tu as lu, il/elle/on a lu, nous avons lu, vous avez lu, ils/elles ont lu*
Imparfait	*je lisais, tu lisais, il/elle/on lisait, nous lisions, vous lisiez, ils/elles lisaient*
Passé simple	*je lus, tu lus, il/elle/on lut, nous lûmes, vous lûtes, ils/elles lurent*
Subjonctif	*je lise, tu lises, il/elle/on lise, nous lisions, vous lisiez, ils/elles lisent*
Futur	*je lirai, tu liras, il/elle/on lira, nous lirons, vous lirez, ils/elles liront*
Conditionnel	*je lirais, tu lirais, il/elle/on lirait, nous lirions, vous liriez, ils/elles liraient*

Autres verbes comme ***lire****: élire* (to elect), *réélire* (to reelect), *relire* (to reread)

manger (*to eat*)

Présent	*je mange, tu manges, il/elle/on mange, nous mangeons, vous mangez, ils/elles mangent*
Impératif	*mange, mangeons, mangez*
Passé composé	*j'ai mangé, tu as mangé, il/elle/on a mangé, nous avons mangé, vous avez mangé, ils/elles ont mangé*
Imparfait	*je mangeais, tu mangeais, il/elle/on mangeait, nous mangions, vous mangiez, ils/elles mangeaient*
Passé simple	*je mangeai, tu mangeas, il/elle/on mangea, nous mangeâmes, vous mangeâtes, ils/elles mangèrent*
Subjonctif	*je mange, tu manges, il/elle/on mange, nous mangions, vous mangiez, ils/elles mangent*
Futur	*je mangerai, tu mangeras, il/elle/on mangera, nous mangerons, vous mangerez, ils/elles mangeront*
Conditionnel	*je mangerais, tu mangerais, il/elle/on mangerait, nous mangerions, vous mangeriez, ils/elles mangeraient*

Autres verbes comme ***manger****: changer* (to change), *nager* (to swim), *ranger* (to arrange), *se venger* (to get revenge), *voyager* (to travel)

mentir (*to lie*)

Présent	*je mens, tu mens, il/elle/on ment, nous mentons, vous mentez, ils/elles mentent*
Impératif	*mens, mentons, mentez*
Passé composé	*j'ai menti, tu as menti, il/elle/on a menti, nous avons menti, vous avez menti, ils/elles ont menti*
Imparfait	*je mentais, tu mentais, il/elle/on mentait, nous mentions, vous mentiez, ils/elles mentaient*
Passé simple	*je mentis, tu mentis, il/elle/on mentit, nous mentîmes, vous mentîtes, ils/elles mentirent*
Subjonctif	*je mente, tu mentes, il/elle/on mente, nous mentions, vous mentiez, ils/elles mentent*
Futur	*je mentirai, tu mentiras, il/elle/on mentira, nous mentirons, vous mentirez, ils/elles mentiront*
Conditionnel	*je mentirais, tu mentirais, il/elle/on mentirait, nous mentirions, vous mentiriez, ils/elles mentiraient*

Verbes irréguliers

mettre (*to put, set*)

Présent	*je mets, tu mets, il/elle/on met, nous mettons, vous mettez, ils/elles mettent*
Impératif	*mets, mettons, mettez*
Passé composé	*j'ai mis, tu as mis, il/elle/on a mis, nous avons mis, vous avez mis, ils/elles ont mis*
Imparfait	*je mettais, tu mettais, il/elle/on mettait, nous mettions, vous mettiez, ils/elles mettaient*
Passé simple	*je mis, tu mis, il/elle/on mit, nous mîmes, vous mîtes, ils/elles mirent*
Subjonctif	*je mette, tu mettes, il/elle/on mette, nous mettions, vous mettiez, ils/elles mettent*
Futur	*je mettrai, tu mettras, il/elle/on mettra, nous mettrons, vous mettrez, ils/elles mettront*
Conditionnel	*je mettrais, tu mettrais, il/elle/on mettrait, nous mettrions, vous mettriez, ils/elles mettraient*

Autres verbes comme ***mettre****:* *admettre* (to admit), *commettre* (to commit an act), *compromettre* (to compromise), *permettre, promettre* (to promise), *remettre* (to put back), *soumettre* (to submit), *transmettre* (to transmit)

mourir (*to die*)

Présent	*je meurs, tu meurs, il/elle/on meurt, nous mourons, vous mourez, ils/elles meurent*
Impératif	*meurs, mourons, meurez*
Passé composé	*je suis mort(e), tu es mort(e), il/elle/on est mort(e), nous sommes mort(e)s, vous êtes mort(e)(s), ils/elles sont mort(e)s*
Imparfait	*je mourais, tu mourais, il/elle/on mourait, nous mourions, vous mouriez, ils/elles mouraient*
Passé simple	*je mourus, tu mourus, il/elle/on mourut, nous mourûmes, vous mourûtes, ils/elles moururent*
Subjonctif	*je meure, tu meures, il/elle/on meure, nous mourions, vous mouriez, ils/elles meurent*
Futur	*je mourrai, tu mourras, il/elle/on mourra, nous mourrons, vous mourrez, ils/elles mourront*
Conditionnel	*je mourrais, tu mourrais, il/elle/on mourrait, nous mourrions, vous mourriez, ils/elles mourraient*

naître (*to be born*)

Présent	*je nais, tu nais, il/elle/on naît, nous naissons, vous naissez, ils/elles naissent*
Impératif	*nais, naissons, naissez*
Passé composé	*je suis né(e), tu es né(e), il/elle/on est né(e), nous sommes né(e)s, vous êtes né(e)(s), ils/elles sont né(e)s*
Imparfait	*je naissais, tu naissais, il/elle/on naissait, nous naissions, vous naissiez, ils/elles naissaient*
Passé simple	*je naquis, tu naquis, il/elle/on naquit, nous naquîmes, vous naquîtes, ils/elles naquirent*
Subjonctif	*je naisse, tu naisses, il/elle/on naisse, nous naissions, vous naissiez, ils/elles naissent*
Futur	*je naîtrai, tu naîtras, il/elle/on naîtra, nous naîtrons, vous naîtrez, ils/elles naîtront*
Conditionnel	*je naîtrais, tu naîtrais, il/elle/on naîtrait, nous naîtrions, vous naîtriez, ils/elles naîtraient*

ouvrir (*to open*)

Présent	*j'ouvre, tu ouvres, il/elle/on ouvre, nous ouvrons, vous ouvrez, ils/elles ouvrent*
Impératif	*ouvre, ouvrons, ouvrez*
Passé composé	*j'ai ouvert, tu as ouvert, il/elle/on a ouvert, nous avons ouvert, vous avez ouvert, ils/elles ont ouvert*
Imparfait	*j'ouvrais, tu ouvrais, il/elle/on ouvrait, nous ouvrions, vous ouvriez, ils/elles ouvraient*
Passé simple	*j'ouvris, tu ouvris, il/elle/on ouvrit, nous ouvrîmes, vous ouvrîtes, ils ouvrirent*
Subjonctif	*j'ouvre, tu ouvres, il/elle/on ouvre, nous ouvrions, vous ouvriez, ils/elles ouvrent*
Futur	*j'ouvrirai, tu ouvriras, il/elle/on ouvrira, nous ouvrirons, vous ouvrirez, ils/elles ouvriront*
Conditionnel	*j'ouvrirais, tu ouvrirais, il/elle/on ouvrirait, nous ouvririons, vous ouvririez, ils/elles ouvriraient*

Autres verbes comme ***ouvrir****:* *découvrir* (to discover), *entrouvrir* (to open a little bit), *offrir* (to offer), *rouvrir, souffrir* (to suffer)

partir (*to leave*)

Présent	*je pars, tu pars, il/elle/on part, nous partons, vous partez, ils/elles partent*
Impératif	*pars, partons, partez*
Passé composé	*je suis parti(e), tu es parti(e), il/elle/on est parti(e), nous sommes parti(e)s, vous êtes parti(e)(s), ils/elles sont parti(e)s*
Imparfait	*je partais, tu partais, il/elle/on partait, nous partions, vous partiez, ils/elles partaient*
Passé simple	*je partis, tu partis, il/elle/on partit, nous partîmes, vous partîtes, ils/elles partirent*
Subjonctif	*je parte, tu partes, il/elle/on parte, nous partions, vous partiez, ils/elles partent*
Futur	*je partirai, tu partiras, il/elle/on partira, nous partirons, vous partirez, ils/elles partiront*
Conditionnel	*je partirais, tu partirais, il/elle/on partirait, nous partirions, vous partiriez, ils/elles partiraient*

Autres verbes comme ***partir****: repartir* (to leave again), *ressortir* (to go out again, emerge), *sortir* (to go out)

peindre (*to paint*)

Présent	*je peins, tu peins, il/elle/on peint, nous peignons, vous peignez, ils/elles peignent*
Impératif	*peins, peignons, peignez*
Passé composé	*j'ai peint, tu as peint, il/elle/on a peint, nous avons peint, vous avez peint, ils/elles ont peint*
Imparfait	*je peignais, tu peignais, il/elle/on peignait, nous peignions, vous peigniez, ils/elles peignaient*
Passé simple	*je peignis, tu peignis, il/elle/on peignit, nous peignîmes, vous peignîtes, ils peignirent*
Subjonctif	*je peigne, tu peignes, il/elle/on peigne, nous peignions, vous peigniez, ils/elles peignent*
Futur	*je peindrai, tu peindras, il/elle/on peindra, nous peindrons, vous peindrez, ils/elles peindront*
Conditionnel	*je peindrais, tu peindrais, il/elle/on peindrait, nous peindrions, vous peindriez, ils/elles peindraient*

Autres verbes comme ***peindre****: atteindre* (to attain), *dépeindre* (to depict), *feindre* (to feign, pretend)

pleuvoir (*to rain*)

Présent	*il pleut*	***Passé composé***	*il a plu*	***Passé simple***	*il plut*	***Futur***	*il pleuvra*
Impératif	*(not usable)*	***Imparfait***	*il pleuvait*	***Subjonctif***	*il pleuve*	***Conditionnel***	*il pleuvrait*

pouvoir (*to can, be able*)

Présent	*je peux (puis-je, inversion irrégulier), tu peux, il/elle/on peut, nous pouvons, vous pouvez, ils/elles peuvent*
Impératif	*(not usable)*
Passé composé	*j'ai pu, tu as pu, il/elle/on a pu, nous avons pu, vous avez pu, ils/elles ont pu*
Imparfait	*je pouvais, tu pouvais, il/elle/on pouvait, nous pouvions, vous pouviez, ils/elles pouvaient*
Passé simple	*je pus, tu pus, il/elle/on put, nous pûmes, vous pûtes, ils/elles purent*
Subjonctif	*je puisse, tu puisses, il/elle/on puisse, nous puissions, vous puissiez, ils/elles puissent*
Futur	*je pourrai, tu pourras, il/elle/on pourra, nous pourrons, vous pourrez, ils/elles pourront*
Conditionnel	*je pourrais, tu pourrais, il/elle/on pourrait, nous pourrions, vous pourriez, ils/elles pourraient*

préférer (*to prefer*)

Présent	*je préfère, tu préfères, il/elle/on préfère, nous préférons, vous préférez, ils/elles préfèrent*
Impératif	*préfère, préférons, préférez*
Passé composé	*j'ai préféré, tu as préféré, il/elle/on a préféré, nous avons préféré, vous avez préféré, ils/elles ont préféré*
Imparfait	*je préférais, tu préférais, il/elle/on préférait, nous préférions, vous préfériez, ils/elles préféraient*
Passé simple	*je préférai, tu préféras, il/elle/on préféra, nous préférâmes, vous préférâtes, ils/elles préférèrent*
Subjonctif	*je préfère, tu préfères, il/elle/on préfère, nous préférions, vous préfériez, ils/elles préfèrent*
Futur	*je préférerai, tu préféreras, il/elle/on préférera, nous préférerons, vous préférerez, ils/elles préféreront*
Conditionnel	*je préférerais, tu préférerais, il/elle/on préférerait, nous préférerions, vous préféreriez, ils/elles préféreraient*

Autres verbes comme ***préférer****: considérer* (to consider), *espérer* (to hope), *posséder* (to possess), *répéter* (to repeat)

Verbes irréguliers

prendre (*to take*)

Présent	*je prends, tu prends, il/elle/on prend, nous prenons, vous prenez, ils/elles prennent*
Impératif	*prends, prenons, prenez*
Passé composé	*j'ai pris, tu as pris, il/elle/on a pris, nous avons pris, vous avez pris, ils/elles ont pris*
Imparfait	*je prenais, tu prenais, il/elle/on prenait, nous prenions, vous preniez, ils/elles prenaient*
Passé simple	*je pris, tu pris, il/elle/on prit, nous prîmes, vous prîtes, ils prirent*
Subjonctif	*je prenne, tu prennes, il/elle/on prenne, nous prenions, vous preniez, ils/elles prennent*
Futur	*je prendrai, tu prendras, il/elle/on prendra, nous prendrons, vous prendrez, ils/elles prendront*
Conditionnel	*je prendrais, tu prendrais, il/elle/on prendrait, nous prendrions, vous prendriez, ils/elles prendraient*

Autres verbes comme ***prendre****: apprendre* (to learn), *comprendre* (to understand), *entreprendre* (to undertake), *reprendre* (to take back, resume), *s'éprendre de* (to fall in love with), *se méprendre sur quelqu'un* (to misjudge someone), *surprendre* (to surprise)

recevoir (*to receive*)

Présent	*je reçois, tu reçois, il/elle/on reçoit, nous recevons, vous recevez, ils/elles reçoivent*
Impératif	*reçois, recevons, recevez*
Passé composé	*j'ai reçu, tu as reçu, il/elle/on a reçu, nous avons reçu, vous avez reçu, ils/elles ont reçu*
Imparfait	*je recevais, tu recevais, il/elle/on recevait, nous recevions, vous receviez, ils/elles recevaient*
Passé simple	*je reçus, tu reçus, il/elle/on reçut, nous reçûmes, vous reçûtes, ils reçurent*
Subjonctif	*je reçoive, tu reçoives, il/elle/on reçoive, nous recevions, vous receviez, ils/elles reçoivent*
Futur	*je recevrai, tu recevras, il/elle/on recevra, nous recevrons, vous recevrez, ils/elles recevront*
Conditionnel	*je recevrais, tu recevrais, il/elle/on recevrait, nous recevrions, vous recevriez, ils/elles recevraient*

Autres verbes comme ***recevoir****: apercevoir* (to perceive), *concevoir* (to conceive, imagine), *décevoir* (to deceive)

rire (*to laugh*)

Présent	*je ris, tu ris, il/elle/on rit, nous rions, vous riez, ils/elles rient*
Impératif	*ris, rions, riez*
Passé composé	*j'ai ri, tu as ri, il/elle/on a ri, nous avons ri, vous avez ri, ils/elles ont ri*
Imparfait	*je riais, tu riais, il/elle/on riait, nous riions, vous riiez, ils/elles riaient*
Passé simple	*je ris, tu ris, il/elle/on rit, nous rîmes, vous rîtes, ils/elles rirent*
Subjonctif	*je rie, tu ries, il/elle/on rie, nous riions, vous riiez, ils/elles rient*
Futur	*je rirai, tu riras, il/elle/on rira, nous rirons, vous rirez, ils/elles riront*
Conditionnel	*je rirais, tu rirais, il/elle/on rirait, nous ririons, vous ririez, ils/elles riraient*

Autres verbes comme ***rire****: sourire* (to smile)

savoir (*to know*)

Présent	*je sais, tu sais, il/elle/on sait, nous savons, vous savez, ils/elles savent*
Impératif	*sache, sachons, sachez*
Passé composé	*j'ai su, tu as su, il/elle/on a su, nous avons su, vous avez su, ils/elles ont su*
Imparfait	*je savais, tu savais, il/elle/on savait, nous savions, vous saviez, ils/elles savaient*
Passé simple	*je sus, tu sus, il/elle/on sut, nous sûmes, vous sûtes, ils/elles surent*
Subjonctif	*je sache, tu saches, il/elle/on sache, nous sachions, vous sachiez, ils/elles sachent*
Futur	*je saurai, tu sauras, il/elle/on saura, nous saurons, vous saurez, ils/elles sauront*
Conditionnel	*je saurais, tu saurais, il/elle/on saurait, nous saurions, vous sauriez, ils/elles sauraient*

Glossaire

This glossary includes all terms presented in the **Vocabulaire** lists and vocabulary-related **Centres d'information.** Serious students should invest in a French-English/English-French dictionary or use one of the free on-line dictionaries suggested in the **Pour vous aider** section of the **Intrigue** Companion Website.

LEXIQUE FRANÇAIS-ANGLAIS

A

à:
- à but non lucratif *nonprofit (organization)*
- à fleurs *floral pattern*
- à la une *front-page story*
- à peine *barely*
- à rayures *striped pattern*
- à tes souhaits *equivalent of "Bless you"*

abasourdi(e) *flabbergasted*
abeille (*f.*) *bee*
aborder *to approach*
accord (*m.*) *agreement*
action (*f.*) *share of stock*
addition (*f.*) *bill*
affaires (*f. pl.*) *business*
- ranger les affaires *to tidy up*
- rompu(e) aux affaires *experienced in business*

affreux/-euse *atrocious*
agité(e) *agitated*
aigle (*m.*) *eagle*
ail (*m.*) *garlic*
aîné(e) *oldest*
ajouter *to add*
aléatoire *risky/uncertain*
allergique *allergic*
aller jusqu'au bout *to go the distance/ to go all the way*
allophone *speaker of languages other than French, English, or Indian (reg. Québec)*
âme (*f.*) *soul*
- âme sœur *soul mate/like-minded person*

amener *to bring (s.o.)*
amère (*adj.*) *bitter*
amorcer *to introduce (a topic of conversation)*
ananas (*m.*) *pineapple*
âne (*m.*) *donkey*
animal (*m.*) familier *pet*
anniversaire (*m.*) *birthday*
anonyme *anonymous*
anorak (*m.*) *winter jacket*
antiquaire (*m.*) *antiques dealer*
apparaître *to appear*
appareil photo (*m.*) *camera*
apporter *to bring (things)*
aquarelle (*f.*) *watercolor*
araignée (*f.*) *spider*
arbre (*m.*) à gomme *rubber tree*
arbrisseau (*m.*) *shrub*
argent (*m.*) *silver*
arrêter *to stop/arrest*
arrière-grands-parents (*m. pl.*) *great-grandparents*
ascenseur (*m.*) *elevator*
aspirine (*f.*) *aspirin*
assiette (*f.*) *plate*
associé(e) *associate*
attaque (*f.*) d'apoplexie *stroke*
atteint(e): être atteint(e) *to suffer from, be stricken with*
attentat (*m.*) *attack*
atterrir *to land (a plane)*
attirer *to attract*
auberge (*f.*) de jeunesse *youth hostel*
aubergine (*f.*) *eggplant*
au bout (de) *at the end (of)*
au cas où *just in case*
aucun(e) *any*
au hasard *by chance*
aujourd'hui *today*
auteur (*m.*) *author*
autochtone *speaker of native American languages (reg. Québec)*
autrefois *in the past*
avare *greedy*
averse (*f.*) *downpour*
avoir:
- avoir honte (de) *to be ashamed (of)*
- avoir la trentaine *to be in one's 30s*
- avoir une bronchite *to have bronchitis*

B

bague (*f.*) *ring*
baguettes (*f. pl.*) *chopsticks*
bail (*m.*) *lease*
baladeur (*m.*) *Walkman™*
balcon (*m.*) *balcony*
baleine (*f.*) *whale*
banane (*f.*) *banana*
bananier (*m.*) *banana tree*
barbe (*f.*) *beard*
basilic (*m.*) *basil*
bavard(e) *talkative*
beau-fils (*m.*) *son-in-law/stepson*
beau-frère (*m.*) *brother-in-law*
beau-père (*m.*) *father-in-law/stepfather*
bégayer *to stutter*
beige *beige*
belle-famille (*f.*) *in-laws*
belle-fille (*f.*) *daughter-in-law/stepdaughter*
belle-mère (*f.*) *mother-in-law/stepmother*
belle-sœur (*f.*) *sister-in-law*
bénéfices (*f. pl.*) *profits*
béquilles (*f. pl.*) *crutches*
bête (*f.*) *animal*
bête (*adj.*) *stupid*
bêtise (*f.*) *mistake, gaffe*

beurre (*m.*) *butter*
bibliothécaire (*m./f.*) *librarian*
bijoux (*m. pl.*) *jewels, jewelry*
blanc(-che) *white*
blesser *to wound*
bleu(e) *blue*
bleuet (*m.*) *blueberry (reg. Québec)*
bœuf (*m.*) *beef*
boire *to drink*
bol (*m.*) *bowl*
bon(ne) *good*
bottes (*f. pl.*) *boots*
bouche bée *open-mouthed*
boucles (*m. pl.*) d'oreille *earrings*
boue: chute (*f.*) de boue *mudslide*
bougainvillée (*f.*) *Bougainvillea flower*
bouillir *to boil*
bouleau (*m.*) *birch tree*
boulot (*m.*) *job, work (slang)*
bouquin (*m.*) *book (slang)*
bouquiniste (*m./f.*) *bookseller*
bourse (*f.*) *stock exchange; fellowship/scholarship*
bout (*m.*) *end*
  aller jusqu'au bout *to go the distance/all the way*
  au bout (de) *at the end (of)*
bracelet (*m.*) *bracelet*
branché(e) *hip*
brancher *to plug in*
brocoli (*m. pl.*) *broccoli*
bronchite: avoir une bronchite *to have bronchitis*
bronzé(e) *bronze*
brosse (*f.*) *brush*
  brosse à cheveux *hairbrush*
  brosse à dents *toothbrush*
brouillard (*m.*) *fog*
brume (*f.*) *fog*
brun(e) *brown*
bruyère (*f.*) *heather*
buanderie (*f.*) *laundry room*
buisson (*m.*) *bush*
bureau (*m.*) *office, desk*
but (*m.*) *goal/objective*
  à but non lucratif *nonprofit (organization)*

C

cacahouète (*f.*) *peanut*
cadeau (*m.*) *present*
cadet(te) *youngest child*
cadre (*m.*) *executive; setting*
cafard (*m.*) *cockroach*
calé(e) *smart/clever (slang)*
canapé (*m.*) *couch*
canard (*m.*) *duck*
canicule (*f.*) *heat wave*
canneberge (*m.*) *cranberry*
cannelle (*f.*) *cinnamon*
canoë (*m.*) *canoe*
canot (*m.*) *canoe (reg. Québec)*
car (*m.*) *intercity bus*
car *for, because*
carie (*f.*) dentaire *cavity (in a tooth)*
carotte (*f.*) *carrot*
carré(e) *square*
cas: au cas où *just in case*
case (*f.*) *hut*
casserole (*f.*) *saucepan*
castor (*m.*) *beaver*
caution (*f.*) *security deposit*
cèdre (*m.*) *cedar tree*
ceinture (*f.*) *belt*
céleri (*m.*) *celery*
cercueil (*m.*) *casket*
cerf (*m.*) *deer*
cerisier (*m.*) *cherry tree*
chair (*f.*) *flesh*
  chair de poule *goose bumps*
  en chair et os *in the flesh*
chaleur (*f.*) *heat*
chaleureux/-euse *warm (personality)*
chambre (*f.*) à coucher *bedroom*
chambre (*f.*) d'hôte *guest room*
chameau (*m.*) *camel*
champêtre *rustic*
chanson (*f.*) *song*
chapeau (*m.*) *hat*
charmant(e) *charming*
chasse (*f.*) *hunting*
chaussette (*f.*) *sock*
chaussures (*f. pl.*) *shoes*
chauve-souris (*f.*) *bat*
chef-d'œuvre (*m.*) *masterpiece*
cheminée (*f.*) *fireplace*
chemise (*f.*) *shirt*
chemisier (*m.*) *blouse*
chêne (*m.*) *oak tree*
cheval (*m.*) *horse*
cheveux (*m. pl.*) *hair*
chèvre (*f.*) *goat*
chèvrefeuille (*m.*) *honeysuckle*
Chin, chin ! *Cheers!*
chômage (*m.*) *unemployment*
chute (*f.*) de boue *mudslide*
cicatrice (*f.*) *scar*
ciel (*m.*) *sky*
cinquantaine (*f.*) (de) *about 50 (of)*
  dans la cinquantaine *in one's 50s*
citoyen(ne) (*m./f.*) *citizen*
citron (*m.*) *lemon*
citronnier (*m.*) *lemon tree*
citrouille (*f.*) *pumpkin*
clair(e) *light (colored)*
clé (*f.*) *key*
  sous clé *under lock and key*
client(e) (*m./f.*) *hotel guest; client*
climatisé(e) *air-conditioned*
cochon (*m.*) *pig*
cocotier (*m.*) *coconut tree*
cœur: de bon cœur *with sincerity*
coin (*m.*) *corner; neighborhood*
collant (*m.*) *pantyhose*
collier (*m.*) *necklace*
colline (*f.*) *hill*
colon (*m.*) *colonist*
colonne (*f.*) de lit *bedpost*
combattre *to fight, battle*
commander *to order*
commode (*f.*) *dresser/chest of drawers*
complet: être au complet *to be full, have no vacancies*
comprimé (*m.*) *tablet/lozenge*
comptable (*m./f.*) *accountant*
comptoir (*m.*) *counter*
concombre (*m.*) *cucumber*
concurrence (*f.*) *competition*
conduire *to drive*
confier *to confide/disclose*
conforts (*m. pl.*) *comforts*
congé (*m.*) *vacation*
congélateur (*m.*) *freezer*
consciencieux/-euse *conscientious*
conseil (*m.*) *advice*
conseiller *to advise*
constitution (*f.*) *constitution*
contagieux/-euse *contagious*
contrefaçon (*f.*) *forgery/counterfeiting*
contrefaire *to forge/counterfeit*
copain (*m.*), copine (*f.*) *friend; boyfriend, girlfriend*
coq (*m.*) *rooster*
coquelicot (*m.*) *red poppy*
corbeau (*m.*) *crow*
costume (*m.*) *man's suit*
coton (*m.*) *cotton*
cougar (*m.*) *mountain lion*
couloir (*m.*) *hallway*
coup (*m.*) de soleil *sunburn*
cour (*f.*) *courtyard*
courbatures (*f. pl.*) *muscle aches*
courgette (*f.*) *zucchini, squash*
courriel (*m.*) *e-mail*
cousin(e) (*m./f.*) *cousin*
couteau (*m.*) *knife*
craindre *to fear*
cravate (*f.*) *tie*
créances (*f. pl.*) gelées *frozen assets*
créateur/-trice *creative*
crédule *credulous*
crème (*f.*) *cream*
crevette (*f.*) *shrimp*

crier *to yell/shout*
crise (*f.*) cardiaque *heart attack*
cru(e) *raw*
cuillère (*f.*) *spoon*
cuillerée (*f.*) *spoonful*
cuir (*m.*) *leather*
cuisine (*f.*) *kitchen, cuisine*
cuisinière (*f.*) *stove*
cyclisme (*m.*) *cycling*

D

danser *to dance*
dauphin (*m.*) *dolphin*
de:
  de bon cœur *with sincerity*
  de mal en pis *from bad to worse*
débarrasser *to clear off*
débat (*m.*) *debate*
décennie (*f.*) *decade*
décevoir (qqn) *to disappoint (s.o.)*
déchiré(e) *torn*
déconcertant(e) *disconcerting, troubling*
décongéler *to defrost*
démangeaison (*f.*) *itch*
déménager *to move (out of a house, apartment, etc.)*
demi-frère (*m.*), demi-sœur (*f.*) *half-brother, half-sister*
démocratie (*f.*) *democracy*
démocratique *democratic*
dentifrice (*m.*) *toothpaste*
déodorant (*m.*) *deodorant*
dépister *to track down*
déprimé(e) *depressed*
dérangé(e) *deranged*
descendant(e) *descendant*
dessin (*m.*) *drawing*
dessus (*m.*) de lit *bedspread*
deviner *to guess*
devoir (de l'argent) *to owe (money)*
dinde (*f.*) *turkey*
discriminiation (*f.*) *discrimination*
disparaître *to disappear*
domestique (*m.*) *housekeeper, servant*
dossier (*m.*) *file*
doux, douce *sweet*
droit (*m.*) *right (legal)*
droite (*f.*) *(the) right (conservative)*

E

ébruiter *to leak (news, information)*
écossais(e) *plaid*
écouteurs (*m. pl.*) *earphones*
écrevisse (*f.*) *crawfish*
écrire (une thèse) *to write (a thesis)*
écriture (*f.*) *writing, handwriting*
écureuil (*m.*) *squirrel*
efficace *efficient*
égalité (*f.*) *equality*
élire *to elect*
émotif/-ive *emotional*
empaqueté(e) *packaged, wrapped up*
emploi (*m.*) *job*
emprunter *to borrow*
ému(e) *emotional/moved*
en:
  en chair et en os *in the flesh*
  en partie *partially, in part*
  en revanche *in return, on the other hand*
  en vouloir à qqn *to hold a grudge against s.o.*
enceinte *pregnant*
endroit (*m.*) *place*
énergique *energetic*
enfer (*m.*) *hell*
ennuyer *to bore*
ennuyeux/-euse *boring*
enquête (*f.*) *inquiry, investigation*
enrhumé(e): être enrhumé(e) *to be sick with a cold*
enterrer *to bury*
entouré(e) *surrounded*
entrepôt (*m.*) *warehouse, storage house*
entreprise (*f.*) *company/business*
entrouvert(e) *half-open, ajar*
envahi(e) *invaded*
environs (*m. pl.*) *surroundings*
épeler *to spell*
épice (*f.*) *spice*
époque (*f.*) *era*
épousseter *to dust*
équitable *fair*
équitation (*f.*) *horseback riding*
érable (*m.*) *maple tree*
escalade (*f.*) de glace *ice climbing*
escalier (*m.*) *stairs*
espèces (*m. pl.*) *cash*
esquisse (*f.*) *sketch*
estimer *to estimate; to think*
étagère (*m.*) *shelf; bookcase*
état (*m.*) *state*
éternuer *to sneeze*
être:
  être à bout de nerfs *to be completely frazzled*
  être abasourdi(e) *to be flabbergasted*
  être allergique *to be allergic to something*
  être atteint(e) de (l'arthrite/de rhumatisme) *to have, suffer from (rheumatoid arthritis)*
  être au complet *to be full, have no vacancy*
  être bien habillé(e) *to be well-dressed*
  être en forme *to be in shape*
  être enrhumé(e) *to have a cold*
  être fichu(e) *to be done for/to have had it*
  être navré(e) *to be sorry*
  être ravi(e) *to be delighted*
  être retardé(e) (de) *to be delayed (flight, transportation)*
évier (*m.*) *large sink*
exigeant(e) *demanding*
exposition (*f.*) *exhibit*
exprès *on purpose*

F

faire:
  faire cuire *to cook*
  faire de son mieux *to do one's best*
  faire do-do *to go night-night (slang)*
  faire du bien à qqn *to do good/to make s.o. feel better*
  faire faillite *to go bankrupt*
  faire la lessive *to wash clothes*
  faire la vaisselle *to wash dishes*
  faire le lit *to make the bed*
  faire le ménage *to do housework*
  faire mijoter *to simmer*
  faire sauter *to sauté*
  faire une excursion *to take a short trip*
fais do-do (*m.*) *dance party (reg. Acadia)*
faits divers (*m. pl.*) *human-interest stories*
fan (*m.*), fanatique (*m./f.*) *fan, a lover of something*
farine (*f.*) *flour*
fauteuil (*m.*) *armchair*
faux, fausse *wrong; fake*
femme (*f.*) *wife; woman*
  femme de ménage *chambermaid, housekeeper*
fer (*m.*) *iron*
  fer à repasser *iron for pressing clothes*
  fer forgé *wrought iron*
feuille (*f.*) *leaf*
feutre (*m.*) *felt*
fiable *reliable*
fiancé(e) (*m./f.*) *fiancé(e)*
fiche (*f.*) *form, sheet*
fichu(e) *ruined*
fier, fière *proud*
fièvre (*f.*) *fever*
fiévreux/-euse *feverish*
filet (*m.*) *net*
filiale (*f.*) *subsidiary*
fille (*f.*) *daughter*
filleul(e) (*m./f.*) *godson, goddaughter*
fils (*m.*) *son*
fleurs: à fleurs *floral patterned*
foie (*f.*) *liver*

fois (*f.*) *a time*
foncé(e) *dark*
fontaine (*f.*) de jouvence *fountain of youth*
forcément *necessarily*
forme: être en forme *to be in shape*
fou, folle *crazy*
foudre (*f.*) *lightning*
fougère (*f.*) *fern*
fouiller *to search through*
foulard (*m.*) *scarf*
foule (*f.*) *crowd*
four (*m.*) *oven*
  four à micro-ondes *microwave oven*
fourchette (*f.*) *fork*
fourmi (*f.*) *ant*
fournir *to furnish/supply*
foyer (*m.*) *entranceway/lobby; home*
fraise (*f.*) *strawberry*
framboise (*f.*) *raspberry*
franchement *frankly*
frappant(e) *striking*
frappé(e) *smacked/hit*
frère (*m.*) *brother*
frissonner *to shiver*
fromage (*m.*) *cheese*
fruits (*m. pl.*) des bois *berries*
fumeur *(adj.) smoking*
funérailles (*f. pl.*) *funeral*
furet (*m.*) *ferret*
fuyant(e) *shifty/receding*

G

gâcher *to spoil, to ruin*
gagner *to win*
garage (*m.*) *garage*
gaspiller *to waste*
gauche (*f.*) *(the) left (liberal)*
gêner *to bother*
gérant(e) (*m./f.*) *manager*
gestion (*f.*) *management*
geule (*f.*)
  gueule de bois *hangover (slang)*
gilet (*m.*) *cardigan*
girafe (*f.*) *giraffe*
glace (*f.*) *ice; ice cream*
gomme: arbre (*m.*) à gomme *rubber tree*
gouverneur (*m.*) *governor*
grande salle (*f.*) *great room, main room, grand hall*
grandes vacances (*f. pl.*) *summer vacation*
grands-parents (*m. pl.*) *grandparents*
gratuit(e) *free*
grave *serious*
gravure (*f.*) *engraving*
grêle (*f.*) *hail*
grenouille (*f.*) *frog*
grève (*f.*) *(workers') strike*
grignoter *to munch, to nibble*
griller *to grill*
grippe (*f.*) *flu*
gris(e) *grey*
gros lot (*m.*) *jackpot*
guerre (*f.*) *war*
guide (*m.*) (touristique) *guidebook*

H

habillé(e): bien habillé(e) *well-dressed*
hall (*m.*) d'entrée *foyer*
haricot (*m.*) *bean*
haut (*m.*) *top (shirt)*
héritage (*m.*) *inheritance*
hibou (*m.*) *owl*
hier *yesterday*
hippopotame (*m.*) *hippopotamus*
hirondelle (*f.*) *swallow*
hockey (*m.*) sur glace *ice hockey*
homard (*m.*) *lobster*
honte: avoir honte (de) *to be ashamed (of)*
hôte: chambre (*f.*) d'hôte *guestroom*
hôtelier (*m.*) , hôtelière (*f.*) *innkeeper, hotel owner*
houx (*m.*) *holly*
huile (*f.*) *oil*
huître (*f.*) *oyster*
hyène (*m.*) *hyena*

I

il vaut:
  il vaut la peine *it's worth the trouble*
  il vaut mieux *it's better, it would be better*
illégal(e) *illegal*
impensable *unthinkable*
imperméable (*m.*) *raincoat*
inconvénients (*m. pl.*) *disadvantages*
indépendance (*f.*) *independence*
infatigable *tireless*
inondation (*f.*) *flood*
investir *to invest*
investissement (*m.*) *investment*
ivoire (*m.*) *ivory*

J

jadis *in the olden days*
jambon (*m.*) *ham*
jaune *yellow*
jean (*m. sg.*) *jeans*
jeu (*m.*) *game*
jogging (*m.*) *sweats*
jonquille (*f.*) *daffodil*
jumeaux (*m. pl.*), jumelles (*f. pl.*) *twins*
jupe (*f.*) *skirt*
jurer *to swear*

K

krach (*m.*) boursier *stock market crash*

L

laid(e) *ugly*
laine (*f.*) *wool*
lait (*m.*) *milk*
lapin (*m.*) *rabbit*
lavabo (*m.*) *small sink*
lavande (*f.*) *lavender*
lave-vaisselle (*m.*) *dishwasher*
lecture (*f.*) *reading*
légal(e) *legal*
lendemain (*m.*) *the next day*
lettre (*f.*) morte *worthless/a dead issue*
lèvres (*f. pl.*) *lips*
liberté (*f.*) *freedom*
lierre (*m.*) *ivy*
lire *to read*
littérature (*f.*) *literature*
livraison (*f.*) des bagages enregistrés *baggage claim area*
livre (*f.*) *pound*
location (*f.*) *rental*
loi (*f.*) *law*
louer *to rent*
loyer (*m.*) *rent*
lunettes (*f. pl.*) *glasses*

M

machine (*f.*) à laver *washing machine*
magie (*f.*) *magic*
maillot (*m.*) de bain *swimsuit*
maire (*m.*) *mayor*
maïs (*m.*) *corn*
maison (*f.*) *company/firm*
majoritaire *majority (adj.)*
majoritairement *in majority (adv.)*
mal:
  de mal en pis *from bad to worse*
  mal (*m.*) à la gorge *sore throat*
  mal à l'aise *uneasy*
  mal (*m.*) au cœur *heartburn*
malade: tomber malade *to get sick*
maladie (*f.*) du cœur *heart disease*
manager (*m.*) *manager*
manifestation (*f.*) *protest*
manigancer *to plot*
manteau (*m.*) *overcoat*
maquillage (*m.*) *makeup*
marbre (*m.*) *marble*
marche (*f.*) *walking*
marée (*f.*) *tide*
marguerite (*f.*) *daisy*
mari (*m.*) *husband*
marié(e) (*m./f.*) *groom/bride*

marketing (*m.*) *marketing*
marmite (*f.*) *cooking pot*
marmotte (*f.*) *groundhog*
marque (*f.*) *brand*
marraine (*f.*) *godmother*
marronnier (*m.*) *chestnut tree*
maussade *gloomy*
mauvais(e) *bad*
mauve *mauve*
mayonnaise (*f.*) *mayonnaise*
méchant(e) *mean*
médicament (*m.*) *medicine*
meilleur(e) *better (adj.)*
mél (*m.*) *e-mail*
mélanger *to mix*
mensonge (*m.*) *lie*
mentir *to lie*
mère (*f.*) *mother*
messe (*f.*) *(religious) mass*
mettre en lumière *to bring to light, to expose*
meuble (*m.*) à tiroirs *cabinet*
meubles (*m. pl.*) *furnishings*
miel (*m.*) *honey*
mien(ne) (pron.) *mine*
mieux *better (adv.)*
  il vaut mieux *it would be better*
mijoter *to simmer; to hatch (a scheme)*
  mijoter un projet *to hatch a scheme*
mince *thin*
ministère (*f.*) *ministry (political)*
ministre (*m.*) *minister (of culture, of foreign affairs, etc.)*
mobilier (*m.*) *furniture*
moche *ugly*
monarchie (*f.*) *monarchy*
montre (*f.*) *watch*
moquette (*f.*) *carpet*
mort (*f.*) *death*
mouche (*f.*) *fly*
mouffette (*f.*) *skunk*
moule (*f.*) *mussel*
mousse (*f.*) *moss; foam*
moustache (*f.*) *mustache*
moustique (*m.*) *mosquito*
moutarde (*f.*) *mustard*
moutarde (*adj.*) *mustard yellow*
mouton (*m.*) *sheep*
moyen (*m.*) *way/means*
moyen(ne) (*adj.*) *medium*
mur (*m.*) *wall*
myrtille (*f.*) *blueberry*

N

n'importe quoi *anything at all*
natation (*f.*) *swimming*
nature (*f.*) morte *still-life painting*
nausée (*f.*) *nausea*
navré(e): être navré(e) *to be sorry*
néanmoins *nonetheless*
neige (*f.*) *snow*
nerveux/-euse *nervous*
nettement *significantly*
neveu (*m.*) *nephew*
nez (*m.*) *nose*
nièce (*f.*) *niece*
noir(e) *black*
noix (*m. pl.*) *walnuts*
non fumeur (*adj.*) *non-smoking*
nouilles (*f. pl.*) *noodles*

O

œuf (*m.*) *egg*
œuvre (*f.*) *work (of art)*
  chef-d'œuvre (*m.*) *masterpiece*
offrande (*f.*) *offering*
oie (*f.*) *goose*
oignon (*m.*) *onion*
oiseau (*m.*) *bird*
olive *olive*
oncle (*m.*) *uncle*
oppressif/-ive *oppressive*
oppression (*f.*) *oppression*
opprimé(e) *oppressed*
opprimer *to oppress*
or (*m.*) *gold*
or (adv.) *now*
orage (*m.*) *storm*
orange (*f.*) *orange*
ordinateur (*m.*) portable *laptop computer*
oreilles (*f. pl.*) *ears*
orgueil (*m.*) *pride*
orignal (*m.*) *moose*
orme (*m.*) *elm tree*
ouragan (*m.*) *hurricane*
ours (*m.*) *bear*

P

pacser *to sign a PACS (civil union document)*
pagaies (*f. pl.*) *paddles*
paille (*f.*) *straw*
palmier (*m.*) *palm tree*
palourde (*f.*) *clam*
pantalon (*m.*) *pants*
papayer (*m.*) *papaya tree*
papillon (*m.*) *butterfly*
paradis (*m.*) *paradise/heaven*
parafe (*m.*) *initials*
parapluie (*m.*) *umbrella*
paresseux/-euse *lazy*
parfum (*m.*) *perfume/flavor*
parier *to bet*
parlement (*m.*) *parliament*
parmi *among*
paroisse (*f.*) *parish/geographical area (reg. Acadia)*
parquet (*m.*) *floor*
parrain (*m.*) *godfather*
part (*f.*) *slice*
partie: en partie *partially, in part*
parti politique (*m.*) *political party*
pas (*m.*) *step*
passer l'aspirateur *to vacuum*
pâte (*f.*) *dough/crust*
pâté (*m.*) *pâté*
pâtes (*f. pl.*) *pasta*
patin (*m.*) en ligne *in-line skating*
patinage (*m.*) *skating*
patron(ne) (*m./f.*) *boss*
pays (*m.*) *country*
paysage (*m.*) *landscape/countryside*
PCV (payable chez vous) *collect call*
PDG (*m.*) *CEO*
pêche (*f.*) *peach*
peigne (*m.*) *comb*
peine:
  à peine *barely*
  ça (il) vaut la peine *it's worth the trouble*
pellicule (*f.*) *film*
péniche (*f.*) *houseboat*
pensée (*f.*) *thought; pansy flower*
pension (*f.*) *bed-and-breakfast*
perdre *to lose*
  perdre confiance en *to lose confidence in*
père (*m.*) *father*
permis de conduire (*m.*) *driver's license*
persil (*m.*) *parsley*
perspicace *perspicacious, shrewd*
pétiller *to crackle*
petite-fille (*f.*) *granddaughter*
petit-fils (*m.*) *grandson*
phoque (*m.*) *seal*
pièce (*f.*) *play (theatrical); room*
pin (*m.*) *pine tree*
pincée (*f.*) *pinch*
piquant(e) *spicy/sharp*
pis:
  de mal en pis *from bad to worse*
  qui pis est *what's even worse*
piscine (*f.*) *pool*
piste (*f.*) *trail*
placer (de l'argent) *to invest (money)*
planche (*f.*) *board*
  planche à voile *windsurfer; windsurfing*
  planche de neige *snowboard; snowboarding*
plastique (*f.*) *plastic*
plat (*m.*) *dish/platter*
platane (*m.*) *plane tree*
plâtre (*m.*) *cast*
pleurer *to cry*

pneumonie (*f.*) *pneumonia*
poêle (*f.*) *frying pan*
poignée (*f.*) *handle, wrist*
pointu(e) *pointy*
poire (*f.*) *pear*
poirier (*m.*) *pear tree*
poisson (*m.*) *fish*
poisson chat *catfish*
poisson rouge *goldfish*
poivre (*m.*) *pepper*
poivron (*m.*) *bell pepper*
polyester (*m.*) *polyester*
pomme (*f.*) *apple*
pomme de terre *potato*
pommier (*m.*) *apple tree*
porc (*m.*) *pork*
porte-documents (*m.*) *briefcase*
portefeuille (*m.*) *wallet*
poste (*f.*) *post office; mail*
poste (*m.*) *job*
potelé(e) *portly*
poulet (*m.*) *chicken*
poupée (*f.*) *doll*
pourboire (*m.*) *tip*
prendre *to take*
prendre feu *to catch fire*
prendre un pot/ un verre *to have a drink*
prétendre que *to claim that*
prétendu(e) *so-called*
prêter *to lend*
privilège (*m.*) *privilege*
procès (*m.*) *trial*
progressiste *progressive*
publicité (*f.*) *advertising*
puissant(e) *powerful*
pull-over (*m.*) *sweater*

Q

quai (*m.*) *embankment, walkway, or roadway next to the river*
qui pis est *what's even worse*
quoiqu'il en soit *be that as it may*

R

raccrocher *to hang up (the phone)*
rafale (*f.*) de vent *gusty wind*
ragoût (*m.*) *stew*
raisin (*m.*) *grapes*
ramasser *to pick up, gather up*
randonnée (*f.*) *hiking*
ranger les affaires *to tidy up*
raquette (*f.*) de neige *snowshoe; snowshoeing*
rasoir (*m.*) *raser*
rater *to miss (a day, a bus, an event, etc.)*
raton (*m.*) laveur *raccoon*
ravi(e) *delighted*
ravissant(e) *ravishing, beautiful*
rayonne (*f.*) *rayon*
rayures: à rayures *striped, patterned with stripes*
réception (*f.*) *check-in desk*
recette (*f.*) *recipe*
recherche (*f.*) *research*
référendum (*m.*) *referendum*
réflexion (*f.*) *reflection*
régime (*m.*) *regime*
reine (*f.*) *queen*
relier *to link together*
rembourser *to reimburse*
remercier *to thank*
remonte-pente (*m.*) *ski lift*
remuer *to stir*
renard (*m.*) *fox*
rendez-vous (*m.*) *date/meeting*
rendre service (à) *to be of service (to)*
renifler *to sniffle*
renne (*m.*) *reindeer*
renseignement (*m.*) *information*
renvoyer *to fire (an employee)*
repas (*m.*) *meal*
repasser *to iron*
reporter (*m.*) *reporter*
repos (*m.*) *rest*
représentant (*m.*) *representative*
république (*f.*) *republic*
requin (*m.*) *shark*
résistence (*f.*) *resistance*
ressentir *to feel strongly*
retardé(e) *delayed*
réunion (*f.*) *meeting/reunion*
revanche: en revanche *in return; on the other hand*
réveil-matin (*m.*) *alarm clock*
rhume (*m.*) *cold (illness)*
ride (*f.*) *wrinkle*
rideaux (*m. pl.*) *curtains*
riz (*m.*) *rice*
robe (*f.*) *dress*
roi (*m.*) *king*
roman (*m.*) *novel*
roman épistolaire *epistolary novel*
roman policier *detective novel*
rompu(e) aux affaires *experienced in business*
ronfler *to snore*
rose *pink*
rôtir *to roast*
rouge *red*
rougir *to redden, to blush*
rouleau (*m.*) de printemps *spring roll*
roulettes (*f. pl.*) *little wheels*
roux, rousse *red (hair)*
ruban (*m.*) *ribbon*

S

s'accroître *to increase*
s'asseoir *to sit down*
s'échapper *to escape*
s'éloigner *to distance oneself*
s'en faire *to worry, get upset*
s'en ficher *to not care*
s'ennuyer *to get bored*
s'étendre *to extend*
s'installer *to settle down, move in*
sable noir (*m.*) *black sand*
sac (*m.*) *bag*
sac à dos *backpack*
sac à main *handbag*
sagesse (*f.*) *wisdom*
saisir *to grasp, understand*
salade (*f.*) *lettuce; salad*
saladier (*m.*) *salad bowl*
salle (*f.*) *room*
salle à manger *dining room*
salle de bains *bathroom*
salon (*m.*) *living room*
sandales (*f. pl.*) *sandals*
Santé ! Chin, chin ! *To your health! Cheers!*
sapin (*m.*) *fir tree*
sauf *except*
saumon (*m.*) *salmon*
savon (*m.*) *soap*
science-fiction (*f.*) *science fiction*
se casser le bras *to break one's arm*
se déguiser *to disguise oneself*
se dérouler *to unfold*
se détendre *to relax, unwind*
se diriger *to head (towards), make one's way*
se fouler la cheville *to sprain one's ankle*
se méfier de *to beware of*
se moucher *to blow one's nose*
se prendre pour *to take oneself for, to think of oneself as*
se reposer *to relax, rest*
se réunir *to get together*
se sentir *to feel*
se serrer la main *to shake hands*
se servir de *to use for/as*
se tromper de *to be mistaken*
sèche-cheveux (*m.*) *hairdryer*
séchoir (*m.*) *(clothes) dryer*
secrétaire (*m./f.*) *secretary*
sel (*m.*) *salt*
sénat (*m.*) *senate*
sénateur (*m.*) *senator*
sensible *sensitive*
sentir *to smell*
serpent (*m.*) *snake*

service (*f.*) de ventes *sales division*
shampooing (*m.*) *shampoo*
short (*m.*) *shorts*
si *if; so; yes*
SIDA (*m.*) *AIDS*
siècle (*m.*) (le 18ème siècle) *century (the 18th century)*
siège (*m.*) *headquarters; seat*
  siège arrière (*m.*) *backseat*
sien(ne) (pron.) *his/hers*
signé(e) *signed*
singe (*m.*) *monkey*
sirop (*m.*) *syrup; cough syrup*
  sirop d'érable *maple syrup*
ski (*m.*) *ski; skiing*
  ski de fond *cross-country skiing*
  ski nautique *waterskiing*
slip (*m.*) *briefs*
société (*f.*) *company, firm*
  société anonyme *public corporation*
sœur (*f.*) *sister*
soie (*f.*) *silk*
sole (*f.*) *sole (type of fish)*
soudain(e) *suddenly*
souhaits: à tes souhaits *equivalent of "Bless you"*
soupçonner *to suspect*
souper (*m.*) *supper*
sourire *to smile*
souris (*f.*) *mouse*
sous-alimentation (*f.*) *malnutrition*
sous clé *under lock and key*
sous-sol (*m.*) *basement*
sous-vêtements (*m. pl.*) *underwear*
soutien-gorge (*m.*) *bra*
souvenir (*m.*) *memory*
souveraineté (*f.*) *sovereignty*
spectacle (*m.*) *show*
stage (*m.*) *internship*
stupéfait(e) *stunned*
succursale (*f.*) *branch office*
sucre (*m.*) *sugar*
sumac (*m.*) vénéneux *poison ivy*
supplier *to beg*
sur-le-champ *immediately*
sur-le-coup *on the spot, instantly*
surlendemain (*m.*) *two days after*
surmonter *to overcome*
syndicat (*m.*) *(workers') union*

T

table basse (*f.*) *coffee table*
tableau (*m.*) *picture*
taille (*f.*) *size, height*
tailleur (*m.*) *women's suit*
talons (*m. pl.*) hauts/plats *high/low heels*
tante (*f.*) *aunt*
tapis (*m.*) roulant *conveyor belt*
tartan *tartan, plaid*
tasse (*f.*) *cup*
tatouage (*m.*) *tattoo*
technicien(ne) (*m./f.*) *technician*
tel(le) *such*
téléphone (*m.*) mobile/portable *cell phone*
téléviseur (*m.*) *TV set*
télé(vision) (*f.*) *television*
témoin (*m.*) *witness*
tempête (*f.*) *storm*
tenace *tenacious, obstinate*
tennis (*m. pl.*) *sneakers*
terrain (*m.*) de camping *campground*
terre (*f.*) *earth, land*
têtu(e) *stubborn*
TGV (*m.*) (train à grande vitesse) *high-speed train*
thématique *thematic*
thèse (*f.*) *thesis*
thon (*m.*) *tuna*
tirer *to fire (weapon)*
toboggan (*m.*) *sledding*
tomate (*f.*) *tomato*
tombeau (*m.*) *grave*
tomber malade *to get sick*
tonnerre (*m.*) *thunder*
tortue (*f.*) *turtle*
tournesol (*m.*) *sunflower*
tourtière (*f.*) *meat pie (reg. Québec)*
tousser *to cough*
tout s'explique ! *everything makes sense!*
toux (*f.*) *cough*
trahir *to betray*
traité (*m.*) *treaty*
traiteur (*m.*) *caterer*
transcrire *to transcribe*
trèfle (*m.*) *clover*
trentaine (*f.*) *about 30 (of something)*
  avoir la trentaine *to be in one's 30s*
trinquer *to toast*
trottoir (*m.*) *sidewalk*
trouvaille (*f.*) *a find*
tuer *to kill*
turquoise *turquoise*

U

une (*f.*): à la une *front page news*

V

vache (*f.*) *cow*
valise (*f.*) *suitcase*
valoir *to be worth*
vaut:
  ça (il) vaut la peine *it's worth the trouble*
  il vaut mieux *it would be better*
vautour (*m.*) *vulture*
veau (*m.*) *veal*
veille (*f.*) *eve/day before*
vélo (*m.*) *biking*
vendeur/-euse *salesperson*
verra: on verra *we'll see*
verre (*m.*) *glass*
vert(e) *green*
vertige (*m.*) *vertigo/dizziness*
vertueux/-euse *virtuous*
veston (*m.*) *men's sport jacket*
vigne (*f.*) *vines*
vinaigre (*f.*) *vinegar*
violet(te) *purple*
visage (*m.*) *face*
vol (*m.*) *flight; robbery*
voler *to fly; to steal*
vote (*m.*) *vote*
voter *to vote*
vouloir *to want*
  en vouloir à qqn *to hold a grudge against s.o.*
  vouloir dire *to mean*
VTT (vélo tout-terrain) (*m.*) *mountain bike*

Y

yaourt (*m.*) *yogurt*
yeux (*m. pl.*) *eyes*

LEXIQUE ANGLAIS-FRANÇAIS

A

accountant comptable (*m./f.*)
add (v.) ajouter
advertising publicité (*f.*)
advice conseil (*m.*)
advise (v.) conseiller
agitated agité(e)
agreement accord (*m.*)
AIDS SIDA (*m.*)
air-conditioned climatisé(e)
ajar entrouvert(e)
alarm clock réveil-matin (*m.*)
allergic allergique
among parmi
animal bête (*f.*), animal (*m.*)
anonymous anonyme
ant fourmi (*f.*)
antique dealer antiquaire (*m.*)
any aucun(e)
appear (v.) apparaître
apple pomme (*f.*)
  apple tree pommier (*m.*)
approach (v.) aborder
armchair fauteuil (*m.*)
arrest (v.) arrêter
arthritis arthrite (*f.*), rhumatisme (*m.*)
ashamed: to be ashamed of avoir honte de
aspirin aspirine (*f.*)
assets créances (*f. pl.*)
associate associé(e) (*m./f.*)
atrocious affreux/-euse
attack attentat (*m.*)
attract (v.) attirer
aunt tante (*f.*)
author auteur (*m.*)

B

backpack sac (*m.*) à dos
backseat siège (*m.*) arrière
bad mauvais(e)
baggage claim area livraison (*f.*) des bagages enregistrés
balcony balcon (*m.*)
banana banane (*f.*)
  banana tree bananier (*m.*)
bankrupt: to be bankrupt faire faillite
barely à peine
basement sous-sol (*m.*)
basil basilic (*m.*)
bat chauve-souris (*f.*)
bathroom salle (*f.*) de bains
bean haricot (*m.*)
bear ours (*m.*)
beard barbe (*f.*)
beaver castor (*m.*)
bed-and-breakfast pension (*f.*)
bedpost colonne (*f.*) de lit
bedroom chambre (*f.*) à coucher
bedspread dessus (*m.*) de lit
bee abeille (*f.*)
beef bœuf (*m.*)
beg (v.) supplier
beige beige
belt ceinture (*f.*)
berries fruits (*m. pl.*) des bois
bet (v.) parier
betray (v.) trahir
better (adj.) meilleur(e)
better (adv.) mieux
beware of (v.) se méfier de
bike vélo (*m.*)
bill addition (*f.*)
birch tree bouleau (*m.*)
bird oiseau (*m.*)
birthday anniversaire (*m.*)
bitter amère
black noir(e)
blouse chemisier (*m.*)
blow one's nose (v.) se moucher
blue bleu(e)
blueberry bleuet (*m.*) (*reg. Québec*), myrtille (*f.*)
blush (v.) rougir
boil (v.) bouillir
book livre (*m.*); (*slang*) bouquin (*m.*)
bookcase étagère (*m.*)
bookseller bouquiniste (*m./f.*)
boots bottes (*f. pl.*)
bore (v.) ennuyer
bored (adj.) ennuyé(e)
  to be bored s'ennuyer
boring ennuyeux/-euse
borrow (v.) emprunter
boss patron(ne) (*m./f.*)
bother (v.) gêner
Bougainvillea (flower) bougainvillée (*f.*)
bowl bol (*m.*)
boyfriend copain (*m.*)
bra soutien-gorge (*m.*)
bracelet bracelet (*m.*)
branch office succursale (*f.*)
brand marque (*f.*)
break one's arm (v.) se casser le bras
bride mariée (*f.*)
briefcase porte-documents (*m.*)
briefs slip (*m.*)
bring (v.):
  bring (s.o.) amener
  bring (things) apporter
broccoli brocoli (*m. pl.*)
bronchitis bronchite (*f.*)
bronze bronzé(e)
brother frère (*m.*)
brother-in-law beau-frère (*m.*)
brown brun(e)
bus (intercity) car (*m.*)
bush buisson (*m.*)
business affaires (*f. pl.*)
butter beurre (*m.*)
butterfly papillon (*m.*)
by chance au hasard

C

cabinet meuble (*m.*) à tiroirs
camel chameau (*m.*)
camera appareil photo (*m.*)
campground terrain (*m.*) de camping
canoe canoë (*m.*), canot (*m.*) (*reg. Québec*)
cardigan gilet (*m.*)
carpet moquette (*f.*), tapis (*m.*)
carrot carotte (*f.*)
cash espèces (*m. pl.*)
cast plâtre (*m.*)
catch fire (v.) prendre feu
caterer traiteur (*m.*)
catfish poisson (*m.*) chat
cavity (dental) carie (*f.*) dentaire
cedar (tree) cèdre (*m.*)
celery céleri (*m.*)
cell phone téléphone mobile (*m.*), portable (*m.*)
century siècle (*m.*)
CEO PDG (*m.*)
chambermaid, housekeeper femme (*f.*) de ménage
charming charmant(e)
check-in desk réception (*f.*)
cheers! Chin, chin ! Santé !
cheese fromage (*m.*)
cherry tree cerisier (*m.*)
chest (of drawers) commode (*f.*)
chestnut tree marronnier (*m.*)
chicken poulet (*m.*)
chopsticks baguettes (*f. pl.*)
cinnamon cannelle (*f.*)
citizen citoyen(ne) (*m./f.*)
civil union PACS (*m.*)
  to enter into a civil union pacser
claim (v.) prétendre que
clam palourde (*f.*)

clever calé(e) *(slang)*
client client(e) (*m./f.*)
clover trèfle (*m.*)
cockroach cafard (*m.*)
coconut tree cocotier (*m.*)
coffee table table (*f.*) basse
cold (illness) rhume (*m.*)
to have a cold être enrhumé(e)
collect call PCV (payable chez vous)
colonist colon (*m.*)
comb peigne (*m.*)
comforts conforts (*m. pl.*)
company entreprise (*f.*), maison (*f.*), société (*f.*), compagnie (*f.*)
competition concurrence (*f.*)
confide (v.) confier
conscientious consciencieux/-euse
contagious contagieux/-euse
conveyor belt tapis (*m.*) roulant
cook (v.) faire cuire
corn maïs (*m.*)
corner coin (*m.*)
cotton coton (*m.*)
couch canapé (*m.*)
cough toux (*f.*), (v.) tousser
cough syrup sirop (*m.*)
counter comptoir (*m.*)
country pays (*m.*)
courtyard cour (*f.*)
cousin cousin(e) (*m./f.*)
cow vache (*f.*)
crackle (v.) pétiller
cranberry canneberge (*m.*)
crawfish écrevisse (*f.*)
crazy fou, folle
cream crème (*f.*)
creative créateur/-trice
cross-country skiing ski (*m.*) de fond
crow corbeau (*m.*)
crowd foule (*f.*)
crust pâte (*f.*)
crutches béquilles (*f. pl.*)
cry (v.) pleurer
cucumber concombre (*m.*)
cup tasse (*f.*)
curtains rideaux (*m. pl.*)
cycling cyclisme (*m.*)

D

daffodil jonquille (*f.*)
daisy marguerite (*f.*)
dance (v.) danser
dark (color) foncé(e)
date rendez-vous (*m.*)
daughter fille (*f.*)
daughter-in-law belle-fille (*f.*)
day before veille (*f.*)
death mort (*f.*)
debate débat (*m.*)
decade décennie (*f.*)
deer cerf (*m.*)
defrost (v.) décongéler
delayed retardé(e)
delighted ravi(e)
demanding exigeant(e)
democracy démocratie (*f.*)
democratic démocratique
deodorant déodorant (*m.*)
depressed déprimé(e)
deranged dérangé(e)
descendant descendant(e)
detective novel roman (*m.*) policier
dining room salle (*f.*) à manger
disadvantages inconvénients (*m. pl.*)
disappear (v.) disparaître
disappoint (v.) décevoir
disconcerting déconcertant(e)
discrimination discriminiation (*f.*)
disguise oneself (v.) se déguiser
dish plat (*m.*)
dishwasher lave-vaisselle (*m.*)
distance oneself (v.) s'éloigner
dizziness vertige (*m.*)
doll poupée (*f.*)
dolphin dauphin (*m.*)
donkey âne (*m.*)
dough pâte (*f.*)
downpour averse (*f.*)
drawing dessin (*m.*)
dress robe (*f.*); (v.) s'habiller
dresser commode (*f.*)
drink (v.) boire, prendre un pot/un verre *(slang)*
drive (v.) conduire
driver's license permis (*m.*) de conduire
dryer (clothes) séchoir (*m.*)
duck canard (*m.*)
dust (v.) épousseter

E

eagle aigle (*m.*)
earphones écouteurs (*m. pl.*)
earrings boucles (*m. pl.*) d'oreille
ears oreilles (*f. pl.*)
earth terre (*f.*)
efficient efficace
egg œuf (*m.*)
eggplant aubergine (*f.*)
elect (v.) élire
elevator ascenseur (*m.*)
elm tree orme (*m.*)
e-mail courriel (*m.*), mél (*m.*)
embankment quai (*m.*)
emotional ému(e), émotif/-ive
end fin (*f.*), bout (*m.*)
energetic énergique
engraving gravure (*f.*)
equality égalité (*f.*)
era époque (*f.*)
escape (v.) (s')échapper
eve veille (*f.*)
except sauf
executive cadre
exhibit exposition (*f.*)
experienced in business rompu(e) aux affaires
expose (v.) mettre en lumière
extend (v.) s'étendre
eye œil (*m.*), yeux (*m. pl.*)
eyeglasses lunettes (*f. pl.*)

F

face visage (*m.*)
fair équitable
fake faux, fausse
fan fan(atique)
father père (*m.*)
father-in-law beau-père (*m.*)
fear (v.) craindre
feel (v.) se sentir, ressentir
fellowship bourse (*f.*)
felt feutre (*m.*)
fern fougère (*f.*)
ferret furet (*m.*)
fever fièvre (*f.*)
feverish fiévreux/-euse
fiancé fiancé(e) (*m./f.*)
fight (v.) combattre
file dossier (*m.*)
film pellicule (*f.*)
fir tree sapin (*m.*)
fire (n.): catch fire prendre feu
fire (v.):
fire (an employee) renvoyer
fire (a weapon) tirer
fireplace cheminée (*f.*)
flabbergasted abasourdi(e)
flight vol (*m.*)
flood inondation (*f.*)
floor plancher (*m.*), parquet (*m.*)
floral pattern à fleurs
flour farine (*f.*)
flu grippe (*f.*)
fly mouche (*f.*)
fog brouillard (*m.*), brume (*f.*)
forge (v.) contrefaire
forgery contrefaçon (*f.*)
fork fourchette (*f.*)
form, sheet fiche (*f.*)
fountain of youth fontaine (*f.*) de jouvence
fox renard (*m.*)
foyer hall (*m.*) d'entrée

frankly franchement
free gratuit(e)
freedom liberté (*f.*)
freezer congélateur (*m.*)
friend copain (*m.*), copine (*f.*)
frog grenouille (*f.*)
front-page stories à la une
frying pan poêle (*f.*)
funeral funérailles (*f. pl.*)
furniture mobilier (*m.*), meubles (*m. pl.*)

G

game jeu (*m.*)
garage garage (*m.*)
garlic ail (*m.*)
gather up (v.) ramasser
get together (v.) se réunir
giraffe girafe (*f.*)
girlfriend copine (*f.*)
glass verre (*m.*)
gloomy maussade
goal but (*m.*)
goat chèvre (*f.*)
goddaughter filleule (*f.*)
godfather parrain (*m.*)
godmother marraine (*f.*)
godson filleul (*m.*)
gold or (*m.*)
goldfish poisson (*m.*) rouge
good bon(ne)
goose oie (*f.*)
  goose bumps chair (*f.*) de poule
governor gouverneur (*m.*)
granddaughter petite-fille (*f.*)
grandparents grands-parents (*m. pl.*)
grandson petit-fils (*m.*)
grape raisin (*m.*)
grasp (understand) (v.) saisir
grave tombeau (*m.*)
great room, hall grande salle (*f.*)
great-grandparents arrière-grands-parents (*m. pl.*)
greedy avare
green vert(e)
grey gris(e)
grill (v.) griller
groom marié (*m.*)
groundhog marmotte (*f.*)
guess (v.) deviner
guest room chambre (*f.*) d'hôte
guidebook guide (*m.*) (touristique)
gusty wind rafale (*f.*) de vent

H

hail grêle (*f.*)
hair cheveux (*m. pl.*)
hairbrush brosse (*f.*) à cheveux
hairdryer sèche-cheveux (*m.*)
half-brother/half-sister demi-frère (*m.*)/demi-sœur (*f.*)
ham jambon (*m.*)
handbag sac (*m.*) à main
handle poignée (*f.*)
handwriting écriture (*f.*)
hangover gueule (*f.*) de bois (*slang*)
hang up (the phone) (v.) raccrocher
hat chapeau (*m.*)
hatch a scheme (v.) mijoter un projet
headquarters siège (*m.*)
heart attack crise (*f.*) cardiaque
heartburn mal (*m.*) au cœur
heart disease maladie (*f.*) du cœur
heat chaleur (*f.*)
  heat wave canicule (*f.*)
heather bruyère (*f.*)
heaven paradis (*m.*)
heels (high/low) talons (*m. pl.*) (hauts/plats)
hell enfer (*m.*)
hike randonnée (*f.*)
hill colline (*f.*)
hippopotamus hippopotame (*m.*)
his/hers (pron.) sien(ne)
hit (adj.) frappé(e)
holly houx (*m.*)
honey miel (*m.*)
honeysuckle chèvrefeuille (*m.*)
horse cheval (*m.*)
horseback riding équitation (*f.*)
hotel owner hôtelier (*m.*), hôtelière (*f.*)
houseboat péniche (*f.*)
housekeeper femme de ménage (*f.*), domestique (*m./f.*)
housework: to do housework faire le ménage
human-interest stories faits divers (*m. pl.*)
hunting chasse (*f.*)
hurricane ouragan (*m.*)
husband mari (*m.*)
hut case (*f.*)
hyena hyène (*m.*)

I

ice glace (*f.*)
  ice cream glace (*f.*)
  ice climbing escalade (*f.*) de glace
  ice hockey hockey (*m.*) sur glace
if si
illegal illégal(e)
immediately sur-le-champ
increase (v.) s'accroître
independence indépendance (*f.*), souveraineté (*f.*)
information renseignement (*m.*)
inheritance héritage (*m.*)
initials parafe (*m.*)
in-laws belle-famille (*f.*)
in-line skating patin (*m.*) en ligne
innkeeper hôtelier (*m.*), hôtelière (*f.*)
intercity bus (auto) car (*m.*)
internship stage (*m.*)
introduce (a topic of conversation) (v.) amorcer
invaded envahi(e)
invest (money) (v.) placer (de l'argent), investir
investigation enquête (*f.*)
investment investissement (*m.*)
iron fer (*m.*) à repasser, (v.) repasser
itch démangeaison (*f.*)
ivory ivoire (*m.*)
ivy lierre (*m.*)
  poison ivy sumac (*m.*) vénéneux

J

jacket (men's) veston (*m.*)
jackpot gros lot (*m.*)
jeans jean (*m.*)
jewelry bijoux (*m. pl.*)
job emploi (*m.*), poste (*m.*); (*slang*) boulot (*m.*)
just in case au cas où

K

key clé (*f.*)
  under lock and key sous clé
kill (v.) tuer
king roi (*m.*)
kitchen cuisine (*f.*)
knife couteau (*m.*)

L

land terre (*f.*)
land (plane) (v.) atterrir
landscape paysage (*m.*)
laptop computer ordinateur (*m.*) portable
laundry room buanderie (*f.*)
lavender lavande (*f.*)
law loi (*f.*)
lazy paresseux/-euse
leaf feuille (*f.*)
leak (news, information) (v.) ébruiter
lease bail (*m.*)
leather cuir (*m.*)
left gauche (*f.*)
legal légal(e)
lemon tree citronnier (*m.*)
lemon citron (*m.*)
lend (v.) prêter
lettuce salade (*f.*), laitue (*f.*)
librarian bibliothécaire (*m./f.*)

lie mensonge (*m.*), (v.) mentir
light (colored) clair(e)
lightning foudre (*f.*)
link together (v.) relier
lips lèvres (*f. pl.*)
literature littérature (*f.*)
liver foie (*f.*)
living room salon (*m.*)
lobster homard (*m.*)
lock: under lock and key sous clé
lose (v.) perdre
lose confidence in (v.) perdre confiance en

M

mad: to be mad at s.o. en vouloir à qqn
magic magie (*f.*)
mail post (*f.*)
majority majorité (*f.*), (*adj.*) majoritaire
make one's way (*v.*) se diriger
makeup maquillage (*m.*)
malnutrition sous-alimentation (*f.*)
man's suit costume (*m.*)
management gestion (*f.*)
manager manager (*m.*), gérant(e) (*m./f.*)
maple tree érable (*m.*)
marble marbre (*m.*)
marketing marketing (*m.*)
mass messe (*f.*) (*religious*)
masterpiece chef-d'œuvre (*m.*)
mauve mauve
mayonnaise mayonnaise (*f.*)
mayor maire (*m.*)
meal repas (*m.*)
mean (adj.) méchant(e)
mean (v.) vouloir dire
medicine médicament (*m.*)
medium moyen(ne)
meeting rendez-vous (*m.*)
business meeting réunion (*f.*)
memory mémoire (*f.*); souvenir (*m.*)
microwave oven four (*m.*) à micro-ondes
milk lait (*m.*)
mine (pron.) mien(ne)
minister (of culture, etc.) ministre (*m.*)
miss (v.) rater, manquer
mistake erreur (*f.*), bêtise (*f.*)
mistaken (v.) se tromper de
monarchy monarchie (*f.*)
monkey singe (*m.*)
moose orignal (*m.*)
mosquito moustique (*m.*)
moss mousse (*f.*)
mother mère (*f.*)
mother-in-law belle-mère (*f.*)
mountain bike VTT (vélo tout-terrain) (*m.*)
mountain lion cougar (*m.*)
mouse souris (*f.*)
move (v.)
move (out of somewhere) (v.) déménager
move toward (v.) se diriger
mudslide chute (*f.*) de boue
munch (v.) grignoter
muscle aches courbature (*f.*)
mussel moule (*f.*)
mustache moustache (*f.*)
mustard moutarde (*f.*)

N

nausea nausée (*f.*)
necessarily forcément
necklace collier (*m.*)
neighborhood coin (*m.*)
nephew neveu (*m.*)
nervous nerveux/-euse
to be nervous être à bout de nerfs
net filet (*m.*)
next prochain(e), suivant(e)
next day lendemain (*m.*)
niece nièce (*f.*)
night-night: to go night-night faire do-do (*slang*)
no vacancy: to have no vacancy être au complet
nonetheless néanmoins
nonprofit à but non lucratif
nonsmoking (adj.) non fumeur
noodles nouilles (*f. pl.*), pâtes (*f. pl.*)
nose nez (*m.*)
novel roman (*m.*)
now maintenant, or
nuts noix (*m. pl.*)

O

oak tree chêne (*m.*)
offering offrande (*f.*)
office bureau (*m.*)
oil huile (*f.*)
oldest (child) aîné(e) (*m./f.*)
onion oignon (*m.*)
on purpose exprès
on the other hand en revanche
on-the-spot sur-le-coup
open-mouthed bouche bée
oppress (v.) opprimer
oppression oppression (*f.*)
oppressive oppressif/-ive
orange orange (*f.*); (*adj.*) orange
order (v.) commander
oven four (*m.*)
overcoat manteau (*m.*)
overcome (v.) surmonter
owe (money) (v.) devoir (de l'argent)
owl hibou (*m.*)
oyster huître (*f.*)

P

packaged empaqueté(e)
paddles pagaies (*f. pl.*)
palm tree palmier (*m.*)
pansy (flower) pensée (*f.*)
pants pantalon (*m.*)
pantyhose collant (*m.*)
papaya tree papayer (*m.*)
paradise paradis (*m.*)
parish paroisse (*f.*)
parliament parlement (*m.*)
parsley persil (*m.*)
partially en partie
party fête (*f.*), soirée (*f.*); parti (politique) (*m.*)
pasta pâtes (*f. pl.*)
peach pêche (*f.*)
peanut cacahouète (*f.*)
pear poire (*f.*)
pear tree poirier (*m.*)
pepper poivre (*m.*)
bell pepper poivron (*m.*)
perfume parfum (*m.*)
pet animal (*m.*) familier
pick up (v.) ramasser
picture tableau (*m.*)
pig cochon (*m.*)
pinch pincée (*f.*)
pineapple ananas (*m.*)
pine tree pin (*m.*)
pink rose
place endroit (*m.*)
plaid tartan, écossais(e)
plane tree platane (*m.*)
plastic plastique (*f.*)
plate assiette (*f.*)
play (theatrical) pièce (*f.*)
plot (v.) manigancer
pneumonia pneumonie (*f.*)
pointy pointu(e)
poison ivy sumac (*m.*) vénéneux
polyester polyester (*m.*)
pool piscine (*f.*)
poppy (flower) coquelicot (*m.*)
pork porc (*m.*)
post office poste (*f.*)
pot (cooking) marmite (*f.*)
potato pomme (*f.*) de terre
pound livre (*f.*)
powerful puissant(e)
pregnant enceinte
present cadeau (*m.*)
privilege privilège (*m.*)

profits bénéfices (*f. pl.*)
progressive progressiste
protest manifestation (*f.*)
proud fier, fière
public corporation société (*f.*) anonyme
pumpkin citrouille (*f.*)
purple violet(te)
purse sac (*m.*) à main

Q

queen reine (*f.*)
quick vite, rapide

R

rabbit lapin (*m.*)
raccoon raton (*m.*) laveur
raincoat imperméable (*m.*)
raser rasoir (*m.*)
raspberry framboise (*f.*)
ravishing, beautiful ravissant(e)
raw cru(e)
rayon rayonne (*f.*)
reading lecture (*f.*)
recipe recette (*f.*)
red rouge; (*hair*) roux, rousse
reflection réflexion (*f.*)
regime régime (*m.*)
reimburse (v.) rembourser
reindeer renne (*m.*)
relax (v.) se détendre; se reposer
reliable fiable
rent loyer (*m.*), (v.) louer
reporter reporter (*m.*)
representative représentant(e) (*m./f.*)
republic république (*f.*)
research recherche (*f.*)
resistance résistence (*f.*)
rest repos (*m.*); (v.) se reposer, se détendre
reunion réunion (*f.*)
ribbon ruban (*m.*)
rice riz (*m.*)
right droite (*f.*); (*legal*) droit (*m.*)
ring bague (*f.*)
risky aléatoire
roast (v.) rôtir
room pièce (*f.*), chambre (*f.*)
rooster coq (*m.*)
rubber tree arbre (*m.*) à gomme
ruin (v.) gâcher
ruined fichu(e)
rustic champêtre

S

salad bowl saladier (*m.*)
salad salade (*f.*)
sales division service (*f.*) de ventes
salesperson vendeur/-euse
salmon saumon (*m.*)
salt sel (*m.*)
sand sable (*m.*)
sandals sandales (*f. pl.*)
saucepan casserole (*f.*)
sauté (v.) faire sauter
scar cicatrice (*f.*)
scarf foulard (*m.*)
science fiction science-fiction (*f.*)
seal (animal) phoque (*m.*)
secretary secrétaire (*m./f.*)
security deposit caution (*f.*)
senate sénat (*m.*)
senator sénateur (*m.*)
sensitive sensible
serious grave
service: to be of service (to) rendre service (à)
setting cadre (*m.*)
settle in (v.) s'installer
shake hands (v.) se serrer la main
shampoo shampooing (*m.*)
shark requin (*m.*)
sharp (tart) piquant(e)
sheep mouton (*m.*)
shelf étagère (*m.*)
shirt chemise (*f.*)
shiver (v.) frissonner
shoes chaussures (*f. pl.*)
shorts short (*m.*)
shout (v.) crier
show spectacle (*m.*)
shrewd perspicace
shrimp crevette (*f.*)
shrub arbrisseau (*m.*)
sick (adj.) malade
  to get sick tomber malade
sidewalk trottoir (*m.*)
signed signé(e)
significantly nettement
silk soie (*f.*)
silver argent (*m.*)
simmer (v.) faire mijoter
sincerely sincèrement, de bon cœur
sink évier (*m.*); lavabo (*m.*)
sister sœur (*f.*)
sister-in-law belle-sœur (*f.*)
sit down s'asseoir
size taille (*f.*)
skating patinage (*m.*)
  in-line skating patin (*m.*) en ligne
sketch esquisse (*f.*)
ski lift remonte-pente (*m.*)
skirt jupe (*f.*)
skunk mouffette (*f.*)
sky ciel (*m.*)
sledding toboggan (*m.*)
slice part (*f.*)
smell (v.) sentir
smile (v.) sourire
smoking (adj.) fumeur
snack (v.) grignoter
snake serpent (*m.*)
sneakers tennis (*m. pl.*), baskets (*m. pl.*)
sneeze (v.) éternuer
sniffle (v.) renifler
snore (v.) ronfler
snow neige (*f.*)
snowboarding planche (*f.*) de neige
snowshoeing raquette (*f.*) de neige
so alors, si (adv.)
soap savon (*m.*)
so-called prétendu(e)
sock chaussette (*f.*)
son fils (*m.*)
song chanson (*f.*)
son-in-law beau-fils (*m.*)
sore throat mal (*m.*) à la gorge
sorry désolé(e), navré(e)
soul âme (*f.*)
  soul mate, like-minded person âme (*f.*) sœur
spell (v.) épeler
spice épice (*f.*)
spicy piquant(e)
spider araignée (*f.*)
spoon cuillère (*f.*)
spoonful cuillerée (*f.*)
sprain one's ankle (v.) se fouler la cheville
spring roll rouleau (*m.*) de printemps
square carré(e)
squirrel écureuil (*m.*)
stairs escalier (*m.*)
state état (*m.*)
steal (v.) voler
step pas (*m.*)
stepdaughter belle-fille (*f.*)
stepfather beau-père (*m.*)
stepmother belle-mère (*f.*)
stepson beau-fils (*m.*)
stew ragoût (*m.*)
still-life (painting) nature (*f.*) morte
stir (v.) remuer
stock exchange bourse (*f.*)
stock market crash krach (*m.*) boursier
stock shares actions (*f. pl.*)
storm orage (*m.*); tempête (*f.*)
stove cuisinière (*f.*)
straw paille (*f.*)
strawberry fraise (*f.*)
strike grêve (*f.*)
striking frappant(e)
striped à rayures
stroke attaque (*f.*) d'apoplexie
stubborn têtu(e)

stunned stupéfait(e)
stupid bête, stupide
stutter (v.) bégayer
subsidiary filiale (*f.*)
such tel(le)
sudden soudain(e)
suddenly soudain
sugar sucre (*m.*)
suit (men's) costume (*m.*); (*women's*) tailleur (*m.*)
suitcase valise (*f.*)
summer vacation grandes vacances (*f. pl.*)
sunburn coup (*m.*) de soleil
sunflower tournesol (*m.*)
supper souper (*m.*)
supply (v.) fournir
surrounded entouré(e)
surroundings environs (*m. pl.*)
suspect (v.) soupçonner
swallow hirondelle (*f.*)
swear (v.) jurer
sweater pull-over (*m.*); (*cardigan*) gilet (*m.*)
sweats jogging (*m.*)
sweet doux, douce
swimming natation (*f.*)
swimsuit maillot (*m.*) de bain

T

tablet comprimé (*m.*)
talkative bavard(e)
tattoo tatouage (*m.*)
technician technicien(ne) (*m./f.*)
television set téléviseur (*m.*)
tenacious tenace
thank (v.) remercier
thematic thématique
thesis thèse (*f.*)
thin mince
think (v.) penser, estimer
thought pensée (*f.*)
thunder tonnerre (*m.*)
tide marée (*f.*)
tidy up (v.) ranger les affaires
tie cravate (*f.*)
time temps (*m.*), fois (*f.*)
tip pourboire (*m.*)
tireless infatigable
toast (speech) (v.) trinquer
today aujourd'hui
tomato tomate (*f.*)
toothbrush brosse (*f.*) à dents
toothpaste dentifrice (*m.*)
top (shirt) haut (*m.*)
torn déchiré(e)
track down (v.) dépister
trail piste (*f.*)
train train (*m.*)
  high speed train train à grande vitesse (TGV)
transcribe (v.) transcrire
treaty traité (*m.*)
trial procès (*m.*)
trip: to take a short trip faire une excursion
troubling déconcertant(e)
tuna thon (*m.*)
turkey dinde (*f.*)
turquoise turquoise
turtle tortue (*f.*)
twins jumeaux (*m.*), jumelles (*f.*)

U

ugly laid(e), moche
umbrella parapluie (*m.*)
uncle oncle (*m.*)
understand (v.) comprendre, saisir
underwear sous-vêtements (*m. pl.*), slip (*m.*)
uneasy mal à l'aise
unemployment chômage (*m.*)
unfold (v.) se dérouler
union (workers') syndicat (*m.*)
unthinkable impensable
use (v.) employer, utiliser, se servir de

V

vacuum (v.) passer l'aspirateur
veal veau (*m.*)
vinegar vinaigre (*f.*)
vine vigne (*f.*)
virtuous vertueux/-euse
vote (v.) voter
vulture vautour (*m.*)

W

walking marche (*f.*)
Walkman™ baladeur (*m.*)
wall mur (*m.*)
wallet portefeuille (*m.*)
war guerre (*f.*)
warehouse entrepôt (*m.*)
warm (personality) chaleureux/-euse
wash (v.) laver
  wash clothes faire la lessive
  wash dishes faire la vaisselle
washing machine machine (*f.*) à laver
waste (v.) gaspiller
watch montre (*f.*)
watercolor aquarelle (*f.*)
waterskiing ski (*m.*) nautique
way moyen (*m.*)
whale baleine (*f.*)
what's worse qui pis est
wheels roues (*f. pl.*), roulettes (*f. pl.*)
white blanc(-che)
wife femme (*f.*)
win (v.) gagner
wind vent (*m.*)
  gust of wind rafale (*f.*) de vent
windsurfing planche (*f.*) à voile
winter jacket anorak (*m.*)
wisdom sagesse (*f.*)
witness témoin (*m.*)
wool laine (*f.*)
work (of art) œuvre (*f.*)
worry (v.) s'en faire
worth (v.) valoir
worthless thing lettre (*f.*) morte
wound (v.) blesser
wounded blessé(e)
wrinkle ride (*f.*)
wrist poignée (*f.*)
writing écriture (*f.*)
wrong faux, fausse
wrought iron fer (*m.*) forgé

Y

yell (v.) crier
yellow jaune
yesterday hier
yogurt yaourt (*m.*)
youngest child cadet(te) (*m./f.*)
youth hostel auberge (*f.*) de jeunesse

Z

zucchini courgette (*f.*)

Credits

Texts

Page 29 «Travailler c'est trop dur», Paroles : Zachary Richard, © Les Editions du Marais Bouleur. **Pages 161–162** Excerpt from *Femmes d'Alger dans leur appartement*, d'Assia Djebar, © 2002 Editions Albin Michel. **Pages 247–248** Excerpt from *Chemin d'école*, de Patrick Chamoiseau, © Editions GALLIMARD. **Pages 284–286** Excerpt from *Une si longue lettre*, de Miriama Bâ, © Les Nouvelles Editions Africaines du Sénégal. **Pages 392–394** Excerpt from *Les Aurores montréales*, de Monique Proulx, © Éditions du Boréal.

Photos

Pages 2, 15, 37, 44, 48 © 1998 Elizabeth A. Blood. **Page 57** © Karen Schneider. **Pages 88, 102** © 1998 Elizabeth A. Blood. **Page 130** © Dana S. Hale (2002). **Pages 143, 151, 168** © 1998 Elizabeth A. Blood. **Page 173** © Ann McBride. **Page 203** © 1998 Elizabeth A. Blood. **Page 216** © T. Gustave. **Pages 220, 228** © T. Gustave. **Pages 254, 283** © Dana S. Hale (2002). **Page 292** © 1998 Elizabeth A. Blood. **Page 301 (top left)** © Claudia Fernandes. **Pages 301 (bottom), 301 (top right), 328, 342, 343, 358, 366, 373, 384, 392** © 1998 Elizabeth A. Blood.

Index

B

C

D

E

F

G

H

I

J

L

M

N

O

P

Q

R

S

T

U

V

W

Y

L'ANGLETERRE
NORD-PAS DE CALAIS
Lille
LA BELGIQUE
L'ALLEMAGNE
Pas-de-Calais
Arras
Nord
La Manche
Somme
Amiens
Charleville-Mézières
LE LUX.
Seine-Maritime
PICARDIE
Laon
Ardennes
Rouen
Beauvais
Aisne
LORRAINE
HAUTE-NORMANDIE
Oise
Metz
Manche
Caen
Pontoise
Châlons-sur-Marne
Meuse
Moselle
ALSACE
Saint-Lô
Calvados
Val-d'Oise
Evreux
Marne
Strasbourg
BASSE-NORMANDIE
Orne
Eure
Yvelines
Paris
ÎLE-DE-FRANCE
CHAMPAGNE-ARDENNE
Bar-le-Duc
Nancy
Meurthe-et-Moselle
Bas-Rhin
Versailles
Évry
Melun
Finistère
St-Brieuc
Alençon
Chartres
Essonne
Seine-et-Marne
Troyes
Chaumont
Vosges
Epinal
Colmar
Côtes-du-Nord
Eure-et-Loire
Aube
Haut-Rhin
Mayenne
Loiret
Quimper
BRETAGNE
Rennes
Laval
Le Mans
Orléans
Auxerre
Haute-Marne
Ille-et-Vilaine
Territoire de Belfort
Morbihan
PAYS DE LA LOIRE
Sarthe
Yonne
Vesoul
Vannes
Blois
Haute-Saône
Loire-Atlantique
Côte-d'Or
Doubs
Angers
Tours
Loir-et-Cher
Dijon
Besançon
Maine-et-Loire
Nantes
CENTRE
Nièvre
FRANCHE-COMTÉ
Indre-et-Loire
Bourges
BOURGOGNE
Nevers
Châteauroux
Cher
Saône-et-Loire
Jura
LA SUISSE
Lons-le-Saunier
La Roche-sur-Yon
Deux-Sèvres
Poitiers
Indre
Moulins
Vendée
Vienne
Allier
Mâcon
Bourg-en-Bresse
Niort
Haute-Savoie
POITOU-CHARENTES
Guéret
AUVERGNE
Ain
Annecy
La Rochelle
Limoges
Creuse
Rhône
Lyon
RHÔNE-ALPES
Seine-Saint-Denis
Clermont-Ferrand
Loire
Chambéry
Nanterre
Bobigny
Charente-Maritime
Haute-Vienne
Angoulême
Puy-de-Dôme
St-Étienne
Isère
Savoie
Paris
Charente
LIMOUSIN
Grenoble
Hauts-de-Seine
Créteil
Val-de-Marne
Périgueux
Tulle
Corrèze
Cantal
Aurillac
Le Puy
Haute-Loire
Valence
L'ITALIE
Dordogne
Hautes-Alpes
Bordeaux
AQUITAINE
Lot
Privas
Drôme
Gap
Ardèche
Gironde
Mende
Lot-et-Garonne
Aveyron
Rodez
Lozère
Digne
Alpes-Maritimes
Agen
Tarn-et-Garonne
MIDI-PYRÉNÉES
Gard
Vaucluse
Avignon
Alpes de Haute-Provence
Landes
Nice
MONACO
Montauban
Albi
Nîmes
PROVENCE-ALPES-CÔTE-D'AZUR
L'océan Atlantique
Mont-de-Marsan
Gers
Auch
Toulouse
Tarn
Hérault
Montpellier
Bouches-du-Rhône
Var
Haute-Garonne
LANGUEDOC-ROUSSILLON
Marseille
Toulon
Pau
Tarbes
Carcassonne
Pyrénées-Atlantiques
Aude
Hautes-Pyrénées
Foix
Ariège
Perpignan
La Mer Méditerranée
L'ANDORRE
Pyrénées-Orientales
Bastia
Haute-Corse
L'ESPAGNE
CORSE
Ajaccio
Corse-du-Sud
Limite départementale
Limite provinciale
Gironde Nomme du département
CENTRE Nomme de la province
0 Kilomètres 200
La France: les provinces les départements

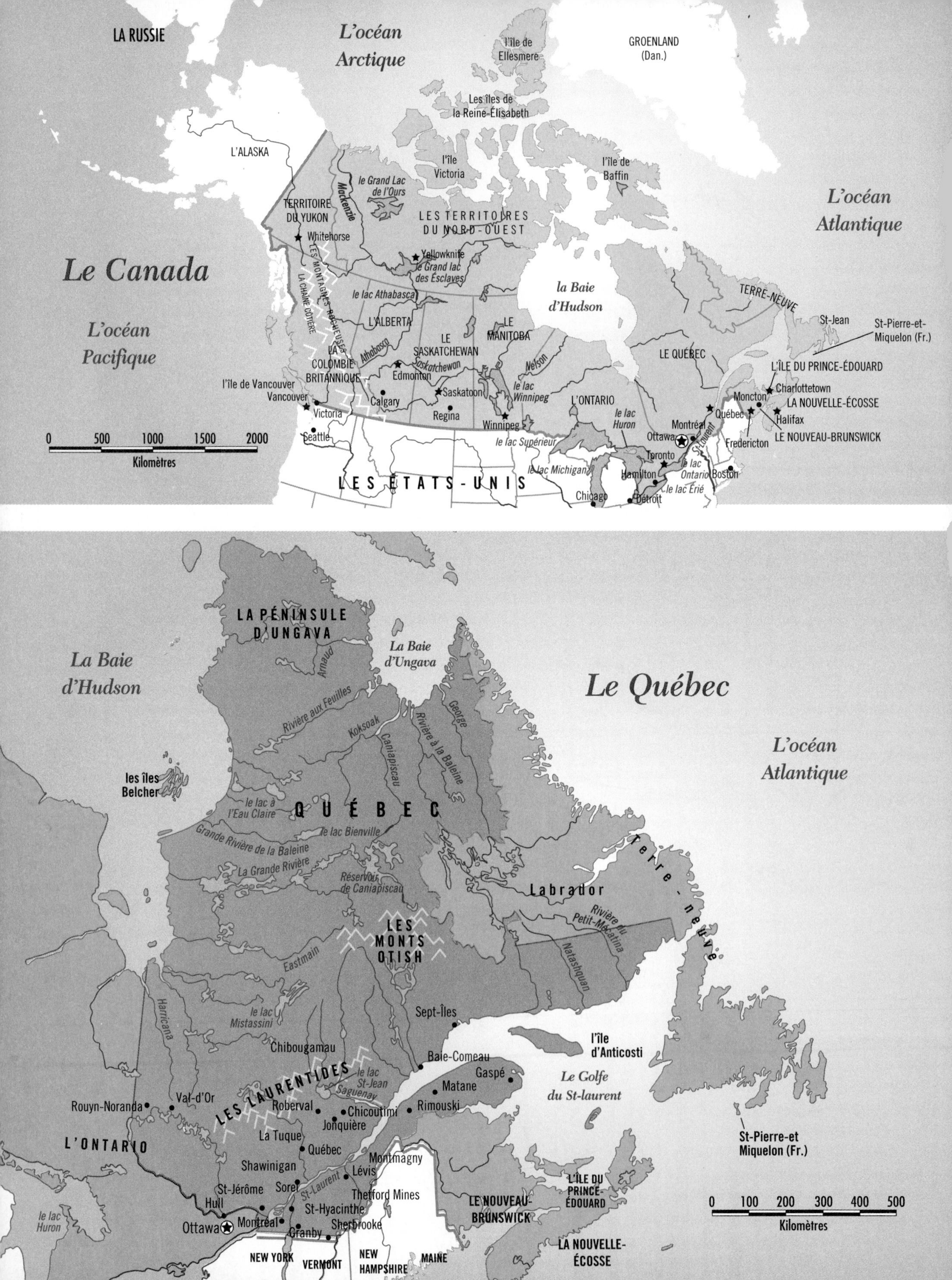

Le Canada
LA RUSSIE
L'océan Arctique
L'île de Ellesmere
GROENLAND (Dan.)
Les îles de la Reine-Élisabeth
L'ALASKA
L'île Victoria
L'île de Baffin
le Grand Lac de l'Ours
Mackenzie
TERRITOIRE DU YUKON
LES TERRITOIRES DU NORD-OUEST
L'océan Atlantique
Whitehorse
Yellowknife
le Grand lac des Esclaves
LES MONTAGNES ROCHEUSES
LA CHAÎNE CÔTIÈRE
la Baie d'Hudson
TERRE-NEUVE
le lac Athabasca
L'ALBERTA
LE SASKATCHEWAN
LE MANITOBA
St-Jean
St-Pierre-et-Miquelon (Fr.)
L'océan Pacifique
LA COLOMBIE BRITANNIQUE
Athabasca
Saskatchewan
Nelson
LE QUÉBEC
L'ÎLE DU PRINCE-ÉDOUARD
Edmonton
le lac Winnipeg
Charlottetown
L'île de Vancouver
Vancouver
Calgary
Saskatoon
L'ONTARIO
Moncton
LA NOUVELLE-ÉCOSSE
Victoria
Regina
Winnipeg
le lac Huron
Montréal
Québec
Halifax
Ottawa
LE NOUVEAU-BRUNSWICK
0 500 1000 1500 2000
Kilomètres
Seattle
le lac Supérieur
St-Laurent
Fredericton
Toronto
le lac Ontario
le lac Michigan
Hamilton
Boston
LES ÉTATS-UNIS
Chicago
Détroit
le lac Érié
Le Québec
LA PÉNINSULE D'UNGAVA
La Baie d'Ungava
La Baie d'Hudson
Arnaud
Rivière aux Feuilles
George
Koksoak
Caniapiscau
Rivière à la Baleine
L'océan Atlantique
les îles Belcher
le lac à l'Eau Claire
QUÉBEC
le lac Bienville
Grande Rivière de la Baleine
La Grande Rivière
Réservoir de Caniapiscau
Terre-neuve
Labrador
Rivière du Petit-Mécatina
LES MONTS OTISH
Eastmain
Natashquan
Harricana
le lac Mistassini
Sept-Îles
Chibougamau
L'île d'Anticosti
Baie-Comeau
LES LAURENTIDES
le lac St-Jean
Saguenay
Gaspé
Matane
Le Golfe du St-laurent
Rouyn-Noranda
Val-d'Or
Roberval
Chicoutimi
Rimouski
Jonquière
L'ONTARIO
La Tuque
St-Pierre-et Miquelon (Fr.)
Québec
Shawinigan
Montmagny
Lévis
St-Jérôme
Sorel
St-Laurent
Thetford Mines
L'ÎLE DU PRINCE-ÉDOUARD
LE NOUVEAU-BRUNSWICK
Hull
St-Hyacinthe
0 100 200 300 400 500
Kilomètres
le lac Huron
Ottawa
Montréal
Sherbrooke
Granby
LA NOUVELLE-ÉCOSSE
NEW YORK
VERMONT
NEW HAMPSHIRE
MAINE